LEBEN?

ODER

THEATER?

EIN SINGSPIEL

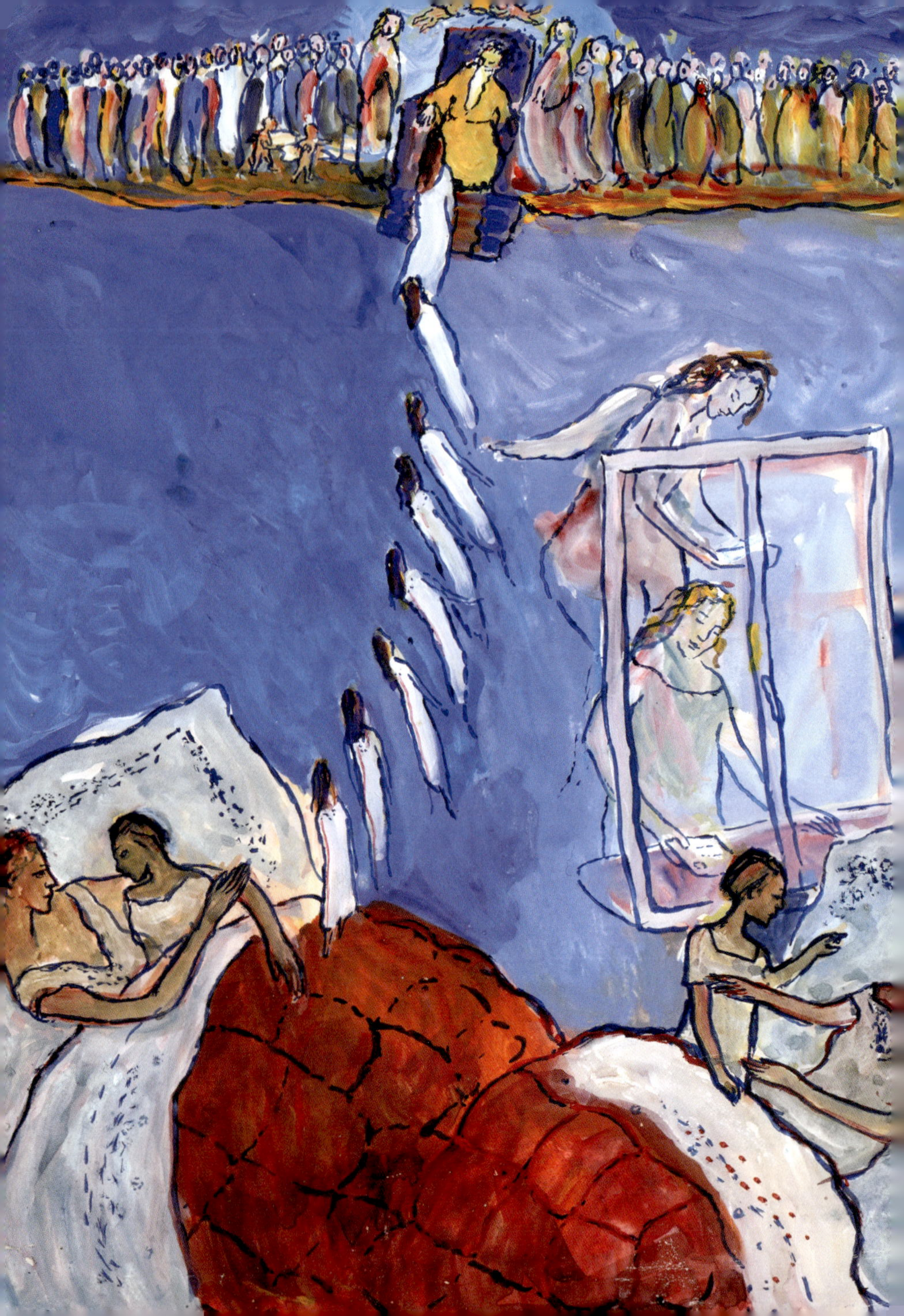

Charlotte Salomon

Life? or Theatre?

A young artist's fight
for survival and hope
1940–1943

Essays by
Judith C.E. Belinfante
and Evelyn Benesch

TASCHEN
Bibliotheca Universalis

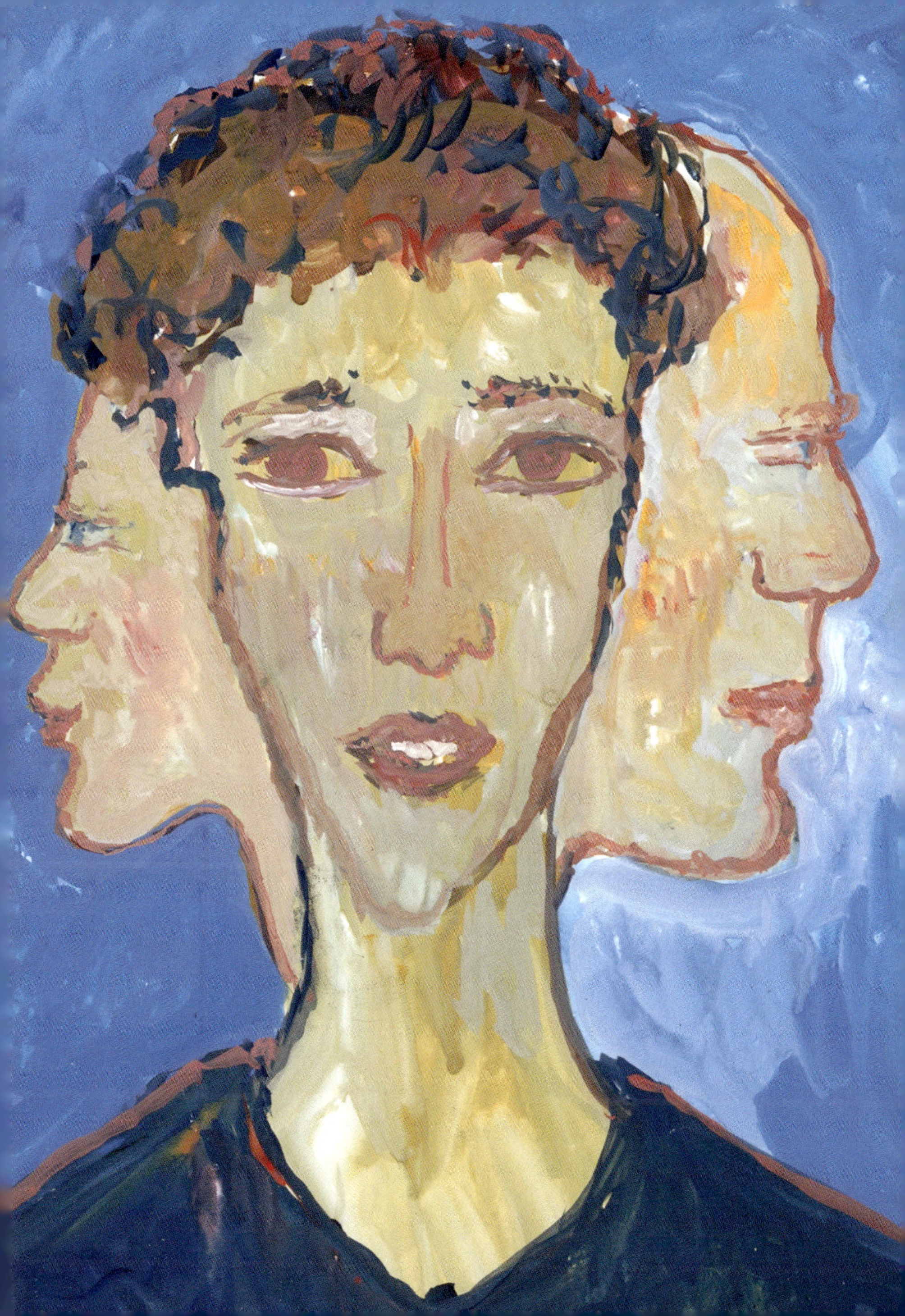

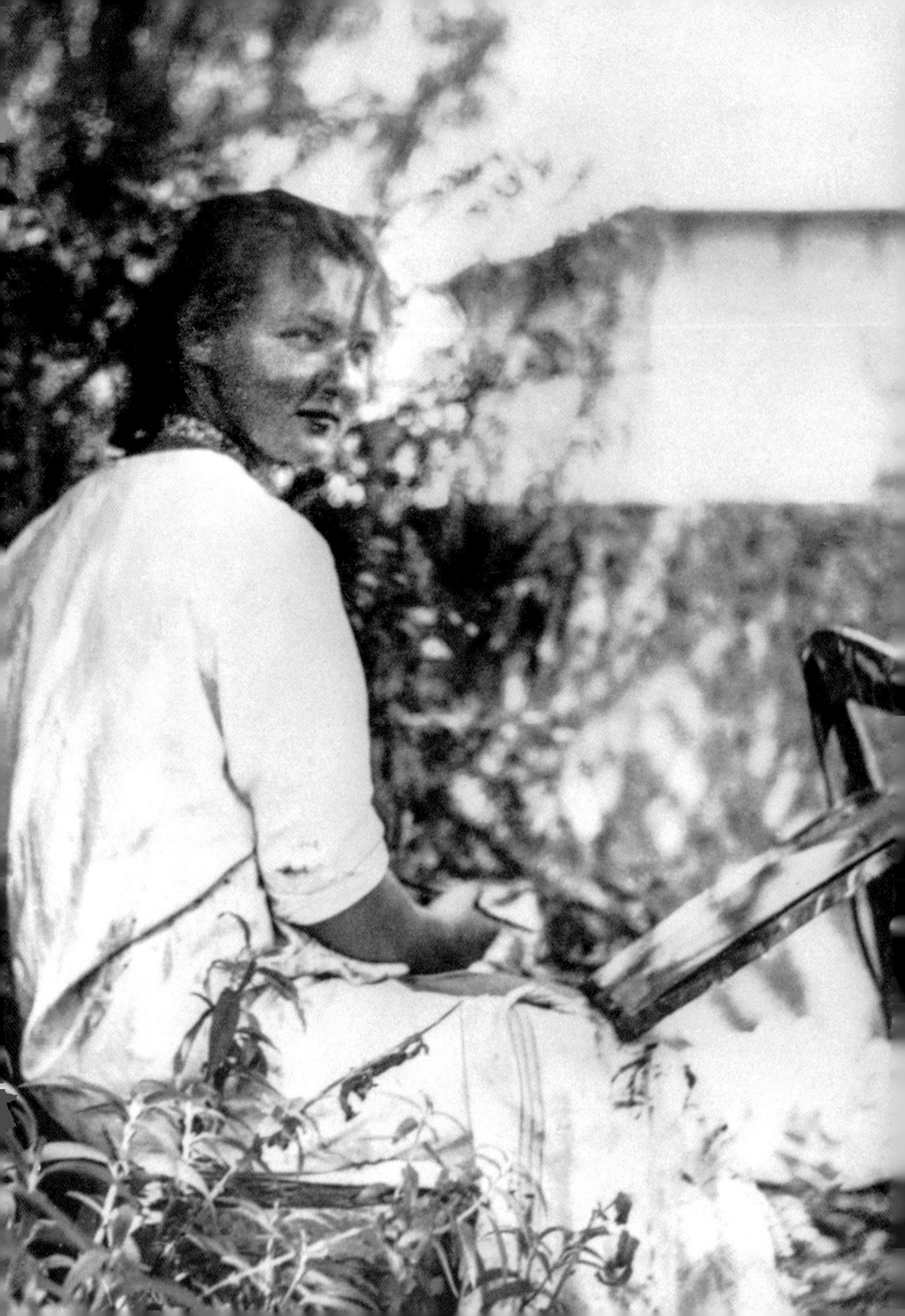

Judith C.E. Belinfante

What is *Life? or Theatre?*?

Death and the Maiden

The Maiden
Away with thee! Let me be!
Get away, thou grisly man of bone!
I am still young. Desist, I beg thee!
And lay not a single finger on me.

Death
Give me thy hand, thou picture of beauty and tenderness!
I come as thy friend, and I mean no harm.
Be of good cheer! I'm not here to scare thee.
Thou shalt sleep sweetly in my arms!

Matthias Claudius, 1774
Franz Schubert, D 531, op. 7, no. 3, February 1817[1]

Among the diverse art works to be produced in the 20th century, *Life? or Theatre?* by Charlotte Salomon (Berlin 1917–1943 Auschwitz) is uniquely all-encompassing. It has been termed a "dramatised autobiography"[2] but also a "semi-autobiography". Its essential subject is the artist's own life in relation to the rise of National Socialism, the encroaching threat of anti-Semitism, and the outbreak of the Second World War. But Salomon uses these developments as a context for an altogether different story. The work is also a vehicle for the author's engagement with herself, and with her determination to avoid the fate of her aunt, her mother, her grandmother, and her great grandmother, all of whom chose suicide as the only way out. Salomon's narrative is only partially chronological; she concentrated instead on seeking out those emotions that had remained concealed from her in the shameful silence of the past.

Charlotte Salomon in France, c. 1939

According to the numbers marked on the sheets of paper, Salomon's work comprises 769 images in gouache, each measuring 32.5 x 25 cm, in addition to 320 pages of text on tracing paper, each of these affixed to the relevant image by means of three narrow strips of gummed paper. *Life? or Theatre?* is divided into three sections: a Prologue, a Main Section, and an Epilogue.[3] Salomon supplied the numbering for each section, that of the Prologue being marked on the pages of text on tracing paper, and that of the other two sections marked on the sheets bearing images. Taking into account surviving preparatory studies, sketches, and drafts of text as well as diverse separate sheets, the total comprises 1,299 images in gouache on 966 sheets of paper;[4] 333 of these used on both sides.[5]

Life? or Theatre? is a multi-layered work, and its "meanings" may be approached from diverse ways. There is no sharp distinction between reality and fiction. Salomon combines images, music, and apparently simple language to give expression to her own personal and artistic struggle. At each point she can be found seeking to achieve a balance between that which she wishes to deal with emotionally, that which she is forced to deal with emotionally, and that which she can bear. This process of development takes on a rhythm of its own thanks to the use of repetitions and variations of form and colour.

In 1961, when Charlotte Salomon's first exhibition of works was presented at the Museum Fodor in Amsterdam, a modest selection of sheets from *Life? or Theatre?* was shown, along with a number of her other drawings and works in gouache. When, in 1963, *Life? or Theatre?* was first published (with the transcribed text in its original German and in an English version) 80 images were presented, and the title was rendered to include the term "diary".[6] As an inevitable result, Salomon's work was soon being compared with *The Diary of Anne Frank* (first Dutch edition 1947); and it was assumed that both conveyed the same optimistic attitude to life. Seemingly not wanting to undermine this impression altogether, Charlotte's stepmother, Paula Lindberg-Salomon (Frankenthal 1897–2000 Amsterdam), requested that the text incorporated within the final gouache (p. 579) of Charlotte's despairing grandfather – "Now conclusively take your life, so this babble finally stops" – be removed, and the sheet with Charlotte's own hopeful exclamation on the beauty of the landscape (p. 575) be presented as the last.

The assumed parallel with Anne Frank (1929–1945), albeit certainly understandable in the 1960s, is inaccurate. Anne Frank was a young girl with a gift for writing who recorded the daily experience of her life in hiding. Charlotte Salomon, by contrast, was a trained artist writing in retrospective contemplation of her entire life and investigating developments and situations. Her own art does not emerge primarily from a direct experience of the Holocaust, even if she had been forced to break off her artistic training. Instead, Salomon sought to make her own life accessible to later viewers and

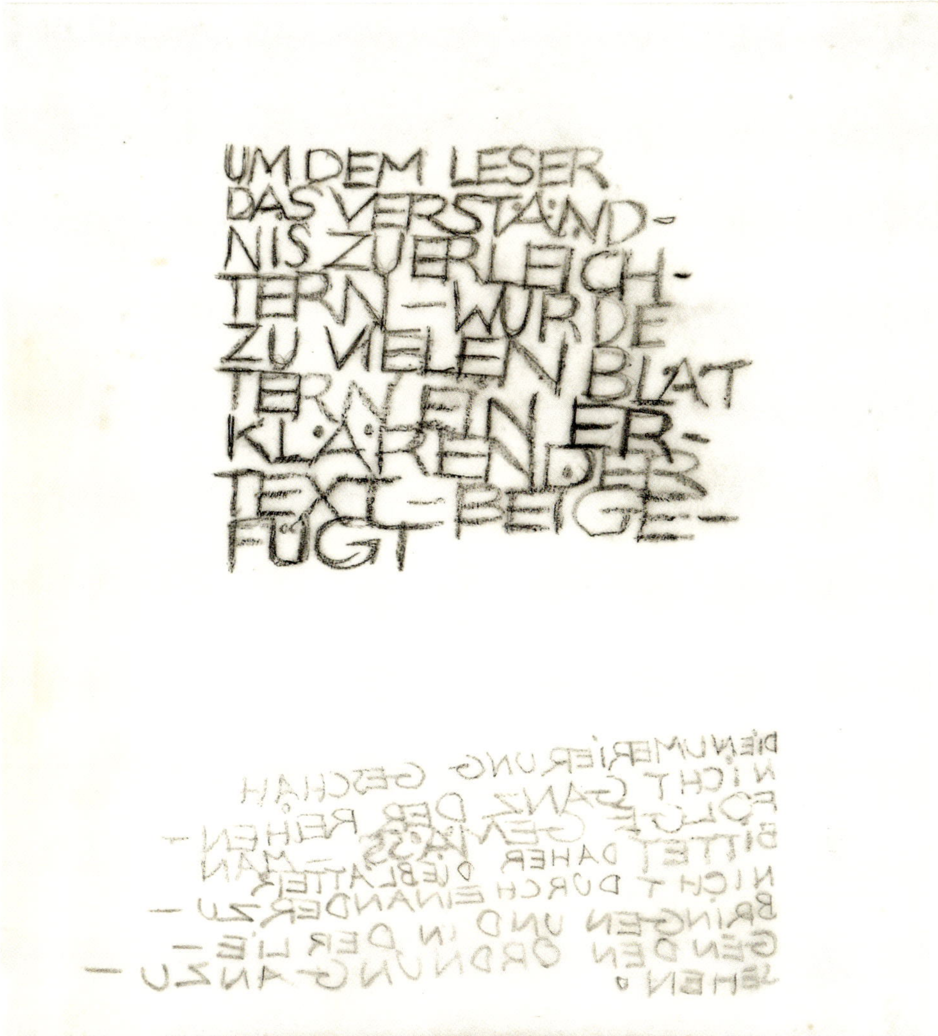

Unnumbered transparent sheet from *Life? or Theatre?* with the explanation of the original sequence of sheets: "In order to facilitate the reader's understanding, an explanatory text has been added to several sheets. [Verso:] The numbering did not take place entirely according to the order – it is therefore advisable not to confuse the sheets and to look at the order in which they are now arranged."

readers, and thus she depicted it as an individual within the context of a specific historical period. In the case of Salomon's work thus, a "diary" is not our concern.

I. Who Was Charlotte Salomon (1917–1943)?

Lotte
"She was like an overcast day in November and, although
she almost never laughed or spoke, she had a terrific gift for observation."
Barbara Petzel, Charlotte's classmate at art school in 1935[7]

Lotte S
"I found it difficult to make close contact with her. She was
extraordinarily taciturn and unable to break through and
emerge from the barrier she had built around herself."
Alfred Wolfsohn on Charlotte in Berlin (1935–38), c. 1946[8]

Charlotte Salomon
"And so one day there she stood in front of me [...] there was
something awkward about her movements and she seemed shy, like
a young deer [...] She lived in her own world of light, air, and
colours, and there were many drawings in pencil and charcoal,
and wash, and crayon and, among them, many a dainty watercolour:
scenes in the garden, on the beach, in the street. Wherever she was
she used to take the drawing pad out of her bag. She had to free
herself, and her pencil or brush supplied the language to do so."
Emil Straus on Charlotte in Villefranche-sur-Mer, 1939[9]

BERLIN 1917–38

During the First World War, Charlotte's father Albert Salomon (Röbel/Müritz 1883–1976 Amsterdam) served at the front as a military surgeon. Among his assistants was the nurse Franziska Grunwald (Berlin 1890–1926 Berlin), whom he married in 1916, although her parents, members of the wealthy Jewish intellectual élite, had disapproved of their daughter's choice. In their eyes, Albert was insufficiently cultivated: he never travelled, rarely went to concerts or to the opera, did not play tennis, and never gave parties. Moreover, on account of his provincial origins and status as an orphan, they found him to be of inadequate social status as a husband for their daughter, even though he had managed to become a physician through sheer hard work, just like his father-in-law.

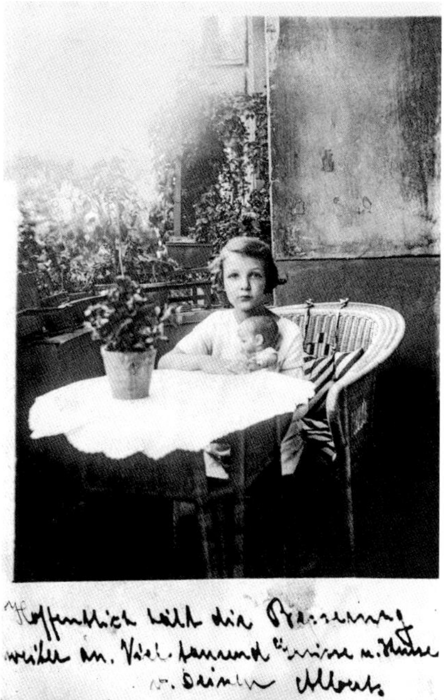

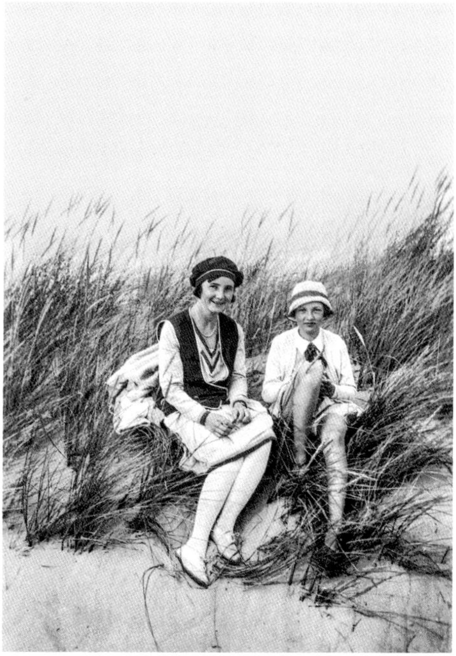

Albert Salomon was, in fact, one of the first to carry out research into breast cancer. In 1921, he joined the teaching staff at the Charité, the University Clinic in Berlin. His daughter Charlotte was born on 16 April 1917.

Charlotte was named after her aunt, her mother's younger sister, who in 1913, at the age of only 18, had committed suicide. Charlotte's mother, the initially vivacious Franziska, had become increasingly distressed over the years and began to suffer from depression. Notwithstanding the love of those around her, in 1926, she threw herself out of a window. Charlotte was not yet nine years old at this point (above, left). In those days suicide was regarded not only as deeply disgraceful, but also as the sign of degeneration of a sort that could infect an entire family. It was also the case that the suicide rate among Jewish women was higher than among the female population as a whole.[10] Charlotte's relatives nonetheless maintained a persistent silence about what had really happened. The little girl was told that her mother had died from influenza.

Charlotte at the age of about eight years, c. 1925
The text signed by Albert Salomon suggests that the photograph was sent to her mother.

Charlotte and "Hase", her governess who inspired her to draw, Sylt, 1928

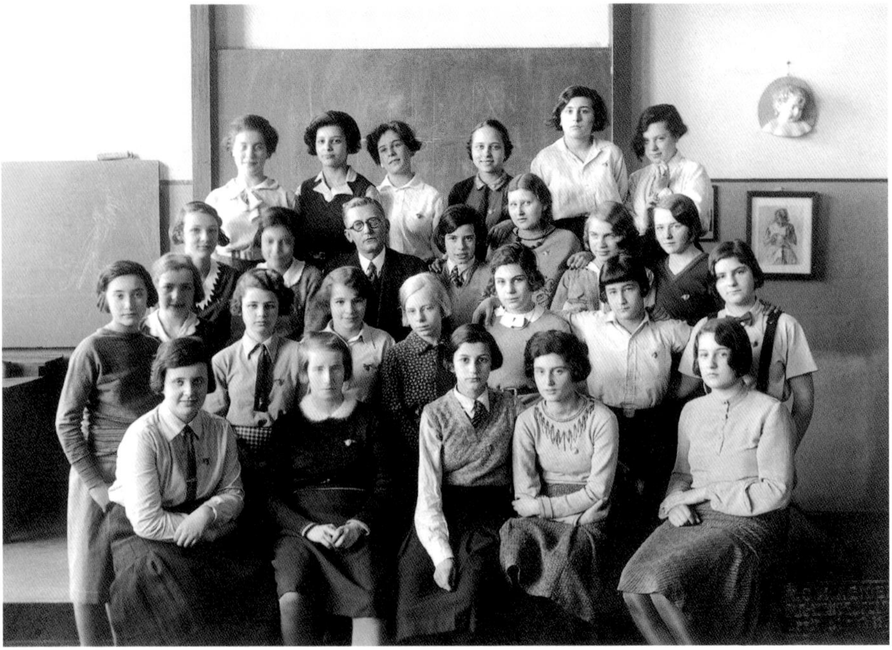

In the following years, a series of governesses attended to Charlotte's upbringing; but it was not until the advent of a cheerful young woman with the last name Hase ("hare") that one succeeded in establishing a genuine relationship with the girl. It was also Ms. Hase who first stimulated Charlotte's interest in drawing (p. 11 right).

In September 1930, Albert Salomon married for the second time: his bride, the singer Paula Levi, had changed her name to make it easier to find work (pp. 16 and 30–31). As Paula Lindberg, she had become a celebrated performer of the vocal music of Johann Sebastian Bach's (1685–1750). Charlotte admired her stepmother very much and idolised her initially. Their relationship was, however, to grow cooler over the years.

During the 1930s, with the rise of National Socialism, Berlin began to change. German attitudes towards the Jews grew increasingly inimical. For Jews, who had fought for Germany during the First World War, this was an especially sad development. In the schools, pupils and even teachers increasingly became followers of Nazi ideology, and

Class photograph of the Fürstin-Bismarck-Gymnasium, Berlin, c. 1932
Charlotte is in the third row, very left.

Students of the Vereinigte Staatsschulen für Freie und Angewandte Kunst (United State Schools for Fine and Applied Arts) painting flowers, c. 1930–39

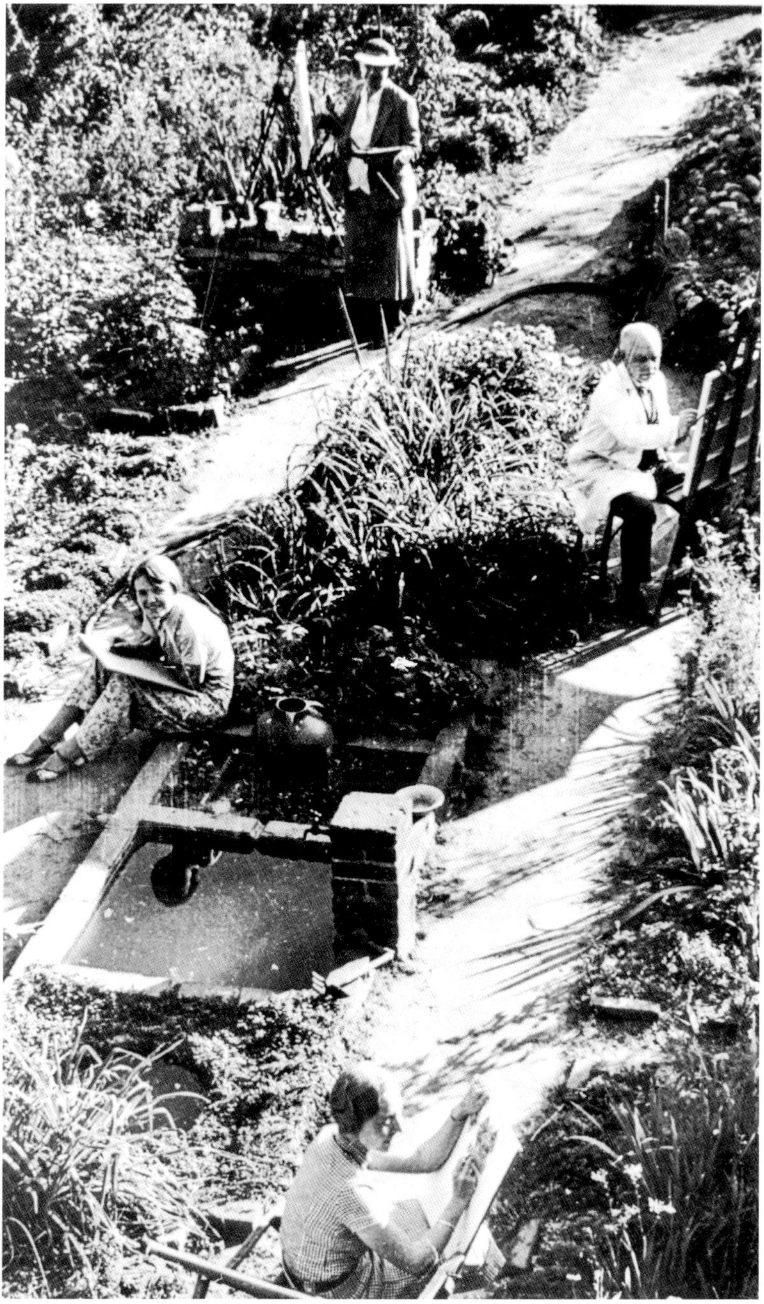

Jewish pupils were, accordingly, bullied and excluded from social life. This was then also the experience of Charlotte who, from 1927, had attended Fürstin-Bismarck-Gymnasium in Berlin's Charlottenburg district, a girls' high school (p. 12).

Following Adolf Hitler's seizure of power on 30 January 1933, Albert Salomon lost his right to work as a teacher. From 1936, he worked at the Jewish Hospital in Berlin. Paula Lindberg-Salomon was now permitted to perform only music written by Jewish composers for Jewish audiences. Her good friend Kurt Singer (1885–1944), who had been dismissed from his post as Musical Director at the Städtische Oper (City Opera House) founded, with permission from the authorities, the Kulturbund Deutscher Juden (Cultural Union of German Jews). Here, Jewish musicians and actors were able to perform together exclusively, and thus to go on earning a modest living. Charlotte's grandparents, Dr Ludwig Grunwald (Berlin 1862–1943 Nice) and Marianne Grunwald, née Bernda (Berlin 1867–1940 Nice) fled Berlin. After a year spent travelling through Italy, they settled in the South of France.

In September 1933, on account of anti-Semitic hostility, Charlotte broke off her studies a year before she was due to take the Abitur, the standard German school-leaving examination. In her last school report her "impeccable conduct" was noted. She therefore continued her studies at home with a series of private tutors.[11] During this time several of her Jewish classmates transferred to private schools. Charlotte preferred instead to work towards acceptance at an art school, which would entail passing an entrance examination. In 1935, she was admitted temporarily and in February 1936 finally to study at the Vereinigte Staatsschulen für Freie und Angewandte Kunst (p. 13). This was only possible because National Socialist laws regarding the permissible percentage of Jews among pupils or students at schools or at places of higher education, which was set at 1.5 per cent, additionally permitted the admission of Jews whose fathers had served at the front during the First World War. Charlotte was the only Jew in her class; she grew increasingly withdrawn and diffident. According to the school's Director, her manner (unappealing as it was to men) had been one of the factors in her favour when her admission had been discussed and then approved – for she was regarded as "posing no danger" to Aryans.[12] Her non-Jewish appearance and her inconspicuous behaviour offered Charlotte a form of protection in a city that was actually precarious for Jews who were identified as such, and in which ever more public amenities – cafés, theatres, park benches – were forbidden to them.

Notwithstanding the intimidating atmosphere even at the art school, Charlotte was happy there. In 1937, she was even sufficiently confident to submit a work (albeit anonymously) in competition for the Sandkuhl Prize, that year's theme being "German Fairy Tales." Her picture *Death and the Maiden* (p. 51) was identified as worthy of the first prize. But it was, of course, clear to all that a Jewish student could not, and thus, would not be allowed to obtain such a distinction. The Sandkuhl Prize was therefore formally "awarded" to Charlotte's classmate Barbara Petzel. After this episode, Charlotte did not return to regular classes at the art school. As she had, however, already matriculated for the academic year 1937/38, she continued to make use of the facilities of this institution in the evenings (p. 468).

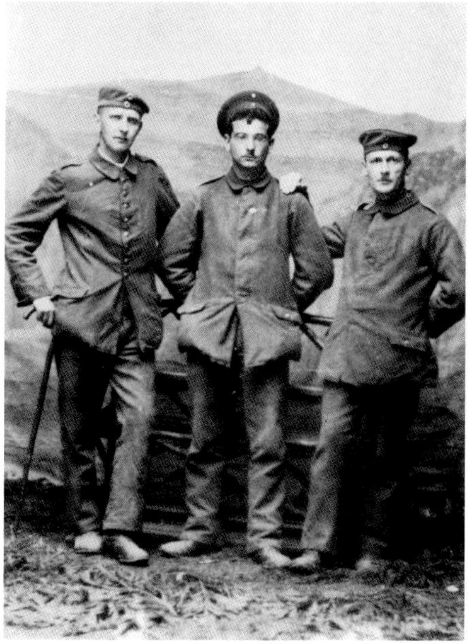

Meanwhile, a man had entered into the Salomon family life who was to play a significant role in Charlotte's future and for her work as an artist: this was the singing teacher Alfred Wolfsohn (Berlin 1896–1962 London; p. 32). He had been sent to Paula Lindberg-Salomon – as a *répétiteur* – through the Jewish organisation Künstlerhilfe (Assistance for Artists), which endeavoured to secure employment for those who found themselves out of work. During this time, Charlotte's stepmother – who was not only a singer – began to commit herself with exceptional energy to assisting her Jewish colleagues to find work or in facilitating their emigration from Germany.

Wolfsohn had served at the front during the First World War (above) from 1914 to 1918. As a stretcher-bearer he had brought those wounded in combat to a field hospital until he himself had been wounded during an offensive, and had been left behind among corpses on the battlefield. Over two million German combatants were killed in action during the First World War. Wolfsohn was one of approximately four million front-line soldiers who returned home disabled and traumatised. He suffered from "shell shock", a form of post-traumatic stress disorder that was manifest in, among other symptoms, uncontrollable shaking. No effective therapies were known at that time. Those affected received inadequate assistance. In his isolation, Wolfsohn devised a method that, in his own estimation, enabled him to look deep within himself and, by this means, to overcome his fear of death. He simultaneously elaborated on a

Alfred Wolfsohn (centre) as soldier in the First World War

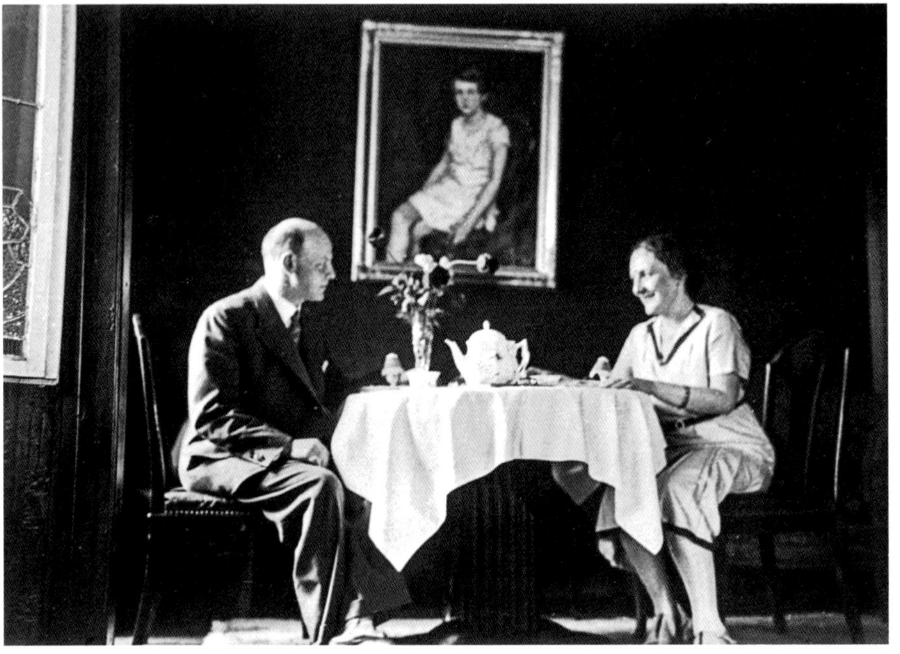

theory relating to the human voice. Through his own experience, he had learnt that a person suddenly placed in mortal danger might well lose his or her voice, but might equally find that this voice had suddenly acquired the unexpected ability to produce a much wider range of sound. In Wolfsohn's view, there existed a connection between death, the human soul, and artistic expression. If a voice was to unleash its maximum range of sound, its owner would not only love life, but would also know death and overcome the fear of death.

Wolfsohn experimented with this method in his work with the singer Paula Lindberg-Salomon. But he also expounded his ideas in his dealings with Charlotte. He was the only one in this young woman's social circle who took a real interest in her and her work. He taught her that a person must dare, in his or her own life, to look danger in the eye. Cultivating a particular relationship with both Salomon women, with Paula as with Charlotte, he played one off against the other. He, in fact, did the same thing with his fiancée (pp. 312–13 and 504). Charlotte saw through this deceit, but she found Wolfsohn's ideas to be fascinating, and she fell in love with him. The Main Section of

Albert and Paula Lindberg-Salomon in their Berlin apartment, c. 1939
Visible in the background is a portrait of ten-year-old Charlotte by Harold Bengen.

Life? or Theatre? – 456 of its 769 images, and by far the most important of these – is concerned with Wolfsohn, his theories, his infidelity, and his interest in women. In a letter of 14 January 1962 Wolfsohn (who had only recently seen an advertisement for the publication of Charlotte's work) wrote to Ruth Liepman that learning of the influence he had had on her had utterly astonished him: "I had never come across a more withdrawn person; never had my endeavours to assist someone with their problems and with the predicaments they had had to overcome in their development seemed to me so hopeless as in this case."[13]

Charlotte greatly admired Wolfsohn, and would wait to intercept him at night at the station from which he travelled home (pp. 458–67). She would hold secret discussions with him in cafés, deceiving both family and friends to do so. Wolfsohn's presence in Salomon's gouaches suggests that, furthermore, there was a sexual element to their relationship (pp. 425–27). Does this reflect the truth of the matter? Paula Lindberg-Salomon never ceased to maintain that such a thing was unthinkable, Charlotte had been, after all, still a child. Alice Croner, however, a pupil of Wolfsohn's, claimed after the Second World War that his commitment to plumbing a person's depths may well have also had a sexual component.[14] In 1946, in his volume *Die Brücke* (The Bridge), Wolfsohn wrote that he believed it to be out of the question that Charlotte had had any experience of physical intimacy with men. But her artistic ability had been such that, even without personal experience of this sort she would have been able to depict passionate physical surrender with as much truth and intensity as if she were drawing from her own experiences.[15] Was he suppressing the truth here? It's likely that we will never know. One thing is, however, for certain: without Wolfsohn, *Life? or Theatre?* would have never come to fruition.

Anti-Semitic discrimination peaked on 9 November 1938 in an explosive outbreak of violence throughout Germany: the so-called "Kristallnacht" (Night of Broken Glass). Albert Salomon was arrested and then interned in the concentration camp at Sachsenhausen. Through her contacts with some engaged in the German resistance, Paula Salomon was able to secure his release. Flight from Germany was now, without doubt, essential to self-preservation, and so the family resolved that Charlotte should leave Berlin as soon as possible. Following his period of incarceration, Albert was still too weak to embark on a journey: but Charlotte had the opportunity to travel to the South of France where she could stay with her grandparents. On 9 December 1938 Charlotte left Berlin on the pretext that she was going to visit her sick grandmother. She would never return. Her father and stepmother fled to Amsterdam in the spring of 1939, and Wolfsohn managed to escape to England. Charlotte would never see them again.

THE SOUTH OF FRANCE 1938–43

Charlotte's grandparents Ludwig and Marianne Grunwald had, in the meantime, found refuge in the Bergerie, the modest guesthouse attached to the Villa L'Ermitage in Villefranche-sur-Mer (pp. 19 and 28). The owner Ottilie Moore (1902–1974) had become acquainted with the Grunwalds years earlier while travelling, and had invited them (p. 20). Moore was the daughter of a very wealthy American entrepreneur, Alfred Gobel, and money for her was no object. She had been widowed while still young but did not enjoy being alone. She was generous and warm-hearted, but could be rather strict on occasion. From 1939, in her secluded villa with its walled garden, she offered shelter to many dozens of refugees, be it for short or longer periods. Among these was Alexander Nagler (1904–1944; p. 34), who had fled Vienna in 1939. In his case the Villa L'Ermitage proved to be the end of his journey. He remained there and was Ottilie Moore's lover for a while.

Charlotte moved in with her grandparents. She felt, almost at once, relieved of the pressure that had weighed her down, the strain of constant fear, and the sense of danger (p. 24). The paintings she did now – of trees, landscapes, the sea – were in a palpably relaxed style (p. 19). It is also possible that she tried to earn money through her painting. Ottilie Moore recognised her talent: she bought landscapes from her and commissioned her to paint the portraits of children and to design New Year's cards (p. 23). Between the two women there evolved a close bond, whereas Charlotte's relationship with her grandfather grew steadily worse. He had no sympathy with her compulsion to paint. But she formed new friendships: with Emil Straus, a friend of her grandparents, who also lived in Villefranche, and with the physician Georges Moridis.

In September 1939, Germany launched an attack on Poland. France and Great Britain, accordingly, declared war on Germany. The Second World War had begun. Charlotte's grandparents suffered greatly from their status as refugees: the dwindling of their savings, and their dependence on Ottilie Moore. And Charlotte was greatly troubled, in turn, by their negative attitude towards her patron, feeling herself unable to deal with this situation. At the start of 1940, she therefore moved with her grandparents to Nice into a small apartment in the Villa Eugénie. By this point Charlotte's grandmother had become so consumed with the fear of the German army's advance that she resolved to take her own life. Her grandparents had taken the precaution of bringing both morphine and the soporific Veronal from Berlin, so that they could end their lives at the time of their own choosing. When Ludwig Grunwald refused to let his wife have any of these medications, Marianne Grunwald tried to hang herself, but this suicide

Landscape with Villa l'Ermitage, Villefranche-sur-Mer, 1939–41
Gouache on paper, 48 x 31 cm. Jerusalem, Collection of the Yad Vashem Art Museum, Gift of Ottilie Gobel Bourne, Washington State

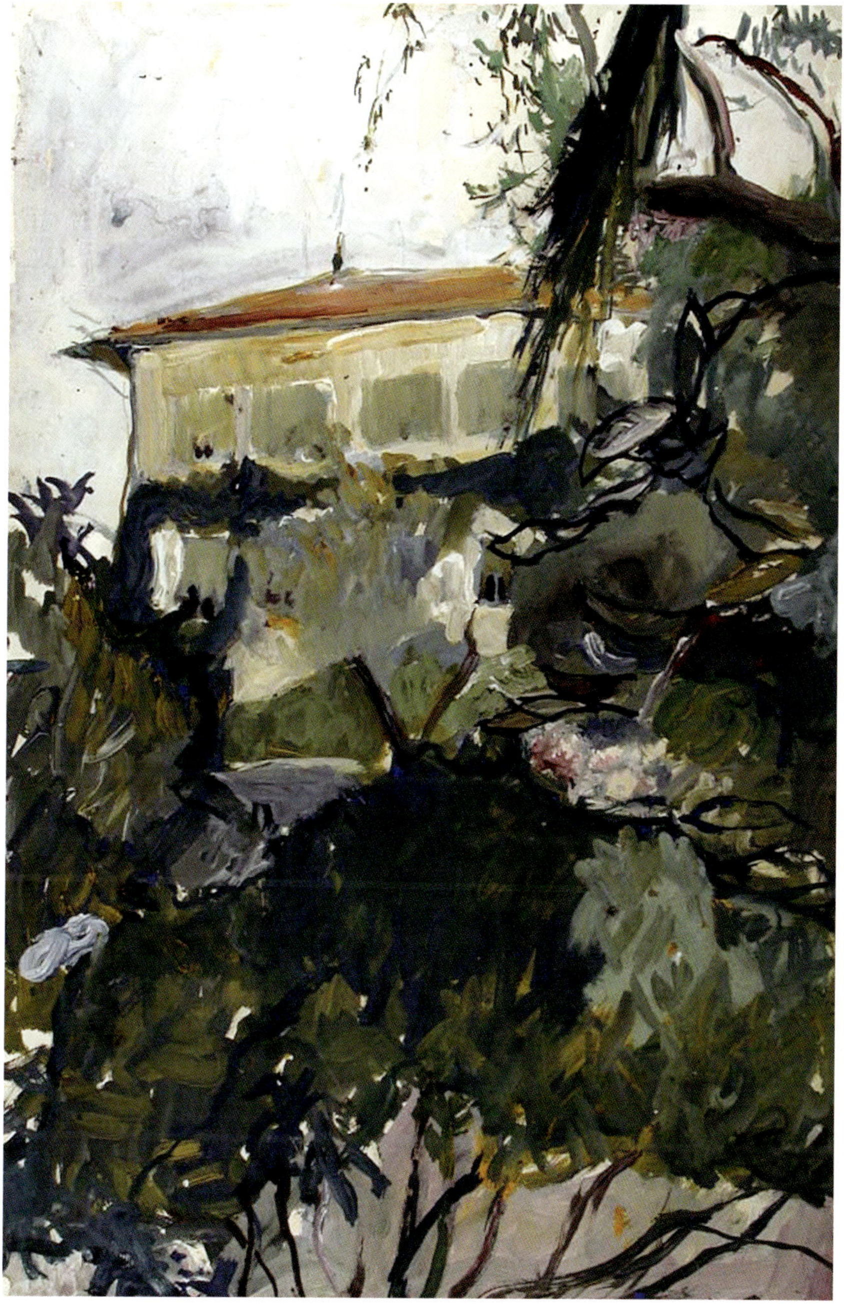

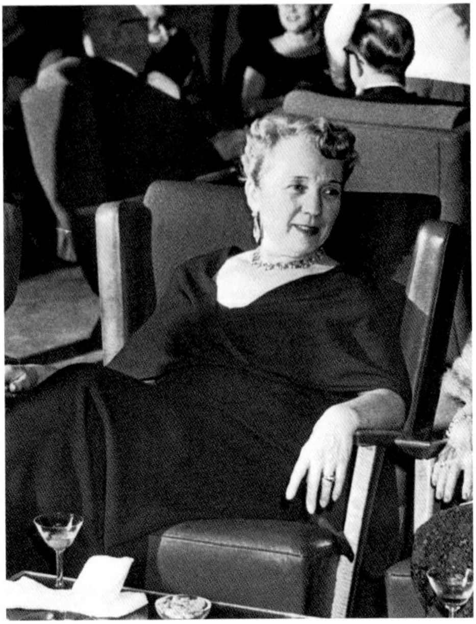

attempt did not succeed. It was only in this situation that Charlotte learnt of her own mother's suicide, and that of other members of the family (pp. 543–48). Deeply shocked at this knowledge, Charlotte endeavoured to do all that was in her power to try to distract her grandmother from the preoccupation with suicide. But these efforts came to a sudden end on 5 March 1940. In a probable attempt to keep her grandmother away from the window, Charlotte was partially dragged through the window, but was able, at the last minute, to cling onto the frame and thus save herself.[16] Then, before her own eyes, her grandmother threw herself out of the window. Charlotte stood back in desperation. Was suicide going to be the only way out for her too?

After France declared war on Germany and French military operations were launched, all alien foreigners were required to report to the authorities. A great many of them were interned. As German nationals, Charlotte and her grandfather were ordered to go to the internment camp at Gurs, in the north-eastern Pyrenees. They arrived there on 27 May 1940. On account, however, of Ludwig Grunwald's advanced age, they were released after only a few weeks, and they returned to Nice.

Although Charlotte's grandfather was infinitely weary of life, he was reluctant to commit suicide, preferring to retreat into his memories as a means of escaping mental decline and a debilitating melancholy. He longed for the now lost world in which he had once felt so secure. For Charlotte, living day in day out with her grandfather became increasingly hard to bear. He demanded care and attention. This emotionally complicated relationship led to the suggestion that her grandfather had violated Charlotte. However, his socially constrained 19th-century Jewish background would have made such behaviour highly transgressive, as social norms and expectations around sexual conduct were strict even for wealthy families. In the last pages of the work we see him in his nightgown, 77 years old, weak, scared and begging Charlotte

Ottilie Moore (1902–1974), Bergquist Collection

for the emotional security he had lost following the death of his wife. But she stays away from him, hardly able to bear her own distress and guilt concerning the death of her grandmother.

Charlotte succumbed to a depression so deep that her parents were sufficiently alarmed by its reflection in her letters to them that they sought the advice of local doctors, psychologists, and graphologists, fearing that she might well kill herself. Those consulted came to the conclusion that their daughter harboured destructive tendencies, but was simultaneously possessed of great talent.[17] Charlotte went to Villefranche as often as possible. It was eventually on the advice of Dr Moridis that she continued to paint as a mean of resisting her sense of distress. Life, as it was in reality – her grandfather growing ever weaker physically, her own sadness about the death of her grandmother, her separation from her parents, and the daily threat of mortal danger – had become simply unbearable, and she recognised that she was in an existential crisis. In this situation two possibilities remained for her: to simply give up and commit suicide, or to oppose the unbearable through daring to embark on "something quite insanely extraordinary" (p. 582).

She resolved to commit herself to the latter option. And here, too, Ottilie Moore was able to offer crucial assistance: above all, through ensuring the peace and space in which Charlotte could re-establish her self-confidence. It is also possible that Ottilie supplied money: for Charlotte to survive and with which she could acquire paper, paints, and brushes. Charlotte's host had, after all, already bought some of her guest's work. Whatever type of support it may have been, it offered Charlotte the opportunity to concentrate almost entirely on her work, the ultimate fruit of this being *Life? or Theatre?* She began to neglect her grandfather, but did, as a duty, go now and then to Nice, being legally compelled as a foreigner to register there regularly with the police. In winter 1941, she moved into the Hotel La Belle Aurore, at Saint-Jean-Cap-Ferrat, remaining there until the spring of 1942. It seems that while there she worked tirelessly, day and night, barely pausing to eat or sleep; and as was later recalled by the hotel's owner Martha Pécher,[18] Charlotte sang to herself while working. By the summer of 1942, *Life? or Theatre?* was completed.

The war, meanwhile, continued and impacted upon every aspect of life. On 27 September 1941, Moore returned to the United States, accompanied by ten of the children (some of them Jewish) who had been living with her. Alexander Nagler remained behind in Villefranche to take care of the villa and four children, while Ottilie paid him 4,000 francs a month for these services. When Ottilie wanted to take her portrait Charlotte had painted, she begged her to leave it: "I want you to stay with me."[19] Charlotte and Alexander gradually fell in love. Had he perhaps agreed to look after her grandfather in her absence so that she could paint in Saint-Jean-Cap-Ferrat? Ludwig

Grunwald's health now continued to deteriorate. One day in Nice he collapsed in the street. He died shortly thereafter on 12 February 1943 after having eaten an omelette laced with Veronal, which Charlotte had prepared for him. This may not have been revenge. After his fall in the street he required constant care, which Charlotte and her husband could not provide while travelling daily between Villefranche-sur-Mer and Nice. Furthermore, as persecuted Jews they had to remain in hiding to avoid being sent to the extermination camps, while the Germans were closing in on southern France, so close to the Italian border. Who would have cared for her grandfather if they were captured, or would he too have faced death? In such circumstances, allowing him to die peacefully could be seen as an act of mercy. Charlotte and Alexander married four months later on 17 June. Dr Moridis, his wife, and Emil Straus served as witnesses. Although food was in short supply, they nonetheless managed a celebratory "wedding breakfast" under parasol pines. In Ottilie's absence, it is possible that Nagler had paid for this with the 600 US dollars he had borrowed from Dr Moridis. Charlotte and Alexander continued living at the Villa L'Ermitage, and became reluctant to leave the house. All around them evidence of anti-Semitism grew apace, and the risk of being betrayed had simply become too great.[20]

What they did not know was that, since April 1943, the police had issued an arrest warrant for "the Jew Nagler."[21] And the Villa, formally registered on 17 January 1942 as a children's home, had aroused the interest of those who coveted the property. The Italian authorities, by now occupying the South of France, had not been at all assiduous in arresting and deporting Jews. But after Italy signed an armistice with its allies in September 1943, the Midi found itself forcibly annexed to the rest of France, which had been under German occupation since 1940. With this, the fate of Charlotte and Alexander was sealed. On 23 September they were arrested at the Villa. The loyal cook Victoria Bravi and her husband heard them shouting as they were led away. (One wonders if Charlotte was able to take her portrait of Ottilie with her). The two were first briefly interned at the transit camp at Drancy, in north-eastern Paris, and were then, on 7 October 1943, deported to the extermination camp at Auschwitz. We may assume that Charlotte, by then five months pregnant, was murdered on the very day of her arrival, 10 October. Alexander is known to have died, exhausted by three months of unremitting forced labour, on 2 January 1944.

After the death of her grandfather, and as she became aware of the increasingly threatening situation, Charlotte had succeeded in getting one more package to Dr Moridis. Wrapped in brown paper, this bore the name of Ottilie Moore (in Alexander's handwriting) as its intended recipient. According to Moridis's daughter, Charlotte handed *Life? or Theatre?* to her trusted friend, begging that he "take good care of it, it is my entire life".[22] We are fortunate that Dr Moridis fulfilled her wish.

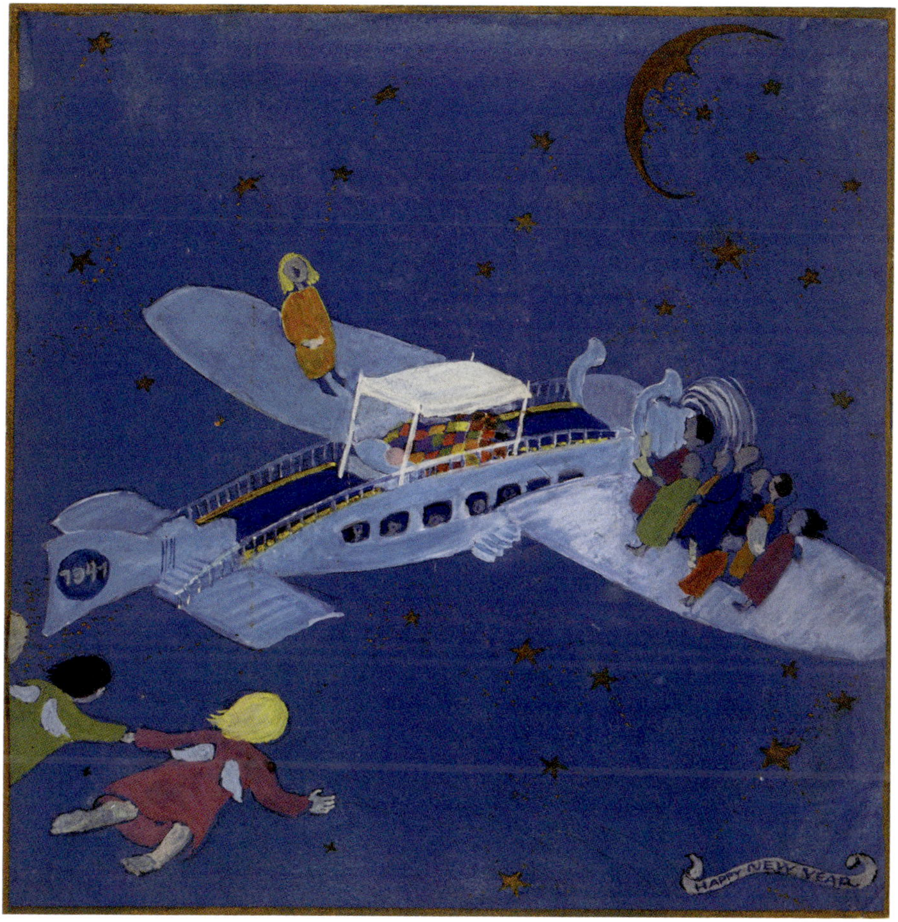

New Year's Card from Charlotte to Ottilie Moore, 1941
Gouache on cardboard, 12 x 12 cm. Private collection

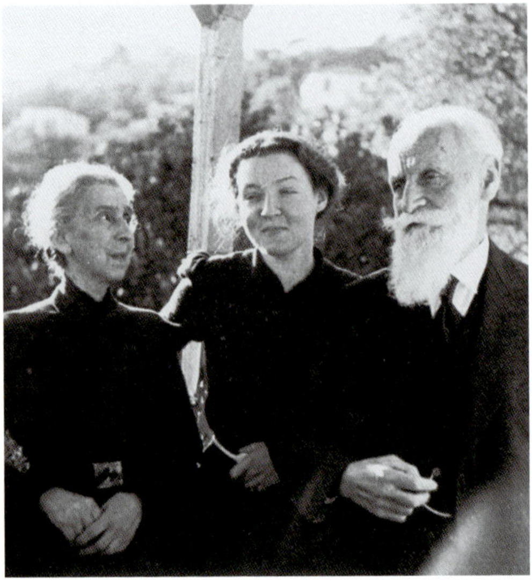 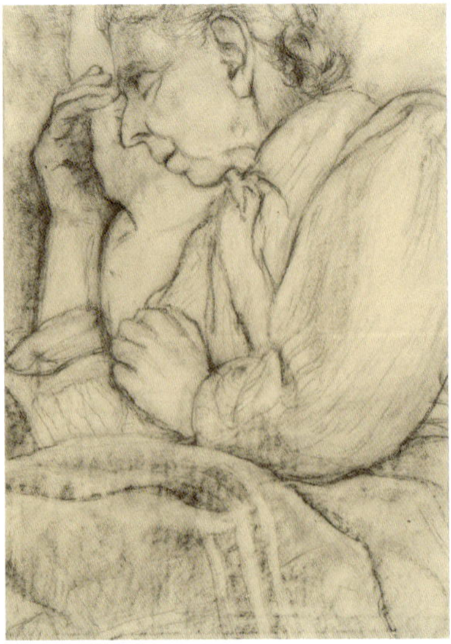

CHARLOTTE SALOMON'S ESTATE

On 8 May 1945 the War in Europe formally ended. Over 50 million people had died, around half of them civilians. In addition there were the six million Jews murdered in extermination camps. Entire cities lay in ruins, reduced to rubble. And millions were now homeless. Only slowly and incrementally did a semblance of "normal life" resume. And neither victims nor perpetrators were willing initially to speak of their wartime experiences.

Paula and Albert Salomon had survived in the Dutch province of Limburg and decided to settle in Amsterdam. To practice as a physician in the Netherlands, Albert (now over 60) agreed to resit the medical examinations. Paula passed the examinations permitting her to work as a nurse and she became Albert's assistant. In addition, she taught singing at the city's Musiklyzeum as she would later at the Mozarteum in Salzburg.

In 1947, it finally became possible for private citizens to acquire foreign currency. Paula and Albert Salomon were thus able to obtain French francs and travel to the South of France in the hope of finding traces of their murdered daughter. They visited Ottilie Moore who had returned from the United States. And it was here in her imposing villa that Albert and Paula discovered pictures painted by Charlotte hanging on the walls. They

Charlotte and her grandparents in Villefranche-sur-Mer, 1939

Portrait of the Sleeping Grandmother, c. 1940/41
Charcoal on paper, 61 x 33 cm. Amsterdam, Joods Historisch Museum

would have, of course, especially liked to have had them. Ottilie was, however, unwilling to part with them. The atmosphere became strained. Paula and Albert did not actually know that it had been Ottilie who had made it possible for Charlotte to commit herself to painting, and had bought the works directly from her. Ottilie Moore did, however, fetch the package wrapped in brown paper, and she presented it to Paula and Albert. They took this back with them to the Netherlands, in addition to Charlotte's *Self-Portrait* (p. 73). It remains uncertain as to whether money had changed hands or whether they had gratefully received it from Ottilie as gift. Thereafter, in any case, Paula only ever spoke negatively of Ottilie Moore.

Since 1947, Charlotte Salomon's *Life? or Theatre?*, along with all its preparatory studies, duplicate images, and accompanying pages of text have been in Amsterdam, where storage was provided in the form of five purpose-designed boxes, covered in gilt-embossed red leather.

Around 1963, Ottilie sold the Villa L'Ermitage, though she remained in Villefranche, moving into an apartment there. The restless life with countless guests, numerous visitors, dinners and parties was now a thing of the past. Yet Ottilie still found loneliness hard to bear. She drank a great deal and gradually got into financial difficulties. Neighbours in the village regarded her with suspicion, although she had, in fact, received official recognition for her contribution to the French Resistance. Around 1965, she received a visit from the journalist, author, and film maker Gerhard Schoenberner. He had been one of the first in Germany to urge an earnest engagement with the crimes of the era of National Socialism. In 1960, he had published *Der gelbe Stern* (The Yellow Star), a book dealing with the persecution of the Jews. In 1966–67, he organised the first exhibition on Charlotte Salomon to be shown in 11 German cities. In 1963, Ottilie Moore impressed him, above all, because she had spoken so lovingly of Charlotte. And he could see the empty space on the wall, from which, according to Ottilie, Charlotte had removed her portrait of her friend to take it with her. Schoenberner even made enquiries as to whether such a portrait had ever been found at Auschwitz. It had not.

II. How Did *Life? or Theatre?* Come about? 1940–47

"The homeless man becomes free in a new sense; and only he who has lost all ties need have no arrière-pensée. And so I hope at least to be able to fulfil one of the chief conditions of my fair portrayal of an era; namely, honesty and impartiality." *Stefan Zweig,* The World of Yesterday, *1942*[23]

"The origin of the following sheets is to be imagined as follows: The person is sitting by the sea. He is painting. A melody suddenly comes into his mind.

As he begins to hum it, he notices that the melody matches exactly what he is trying to put to paper. [...] The differences of the sheets should rest less on the author than on the differences of the characters being developed. The author endeavours [...] to go completely out of herself and to let the characters sing or speak in their own voices. In order to achieve this, much of the artistic values had to be dispensed with, for which I hope will be forgiven for the work of the soul."
Charlotte Salomon, Life? or Theatre?

MUSIC, TEXT, AND IMAGE

Thanks to the "breathing space" that Ottilie Moore had offered her in Villefranche, from the summer of 1940, Charlotte gradually began to find both time and motivation to reflect on everything that had occurred to her, and on those individuals she loved and hated. During this process of self-interrogation she vividly recalled her work *Death and the Maiden*, which had been thought worthy of being awarded the Sandkuhl Prize, and she suddenly recognised that this had really been about her and Wolfsohn together. She understood that she did not need to have any fear of death or committing suicide. Just as one might delve deep into one's emotions, so too might one be in a position to free oneself from death, to – as it were – rise again and overcome one's fear. To be able to love life once again one had to, indeed, as Wolfsohn had himself understood it, first, in a sense, have already "died." As Charlotte came to realise the truth of this, there arose again within her a great love for Wolfsohn, and it was clear to her: "[...] she had to vanish for a while from the human plane and make every sacrifice in order to create her world anew out of the depths" (p. 589). And this is what she did.

Taciturn and inconspicuous though she was, Charlotte had an inner strength and great talent, a capacity for precise observation, and an extraordinarily good visual memory. She was capable of paying particular attention not only to faces, but also to characteristic forms of movement, poses, and facial expressions. During the 1990s, Charlotte's cousin Helen Salomon, daughter of the brother of Charlotte's father, recalled her aunt Franziska, who by that date had been dead for over 70 years, and wrote of how accurate Charlotte's portrayals were of this woman in *Life? or Theatre?*: "They are very akin to the resemblance of her."[24] Anyone who had known Paula and Albert Salomon can confirm that they too can be recognised even decades later in some detail in Charlotte's work, and that Charlotte was very much like her father. Like him, she was taciturn, shrewd, sarcastic, witty, and alert.

In the Salomon household music was clearly of importance, even before Paula Lindberg had come into their lives. In Charlotte's work we encounter a pregnant Franziska seated at a grand piano and playing for herself while awaiting the arrival

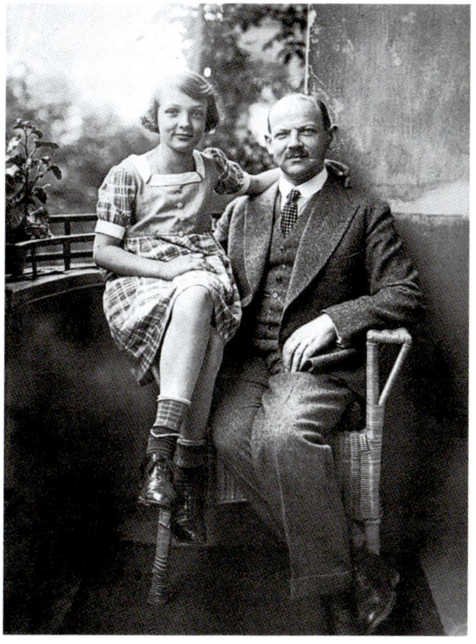

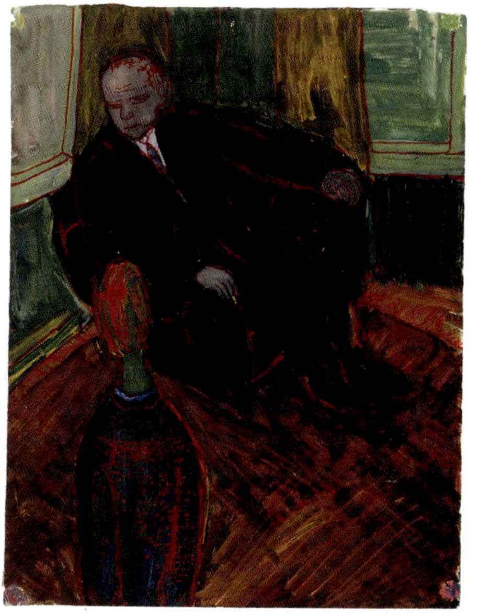

of her husband (p. 116). Charlotte also played the piano, sometimes as an accompanist for Paula.[25] As in every German family of the cultivated, upper-middle class, music was an indispensable component of life for the Salomons. A grand piano was also at the Villa L'Ermitage. One naturally wonders if Charlotte had ever played it.

Charlotte described her grandmother as possessed of the "exacting soul of a gifted woman."[26] As indeed documented in one of Charlotte's images, her grandmother wrote poems in which she recorded her thoughts on the so-called "Kristallnacht" (pp. 490–91). The texts in *Life? or Theatre?* – written at times in somewhat clumsy rhyming verse – reflect Charlotte's own education and her knowledge of German literature. Like music, a love of language and literature was something she had imbibed at home. While the school had enabled her to enrich her knowledge, the art school had given her the technical capacities to realise images exactly as she wished them to appear. It is the union of these three elements – music, text, and image – that constitutes the essence of her work.

Charlotte and Albert Salomon, Berlin c. 1927

Gouache with Charlotte and Albert Kann from *Life? or Theatre?* (see also p. 139)

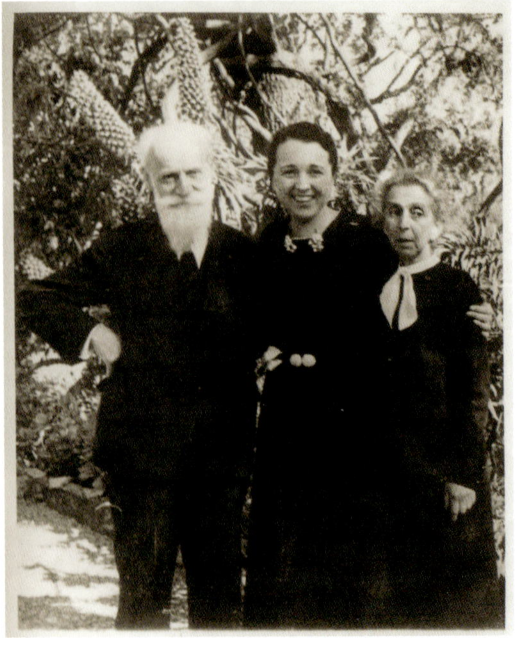

THE ORDERING OF THE IMAGES

We are in Amsterdam. It is five o'clock in the afternoon, and the Stedelijk Museum is closing for the night. After the departure of the wardens, only two people remain in the securely locked building. The curator Ad Petersen had been asked to organise an exhibition of Salomon's work. This was scheduled to run at the Museum Fodor (in those days a dépendance of the Stedelijk Museum, and known for its promotion of the work of young, local, artists) from 2 February to 5 March 1961. In collaboration with the poet Judith Herzberg, Petersen was at the Stedelijk to agree on which of Charlotte's hundreds of gouache sheets were to be included in the forthcoming show. During this one night, the two of them laid out images (which were no longer in the sequence the artist had envisaged) on the steps of the monumental staircase leading up from the museum's entrance hall.[27] They noticed that some of the sheets bore numbers, but decided to pay no more attention to them. Their aim was to agree upon a relatively small number of images that, as a group, would convey the expressive power of Charlotte's work as an artist. In this first exhibition the selection included 17 drawings and gouache sheets supplemented from the collection of Ottilie Moore. After its showing in Amsterdam, this exhibition toured in a modified form in Locarno and Tel Aviv. It also became the conceptual starting point for the show subsequently organised by Gerhard Schoenberner, although this was supplemented with photographs illustrating the context in which Charlotte's own work had been produced.

During a weekend towards the end of December 1960, Paula and Albert Salomon met with Ad Petersen, the German publisher Kurt Wolff (1887–1963) and his wife, and the

Ottilie Moore with the Grunwald grandparents,
Villefranche-sur-Mer, before March 1940

Unnumbered gouache with Ottilie Moore and the grandparents

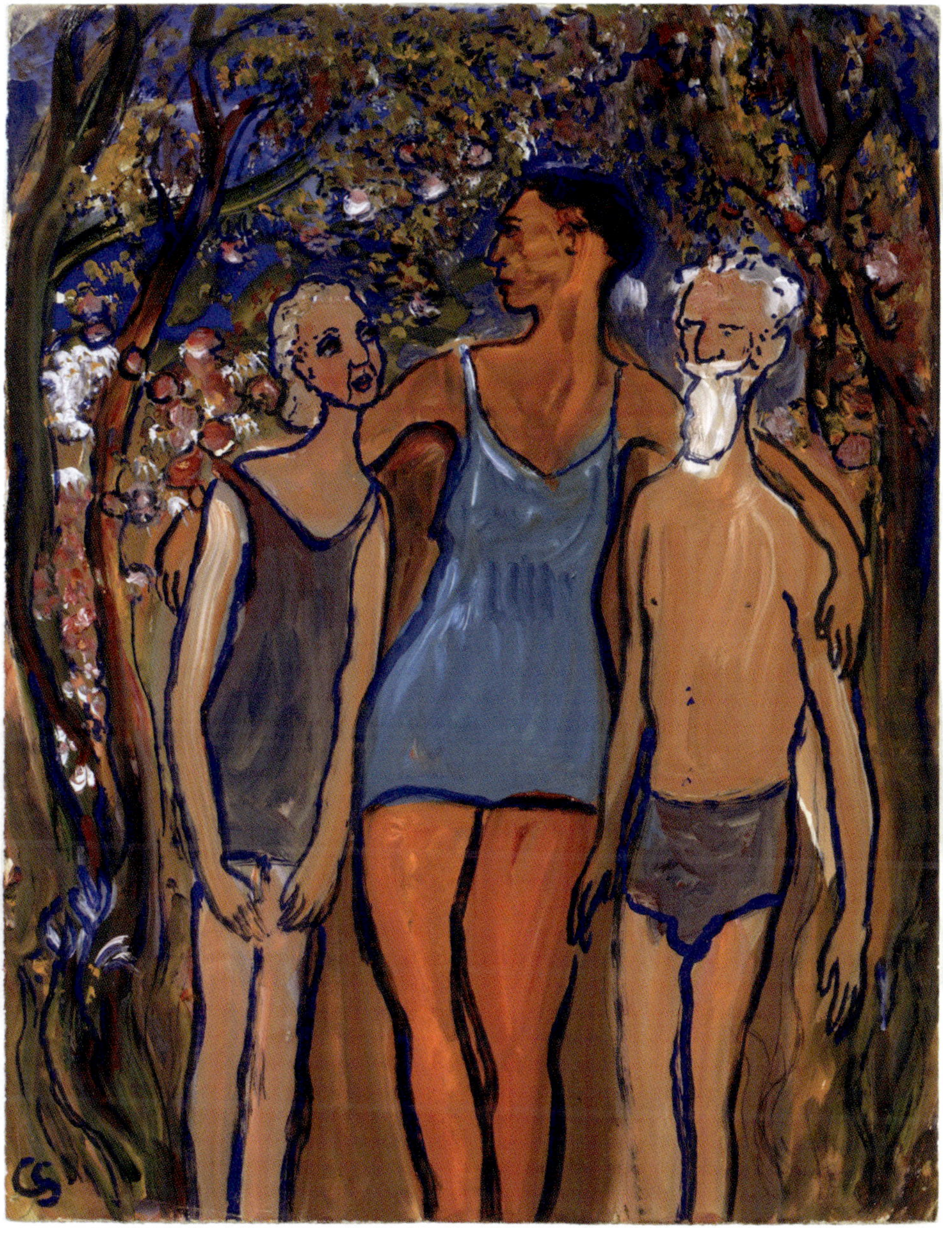

literary agent Ruth Liepman (1909-2001) at the Grand Hotel Dolder in Zurich to agree on a selection of 80 of Charlotte's images to be published as a book. The resulting publication appeared in 1963, in Dutch, German, English, and Italian editions.

In 1971, Albert Salomon, by now 88 years old, was concerned with ensuring that his daughter's work would remain in good hands after his death. Neither the Stedelijk Museum in Amsterdam had an interest in acquiring her work nor the Tel Aviv Museum of Art. Albert Salomon was advised therefore to donate the art to the still small Joods Historisch Museum (JHM), Amsterdam's museum of Jewish history. In early November 1971, the Museum's Director H.L.C. Jaffé and the assistant to its Chief Curator visited Albert and Paula Salomon. On the table around which they sat in the Salomons' living room were the five purposed designed boxes covered in red leather that had been made in the late 1940s to store Charlotte's texts and images. The only condition that Albert and Paula Salomon attached to their donation was that an exhibition of their daughter's work be organised as soon as possible.

It was thus necessary first of all to carry out a careful inspection and registration of the contents of each of the five boxes. By coincidence, the house next door to the Museum Fodor – Keizersgracht 611 – was unoccupied at this time. Two members of the Joods Historisch Museum staff – the Curator Eva Ornstein-van Slooten and her assistant – spent six weeks laying out, row by row, every one of Charlotte's gouache images, together with the sheets of tracing paper bearing related text (p. 9), gradually working their way down through the house from attic to cellar. This is how *Life? or Theatre?* assumed the arrangement we know today. During these worthy efforts the text on one small, unnumbered sheet of tracing paper had, however, been overlooked. It read: "In order to facilitate the reader's understanding, an explanatory text has been added to several sheets. The numbering did not take place entirely according to the order – it is therefore advisable not to confuse the sheets and to look at the order in which they are now arranged". This "order in which they are now arranged"[28] had, however, already been lost sight of in 1960, when a selection of images had been extracted for the purposes of the first exhibition. No one who has subsequently been involved with Charlotte Salomon's work has ever seen her images in the order that Charlotte had envisaged.

NO TITLE PAGE, BUT A PROGRAMME

There is, in essence, no such thing as the six-sheet "title page" of *Life? or Theatre? A Singspiel*. Instead it resembles a programme (pp. 83–93). This confronts the viewer immediately with the paradoxical way in which Charlotte sought to make her own feelings at all bearable. A "Singspiel", the term that serves as the work's subtitle, is suggestive of an already old-fashioned sort of frivolous theatrical entertainment, comprising music, song, and spoken dialogue.

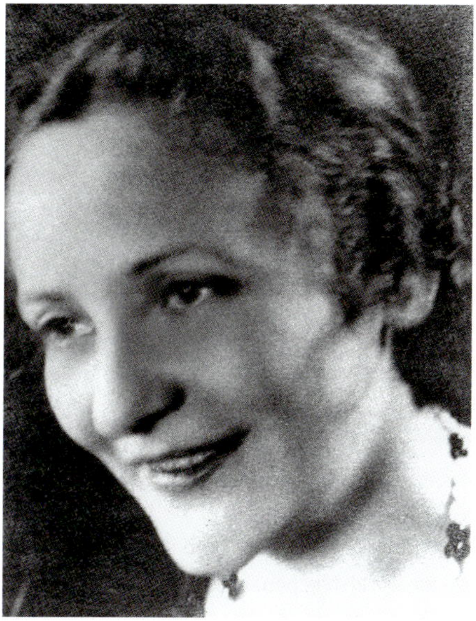

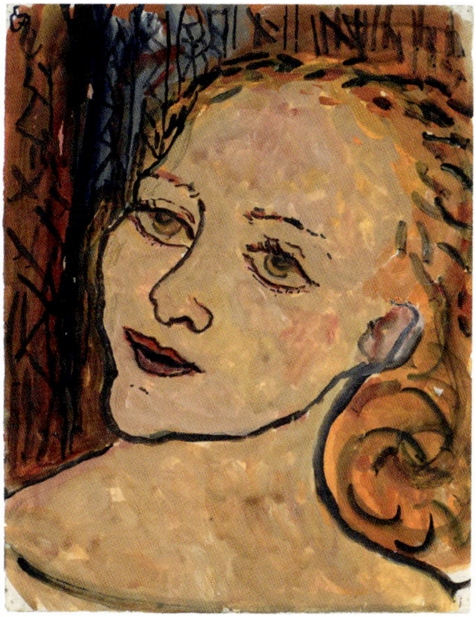

As for the equally baffling main title *Life? or Theatre?*: Charlotte formed the last one in a way that might be (mis-)read as "*Teleater*?" In so doing she expressly introduced a further level of meaning, a play on words, such as she would employ more and more frequently. The term "*teleater*" alludes to the name given to the first opera glasses that were marketed by the Zeiss company until the late 1920s.[29] Employed by Charlotte as a metaphor, in the early 1940s, she was looking back on her own life from a certain distance, as if she were observing it enacted upon a stage, and was making use of opera glasses to bestow sharper clarity on what she saw. Was she devising this artistic work in the hope of being able to answer questions she had always asked herself? There are two further gouache images on which the title is to be found: the last sheet and the corresponding sheet of tracing paper (p. 591). This text reads: "And from that came: *Life or Theatre???*" In the corresponding image we see the artist painting, dressed in a swimming costume, her gaze fixed on the sea. On her back, which is turned towards us, we read the words "*Life or Theater*". Here the title dispenses with its question marks. Does that mean that the artist had at last found the peace that she had sought?

Paula Lindberg-Salomon, c. 1929

Gouache of Paulinka Bimbam

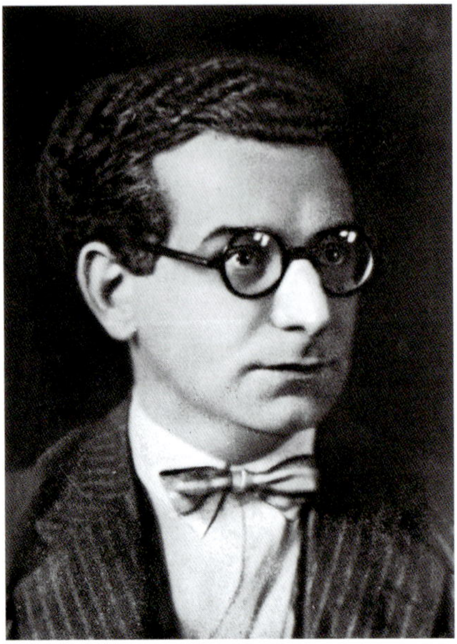

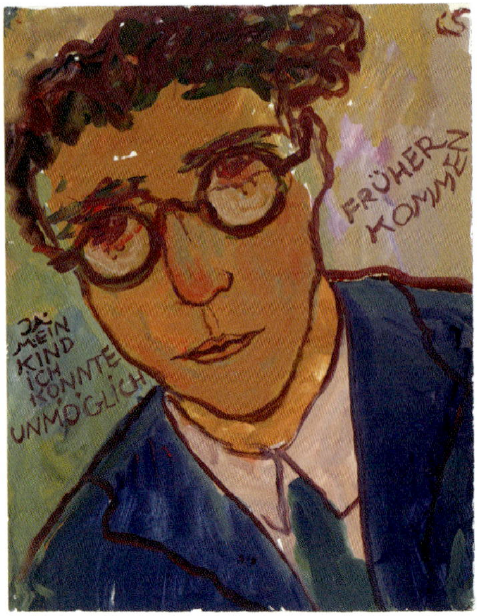

Charlotte did not sign any of her gouache images with her full name, using instead the initial "C" entwined with the initial "S". This monogram initially occurs on the cover of the "programme", where it is enclosed within a yellow and blue line, which is itself enclosed between the words "Ein Singespiel". There is no doubt that "CS" is the author as she indeed describes herself on the sixth and last page of the programme. An inscription in the programme indicates that the work as a whole is dedicated to Ottilie Moore (p. 85). It is striking that Ottilie appears only once in all 1299 images, and on an unnumbered sheet which shows her in the company of Charlotte's grandparents, around each of whom Ottilie has gently placed an arm (p. 29). The scene is rendered to suggest that the protective gesture also embraces Charlotte. And it is clear that we, as viewers, should recognise this sense of security as a sheltering space. It is on the programme's third page that the "the tri-coloured Singspiel" – featuring the primary tones red, yellow, and blue – properly begins. Research has revealed that all the colours employed by Charlotte in *Life? or Theatre?* are derived

Alfred Wolfsohn, Berlin 1932

Gouache of Amadeus Daberlohn from *Life? or Theatre?*:
"Yes, my child, I couldn't possibly get here any earlier." (see also p. 313)

from these three primary tones. Occasionally, white is added to lighten certain colours. Black, on the other hand, is never used. The colours are true, the paint of good quality, and this is also true of the paper, with the exception of only 49 sheets (none of these being numbered). Charlotte's division of her work into a Prelude, a Main Section, and an Epilogue is emphasised through the use of a different colour for the figures appearing in each.

It is by no means difficult to relate the characters of the "Singspiel" with their real-life models, not least on account of the meaningful, (semi-)onomatopoeic pseudonyms that Charlotte has given to each of them. Her grandparents become "Dr and Mrs Knarre – a married couple" (p. 29). The German term "Knarre" means a rattle, a small musical instrument that, through a turning movement, may be induced to emit a scraping sound, devoid of resonance or harmony, and which cannot be played alongside other instruments.

The fictional versions of the Knarres' "daughters Franziska and Charlotte" (p. 218) retain their own real-life first names and identities. The family name "Knarre" is not used together with those first names. As yet, no photograph of either of these two women has been discovered.

Charlotte's father becomes "Dr Kann – a physician" (p. 27). She herself becomes "Charlotte Kann – his daughter"; the artist appearing within her own work. Like her mother and aunt, she retains her own name. The German term "Kanne" means jug with a lid, here doubtless intended as a symbol of a withdrawn personality – be it Charlotte's or her father's. Or perhaps we may be inclined to read "Kann" as in the singular, first and third person, present tense form of the verb "können" (can): to be able to.

Charlotte's stepmother, Paula Lindberg-Salomon, becomes "Paulinka Bimbam – a singer". This name conveys its owner's profession through its distinctive sound (p. 31). Alfred Wolfsohn, as he appears in the Main Section, is "Amadeus Daberlohn – a singing teacher", of whom Charlotte is greatly enamoured. The first name clearly alludes to Mozart while the surname hints at a lack of income (p. 32).

In one of the five boxes, right on the top of the pile of sheets, one page was unlike the others: it was a watercolour measuring 25.2 x 16.4 cm. And in an old file at the Joods Historisch Museum there is a related scrap of paper bearing the inscription: "Who is this supposed to be? Alexander Nagler, Charlotte's husband?" That was indeed the case. Nagler does not, in fact, appear in *Life? or Theatre?* but he did, of course, feature very much in Charlotte's real life. Charlotte included the portrait of her husband for this reason (p. 35).

COLOUR

After he had seen the first published version of Charlotte's work the Dutch printmaker and typographer Willem Sandberg, who was Director of the Stedelijk Museum in Amsterdam until 1962, wrote in November 1963 that he had initially thought that these were not the sort of colours one would readily associate with a young girl, "but now that I see them all together here in this book, used on such a varied scale and applied so diversely – now [I see] it is the colour that held everything together, as if this had become the keynote of the book, [and] perhaps its very essence lies in its colour."[30]

For Charlotte, colour was indispensable to the expression of feeling. This is also apparent if one considers the sequential arrangement of those images in which Daberlohn (supposedly "pressed for time") pays not the slightest attention to his birthday present on which she has lavished such care. The initially warm tones become increasingly colder the greater Charlotte's fury grows (pp. 434–45). In the several image sequences featuring a monologue by Daberlohn, this shifting mood is conveyed through the colour used for his figure and his face (e.g. pp. 325–39). This is perhaps most obvious in the two versions of the image, a lighter and a darker one, in which Charlotte, consumed by despair, utters the words: "I have enough of this life. I have enough of this time" (p. 485).[31] Her father has been arrested, she can no longer endure staying at home and observing Daberlohn and Paulinka; an argument ensues, leading Paulinka to fear that Charlotte might commit suicide herself. Paulinka and Charlotte resolve their argument, but the tension between them persists. This is the first image in which the figure of Charlotte Kann utters the word "I." But we do not know which image Charlotte Salomon painted first. She incorporated the brighter version into the sequence.

CHARLOTTE SALOMON'S WORKING METHOD

To produce so inclusive a work, one would need time: time to think about form, content, characters, and the sequence of events. On the very last pages of the programme an inscription informs us that "the author" had been at work from 1940 to 1942. But if we look carefully we recognise that the "0" of "41" was painted over an earlier indication of the figure "1" (p. 93) This would then indicate that Charlotte produced *Life? or Theatre?* within a single year. On the concluding sheets (pp. 580ff), Salomon inscribed the last conversation that Charlotte Kann had with her grandfather in July 1940 in Nice. It was a year later that Salomon resolved to dare embark on "something quite insanely extraordinary." But first it was essential that she sufficiently overcome her depression so that she could work again. What can one see of this struggle in the work itself?

Charlotte first needed to find her right format. Among the unnumbered sheets there are around 15 sketches of what would later unfold in detail in the sequences of images.

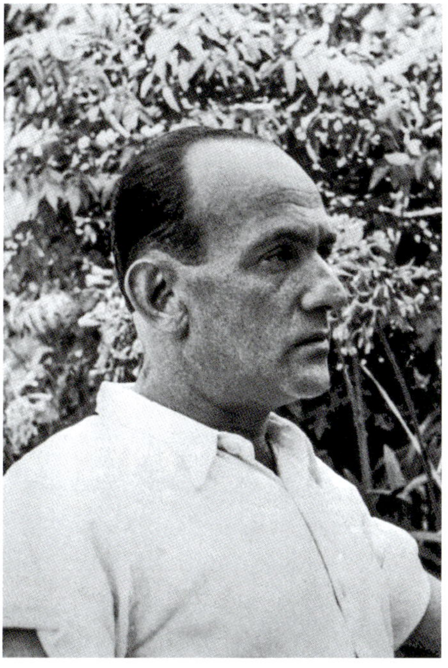

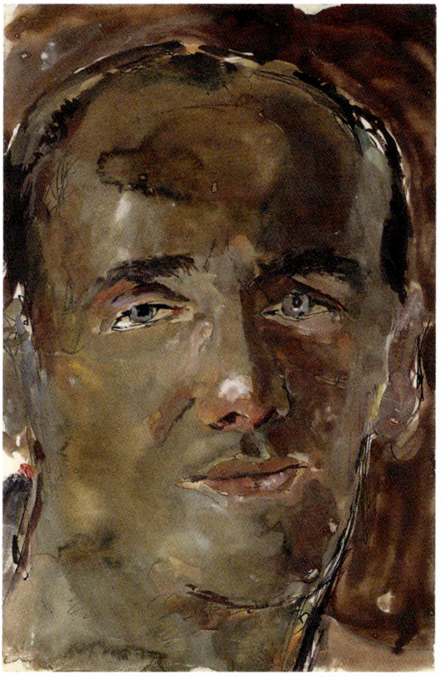

She repeated some ideas, tested out others, sought for something new (pp. 42 and 43). At the art school Charlotte Salomon had already worked on images that were arranged in series, as her classmate Barbara Petzel recalled.[32] Were these images at all comparable with the small book that Charlotte prepared as a gift for her grandparents on the occasion of their Golden Wedding (p. 37)?

Certain situations may have been rendered in various versions. On occasion, Charlotte may have sought to express something which did not always succeed. Upon hearing from Daberlohn an account of his own experiences during the war, for example, Charlotte wanted to illustrate this for him as a birthday present. Salomon made a number of related illustrations, but none of these were incorporated in the final version of the work. One sheet shows Charlotte sitting in her pyjamas, within her lap a book from which she appears to be reading (p. 38). Yet, in response to the violence of the battlefield, she keeps her eyes shut. In *Life? or Theatre?* this episode is retained as

Alexander Nagler, Charlotte's husband, Villefranche-sur-Mer, c. 1938

Portrait of Alexander Nagler, c. 1940
The watercolour differs in size and technique from the gouaches in *Life? or Theatre?*

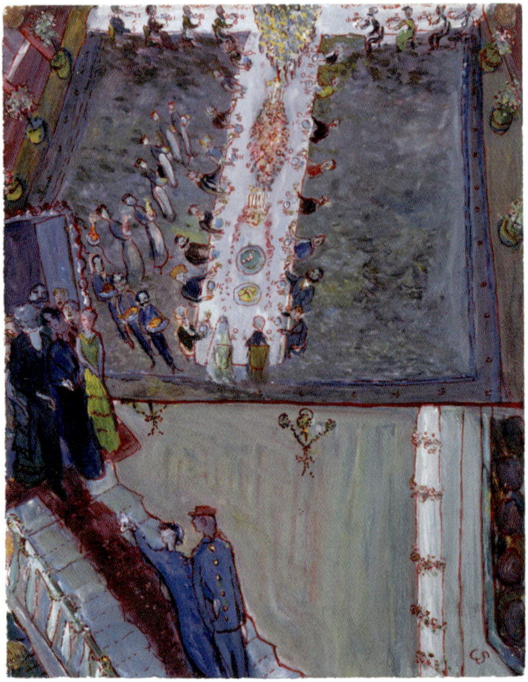

text alone, in the form of a conversation in which Daberlohn narrates his war-time experience to Paulinka (pp. 305–10). Daberlohn's text *Orpheus or the Way to a Mask*, an exposition of his theory that will prove of enormous significance for Charlotte, is depicted as an open book, the easily legible text of which we see Daberlohn still writing (pp. 447–56).

Were the images painted in the order familiar to us now? We will never know. As we can see, the Prelude is stylistically distinct from the Main Section and the Epilogue. It is customary, for instance, that a number of scenes are presented on a single sheet, and that the action sometimes continues onto the next sheet. Only in sequences from the life of Charlotte's grandmother are there several striking scenes that occupy an entire sheet (pp. 207–26). Each sheet bears an indication of the piece of music that belonged with it. Because each of the images drawn is in such detail, there is little scope for text to be incorporated. The Prelude is therefore supplied in its entirety with a separate series of tracing paper sheets bearing related text. Each of these is attached to the relevant image sheets by means of three narrow paper strips. This makes it clear that the images were painted first and the corresponding text subsequently added to it – a rather time-consuming way of working.

In the Main Section the same procedure is employed for the first six images. Thereafter, the images are more expansively composed and the text is written directly into the pictorial structure. Not least on account of this sudden change, it is plausible that we are dealing here with two distinct periods of work. The Prelude is divided into two "Acts", and the first of these is divided into five scenes. In the Main Section, however, the narrative is divided only into chapters. And only a single piece of music is specifically identified. This is the "March of the Toreadors" from Georges Bizet's *Carmen*, which is mentioned on the first page. This page recounts the

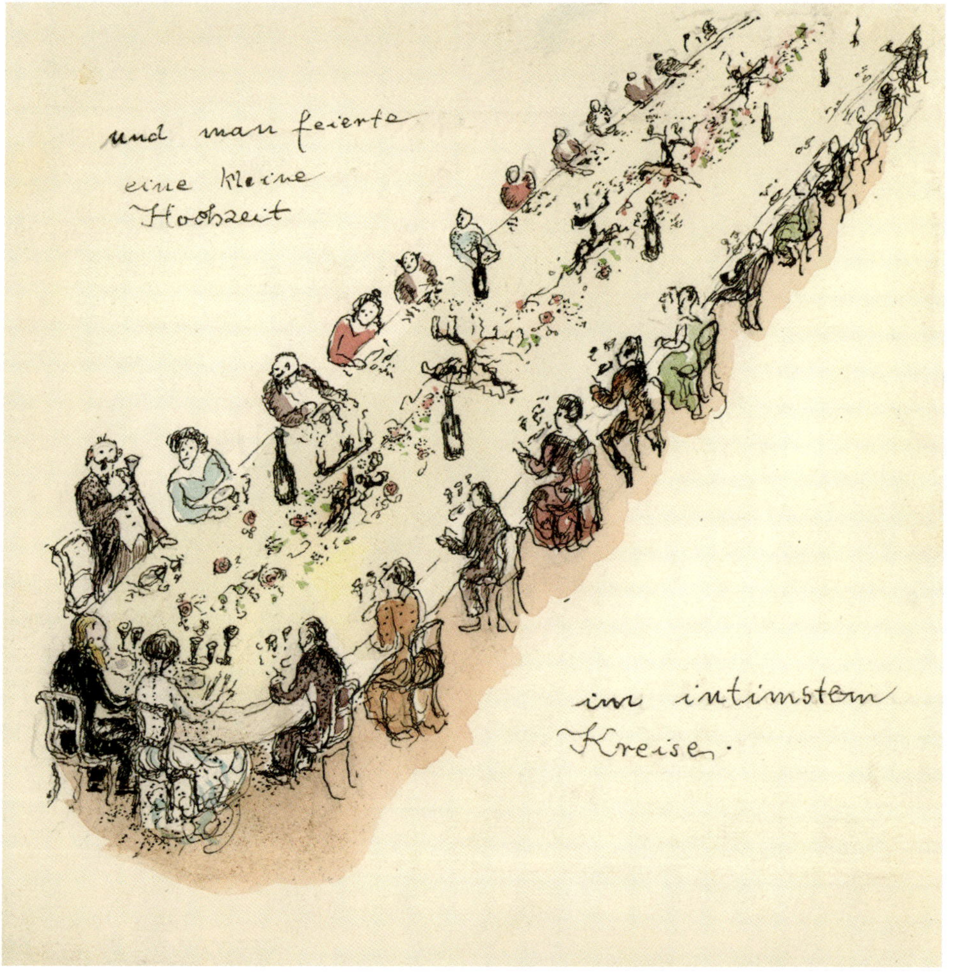

The gouache with the wedding feast of her parents in *Life? or Theatre?* shows a striking similarity to the sketch of 1939 (see also p. 110).

Charlotte was already working in small series at the academy. This depiction of a party comes from a small book that Charlotte painted in 1939 for the 50th wedding anniversary of her grandparents.

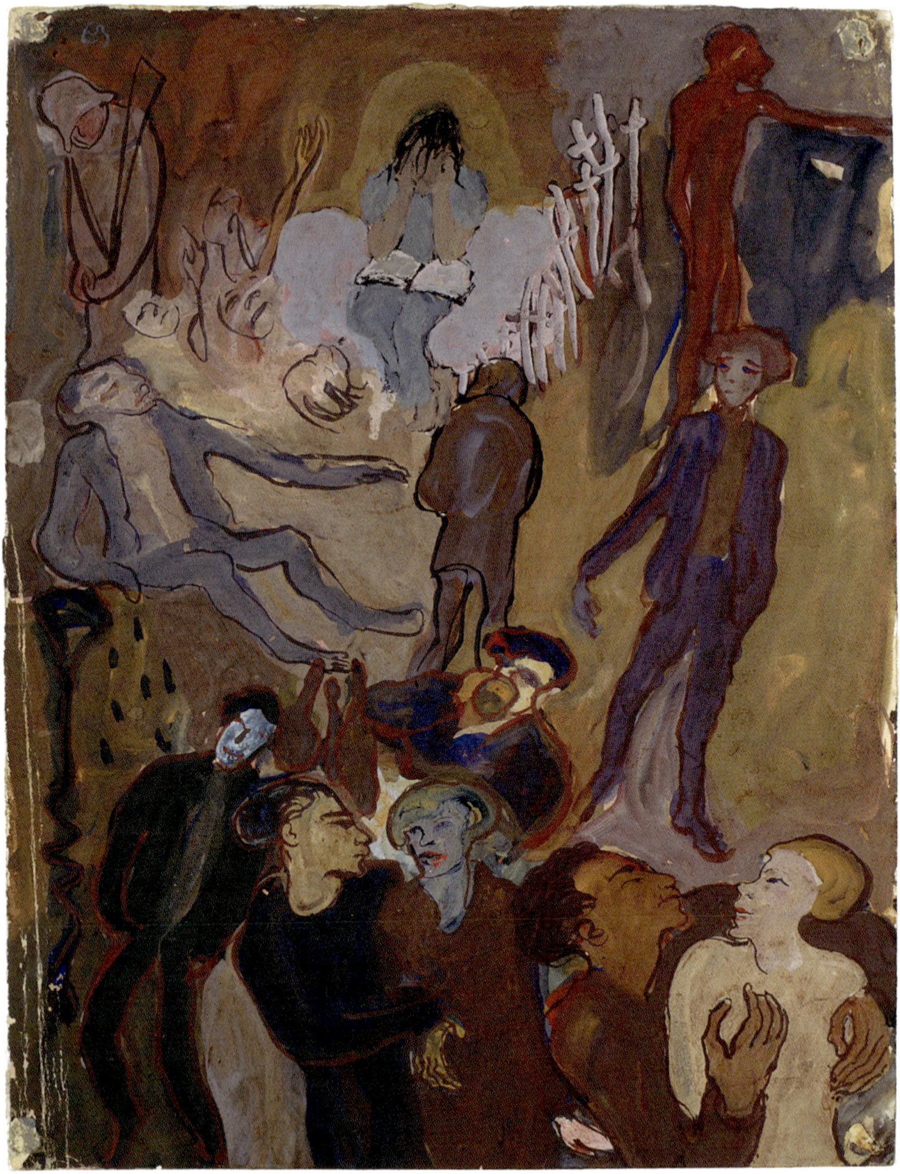

Unnumbered sheet from *Life? or Theatre?*: Charlotte reads Daberlohn's book in which he describes his experiences in the trenches.

arrival of Daberlohn (p. 280). Other pieces of music occur only incorporated within the narrative.

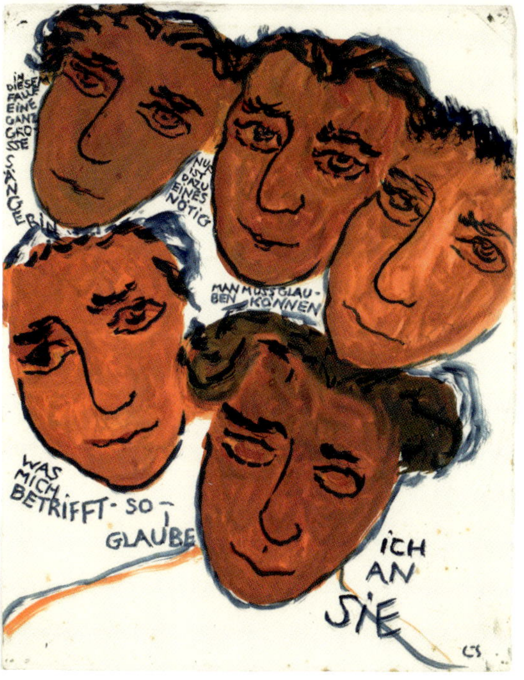

Now we no longer find several scenes appearing on the same sheet. On the contrary, a notable feature is an entire series of faces, most particularly that of Daberlohn taking up a series of sheets, which is repeated dozens of times (right). By this we are able to participate in the conversation that Charlotte has with him, and are thus introduced to those theories that she will apply to her own work. In *Die Brücke* Wolfsohn writes that when he spoke with Charlotte and tried to help her, she looked at him with an intent and attentive gaze that "[made] me play the fool and finally allow[ed] my own words to unravel so that I was sharing with her every deep insight into my own experience [...]."[33] Both individuals went to the absolute limit to seek out the truth of their lives, even if this method proved to be bitter, harsh, and frightening.

The Epilogue treats in a very sketchy manner the suicide of her grandmother, the role suicide had played in the family's history, the outbreak of the Second World War, and the return to Nice from the internment camp at Gurs. The death of her grandmother has an enormous intensity as well as deep emotional resonance, its unbearable quality making it necessary that Salomon work through it with some speed. This episode is the apotheosis of *Life? or Theatre?* It freed Salomon from the apparent necessity of committing suicide.

Gouache depicting Amadeus Daberlohn and his theories:
"In this case a really great singer, but just one thing is necessary: one should be able to believe. As for me, I believe in you."

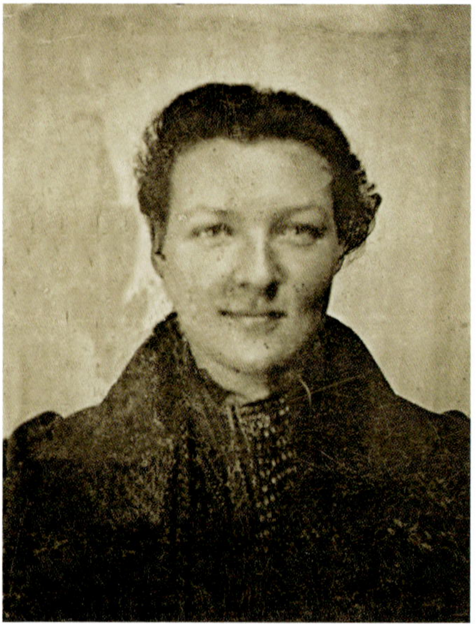

THE PRINCIPAL THEMES: LIFE AND DEATH

Life? or Theatre? covers the years 1913–40, a period encompassing both the First and Second World Wars. The first two pages deal with the suicide of Charlotte's aunt Charlotte in 1913 (pp. 96 and 99), the third shows her mother Franziska, who had wanted to become a nurse (p. 100) at the outbreak of the First World War. The last image shows a conversation between Charlotte and her grandfather in Nice after they had been released from the internment camp at Gurs: "You know, Grandpa," she says, "I feel as if the whole world needs to be put together again." To which her grandfather's answer is: "Now conclusively take your life, so this babble finally stops" (p. 579). It is not war alone that frames the story, but, and above all, the question of life and death.

In the Main Section everything hinges on the increasing dangers of life in Germany and the insidious approach of death. Only two pieces of music are featured in this part of the work. And both – the aria "Bist du bei mir" ("When you are with me") by J. S. Bach, and the opera *Orpheus and Euridyce* by Christoph Willibald Gluck (1714–1787) – are concerned with the need of coming to terms with death and loss. Here, this is the music that accompanies the exposition of Daberlohn's theories. Other themes of indubitable importance from the period to which Charlotte Salomon belongs – the obtrusive "modernity" of life, in which new media such as film and radio played quite a part – are barely touched upon, although they are acknowledged in the unnumbered sheets. Significantly, however, she does adopt the film and comic strip format, perhaps making it unnecessary for them to become explicit "subjects" in their own right. Or would the incorporation of further aspects perhaps have distracted too much from Salomon's central theme? And might this also have been the case with other emotional developments, such as Charlotte's reluctant decision to break off her studies at the art school?

Two sheets (pp. 372 and 374) are the heart of the work. Here, one of the drawings that Charlotte shows to Daberlohn is called *Death and the Maiden* (p. 50). "That's the two of us," he says (p. 51). But nowhere in *Life? or Theatre?* does one learn that this is

Passport photograph of Charlotte, c. 1939

indeed the prize-worthy picture which indirectly leads Charlotte to break off her studies. The threat posed by the rise of National Socialism is vividly evoked. A group of splendid unnumbered sheets capture Charlotte's abhorrence: she draws the Nazi swastika in reverse – an almost imperceptible yet highly significant detail (pp. 239 and 472). Yet there is no record of the chaos at the internment camp at Gurs. This, too, was perhaps perceived as a distraction from the principal theme, from what really concerned her most.

For veritably engraved on her memory is the sight of her grandmother throwing herself out of the window, one foot in the air still quivering. This image cries out for processing. In the sheet depicting the suicide of Charlotte's mother (p. 131), the open window is shown twice; and below, and barely perceptible at the centre of the window frame, a foot is again to be seen. In one sheet (p. 133) we find the mother in the very same pose, throwing herself out the window like the grandmother in another sheet.[34] Death is powerful – even during the inter-war years. Charlotte painted this to be better able to accept it. Only when she had tried out everything and was satisfied did she number in blue paint each of the selected sheets. If we are to believe what we are told in the programme, this numbering procedure would have been carried out in 1942. This would mean that Charlotte produced *Life? or Theatre?* between July 1941 and an unknown date in 1942, that is, in not much more than a year and a half. It would only have been possible for a work of such scope to be produced in such a short time had the author disappeared as it were, from the surface of the earth and had worked incessantly, day and night. Her absorption in her work, her obsessive preoccupation with death, and her understanding of the world that was collapsing around her made her increasingly alienated from her grandfather. As a refugee, he had lost so much: his possessions, his authority, his dignity. And as a widower, he was unable to accept his lifelong pain. He clung to the world of his own past, which was already hastening towards its own end. For Charlotte, this way of thinking had become unbearable. Yet it was her duty to go on caring for him, the only alternative being to return to the internment camp at Gurs.

III. Making a Name for Oneself: from 1960 to today

"I firmly believe – that this war represents a sort of biblical deluge. It will once and for all be revealed that humanity's culture and education are laughable entities that we have ourselves constructed only to see them helplessly destroyed by a ferocious power through their own inadequacy. Are war and destruction perhaps the evidence of how exhausted our culture is? And what does all this signify when set against the supreme power that controls our lives? [...] Perhaps, my dearest, it is truly the case that,

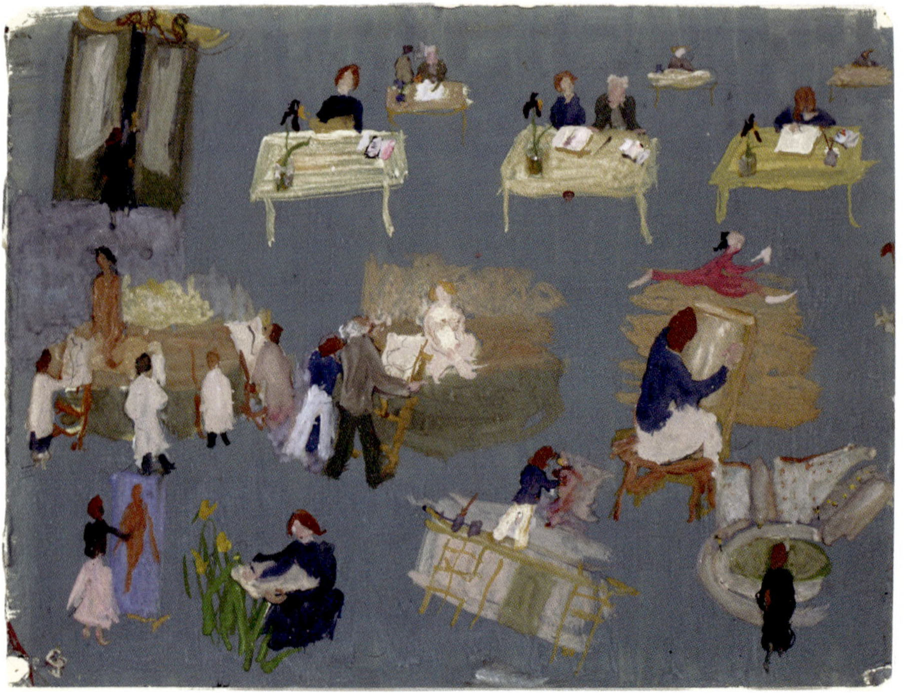

with this present war, even that theatre in which humanity has always enacted itself is on the way out – that all of humanity is now tested through the most difficult sorrow and experience in order to move towards a more truly vital form of existence. Thank you. I would almost like to say: Amen."
Charlotte Salomon, Letter to Alfred Daberlohn, Februar 1943[35]

"Her aim was 'to cleanse' the world [...] by using all the disciplines and senses available to her in order to set free the cathartic power that comes with the making and contemplation of art. [...] Life? or Theatre? is indeed a great opera of the mind and eye, a record of an epic modern tragedy that demands concentration and deserves eternal applause."
Norman Rosenthal, Royal Academy of Arts, London, 1998[36]

Charlotte executed about 15 such sketches to prepare for the series on which she subsequently elaborated.

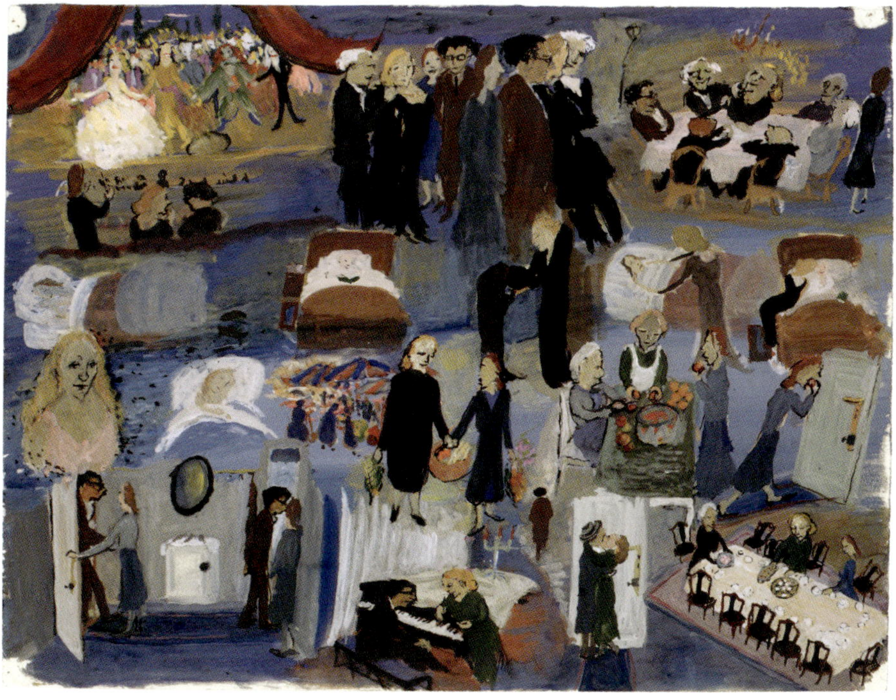

THE BEGINNINGS OF INTERNATIONAL RECOGNITION, 1981

The exhibition staged at the Joods Historisch Museum in Amsterdam in 1972 showed, for the first time, 250 gouaches in a sequence that reflected Charlotte Salomon's own numbering of the sheets. This show attracted many thousands of visitors, and two newspaper articles were devoted to it. When the museum was about to close on the final afternoon, one visitor had to be persuaded to leave. This was the filmmaker Frans Weisz. He finally made a formal request for approval of his plan to make a feature film about Charlotte Salomon. Also contributing to the screenplay was Judith Herzberg. A few years later, with the additional collaboration of Gary Schwartz (who wished to publish an edition of all 769 numbered gouache sheets), the project became an international co-production. An agreement was reached that the film and book should appear at the same time, and that a new Charlotte Salomon exhibition at the Joods Historisch Museum should be staged simultaneously. By 1981, this triple project was complete. The book appeared in German, Dutch, and English editions. The museum, meanwhile, was seeking to exhibit the work of Charlotte as if it were that of an autonomous artist, not of a victim of the Holocaust, even though she had been murdered in Auschwitz. As no work by her was,

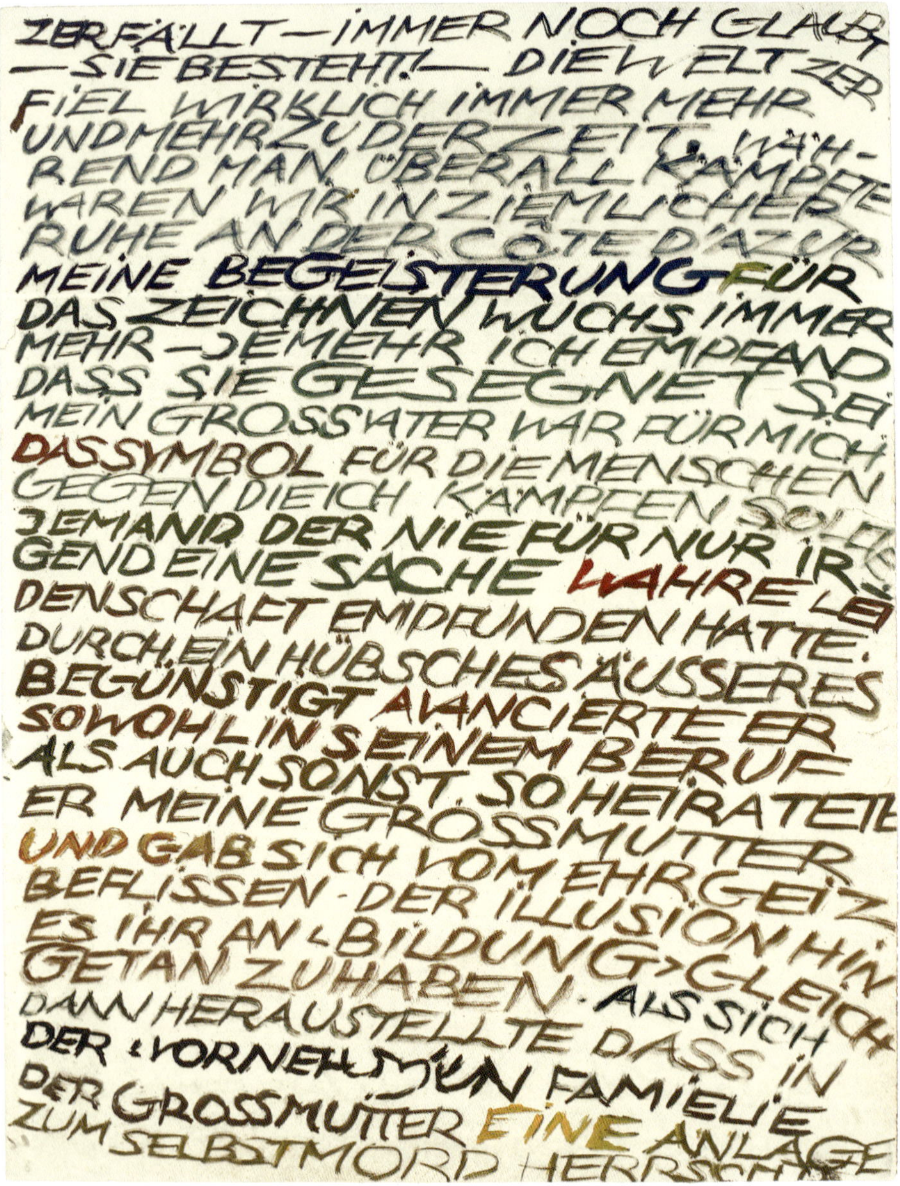

ZERFÄLLT – IMMER NOCH GLAUBT
– SIE BESTEHT! – DIE WELT ZER
FIEL WIRKLICH IMMER MEHR
UND MEHR ZU DER ZEIT. WÄH-
REND MAN ÜBERALL KÄMPFTE
WAREN WIR IN ZIEMLICHER
RUHE AN DER CÔTE D'AZUR
MEINE BEGEISTERUNG FÜR
DAS ZEICHNEN WUCHS IMMER
MEHR – JE MEHR ICH EMPFAND
DASS SIE GESEGNET SEI
MEIN GROSSVATER WAR FÜR MICH
DAS SYMBOL FÜR DIE MENSCHEN
GEGEN DIE ICH KÄMPFEN SOLLTE
JEMAND DER NIE FÜR NUR IR-
GEND EINE SACHE WAHRE LEI
DENSCHAFT EMPFUNDEN HATTE.
DURCH EIN HÜBSCHES ÄUSSERES
BEGÜNSTIGT AVANCIERTE ER
SOWOHL IN SEINEM BERUF
ALS AUCH SONST. SO HEIRATETE
ER MEINE GROSSMUTTER
UND GAB SICH VOM EHRGEIZ
BEFLISSEN – DER ILLUSION HIN
ES IHR AN «BILDUNG» GLEICH
GETAN ZU HABEN. ALS SICH
DANN HERAUSSTELLTE DASS IN
DER «VORNEHMEN» FAMILIE
DER GROSSMUTTER EINE ANLAGE
ZUM SELBSTMORD HERRSCHTE

A sheet of Charlotte's *Letter to Amadeus Daberlohn.* Of the original 25 sheets only 16 are preserved (translation see p. 598, note 37).

at that point, to be found on the art market, and there was as yet no widely available "guidance" as to how to approach her achievement, publishing and exhibiting her work, researching it, and making films about it were the only means of achieving a modicum of international recognition for Salomon.

Thanks to the book and the screening of the film, important new contacts were established. In 1983/84, an exhibition was organised that toured America and Israel, where it was chiefly shown in museums devoted to Jewish history, culture, and art. In Berlin, Christine Fischer-Defoy researched Charlotte's time at the art school and the career of Paula Salomon in the context of Jewish cultural life after 1933. Her research made possible the inclusion of a documentary section into the Charlotte Salomon exhibition at the Akademie der Künste in Berlin in 1986.

Around 1985, Norman Rosenthal, Exhibitions Secretary at the Royal Academy of Arts in London, happened to meet Paula Lindberg-Salomon at the Salzburg Festival. She told him about her stepdaughter's work. This prompted him to travel to Amsterdam to see the art for himself – and to fall at once under its spell. It was, however, to require a full 14 years before Rosenthal was able to secure the funding, in 1998, of an exhibition of Charlotte Salomon's work at the Royal Academy, thereby honouring this as yet little-known female artist at an illustrious venue more readily associated with established art world "stars" such as Claude Monet, George Grosz, and Joseph Beuys. The exhibition was a great success, although it was not until the presentation of images from *Life? or Theatre?* at dOCUMENTA (13) in Kassel in 2012 that Charlotte Salomon's place was truly secured in the canon of 20th-century art.

The now, far greater visibility of Charlotte Salomon's work ensured that many more art historians took a scholarly interest in her. In 1994, Mary Lowenthal Felstiner, Professor of History at San Francisco State University, published a biography: *To Paint Her Life: Charlotte Salomon in the Nazi Era*. With extraordinary patience Felstiner had sought out individuals – be it in Berlin, France, or the United States – who had known Charlotte Salomon and the context in which she had lived. This effort was rewarded by the discovery of a great deal of new information. In 2013, Darcy C. Buerkle, Professor of History at Smith College (Northhampton, Massachusetts), published her own volume: *Nothing Happened: Charlotte Salomon and an Archive of Suicide*, which succeeded in throwing valuable light on a difficult but crucial aspect of Charlotte's career.

In the unabridged edition of *Life? or Theatre?* published in France and the Netherlands in 2015, the original sheets of text were published for the first time, being provided alongside the images, albeit on a smaller scale. This encouraged a new intensity in general interest in Charlotte Salomon's work. In 2015/16, there was an exhibition in Nice at the Musée Masséna, in part encouraged by the success of David

Foenkinos's novel *Charlotte* (2014). Currently, Batya Wolff is carrying out archival research when precisely Charlotte Salomon worked on *Life? or Theatre?*

In 1984, the first theatre piece to be based on Charlotte Salomon's *Life? or Theatre?* was staged in Jerusalem, directed by Rinath Joyce Miller and Marc Rittenberg. Soon, numerous stage adaptations were being prepared. Among these was *Charlotte, Life? or Theatre?* staged by Elise Thoron in 2001 in Philadelphia. And an opera *Charlotte Salomon*, with music by Marc-André Dalbavie, received its première at the Salzburg Festival in 2014. The ballet *Charlotte Salomon: Death and the Painter*, with choreography and staging by Bridget Breiner and music by Michelle DiBucci in 2015 was presented in Gelsenkirchen.

A DOCUMENTARY, AND NEW DISCOVERIES CONCERNING DATING

In 2000, Paula Lindberg-Salomon died at the age of 102. She had been the supreme source of information on the life of her stepdaughter. In 2010, the Joods Historisch Museum commissioned Frans Weisz to shoot a documentary based on discussions with witnesses of Charlotte's life and work. In 2012, this film – *Leven? of Theater?* – had its première. The film together with all the footage shot, could be seen as marking the end of an era as well as constituting a unique body of source material on which scholars might draw in their research.

During the course of the negotiations that preceded work on the documentary, an especially interesting piece of information came to light. In the 1970s, Frans Weisz and Judith Herzberg had painstakingly gone through Charlotte's work, sheet by sheet, together with Paula Lindberg-Solomon. During these meetings that lasted for weeks the latter had made available to them a series of sheets with text that had never formed part of the collection of Lindberg-Solomon's work in the Joods Historisch Museum. While Weisz and Herzberg were permitted to examine these, they had to promise to divulge their content. Herzberg compared her own transcription of the pages of text in the possession of Paula Salomon with those in the collection of the Museum and discovered that they complemented each other. The only other person permitted to know of this situation was the Director of the Museum. To make doubly sure that the information remained secret, the transcript was not made available to the Museum at the time. After Paula Lindberg-Solomon's death, however, the Museum collection was not enriched by the addition of these papers from her estate. And no one knows where they are now to be found. The complete text of what has, in the interim, come to be called the "Letter to Amadeus Daberlohn", is known only in the form of a typed transcript now in the possession of Frans Weisz. And, of the initial 25 sheets of this letter, only 16 are present in the Museum (p. 44).[37]

The question arose as to whether the text that did not belong to the Museum ought to be used by Weisz in preparing his documentary. The "letter" appears to have been written by Charlotte to Daberlohn in February 1943, even though his name is not mentioned. She tells him she has been drawing her utterly exhausted grandfather (right), whom she knows to be dying because she had laced the omelette he has just eaten with Veronal and this had already begun to exert its deadly effect. Did Charlotte wish to spare her grandfather the agonies and indignities of an extended old age? For Paula Lindberg-Solomon and her own generation, conduct of this sort was just as morally reprehensible, and thus, unacceptable, as was suicide; and this makes her request that the content of the texts in her own possession be kept secret quite comprehensible. Over the decades since, however, and in very many countries, attitudes to the care of the terminally ill have evolved, in most cases in the direction of a concern that such patients be assured of freedom from pain, respect for their personal dignity, and the presence of those in whose company they wish to spend their last hours. Measures have been taken in some countries to secure such benefits as a legal right, and to ensure legal protection for the others involved in each case, be it as medical staff or professional carers, as family members or close friends. The ethically problematic subject of assisted dying is, nonetheless, still a subject of heated debate.

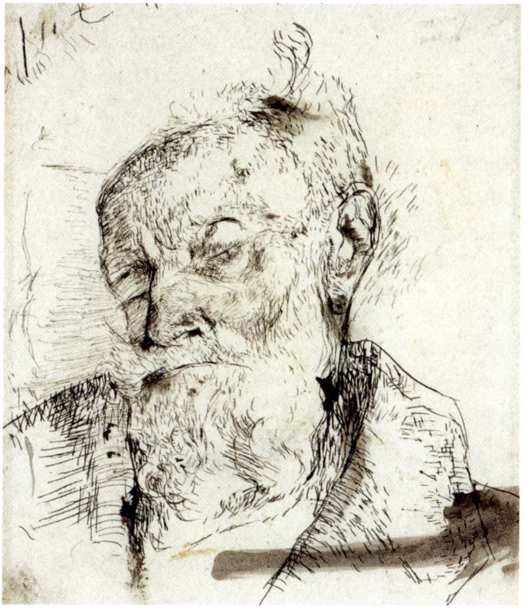

Charlotte writes that the care of her grandfather, a task imposed upon her, is repeatedly forcing her back into a world that had been smashed to smithereens and thus no longer existed – into a theatre in which she could no longer live. For three whole years she has been doing everything to be free of this burden. She would be unable to withstand the experience of falling back into this depression, even though the effort to resist is a great drain on her energy – energy that had given her a summer during which

Portrait of Dr Ludwig Grunwald (detail), 1939–41. Ink and wash on paper, 35.6 x 28.2 cm
Jerusalem, Collection of the Yad Vashem Art Museum, Gift of Dr Miri and Sheldon Adelson

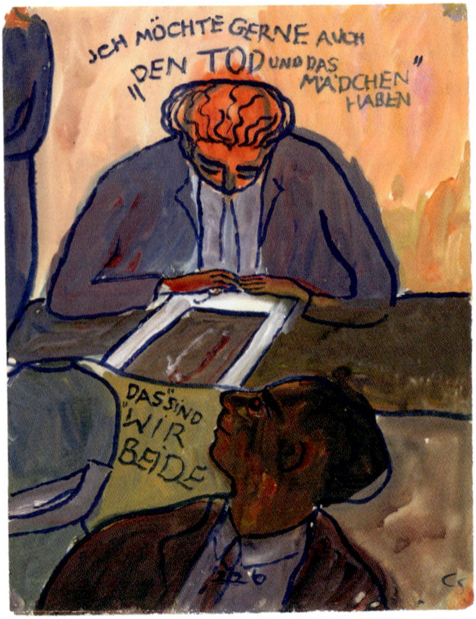

she was able to work in great happiness, above all, on *Life? or Theatre?*

With its characteristically formed letters, the letter adopts again the style of handwriting found in the texts of *Life? or Theatre?* In arming herself to take the difficult decision that lay ahead of her, Charlotte once again looked to the strength that she still believed she could derive from her great love. At some point after February 1943, she had added this "letter" to the rest of her work, where it nevertheless remained an evident "appendix", written on an unnumbered sheet of poor quality paper. She thus left open the question of whether the contents of the letter constituted reality or fiction. Do the numbered sheets require this supplementary information? This text of the "letter" is distinct in several respects from the main work. The artist, in the former, appears to be writing entirely from her own point of view, frequently employing the word "I". This question is ultimately impervious to a definitive answer. Nonetheless, as was also the case with her portrait of Alexander Nagler, Charlotte seemingly wished her "Letter to Amadeus Daberlohn" to have an evident connection with *Life? or Theatre?* and at the very least, that it be recognised as her work. And on that account, we must recognise that *Life? or Theatre?* should yet again be redated to 1940–43.

The text of the letter throws light, moreover, on the background of the work. It reveals that *Life? or Theatre?* was itself completed in August 1942, that is to say 14 months after Charlotte had embarked upon it. She here speaks of Nice and Villefranche and tells how, in the spring of 1942 she had been able to work for three months at the Hotel La Belle Aurore. Was it there perhaps that she worked on the Main Section and the Epilogue, so distinct in character to the Prologue? Was it Nagler who paid for Charlotte's stay at this hotel, perhaps with the money he had received from Ottilie Moore? And was it he who had, meanwhile, cared for Charlotte's grandfather in her

Daberlohn about Charlotte's drawing *Death and the Maiden*:
"I'd like to have *Death and the Maiden*, too. 'That's' the two of us." (see also p. 374)

absence? And just as Wolfsohn was a source of inspiration for Charlotte, was Nagler too, albeit distinctly, essential for her artistic work? And was it this that had initially brought Alexander and Charlotte together? This too is something that we will never know. What is certain, however, is that by August 1942, and her return to Villefranche and Nice, the definitive version of her *Life? or Theatre?* had been completed.

And so we finally come to recognise that the term "theatre" in Charlotte's title assumed, as time went on, another meaning, and not least through Charlotte's own spiritual and intellectual development, hastened as this was through her intensive engagement with writing and painting. In the Prelude, "theatre" signifies a form in which her emotions can be securely expressed. In the Main Section, Charlotte frees herself from this meaning. She is concerned here with more than just the paradoxical co-existence of reality, fiction, and imagination and, as a result, attained a greater creative power. She is, above all, concerned with her recognition that human culture and civilisation can, over the course of time, bring utter destruction and annihilation in its wake. Whoever fails to recognise this may be said to be living in a "theatre", removed from all that is unbearable in reality. In Charlotte's view, a "theatre" that denies reality also extinguishes life; and reality, that is to say real life, must therefore be created anew, just as she was recreating her own life.

POSTSCRIPT

Since 1961, Charlotte Salomon's *Life? or Theatre?* has brought inspiration to many people. Each approaches the work on his or her own terms and brings to it his or her own point of view and range of interpretations. It will never be possible for the "last word" to be spoken about this work of art, for it is one that may be said to evolve along with those who observe it and who, in doing so, bring to it their own emotions and the experience drawn from their own lives. Since 1971, I have taken a serious interest in the work of Charlotte Salomon, and have thus worked closely with all those who, over many years, have brought scholarly engagement, meticulous attention, and infinite patience to the study of her "bequest" to the Joods Historisch Museum, under the direction of Stephen Hartog and Irene Faber. Over the same period, I have spoken with numerous other people who have brought intense interest and endeavoured scholarly focus to the subject of Charlotte's life and her work. In the present essay, I have sought to assemble the insights I have gained over the course of years into a coherent narrative. It is with both gratitude and affection that I recall the many hours that we spent – discussing, narrating, discovering – deeply absorbed with that which we all so loved – Charlotte Salomon's *Life? or Theatre?*

In the end, Daberlohn had proved to be right in his belief in Charlotte Salomon. When seated together in a café, he says to her: "One day people will be looking at us two" (p. 467). At this point in the story he could not have possibly known that Charlotte Salomon would become so famous. Through working with devotion, and delving deep into her innermost being, Charlotte Salomon evolved from the little girl who had been seen as "not very gifted, not very pretty, not very energetic, rather indolent, lacking in self-control, and egoistic"[38] to an artist with a remarkably strong personality – the artist Wolfsohn saw in her and that she so much wanted to be.

When the "Letter to Alfred Daberlohn" was published for the first time in the Le Tripode edition in 2015, it was accompanied by a sense of trepidation; there was a slight fear of trespassing on the family's wishes. By that time, none of the Benda family members, nor the close Salomon relations, were still alive. As noted previously, the last sentences in the letter contain the deeper meaning of the work in Charlotte's own words. She first describes her despair when her permission to stay in Nice is again linked to the care she is giving to her weak 80-year-old grandfather, Ludwig Grunwald. She thoroughly dislikes him and his attitude of "playing the theatre of the civilised man of culture". Underneath this theatrical performance she sensed something was wrong, as his presence made her feel deeply depressed. This was the denial of the reality of her grandparents' life, full of pain and grief. For Charlotte, her grandfather's public reality was all theatre – a façade. After her painstaking self-examination through her art, her life had become real, and she had accepted the pain of her mother's suicide, as well as the suicides of her aunt and her beloved grandmother. She was the last living member of the Benda family. Her grandfather did not understand her struggle with the choice of life or death, nor her courage or her talent to act upon it by painting. In her relationship with him, he denied her the life, the reality she craved in order to be able to embrace life.

Daberlohn taught her to recognise this, to see the reality of life, and not only the pain and suffering but also what life was as well: the beauty, the love, the power of creation. Her grandfather's presence brought her back to the misery she had escaped while painting *Life? or Theatre?* And she wrote, to Daberlohn, in the third person without mentioning the word "murder":

> "Desperate, she mixes the Veronal, a poisonous medicine her grandparents had taken from Germany, in case they ran out of money, into an omelette. When he, grandfather, was feeling the effects of the 'Veronal omelette' and I was drawing him, it was as if a voice called to me: the theatre is dead! Perhaps, beloved, it is really the case that with this war the theatre that humanity has imagined for itself is also coming to an end, that the whole of humanity, through suffering and experience, is moving towards a truer life. I thank you. Almost wanted to say. Amen."
> *Charlotte Salomon, Letter to Alfred Daberlohn, February 1943*

Not long after the Le Tripode publication, Toni Bentley, the writer and former dancer in the New York City Ballet, wrote an article in *The New Yorker* of 15 July 2017 in which she describes Charlotte as having killed her grandfather. A few pages later, she suggests that, on the basis of two enigmatic final pages of *Life? or Theatre?* (II 538, 539; see p. 573), Charlotte, her mother, and her aunt may have been molested by their father and grandfather – an interpretation offered as a possible explanation for their suicides. She shares this opinion with Griselda Pollock, a retired professor of Feminist Studies in the Visual Arts at the University of Leeds, who published *Charlotte Salomon and the Theatre of Memory* in 2018. Her conclusion is likewise based on the same two pages of the work. Over three generations, eight members of grandmother Benda's family took their own lives, indicating that genetic and social factors may have been highly influential. Any suggestion of sexual misconduct by the grandfather is drawn from only two pages of the 769 gouaches, and its significance relative to these broader familial circumstances remains uncertain.

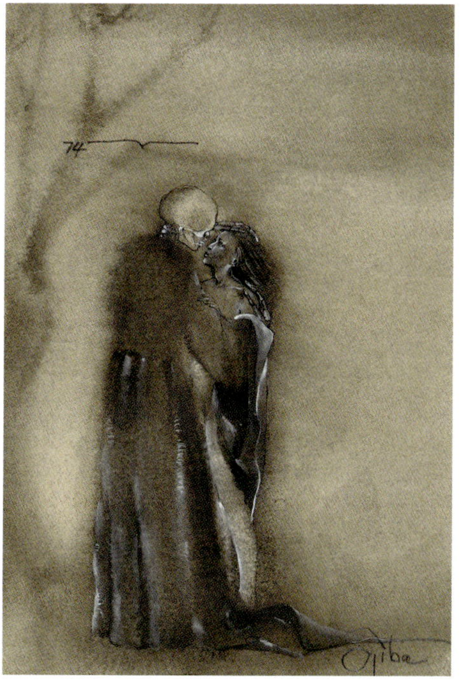

All of this shows that as time passes and ideas, social circumstances, and opinions evolve, *Life? or Theatre?* remains an important work of art. New notions are tested, new ideas developed, but Charlotte Salomon remains an artist who created a unique work for later generations. Over the course of 60 years in the public realm, her work continues to fascinate, move, and inspire new research, prompting discussion, reassessment, or further interpretation of her ideas in the context of the present. It is hoped that this will continue to be the case for years to come. Salomon's 35-page confessional letter regarding her grandfather's death reminds us that interpretations of her life and work remain open, and that no conclusive opinion can be drawn about the controversy surrounding these events.

Death and the Maiden, c. 1938. Ink on paper, 22 x 15 cm. Donation from the estate of Dr Thorbjorg (Sig) Sigurdson and Ottilie (Didi) Gobel Bourne

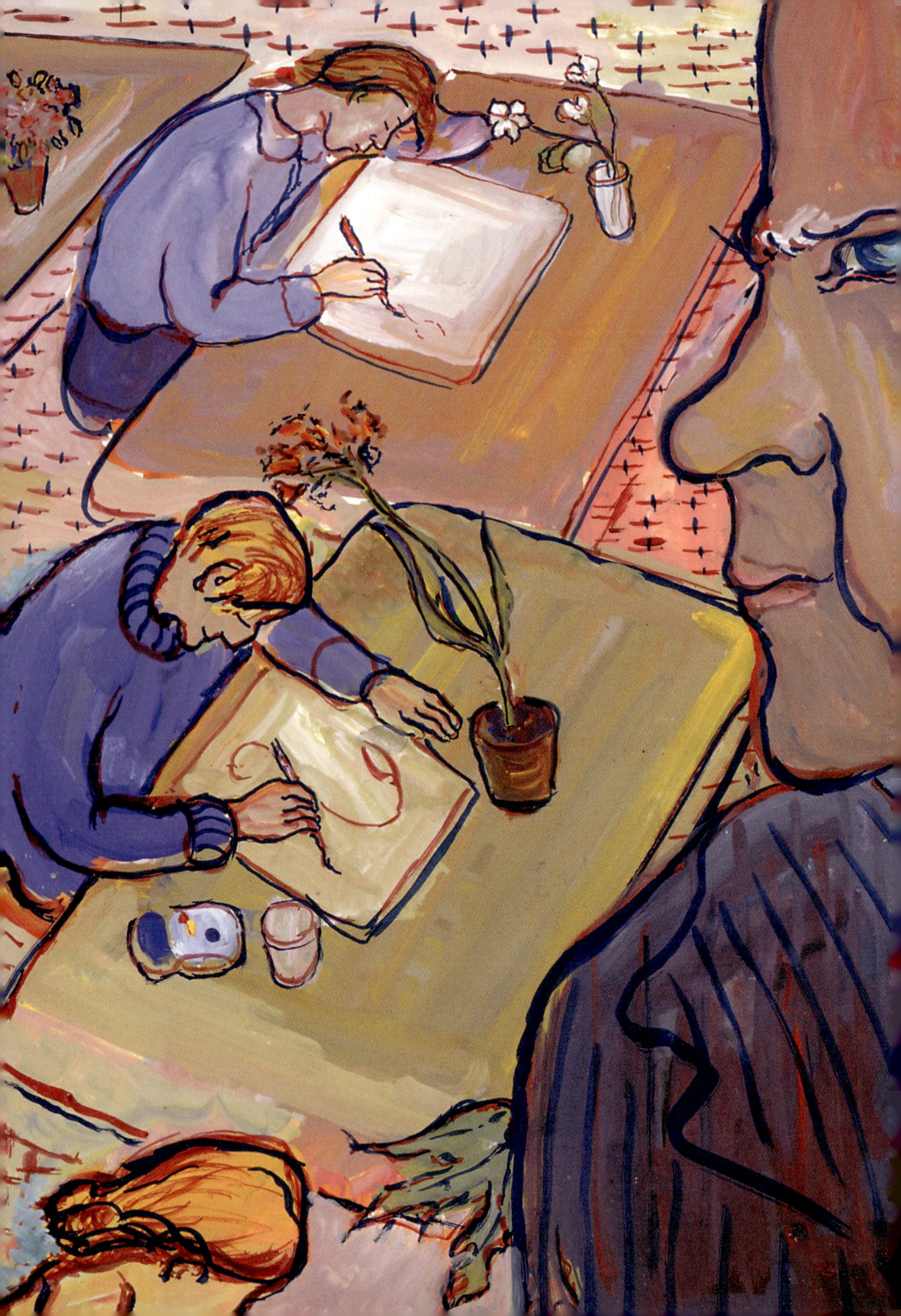

Evelyn Benesch

Life? or Theatre? as a Mirror of Art and Culture in Berlin in the 1920s and Early 1930s

In *Life? or Theatre?* Charlotte Salomon's image-and-text narrative, which she termed a "Singespiel", we find the story of her own childhood in Berlin – which is simultaneously the history of an assimilated upper-middle-class Jewish family. Beginning with the First World War, it goes on to tell of the inter-war years, then of the seizure of power by the National Socialists, and ends with Charlotte's emigration to the South of France in early 1939. It was here in 1941/42 that Salomon produced over a thousand images in gouache that make up *Life? or Theatre?*[1]

Salomon's lyrical drama is divided into three large parts, not unlike the acts of a play. These she introduces in a form of a colophon, as "comprising a Prelude, a Main Section, and an Epilogue". On the next sheet, using capital letters and forceful brushstrokes of red, blue, and yellow gouache, she lists her protagonists, each of whom is a poetically and allusively renamed version of a member of her family or of the circle of her closest friends (p. 87). The most important of these are: "Dr and Mrs Knarre – a married couple" (Salomon's grandparents, the Grunwalds), "Franziska and Charlotte – their daughters", "Dr Kann – a physician" (Dr Albert Salomon), "Charlotte Kann" (Charlotte Salomon), "Paulinka Bimbam – a singer" (Paula Lindberg-Salomon), "Amadeus Daberlohn – a singing teacher" (Alfred Wolfsohn), and "Dr Singsang – a versatile person" (Kurt Singer). In the style of a revue, Salomon integrates musical compositions of diverse styles into her work: arias such as Paula Lindberg-Salomon had sung by Johann Sebastian Bach and Christoph Willibald Gluck, *Lieder* by Franz Schubert (1797–1828) and Robert Schumann (1810–1856), excerpts from the operettas of Johann Strauss (1825–1899), Emmerich Kálmán (1882–1953), and others, and both German and Jewish folk songs – but also songs from the National Socialist period in Germany.[2]

Charlotte at work in the studio of the United State Schools in Berlin (detail, see also p. 269)

The gouaches are all more or less equal in size and are numbered in a sequence probably established at the start, though evidently later altered.[3] Both compositionally and formally, they change significantly as the narrative progresses, becoming increasingly freer and more open, which would lead one to assume that the images were produced in tandem with the story. Salomon employs only three primary colours – red, blue, and yellow – mixing them to obtain a great variety of intermediate tones.[4] In view of the situation in which Salomon was working, necessity is perhaps the more likely explanation. In her Prelude Salomon supplements each image with an explanatory text inscribed on an accompanying sheet of tracing paper; but the text in the Main Section is incorporated within the images, in the form of blocks of script placed between and/or sometimes around figures in a calligraphic manner. The text is written in large capital letters with a brush, each of the distinct speakers or their respective thoughts are chromatically distinct.

In attempting to understand Salomon's lyrical drama, it is essential that we recognise that text, image, and music are of equal importance, a point emphasised by Salomon in her Introduction: "The origin of the following sheets is to be imagined as follows: The person is sitting by the sea. He is painting. A melody suddenly comes into his mind. As he begins to hum it, he notices that the melody matches exactly what he is trying to put to paper. A text forms within him and he begins to sing the melody with his own text, innumerable times in a loud voice until the sheet appears to be finished. Frequently, several texts take shape, and the result is a double song, or it..." (p. 91).

To grasp the narrative structure of *Life? or Theatre?* we shall consider the thematic contents of this lyrical drama. In so doing we shall identify the protagonists – derived, as has been explained, from Salomon's family and friends – by their aforementioned dramatic appellations.

The Prelude

The first section of Salomon's work, the Prelude, consists of 250 sheets of images, in addition to the accompanying sheets of tracing paper bearing explanatory text. It tells of the childhood of Charlotte Kann, starting with a reminiscence of 1913 and ending with the seizure of power by the National Socialists in January 1933. The narrative opens very immediately and suddenly – dramatically with the suicide of Charlotte's aunt Charlotte, her mother's sister, in 1913 (a real-life event of which Charlotte Salomon learnt about only many years later through her grandfather). Charlotte then turns to the story of her parents, beginning in a military hospital during the First World War where her father Albert Kann is a surgeon and her mother Franziska Knarre works as a nurse. There follows a detailed and affectionate account of the parents' marriage (1916) and her father's return to the front. There

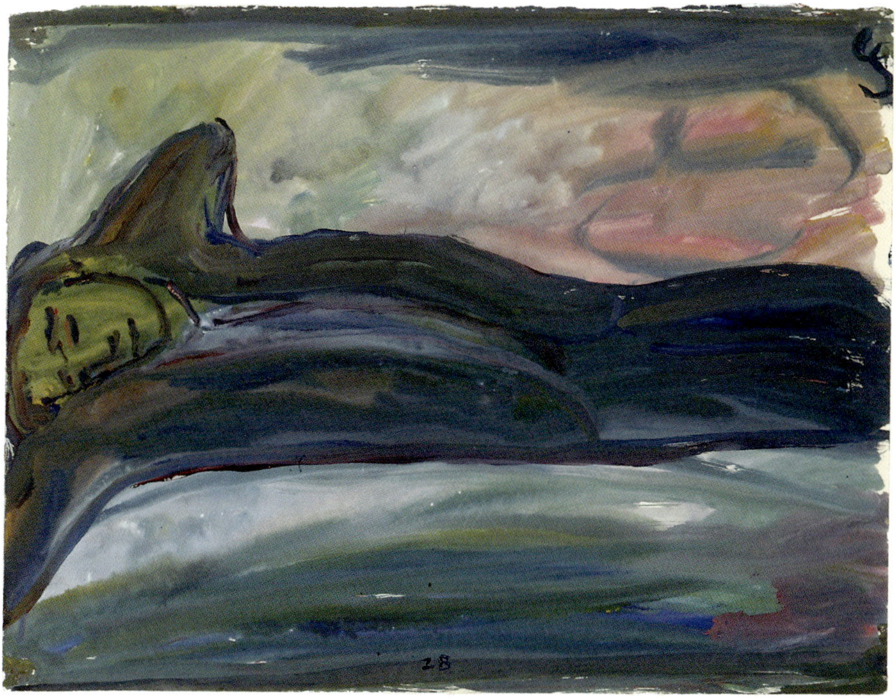

is a minutely detailed description of the upper-middle-class apartment in the Charlottenburg district of Berlin, in which Charlotte in due course enjoys a sheltered upbringing. But into the account of the family's contented daily life and the father's new teaching career at Berlin University, there soon creeps in evidence of the despair and depression felt by Charlotte's mother. Despite every effort on the part of family members to help her, she eventually throws herself out of a window, her death being explained to her young daughter as the outcome of severe influenza. The child's dismay and ensuing loneliness are as carefully documented as is the attention she then receives from a succession of governesses and from her grandparents, who take her with them on holidays spent in the mountains, at the sea, and in Venice. At the end of the first act, the celebrated alto Paulinka Bimbam enters the narrative, marrying Charlotte's father in 1930. Adored by the young Charlotte, Paulinka Bimbam introduces music and culture and a social life into the Kann household.

The second act of the Prelude opens on 30 January 1933 (p. 238) and deals with the life of the Kann family in Berlin of the National Socialists: Charlotte's father

Daberlohn as a reclining figure (see also p. 302)

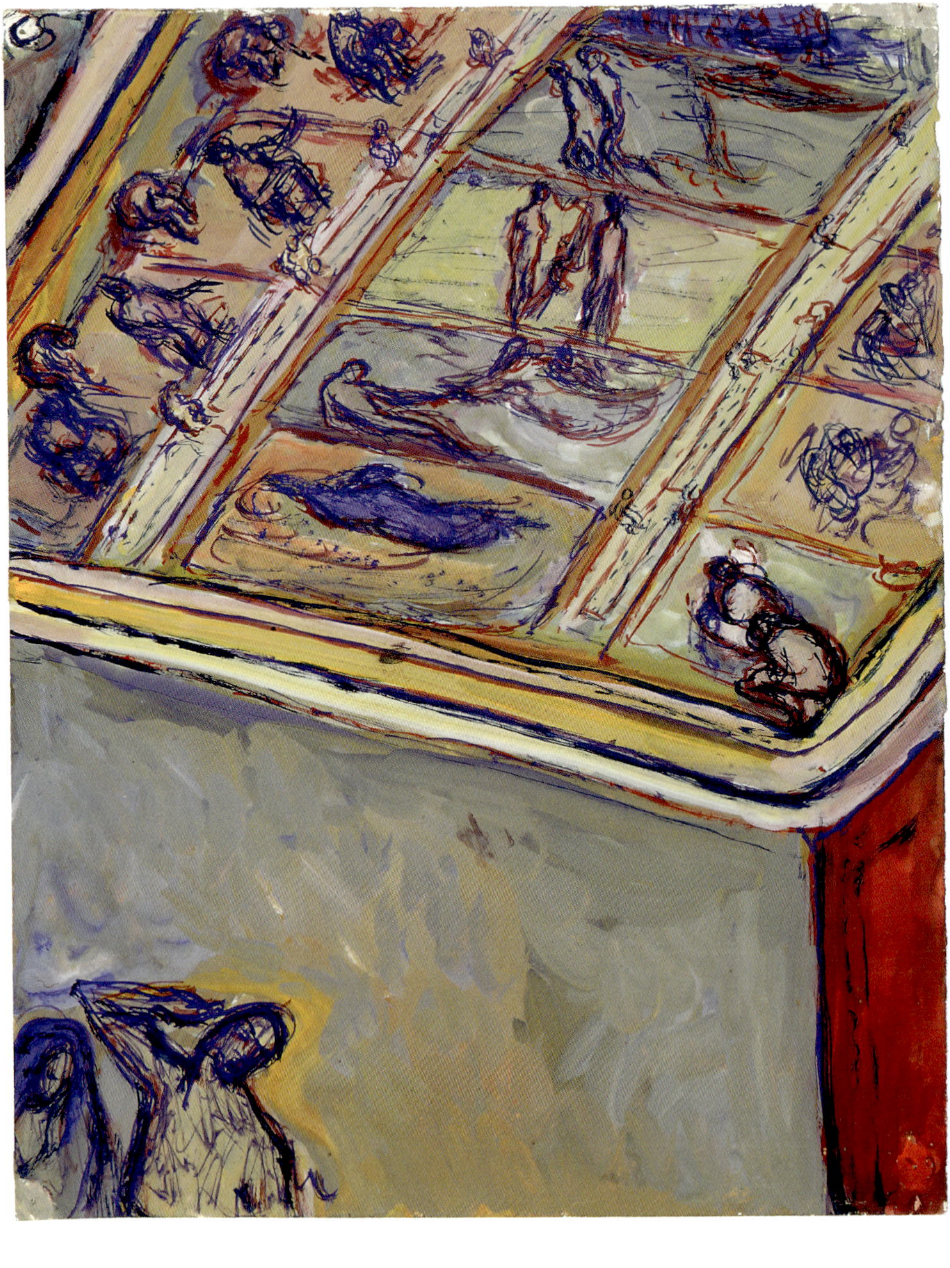

loses his post at the university (p. 242), and Paulinka Bimbam is assailed at a concert by shouts of "Out – get out" (p. 244). We learn of the founding of the Kulturbund Deutscher Juden (Cultural Union of German Jews), where Paulinka works in close collaboration with Dr Singsang, as also of Dr Kann's work in his new post at the Jewish Hospital. A short chapter is devoted entirely to Charlotte's grandparents Dr and Mrs Knarre, who had already emigrated to Italy in 1933, and who invite their granddaughter to Rome. Her fascination with the city and its works of art are recorded in both the images and the commentary related to this episode: "And then: this Michelangelo, I find him extremely magnificent – there really is a sovereign power in them" (pp. 56 and 259). After her return from Rome, Charlotte (having left school) endeavours to gain admission to the Berlin Academy of Arts – where her application is initially rejected on account of her Jewish origins. Later, however, we encounter her with colleagues in a drawing class at the Academy (pp. 52, 267–69 and 273). The Prelude to *Life? or Theatre?* ends with a consideration of the voice of Paulinka Bimbam, which now seems to Charlotte to have lost the sparkle of earlier years (pp. 276–77).

Within the densely narrated Prelude there are a number of richly detailed "set pieces", among them Charlotte's visit to Venice with her grandparents, the time spent in the Swiss Alps, her relationships with her several governesses, and her stay in Rome. Also incorporated are subsidiary narrative strands touching on, by way of a further reminiscence, the life of Paulinka Bimbam (pp. 180–93) or of Charlotte's grandmother (pp. 206–37). A number of scenes are evidently included in the allusion to the contemporary events of Berlin in the mid-1930s: They include Paulinka's negative experiences following the ban of performances by Jewish singers, musicians, and actors, and Charlotte's father losing his professorship after Jewish physicians are banned from working in public institutions.

In other respects the narrative pays less attention to Salomon's own experiences: although she was, in fact, a pupil at the Vereinigte Staatsschulen für Freie und Angewandte Kunst (United State Schools for Fine and Applied Arts) from autumn 1935 until at least summer 1937, Charlotte barely mentions any equivalent to this.[5] She was admitted "on a provisional basis" to the institution in the winter semester of 1935, but was permitted to matriculate in the usual way in February 1936.[6] This was possible because her father had served as a military doctor at the front during the First World War. As a fellow pupil of Charlotte Salomon later observed, her friend's Jewish parentage was not discussed in their class.[7] In winter 1937, however, Salomon was not awarded the Sandkuhl Prize, which she had been informally led to expect. This

Depiction of Michelangelo's ceiling fresco
in the Sistine Chapel (see also p. 259)

was probably to protect her, given that she had been known up to this point at the school merely as "Lotte". Had she been formally granted the prize it would have been imperative to identify her in full, thereby revealing her Jewish origin. Charlotte Salomon nonetheless left the school then.[8]

Also worth noting are the activities of the aforementioned Cultural Union of German Jews, which certainly had a significant impact on Salomon. This had been established in 1933 by Kurt Singer. Especially striking is Salomon's acute characterisation, in her account of the founding of the institution, of Singer in conversation with the National Socialist Minister for Propaganda Joseph Goebbels (whose words she mocks on one of the accompanying sheets of tracing paper, imputing to him the pompous declaration: "I am the Minista for Propaganda!"; pp. 248–51). Paula Lindberg-Salomon was particularly close to Singer and became a founding member of the Cultural Union, taking part in many of its performances, some of which Singer conducted. These events, without doubt, aroused an interest in the world of the oratorio and classical music of every sort for her stepdaughter, an interest still detectable in some of the musical compositions cited in *Life? or Theatre?*[9]

In her Prelude Salomon frequently arranges her pictorial narrative into a number of superimposed image rows, with several juxtaposed scenes running customarily from left to right (pp. 122, 169, 178, 181, and 194). This enhances our sense of both continuity and speed. Some sheets are more loosely composed, with several scenes each resembling a small island, distributed across the page in a seemingly incidental fashion (for instance pp. 173 and 174). Salomon likes to combine this sort of pictorial composition with a more complex representation of space and an extreme form of the bird's-eye view; this results not only in a diminution in the size of those depicted, but also in the scope for the inclusion of more figures and episodes (pp. 114, 121, 155, 165, and 166). Over the course of the narrative (and in a few cases also near its opening) we find motifs that fill out an entire sheet, even implicitly extending beyond it: this may be the case with individual figures, figural groups, even single portraits (pp. 133–37, 187, 212, 218–21). Particularly notable in this respect is the rendering of Charlotte's deceased mother, which is the first figure to fill an entire sheet (p. 133): a drastic scene, presenting the corpse as a shapeless mountain of flesh, as viewed slightly from above, and defined only through its rough outline.

The Main Section

The Main Section of Salomon's lyrical drama opens with the first appearance of Amadeus Daberlohn, a frequent visitor to the Kann household from 1937 in his role as a singing teacher. It is to Daberlohn and his ideas that this part of Salomon's narrative is largely devoted. The aftermath of the notorious "Kristallnacht" (Night of Broken

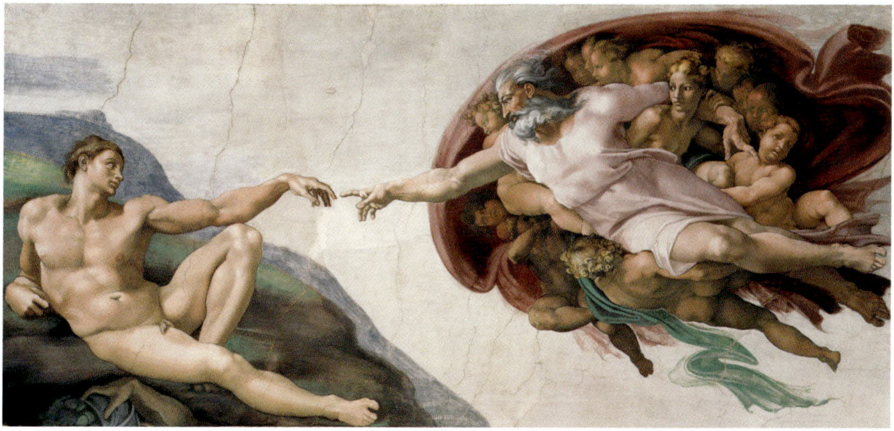

Glass, 9 November 1938) and the months preceding her own departure on 9 December 1938 for the South of France are the subjects in over 400 images. Paulinka's singing sessions with Daberlohn (who serves as her *répétiteur*) are accompanied by comprehensive discussions of music and art, in the course of which Daberlohn frequently engages in monologues on his idealising vision of a future union of singing and life.

What is striking within this particular sequence of images is Salomon's account of the celebration of Christmas Eve, to which Paulinka had invited Daberlohn and his fiancée. Salomon supplies a detailed description of those gathered around the dining table on this occasion, with them engaging in a game of dice, and finally Paulinka's performance of a Bach cantata (pp. 317–24). The subsequent dialogue between Daberlohn and his sculptor friend is of central importance within Salomon's overall narrative. As they drink, they philosophise: "The searching and striving for the ideal that is so strong in him that he'll leave everything to follow his Master..." (pp. 325–26). Of particular importance here is Daberlohn's thesis (also voiced elsewhere in the narrative) "that, apart from great technical ability, the emotional life of the singer must suffer a great upheaval to enable that singer to achieve exceptional results" (p. 335). He also praises the mythical figure of Orpheus (Paulinka, for whom he had a great admiration, was about to appear in this role in a production of Gluck's *Orpheus and Euridyce*), "... in order to regain his lost beloved, must descend – symbolically, of course – into the underworld, into his own depths, for which he needs the help of Cupid or Eros" (p. 334). Orpheus embodies Daberlohn's own conviction that an emotional

Michelangelo, *The Creation of Adam*, 1512. Part of the ceiling fresco of the Sistine Chapel. Fresco, 40.5 x 13.2 m (total). Rome, Vatican, Sistine Chapel

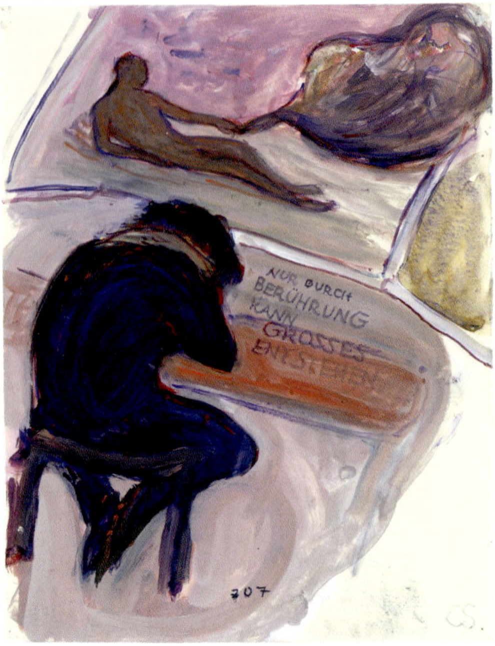

basis is required for the exercise of every art. It is out of the themes addressed in these nocturnal conversations that Daberlohn goes on to develop the thesis of his book, "Orpheus, or the Way to a Mask. Learn to sing, O my Soul (Nietzsche)" (p. 447). A further chapter within the Main Section of Salomon's narrative is concerned with Charlotte's own dealings with Daberlohn, whom she passionately admires and who, in turn, encourages her to continue with her drawing: "In my opinion you are destined to create something above average" (pp. 366–67). It is at Daberlohn's expressed wish that Charlotte begins to illustrate a book for him. In the images that follow we learn of the young girl's emotional instability as reflected in a closely packed sequence of incidents and corresponding emotions: of conversations both exciting and encouraging, of disappointment over affection not returned or of a lack of response to her work, and of joy felt during a high-spirited boat trip.

With 9 November 1938 Charlotte explicitly embarks on a "new section, chapter one" under the title "And time goes on" (p. 472). The aftermath of the infamous night is vividly illustrated: in Dr Kann's internment in the prison at Sachsenhausen (though he is later freed, thanks to the intervention of Paulinka), in Daberlohn's decision to move in with the Kanns, in Paulinka's concern for Charlotte, and in the anxiety of the latter's grandmother, now in the South of France, who learns through radio broadcasts of the violent measures being taken against Jews in Germany – which, here again, enters the narrative as a subsidiary thread – and which resolve to ensure that Charlotte comes to live with her grandmother. The Main Section ends with Charlotte leaving Berlin. Daberlohn sends her on her way with the heartening words: "May you never forget that I believe in you" (p. 508).

"Only by touching can greatness be achieved."
(see also p. 412)

While covering a much shorter period than does the Prelude,[10] the Main Section delivers a great deal more specificity in terms of narrative. At the same time it engages far more in the evocation of emotional states and moods, in detailing the themes and the character of conversations and in the exposition of convictions and ideas. It is the longest part of *Life? or Theatre?*, extending across over 400 sheets. Salomon now eschews the use of supplementary commentary on sheets of tracing paper, and incorporates her explanatory texts into her images. As a result of this device, the protagonists' thoughts and statements move closer to the depicted figures themselves, thereby heightening the emotional intensity of the conversations in which they engage. When Salomon does still employ tracing paper occasionally, this is intended to supply a sort of stage direction, as in the words: "he falls asleep, and sees in his dream how Paulinka sings" or in the authorial explanation: "here the author cannot help but abandon Daberlohn's soul and enter that of his partner".[11] The sheets of tracing paper used at this point are just large enough for the information imparted on them, and are in each case glued on to the back of the corresponding illustration.

The change in narrative style is, above all, apparent in compositional structure: individual scenes are now no longer arranged in superimposed horizontal rows; no longer are there bird's-eye views of detailed or repeated events. There is also a change in Salomon's formal language: We find a shift from detailed description to an open, far more painterly mode that conveys the atmosphere of a scene by way of broad brushstrokes and sketchy contours. Her chief interest now lies in her treatment of the figure of Daberlohn/Wolfsohn, whose theories and thoughts on synaesthesia are often allowed to extend over several sheets. Salomon's concern with Daberlohn/Wolfsohn reaches its climax in her affirmation of the central mission of the book on which Wolfsohn was then working: *Orpheus, or the Way to a Mask* (for Salomon, a life-affirming and ultimately indispensable text). It argues that one may, by means of a "descent into the unconscious", achieve a new form of creativity. This conviction later saves her from the temptation to commit suicide.[12]

Exceptional are the several sequences comprised entirely of repeated faces, sometimes a dozen or more to a sheet, and reminiscent of hovering masks which engage in "persuading" an interlocutor whom we do not necessarily see. Salomon first employs this device when Daberlohn tells of his own traumatic experiences at the front during the First World War (pp. 305–10). This sequence extends over several sheets, the speaker's face painted in bold, opaque gouache, from an olive green to a powerful orange, and appearing gradually ever closer to the listener, in this case Charlotte (and, indeed, the observer). By this means, as also through the positioning of each segment of text directly below each recurrence of the speaker's face,

Salomon intensifies what is stated in each case. She also incorporates into several multi-sheet sequences the repeated motif of the reclining figure with arms crossed behind the neck (pp. 325–35), which she had indirectly derived from Michelangelo's reclining figures on the Sistine Chapel ceiling, and which she had initially employed for the single figure of Daberlohn shown dreaming of Paulinka (p. 55). In her rendering of the nocturnal conversation between Daberlohn and the sculptor, Salomon gradually simplifies each figure until they are reduced to a vigorous diagrammatic scrawl, the impact further enhanced through her use of significantly intense colour, so as to achieve a rhythmic sequence of enormous excitement: an apt pictorial equivalent for Daberlohn's emotional, almost frenzied exclamations.

The Epilogue

The Epilogue is the shortest continuous sequence in Salomon's lyrical drama, comprising of only 90 sheets. It opens in December 1938 with Charlotte's arrival in Villefranche-sur-Mer, near Nice, to live with her grandparents, and ends with her return there in July 1940, after a short absence in Gurs. The sequence begins with sheets bright with glowing colour, almost bucolic in character: We see Charlotte in a swimsuit, under a blue sky, painting and talking with her grandparents in a garden (pp. 527–29) – only for this to give way suddenly to a deeply oppressive mood when the grandmother learns through a radio news broadcast that German troops have crossed the French frontier (p. 530). This news leads to the first narrative climax in this chapter, when the old woman resolves, out of fear, to hang herself. In the ensuing scenes the overall structure loosens, composition is disordered, and both figural and other forms become large and ill-defined. The accompanying script is far more urgent, and is applied in thick red brushstrokes. Especially striking is the passage in which Charlotte tries to stop her grandmother from making another suicide attempt by drawing her attention to the light: "look how the sun is shining", and singing to her a passage from Beethoven's Ninth Symphony (pp. 538–42). The girl's efforts are emphasised through the expansive gestures of her raised arms while the bodies are reduced to roughly outlined, reddish orange shapes to further enhance expression.

It is at this extreme moment in the story that Charlotte's grandfather tells her of the recurrence of suicide in their family (pp. 543–48), revealing that her own mother had, in fact, killed herself, as also her mother's sister, her grandmother's brother and his daughter. Charlotte's shock at what she only now learns is conveyed in the transformation of the colouring of her face, from a normal flesh tone to a glowing orange. Her – eventually unsuccessful – battle for the life of her grandmother is treated in a long sequence (of over forty sheets) in which the formal language becomes increasingly incoherent, eventually comprising little more than

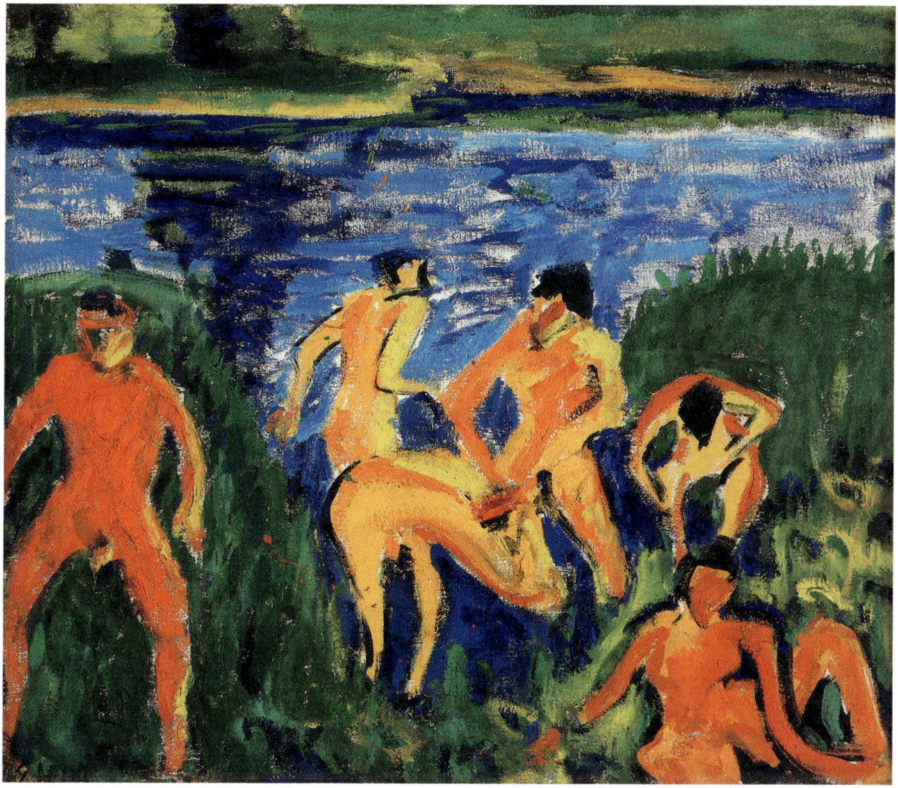

non-representational brushstrokes. In rendering the body of the dead grandmother, Salomon alludes to her similar treatment of Charlotte's dead mother in the Prelude (p. 133). She here powerfully conveys the girl's despair in the expressive and chromatic intensity of the inscribed image: "Dear God, please don't let me go mad" (p. 69). The concluding chapter is devoted to the time after the occupation of France by Germany in May 1940, the subsequent internment of Charlotte and her grandfather in the labour camp at Gurs, in the Pyrenees, and their return to Nice in July 1940, which was permitted on account of her grandfather's old age. Thus ends the pictorial sequence of Salomon's *Life? or Theatre?*

In this final part of the lyrical drama the emotional demands on Charlotte reach an unprecedented intensity: At one and the same time she is confronted with her

Erich Heckel, *Bathers in the Reeds*, 1909
Oil on canvas, 71 x 81 cm. Düsseldorf, Museum Kunstpalast

grandmother's attempted suicide, the belated discovery of her own mother's suicide, and that of other family members. In addition, she has to now also contend with the start of the persecution of those Jews resident in the South of France as well as the evidently traumatic experience of internment in the camp at Gurs in the early summer of 1940:[13] All of these were, as can be imagined, extreme situations that had a direct impact on Charlotte. In the corresponding passages of narrative, her pictorial language is at its most emotional, and is also markedly expressive and gesturally very free, now altogether eschewing the use of internal contours and outlining the figures with roughly marked lines brushed around large, aggressive planes of colour (pp. 538–41). A number of gouaches are made up of no more than broad bands of reddish orange, altogether abandoning objective representation (pp. 67 and 559). Also extreme in their colouring are the sheets steeped in an intensely glowing red: "Another night like that will be more than I can take" (p. 562), and the aforementioned image inscribed: "Dear God, please don't let me go mad" (pp. 69 and 567), in which the figure, as if it were a caricature, is indicated only through its outline. Here, the underlying structure in the manner of a lattice reduces script and figure to effective compositional equivalents.

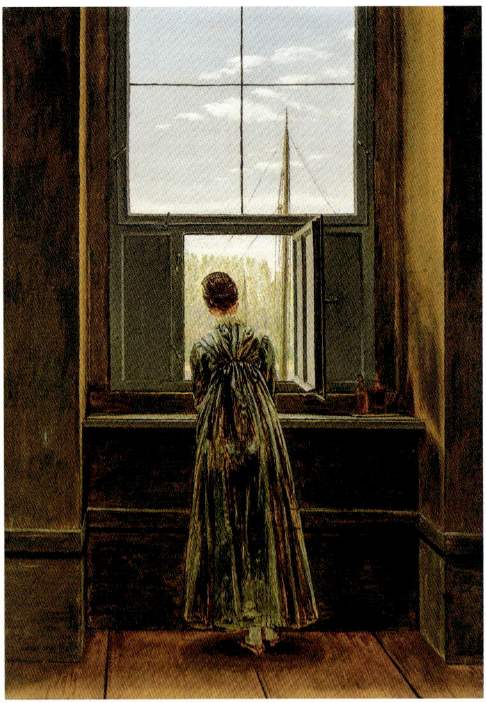

Formal Language and Inspiration[14]

Salomon's formal narrative language evolves during the course of the work, as though through the interactive means of expression and contents. While Salomon narrates in a dense and detailed manner at the beginning, she subsequently focuses more and more on moods and conversations, which she conveys through corporeal gestures, signs, and colours. From an initially precisely ordered, and richly detailed style of drawing, there gradually emerges an emotional fluidity. The increasingly emotional quality of the work goes hand in hand with a decline in description – a distinction also

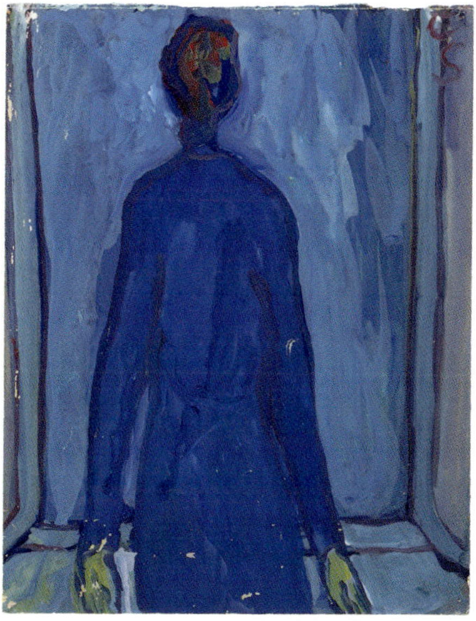 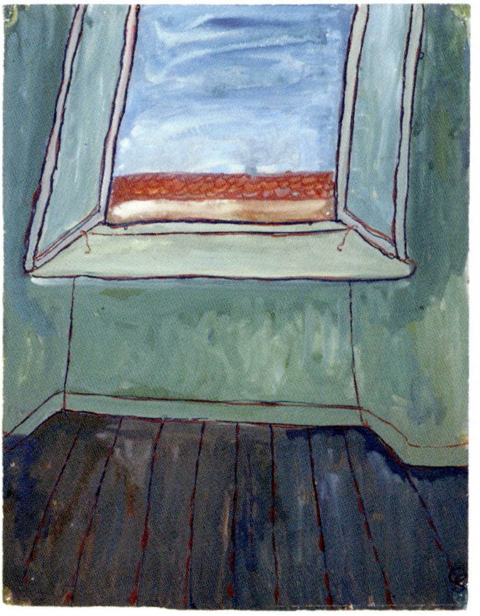

reflected in the number of sheets devoted to any given episode. Thus, the passages recounting Charlotte's childhood contain many descriptions, such as her parents' Berlin apartment and a trip to the Swiss Alps. But the narrative tone is relatively cool for a descriptive point of view, and it is attentive to the colour and detail of a still safe world. Particularly notable is the fact that, in the sheets to be found at the end of the Main Section, which cover Charlotte's precarious departure from Berlin, Salomon returns to the detailed, and yet bird's eye views of the Prelude (pp. 510–23). Even when Salomon recounts what is to prove a fateful event in Charlotte's life, and she (surreptitiously) attends to (and looks beneath) the representation of the facts, she does so without appropriating the emotional significance of the moment – for which one would have expected an engagingly close-up view.

Much of *Life? or Theatre?* is dominated by a formal vocabulary that intensifies expression through a simplification of form, open contours, the omission of detail, and a great deal of colour while negating a connection with any specific tradition or stylistic classification. Salomon's style is indeed characterised by "stylelessness",

Caspar David Friedrich, *Woman at the Window*, 1822
Oil on canvas, 44 x 37 cm. Berlin, Nationalgalerie, Staatliche Museen zu Berlin

Figure of the grandmother seen from behind (see also p. 230) and an open window (see also p. 231)

not unlike that identified by Werner Hofmann many years ago in the work of the Brücke artists: "The conventional tradition of painting was then thrown overboard, in the interests of achieving a 'decivilising' of the means of expression: that extreme point at which action painting was to arrive around forty years later."[15] In Hofmann's view, "the desire for expression, to which one seeks to submit oneself, is itself subject to a certain degree of formal reserve."

In many passages in *Life? or Theatre?* Salomon's own formal language also seems to be borne by the power of expression, and the sheer will to express herself. With her open, expressive style, which negated traditional preoccupations with the "craft" of painting, she was not seeking to transmit a message, such as formulated by artists of the Brücke as they strove for a conscious turning away from tradition in the sense of a rejection of conventionally understood aesthetic and social norms. Instead, she was driven by a desire to recount her story and, to this end, made use of an expressive means that became ever more expressive as her narrative progressed. One is, indeed, almost inclined to speak of an "incidental" formal language, made up of elements that seemed to call out to her from the very subjects she addressed.[16] This is a formal language that, in spite of everything, can, in retrospect, be pinned down and shown to comprise elements of all that Salomon had been able to absorb in Berlin during the years before her departure to the South of France. One thinks, above all, of aspects of German Expressionism, but also of much else – of paintings in the Berlin collections, of inspiration drawn from reproductions such as she might have seen in volumes from her father's own library, but also of those from the Vereinigte Staatsschulen. Such impressions would have been combined with "literal" quotations from the literature of classical art history.[17] Salomon evidently possessed an extraordinary capacity for absorbing and retaining visual stimuli – although one should not forget that, born only in 1917, she would have encountered these as a very young girl. It would have been essentially a cumulative impression that we should expect to have influenced her work.

In first place among Salomon's sources of inspiration, however, must by any reckoning be Michelangelo (1475–1564), whose work partially came to signify not only a formal, but also a thematic reference point: a testament to the awakening of an artist's creative capacities. Her initial enthusiasm for his work arose during her visit to Rome. Charlotte records her own response when in the Sistine Chapel: "And then: this Michelangelo, I find him extremely magnificent – there really is a sovereign power in them. One must, however, twist one's neck a lot to see anything at all. He hovers too high in God's Highness, however, ça vaut la peine!" (p. 56). It was principally the reclining figures found in a *Last Judgement* that Salomon cites on the aforementioned sheet (p. 55) in the figure of the sleeping Daberlohn and to which she often returns thereafter. The work of Michelangelo is, however, absorbed into Salomon's art most

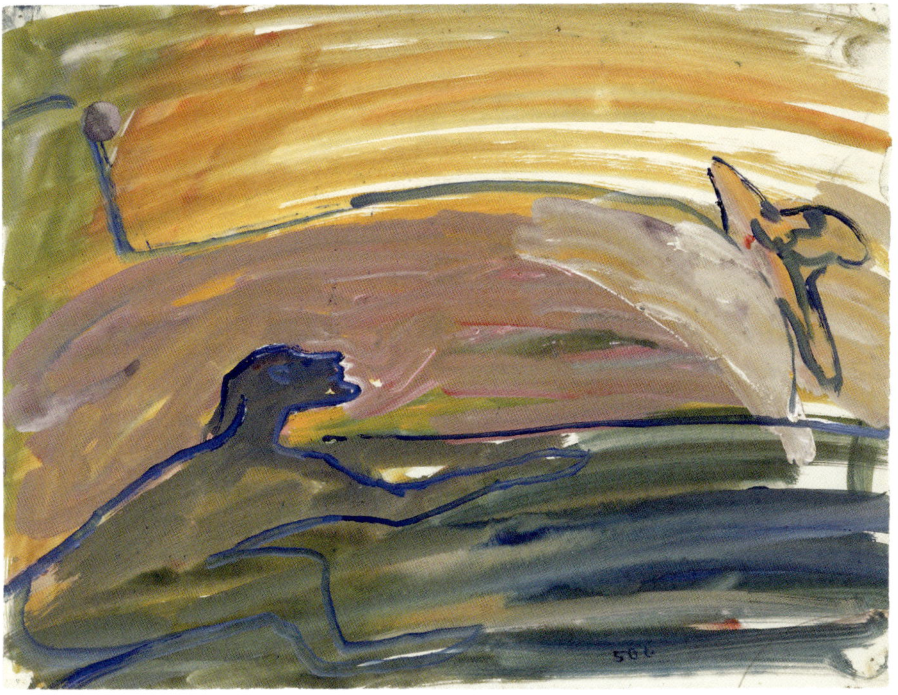

markedly in the sequence of sheets devoted to Daberlohn's work on his own book, which is central to *Life? or Theatre?* As Salomon remarks on the sheet of tracing paper (p. 60) that directly precedes this sequence: "The following sheets are those that to the author seem the strangest. Without doubt they have their origin in the Michelangelo Rome series of the Main Section..." In the text incorporated within the image, Salomon refers to *The Creation of Adam* (p. 59) – in connection with the creative process of her hero Daberlohn whom she here has observed: "The creation of Adam is God's final act which He hurls from His heights into the depths" (p. 416).[18]

Salomon's references to other works from the history of art are less direct, although they deliberately selected and knowingly employed Caspar David Friedrich's (1774–1840) *Woman at the Window* which may have served as a model for the "diverse" figures hurling themselves out of windows (pp. 64 and 65), and Rembrandt's (1606–1669) *Anatomy Lesson of Dr Nicolaes Tulp*, which Salomon probably knew from reproductions in books. It is an image that she cites as "crossed out", in allusion to her father's loss

Expressively executed gouache with wide brush strokes on the death of Charlotte's grandmother, an episode of great emotionality

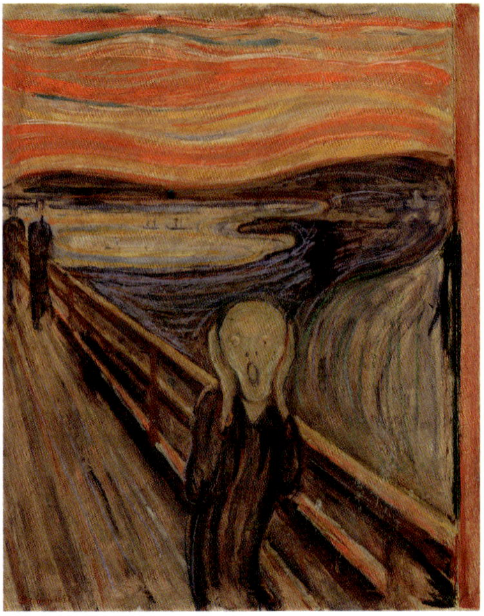

of his university teaching post in March 1933 (p. 242).[19]

Salomon often drew inspiration from German or Northern European Expressionism, from which she quotes directly on occasion, its bold colouring and powerful forms easily leaving their mark on the imagination of a young girl. And the optically precocious Charlotte could have evidently seen such work in the Berlin collections and great exhibitions of the late 1920s and early 1930s, since Berlin had become a centre for the emerging Modernist avant-garde during the years around 1900 – thanks initially to exhibitions staged by the Berlin Secession, and later, on account of Herwarth Walden's (1878–1941) gallery Der Sturm and the First German Autumn Salon (Erster Deutscher Herbstsalon) of recent international progressivist art, which he staged in 1913. Over the same period Hugo von Tschudi (1851–1911), Director, from the late 1890s, of the Berlin Nationalgalerie, was able to establish the beginnings of a public collection of modern and contemporary art through important acquisitions of works by French Impressionist painters. Tschudi's successor Ludwig Justi was initially committed to the same goal: In 1919, he created a new department of the Nationalgalerie, housed separately in the Kronprinzenpalais, and he embarked on acquiring works by artists associated with German Expressionism: members of the Brücke, Oskar Kokoschka (1886–1980), and Franz Marc (1880–1916) among others. Justi's commitment to this cause also went beyond enlarging the collection: In a series of exhibitions he introduced the Berlin public to contemporary art, both German and foreign: Ernst-Ludwig Kirchner (1880–1938) in 1921, Marc in 1922, Edvard Munch (1863–1944) in 1927 (a show of over 200 paintings), and Vincent van Gogh (1853–1890) in 1928. Further exhibitions held in the Kronprinzenpalais were devoted to Lyonel Feininger (1871–1956) in 1931, and Emil Nolde (1867–1956) in 1932. In 1933, moreover,

Edward Munch, *The Scream*, 1893
Oil, tempera, and pastel on cardboard, 91 x 73.5 cm. Oslo, Nasjonalgalleriet

an entire room in the collection was devoted to work by Max Beckmann (1884–1950). Justi was, however, dismissed from his post in July 1933, and all paintings in this collection found unacceptable to the National Socialist regime (examples of Expressionism, as well as various forms of abstract art) were then removed from public display. In 1936, the Nationalgalerie's new department was closed to the general public. Paradoxically, the last chance to see Expressionist painting (and especially German Expressionist painting) on public display in Berlin was between 26 February and 8 May 1938, when the city served as a venue for the infamous touring "Degenerate Art" (Entartete Kunst) exhibition.[20] This show is, moreover, the only one that we can be certain that Charlotte Salomon visited.[21]

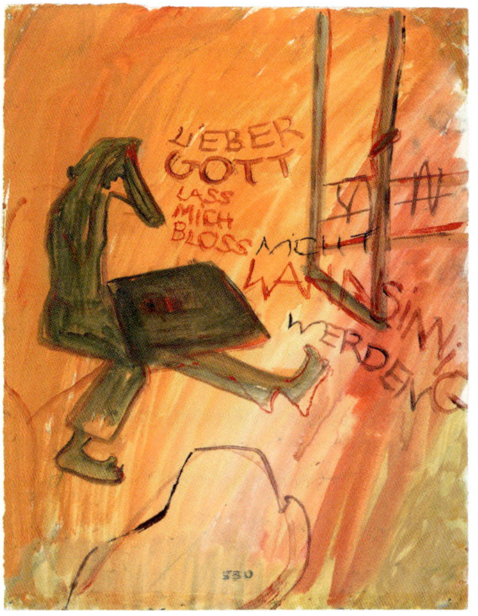

From the vast range of contemporary art "on offer" that may have supplied inspiration for Salomon, we should be especially attentive to Munch. For it is conceivable that she saw the large Munch exhibition at the Kronprinzenpalais in 1927. In that case she may have well been struck not only by the Norwegian artist's glaze-like application of subdued colour or the firm outlines drawn around his figures in dark brushstrokes, but also his treatment of emotions and states of mind – fear, illness, uneasiness. In her own work Salomon may well be reflecting on her recollection of particular images by Munch or compositional arrangements readily associated with him, such as is found in *The Scream* (p. 68), *Madonna*, or *The Sick Child*. She may have even been more or less consciously following Munch in seizing on both compositional and gestural motifs suited to evoking particular moods: One thinks, for example, of the long, threatening corridor in Salomon's grandparents' apartment, along which Charlotte walks when she has just learnt of her mother's death (p. 147), or the later, slumped figure of the grandmother, or the abandoned and despairing child sitting on

The pictorial composition and figurative language of this gouache express Charlotte's inner despair: "Dear God, please don't let me go mad." (see also p. 567)

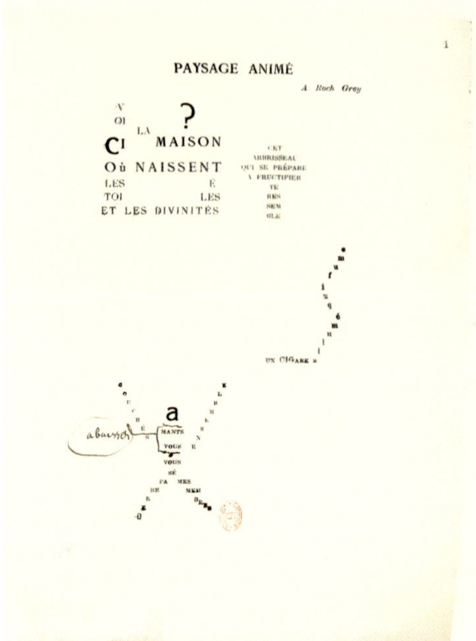

the edge of her bed – and, ultimately, Charlotte sitting with her open case on the eve of her departure for the South of France (p. 514).

Salomon may well, however, have been impressed by the work of other artists on display at the Kronprinzenpalais – we have already noted the similarities between her own work and the open, caricatural pictorial language of the artists of the Brücke (p. 63). One is also inclined to point to the paintings of Beckmann, on account of their powerful figures with emphatic black outlines and the prevalence of the primary colours red, blue, and yellow. Equally possible sources of influence may have been works by artists associated with the *Der Blaue Reiter* almanac: There is a suggestive similarity between Salomon's *Self-portrait* (painted only shortly before *Life? or Theatre?*), with its planes of colour outlined by a dark, broken contour, and Gabriele Münter's (1877–1962) own images that evoke the cloisonné technique (pp. 72 and 73).[22] Salomon would certainly have been aware of Marc Chagall's (1887–1985) work, whose hovering outstretched figures are reflected, in their tender corporeality, in Salomon's record of her parents' wedding, or in the ascent of the angels in the sky in a scene in the Prelude to *Life? or Theatre?* (pp. 108 and 125). Although no work by Chagall was to be found in the collection of the Berlin Nationalgalerie's new department, paintings by him had been temporarily on view at the commercial gallery of Paul Cassirer (1871–1926) who, in 1923, had, moreover, commissioned the series of etchings that became *My Life*. Further stimulus may have been found in the work – possibly encountered by Salomon only after her arrival in the South of France – of Henri Matisse (1869–1954): among other examples, one thinks in particular of the emphatically outlined portraits of Lydia Delectorskaya, on which he embarked in the mid-1930s (pp. 78 and 79).

Guillaume Apollinaire, *Poèmes de la paix et de la guerre*, 1913–16
Calligram "Paysage", folio 1r. Paris, Bibliothèque nationale de France, NAF 25610

It appears that the work of Vincent van Gogh had a distinct relationship to Charlotte Salomon – beside Michelangelo he is the only artist to be explicitly mentioned in her narrative. On the verso of a subsequently discarded sheet[23] she wrote: "I have already achieved that which Van Gogh in his own time achieved, that is to say that extraordinary lightness of touch in my brushstrokes, which sadly has a lot to do with the pathological." We are probably concerned less here with the sense of a formal than with an emotional proximity, it being hard to detect any real formal similarity between the two artists. A single exception might perhaps be the alienatingly cuboid rendering of the building of the Jewish Hospital on a sheet (p. 243), which might be found to recall that of the prison yard in Van Gogh's *Prisoners' Round*.[24] Looking for parallels between Salomon's work and that of artists active many years after her death, one may well be struck by those between the image depicting the formless body of a woman who has just hurled herself out of a window and some of the drastic "body-awareness pictures" painted by Maria Lassnig (1919–2014; p. 133).[25]

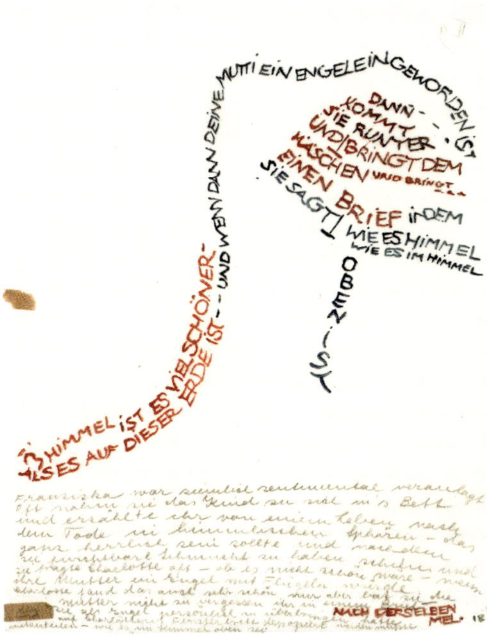

Calligraphic text on one of the transparent sheets (see also p. 124)

Interviews with Paula Salomon and Barbara Petzel, Salomon's former fellow student at the Vereinigte Staatsschulen, substantiate the artist's own account as a young woman brought up in an upper-middle-class cultural ambience.[26] She had received a good education in art history – acquired through visits to the Berlin collections and exhibitions, and probably also through visits to exhibitions at commercial galleries such as those of Alfred Flechtheim (1878–1937) or Cassirer, and/or through publications found in her father's library, and the library at the Vereinigte Staatsschulen. From at least the date of her father's marriage to Paula Lindberg, Charlotte also began to acquire a familiarity with classical music, such as is attested by the

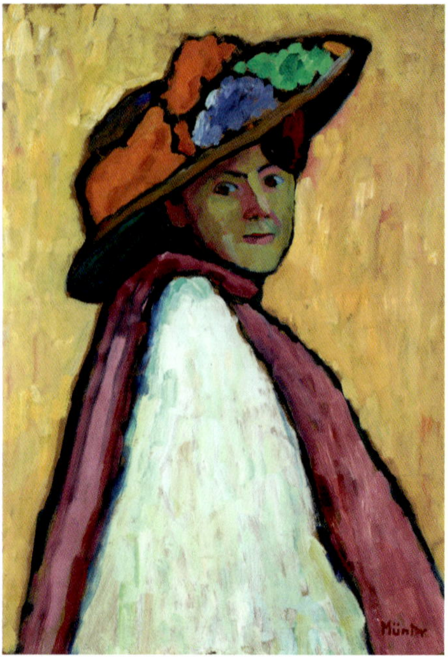

carefully chosen musical examples that feature in *Life? or Theatre?* To these we must, of course, add a sound knowledge – indispensable for any "girl from a good family" – of German literature, and, above all, of German poetry, as evinced by the quotations from the work of Christian Morgenstern (1871–1914; p. 274), Rainer Maria Rilke's (1875–1926) short story of *Cornet Christoph Rilke* (p. 434), or Joseph von Eichendorff's (1788–1857) *Moonlit Night* (p. 453). In all probability, Salomon also had some knowledge of foreign literature: The calligraphically formed texts arranged in arabesques of the words spoken by her protagonists recall the calligrammes of Guillaume Apollinaire (1880–1918; pp. 70–71 and 124).

Salomon's own observations on the psychological context of her work and the effect of her use of colour presuppose an interest in the psychology of colour – as employed by numerous writers and artists, from Antoine Artaud (1896–1948) to Wassily Kandinsky (1866–1944). It would also seem that Salomon was possessed of a certain awareness of psychoanalysis, which may have been imparted to her by Wolfsohn, who appears to have been a follower of C. G. Jung (1875–1961). Significantly, Salomon has Daberlohn explain that "a celebrated professor… on account of his calling – he is a psychoanalyst – is bound to be interested in this work" (p. 471), that is to say, the evolving text of *Orpheus, or the Way to a Mask*.

Narrative Style and the Structure of the Work

The narrative style and structure of *Life? or Theatre?* are so specific and so insistent that one cannot avoid scrutinising Salomon's approach in relation, yet again, to a number of possible art-historical or contemporary (namely relating to life in Berlin in the 1920s and 1930s) sources of inspiration. One becomes utmostly aware of the co-existence of two types of narrative structures employed by Salomon in the

Gabriele Münter, *Portrait of Marianne von Werefkin*, 1909
Oil on cardboard, 81 x 55 cm. Munich, Städtische Galerie im Lenbachhaus

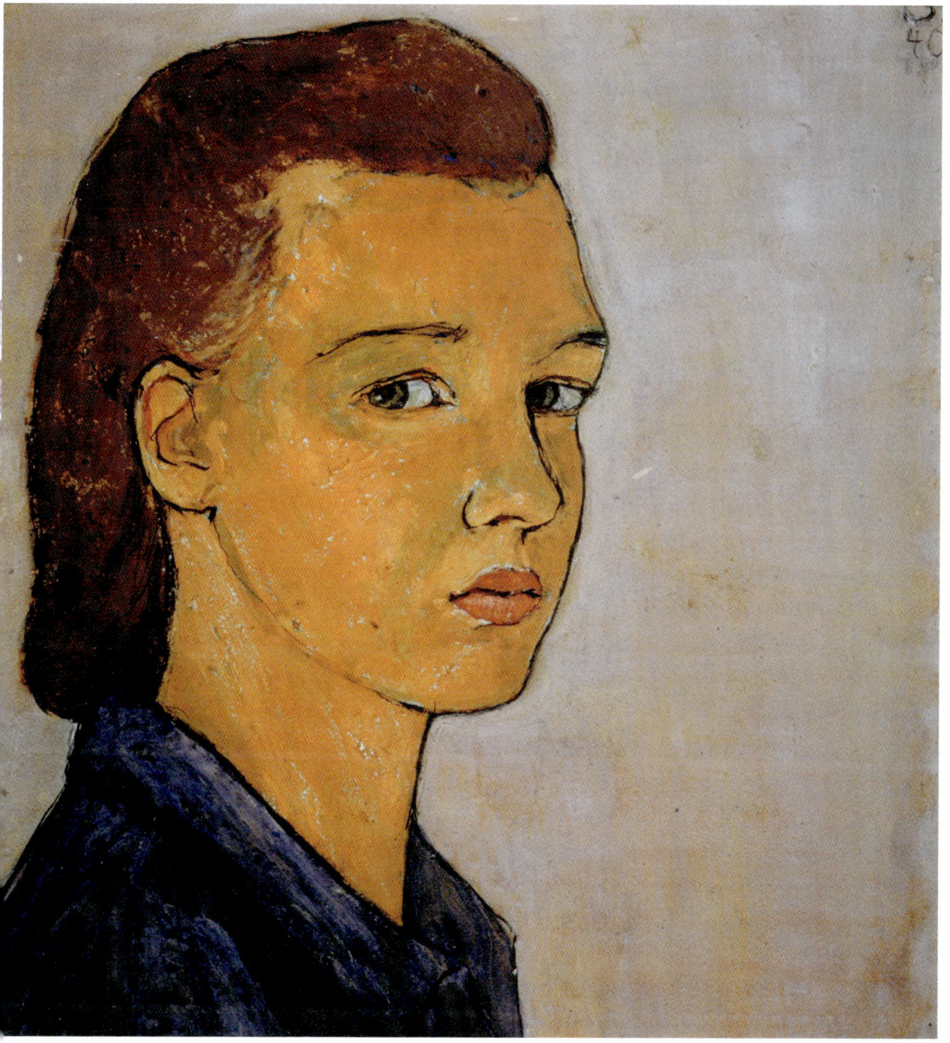

Self-Portrait, 1940
Gouache on cardboard, 54 x 49 cm. Amsterdam, Joods Historisch Museum

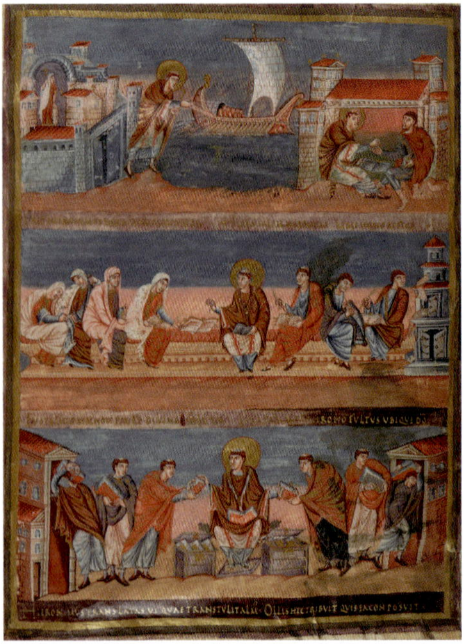

detailed account of her still unscathed childhood in the first two sections of *Life? or Theatre?* On one hand, we encounter scenes following one after the other rapidly, each occupying superimposed rows, and mostly distinguished only through an alteration in the background colour in one image. This occurs primarily in the Prelude (pp. 169, 178, and 197). Opposed to these are sheets across which several isolated images are distributed in the manner of islands (pp. 155–58). Salomon's narrative structure here recalls that which can be found in the art of Late Antiquity or the era of Charlemagne, especially in illuminated manuscripts (left), and which had only been subject to a thorough art-historical analysis by Franz Wickhoff in 1895. He had identified them as a fundamental form of art-historical narration.[27] In the sheet that illustrates Charlotte's childhood (pp. 75 and 122), Salomon may be found employing the first "continuous" form of narrative structure, with individual figures, presented repeatedly within one and the same image. She also uses this form of narration, if in a somewhat modified fashion, in the long passages of conversation to be found in the Main Section and the Epilogue. The second narrative form Salomon employs is derived from that which Wickhoff termed "supplementary". This form unites several scenes on a single sheet that are essential to the narrative but do not, strictly speaking, occur simultaneously. Salomon employs this method on the sheet illustrating Charlotte's trip to the Swiss Alps (p. 155). Although the protagonists do not usually recur in work following this approach, Salomon does in fact allow several of them to do so.

Both the subsequent quick scenes, placed in rows stacked one on top of another, and the sequences of heads with accompanying spoken text inevitably also recall a far more modern pictorial narrative form: the comic strip – the dependence of which on the aforementioned "continuous" (or, in subsequent art-historical terminology, "sequential") narrative style has frequently been emphasised.[28] While it is true that the comic strip, in the strict sense of the term, was not to flourish in Germany until after 1945, it is nonetheless the case that earlier visual narratives such as Wilhelm Busch's *Max and Moritz* books (to be found in every well-equipped German nursery) evince comparably arranged sequences of images, each accompanied by text. In addition, there arises in the sketchy or caricatural renderings of Salomon's figures – with their emphatic outlines and partial absence of internal contours – a style comparable to what one finds in a comic strip or in early pictorial narratives.

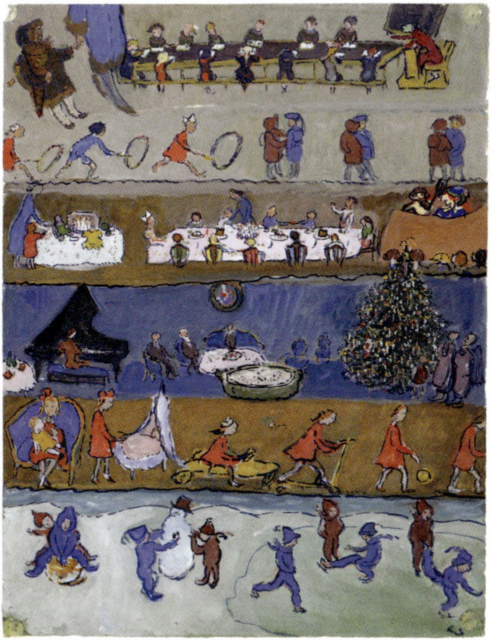

The further important parallel to Salomon's sequential form of narrative is film, which may well have offered her inspiration regarding the thematic as well as the structural aspect of her work.[29] *Life? or Theatre?* does of course reflect the cinema's rapid sequence of images and its tempo; but there would also seem to be a general cinematic dimension to the structure of Salomon's "plot", with the overall narrative arc interrupted and complicated through flashbacks that introduce developments extraneous to it, the whole accompanied by music – as was usual in the case of silent cinema of the 1920s. The film industry was, in fact, enjoying somewhat of a boom in Germany in the late 1920s, and visits to the cinema would certainly have featured among the leisure activities of most, including Charlotte.[30]

We do not know, however, precisely which films she saw. Perhaps she may have felt drawn to comedies and revue films of the years after 1933;[31] it is possible that she may have also seen Fritz Lang's *Metropolis* (p. 77), although in the year of its release, 1927, it was only very briefly shown in cinemas in Berlin. Its striking crowd scenes must have remained vividly fixed in the memories of all those who had seen this film,

Vivian Bible, so-called First Bible of Charles the Bald, Tours, 845–46
Frontispiece of the Prologues of St Jerome, folio 3v
Paris, Bibliothèque nationale de France, Ms. Lat. 1

Episodes from Charlotte's childhood (see also p. 122)

and may have possibly had an influence on Salomon's rendering of the enthused crowds to be encountered in Berlin on 30 January 1933 (p. 239), which she, after all, had undoubtedly experienced herself.

For Salomon, film was to have a further metaphysical significance for reasons she has Amadeus Daberlohn explain, once again. In it is to be found an embodiment of public desire: "At the movies, he [Daberlohn] feels, on an equal level with the hero passing before his eyes, equal of his ideal. At the movies he follows his path to the heights, to his refuge, the dream world that is to help him ignore the grey blackish harshness of daily life" (tracing paper accompanying sheet p. 421).

In an essay both interesting and compelling, which sets Charlotte Salomon in relation to Walter Benjamin's (1892–1940) preoccupation with Berlin, Griselda Pollock has argued that *Life? or Theatre?* should be understood as a sort of Theatre of Memory.[32] In his own *Chronicle of Berlin*, and later in the volume *Berlin Childhood*, Benjamin trains a sort of spotlight on diverse locations in this city, thereby evolving a topography of memory while also ventilating the process of writing an autobiography by reference to a map of the city.[33] In the radio broadcasts of 1929–33, he proceeded with *Explanations for Children* in a similar fashion, to which the young Charlotte may have listened.[34] Benjamin's focus on a sequence of individual subjects may have eventually influenced Salomon's own approach to narrative, in which a collection of sketchily rendered fragments and/or rapidly shifting and ostensibly unrelated scenes and images match the tempo and complexity of the metropolis. Not only do a number of scenes, especially in the Prelude and Epilogue of *Life? or Theatre?* narrate the history of the Salomon family, but they serve as a certain type of memory work. This functions here through specific locations – the parental apartment, the Vereinigte Staatsschulen the station that is the setting for the scene of leave-taking – which are comparable to the entities that jog Charlotte's memory (similar to smells and moods in Marcel Proust's (1871–1922) writings).

The Lyrical Drama II

At a first glance the corpus of *Life? or Theatre?* may be said to function in the manner of a conventional storyboard, with distinct acts and scenes, the introduction of music, and directions, as if for a revue – for a lyrical drama – in which the most varied stimuli and impressions from Berlin of the Weimar Republic are amalgamated. One must, however, always bear in mind how young Charlotte Salomon was during this period, having been born only in 1917, and the fact that we have no concrete information in terms of which, if any, theatrical or musical performances she witnessed first-hand or how intense such experiences were for her.

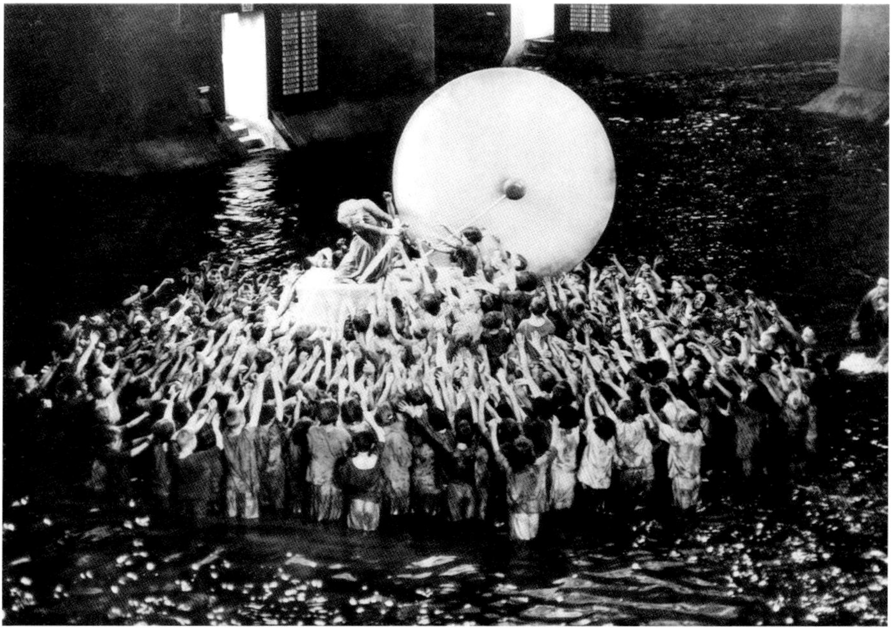

What is especially extraordinary in *Life? or Theatre?*, in both an artistic and emotional sense, is the frequent extremity of its thematic content, which goes far beyond the possible sources of inspiration we have proposed here; the author's own experiences both inform and weigh upon her narrative, transposing its formal language into something powerfully harsh and wilful. In this respect, Salomon's narrative may be said to transgress the borders between high and low – with a formal vocabulary drawing on Michelangelo, German Expressionism, and the comic strip, and allusions to music that appropriates Bach's cantatas, chansons of the 1920s, operettas – just as she mixes reality with fiction, her own autobiography with history, and history with individual stories.[35]

A final, important consideration for an understanding of *Life? or Theatre?* is that Charlotte Salomon herself regarded the work on her images in gouache as a form of therapy – and was also conscious of the need for this therapy – after her traumatic experience. As she noted in her Epilogue: "Yet, in the long run, such a day-nightish life like this became intolerable even to a creature thus "predisposed." And she found herself facing the question of whether to commit suicide or to undertake something quite insanely extraordinary" (p. 582).

Fritz Lang, *The gong in the workers' city*, 1927. Still from *Metropolis*

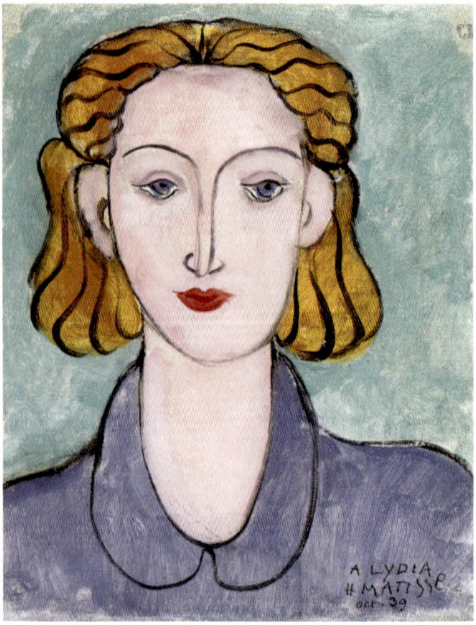

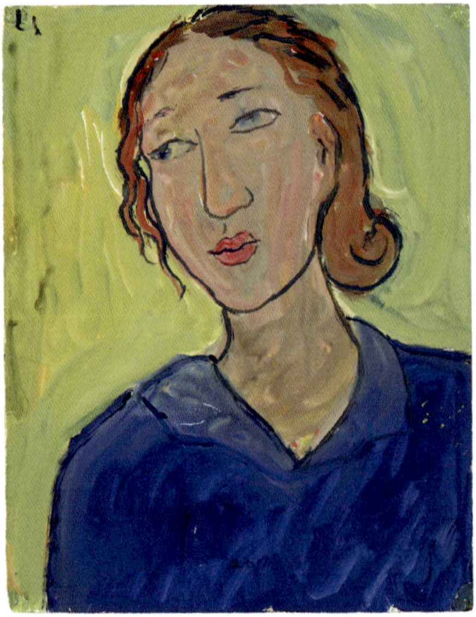

In the end it did prove possible for Charlotte Salomon to achieve this "something quite insanely extraordinary" – that is to say, to draw and to narrate *Life? or Theatre?* This she reflects in a sort of closing statement, in memory of the mission that her idealised version of Alfred Wolfsohn had formulated in the manuscript of his *Orpheus, or the Way to a Mask*:[36] "Thus facing the most ardent sun, blue-red sea, and the most blossoming trees, she remembered an old experience of her most glowing former love [...] For she discovered that this figure [...] might possibly preserve her from suicide inasmuch as she remembered one of Amadeus's main clauses which he was always ready to utter: Love, know thyself first in order to love thy neighbour [...] And, with dream-awakened eyes, she saw all the beauty around her, saw the sea, felt the sun, and knew: she had to vanish for a time from the human surface and make every sacrifice to create her world anew out of the depths. And from that came: Life or Theatre??? (pp. 584–89). By way of the metaphor of the descent of Orpheus into the Underworld – in other words the search for one's own subconscious – Charlotte Salomon discovered an artistic process: the possibility of truly knowing more of the world around her and thereby – in her case, at least – gaining the strength to go on with life.

Henri Matisse, *Portrait of Lydia Delectorskaya*, 1936
Oil on canvas, 35.4 x 27.3 cm. St Petersburg, The State Hermitage Museum

Charlotte's self-portraits (see also pp. 370 and 395)

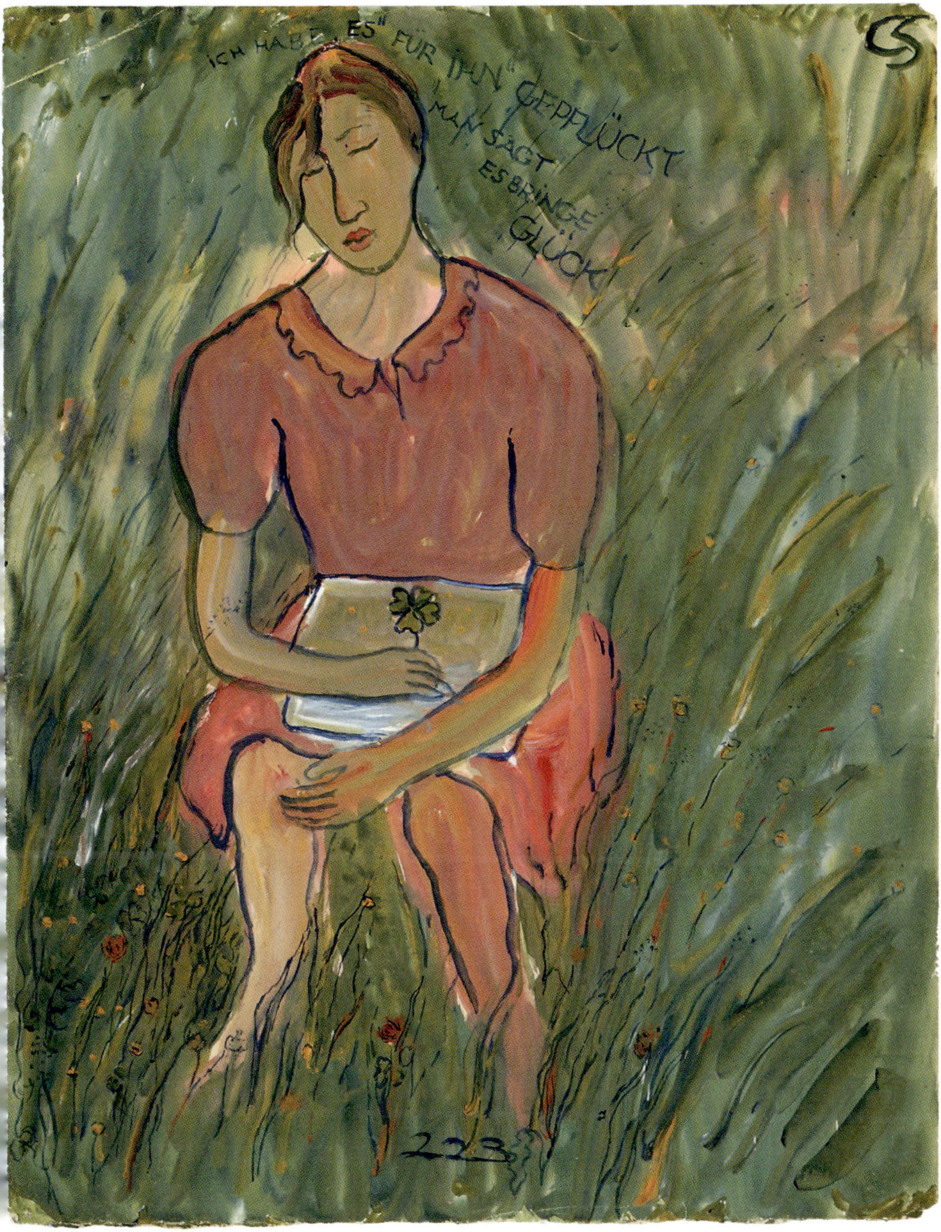
ICH HABE „ES" FÜR IHN" GEPFLÜCKT
MAN SAGT
ES BRINGE
GLÜCK
CS
223

PROGRAMME

Life?
or Theatre?

A Singspiel
[play with music]
CS

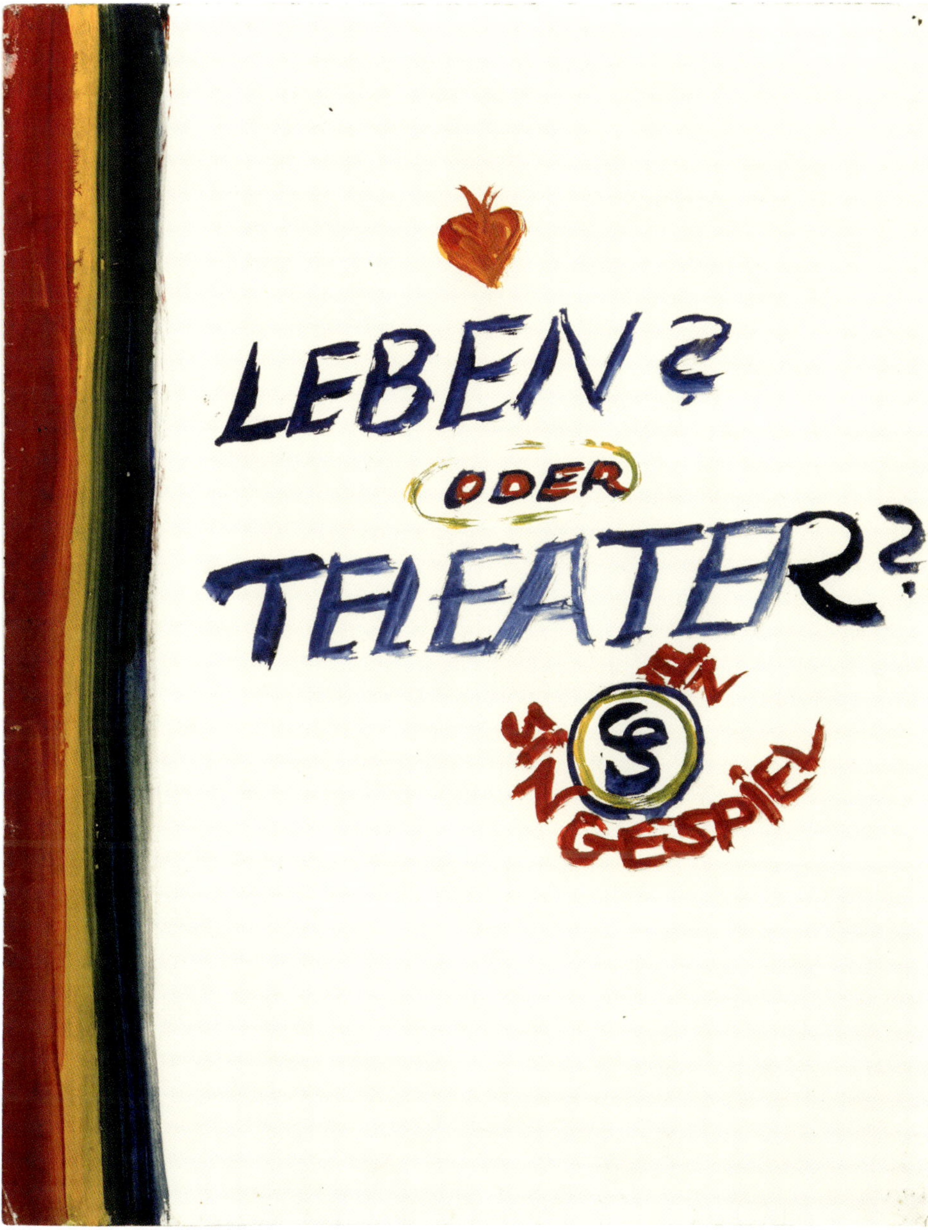
LEBEN?
ODER
THEATER?
EIN
SIN
S
GESPIEL

Ascribed to Ottilie Moore

Consisting of a Prelude,
a Main Section,
and an Epilogue!

OTTILIE MOORE ZUGESCHRIEBEN

BESTEHEND AUS EINEM VORSPIEL EINEM HAUPTTEIL UND EINEM NACHWORT

The tricoloured Singspiel begins.

The performers are as follows:

Dr and Mrs Knarre......... a married couple
Franziska and Charlotte.... their daughters
Dr Kann ....a physician
Charlotte Kann .... his daughter
Paulinka Bimbam....................a singer
Dr Singsang ....a versatile person
Professor Klingklang.... a famous conductor
A drawing teacher
Professor and students at a drawing academy
and chorus.

In the Main Section appears:
Amadeus Daberlohn........ a singing teacher
His fiancée
A sculptor
Paulinka Bimbam
Charlotte Kann
Related material

In the Epilogue appears:
Mrs Knarre
Mr Knarre
Charlotte Kann and others.

The piece plays during the time from 1913
to 1940 in Germany, later in Nice.

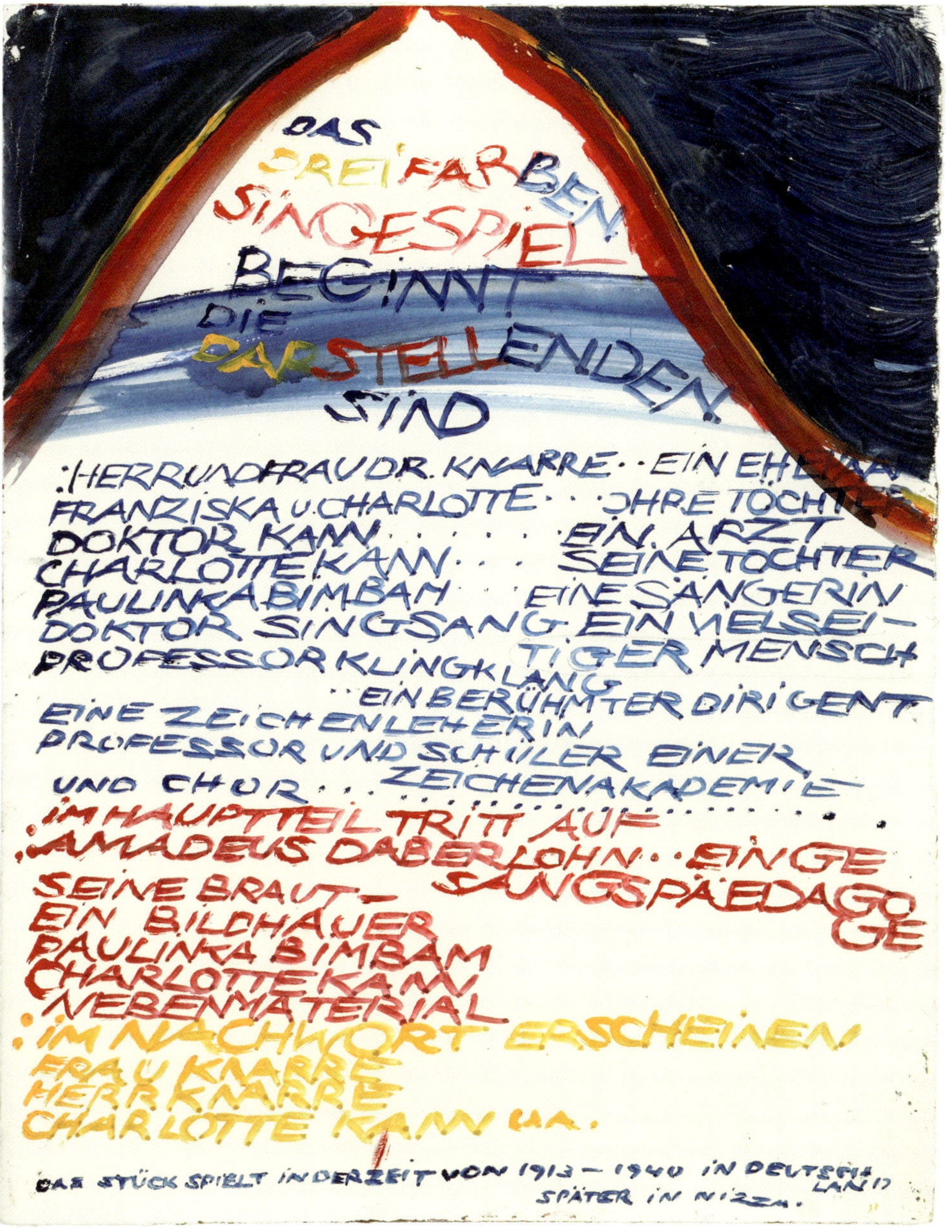
DAS
DREI FARBEN
SINGESPIEL
BEGINNT
DIE
DARSTELLENDEN
SIND
:HERR UND FRAU DR. KNARRE . . EIN EH
FRANZISKA U. CHARLOTTE . . . IHRE TÖCHT
DOKTOR KANN . . . . EIN ARZT
CHARLOTTE KANN . . . SEINE TOCHTER
PAULINKA BIMBAM . EINE SÄNGERIN
DOKTOR SINGSANG EIN VIELSEI-
TIGER MENSCH
PROFESSOR KLINGKLANG
. . EIN BERÜHMTER DIRIGENT
EINE ZEICHENLEHERIN
PROFESSOR UND SCHÜLER EINER
ZEICHENAKADEMIE
UND CHOR . . . .
:IM HAUPTTEIL TRITT AUF
:AMADEUS DABERLOHN . . EIN GE
SANGSPÄEDAGO
GE
SEINE BRAUT –
EIN BILDHAUER
PAULINKA BIMBAM
CHARLOTTE KANN
NEBENMATERIAL
:IM NACHWORT ERSCHEINEN
FRAU KNARRE
HERR KNARRE
CHARLOTTE KANN U.A.
DAS STÜCK SPIELT IN DER ZEIT VON 1913 – 1940 IN DEUTSCHLAND
SPÄTER IN NIZZA.

What is man, that thou be mindful of him, the earthly worm, to which thou doth pay attention?

Since I myself needed a year to find out what this strange work is about to me, especially in the first sheets, many of the texts and tunes have been omitted and must – it seems to me – remain shrouded in darkness, like the creation as a whole.

CS

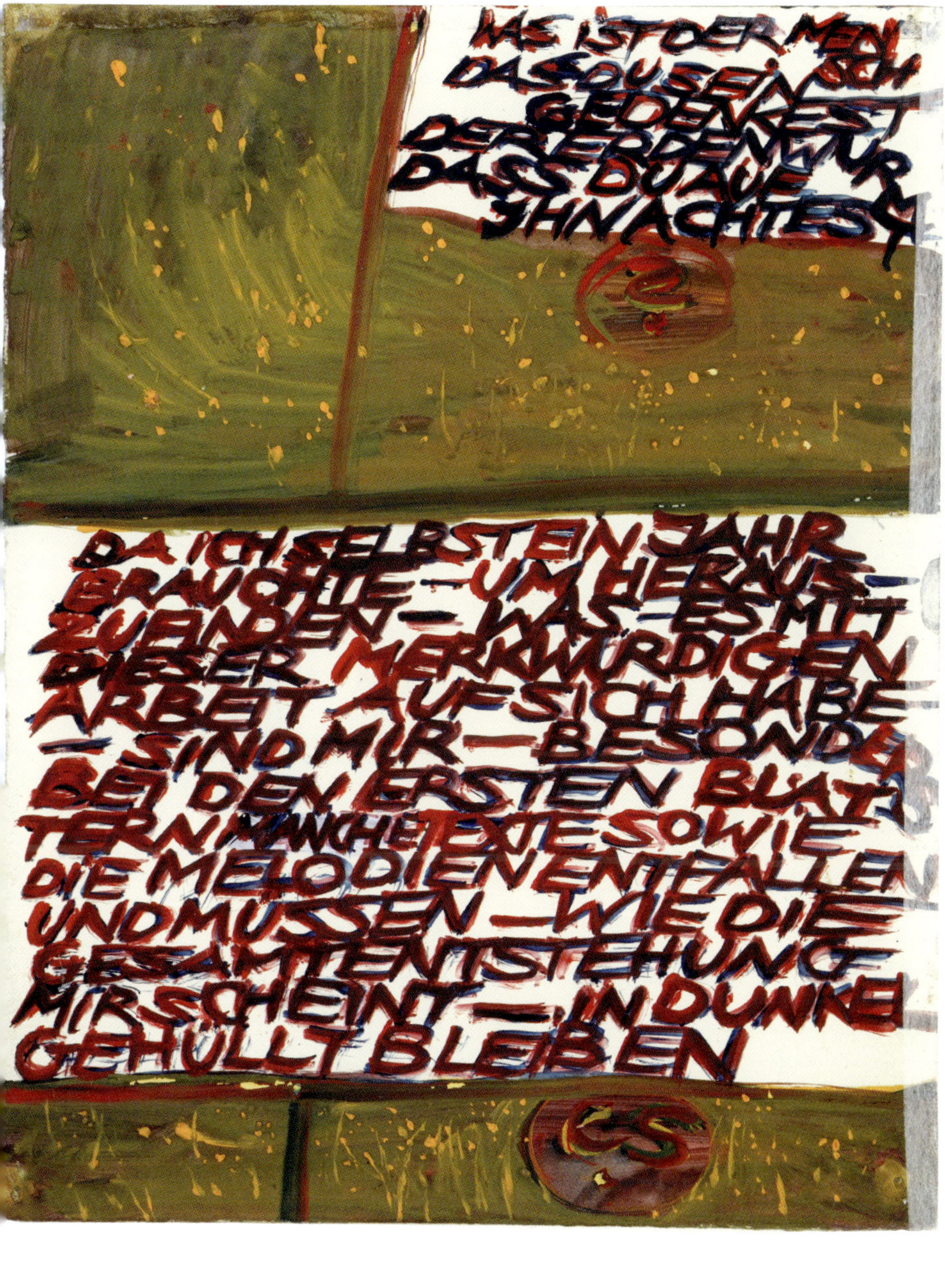
WAS IST DER MEN
DASS DU SEIN SCH
GEDENKEST
DER ERDENWURM
DASS DU AUF
IHN ACHTEST
DA ICH SELBST EIN JAHR
BRAUCHTE – UM HERAUS-
ZUFINDEN – WAS ES MIT
DIESER MERKWÜRDIGEN
ARBEIT AUF SICH HABE
– SIND MIR – BESONDE
BEI DEN ERSTEN BLAT-
TERN MANCHE TEXTE SOWIE
DIE MELODIEN ENTFALLEN
UND MÜSSEN – WIE DIE
GESAMTENTSTEHUNG
MIR SCHEINT – IN DUNKE
GEHÜLLT BLEIBEN

The origin of the following sheets is to be imagined as follows: The person is sitting by the sea. He is painting. A melody suddenly comes into his mind. As he begins to hum it, he notices that the melody matches exactly what he is trying to put to paper. A text forms within him and he begins to sing the melody with his own text, innumerable times in a loud voice until the sheet appears to be finished. Frequently, several texts take shape, and the result is a double song, or it...

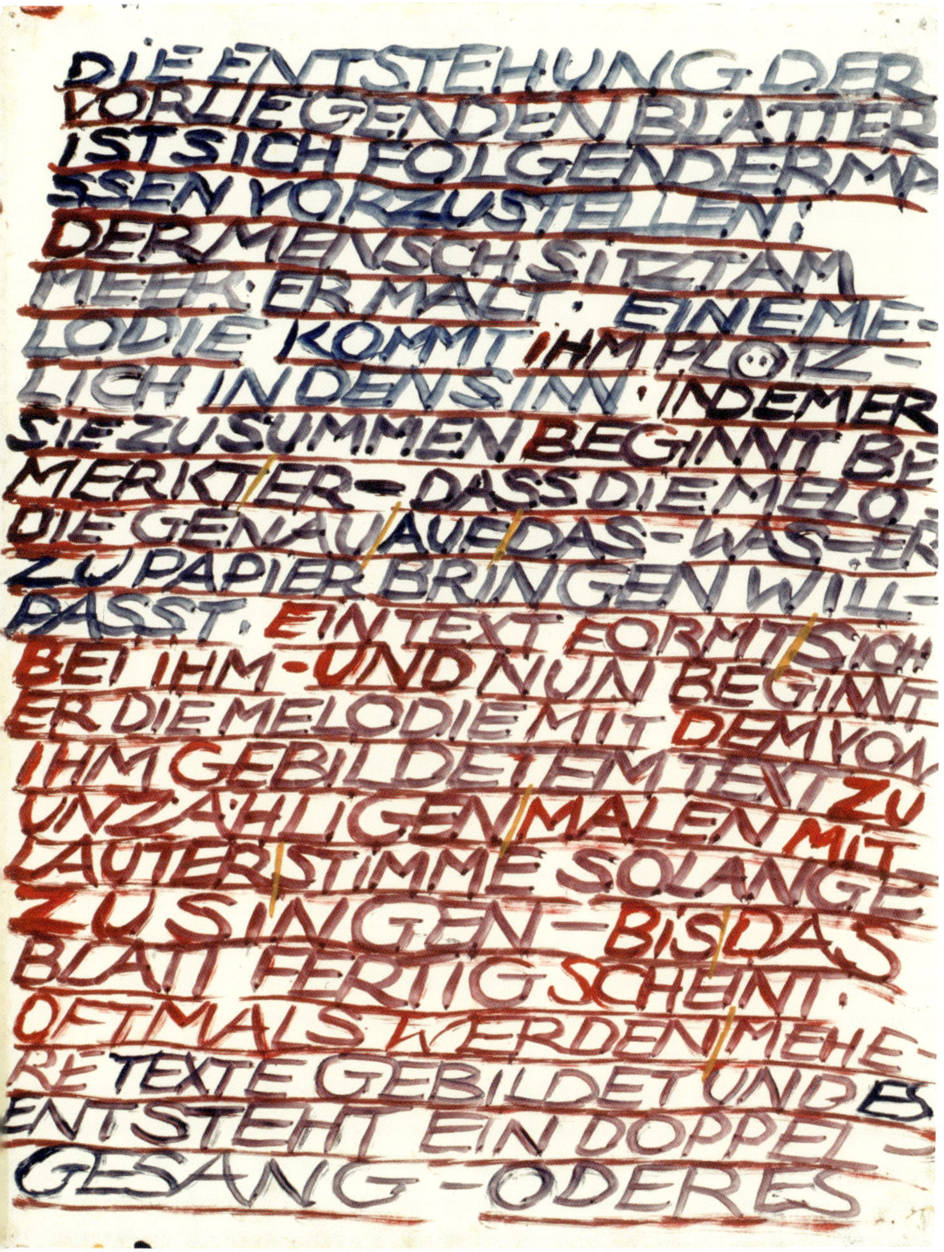
DIE ENTSTEHUNG DER
VORLIEGENDEN BLÄTTER
IST SICH FOLGENDERMA
SSEN VORZUSTELLEN:
DER MENSCH SITZT AM
MEER. ER MALT. EINE ME-
LODIE KOMMT IHM PLÖTZ-
LICH IN DEN SINN. INDEM ER
SIE ZU SUMMEN BEGINNT BE
MERKT ER - DASS DIE MELO-
DIE GENAU AUF DAS - WAS ER
ZU PAPIER BRINGEN WILL -
PASST. EIN TEXT FORMT SICH
BEI IHM - UND NUN BEGINNT
ER DIE MELODIE MIT DEM VON
IHM GEBILDETEM TEXT ZU
UNZÄHLIGEN MALEN MIT
LAUTER STIMME SOLANGE
ZU SINGEN - BIS DAS
BLATT FERTIG SCHEINT.
OFTMALS WERDEN MEHE-
RE TEXTE GEBILDET UND ES
ENTSTEHT EIN DOPPEL-
GESANG - ODER ES

... even happens that all the people to be depicted have to sing a different text, resulting in a choral song. The differences of the sheets should rest less on the author than on the differences of the characters being developed. The author endeavours to discover – perhaps what is most clearly felt in the Main Section – to go completely out of herself and to let the characters sing or speak in their own voices. In order to achieve this, much of the artistic values had to be dispensed with, for which I hope will be forgiven for the work of the soul.

The author
St Jean,
August 1940/42

Or between heaven and earth beyond our time in year 1 of the new salvation.

PASSIERT SOGAR – DASS
ALLE DARZUSTELLENDEN PER-
SONEN EINEN VERSCHIEDENEN
TEXT ZU SINGEN HABEN, WO-
MIT EIN CHORGESANG ENT-
STEHT. DIE VERSCHIEDEN-
HEIT DER BLÄTTER SOLLTE WENI-
GER AM VERFASSER LIEGEN – ALS
AN DER VERSCHIEDENHEIT DER
CHARAKTHERE DER ZU GEBILD-
ET WERDENDEN PERSONEN. DER
VERFASSER BEMÜHT SICH – WAS
AM DEUTLICHSTEN VIELLEICHT IM HAUPT-
TEIL ZU SPÜREN IST – VOLLSTÄNDIG
AUS SICH SELBST HERAUSZUGEHEN
UND DIE PERSONEN MIT EIGENER STIMME
SINGEN ODER SRECHEN ZU LASSEN.
UM DAS ZU ERREICHEN – WURDE
AUF VIEL KÜNSTLERISCHES VERZICH-
TET. WAS MAN JEDOCH – SO HOFFE
ICH – IN HINSICHT DER SEELENEIN-
DRÄNGERISCH GELEISTETEN
ARBEIT – VERZEIHEN
WIRD.

DER VERFASSER
ST. JEAN AUGUST 1940/41
ODER ZWISCHEN HIMMEL
UND ERDE AUSSERHALB
VON UNSERER ZEIT IM JAHR
1 DES
NEUEN HEILS

PRELUDE

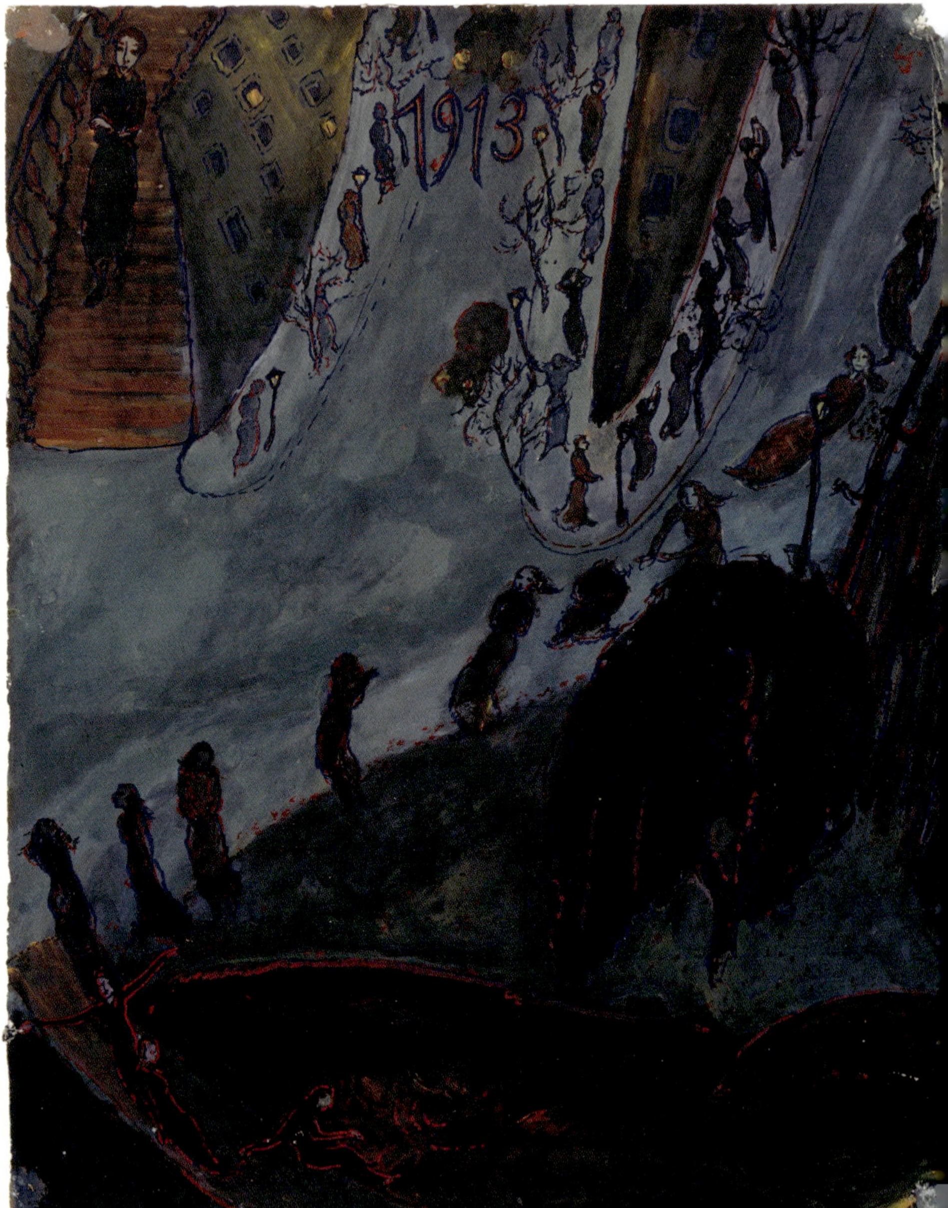
1913

SCENE 1
1913

On a November day, Charlotte Knarre left her parents' home and threw herself into the water.

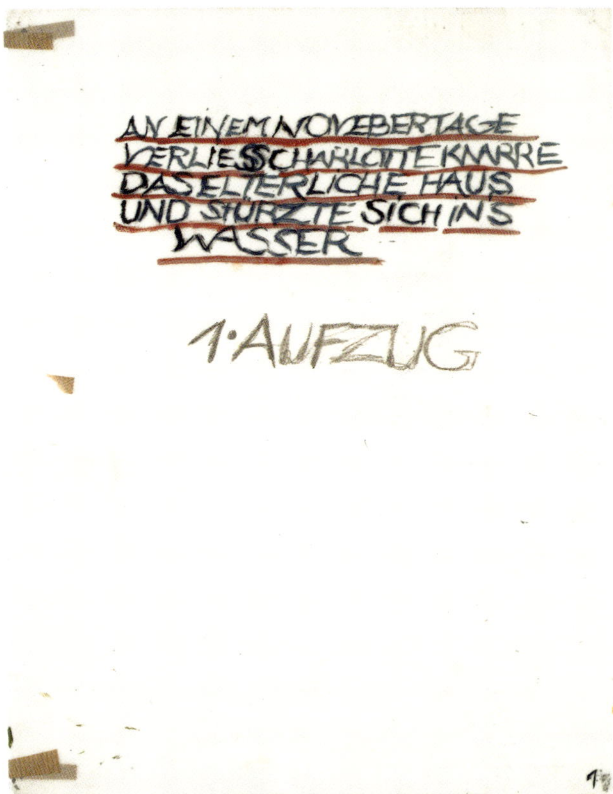

SUICIDE OF AN EIGHTEEN-YEAR-OLD!
CHARLOTTE SEEKS DEATH IN LAKE SCHLACHTENSEE!

Last night a young girl drowned herself in the Schlachtensee. The recovered body was identified by her father this morning at the morgue. We say to her parents our deepest sympathy and trust they will find consolation in their older daughter.

Vossische Zeitung [newspaper].

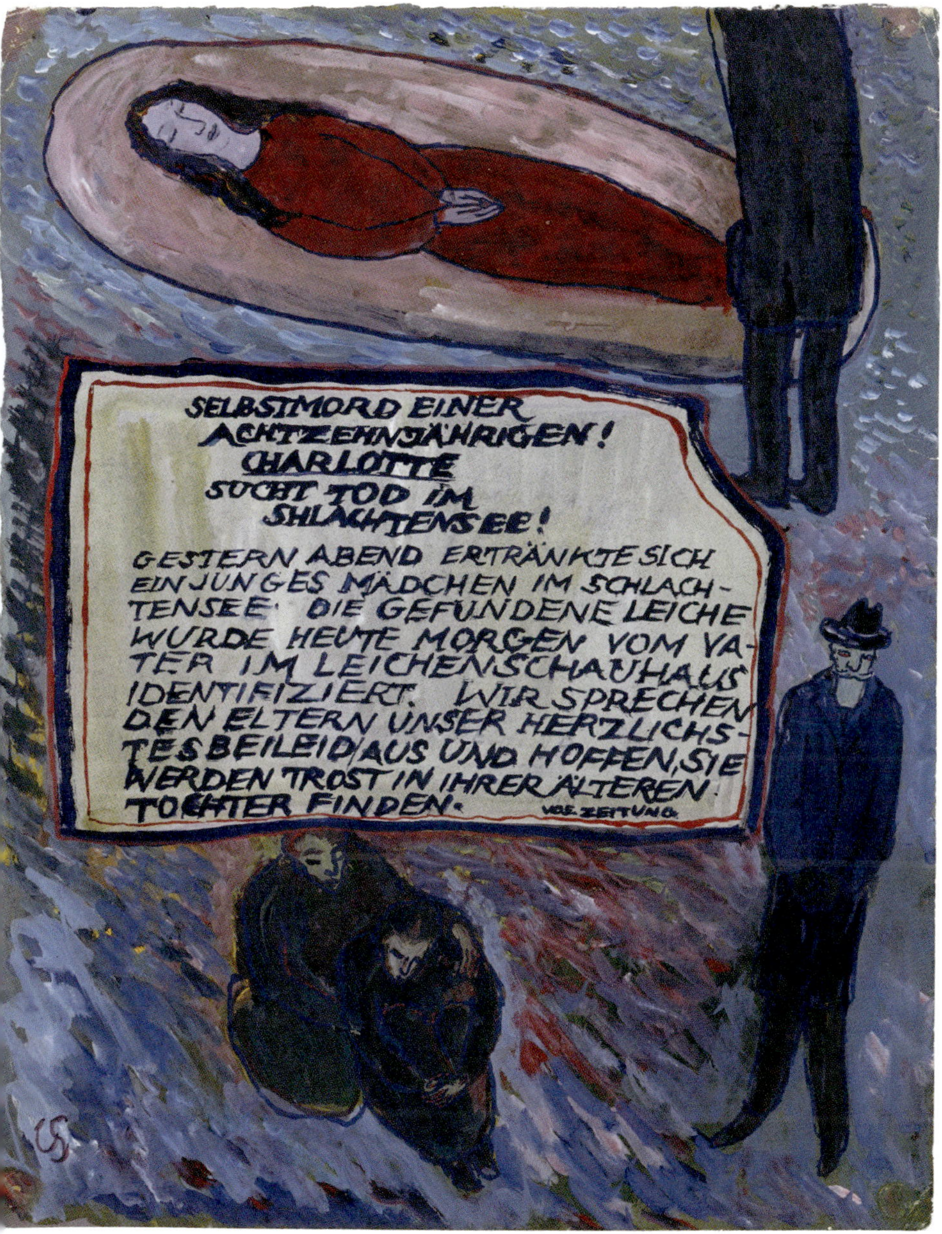
SELBSTMORD EINER
ACHTZEHNJÄHRIGEN!
CHARLOTTE
SUCHT TOD IM
SCHLACHTENSEE!
GESTERN ABEND ERTRÄNKTE SICH
EIN JUNGES MÄDCHEN IM SCHLACH-
TENSEE. DIE GEFUNDENE LEICHE
WURDE HEUTE MORGEN VOM VA-
TER IM LEICHENSCHAUHAUS
IDENTIFIZIERT. WIR SPRECHEN
DEN ELTERN UNSER HERZLICHS-
TES BEILEID AUS UND HOFFEN, SIE
WERDEN TROST IN IHRER ÄLTEREN
TOCHTER FINDEN.
VOS. ZEITUNG.

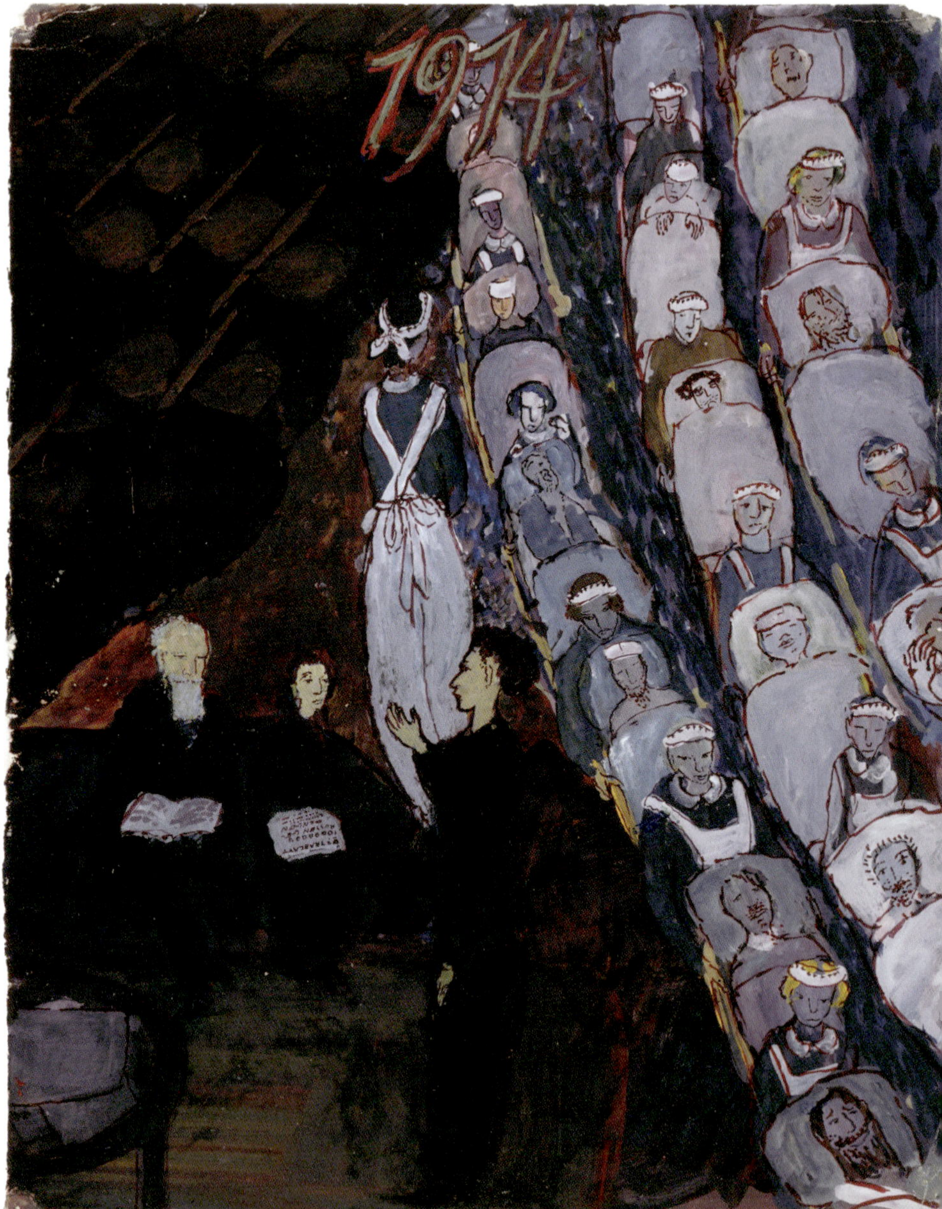
1914

1914

FRANZISKA
"I have to be a nurse!"

With this emotional outburst and the allusion to the needs of the Fatherland for more helping hands, Franziska surprises her parents one day while they are engrossed in the "newspaper extras" to which they are not very appreciative, especially since their little daughter wishes to go to the front.

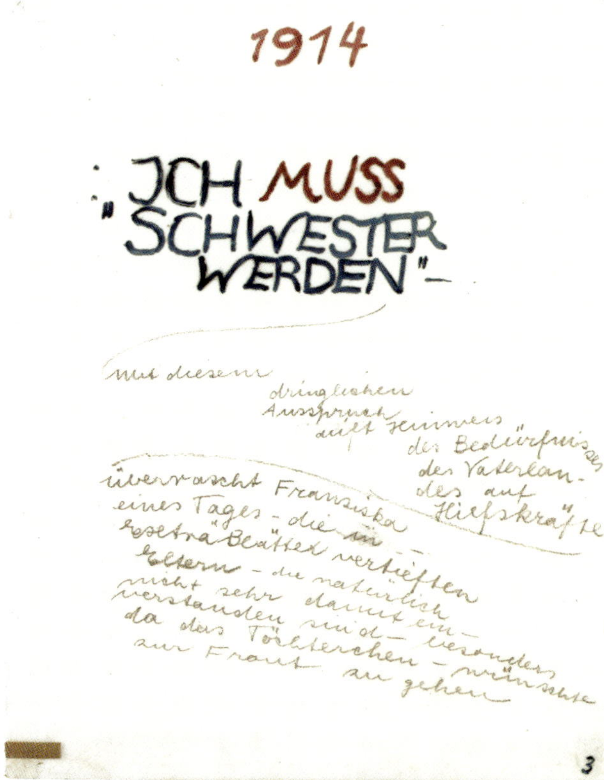

1915

... she became a very efficient ward and operating nurse. She was especially fond of assisting one young surgeon. As he had the sniffles, she had to wipe his nose during the operation. After the operation they parted, and Franziska made her rounds. But then they met again and had a little chat.

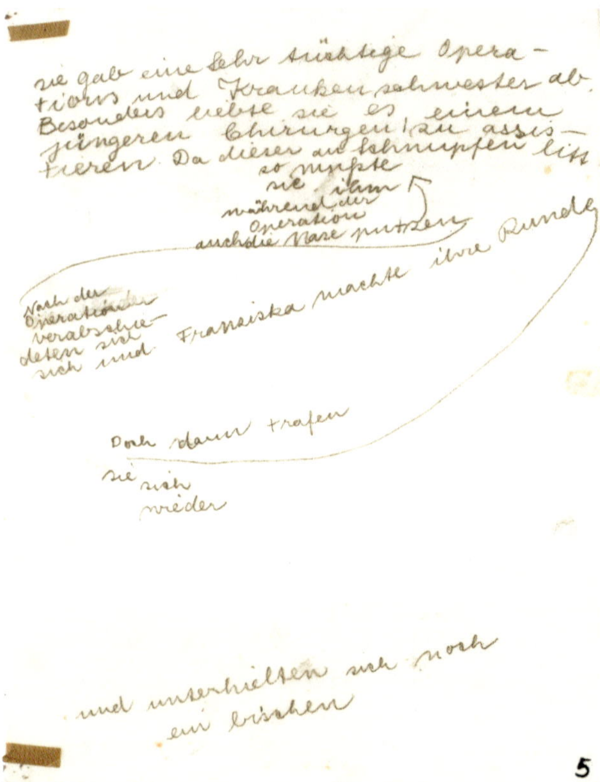
sie gab eine sehr tüchtige Opera-
tions und Krankenschwester ab.
Besonders liebte sie es einem
jüngeren Chirurgen zu assis-
tieren. Da dieser an Schnupfen litt
so mußte
sie ihm
während der
Operation
auch die Nase putzen

Nach der
Operation ver-
abschie-
deten sich
sich und Franziska machte ihre Runde

Doch dann trafen
sie sich
wieder

und unterhielten sich noch
ein bißchen

5

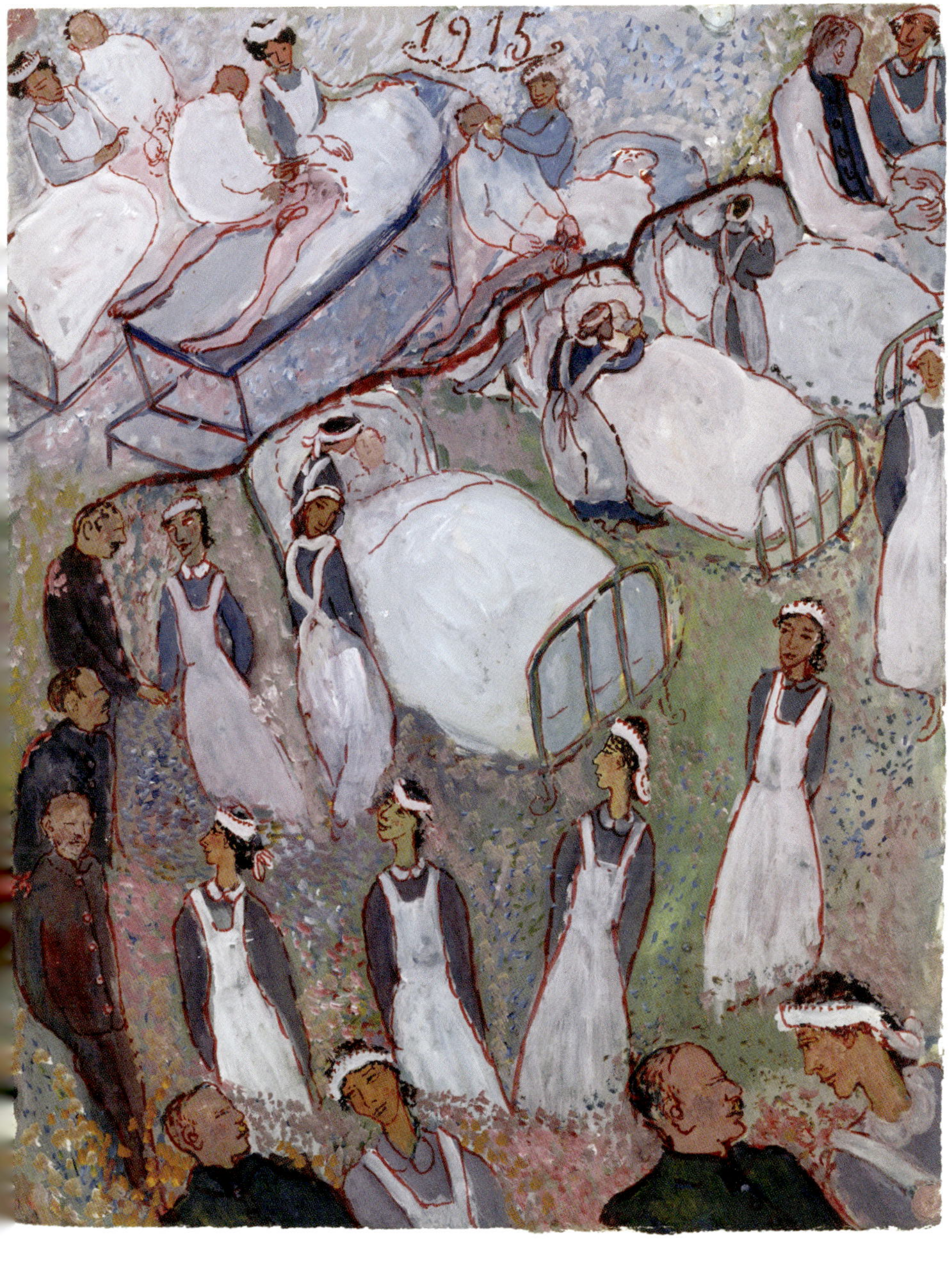
1915

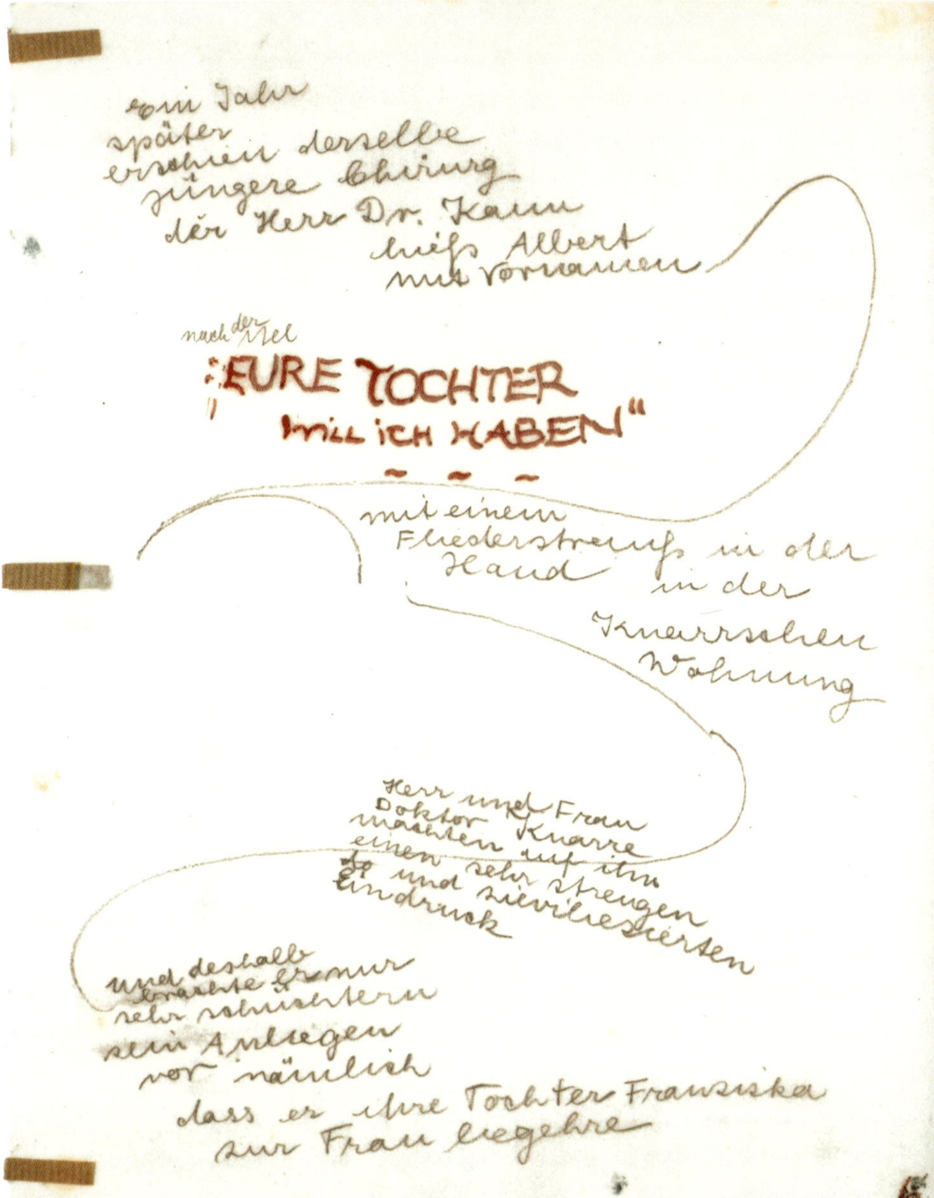
ein Jahr
später
erschien derselbe
jüngere Chirurg
der Herr Dr. Kann
hieß Albert
mit Vornamen
nach der Mel
„Eure Tochter
will ich haben"
mit einem
Fliederstrauß in der
Hand in der
Knarrschen
Wohnung
Herr und Frau
Doktor Knarre
machten auf ihn
einen sehr strengen
und zivilisierten
Eindruck
und deshalb
brachte er nur
sehr schüchtern
sein Anliegen
vor nämlich
dass er ihre Tochter Franziska
zur Frau begehre

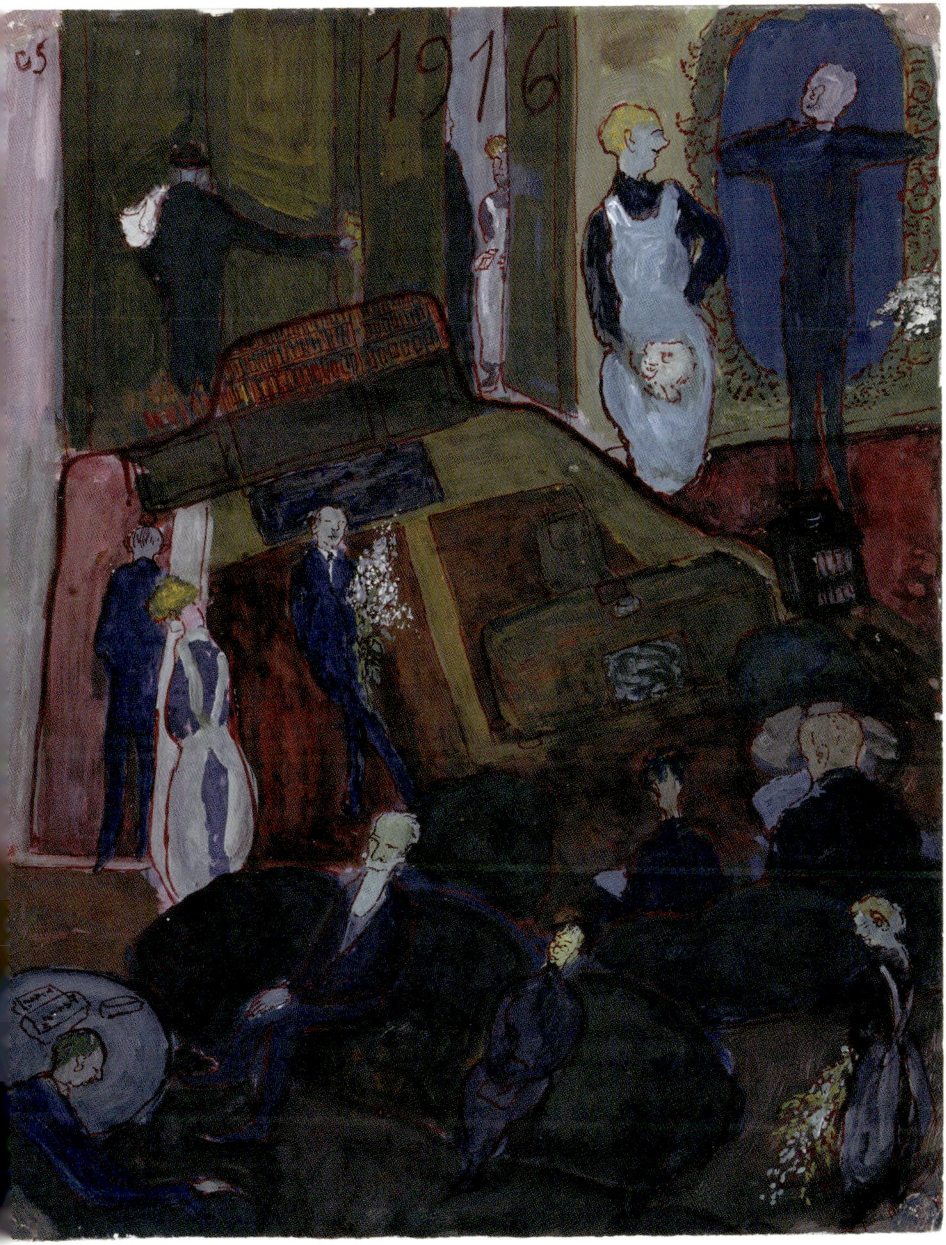
1916

(previous pages)

1916

One year later, this young surgeon, whose name was Dr Kann – with the first name Albert – turned up at the Knarres' apartment with a bunch of lilacs in his hand. Dr and Mrs Knarre made a very stern and civilised impression on him, and that is why he brought up his request in an extremely timid manner, namely, that he coveted their daughter Franziska to be his wife.

To the melody: Eure Tochter will ich haben
[It's your daughter I desire]

(opposite)

PARENTS
"Yes, you should have her, but it is a most precious good that we are entrusting to you there."

Mr Knarre, while expressing the long-awaited-for consent, explains to Albert Kann that his daughter – quite apart from the respectable dowry he is prepared to give her – is an especially precious commodity that has to be handled very gently and affectionately. Albert seems to know this.

In the dark, large, high-ceilinged dining room, they have supper. Dr Kann is somewhat uncomfortable. Mrs Knarre's glances in particular disturb him. He would prefer to be alone with Franziska. Then, she embraces him tenderly, and he walks down the red-trimmed, white marble stairs, not quite sure whether he has done the right thing; he finds Franziska charming, but the atmosphere of her parents' home makes an eerie impression.

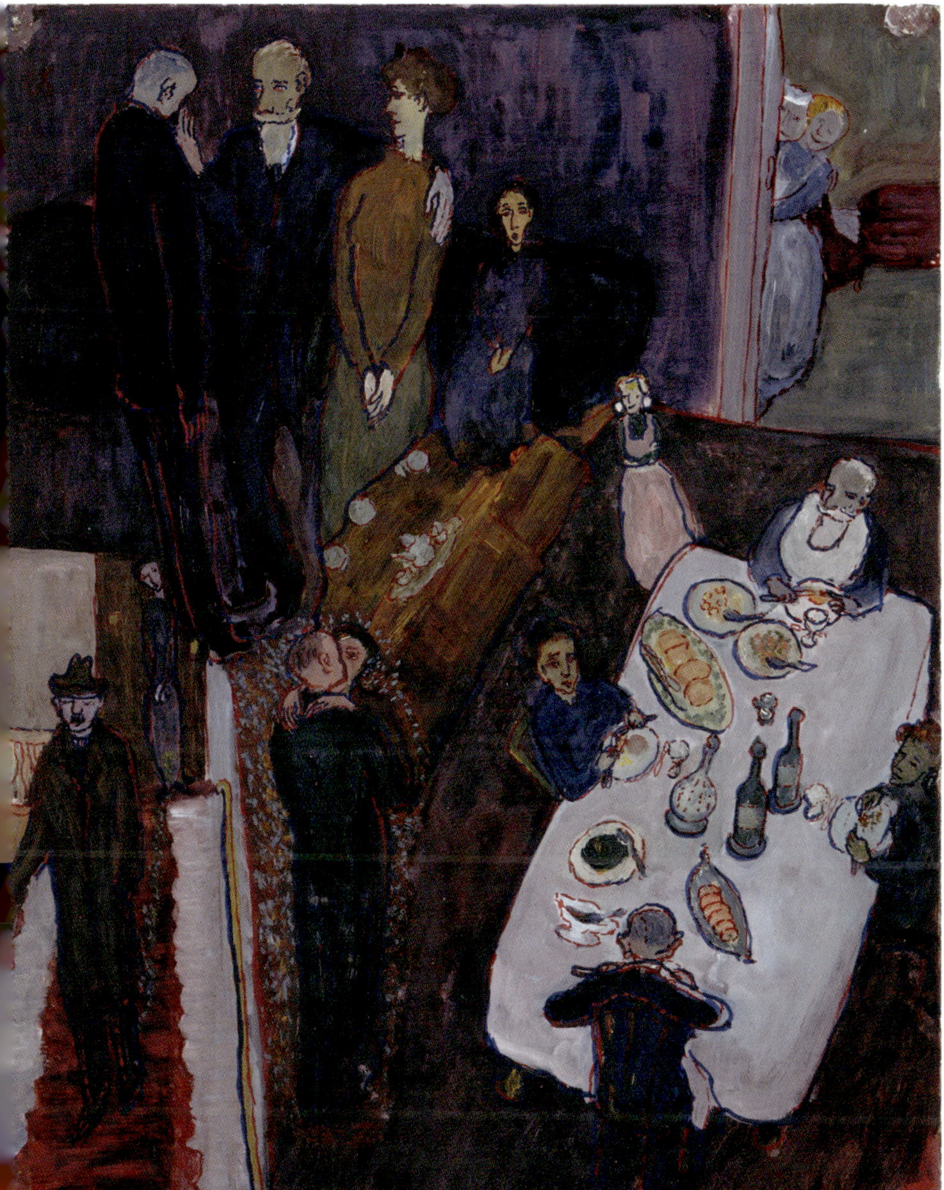

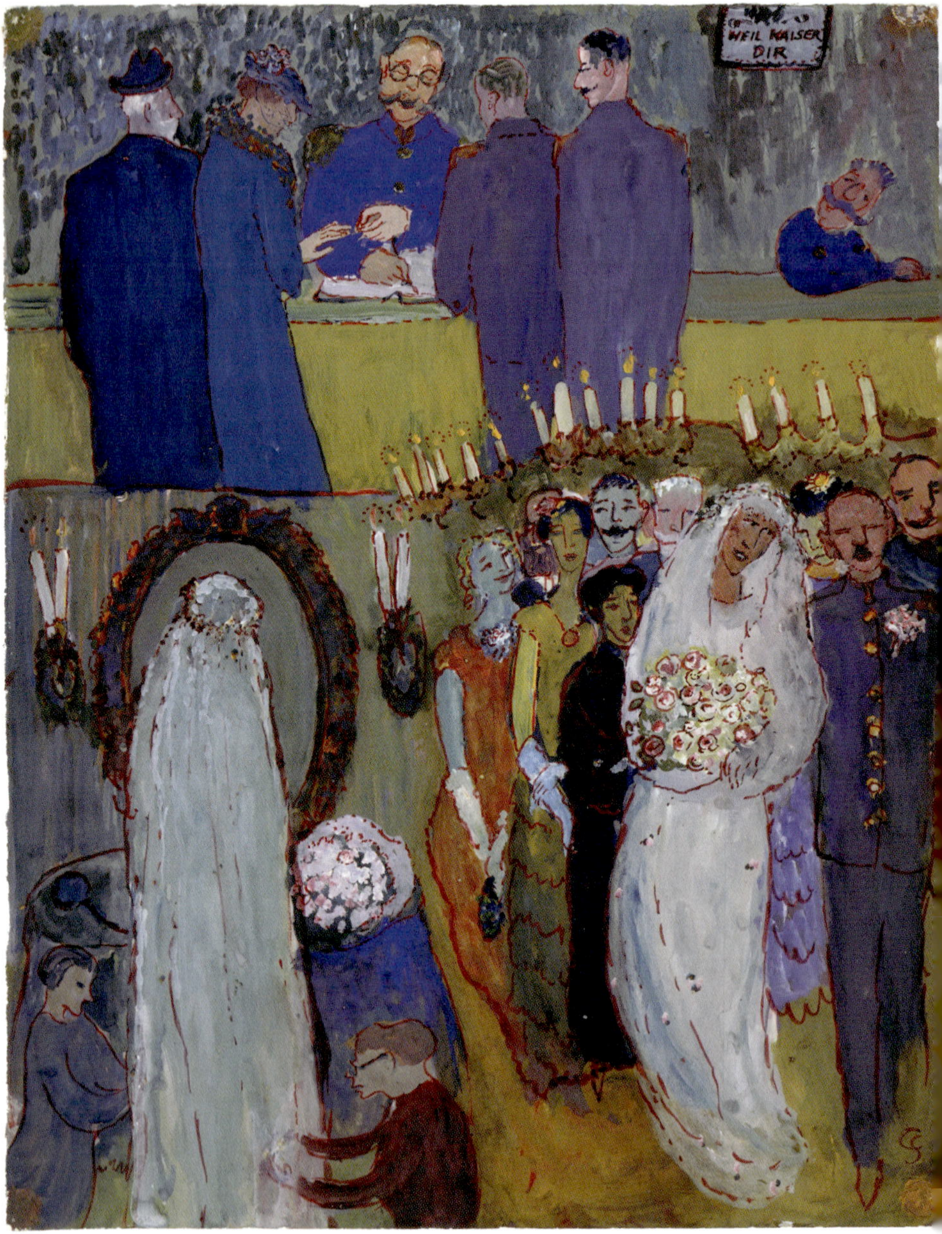
HEIL KAISER
DIR

But, it is too late for such reflections. The registry office official of the German Empire places the ring in the presence of the witnesses Mr Knarre and Albert's brother – Albert's parents having since long been dead – on the ring finger of the happy bride's slender, long right hand.

After the civil ceremony, the dressmaker and her assistant busily dress Franziska. She looks really enchanting and is truly happy as she walks on the arm of her beloved before the many members of the wedding party.

Mr Knarre, but especially Mrs Knarre seems to be thinking of something very sad and make a depressing impression in the midst of the cheerful throng.

To the melody: Wir winden dir den Jungfernkranz
[We twine for thee the maiden's wreath]

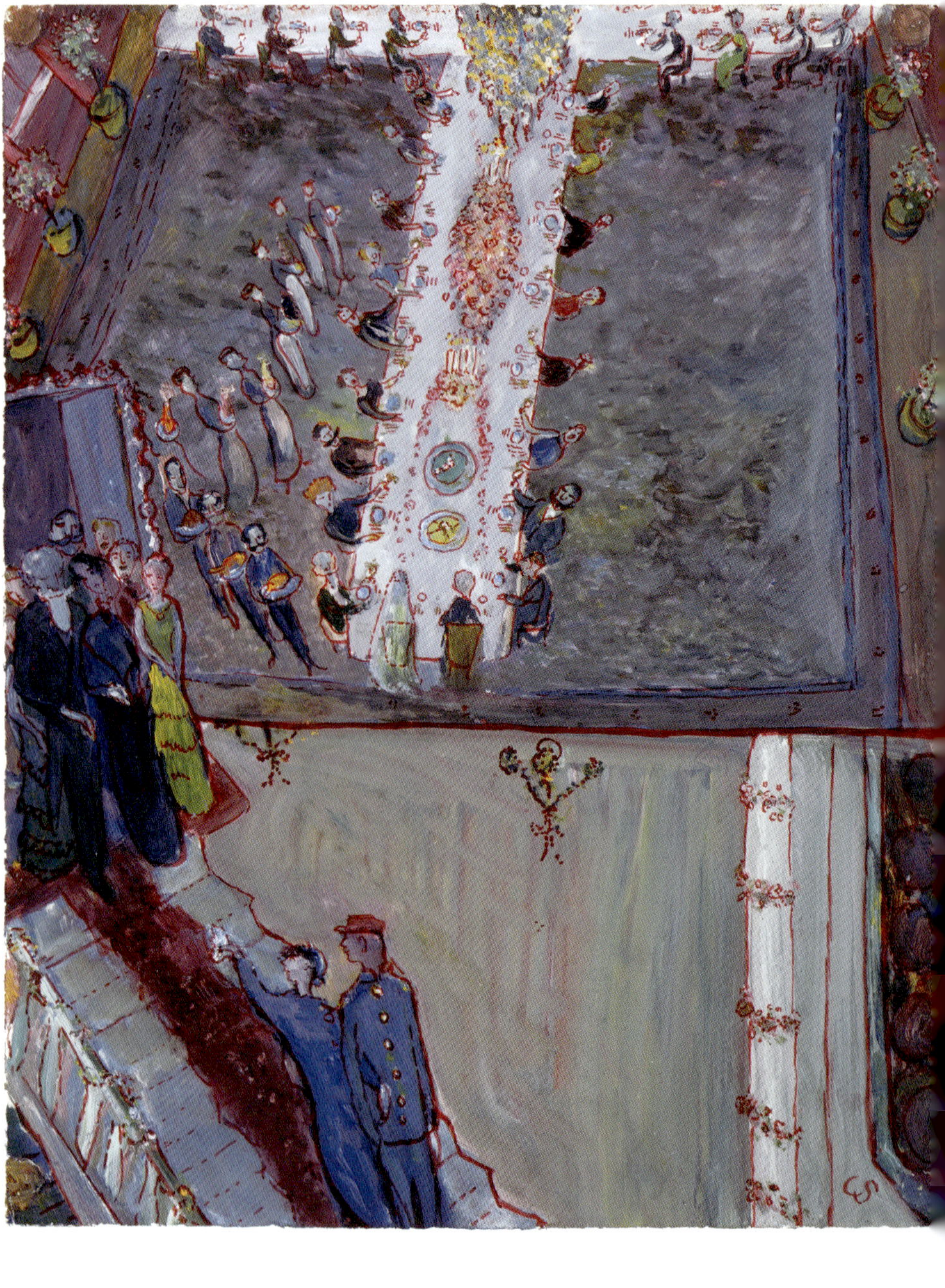

(opposite)

The wedding banquet, served in the tall, large, completely cleared out study now decorated with little tubs of rose trees, is excellent, and does nothing to remind the gathering of the war that is still raging.

Later the bridal couple leaves the house accompanied by the good wishes and blessings of parents and guests.

Melody is missing.
Presumably: Wir winden dir den Hochzeitskranz

(right)

For his first night Albert has chosen the finest hotel in the city. He very much loves the comfort of grand hotels and even as a boy had a soft spot for them.

The room they enter is charmingly furnished in the Empire style. The wide bed is adorned with a cherub's head carved out of wood.

The bed cover is pleasantly silky-downy soft. It seems to be a full moon. The wide window frames cast a shadow onto the bed and the thick plush carpet.

Melody is missing.

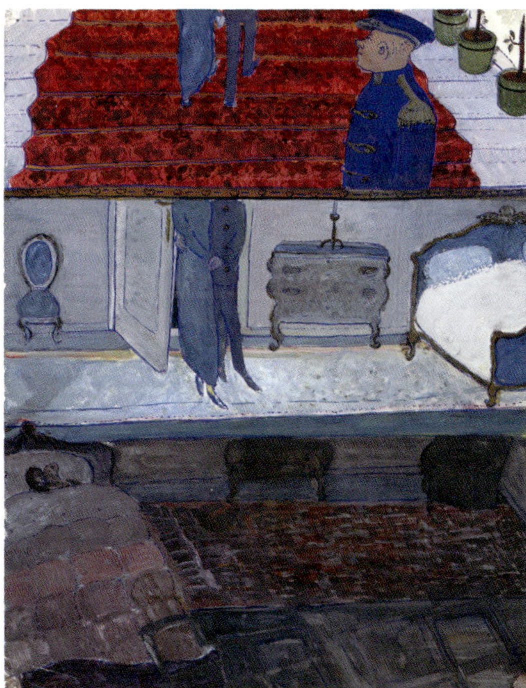

"Goodbye, my litte darling."

Unfortunately Albert, being a soldier, must leave the city the next morning. Mr and Mrs Knarre, who have come to the station to see him off, want Franziska to come home with them. Franziska, however, prefers to drive to her own, new home which is situated somewhat beyond the bustle of the city. She is sad that her beloved has gone away – but happy in the anticipation of taking possession of her apartment, which has been furnished with so much love and taste.

Mr and Mrs Knarre are horrified over this first act of disobedience of their daughter.

To the melody: <u>Wir</u> <u>winden</u> <u>dir</u>...

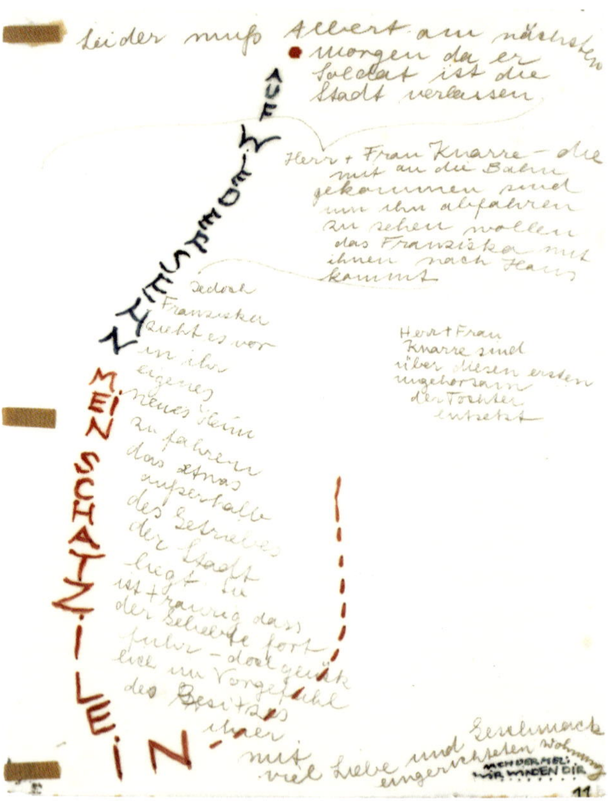

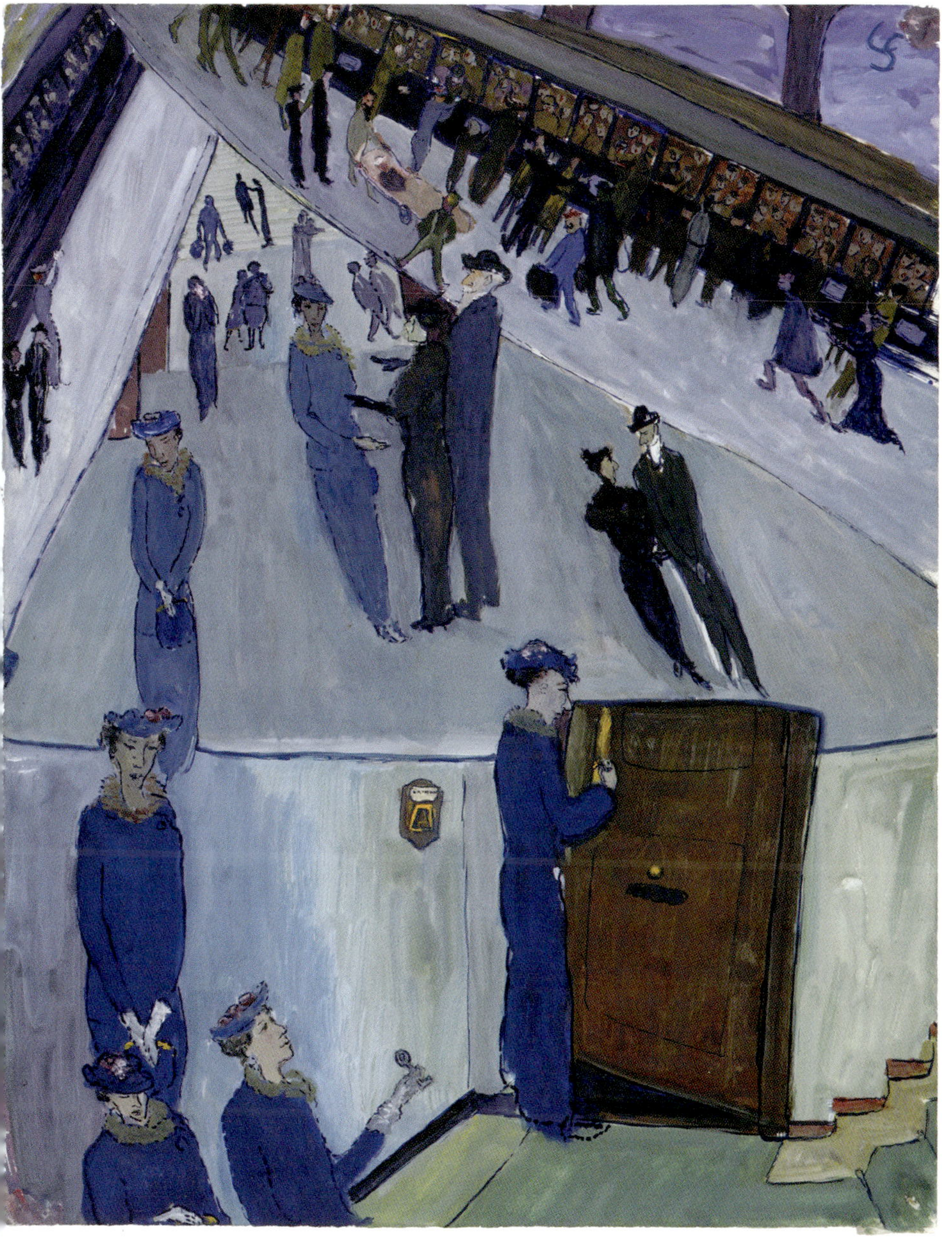

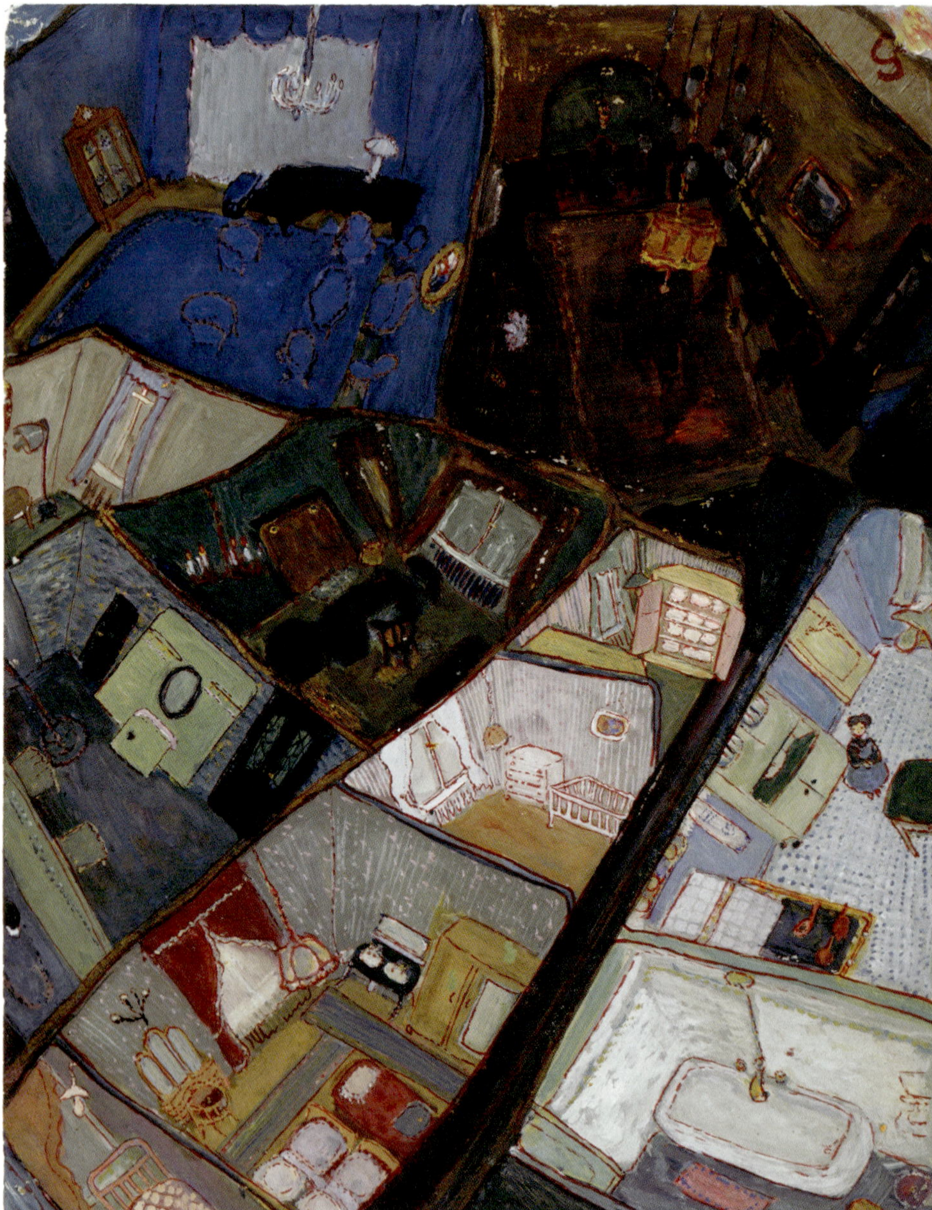

1 The apartment is really – one might almost say, beautiful. There is
2 the study with an adjoining consulting room for Albert;
3 a salon all in blue where Franziska's grand piano stands;
4 the big dining room with a small alcove in the background for such lesser meals: breakfast, coffee, etc.;
5 a long corridor that leads to the back of the apartment;
6 There is the wardrobe room with the well-stocked linen cabinets;
7 the nursery for the expected offsprings;
8 the bedroom;
9 the kitchen – where Augusta is already sitting waiting for the orders of the housewife;
10 the pleasant bathroom;
11 and Augusta's little room.

To the melody: Wir winden dir...

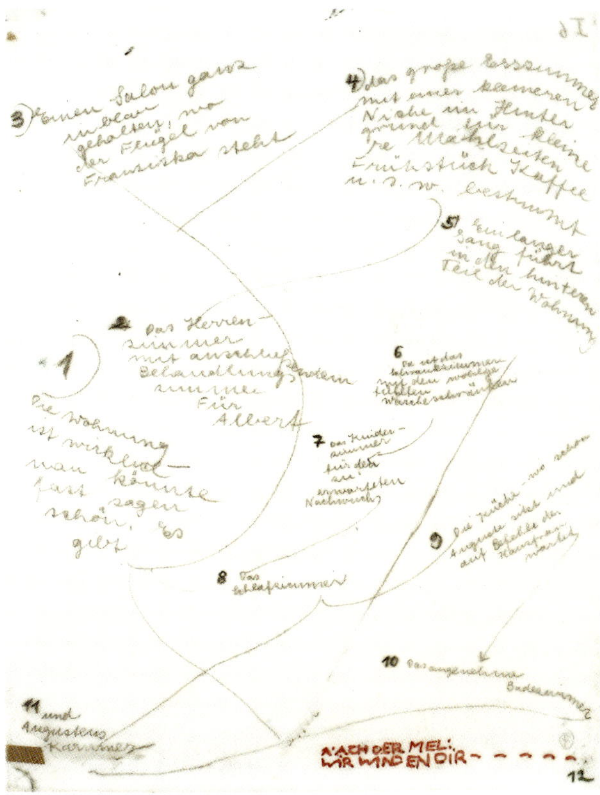

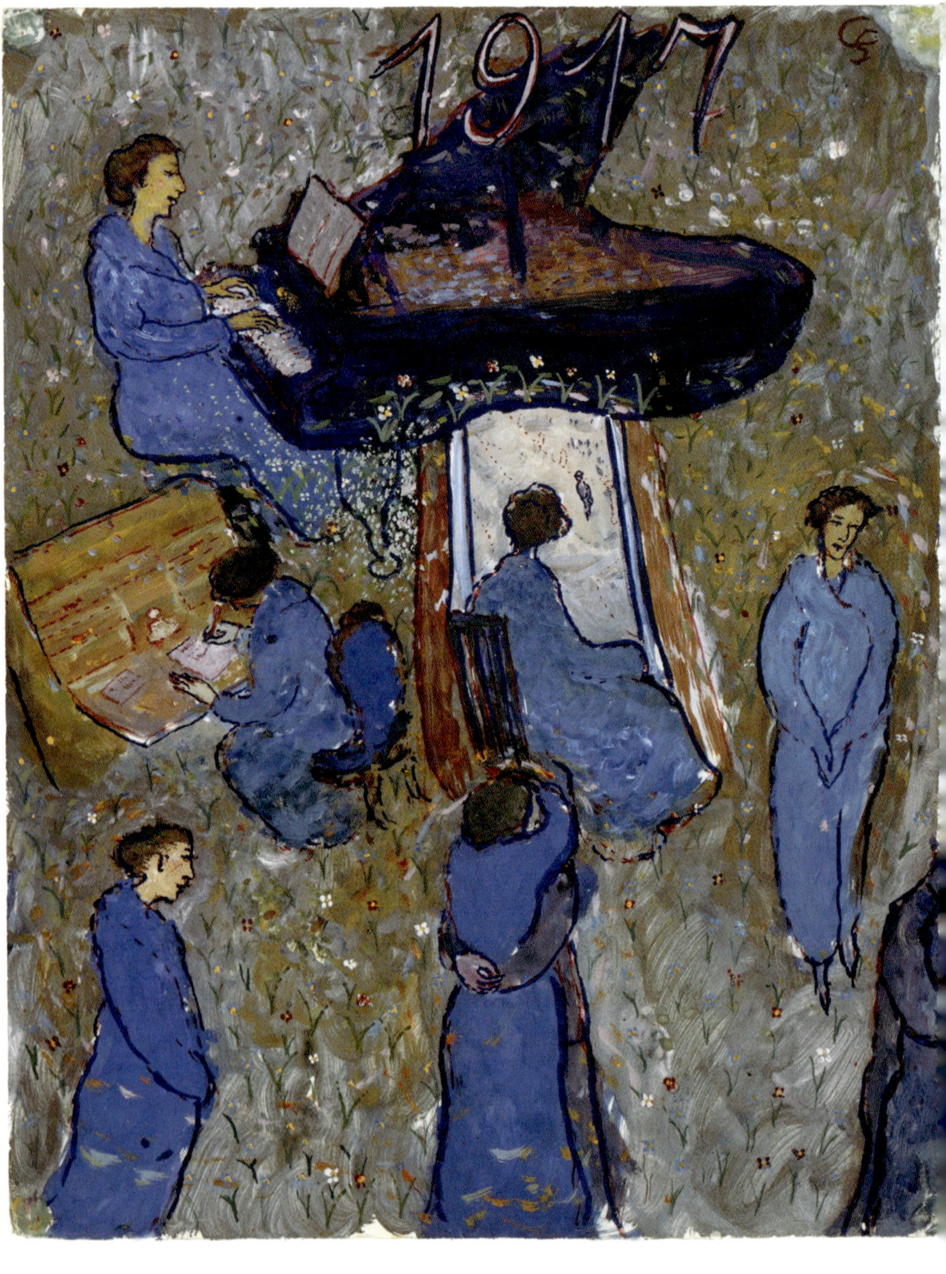
1917

(opposite)

1917

A short year later and the war is at an end, and still unexpectedly for Franziska Albert suddenly returns, just before the birth of their first child, to whom she gives the name Charlotte in memory of her younger sister.

Birth announcements are sent to all their friends and acquaintances.

No melody

(bottom)

Dr A. Kann and Mrs F. Kann, née Knarre, announce the birth of a girl, yesterday, named Charlotte.

April 1917

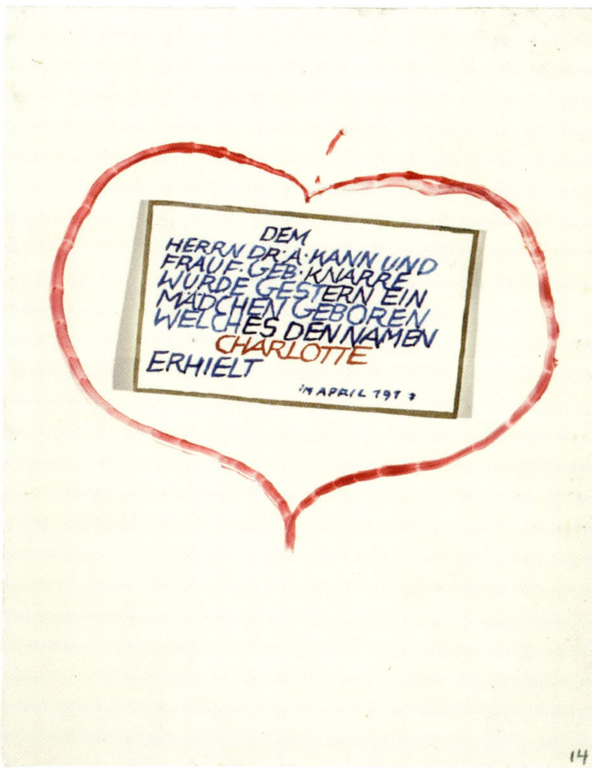

(bottom)

Although little Charlotte did not seem to agree at all with being born – she cried miserably day and night – Franziska was very happy with her.

She nurtured her herself and was very downcast each time the almighty infant nurse took her baby away.

With the new Charlotte's head like a pin, she always pushed the tall, white baby carriage herself.

(opposite)

1922

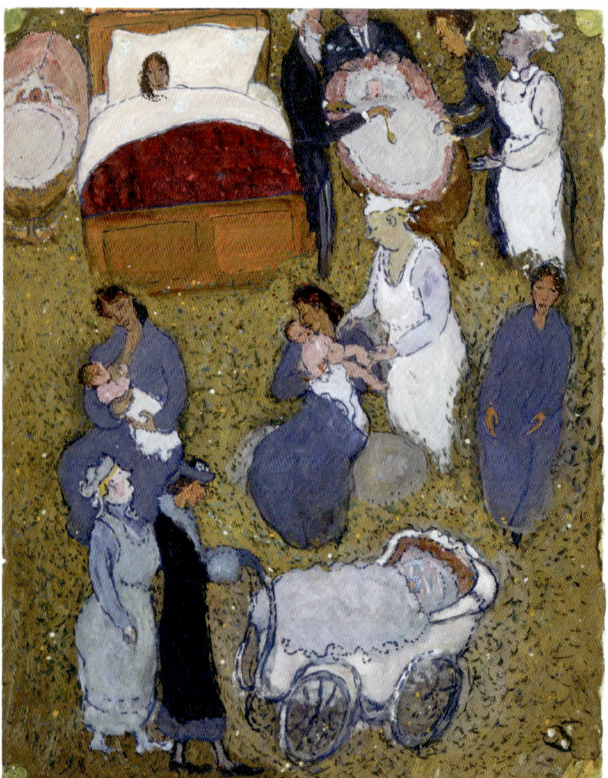

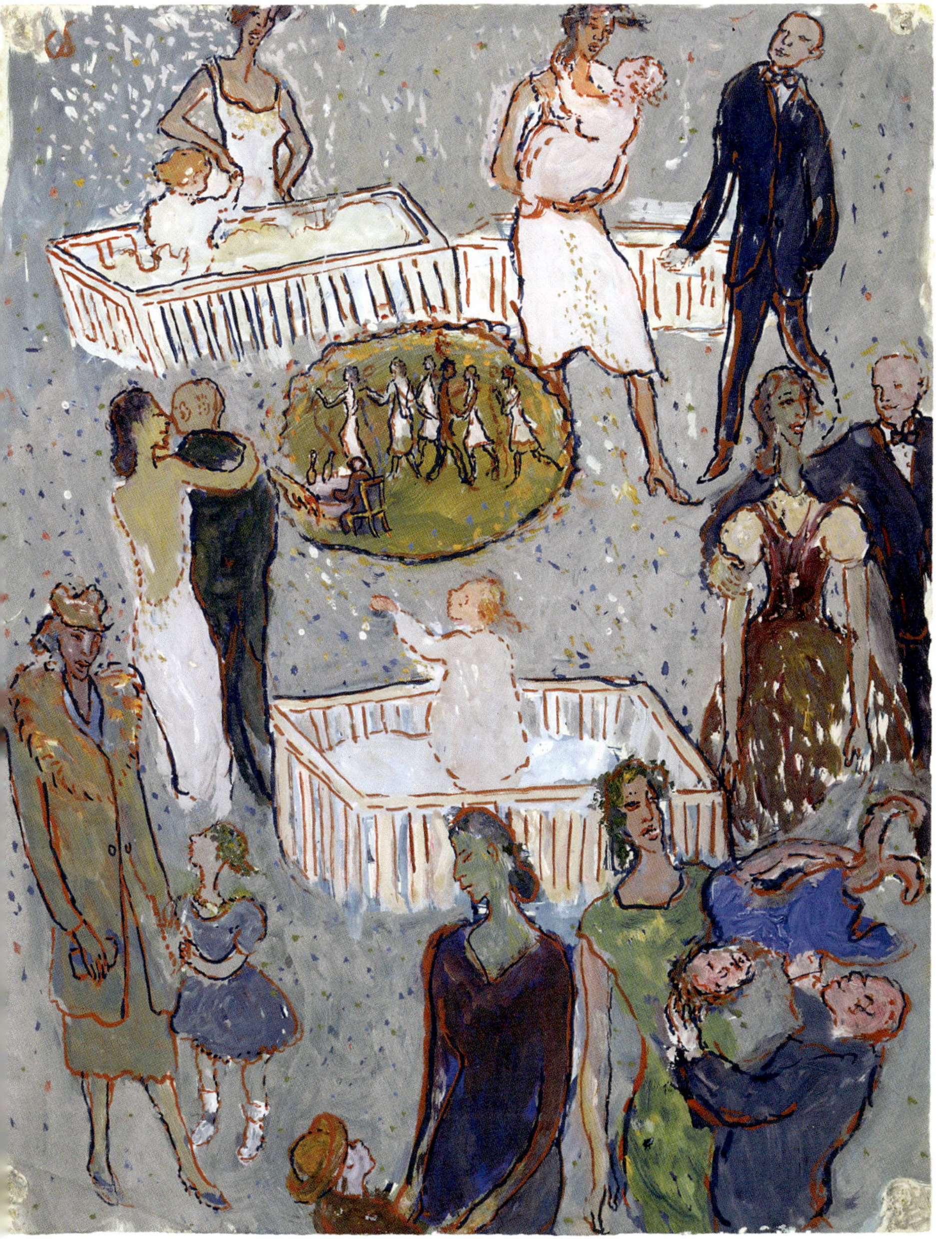

Charlotte's first journey was to the Bavarian mountains. Later she often recalled it. Her mother was terribly funny and sang and jumped around with her everywhere. Her father was serious. But he was very happy with his family. They also went in a boat and climbed way up onto the mountains.

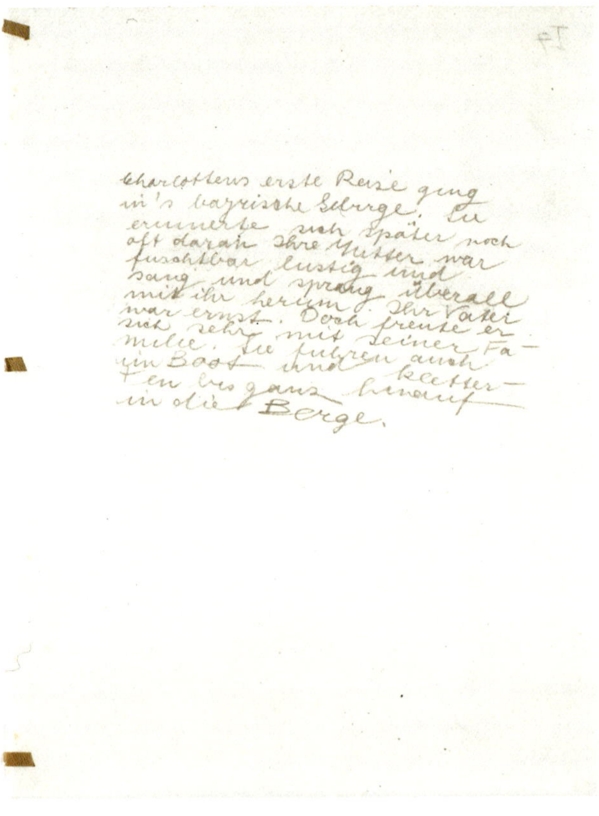
19

charlottens erste Reise ging
in's bayrische Gebirge. Sie
erinnerte sich später noch
oft daran Ihre Mutter war
furchtbar lustig und
sang und sprang
mit ihr herum überall
war ernst. Doch Ihr Vater
sich sehr mit freute er
milie. Sie fuhren seiner Fa-
ein Boot und auch
ten bis ganz kletter-
in die Berge. hinauf

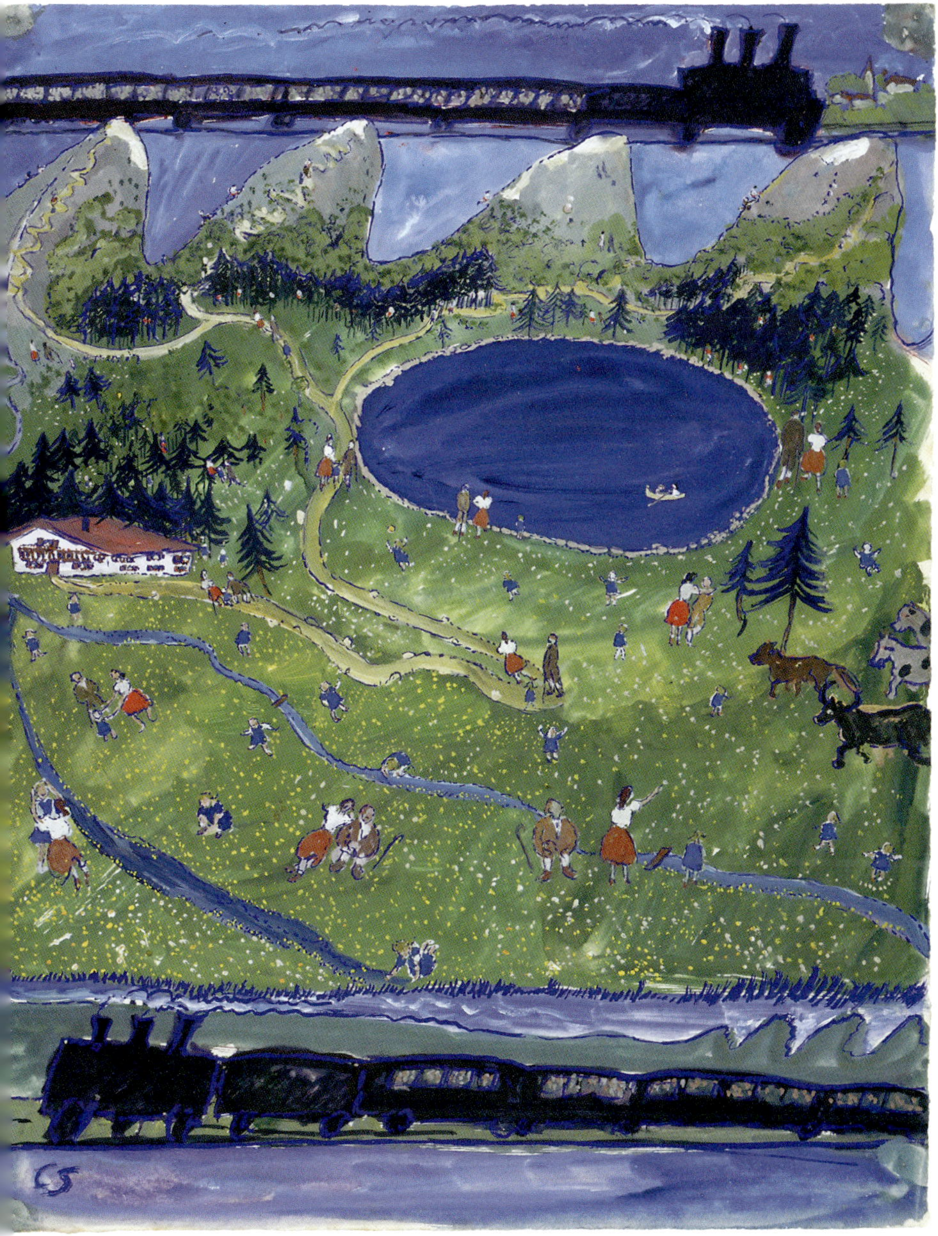

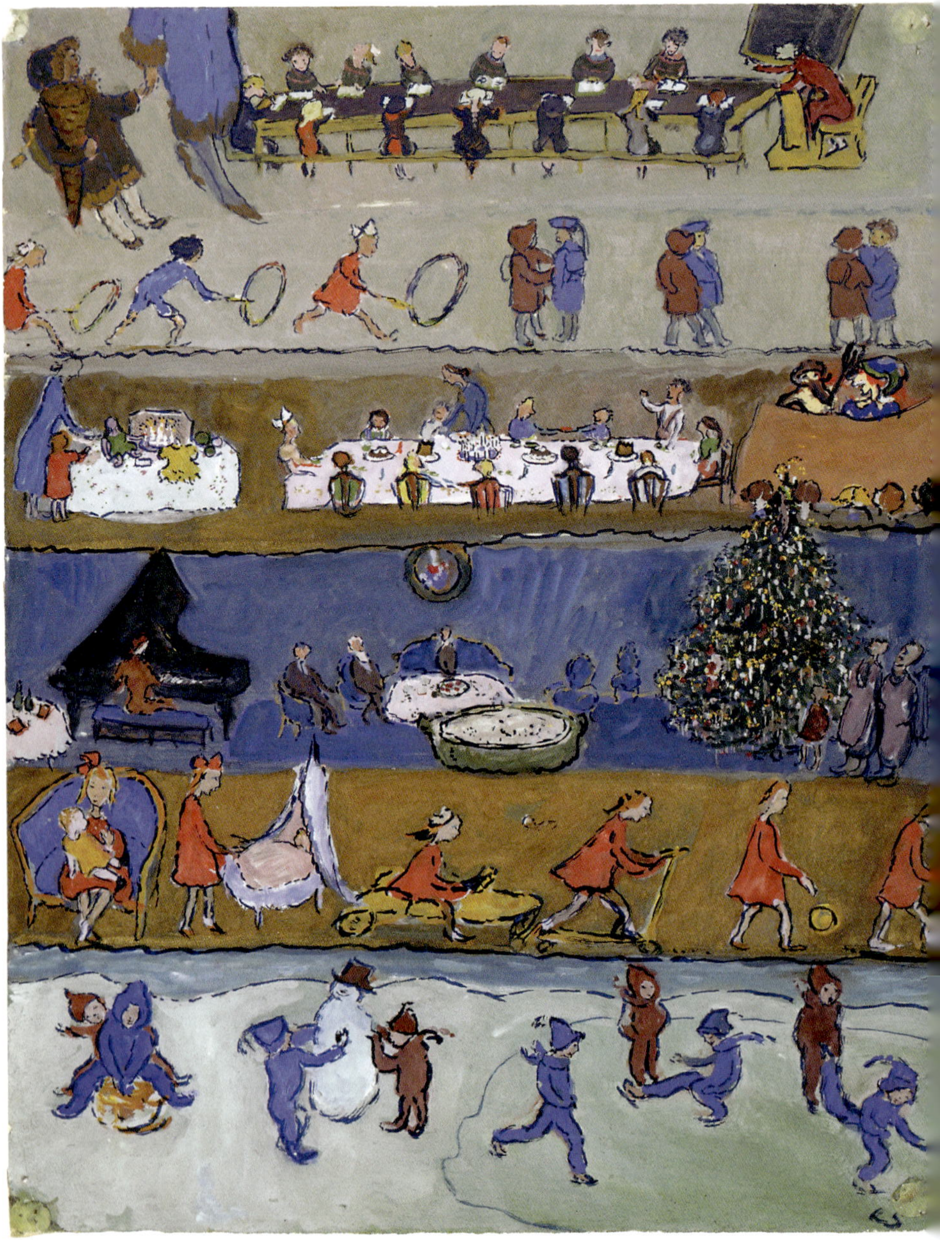

One day Franziska went with Charlotte to school. She didn't like it there much, since she wasn't allowed to look around without the teacher getting very cross with her. But she had a friend, Kurt, with black ruffled hair whom she loved very much.

Her birthday was always a big celebration. The whole class was invited for coffee and supper, and Kurt made a great speech in which he invited the guests to toast to the well-being of the birthday girl.

But Christmas was almost more beautiful. The mother sat at the grand piano and sang Stille Nacht, Heilige Nacht [Silent Night] or Am Weihnachtsbaum die Lichter brennen [With lighted candles the Christmas tree], and father and grandparents also sang, as did Charlotte and Minna and Augusta standing beside Franziska's magnificently decorated tree. While they were still singing, Charlotte took a furtive glance at the large laundry basket standing in the middle of the room.

As in every other year, it contained once again the most unbelievable gifts.

Charlotte was a great friend of winter sports. With her friend Kurt she went tobogganing, built snowmen, but in figure skating she was an exceptional artist.

To the melody: Am Weihnachtsbaum die Lichter brennen

FRANZISKA
"In heaven everything is much more beautiful than here on earth – and when your Mummy has turned into a little angel she'll come down and bring to the little bunny and bring a letter, in which she will say, what it is like in heaven, what it is like up there in heaven."

Franziska had quite a sentimental disposition. She often took the child to bed, and told her about a life after death in heavenly spheres – which was supposed to be absolutely glorious and afterward she seemed to have a terrible yearning, and often asked Charlotte if it wouldn't be wonderful if her mother were to be an angel with wings. Charlotte also found this to be very beautiful, but she only begged her mother not to forget to tell her how it was up there in heaven in a letter – which she had to deliver personally as an angel and it had to be deposited on Charlotte's window sill.

To the same melody.

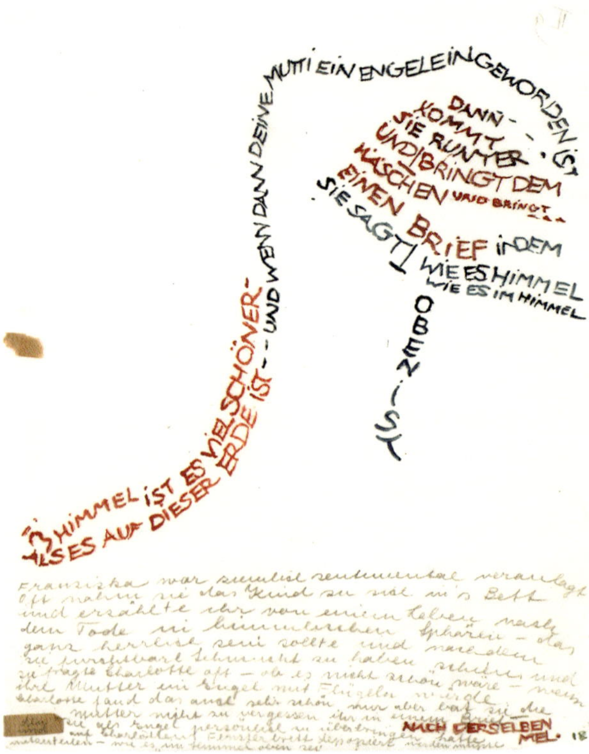

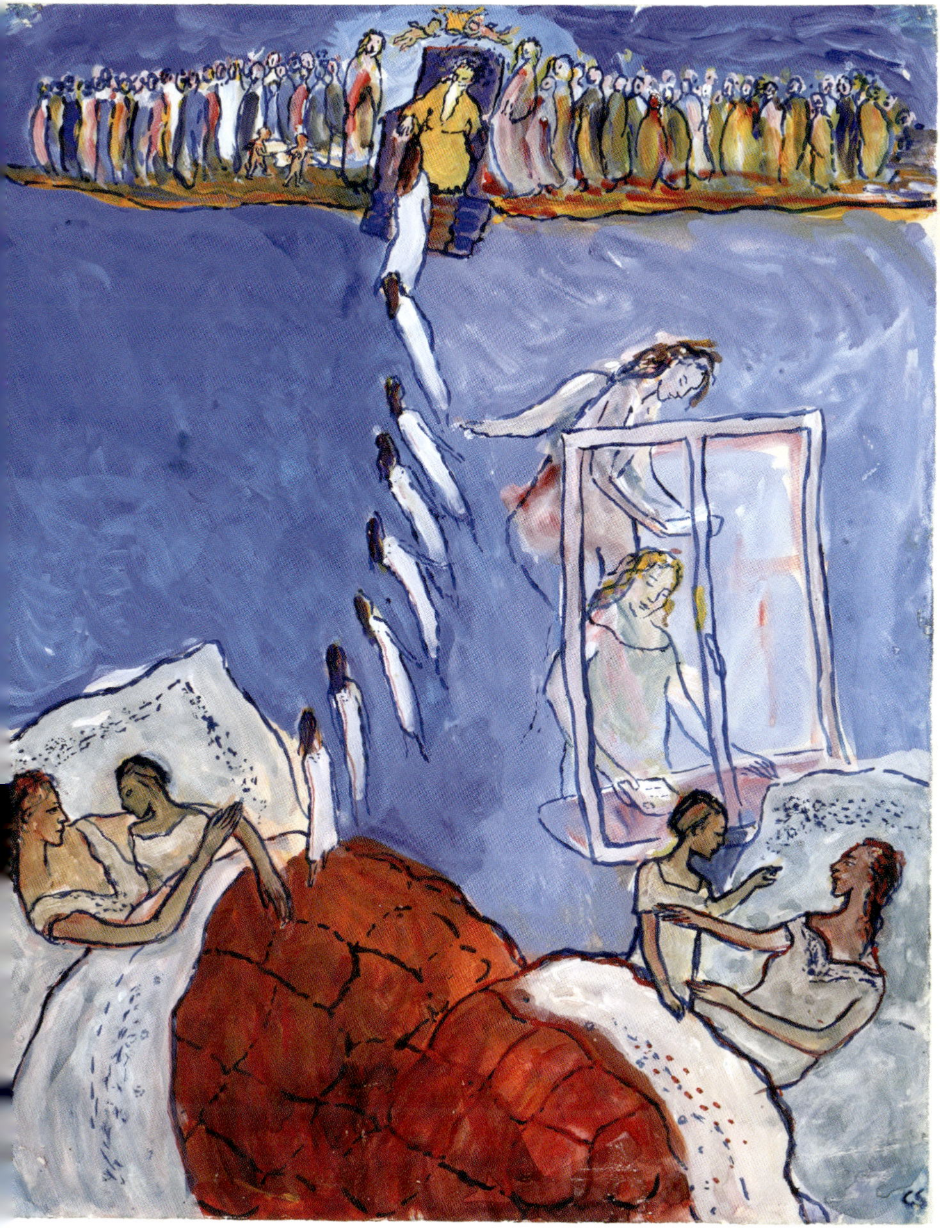

SCENE 2

For inexplicable reasons, Franziska suddenly cannot find any happiness. She still has her singing lessons with Mrs Klatte as before, is allowed to accompany Charlotte, she plays the piano, she helps her husband, she continues as always to keep entire dinner parties entertained with her high spirits, and accompanies Charlotte's gymnastics lessons on the grand piano. But none of it gives her any pleasure. She is desperate.

Her expression has completely changed. She speaks only of death. Albert tells her he still needs her, and Charlotte would also need her mother. She was still so young, just eight years old, but it did not help. Franziska did not have the slightest desire to go on living, and one night she got out of bed, took a strong dose of opium from her husband's medical kit, which she swallowed and then went back to bed.

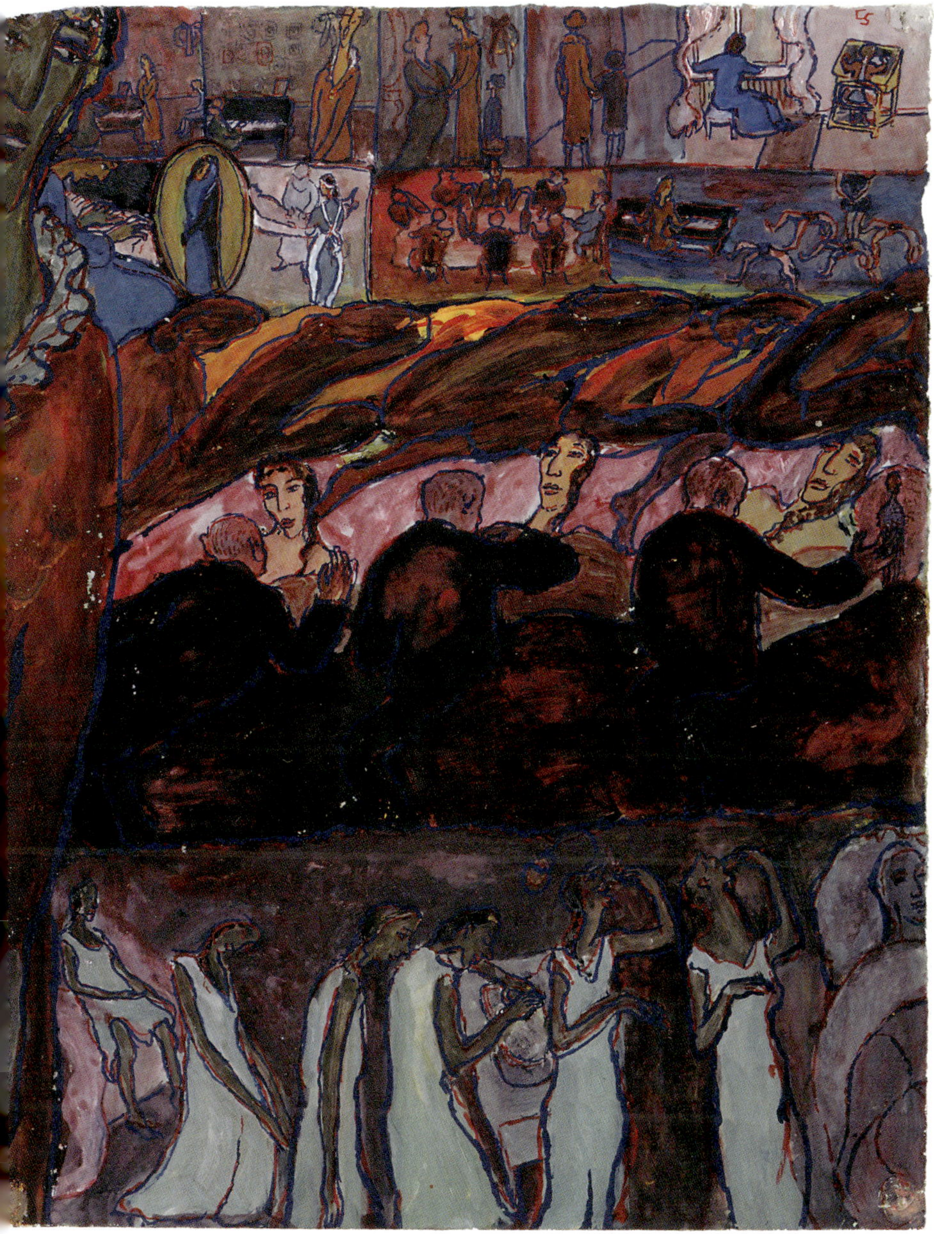

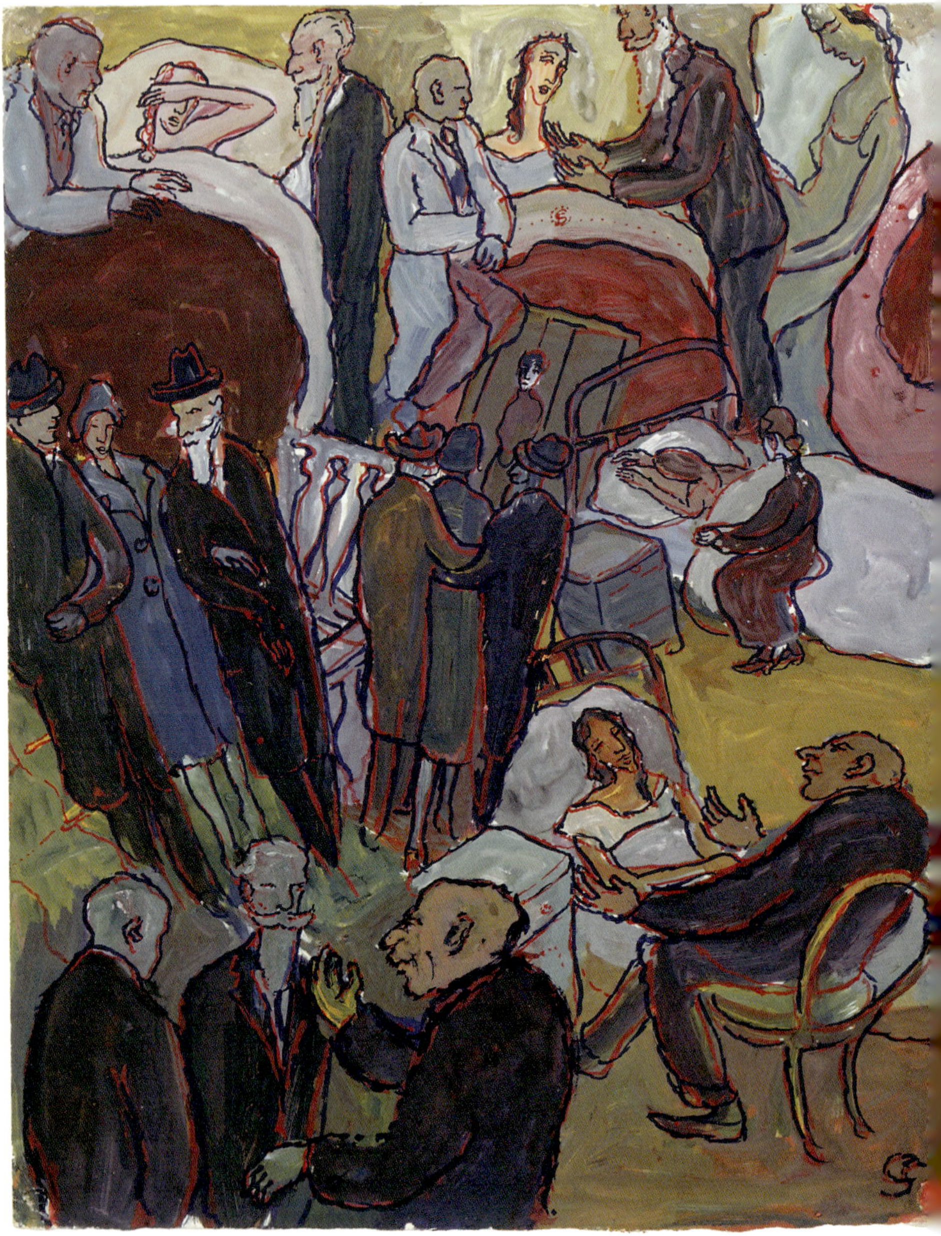

(opposite)

ALBERT KANN
"But what is it then with all this drama you are making here? How can you only poison yourself? Well, thank God it did not work!"

Thank God the dose was not strong enough and Albert's efforts succeeded in bringing her back to life.

It was thought that she would be better taken care of in her parents' home than in her own, so her husband and Mr Knarre took her to the Knarres' place. A neurologist is called in but he declares her perfectly healthy and considers the attempted suicide to be merely momentary sentimentality.

(following pages)

The nurse also shares this opinion. Only she confuses optimism for the future with the actual present and leaves the room for a moment – which Franziska seizes upon to throw herself out the window.

FRANZISKA
"I cannot bear it. I'm so alone."

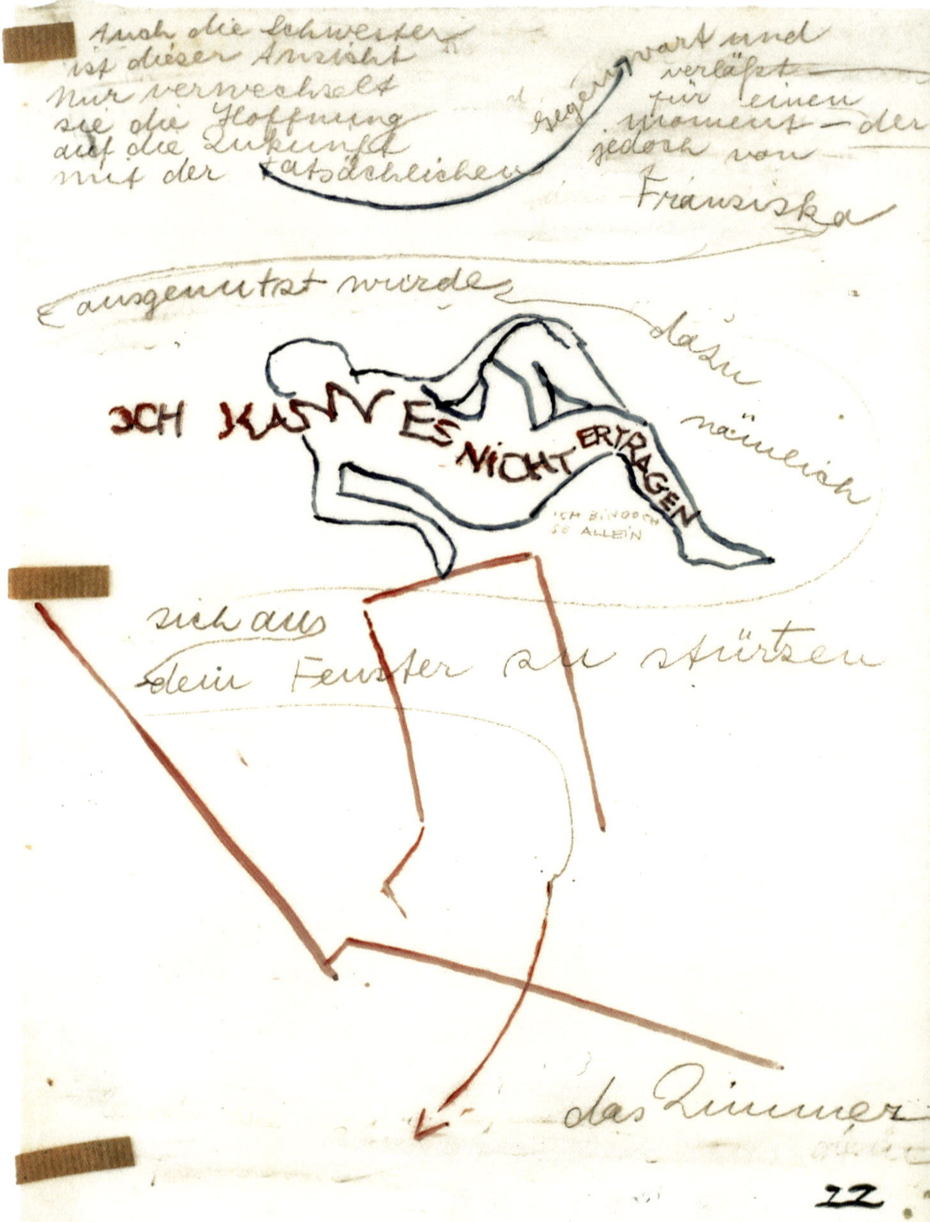
Auch die Schwester
ist dieser Ansicht
nur verwechselt
sie die Hoffnung
auf die Zukunft
mit der tatsächlichen
Gegenwart und
verläßt
für einen
Moment – der
jedoch von
Franziska
ausgenutzt würde
dazu
nämlich
ICH KANN ES NICHT ERTRAGEN
ICH BIN DOCH SO ALLEIN
sich aus
dem Fenster zu stürzen
das Zimmer
22

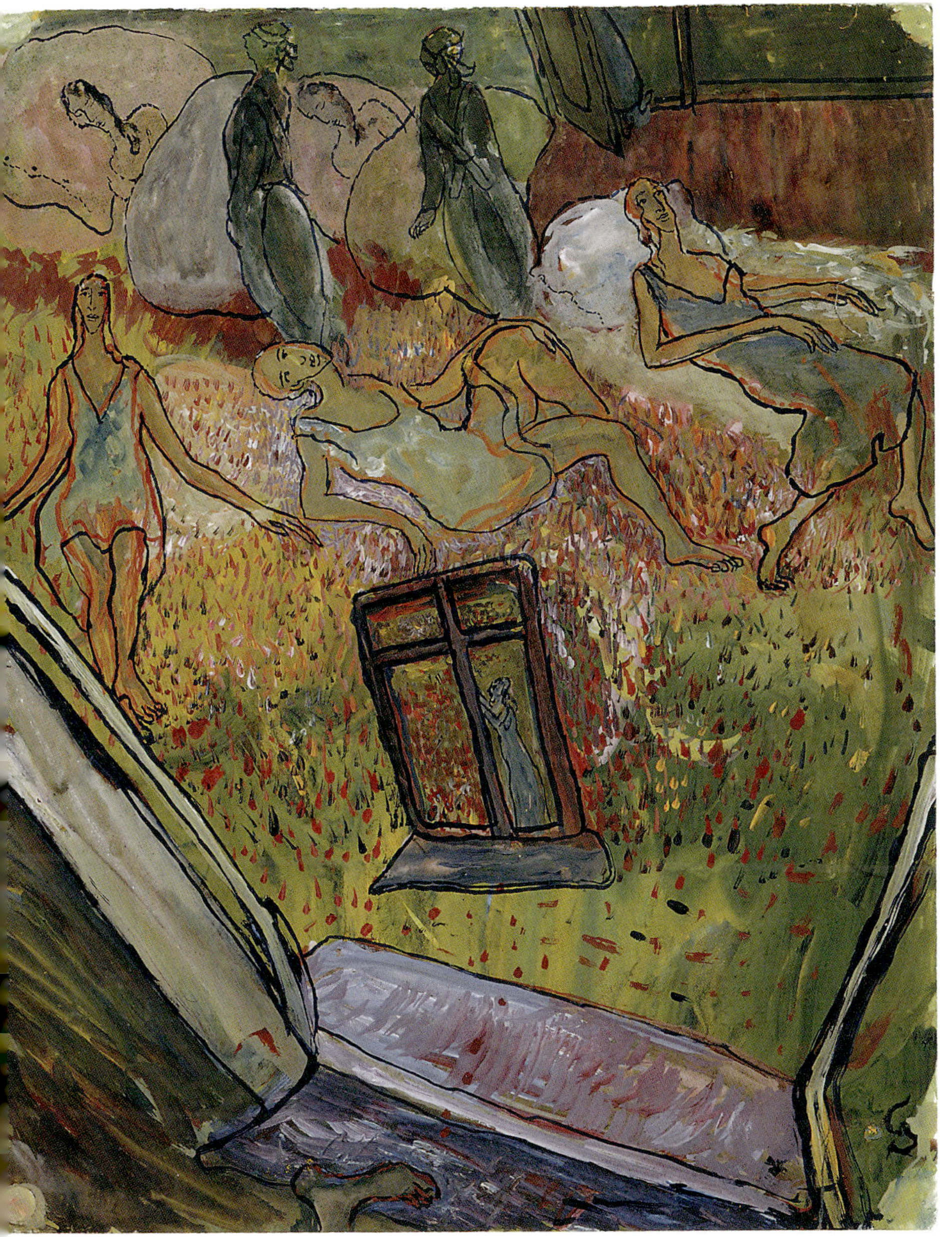

Wir winden dir den Jungfernkranz mit veilchenblauer Seide
[We twine for thee the maiden's wreath with violet-blue silk]

Franziska dies immediately, because the apartment is on the third floor. There is nothing more to be done to change the misfortune.

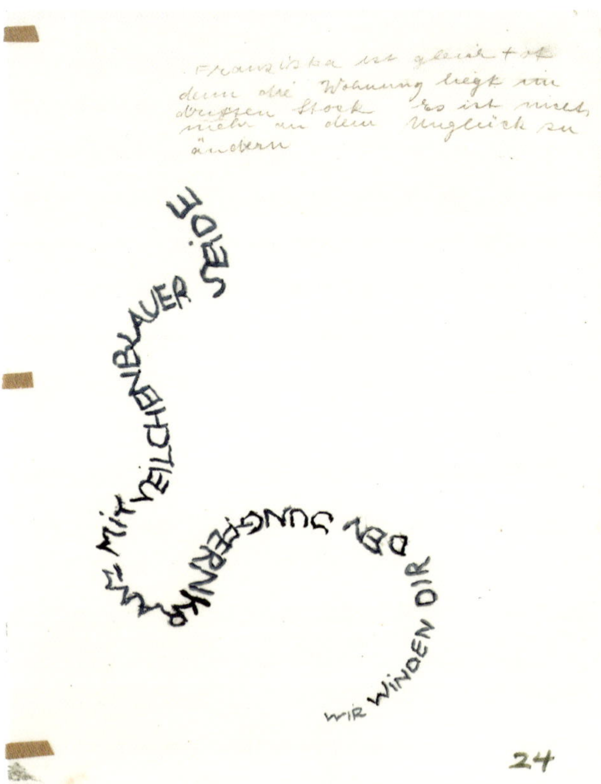

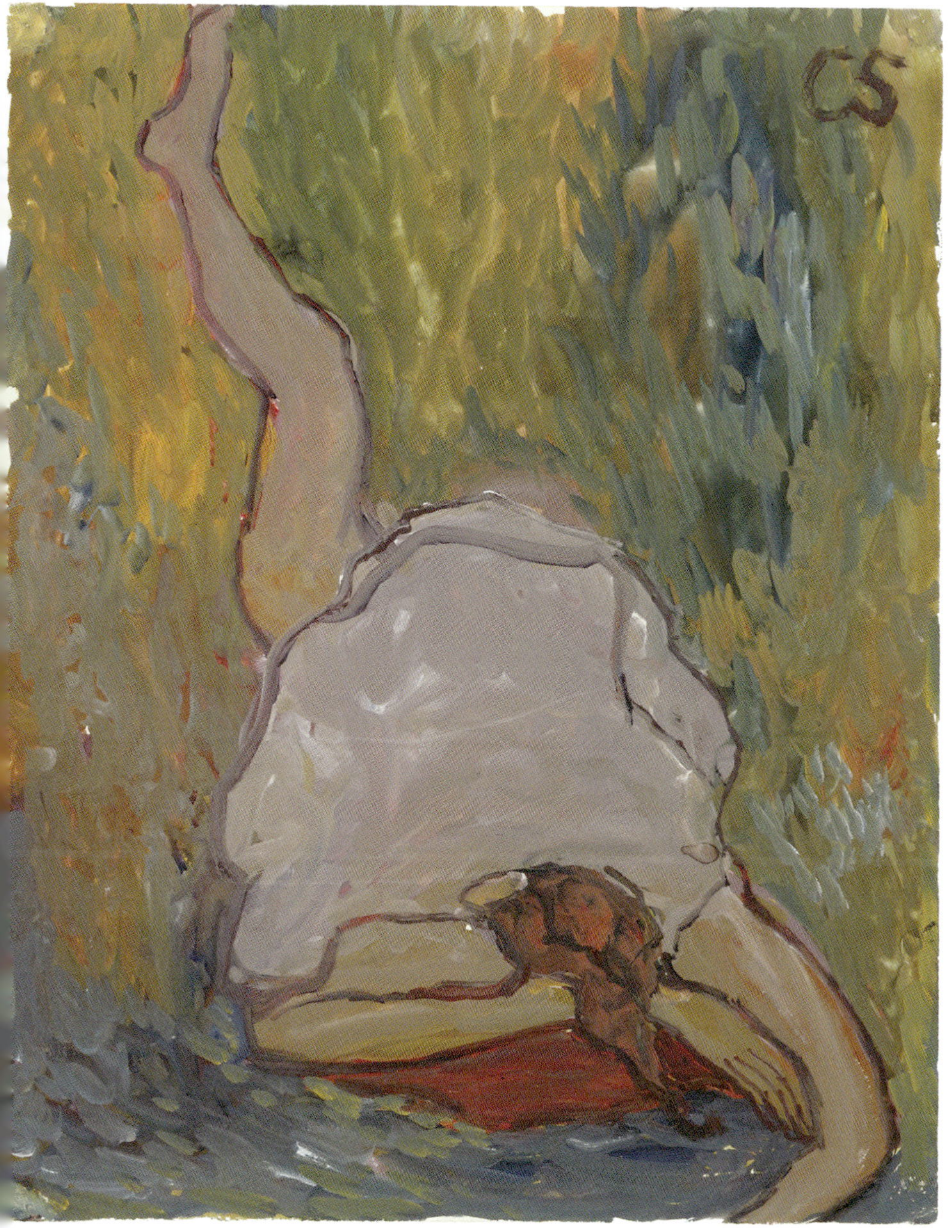
CS

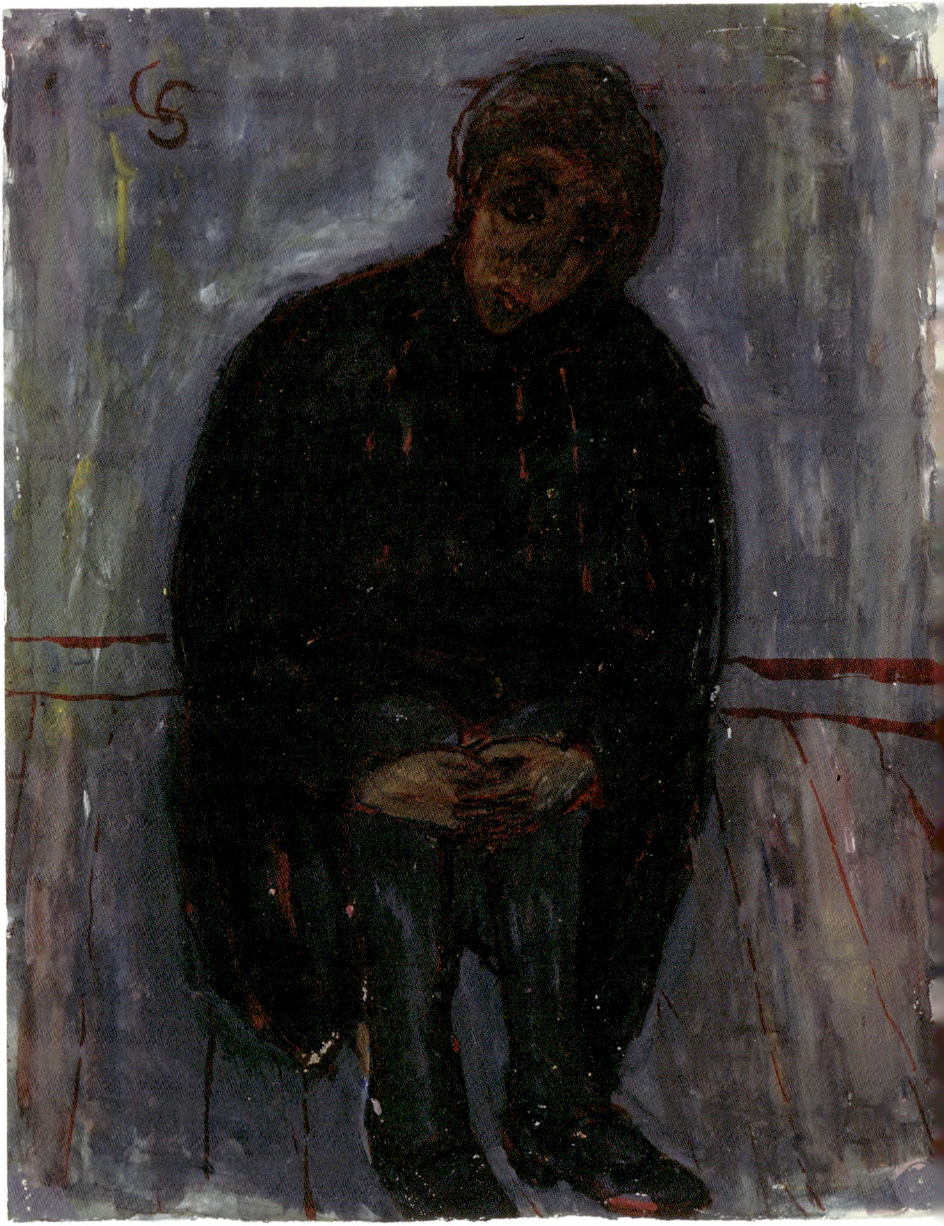

Mrs Knarre does not cry, but her gaze seems to penetrate the deepest depths of the world. From the topmost tips of her hair down to the farthest joints of her small feet, her grief spreads. – It goes beyond her own suffering. It is the suffering of the world, the suffering of destiny that Mrs Knarre, born Bend, has been chosen to bear.

MRS KNARRE
"Now also my little Franziska."

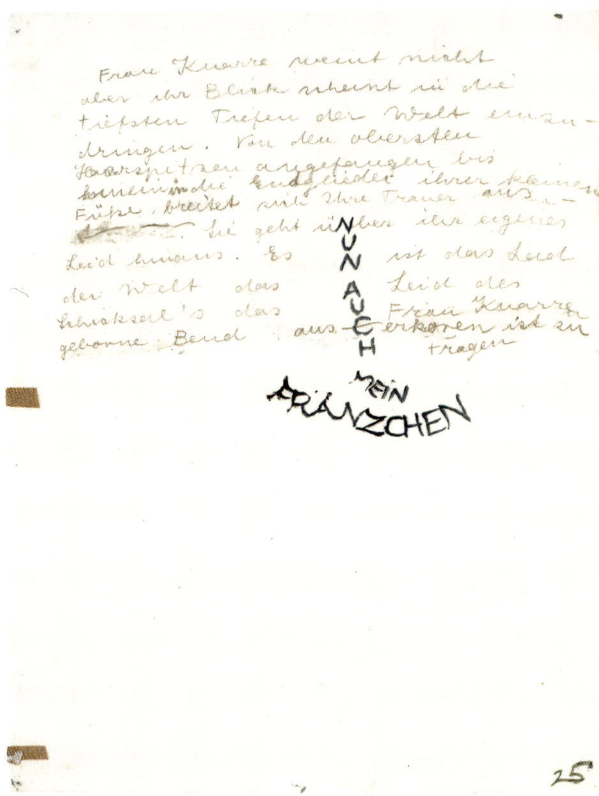

Frau Knarre weint nicht
aber ihr Blick scheint in die
tiefsten Tiefen der Welt einzu-
dringen. Von den obersten
Haarspitzen angefangen bis
hinein in die Endglieder ihrer kleinen
Füße, breitet sich ihre Trauer aus. –
Sie geht über ihr eigenes
Leid hinaus. Es ist das Leid
der Welt das Leid des
Schicksal's das Frau Knarre
geborne Bend auserkoren ist zu
tragen

NUN AUCH MEIN FRÄNZCHEN

25

ALBERT
"Oh, I have lost her,
all my happiness is now gone!"

Albert as well is heartbroken. He sits on his lonely red down-filled blanket and is ready to make any sacrifice to win back his lost one.

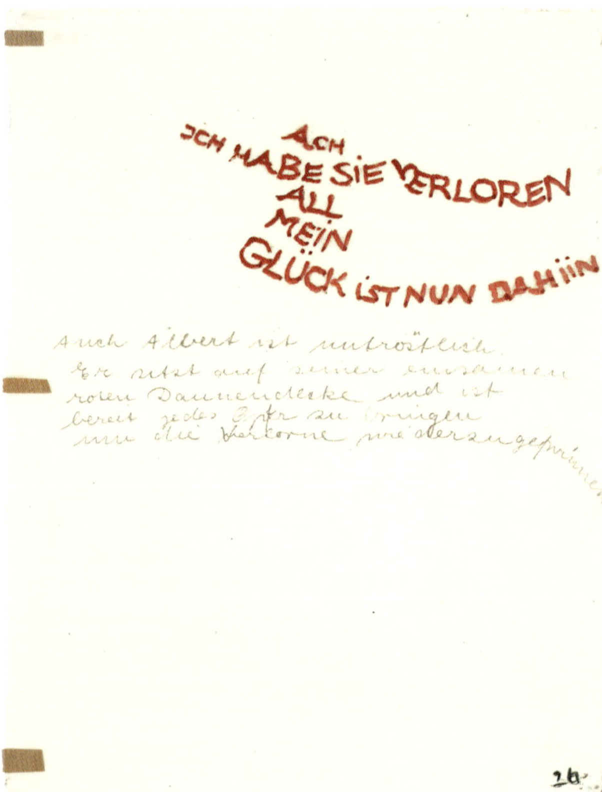

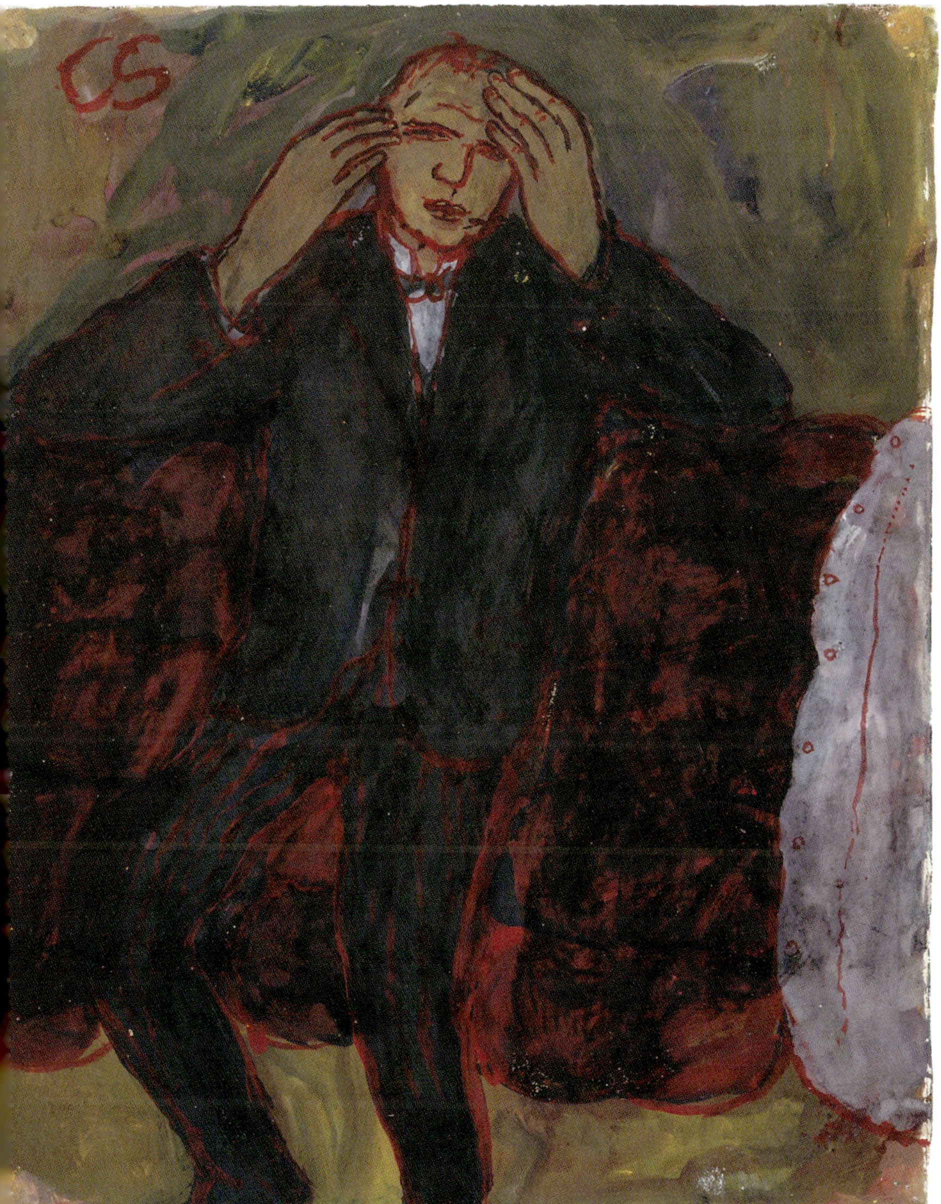

(bottom)

On Monday, 22 February, after a brief illness, our dearly beloved daughter – wife and mother – Franziska Kann née Knarre, passed away. We kindly ask you to refrain from condolence visits. Cremation has already taken place.

The ones to suffer:
Medical Consultant Dr L. Knarre
and wife Marianne, née Bend,
private lecturer Dr A. Kann,
Charlotte Kann

February 1926

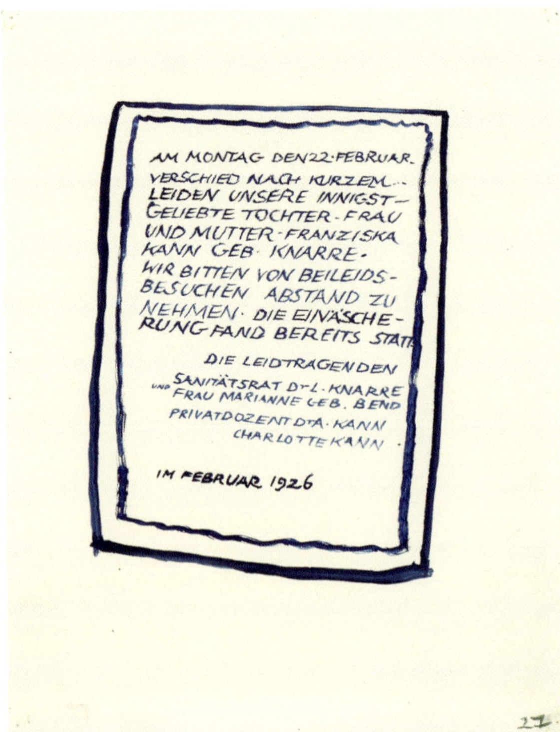

(opposite)

When Charlotte who, one obviously tells that her mother has died of influenza, sees him, she has the impression that he has scratched his whole head.

Wir winden dir den Jungfern...

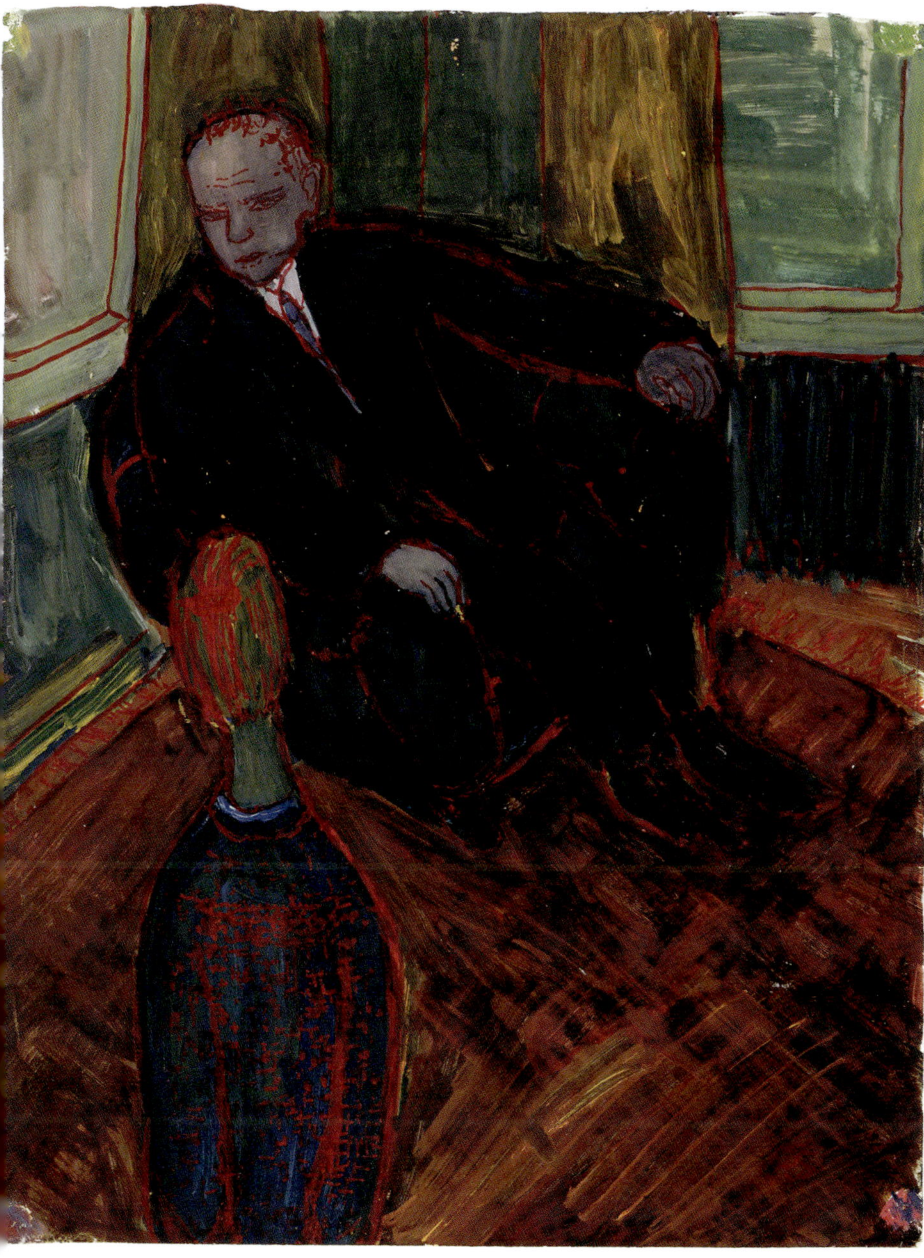

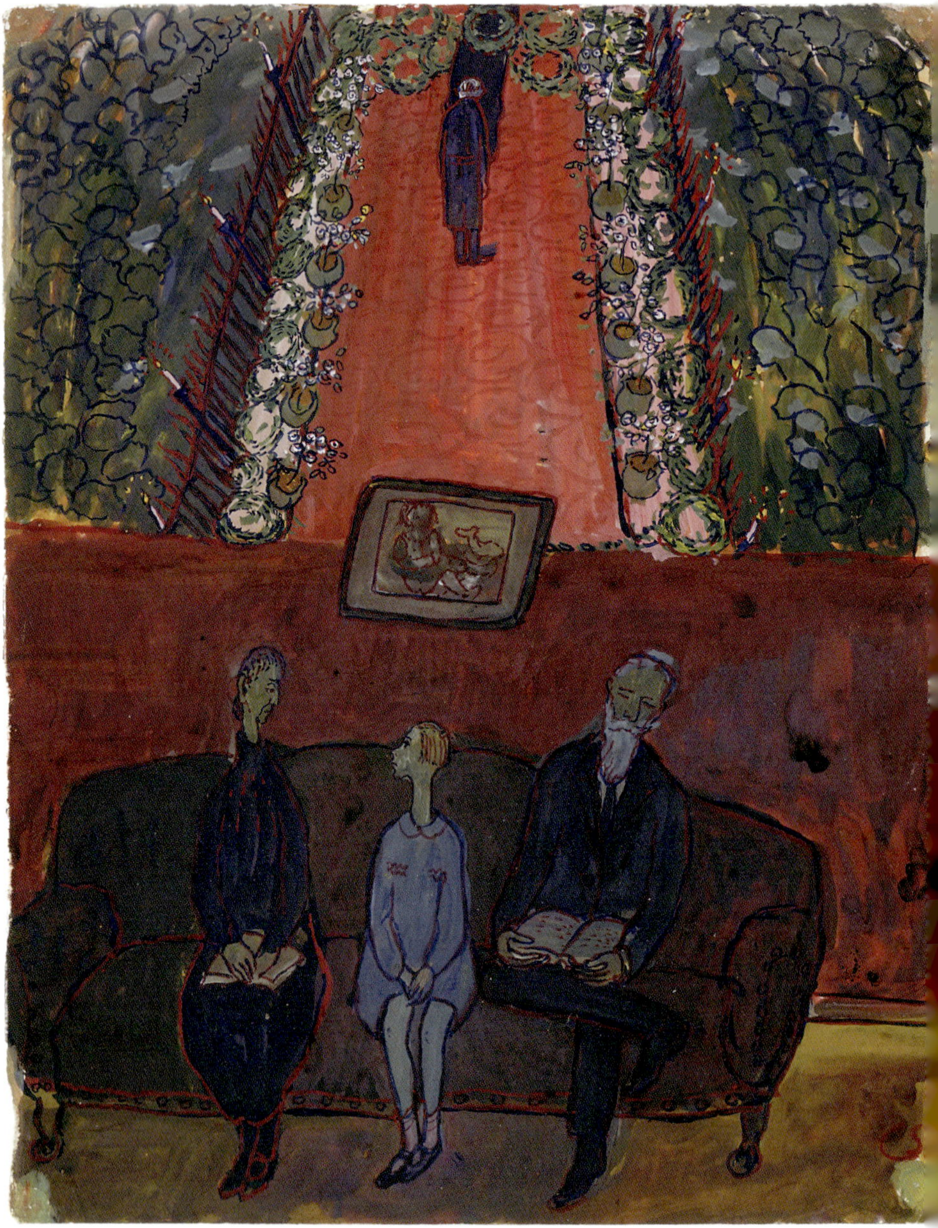

CHARLOTTE
"Oh, I have lost her!"

GRANDPARENTS
"Oh, we have lost her!"

The funeral is attended by a tremendous crowd of people. Yet Albert feels as though he is entirely alone as he stands by her coffin, which is about to be burned.

Mr and Mrs Knarre and Charlotte are not at the funeral. Charlotte asks her grandmother why everyone is crying; since "her Mummy had now become a little angel in heaven", they must grant her this stroke of luck and not cry. Mrs Knarre is strangely moved by this observation.

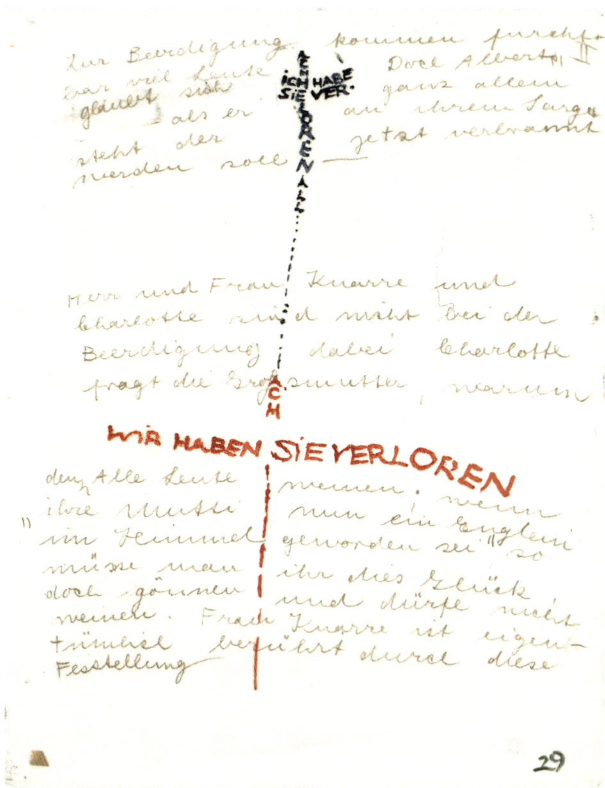

CHARLOTTE
"My Mummy, write me again."

When they all go to the grave a few weeks later where Charlotte Knarre already rests, the little girl brings along a letter for her mother, in which she asks her not to forget her promise to tell her as soon as possible and in detail, "how it is in heaven above". Albert is, for the first time in a while, slightly amused.

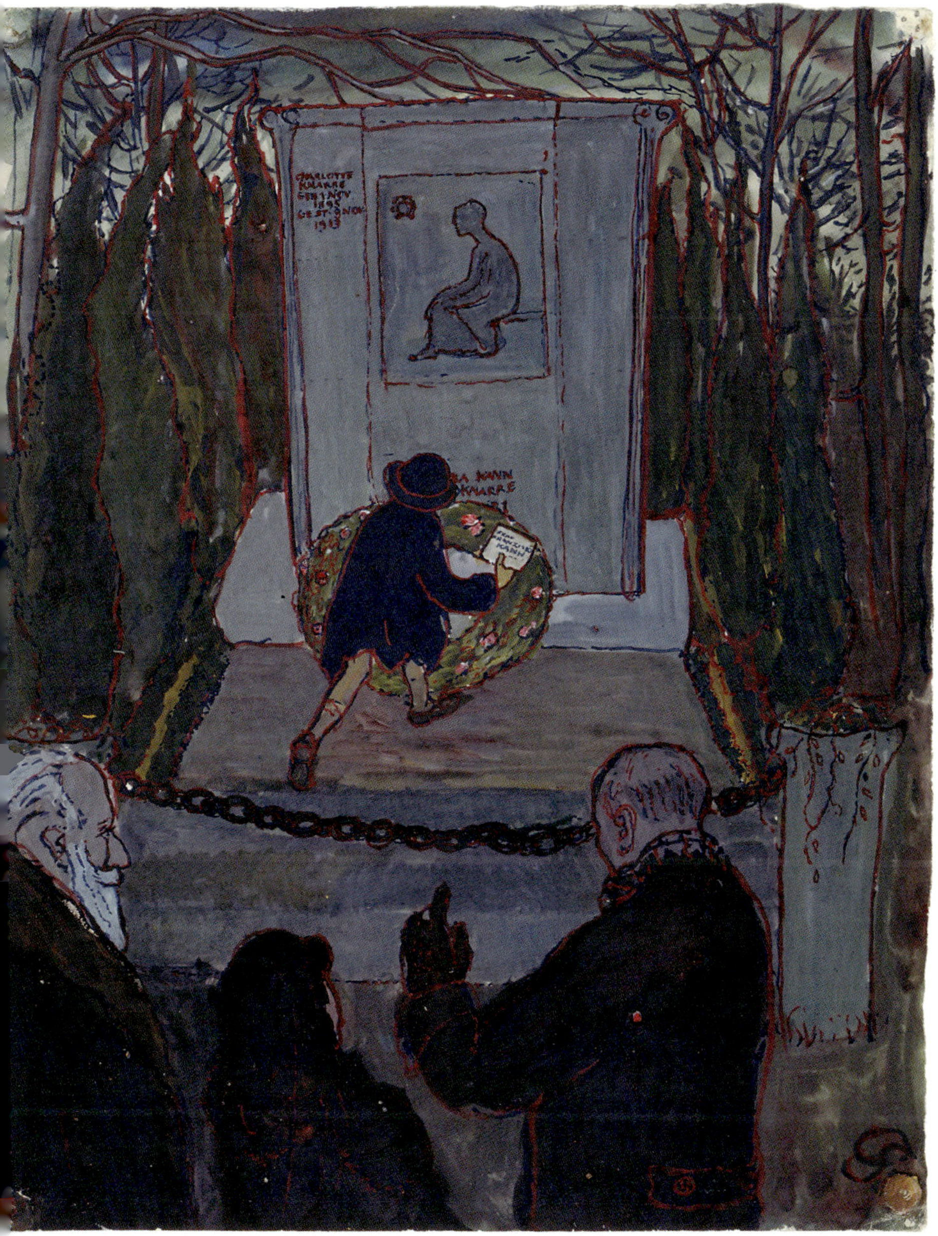

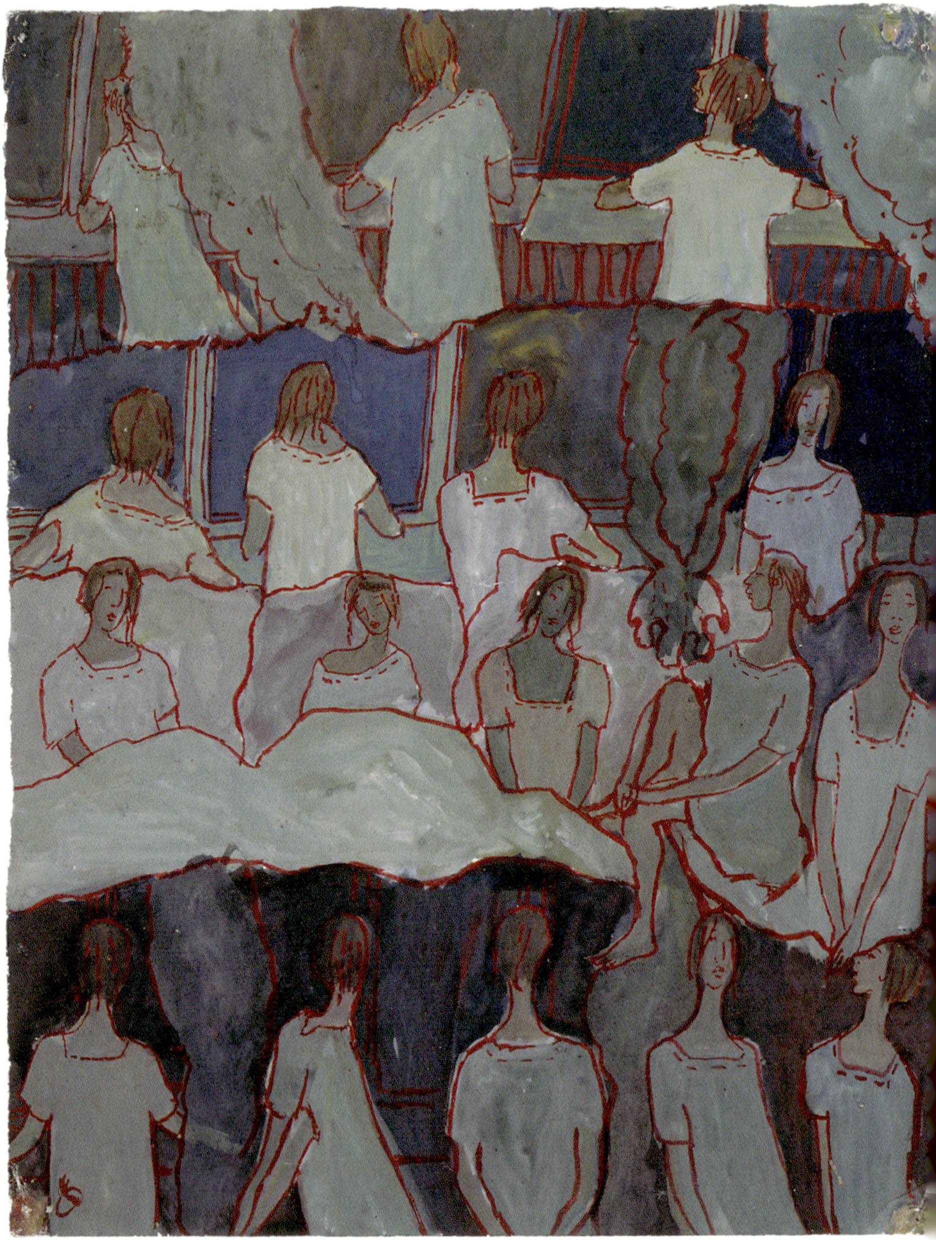

(opposite)

CHARLOTTE
"Why does she not come, my Mummy – she promised."

Charlotte cannot sleep well at all any more. Ten times a night she gets up to see whether there is any angelic trace or at least find a letter lying on the windowsill. She is very disappointed.

(following pages)

Wir winden dir den Jungfernkranz mit veilchenblauer...

And each time she has to walk along the endless, wide, high, dark corridors in her grandparents' home, she has the idea of something wholly terrible with skeleton's limbs, which has something to do with her mother. Then she gets fear-stricken and begins to run – run – run...

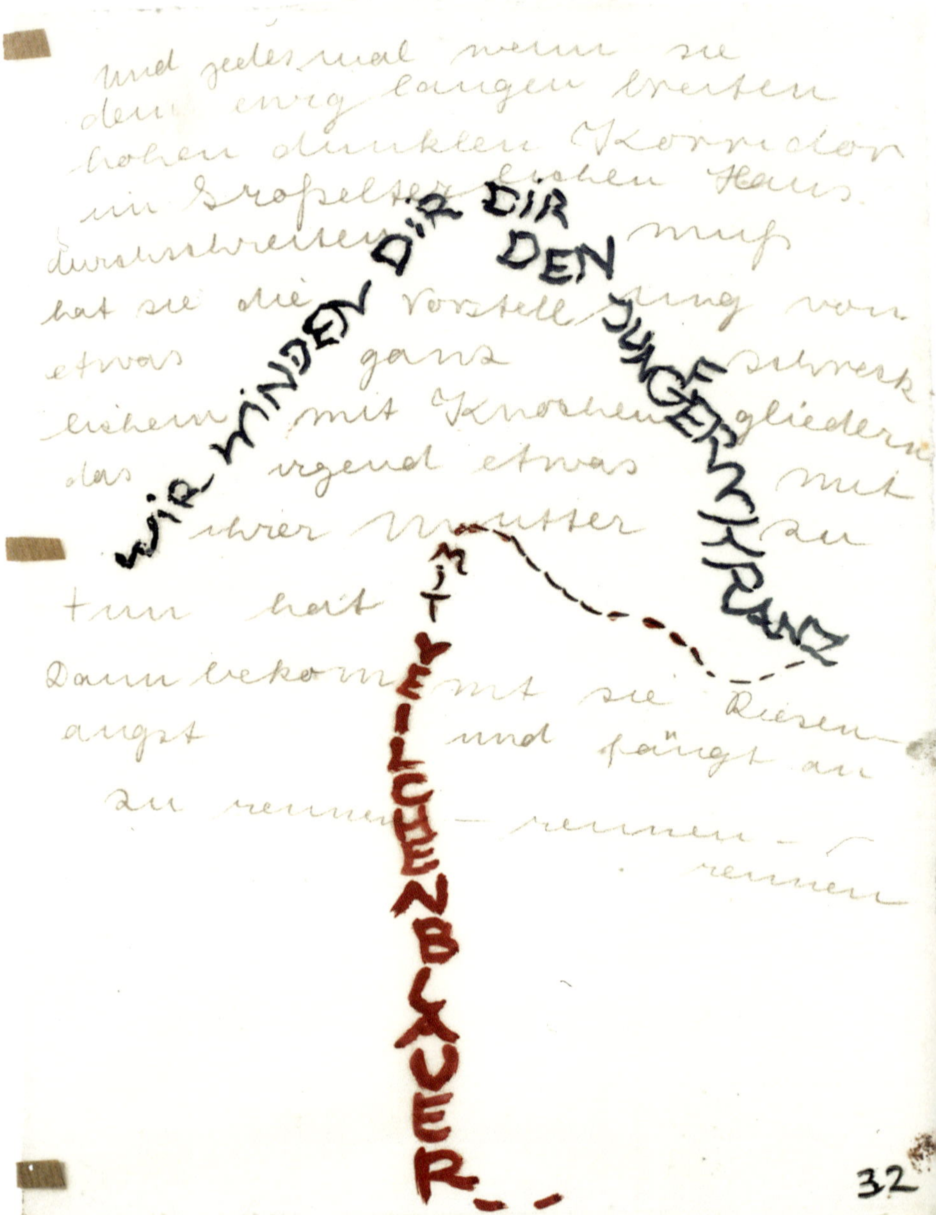
und jedesmal wenn sie
den ewig langen breiten
hohen dunklen Korridor
im Großelterlichen Haus
durchschreiten muß
hat sie die Vorstellung von
etwas ganz schreck-
lichem mit Knochengliedern
das irgend etwas mit
ihrer Mutter zu
tun hat
Dann bekommt sie Riesen-
angst und fängt an
zu rennen – rennen –
rennen
WIR WINDEN DIR DIR DEN JUNGFERNKRANZ
MIT VEILCHENBLAUER
32

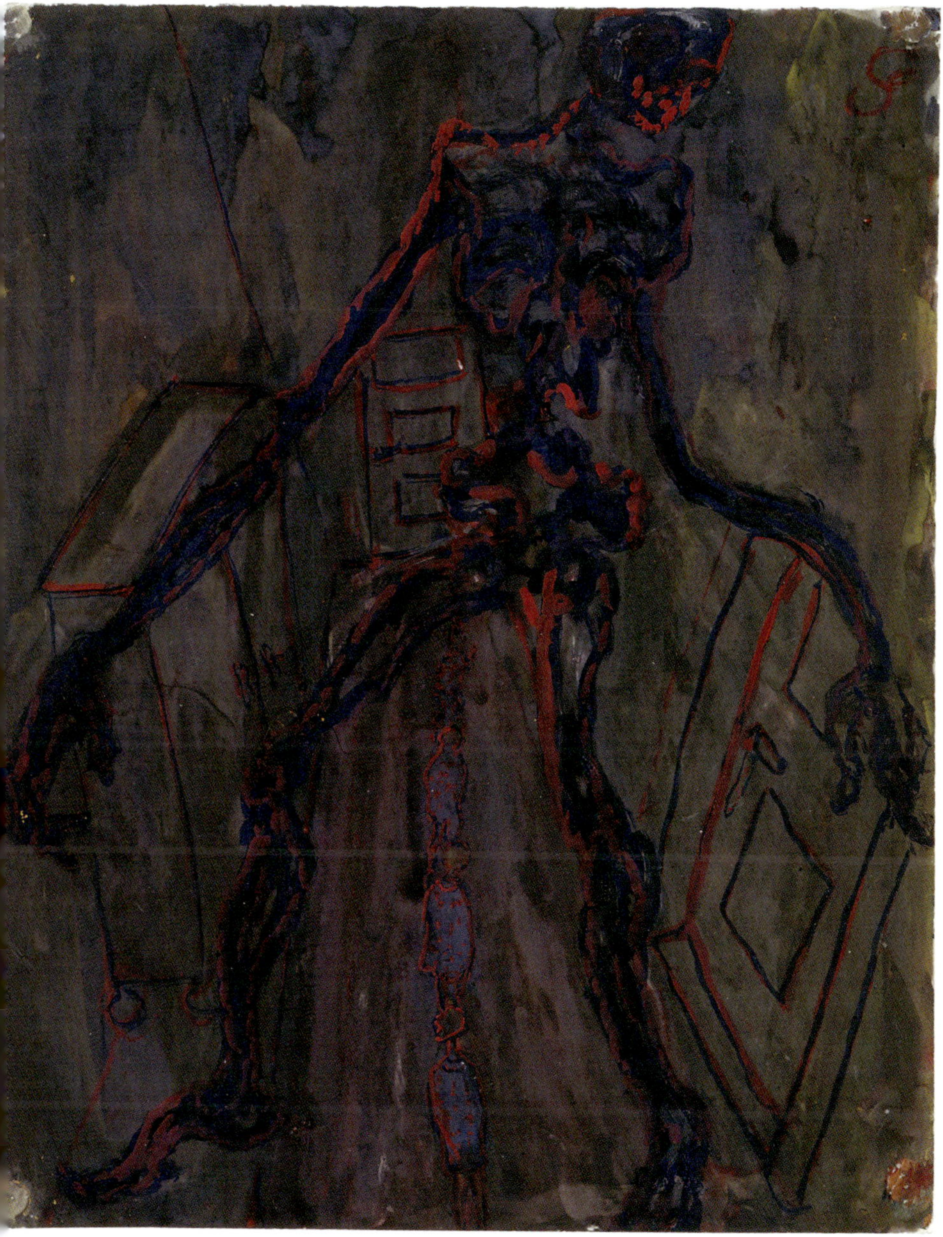

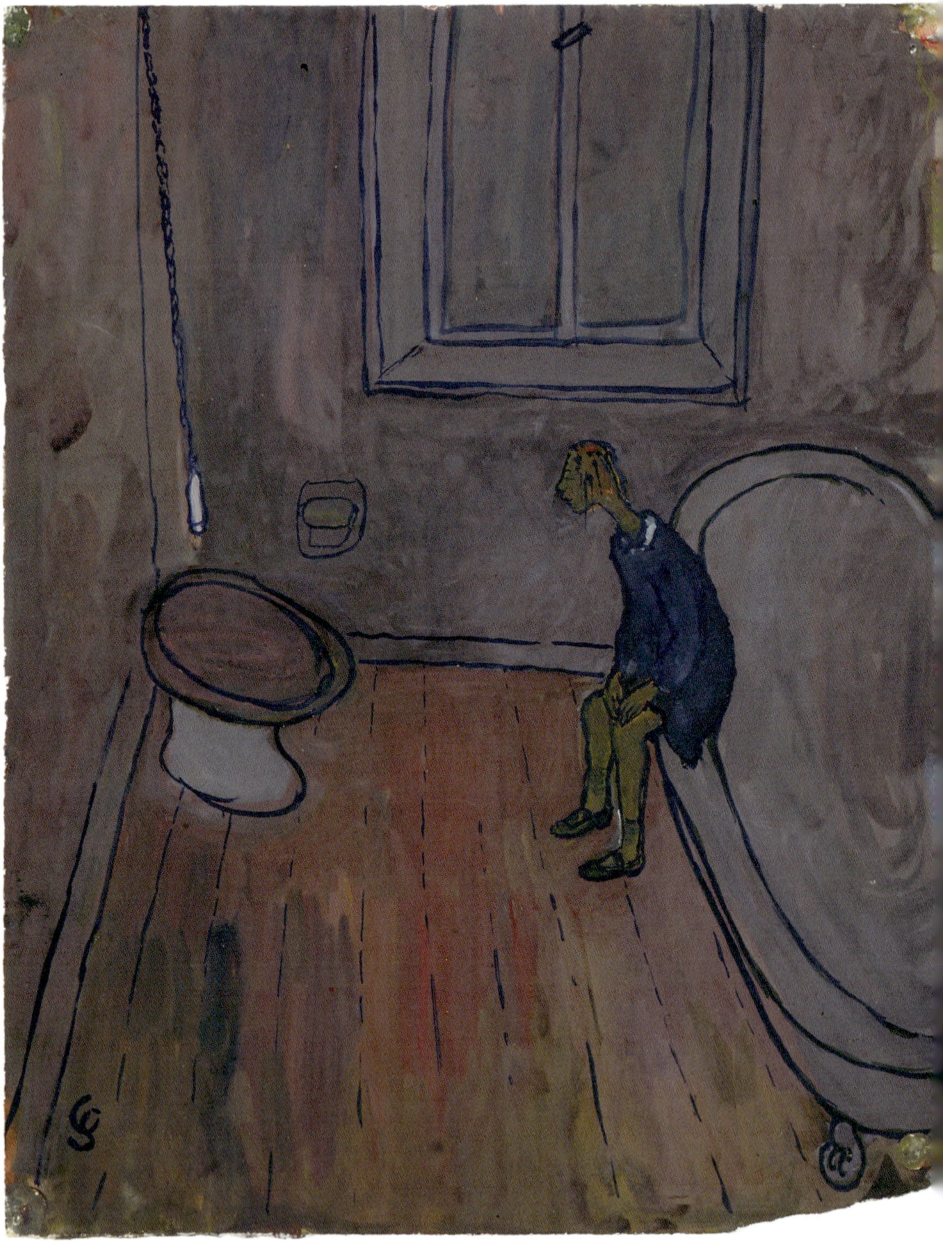

... until she finally locks herself in the bathroom and begins to think about life.

CHARLOTTE
"Now this is what is called life."

To the same melody.

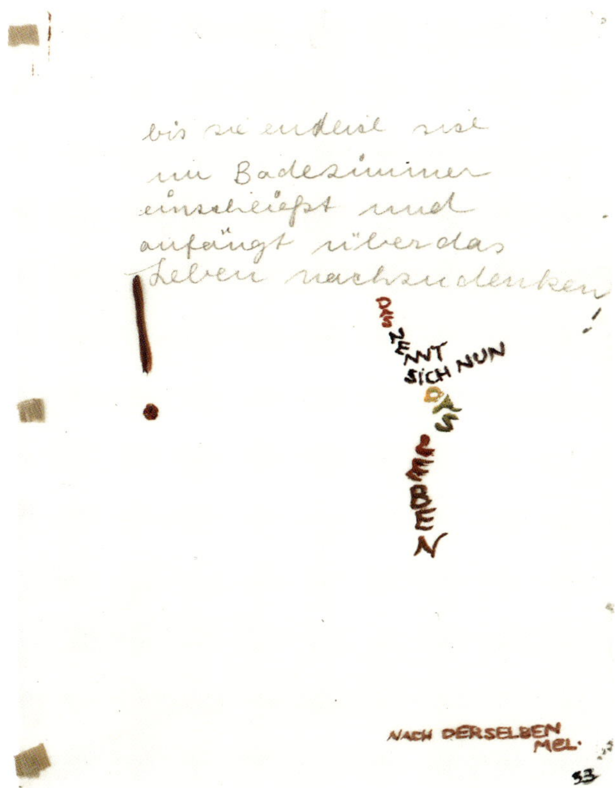

CHARLOTTE
"I don't need any governesses,
I alone know what I want!"

A governess arrives. Charlotte goes through the greatest of pains to annoy her and becomes the inventor of all sorts of naughtiness.

When she is then slapped in the face, her grandmother will be informed by telephone right away. She then comes straight to the Kann apartment and is told that no one can possibly cope with such a brat, and Charlotte is thereby enchanted.

To the same melody.

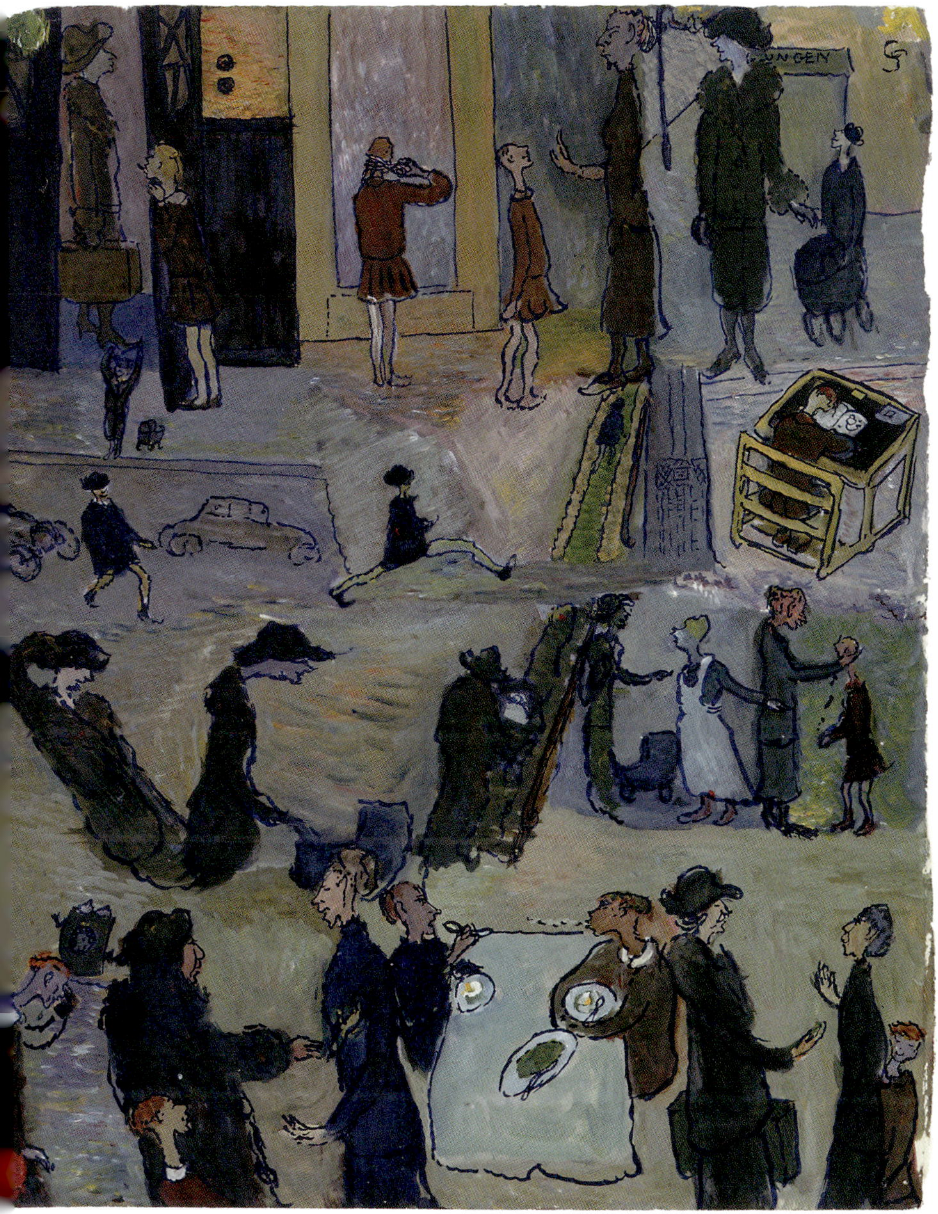
UNGEN

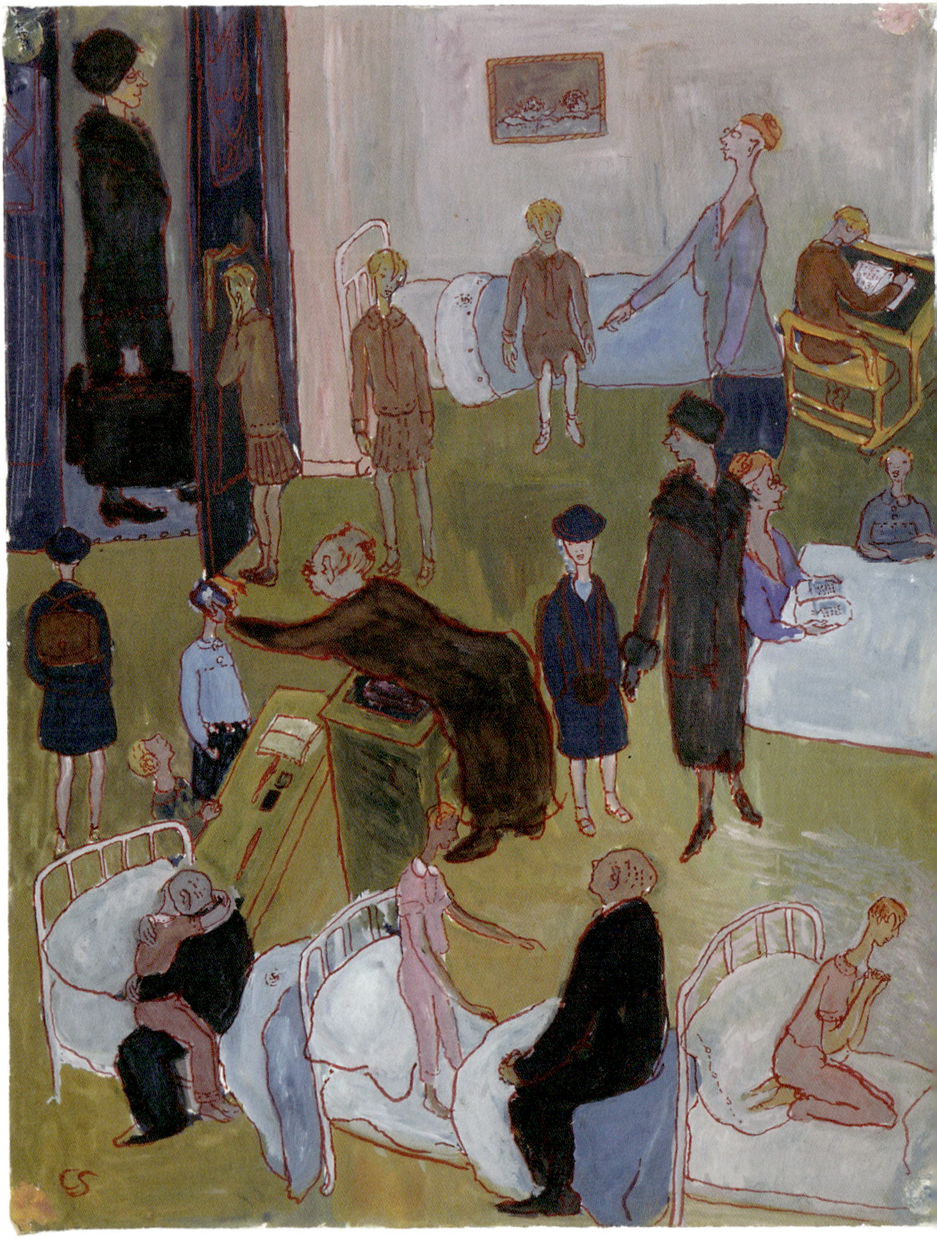

But, oh horrors, a new one appears! Compared to Elfriede Wolf, the one who left was pure gold.

GOVERNESS
"Now you do that – right now
you do that – finally."

Charlotte is extremely unhappy. In school, too, she gets slapped all the time.

Albert is sad as well, but he can do nothing about her suffering.

Still: Wir winden dir...

Charlotte's tormenting had succeeded in driving Elfriede Wolf away, too, and a new horror begins with Miss Stargard.

But Charlotte is compensated by a beautiful trip to Engadine, where they all stay in a large hotel and even do a glacier tour, properly roped up with a guide. When, after a terrible thunderstorm – where one has to lie flat on the ice – Miss Stargard falls into a snowpit and screams uncontrollably, Charlotte is delighted.

Proud like a heroine, she re-enters the village on the guide's shoulders at the end of the tour.

To the melody: Das Wandern ist des Müllers Lust
[The Miller's Joy is Wandering]

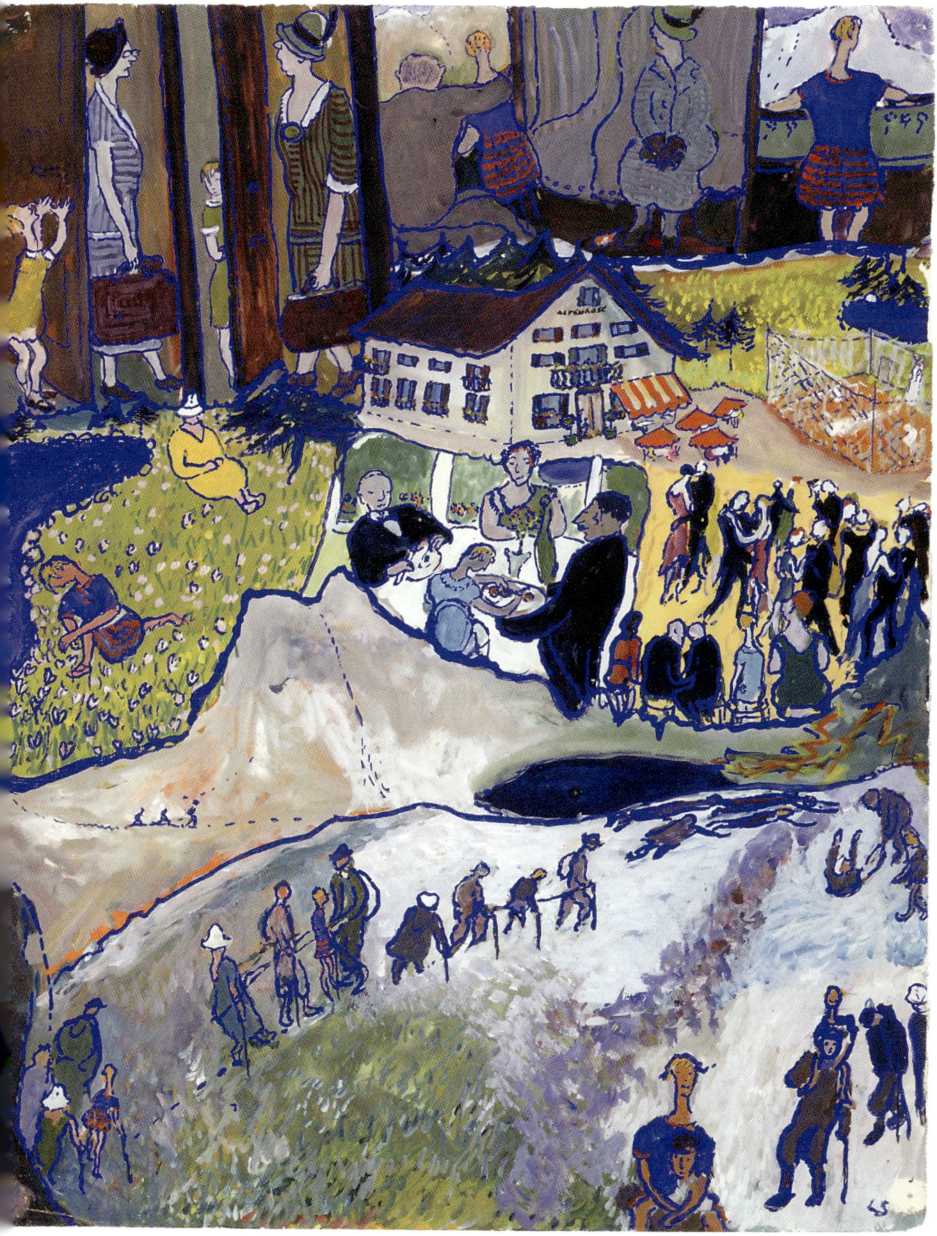

GRANDPARENTS
"Our travels took us to Greece and then to Turkey. To Africa on a camel and then on to Spain. And then we went homeward..."

Mr and Mrs Knarre travel a lot, and from each place they visit they bring something home for Charlotte. She cannot get enough of hearing her grandmother tell her about all the glorious things she has seen.

To the same melody.

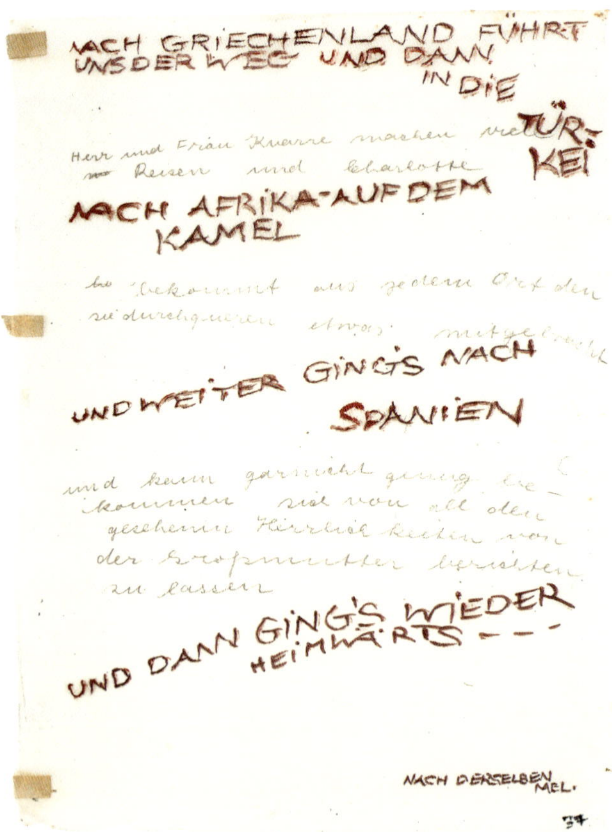

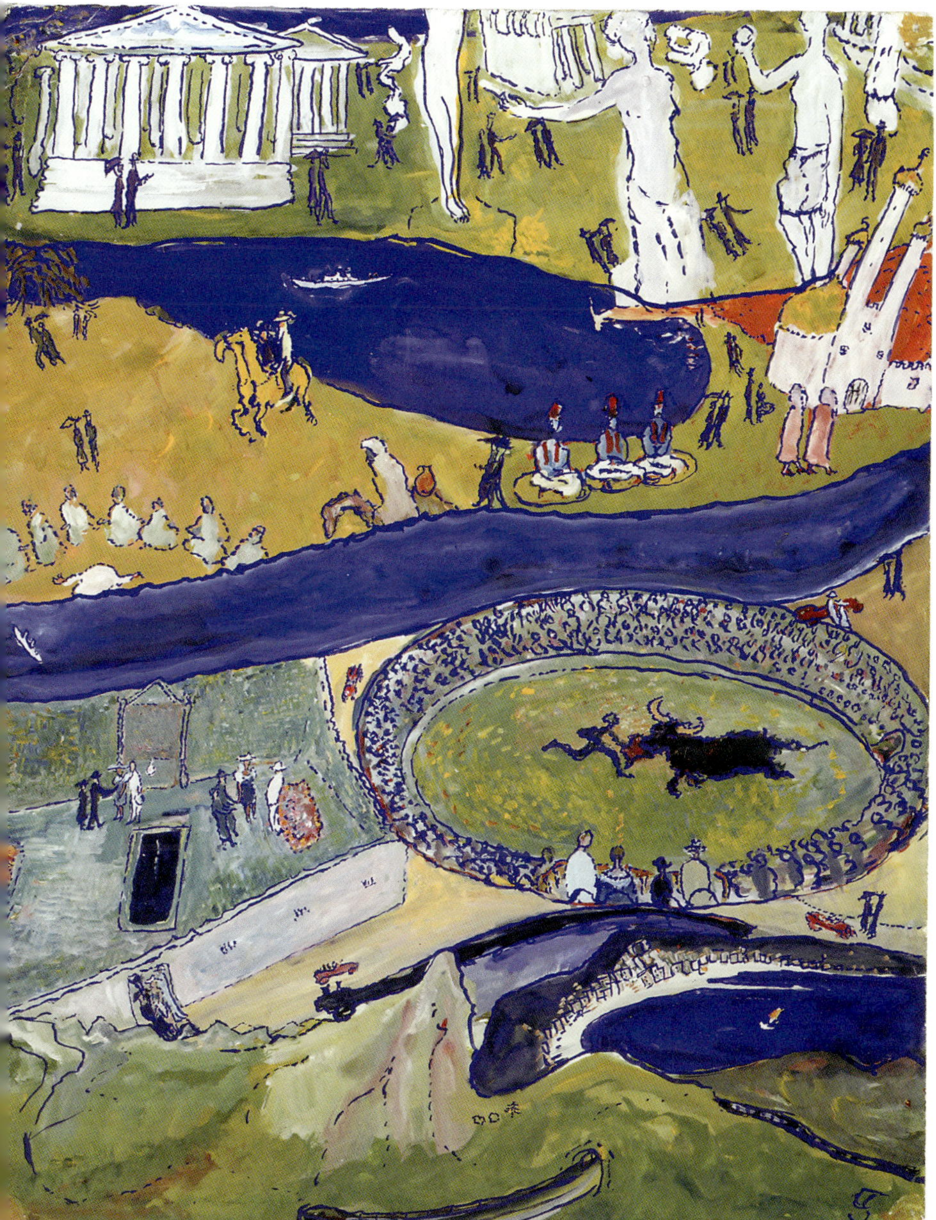

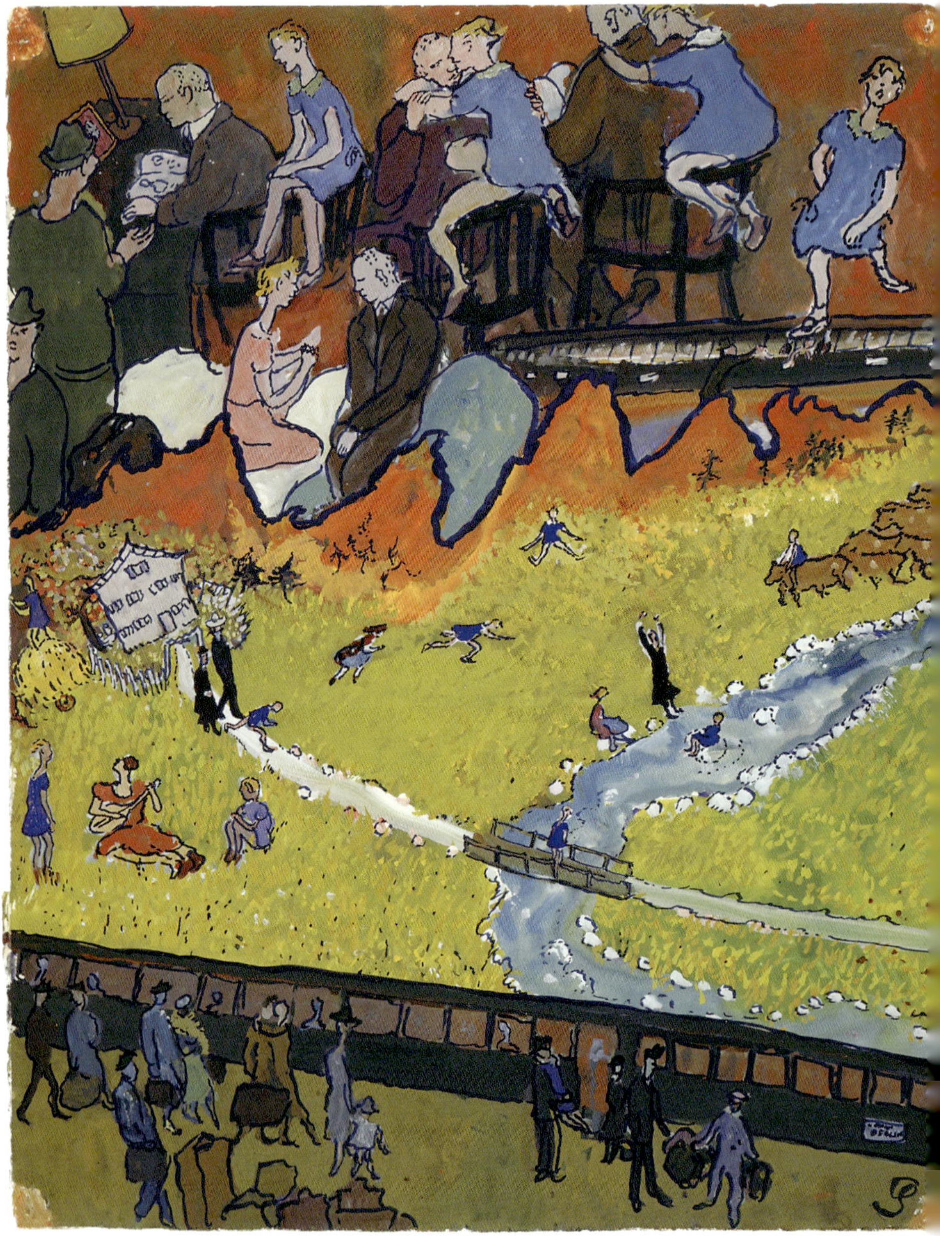

Miss Stargard also says that Charlotte is the naughtiest creature in the whole world and that she cannot hold out any longer.

CHARLOTTE
"Today I am so happy. Today I am so glad!"

Charlotte's father is not exactly thrilled about this, but Charlotte is in an especially good mood, and then she is very nice, and everybody loves her.

The good mood is because of an impending trip with the grandparents to the Dolomites. A small house in quite a remote place has been rented, and all three live there. Charlotte's wildness greatly agitates Mrs Knarre.

One day on a meadow she meets a girl playing a lute with a child. By chance she is the governess of a family friend of the Knarres. Charlotte explains that she must have "this governess" for herself.

The same melody: Das hat nicht Ruh bei Tag und Nacht, ist stets auf Wanderschaft bedacht – das Wasser [That has no rest by night or day, continuously on its way – the water].

And indeed her strong-headedness wins. A month later the young woman named Hase joins Dr Kann.

Charlotte is very pleased with her new governess, and since Hase finds that she has a gift for drawing – here you see her first painting, "a little boy" running behind "a big bell" – she also does her portrait.

As always Christmas is a glorious celebration with many gifts and with a Christmas tree.

Melody: <u>Am</u> <u>Weihnachtsbaum</u> <u>die</u> <u>Lichter</u> <u>brennen</u>, <u>die</u> <u>Lichter</u> <u>brennen</u> – <u>wie</u> <u>glänzt</u> <u>er</u> <u>ruhig</u>, <u>lieb</u> <u>und</u> <u>mild</u> [The Christmas tree is bright with candles, bright with candles – how soft it shines, serene and mild].

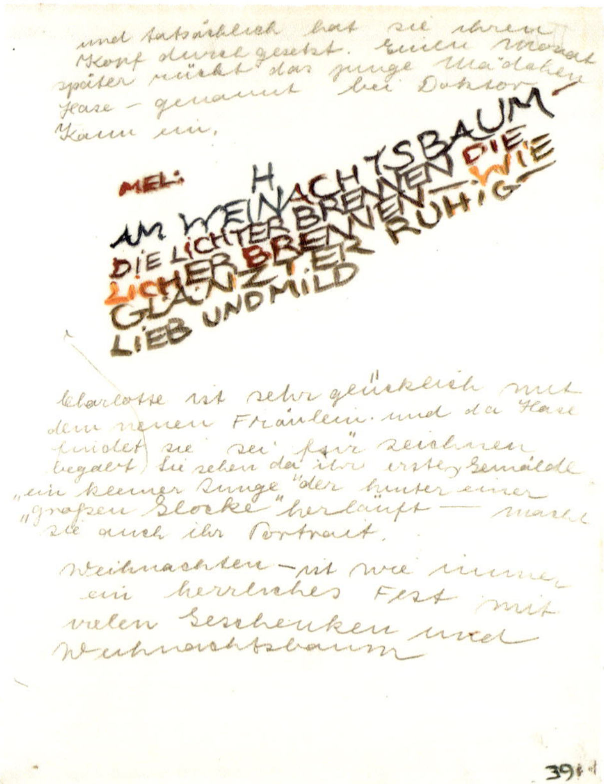

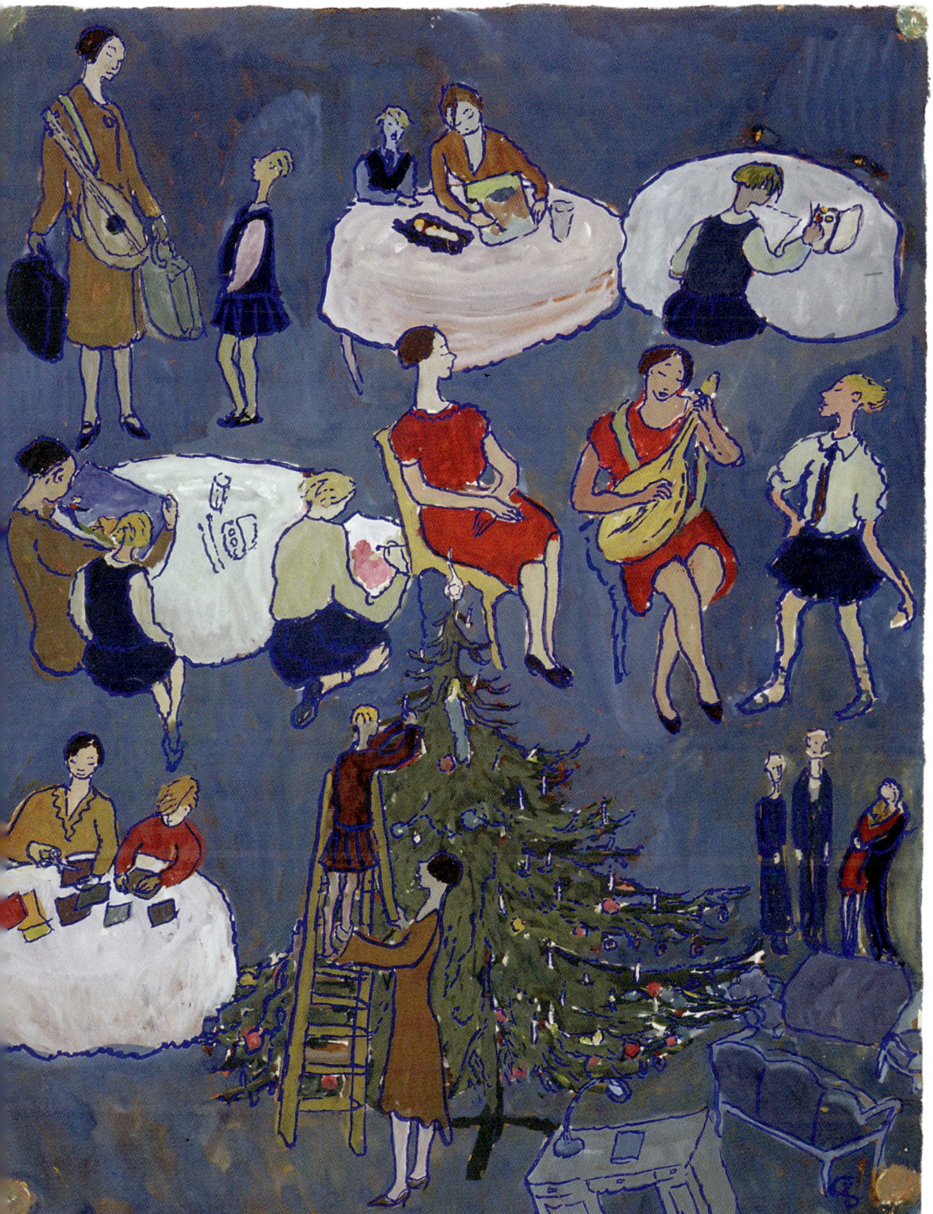

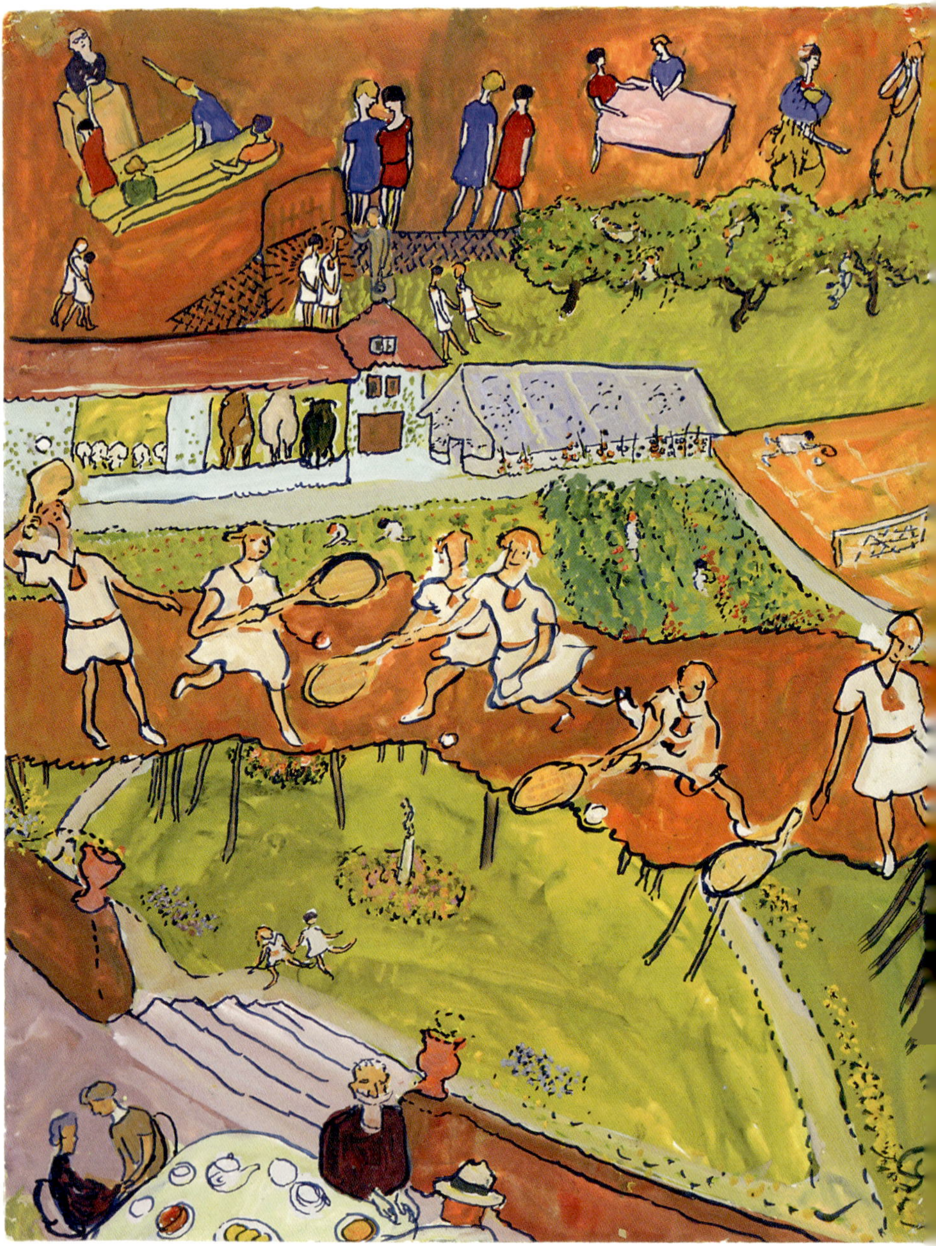

Charlotte is very pleased; she is also making good progress in school. Hilde is her best friend. In the afternoons they go to Aunt Martha's beautiful garden where they are allowed to eat fruit as long as they like and even milk cows.

CHARLOTTE
"Oh, my future still lies ahead of me."

Charlotte likes to play tennis tremendously, sometimes amazingly good for her age.

Aunt Martha is grandma's best friend and while the children play together, the adults drink coffee on the terrace.

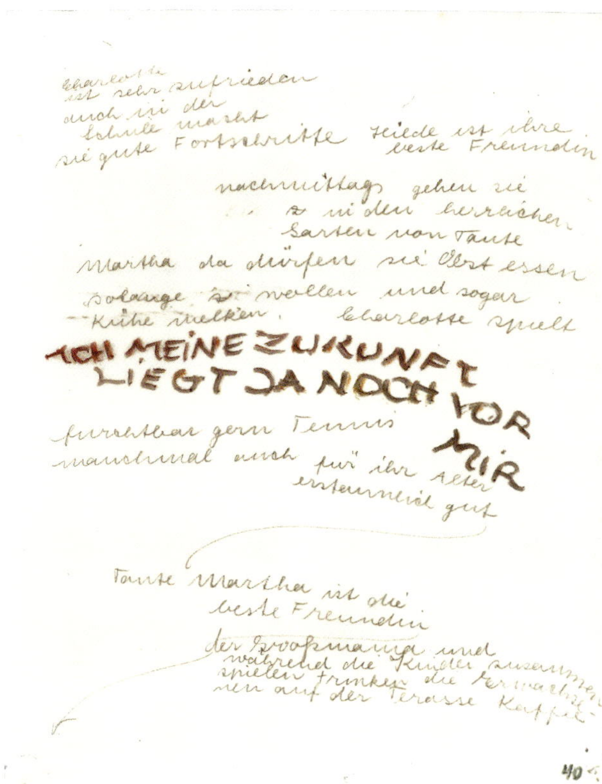

CHARLOTTE
"What will she bring?"

Charlotte goes with Hase to the North Sea and finds it glorious there. She is even allowed once to ride, and the back of the horse arouses in her a particularly tender feeling.

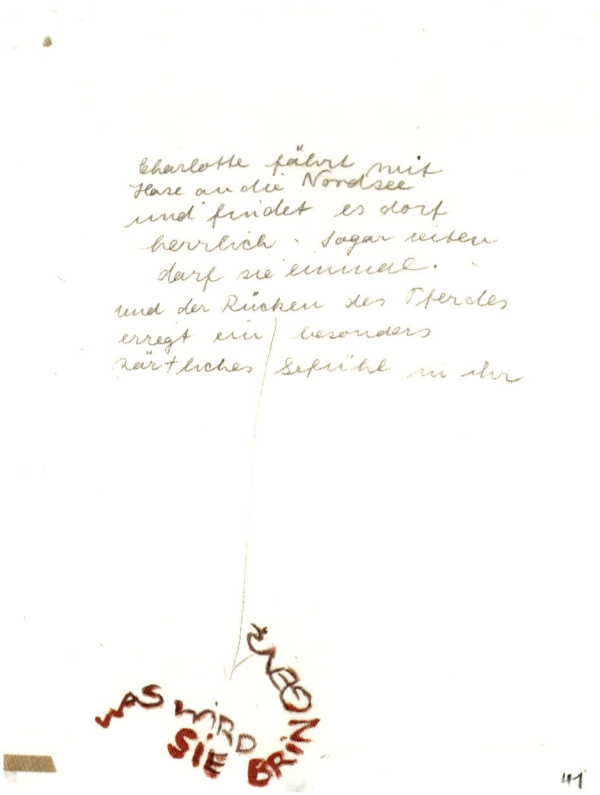

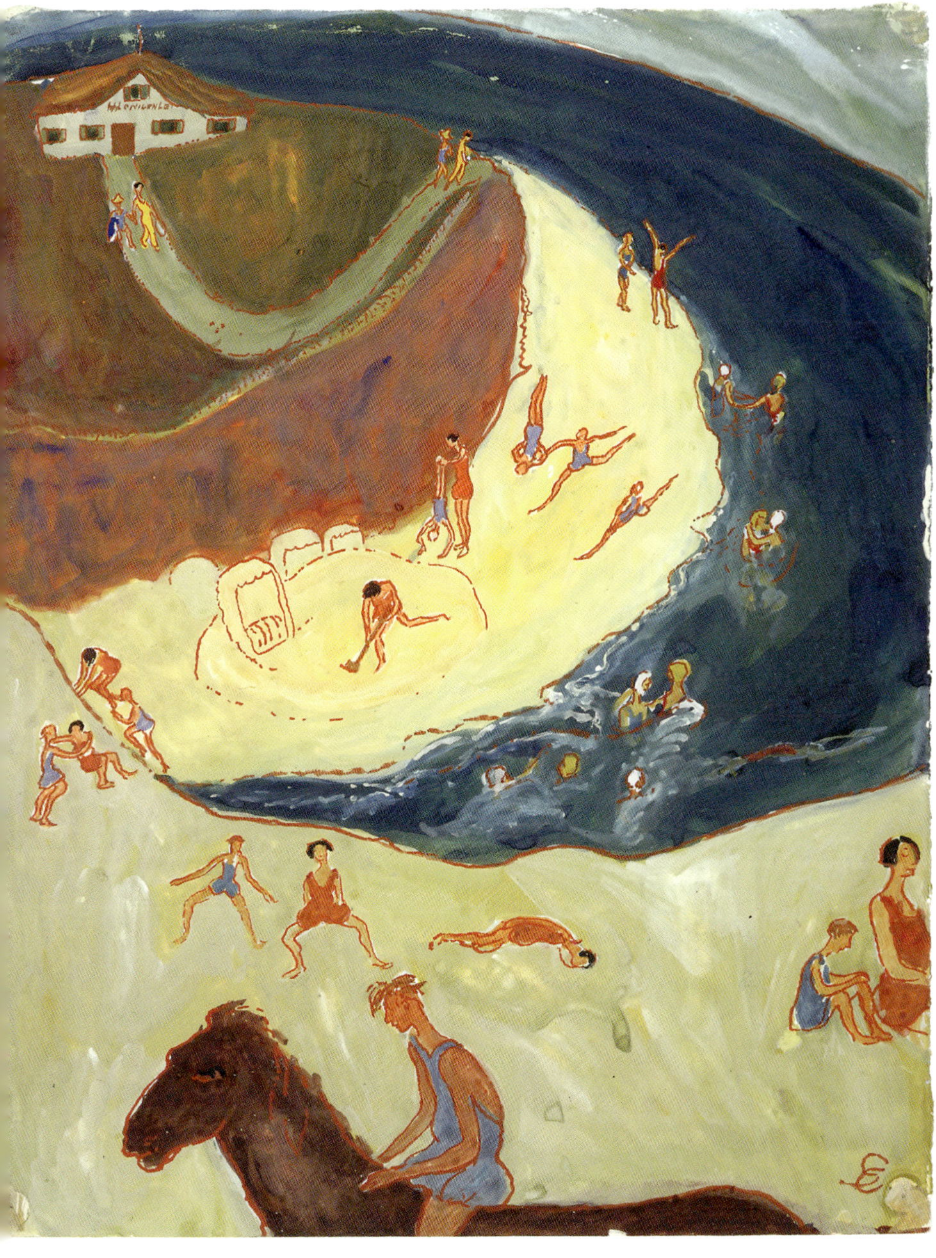

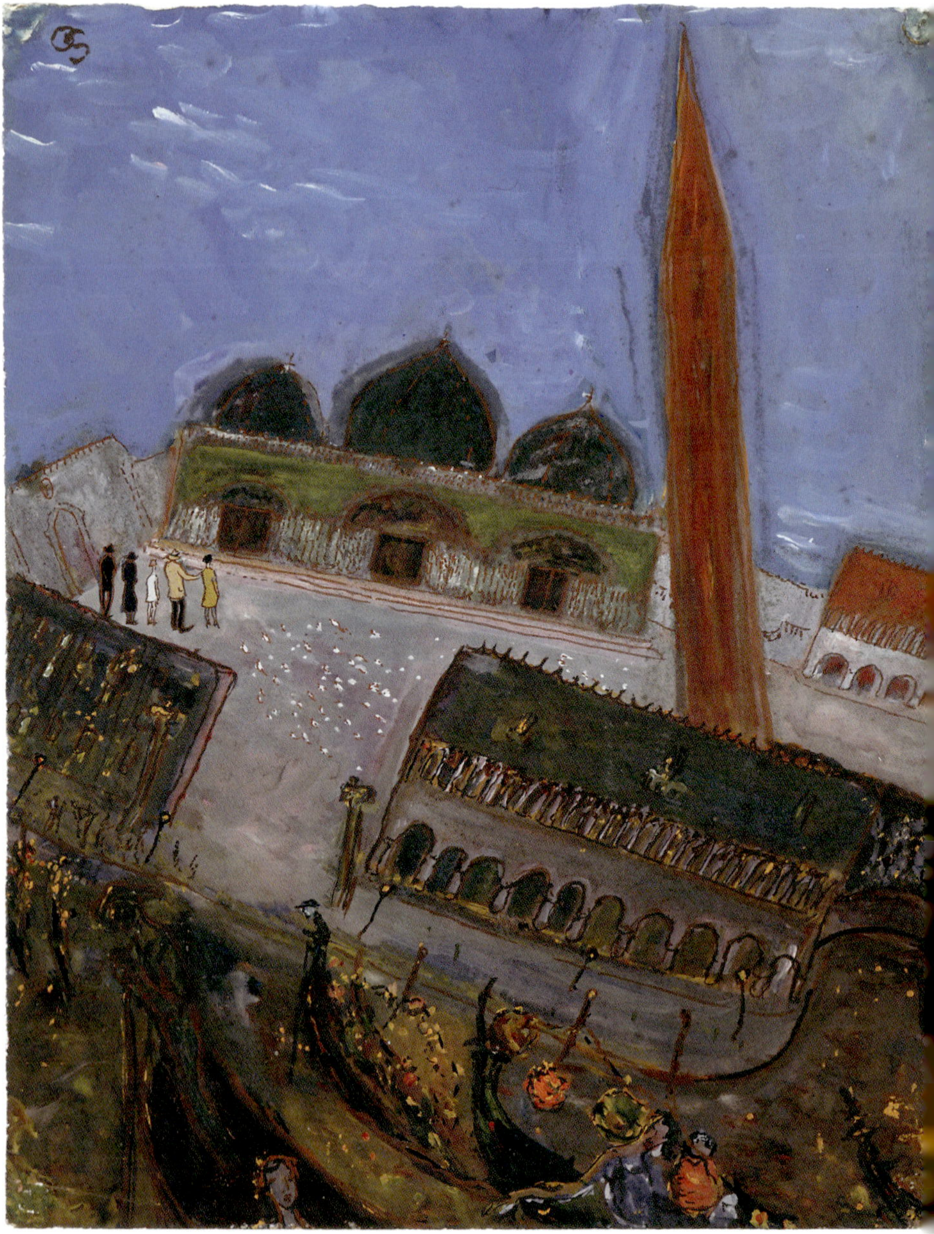

“And only wait – wait till the shadows darken passing to the warm, brown night.”

The following year the whole family goes to Venice. Charlotte can hardly believe that she is actually standing on Saint Mark’s Square. Since Mr and Mrs Knarre have been preparing her well for a long time for the beautiful sights they are going to see, Charlotte therefore knows Venice very well.

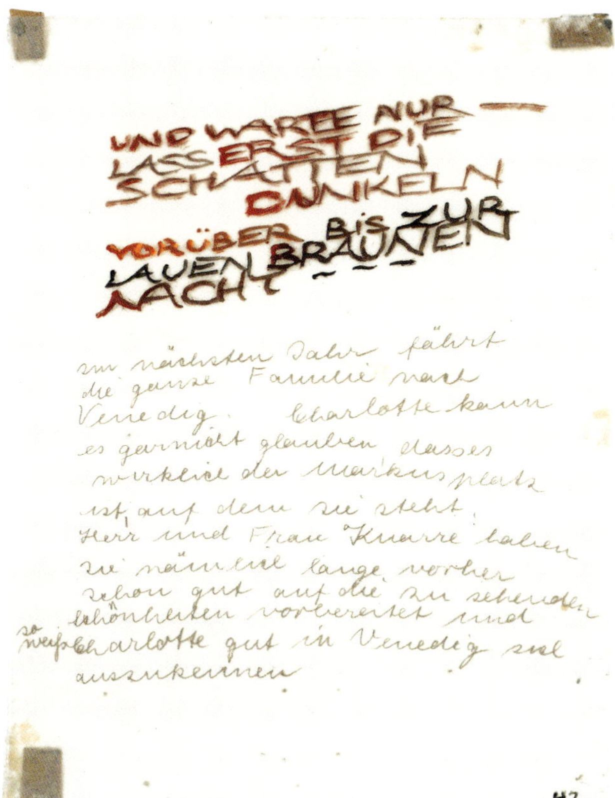

“Les sanglots longs des violons de l’automne blessent mon cœur dans une langueur monotone – tout suffoquant et blême quand sonne l’heure et je me souviens des jours anciens et je pleure.”

This is why, on the morning of departure, she sneaks out of the hotel in order to solidify certain beauties of the city in her memory. She tries to draw Saint Mark’s Cathedral.

On her way she meets Albert who, armed with his camera, has left the hotel for the same reasons.

Meanwhile Mrs Knarre at the hotel already sees Charlotte’s dead body before her eyes. She brings everyone around her into a state of commotion. To Albert and Charlotte her behaviour seems ridiculous when they see her in the distance standing on a bridge outside the hotel in a posture that Charlotte will never forget as long as she lives. She makes the most vehement reproaches to her son in-law about his behaviour, for having run off without breakfast prior to departure.

They are all offended and angry with one another as they get into the gondola that goes to the station. This state of affairs continues all the way to Milan.

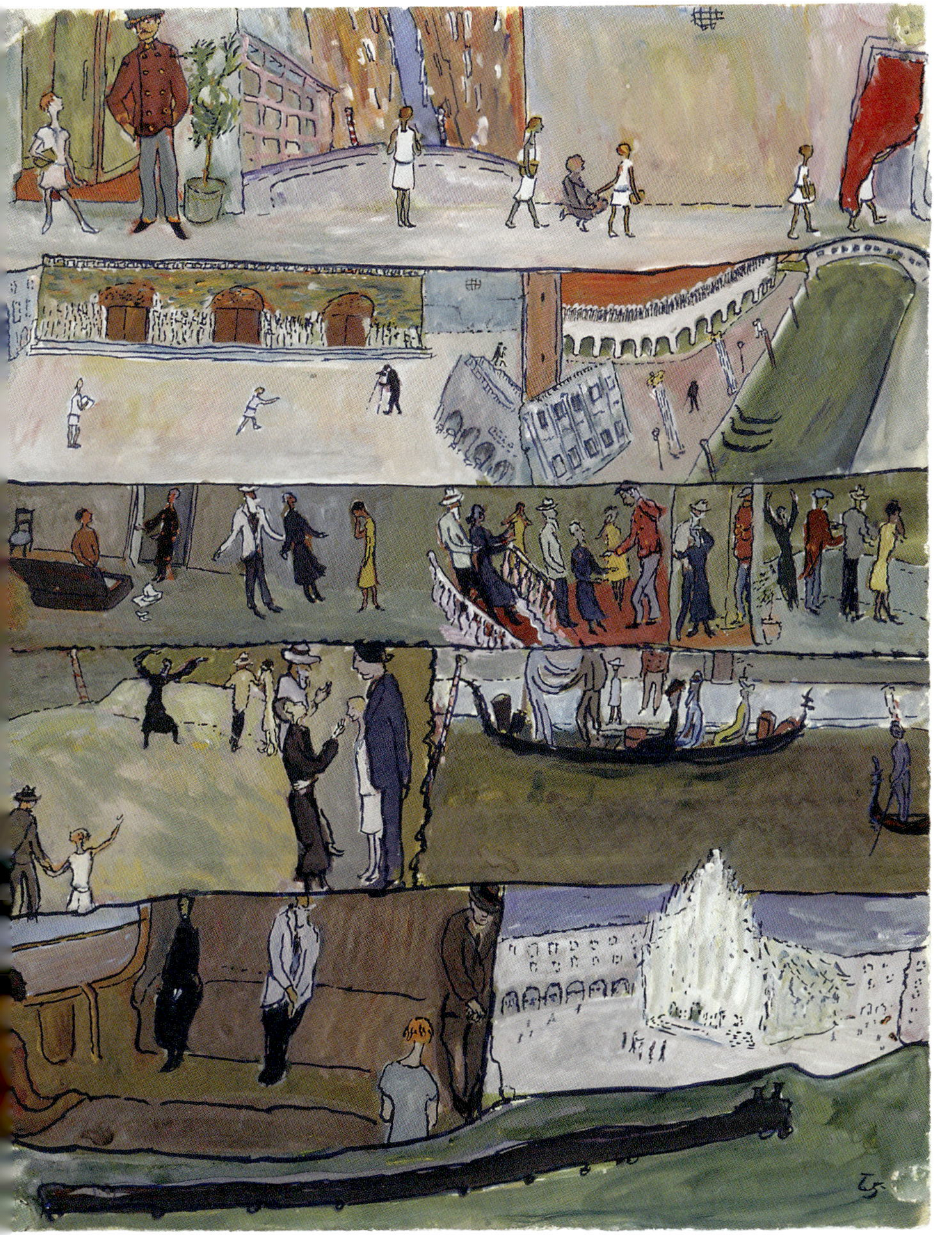

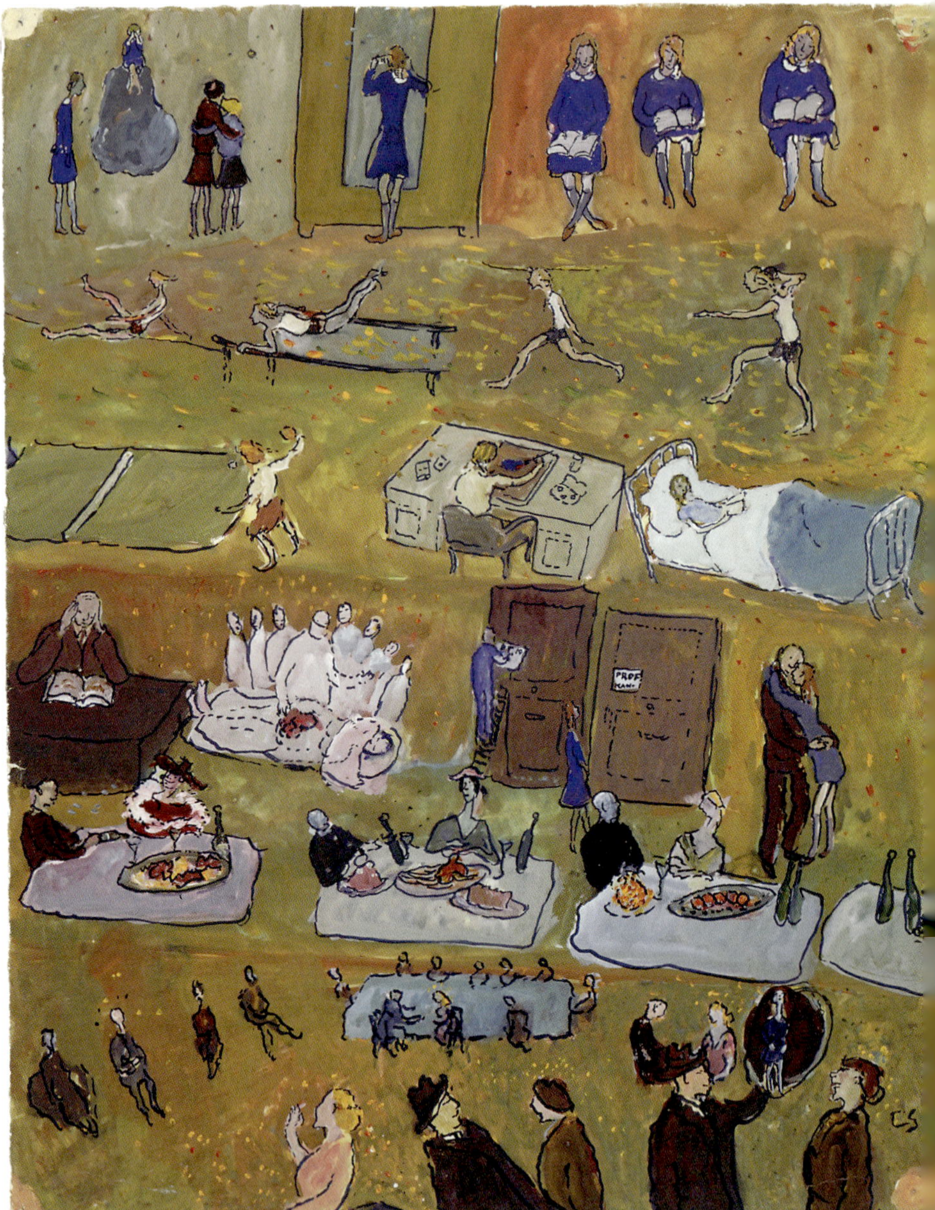
PROF

"I know not what this yearning is, the sadness filling my heart, I seem to hear church bells ringing – and never from that sound can I part."

Charlotte has reached a melancholy age. Her friend Hilde has found another, much prettier friend than Charlotte, and during recess she now goes around with Marianne while Charlotte trails sadly behind or sits on the stone cairn that stands in the middle of the playground.

She lets her hair grow and stands for hours in front of the mirror. She loves to read very romantic stories. Gym and playing ping-pong cheer her up somewhat. Drawing is one of her favourite occupations.

Albert Kann, meanwhile, has been studying a lot. He has been offering up some interesting works on organic disorders in the lower extremities of the human body. He received the professor title and a chair for minor surgery. Charlotte is very proud of her father.

He loves very fine food and thinks that it would also be good to remarry, only that the choice, because of the great variety of offers, is quite difficult.

At a party he meets a singer who sings a song by Schubert: Was vermeid ich denn die Wege, wo die anderen Weiser stehn. [Why do I avoid the pathways where the other signposts stand?]. Her singing impresses him very much. Afterwards they talk, and he tells her that he has a small daughter. She says she finds that charming.

(opposite)

<u>Last night I had a dream of you, you sweet little lady</u>.

The singer has the glorious name of Paulinka Bimbam. She comes almost every evening to them – longingly awaited by both Charlotte and Albert. On one occasion she invites Charlotte with Hase the governess to the opera.

Charlotte thinks of nothing but Miss Paulinka Bimbam, but she is terribly embarrassed to let her or anyone else know.

She goes with Hase the governess to the seaside, and the windmills, houses, lighthouse, airplanes, sea seem to whisper "her" name in her ear.

Meanwhile Albert and Paulinka Bimbam decide to get married.

(page 174)

"I seem to hear church bells ringing – and ne'er from that sound can I part... and quiet flows the Rhine."

Charlotte, too, has many opportunities to meet the singer. On a trip to the Rhine with Albert she suddenly turns up in the red-carpeted lobby of the hotel.

They spend an evening together when Charlotte, probably stimulated by the uncustomary pleasure of alcohol, tells the singer about her father's various female acquaintances who have bombarded her with presents, which is understandably very unpleasant for Albert – but is, however, extremely funny to the singer.

They also have a beautiful rowing trip together on the deep, blue-black Laach Lake. Charlotte does the rowing. Then the singer leaves again.

Albert and Charlotte continue their journey but at each mealtime never fail to drink to the health of the singer, who also seems to have made a deep impression on Charlotte.

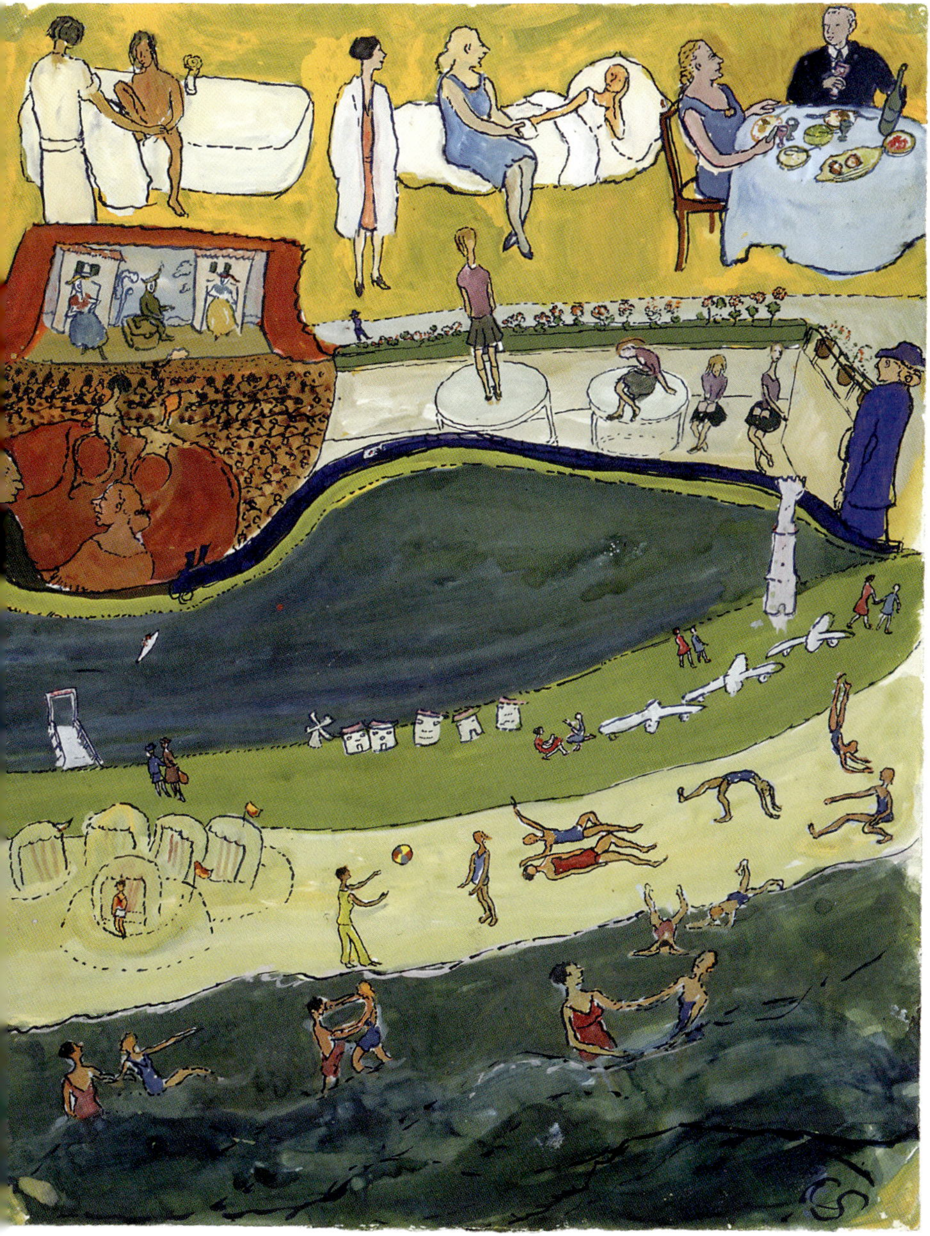

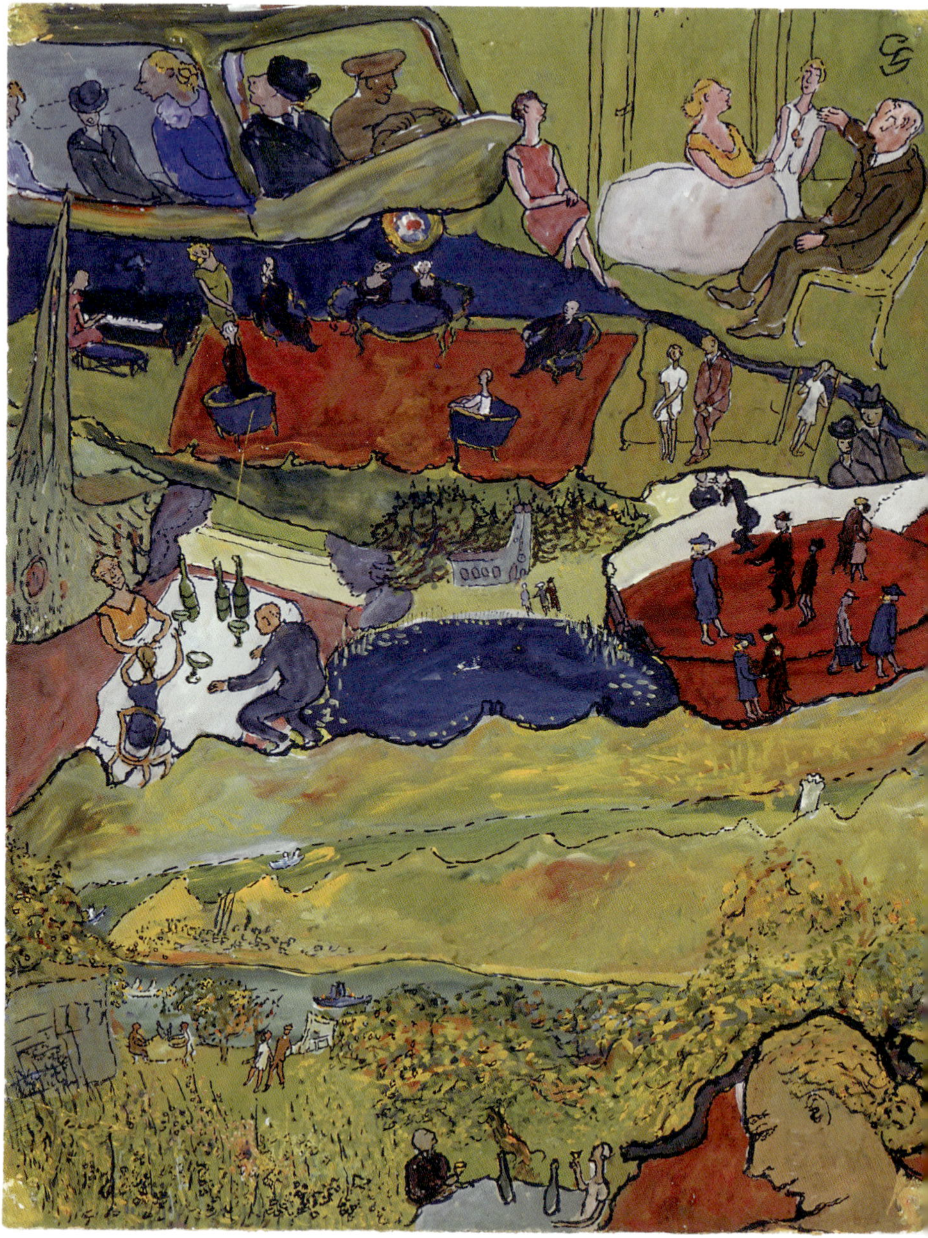

(bottom)

We announce our marriage.

Professor Albert Kann
Paulinka Bimbam

September 1930

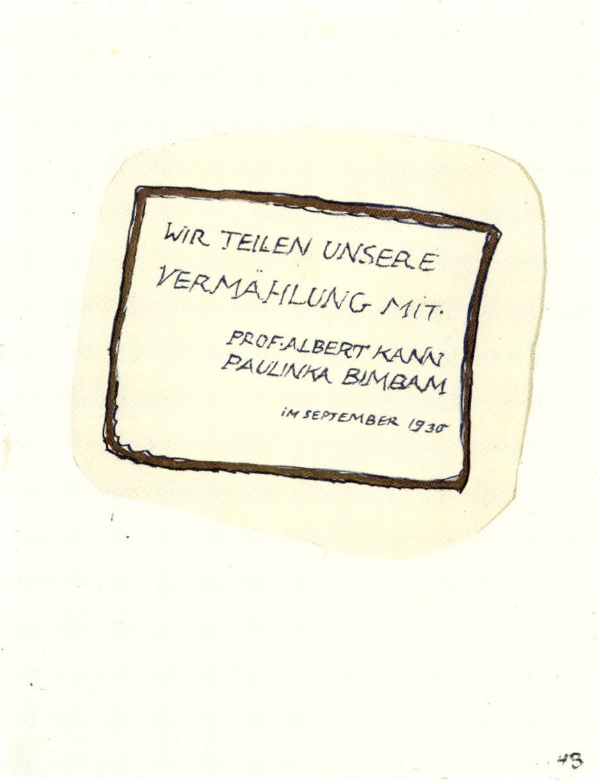

L'amour est enfant de Bohème, il n'a jamais connu de loi. [Love is a gypsy's child, it has never known the law].

The wedding was celebrated in Paulinka's hometown of Kurzenberg-on-the-Rhine. Her father had been dead for a long time. But her mother was still alive and was moved to tears often at the wedding.

Then Albert and Paulinka went off to Italy. Charlotte celebrated the wedding with Hase the governess and the Knarre grandparents. She was given a phonograph record of Paulinka singing in her glorious contralto L'amour est un oiseau rebelle from Carmen. The record was played so often that it remained on the same spot every third note and would repeat countless times unless one lifted it and moved it on.

Meanwhile, a very good friend of Paulinka's, an extremely famous man, the general manager of an opera house, sat in his box listening with a critical ear for a new production of Orpheus and Eurydice. Orpheus's aria Ach, ich habe sie verloren [Oh, I have lost her] seemed to be sung especially with much expression and feeling.

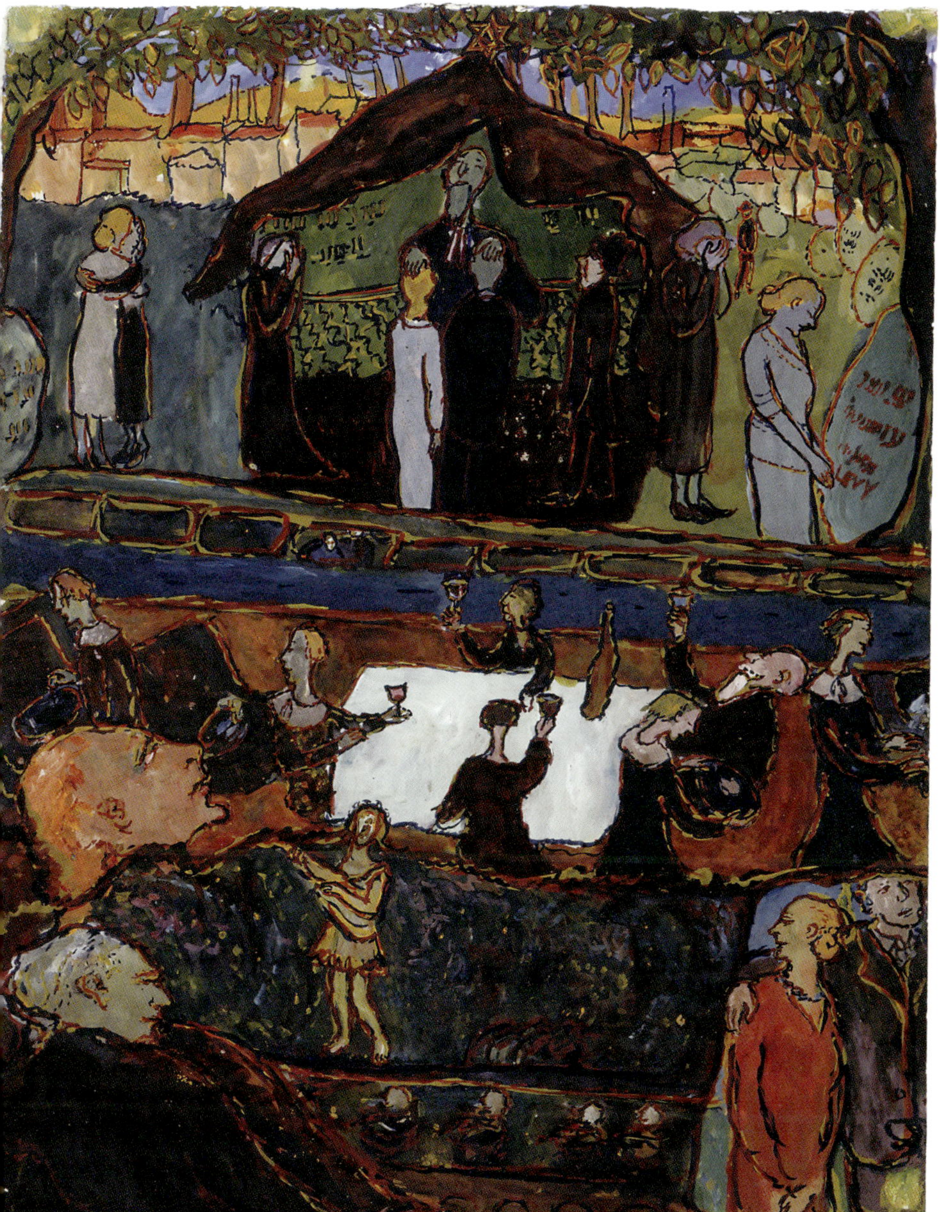
LEVY

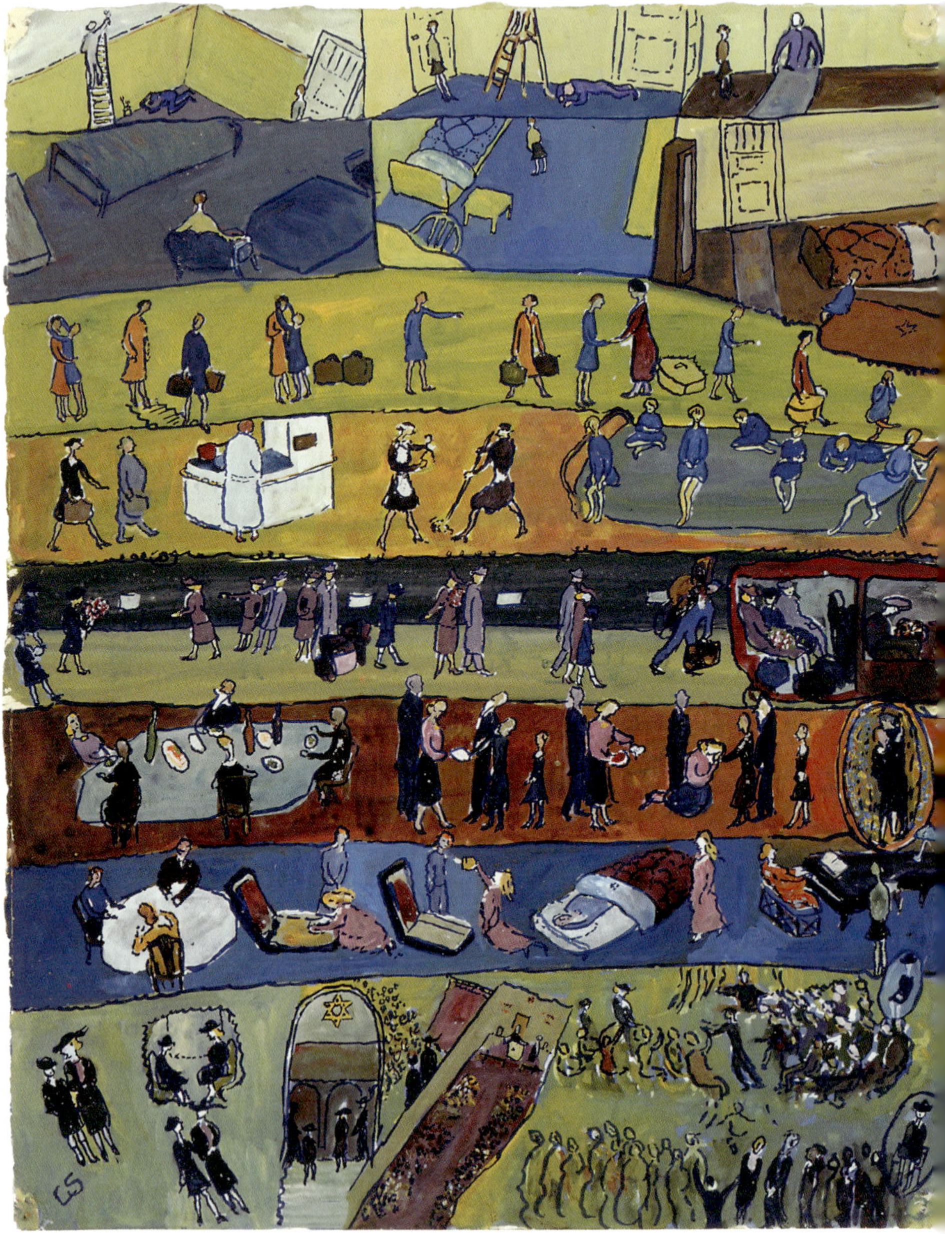

(opposite)

Now comes the last sheet of Scene 2. From now on, Charlotte's feelings are expressed in "songs".

CHARLOTTE
Oh dear – our home is being all changed around, and I have to give up my room to her, and my dear Hase is going away from me, and Anna is leaving too, and these new ones are coming – I have to go to the station. Oh dear, how reluctantly, oh how reluctantly do I do that. Oh, my Mummy...
Oh, isn't it nice of Grandmother to give her such a beautiful piece of jewellery.
But they've brought me something too, and she is indeed my beloved little woman too, and everyone loves her as well – but no one as much as I do."

(following pages)

And soon she [Paulinka] became a teacher herself, adored by all her pupils. Two almost killed themselves for her. So she then ran away.

You see her here at her father's grave, and she makes the decision to leave her home country and go to the big city to establish her path with the wits of her father (who, with all his talents had never left his little town,
where one could live – love – sing – talk and drink,
so comfortably).

That's how she came to a great lady, known throughout the city as a beauty. Here she had first to wash, iron, mend – but at night she never forgot her true calling.

She listened to a famous professor of music lecturing on The Art of the Fugue, and once, when something slipped the professor's memory, she even dared to supplement him.

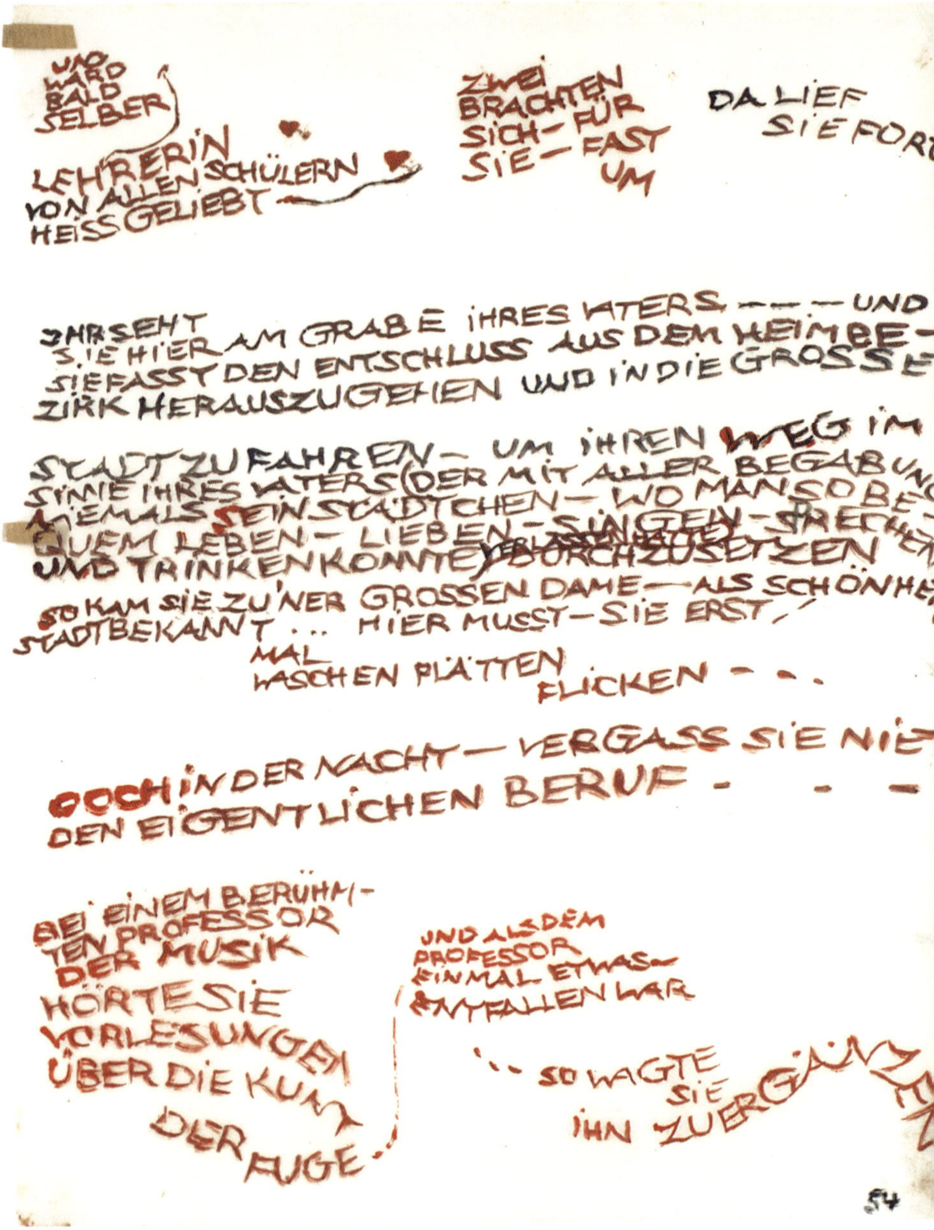
UND WARD BALD SELBER
LEHRERIN VON ALLEN SCHÜLERN HEISS GELIEBT
ZWEI BRACHTEN SICH - FÜR SIE - FAST UM
DA LIEF SIE FORT
IHR SEHT SIE HIER AM GRABE IHRES VATERS - - - - UND SIE FASST DEN ENTSCHLUSS AUS DEM HEIMBEZIRK HERAUSZUGEHEN UND IN DIE GROSSE STADT ZU FAHREN - UM IHREN WEG IM SINNE IHRES VATERS (DER MIT ALLER BEGABUNG NIEMALS SEIN STÄDTCHEN - WO MAN SO BEQUEM LEBEN - LIEBEN - SINGEN - SPRECHEN UND TRINKEN KONNTE) VERLASSEN HATTE DURCHZUSETZEN
SO KAM SIE ZU'NER GROSSEN DAME - ALS SCHÖNHEIT STADTBEKANNT ... HIER MUSST - SIE ERST MAL WASCHEN PLÄTTEN FLICKEN - - .
OOCH IN DER NACHT - VERGASS SIE NIE DEN EIGENTLICHEN BERUF - - -
BEI EINEM BERÜHMTEN PROFESSOR DER MUSIK HÖRTE SIE VORLESUNGEN ÜBER DIE KUNST DER FUGE ...
UND ALS DEM PROFESSOR EINMAL ETWAS - ENTFALLEN WAR
... SO WAGTE SIE IHN ZU ERGÄNZEN
54

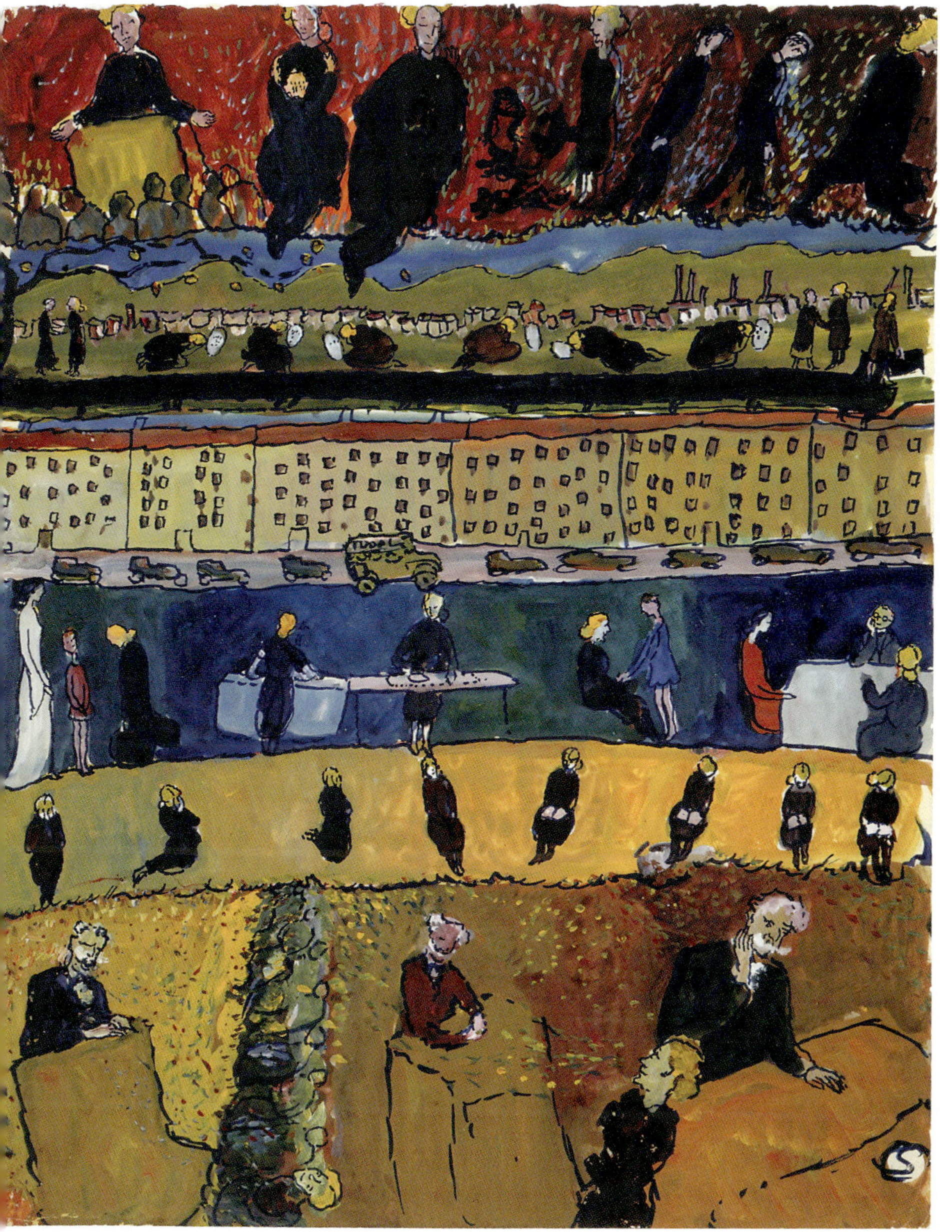

"Hello, hello, my young lady!" the Professor called her back as she wanted to leave the hall after the lecture. "Here, have a ticket for my concert tonight."

And she sits in the concert and listens with devotion; and afterwards brings him a bouquet of violets. "No, Professor, it was wonderful!" And he invited her to visit him sometime.

"We are the family of the famous Professor Klingklang. Who is this then?" – "We are the daughters of..." – 'I am t..." – "I am the son of the famous..." – "And that is my wife."

And he wanted to evaluate her voice and found out that in her throat lay a glorious aptitude for singing.

Melody: Kommt all ihr Seraphim mit...
[Come all ye seraphim with...]

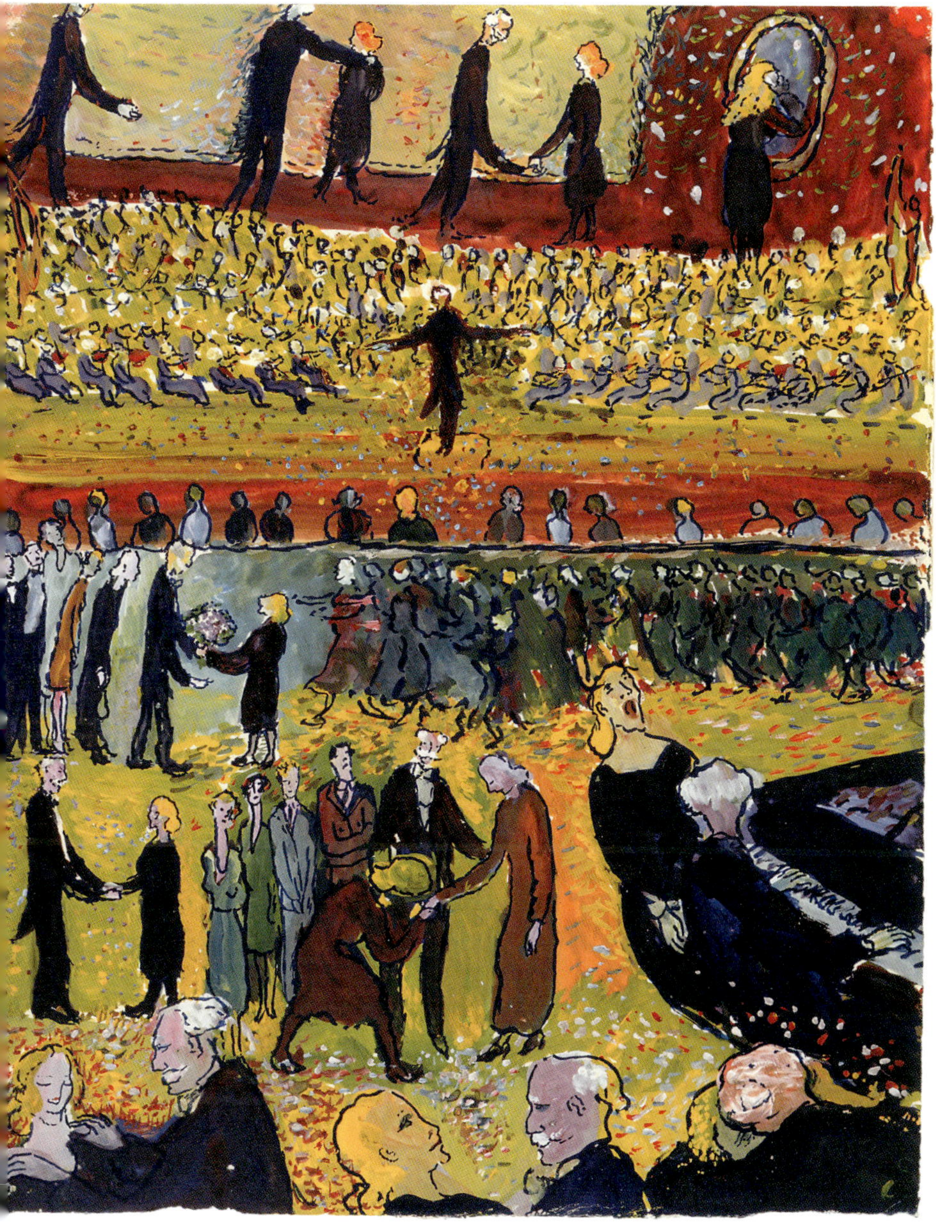

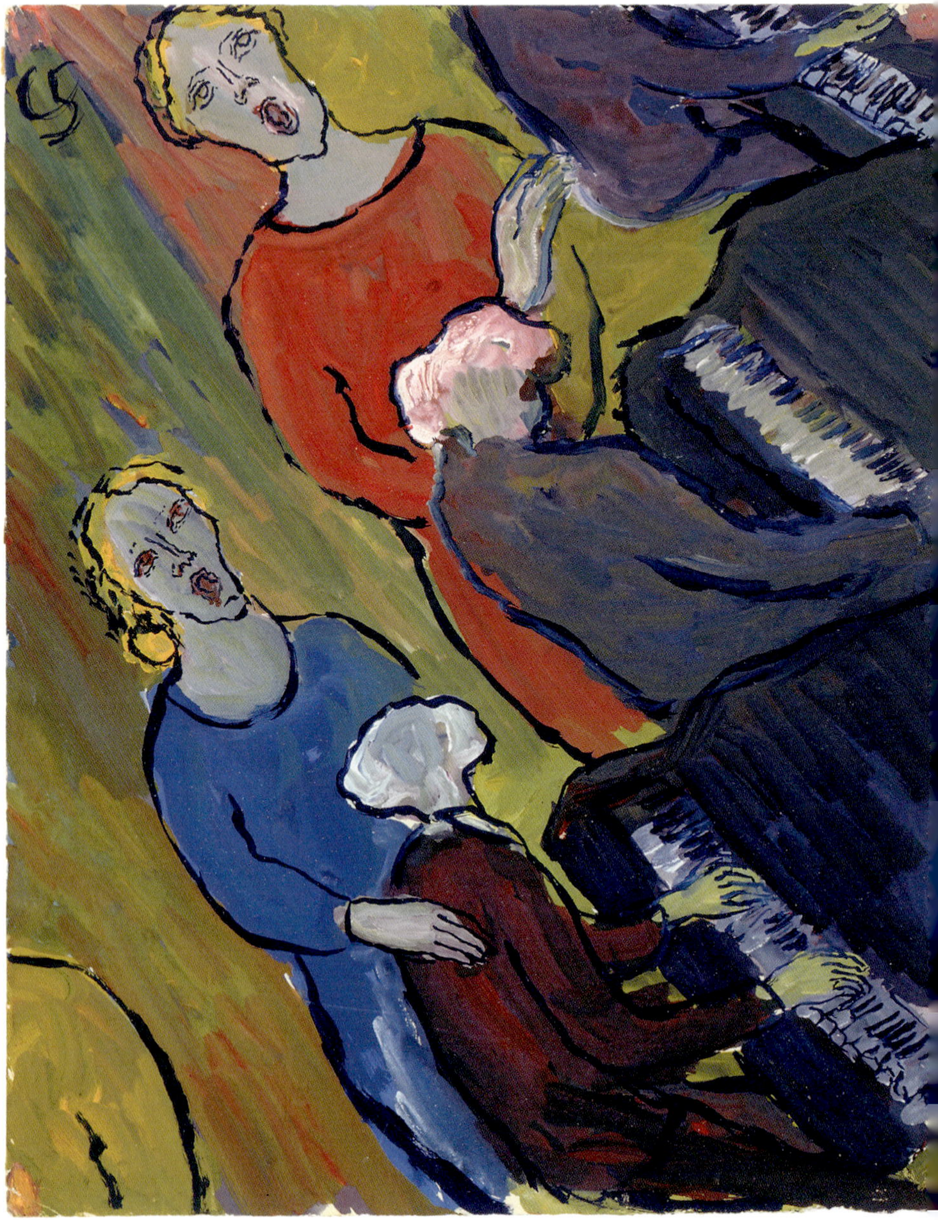

PAULINKA
“Ha, ha, ha, ha, ha, ha, ha, ha, ha, ha,
ha, ha, ha, ha, ha, ha, ha, ha, ha...”

Therewith she spent the most wonderful hours of her life in the most ardent singing work with her beloved and revered Professor.

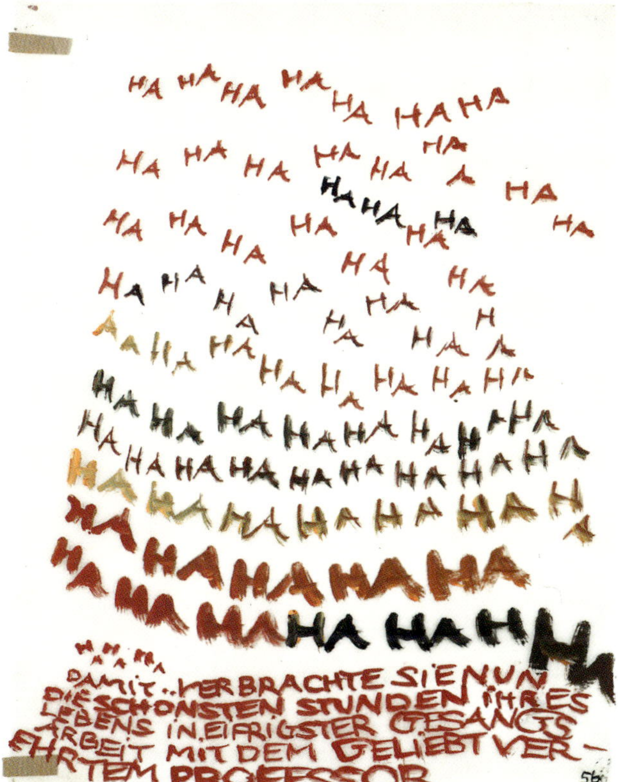

And she sang
more beautifully than ever.

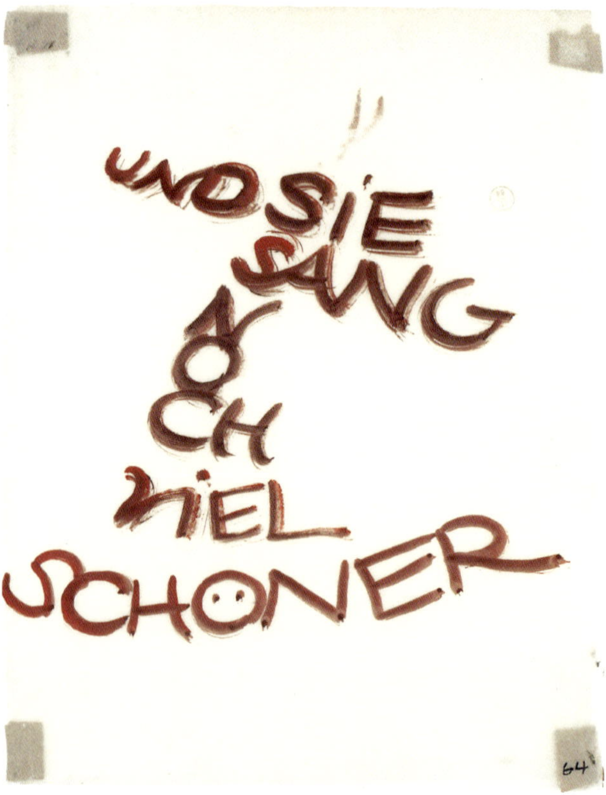

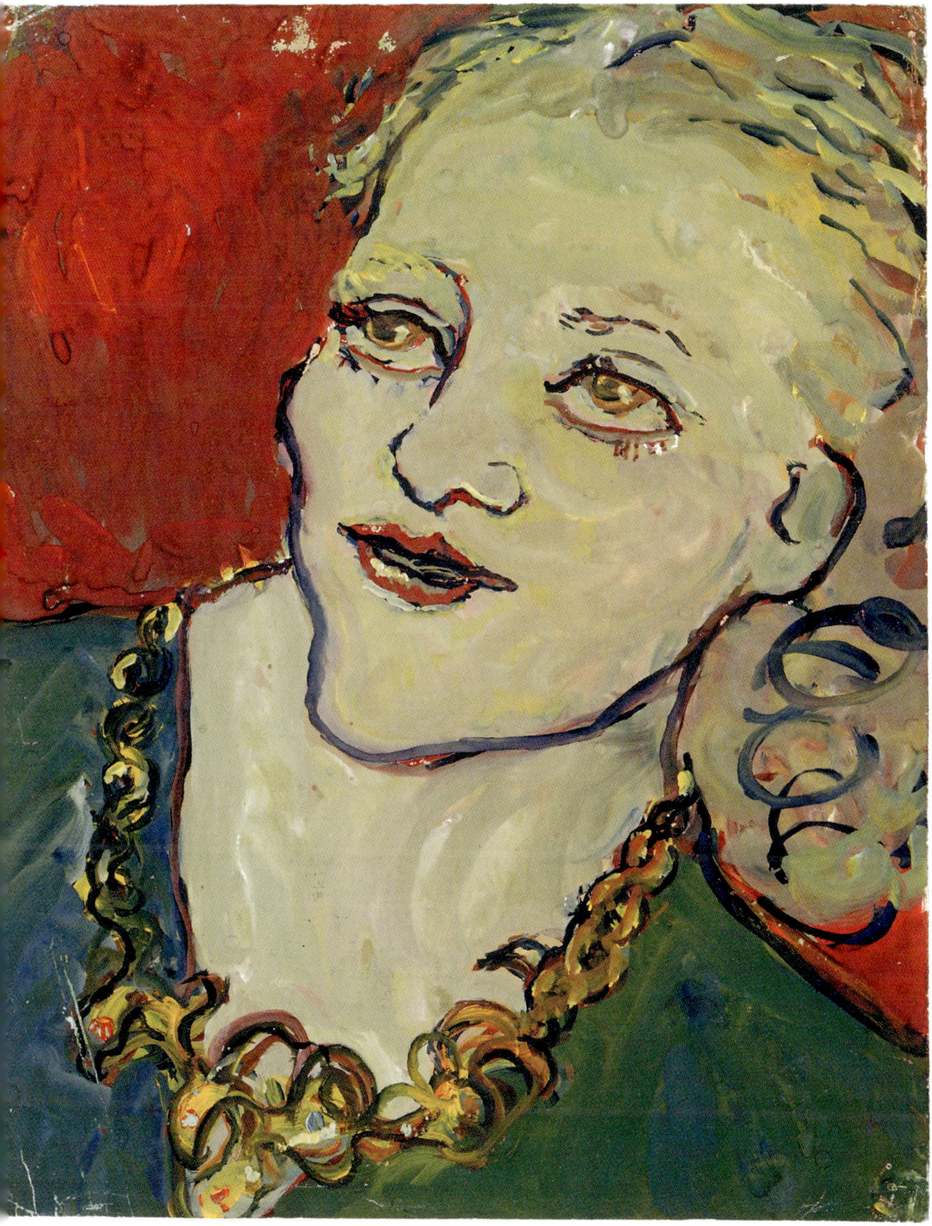

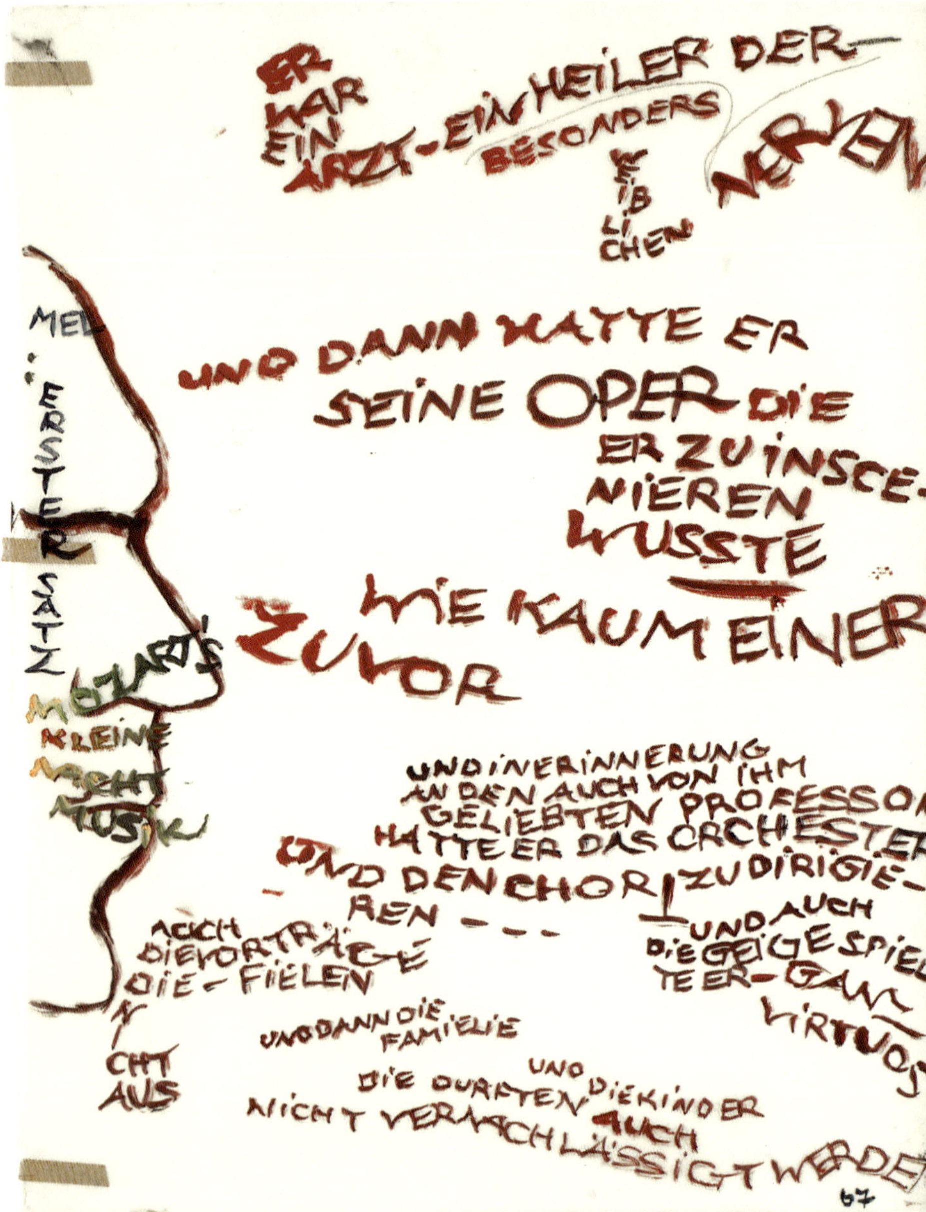

ER WAR EIN ARZT - EIN HEILER DER BESONDERS WEIBLICHEN NERVEN
UND DANN HATTE ER SEINE OPER DIE ER ZU INSCE-NIEREN WUSSTE WIE KAUM EINER ZUVOR
UND IN ERINNERUNG AN DEN AUCH VON IHM GELIEBTEN PROFESSOR HATTE ER DAS ORCHESTER UND DEN CHOR ZU DIRIGIE-REN - - -
UND AUCH DIE GEIGE SPIELTE ER - GANZ VIRTUOS
AUCH DIE VORTRÄGE DIE - FIELEN NICHT AUS
UND DANN DIE FAMILIE UND DIE KINDER DIE DURFTEN AUCH NICHT VERNACHLÄSSIGT WERDEN
MEL: ERSTER SATZ MOZART'S KLEINE NACHT MUSIK
67

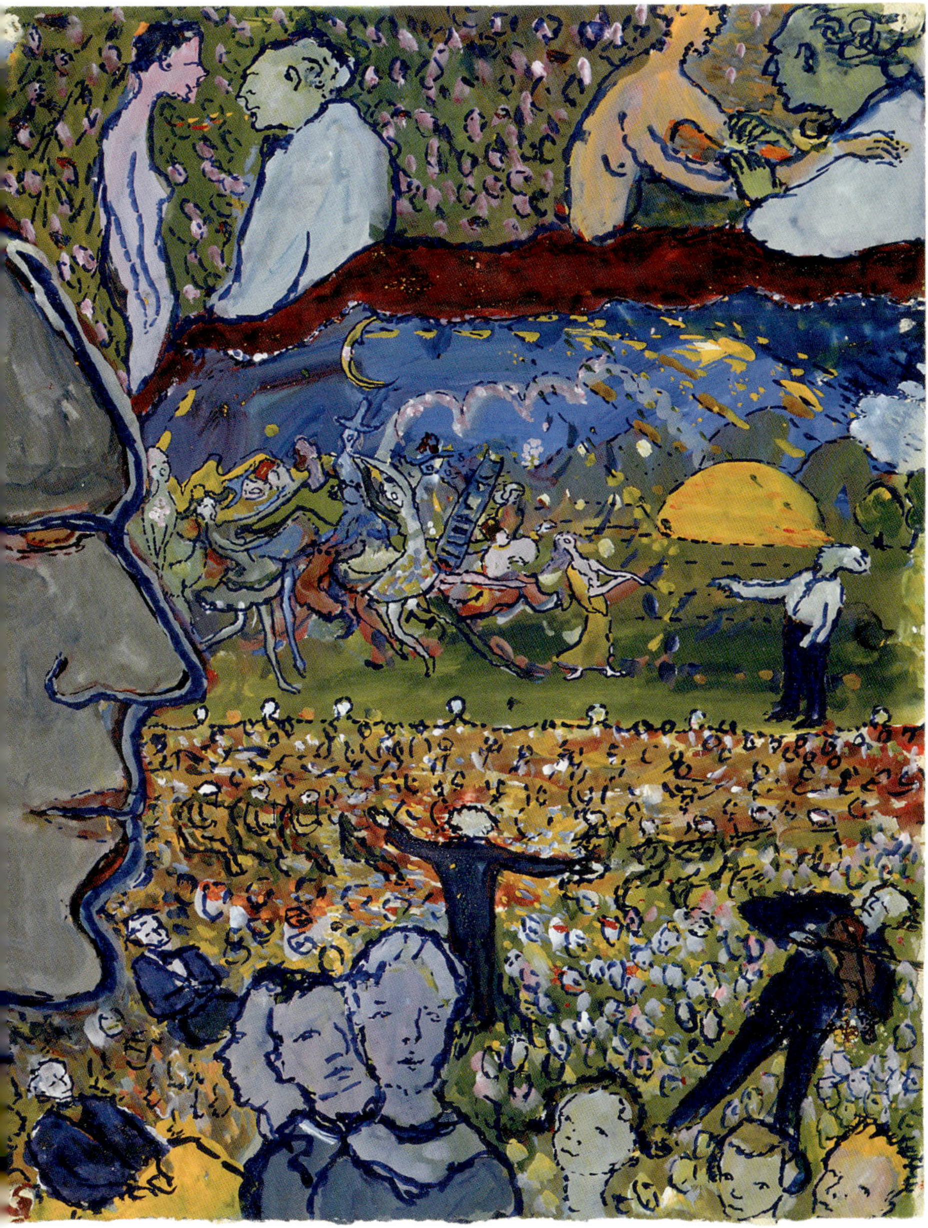

(previous pages)

He [Dr Singsang] was a doctor, a healer of – especially female – nerves. And then he had his opera, which he knew how to produce like hardly none before. And in memory of the professor, also beloved by him, he had to conduct the orchestra and the choir. – He also played the violin quite masterly.

The lectures too, were not canceled. And then the family and the children, they also cannot be neglected.

Melody: first movement of Mozart's Eine kleine Nachtmusik

(opposite)

Such a man demands from respectable women the entire devotion of their time – and so this was her line of thought: Gone is the dream of the singer if I am with him; and, although deeply touched, she remained steadfast not to marry him.

To the melody: Paulinkaa, I love you, oh will you be my wife

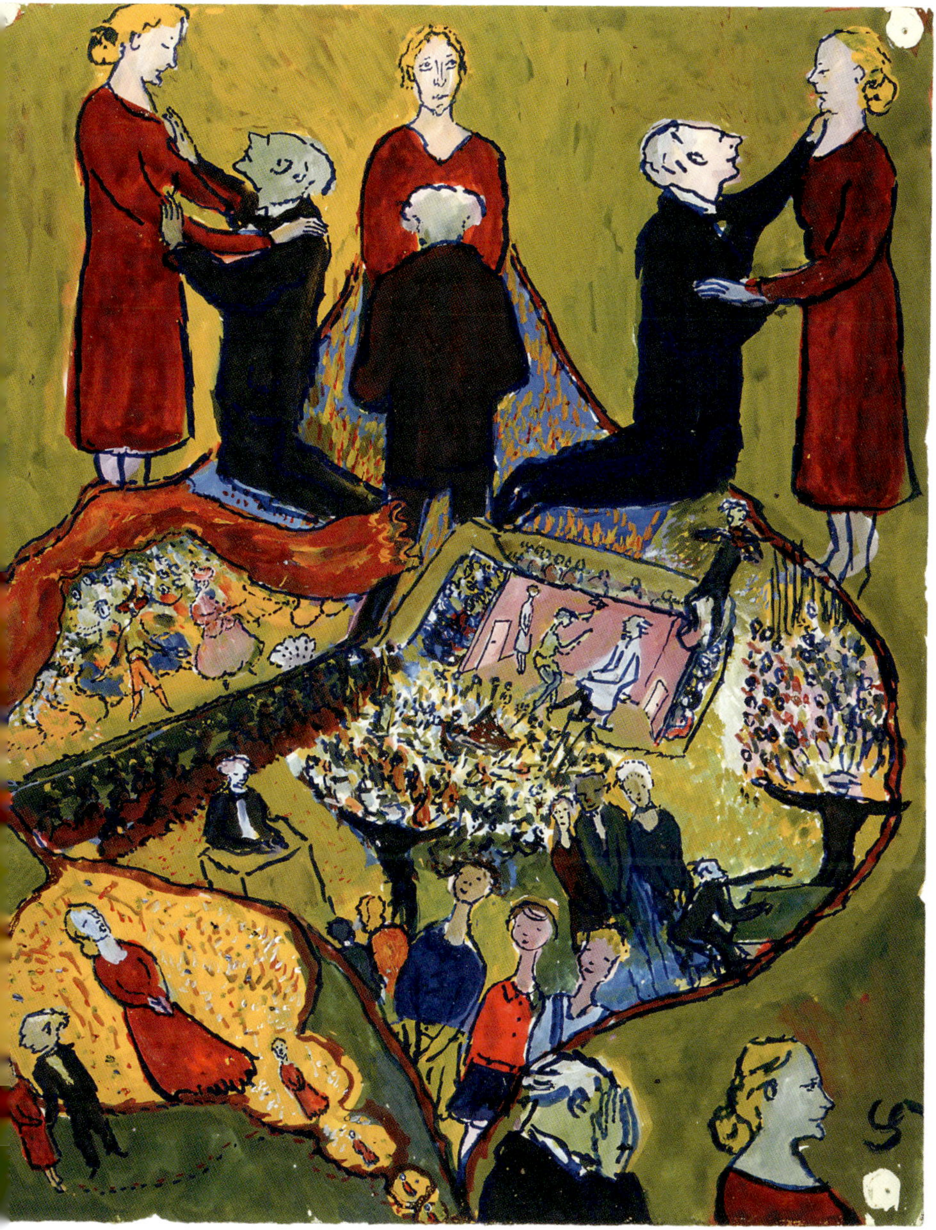

(bottom)

And the career continued. In 1930 Paulinka Bimbam sang in Königsberg, Berlin, Cologne, Hamm, Vienna, Basel, Lucerne, Bern, Geneva, Amsterdam, Wroclaw, Munich, Frankfurt ... for the next season she has engagements in Paris, Budapest, Vienna, Bucha...

(opposite)

But love as well was not to dry up so fast.
He followed her to all the cities, until one day she also forbade this.

To the melody: L'amour est un oiseau rebelle

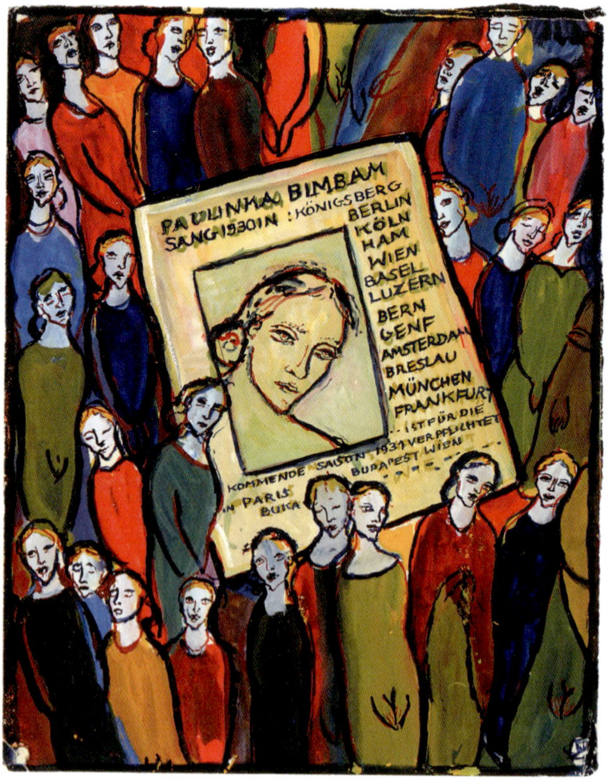

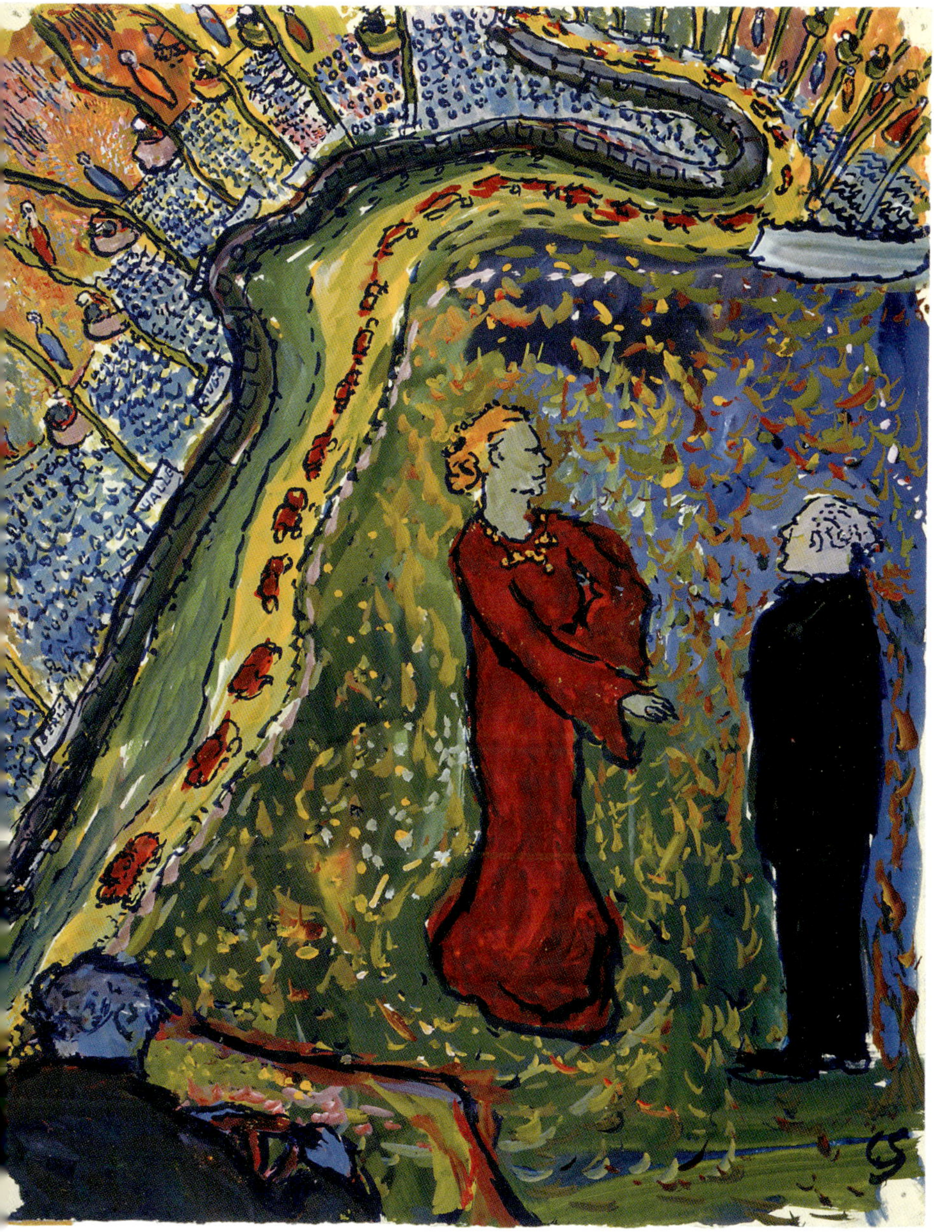

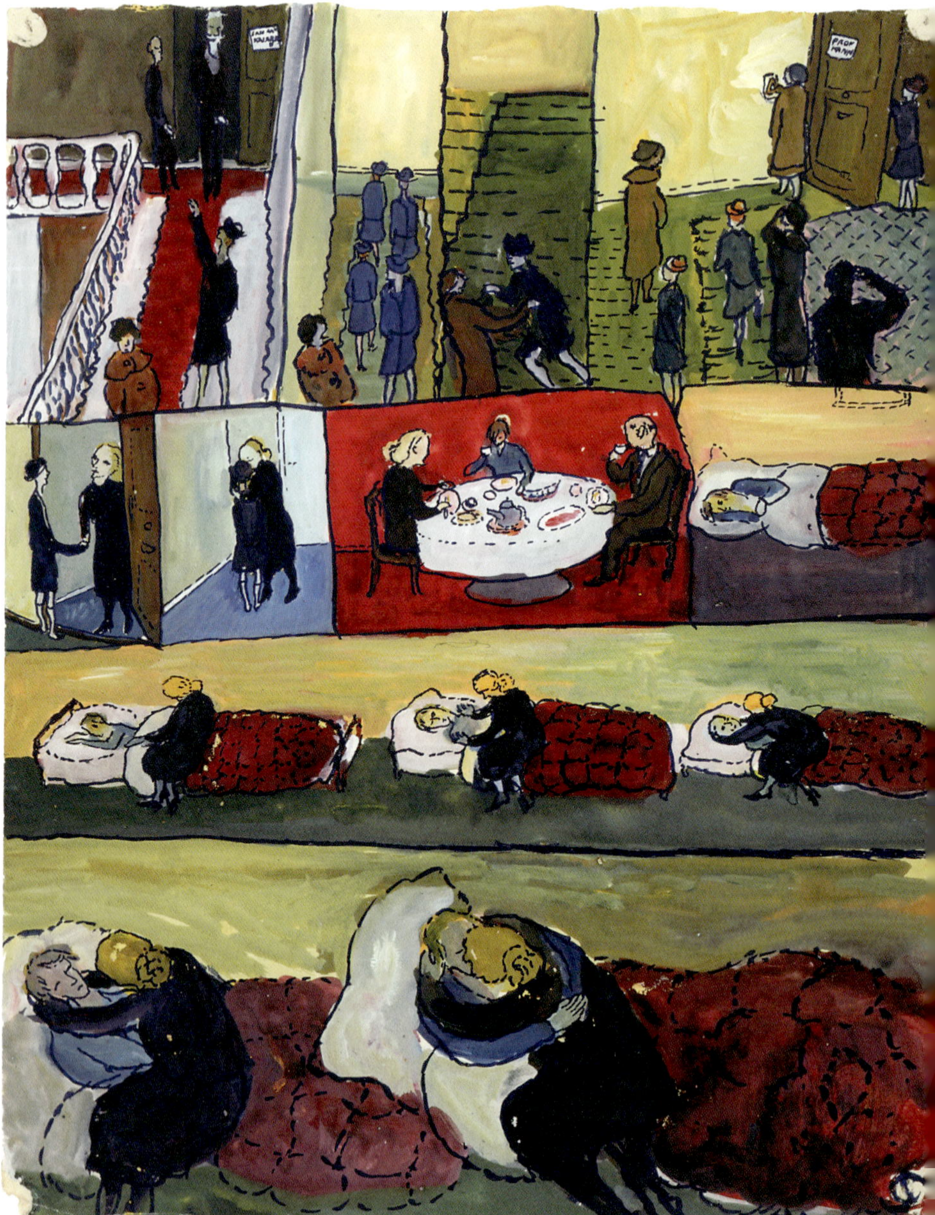

SCENE 4

Meanwhile little Charlotte Kann has been with her Knarre grandparents and is now being taken home, where she doesn't dare pull the bell, for unexplored reasons and instead contends in a battle with the person accompanying her until the latter angrily goes upstairs and rings the bell herself.

But now shame befalls our model, and with hurrying steps she goes up where the beloved in the black dress tenderly welcomes her.

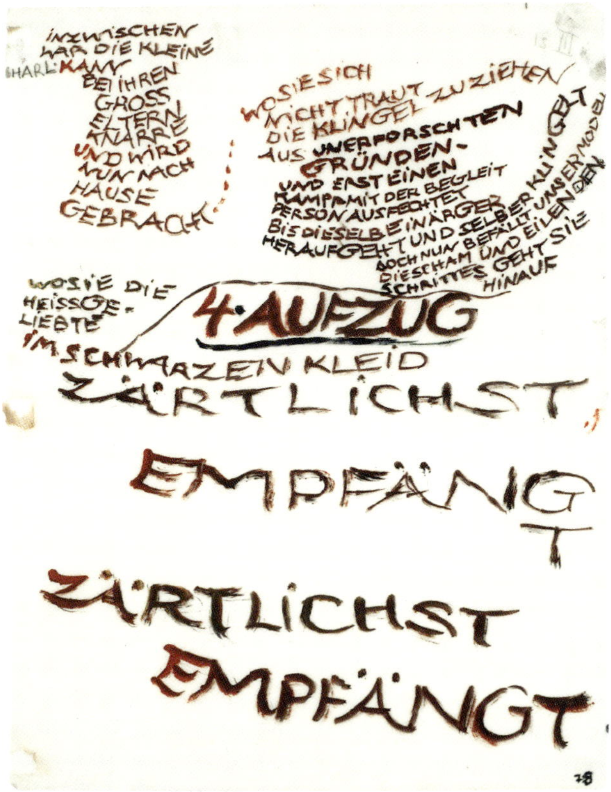

And in school as well, she is only thinking of her. Only very rarely does one succeed in wrenching her out of her lethargy. But now she has another friend and also likes going to the movies. However, the first question when she comes home is: “Is ‘she’ (for she hasn’t been capable of giving her a name) at home?!!”

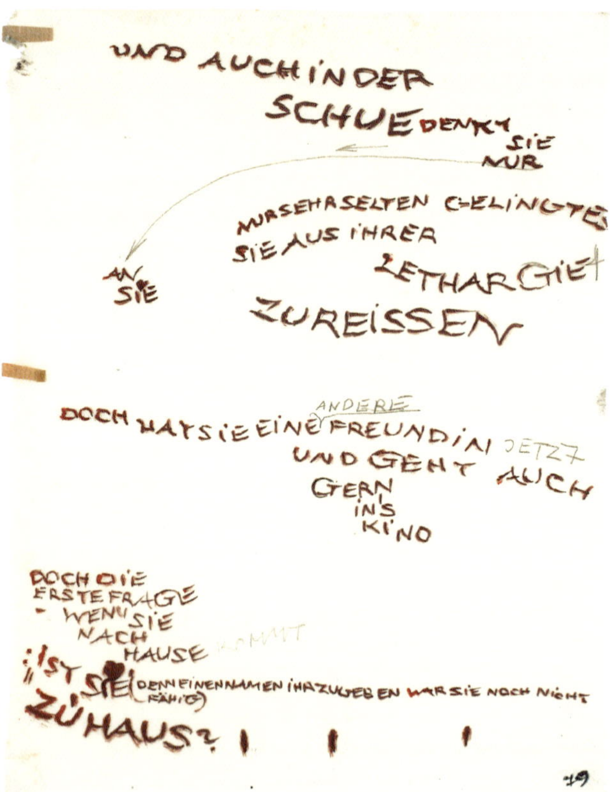

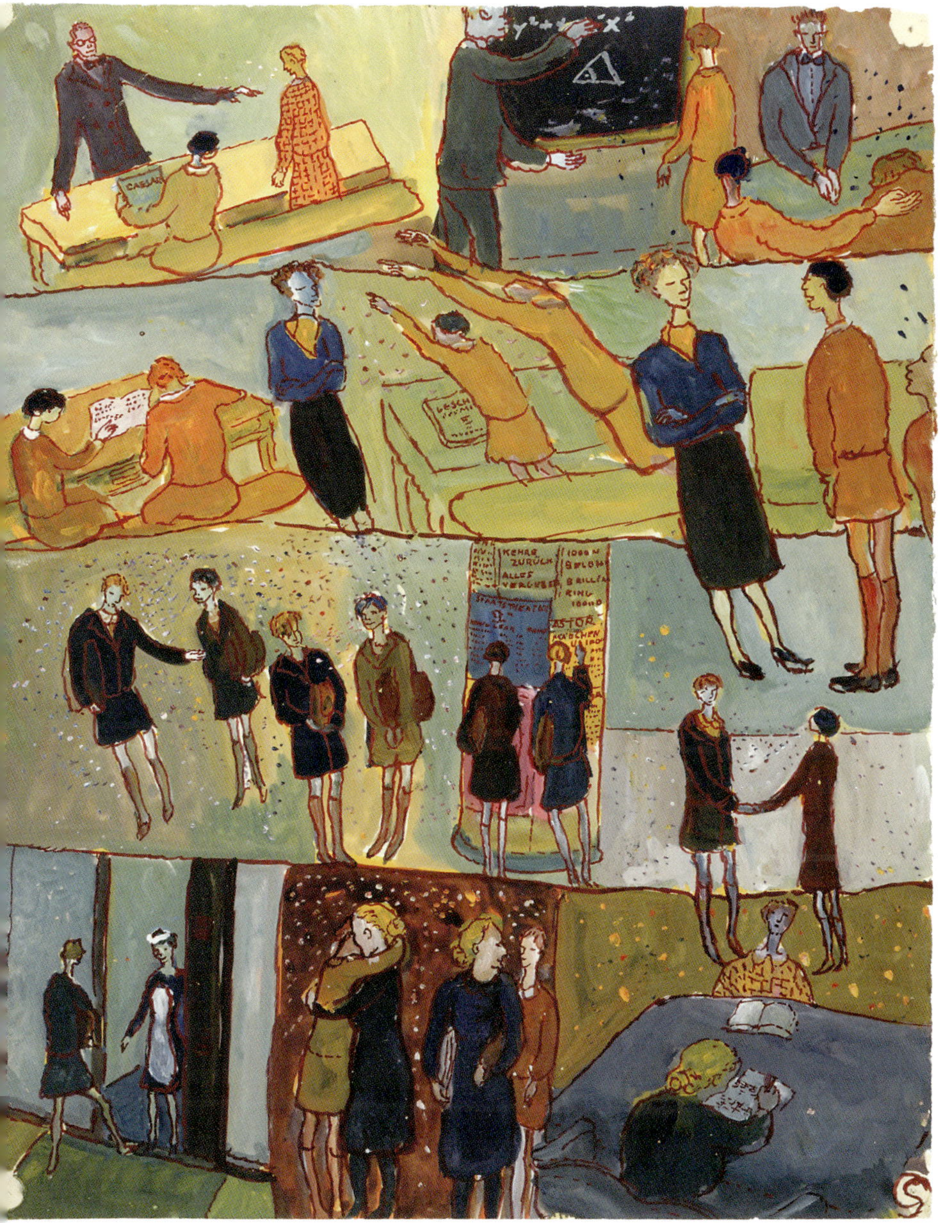
KEHRE ZURÜCK
ALLES
ASTOR

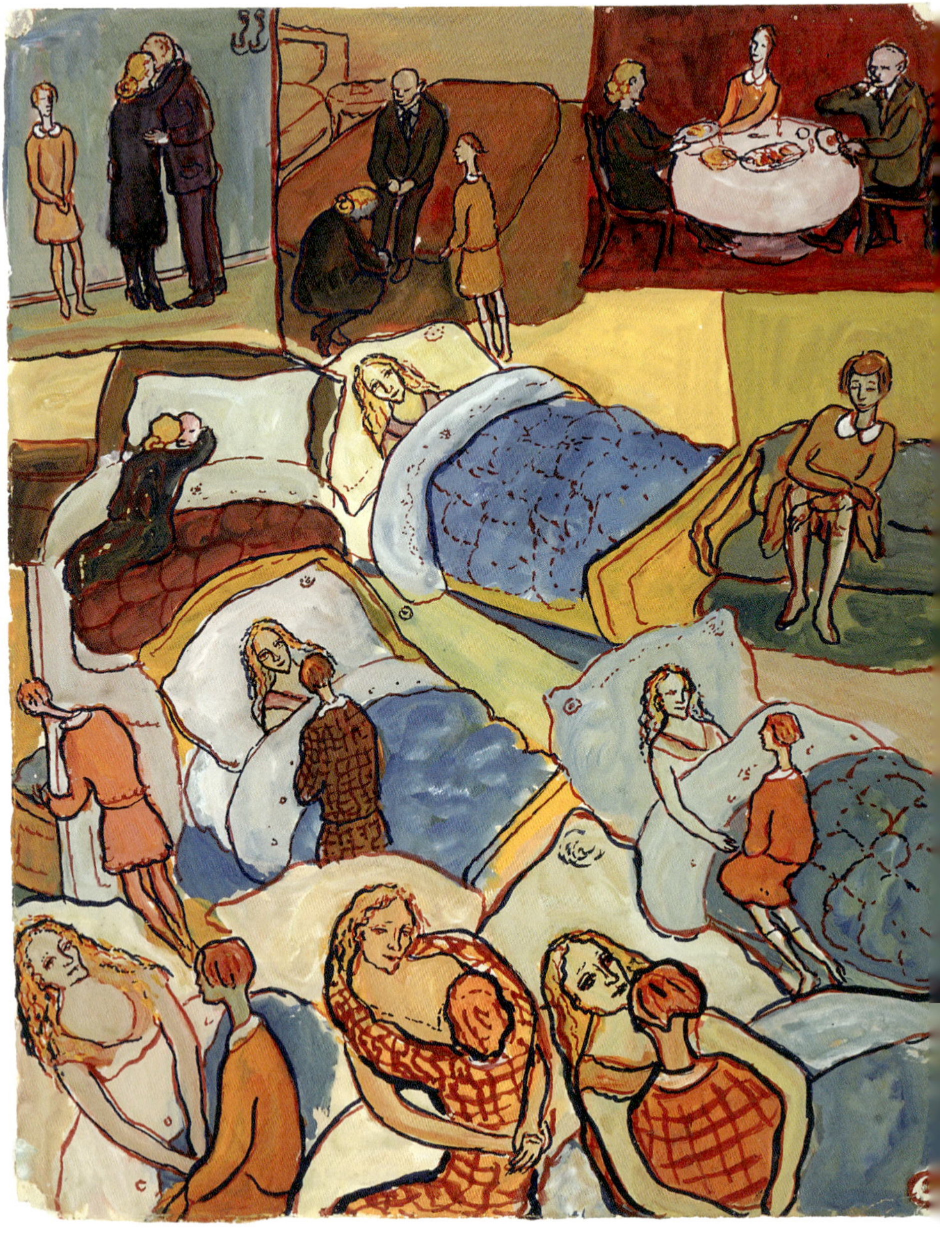

(opposite)

The little girl – you will laugh – was even jealous of her father.

And Paulinka was not happy. Also the sudden death of her mother had weakened her.

And she wasn't dissatisfied with the little girl's fervent hidden love (for, of course, no one knew anything about it).

(bottom)

Here you see them both at a home concert, singing: Schlage doch, gewünschte Stunde, brich doch an, gewünschter Tag [Strike, oh strike, thou yearned-for hour; break, oh break, thou yearned-for day!]

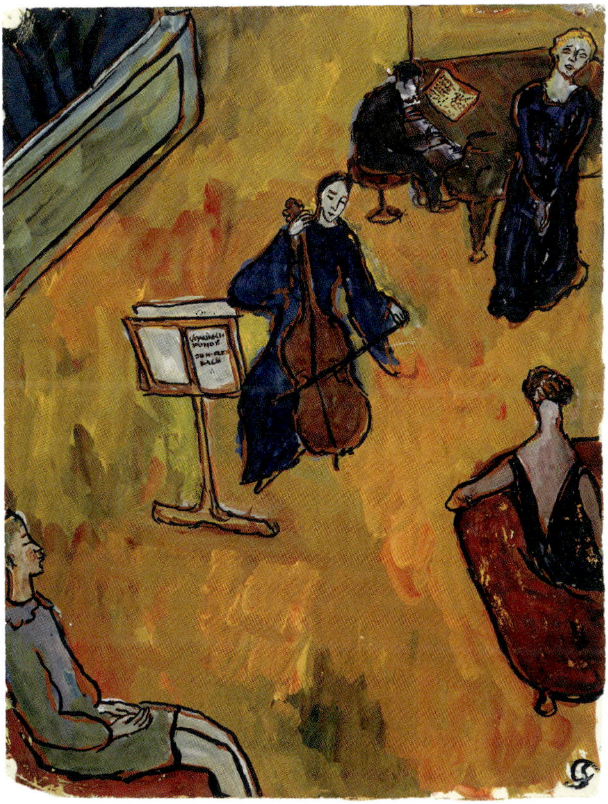

(these pages)

And this sheet actually emerged after the melody:
In einer kleinen Konditorei, da saßen wir zwei bei Kuchen und Tee [In a small café, we sat one sunny day, over a cup of tea]. Not one word did you say, but you knew right away that all was understood. And the electric piano tinkled soft, a tune of love we'd heard so oft...

(following pages)

And Paulinka sings: Bist du bei mir, geh ich mit Freuden zum Sterben und zu meiner Ruh [When thou art near, I go with joy to my death and to my rest].

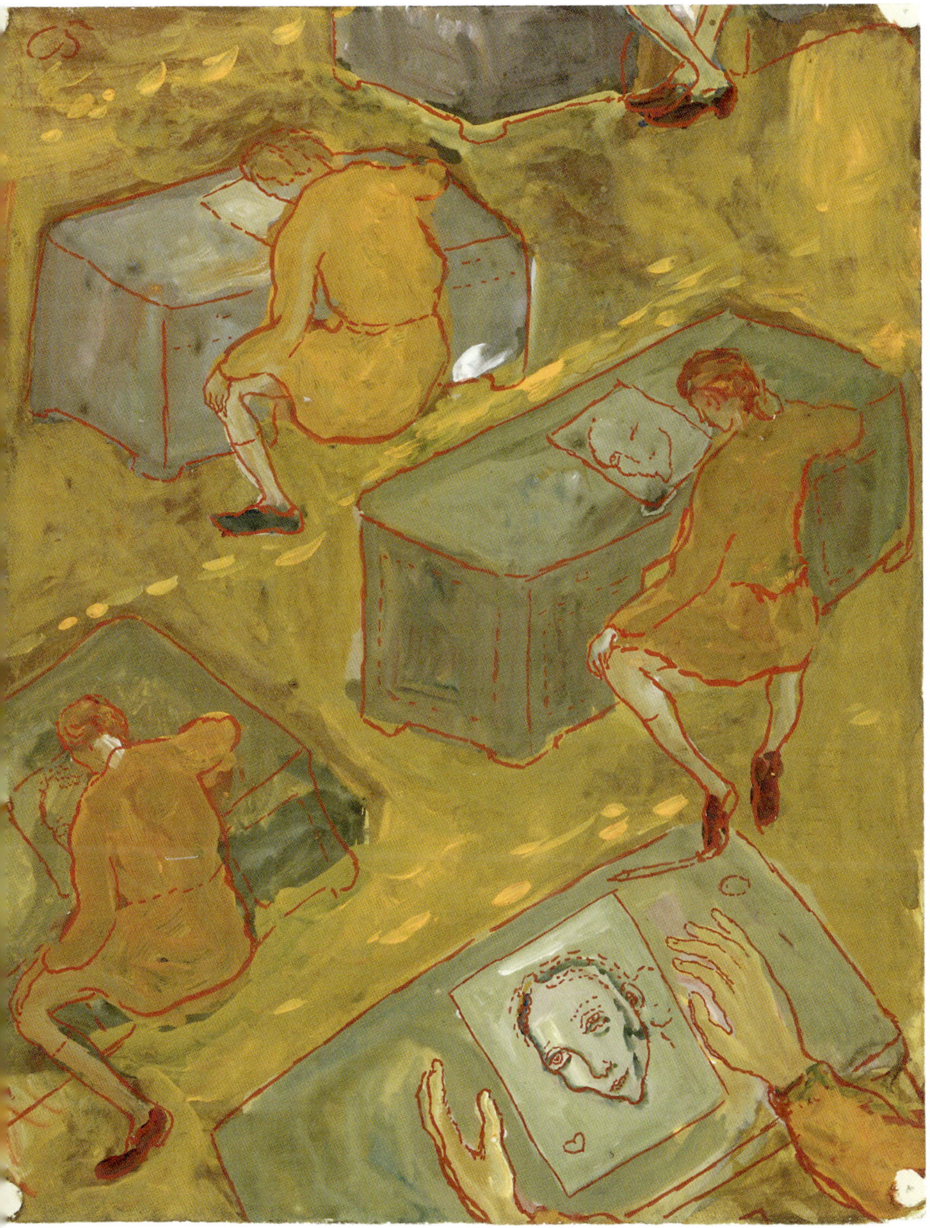

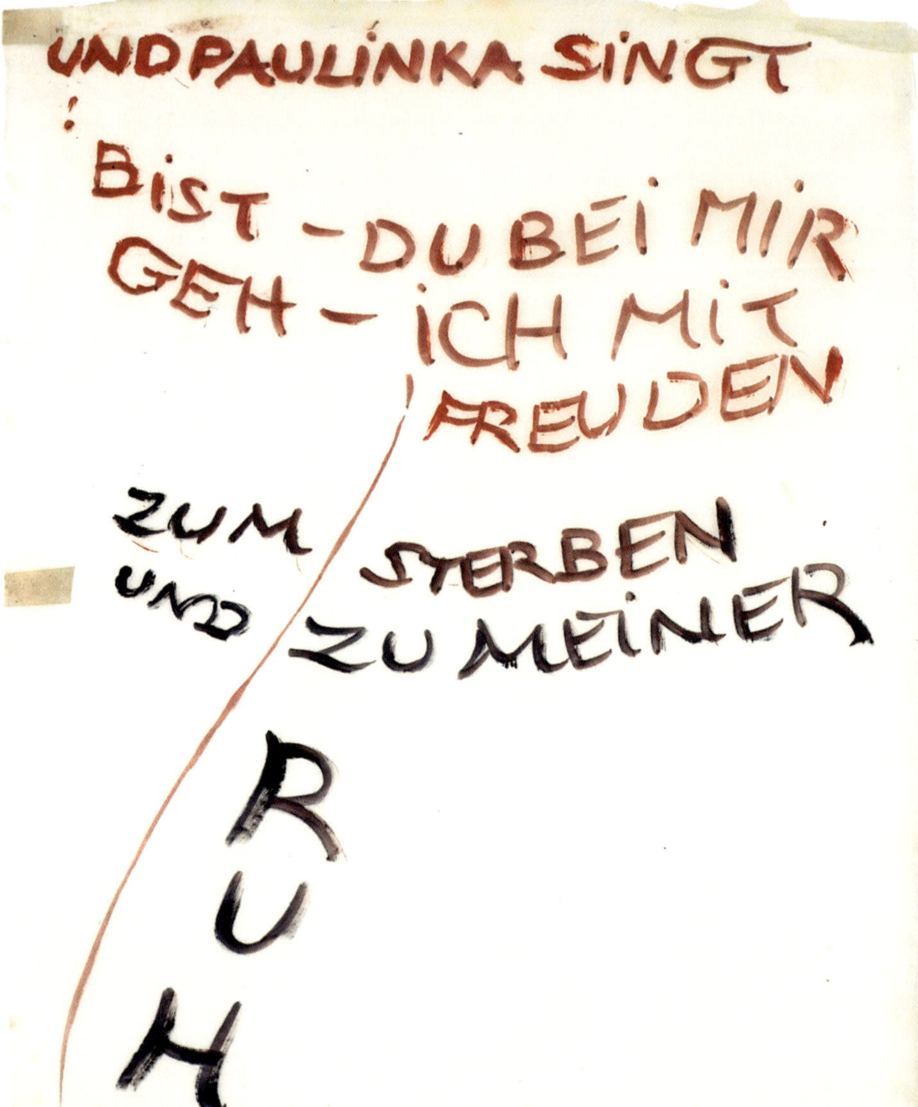
UND PAULINKA SINGT
:
BIST - DU BEI MIR
GEH - ICH MIT
FREUDEN
ZUM
STERBEN
UND
ZU MEINER
RUH
93

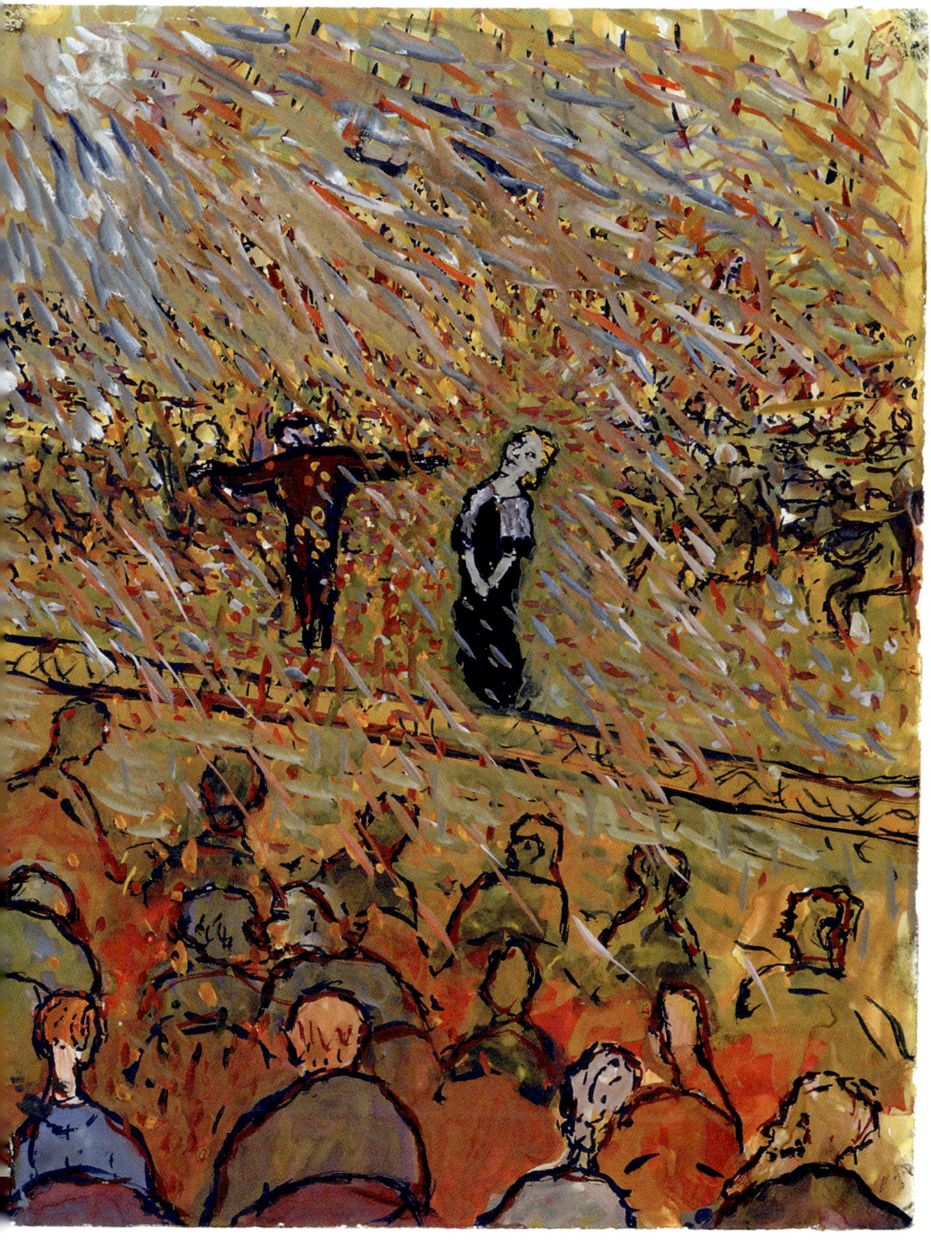

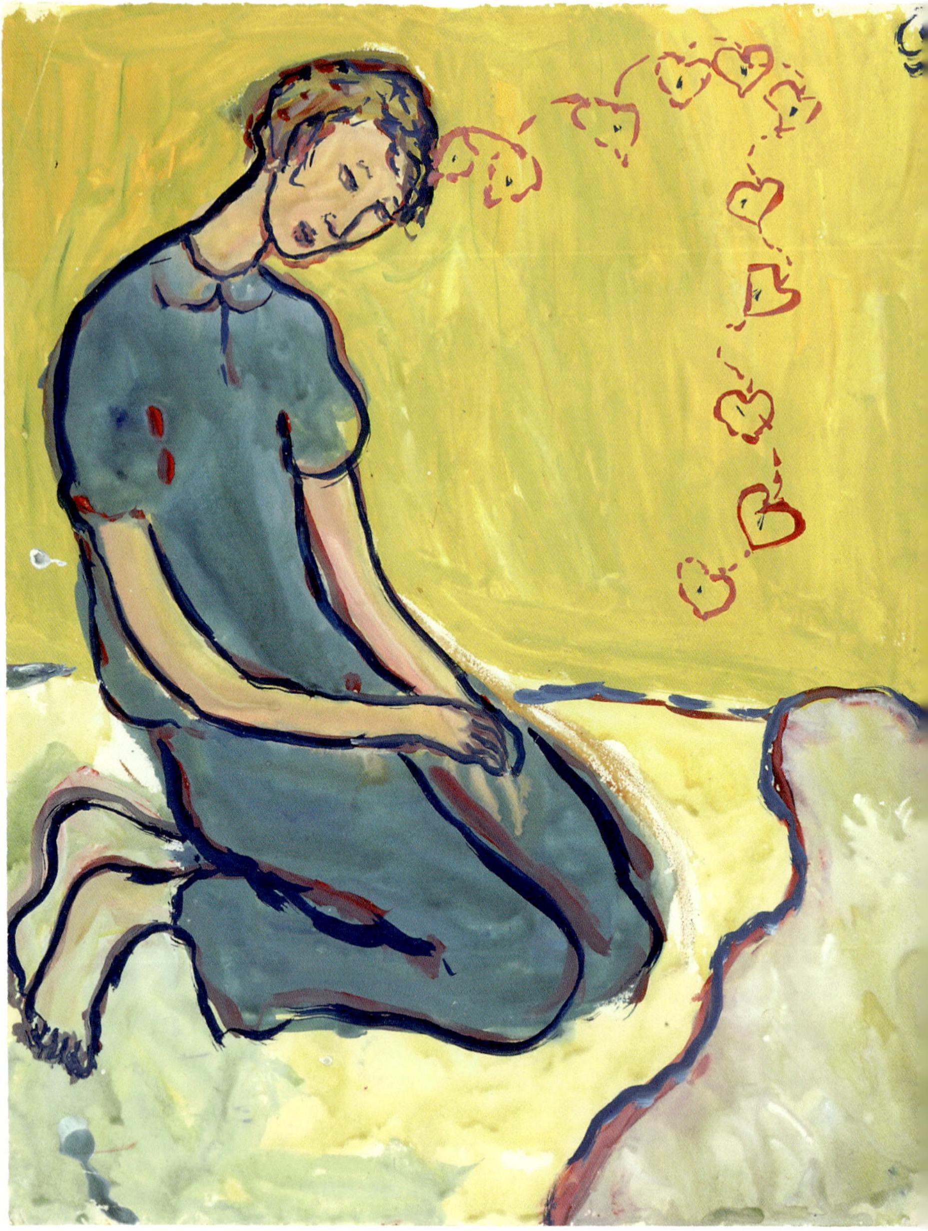

In the meantime, to the melody:
L'amour est un oiseau rebelle,
Charlotte is sitting on her bed.

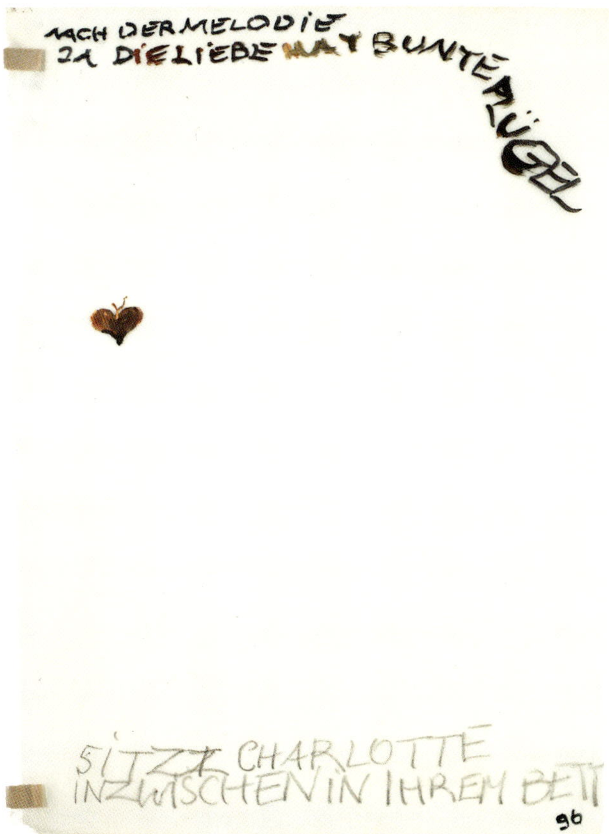

SCENE 5

Meanwhile, Mrs Knarre has withdrawn entirely into herself and lets her tragic, emotional life pass before her in her own poetic form.

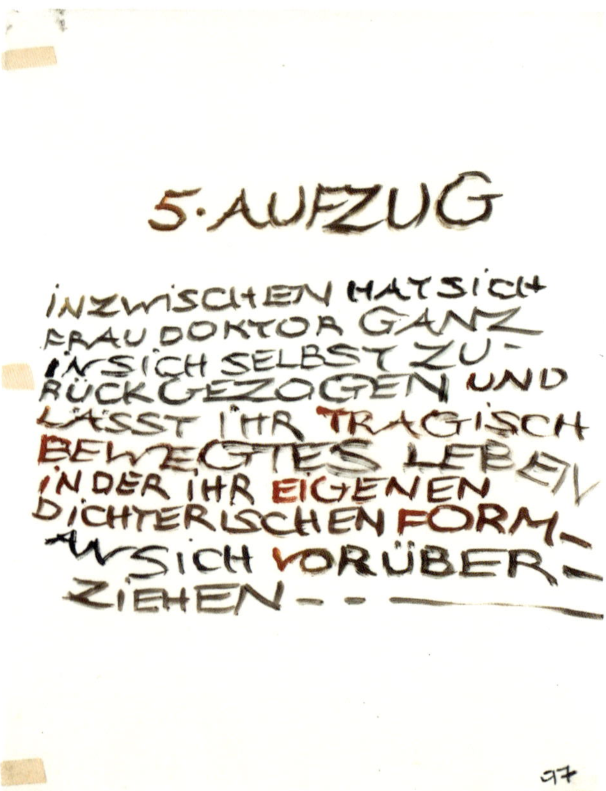

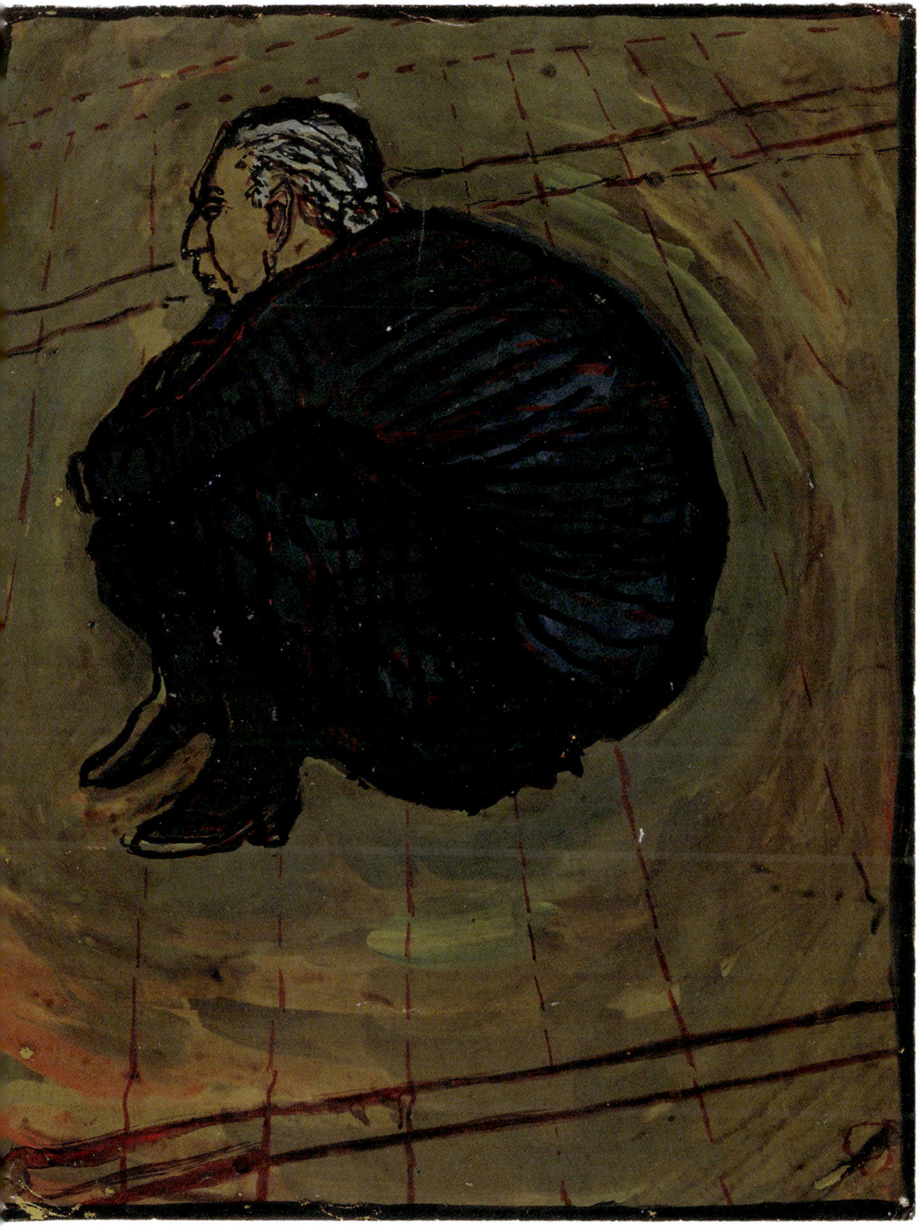

(bottom)

MRS KNARRE
"It's almost forty-five years since I was
a girl. We were three, and when I was happily
married to my dear husband my mother forced
my brother to marry a dowry."

(opposite)

"My poor brother became very unhappy with her!!!
And he was more with us than with himself."

Mr and Mrs [...] Bend are honoured to announce the [...]
their first daught [...] Franziska Knarre. July 1890

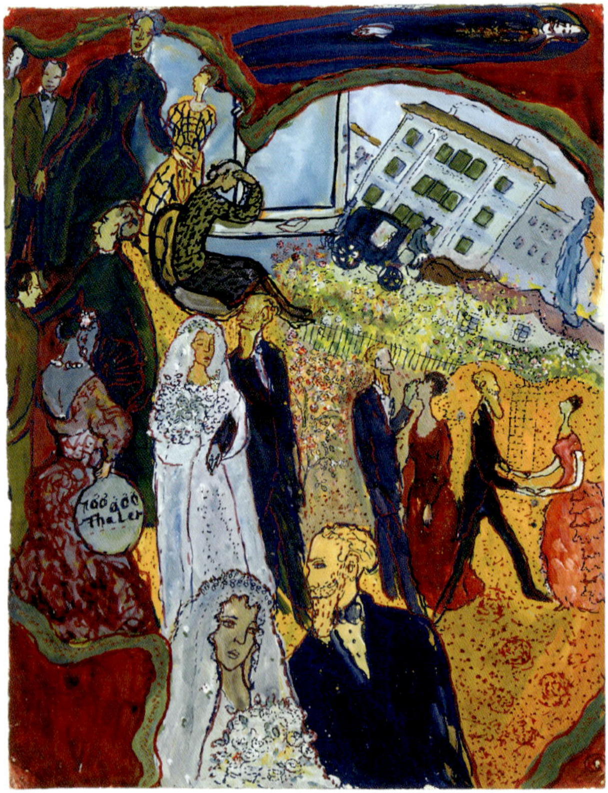

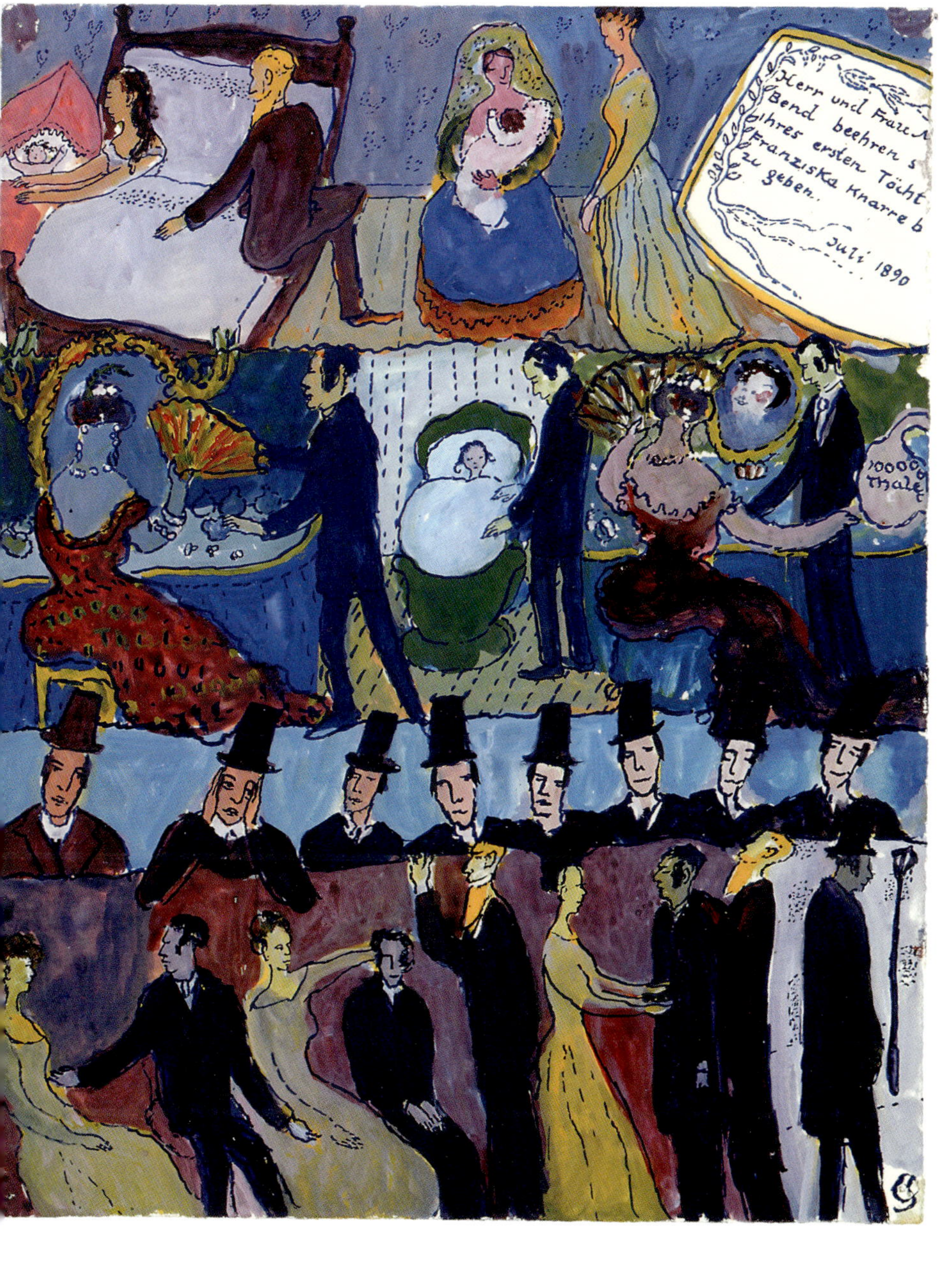
Herr und Frau
Bend beehren
ihres ersten Töcht
Franziska Knarre
zu geben.
Juli 1890

"As a result, my mother became insane and..."

This morning the body of twenty-eight-year-old Doctor of Law Georges Bend was found on the banks of the River Spree. The body was identified by his brother-in-law and transferred to his maternal house, where the solemn laying out took place. – An unhappy marriage is thought to be the reason for the suicide.

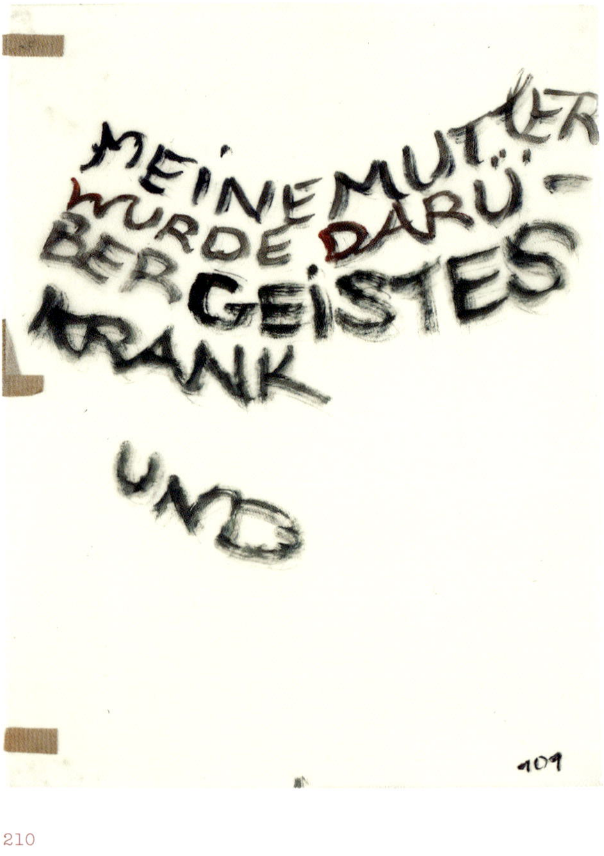

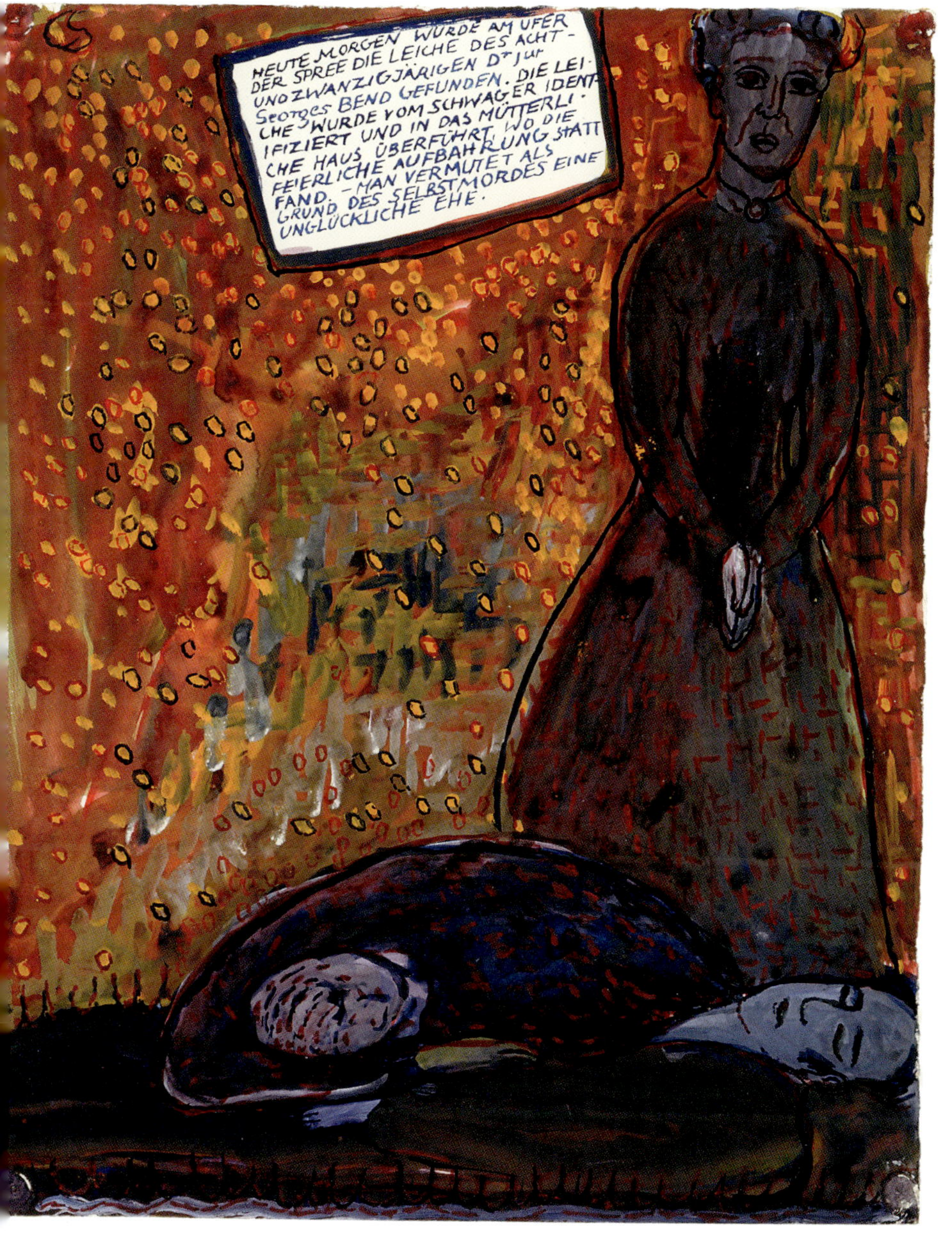
HEUTE MORGEN WURDE AM UFER
DER SPREE DIE LEICHE DES ACHT-
UNDZWANZIGJÄRIGEN Dr Jur
Seorges BEND GEFUNDEN. DIE LEI-
CHE WURDE VOM SCHWAGER IDENT-
IFIZIERT UND IN DAS MÜTTERLI-
CHE HAUS ÜBERFÜHRT, WO DIE
FEIERLICHE AUFBAHRUNG STATT
FAND. - MAN VERMUTET ALS
GRUND DES SELBSTMORDES EINE
UNGLÜCKLICHE EHE.

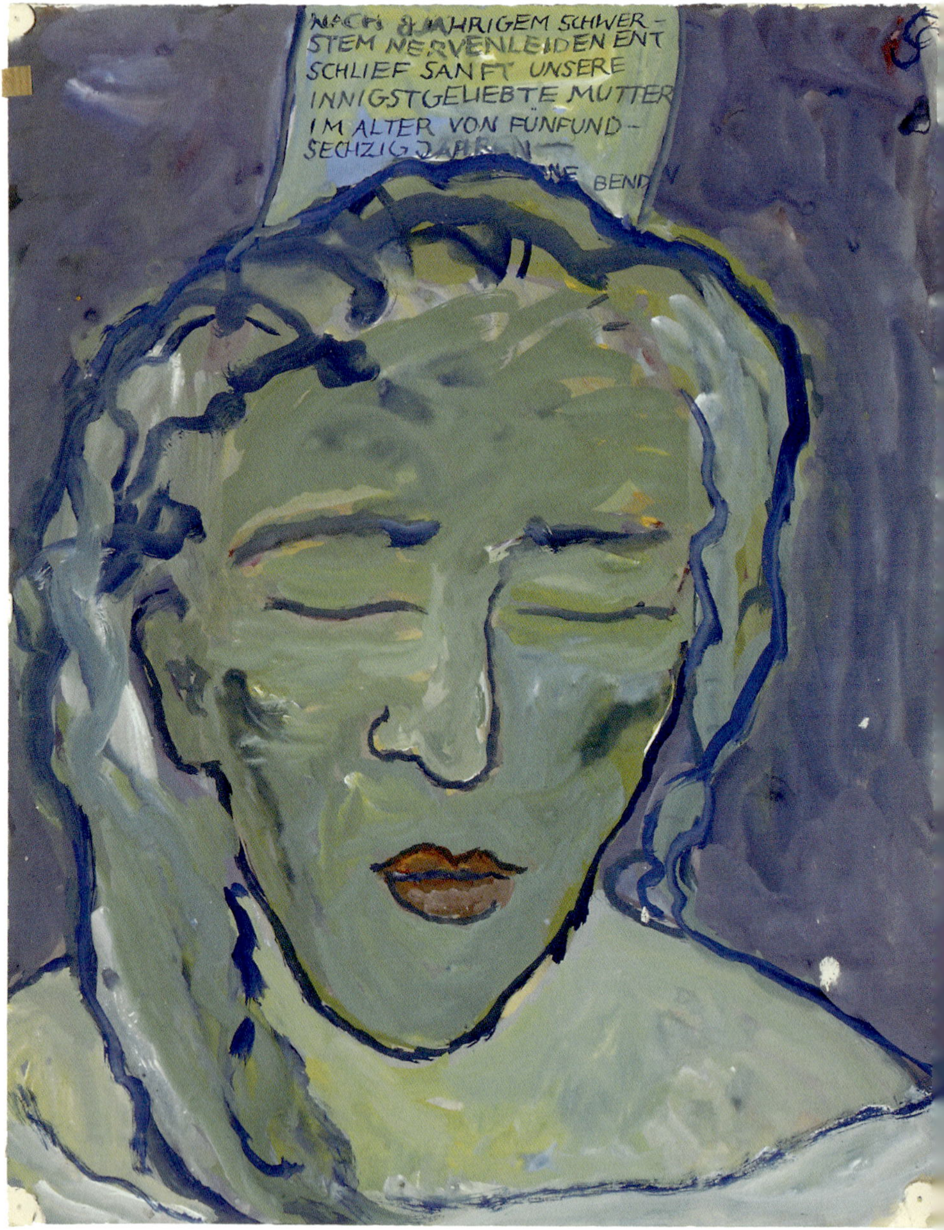
NACH 8JAHRIGEM SCHWER-
STEM NERVENLEIDEN ENT
SCHLIEF SANFT UNSERE
INNIGSTGELIEBTE MUTTER
IM ALTER VON FÜNFUND-
SECHZIG JAHREN

MRS KNARRE
"I believe that she cursed us."

Melody: Und ich verfluche Euch, die Ihr mir meine Ruhe nicht gönnen wolltet – und Eure Kinder
[And I curse you all who would not let me rest – and your children].

After eight years of extreme mental suffering, our dearly beloved mother passed away peacefully at the age of sixty-five.

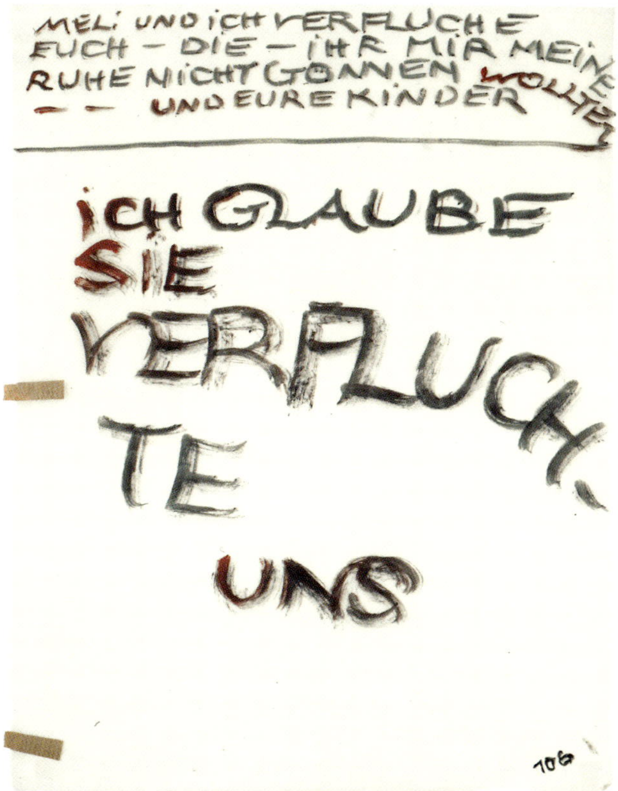

(bottom)

MRS Knarre
"I had my children."

(opposite)

"And this one was my friend."

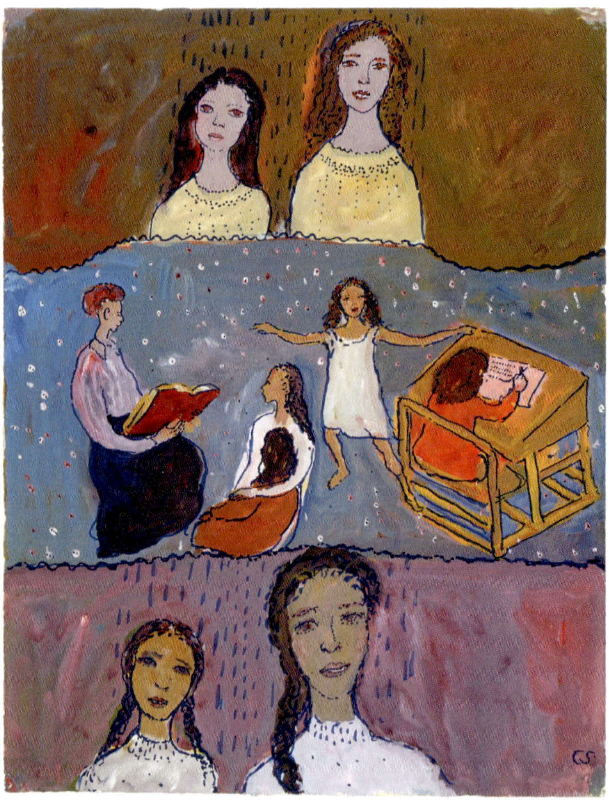

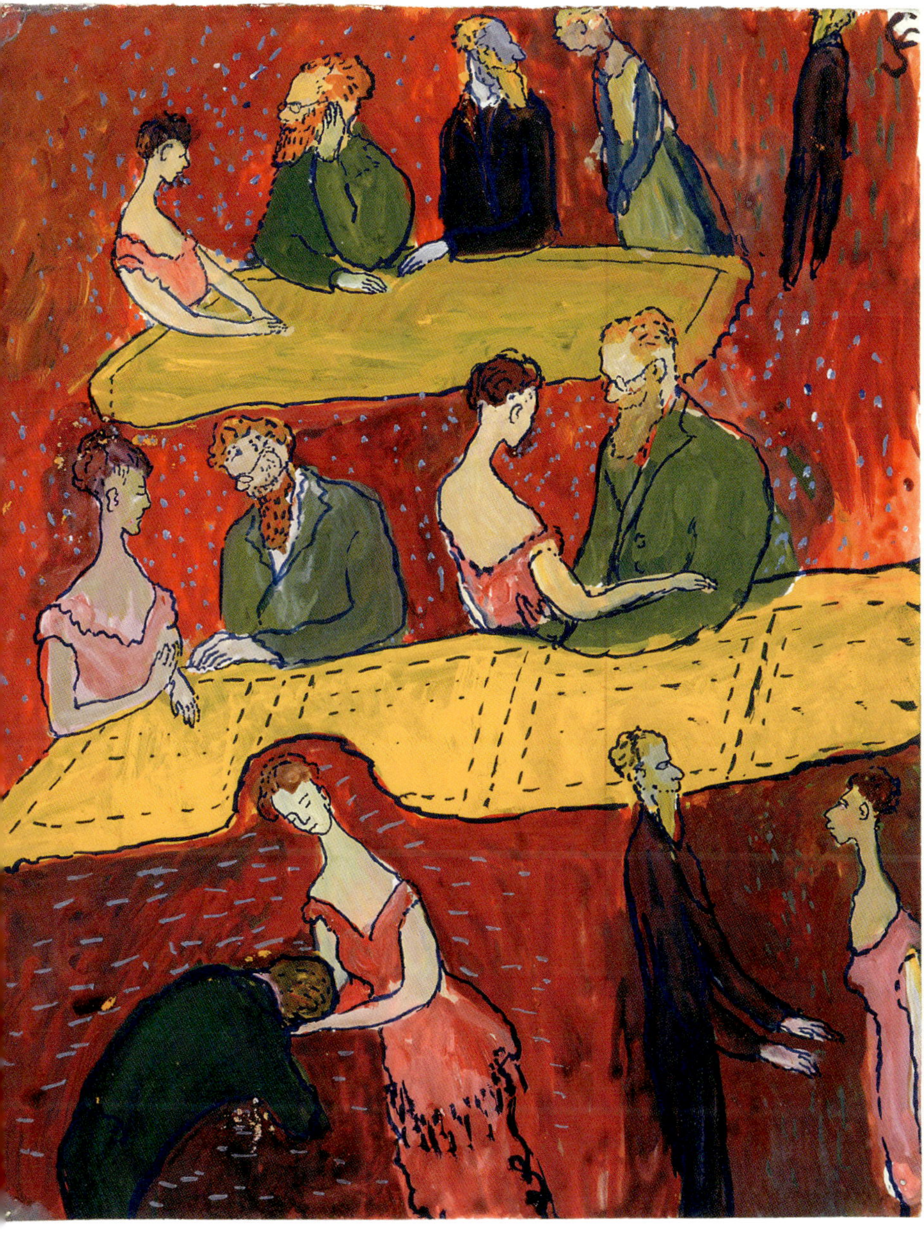

(bottom)

"'Many people break down,' then said my dear, brave husband, whose best friend was hence also snatched away."

(opposite)

"We made beautiful journeys.
We were drawn to the South."

To the melody: Napoli vedere e morire

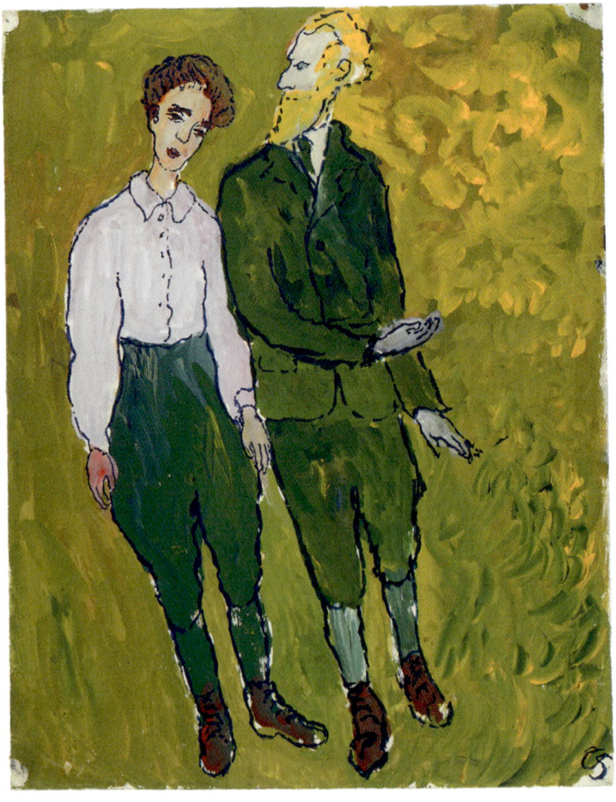

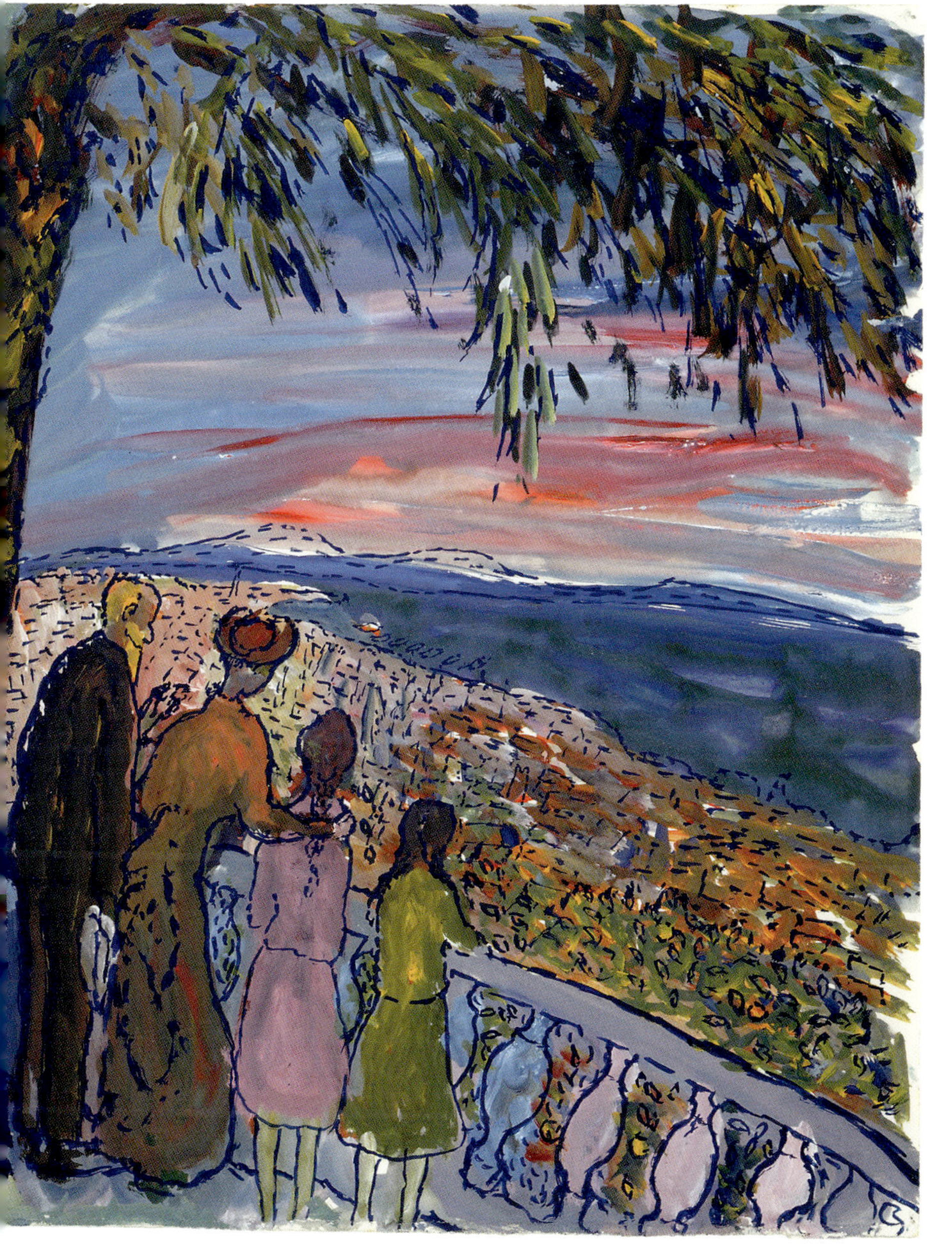

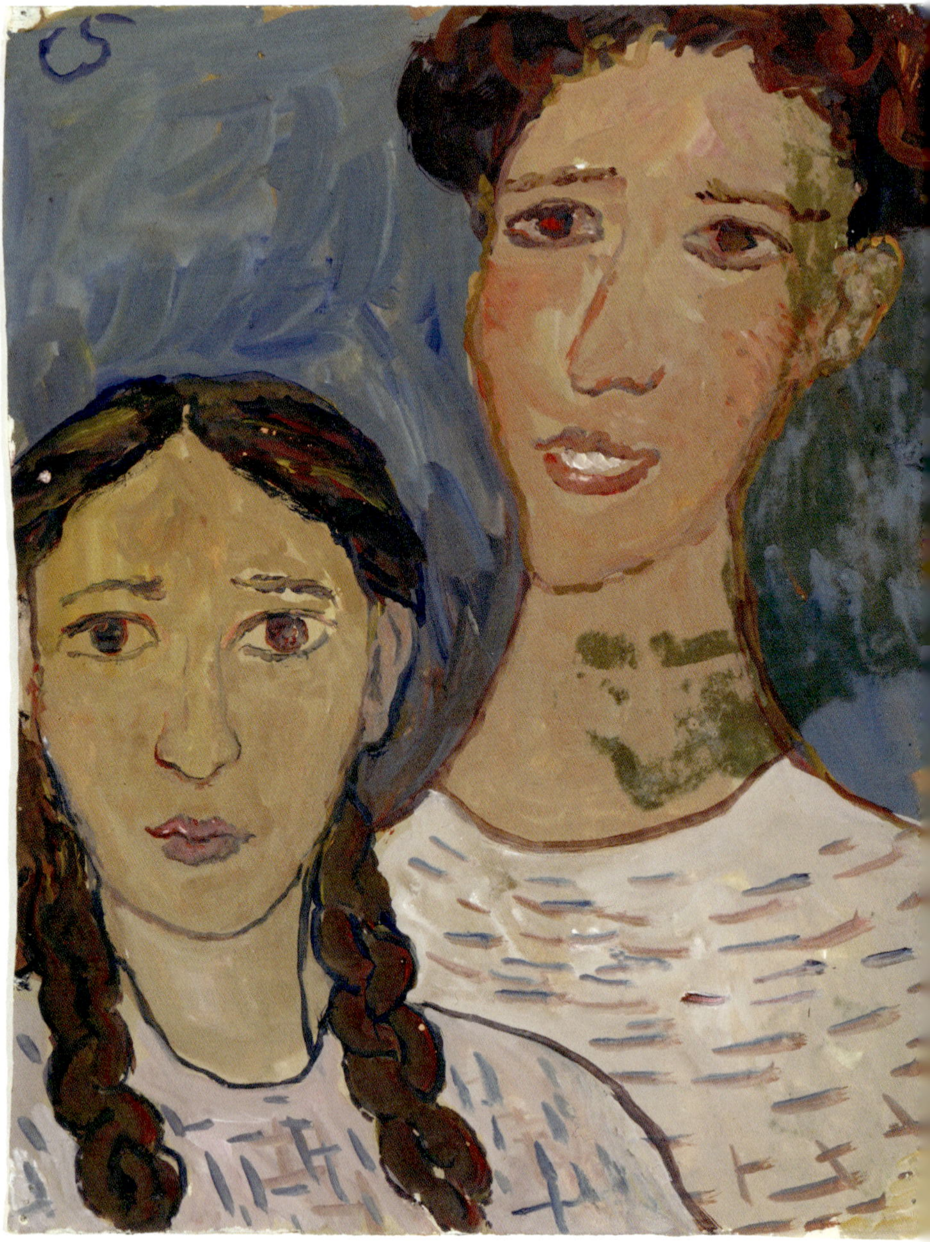
CS

MRS Knarre
“And meanwhile my children grew up.
One sad and one happy.”

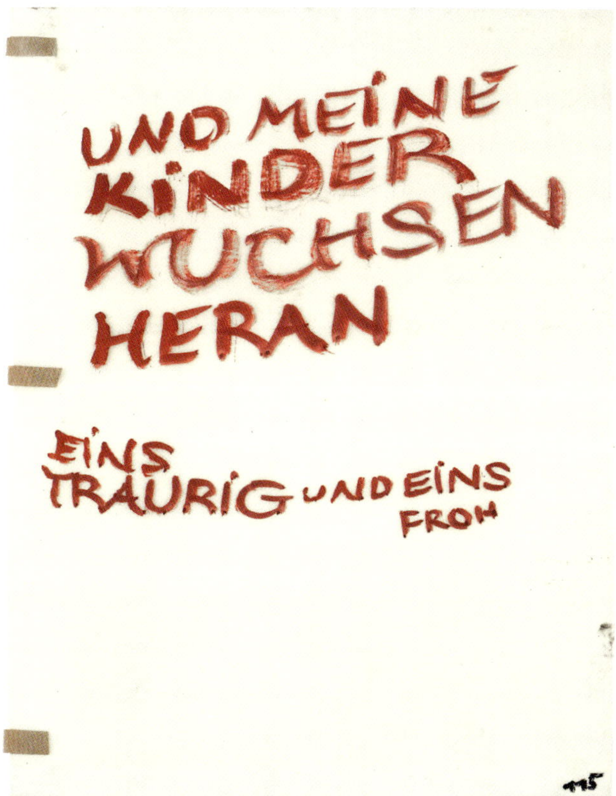

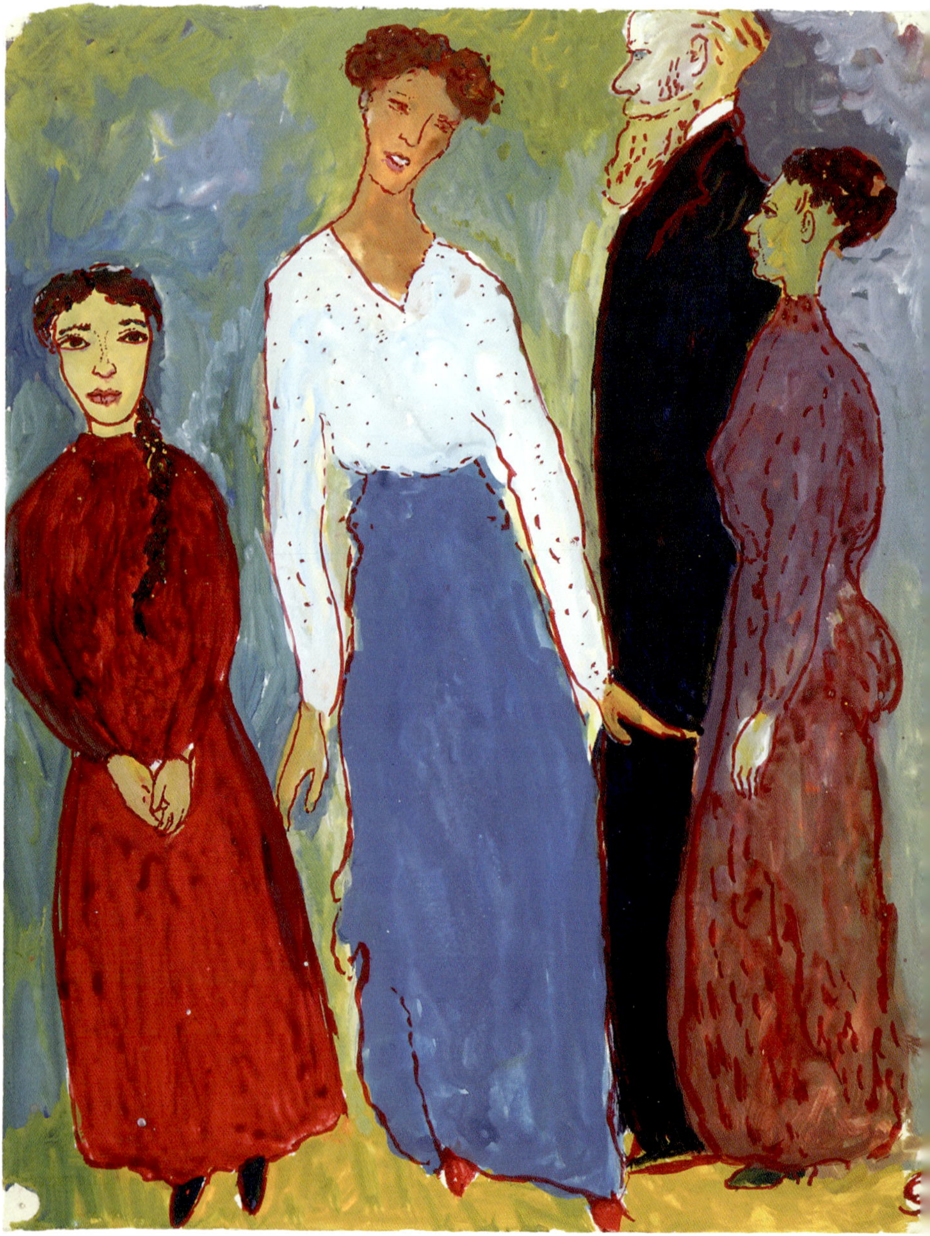

(opposite)

“And we were standing before the phenomenon of light full of admiration. And there we failed to notice that our little Lottchen was sad, oh so sad.”

(bottom)

“She always saw her happy sister’s face in front of her.”

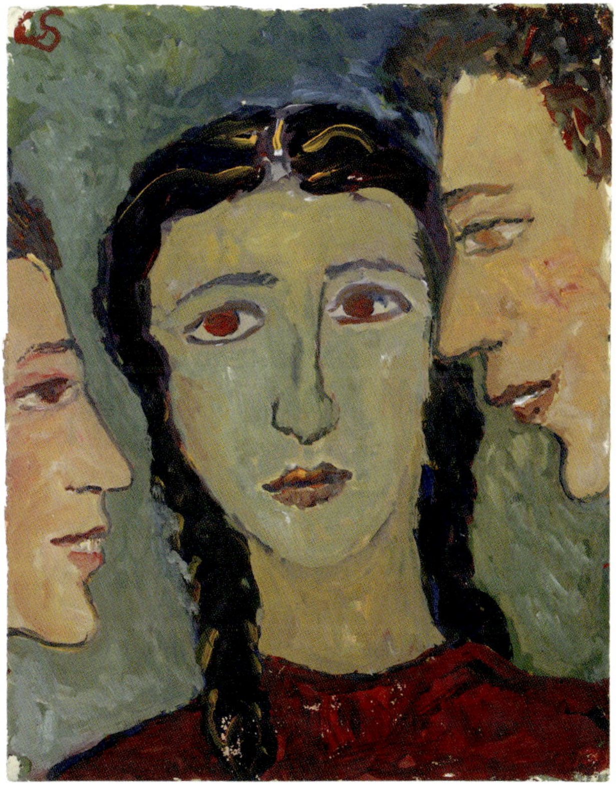

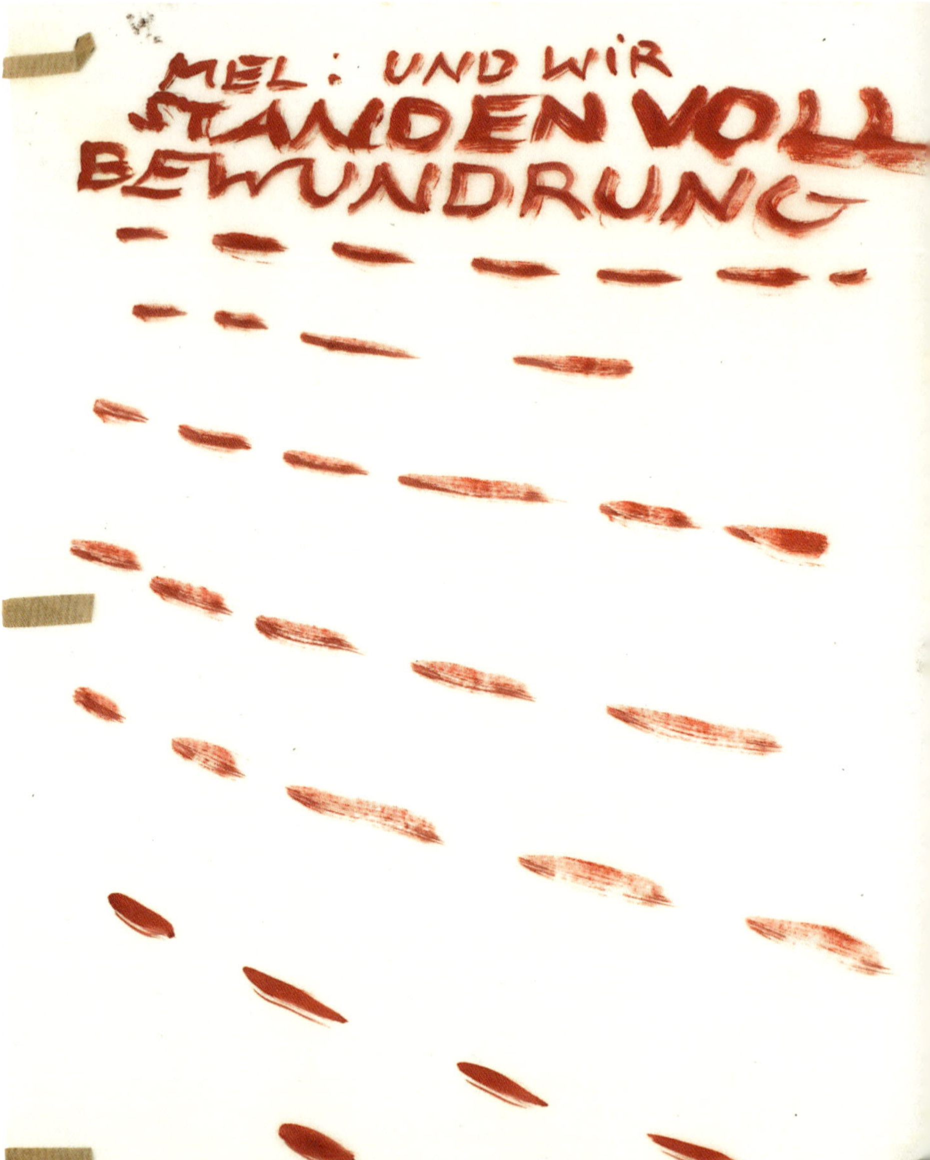
MEL : UND WIR
STANDEN VOLL
BEWUNDRUNG

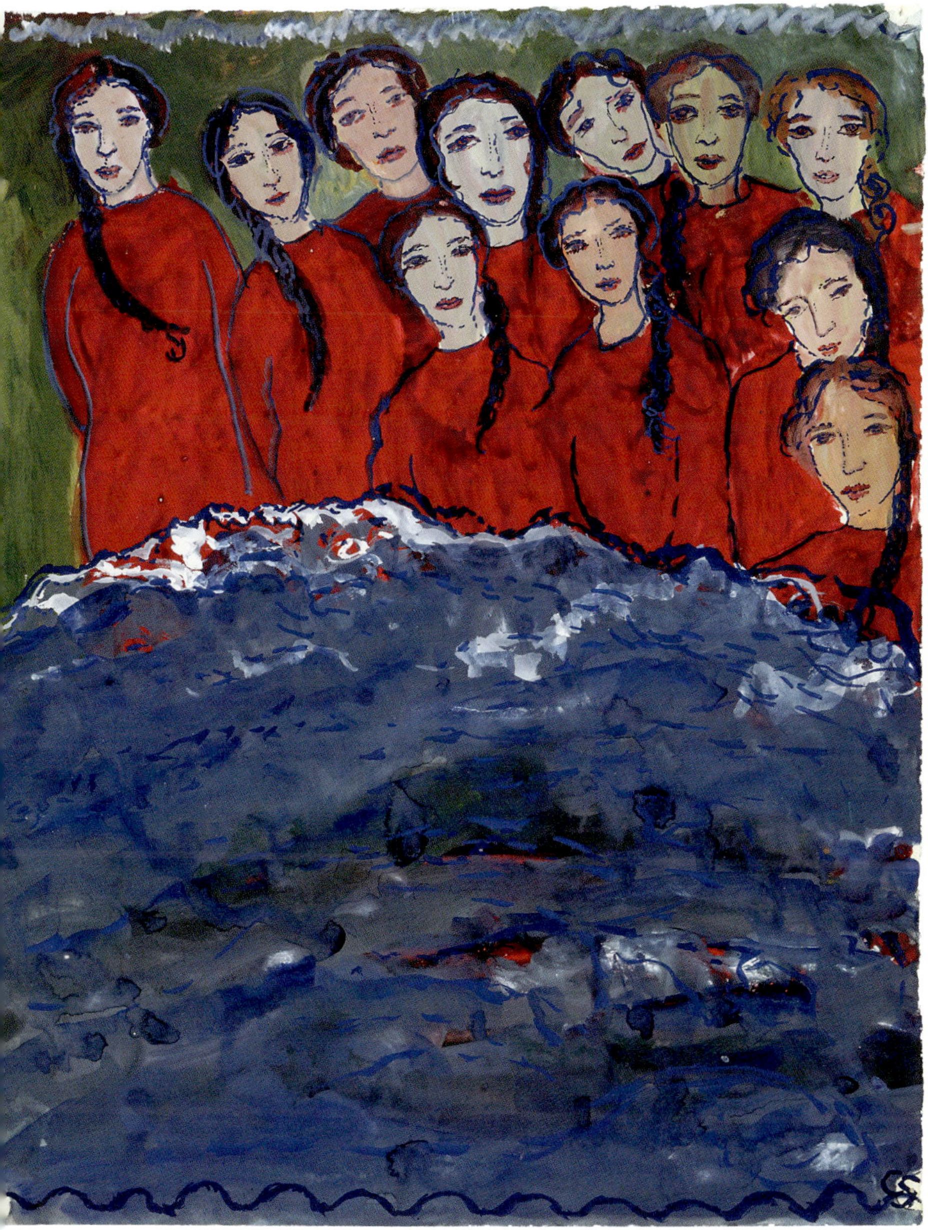

(previous pages)

Melody: Und wir standen voll Bewundrung...
[And we were standing full of admiration...]

(these pages)

MRS KNARRE
"'Am I to be blamed for her death?'
my little Franziska asked herself."
sagte sich mein Fränzchen dann."

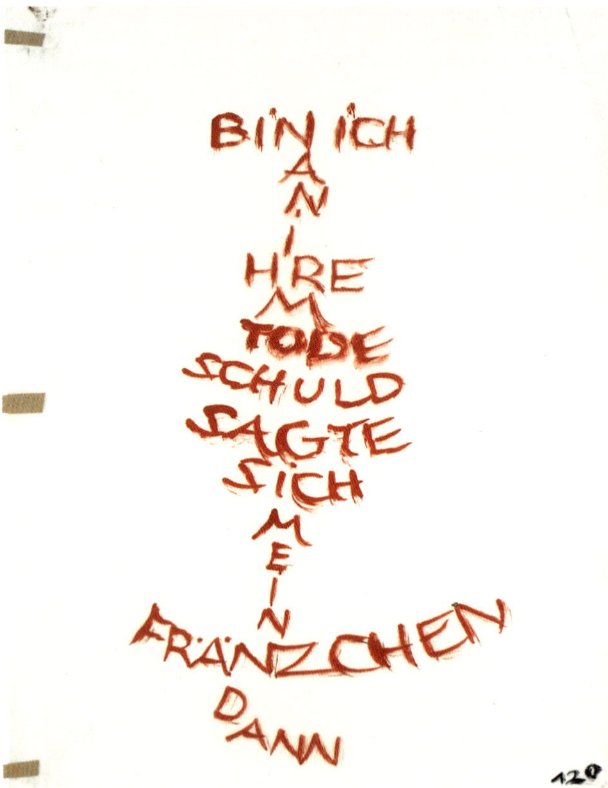

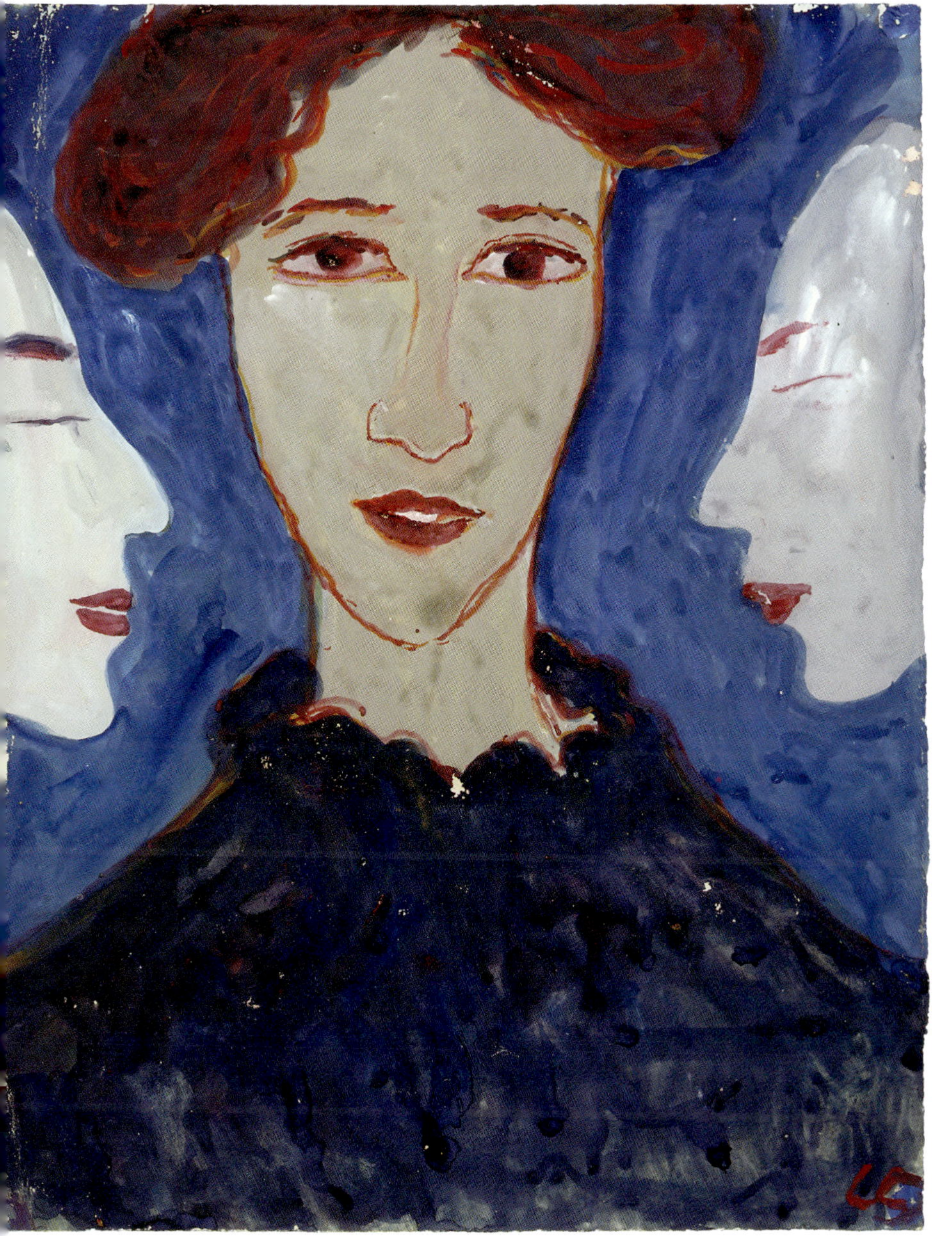

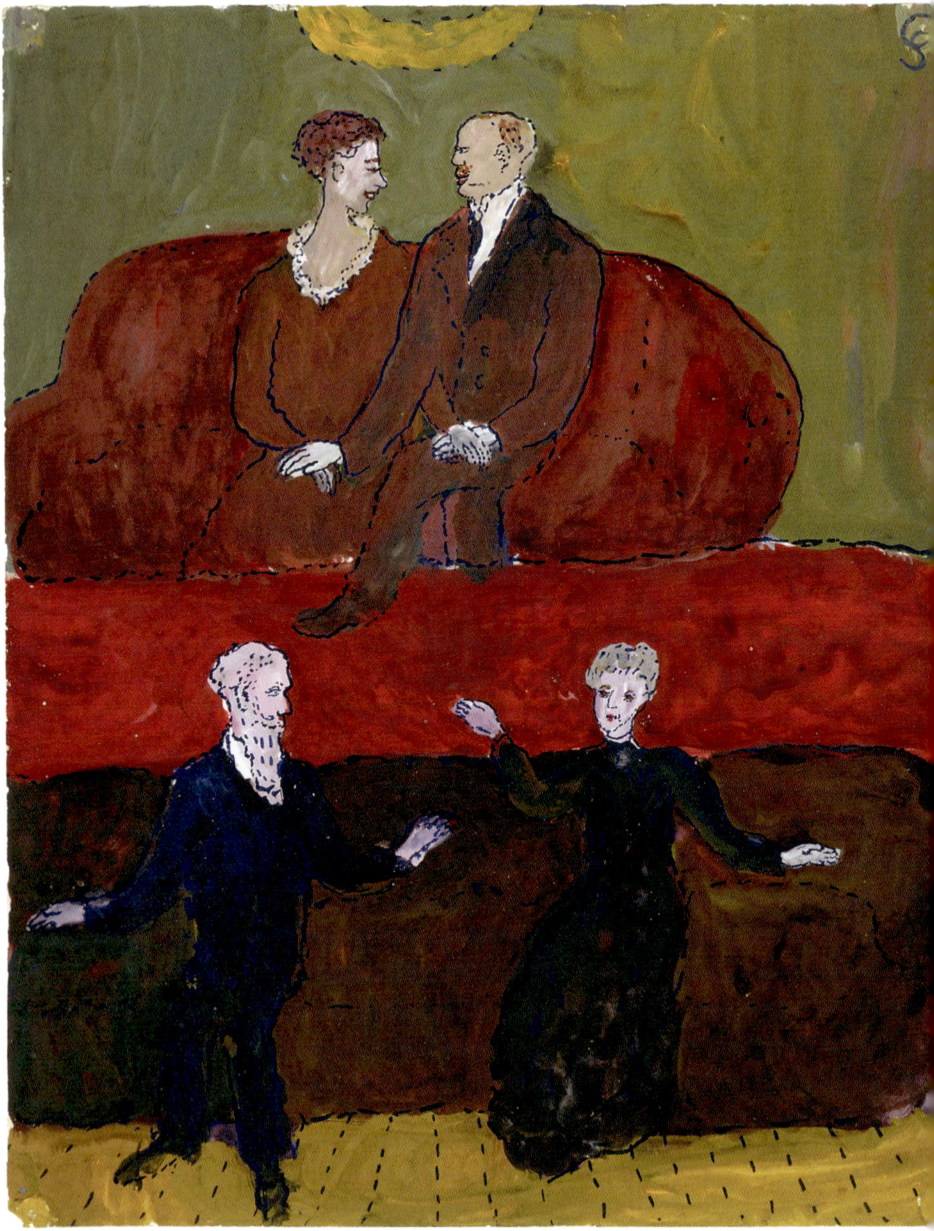

"All he ever thought of was his career.
But what were we to do – since she really
loves him dearly."

Melody: And I will become Professor
and I Mrs Professor

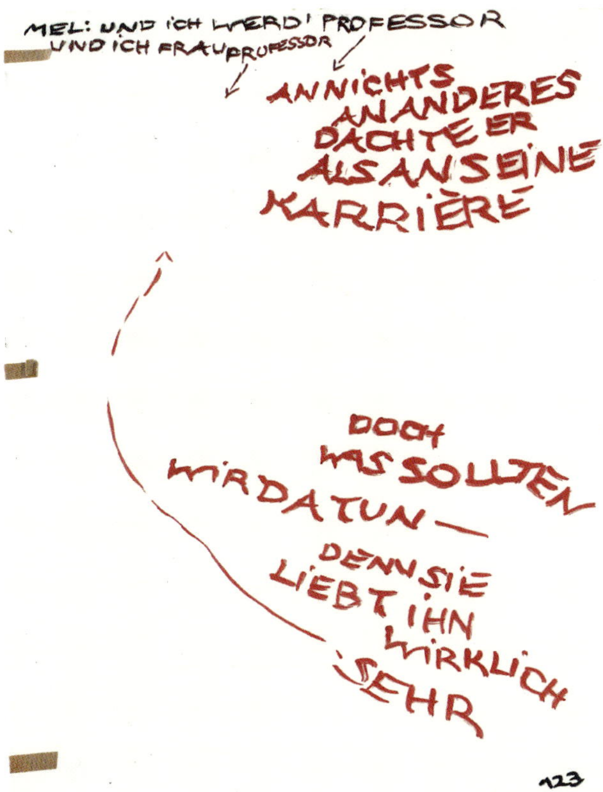

Melody: And my husband – he loves me not.
And my child – she needs me not.
Why, oh why, am I living

“So was the line of thought.”

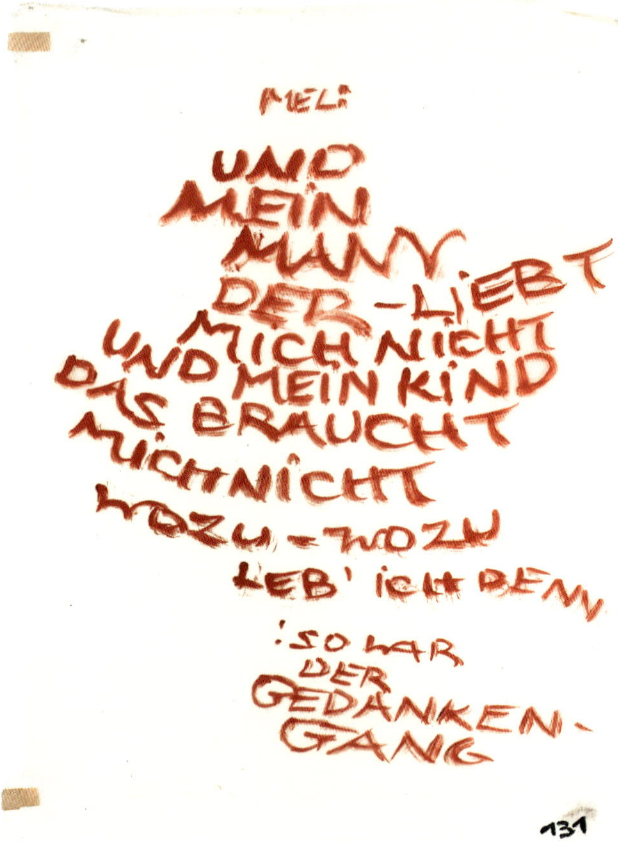
MEL:

UND
MEIN
MANN
DER – LIEBT
MICH NICHT
UND MEIN KIND
DAS BRAUCHT
MICH NICHT
WOZU – WOZU
LEB' ICH DENN

!SO WAR
DER
GEDANKEN-
GANG

131

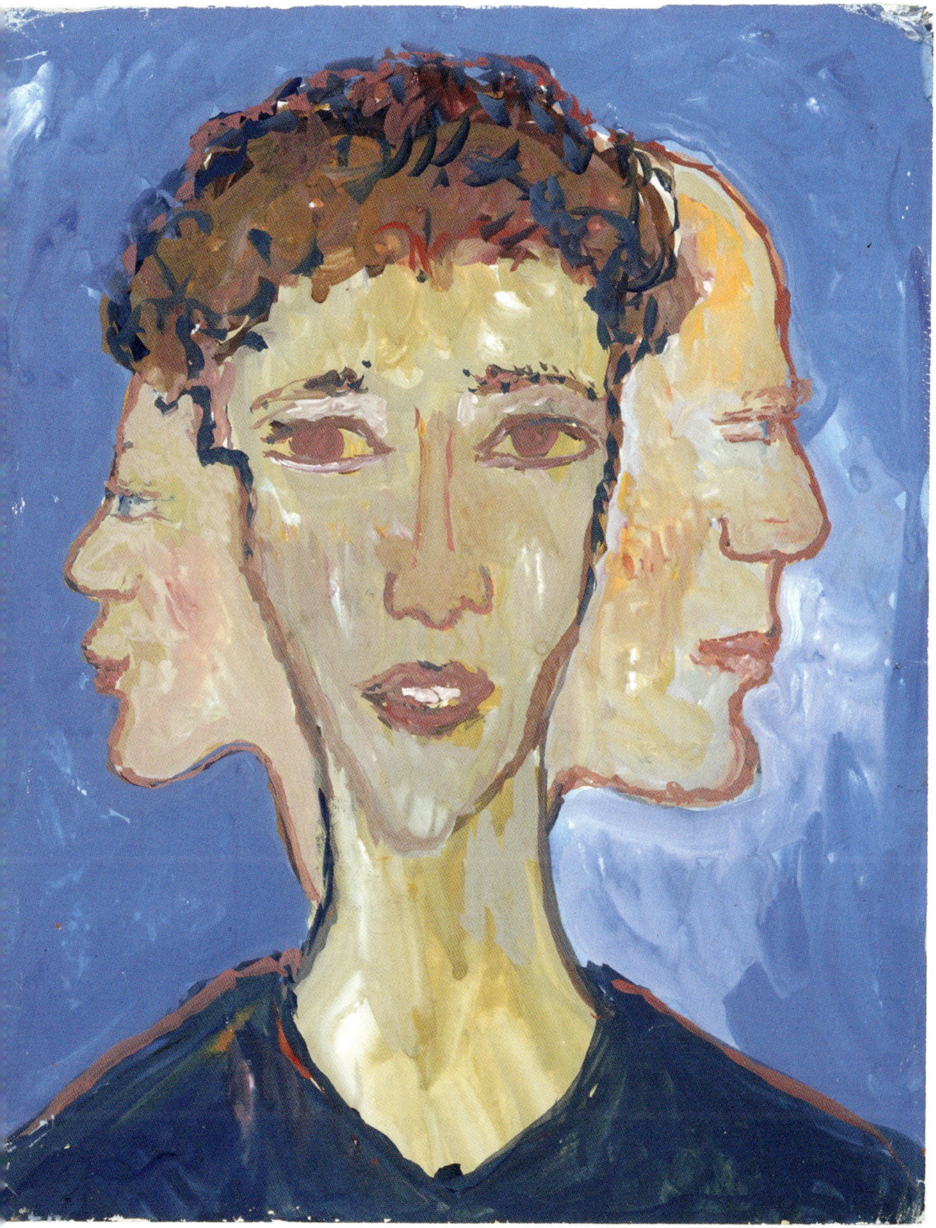

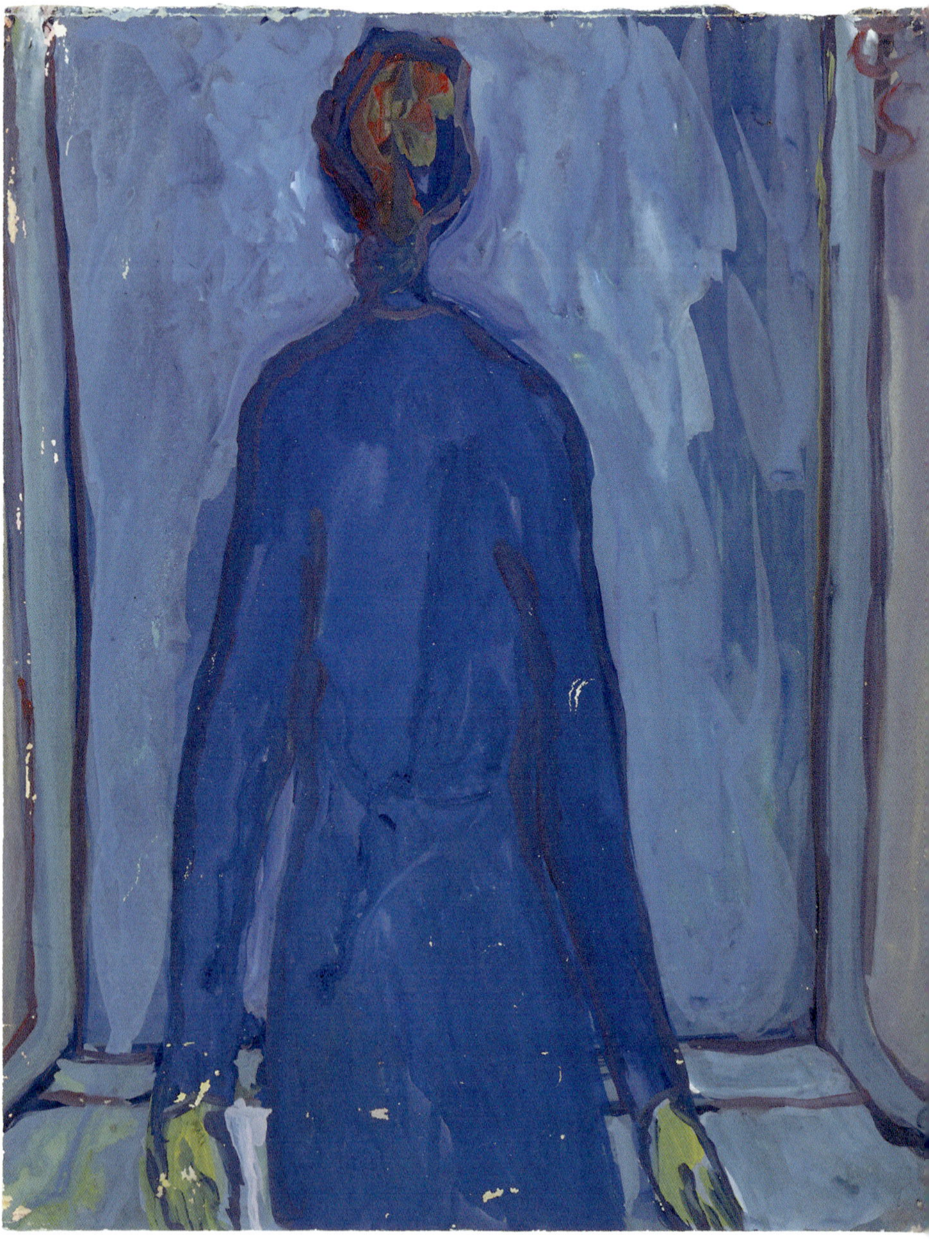

(opposite)

"For a long time she stood like this –
Yes, she stood at this window, for – "

(bottom)

"Now she stands there no more –
Ah, in a different place – she now abides."

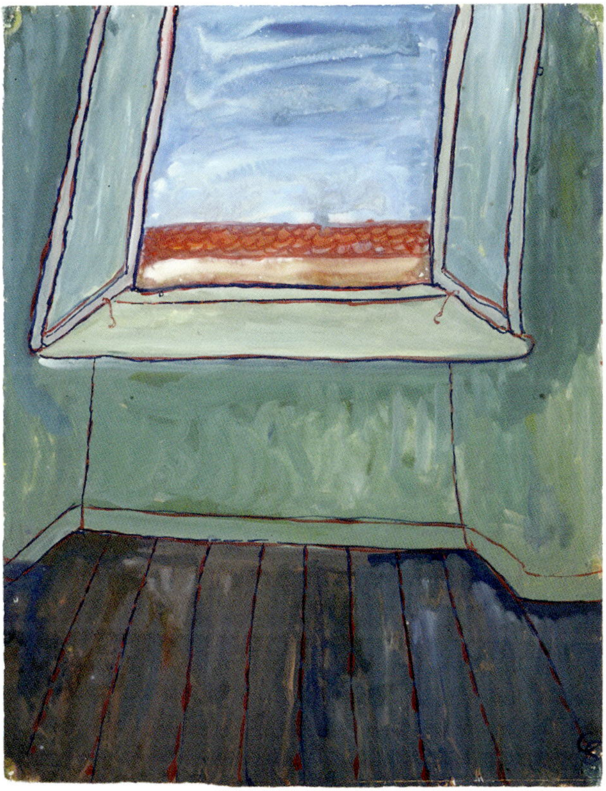

(bottom)

Melody: <u>She was but part of nature's heart, and earth again has claimed her</u>

(opposite)

MRS KNARRE
"Then my sister and my brother's
only daughter took their lives."

[...] inform you [...] your young [...] sister [...] poisoned with gas [...] left behind a son Franz.

I inform y(ou) [...] the only [...] of your brother Georges Bend [...] life with Veronal.

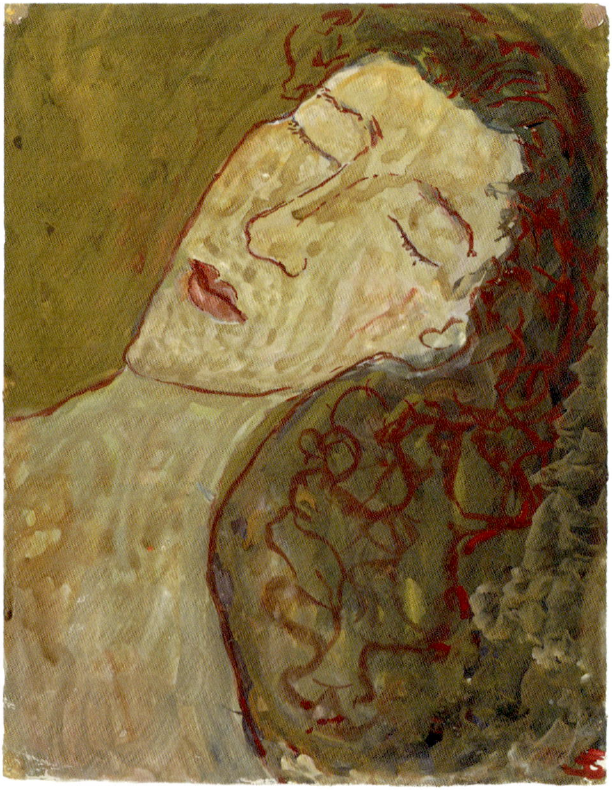

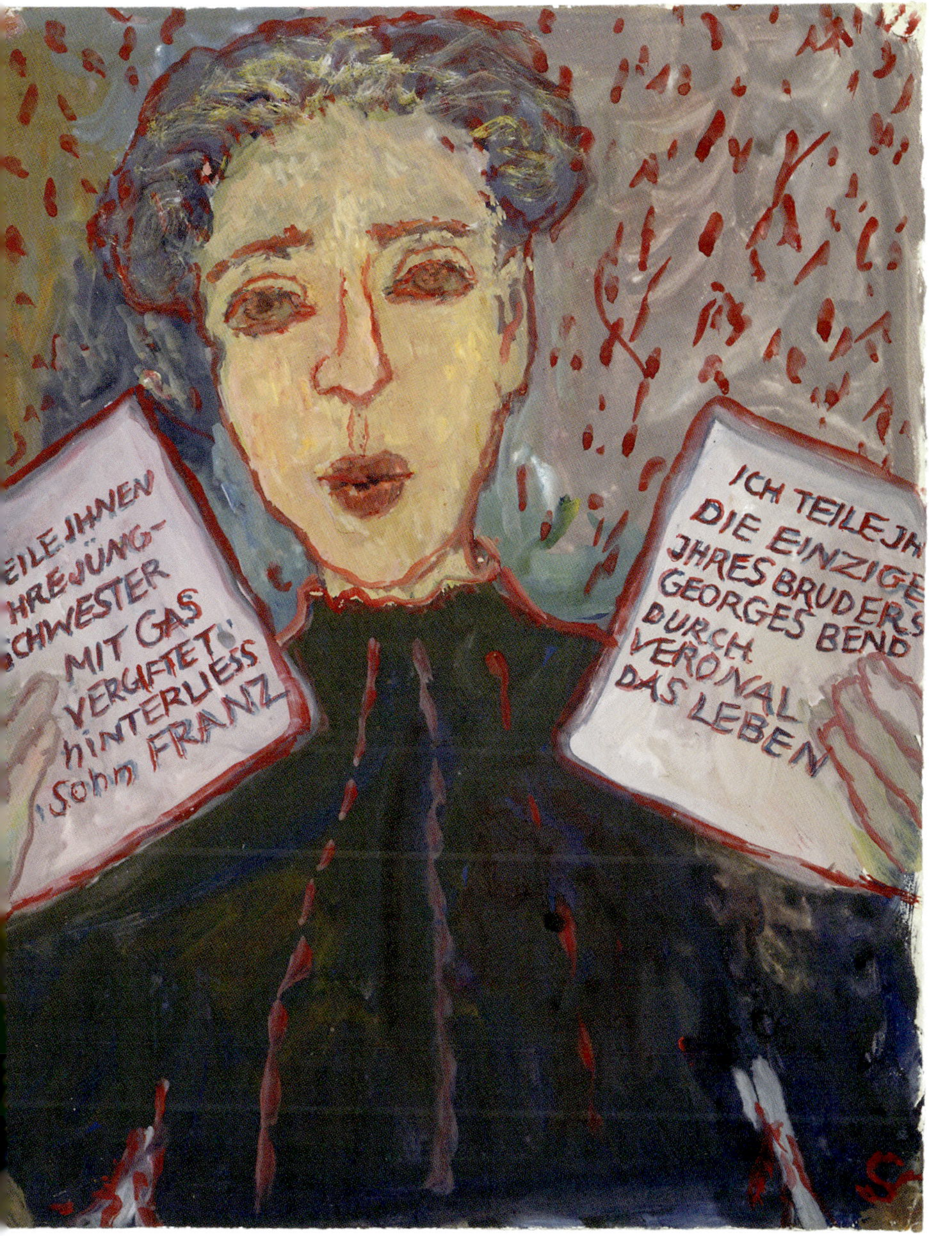
EILE JHNEN
HRE JÜNG-
CHWESTER
MIT GAS
VERGIFTET
hinterLIESS
1 Sohn FRANZ
ICH TEILE JH
DIE EINZIGE
JHRES BRUDERS
GEORGES BEND
DURCH
VERONAL
DAS LEBEN

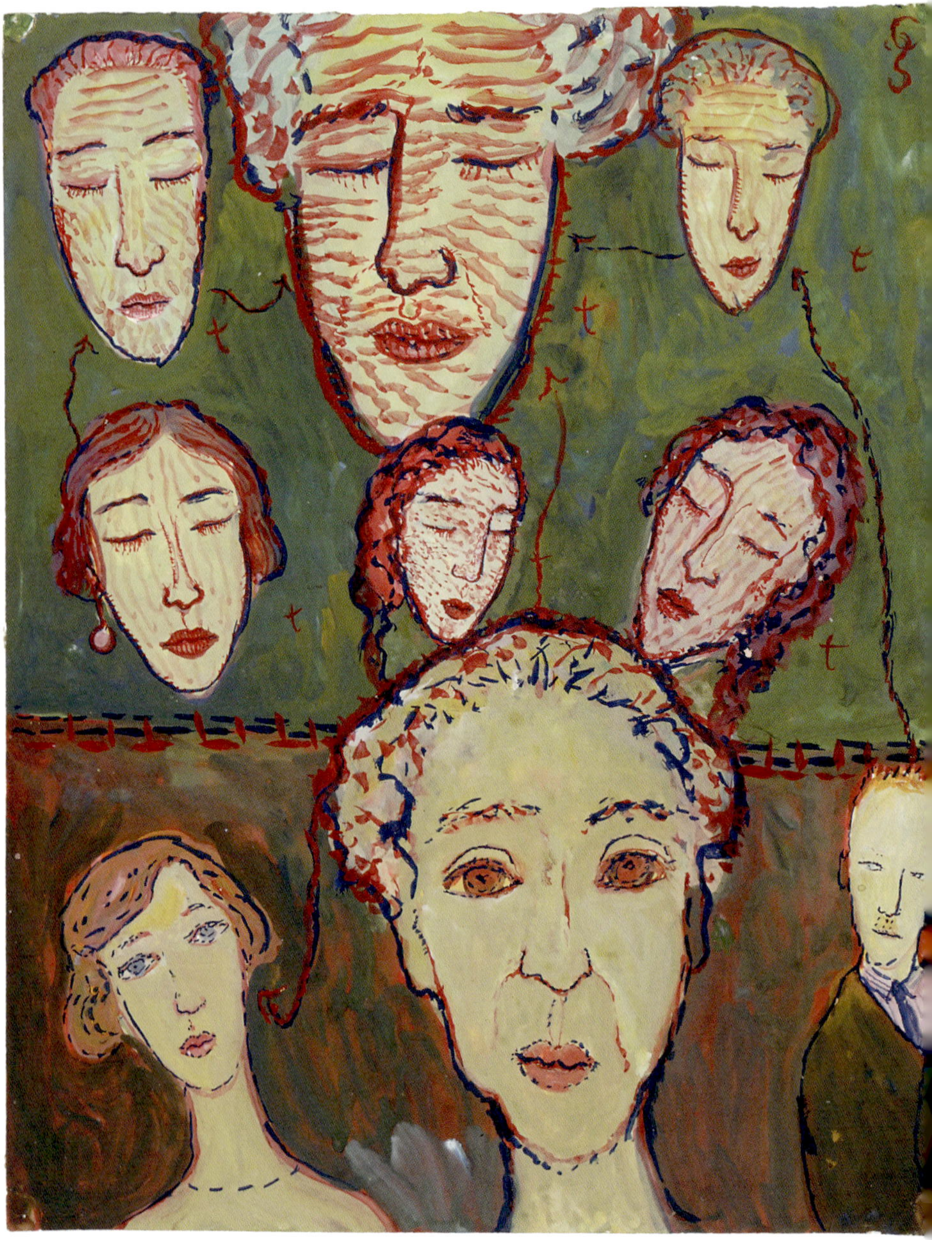

"One, two, three, four, five, six,
do you play witch's tricks?
Now we are only three."

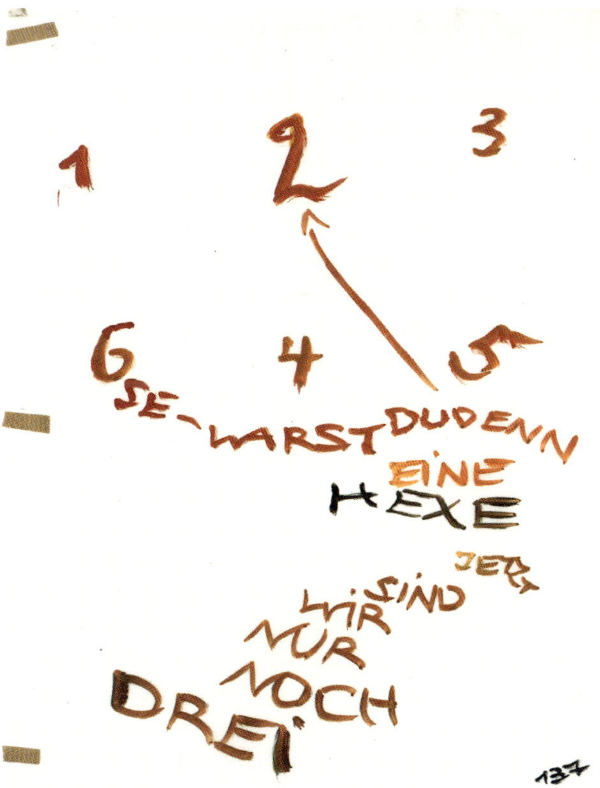

(bottom)

MRS KNARRE
"But then when he married Paulinka I gave her my finest jewelry. My husband was not pleased with it at all, but I gave it to her and..."

(opposite)

"... Now I don't have anybody anymore. Fate, fate, how harsh you are. And..."

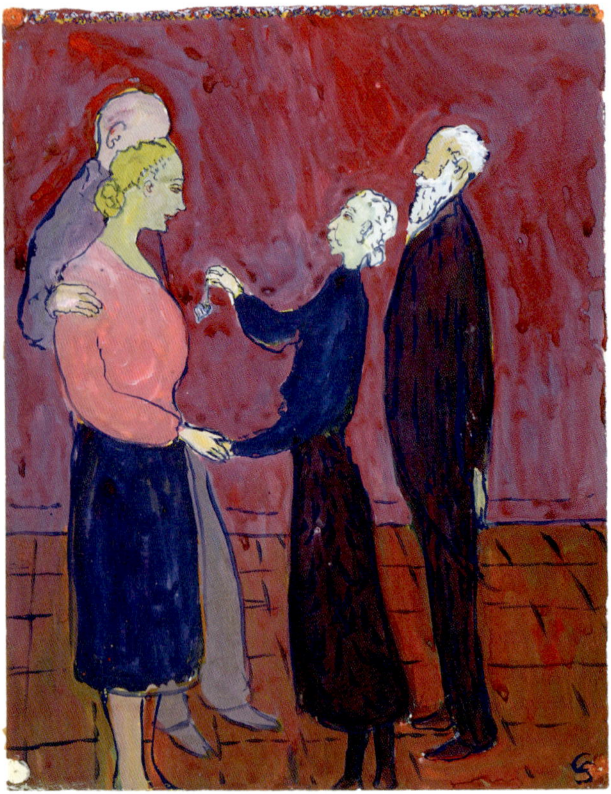

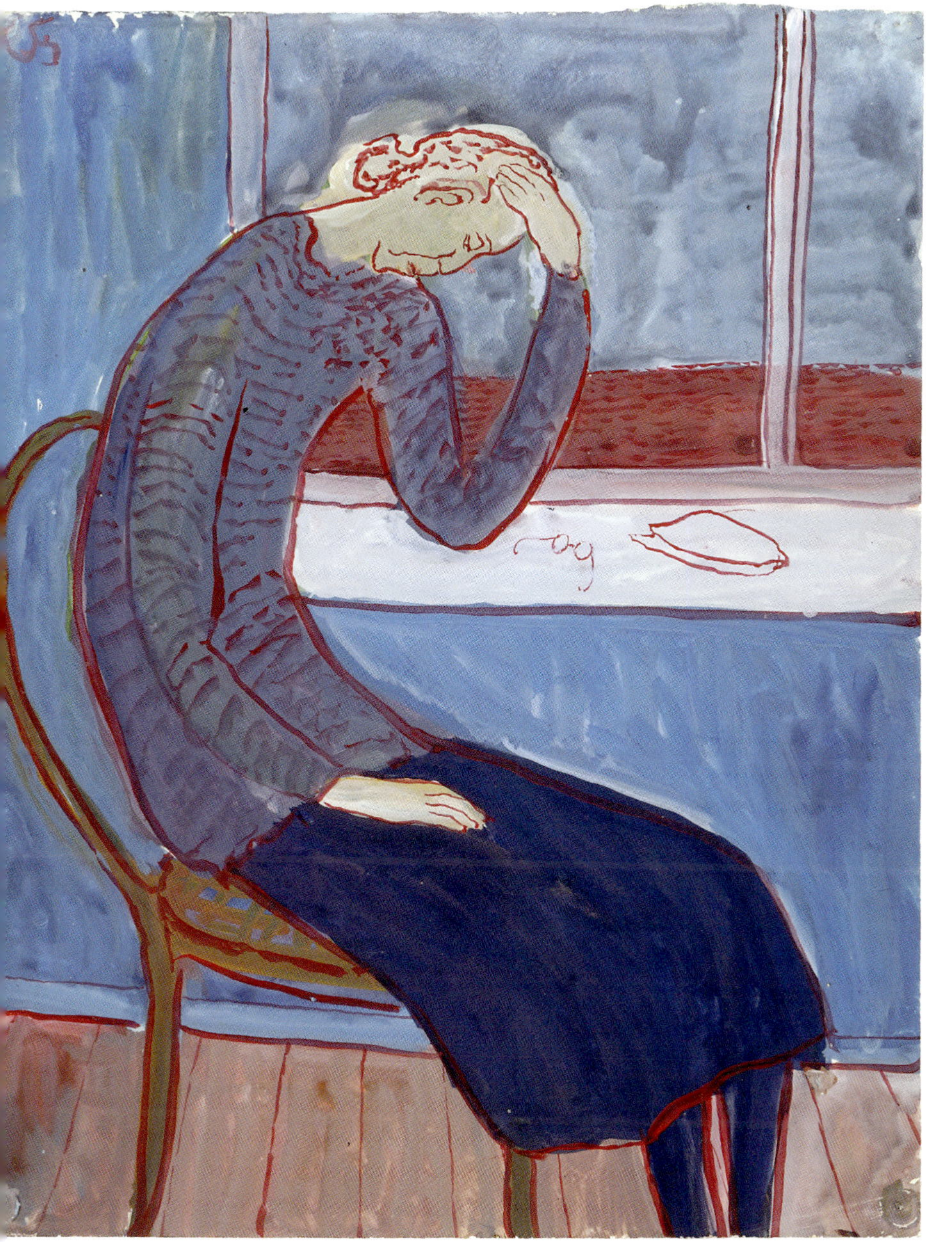

ACT TWO
30 JANUARY 1933

Es schaun aufs Hakenkreuz voll Hoffnung schon –
Der Tag für Freiheit und für Brot bricht an –
[People look at the swastika – full of hope –
The day of freedom and of bread dawns...]

Just at this time, many Jews – who, with all their often undesirable efficiency, are perhaps a pushy and insistent race, happened to be occupying government and other senior positions – and after the Nazi seizure of power they were all dismissed without notice.

You now see how this affects the different human-Jewish souls!

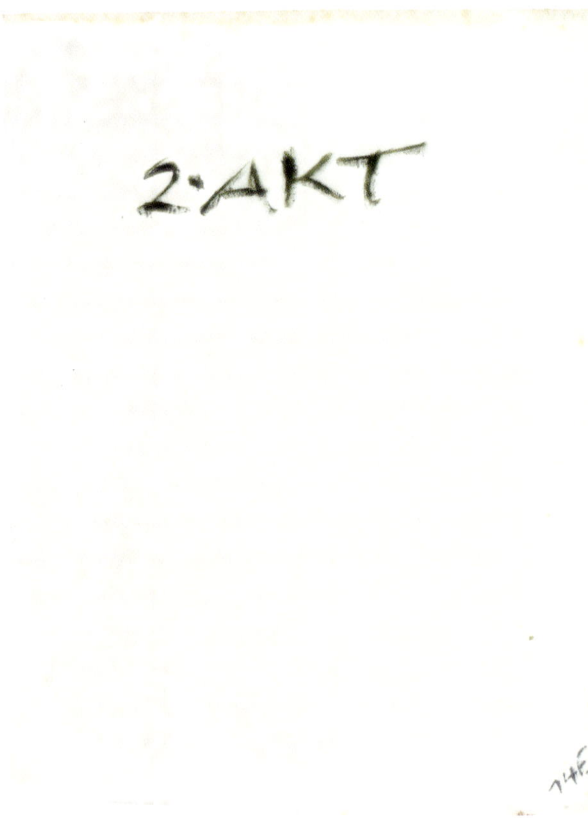

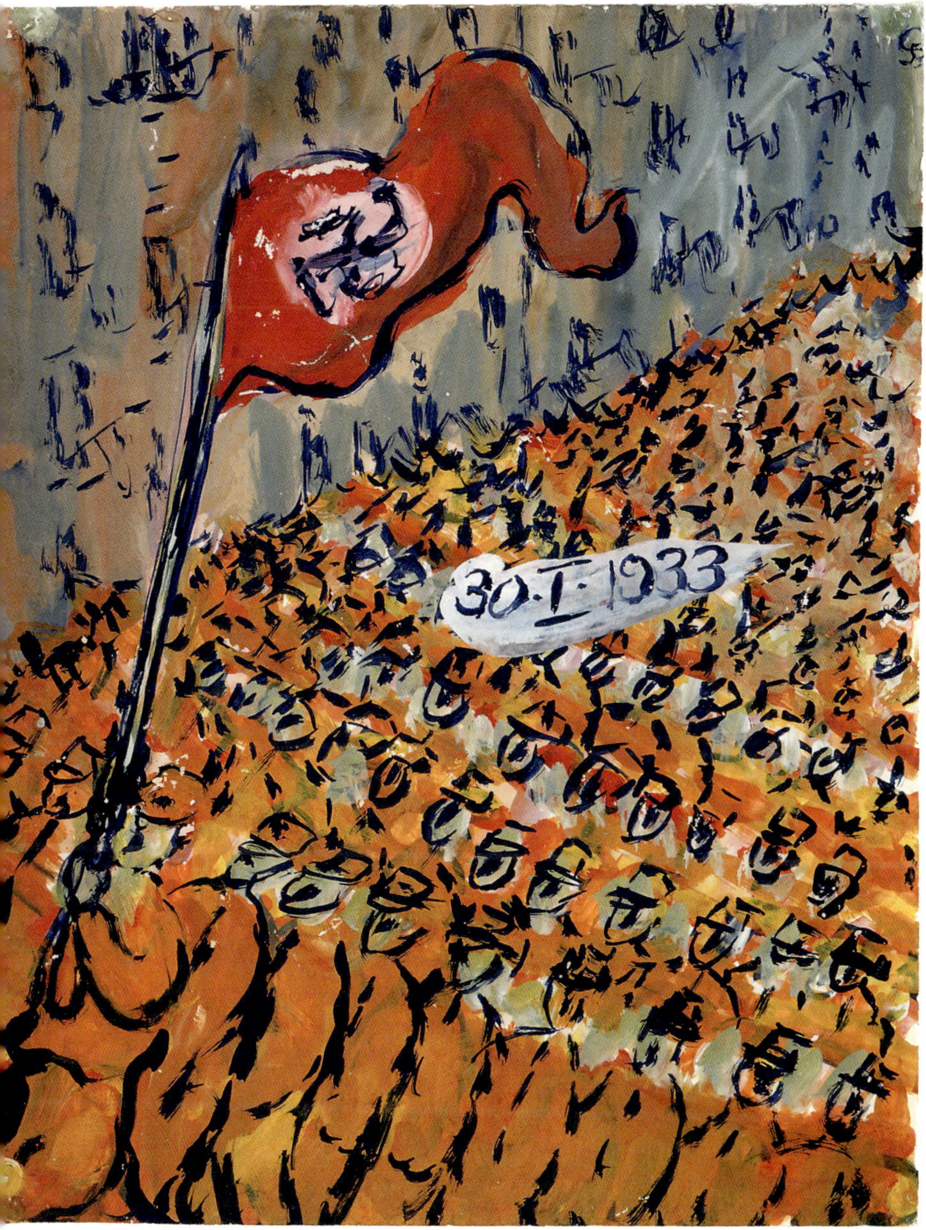
30·I·1933

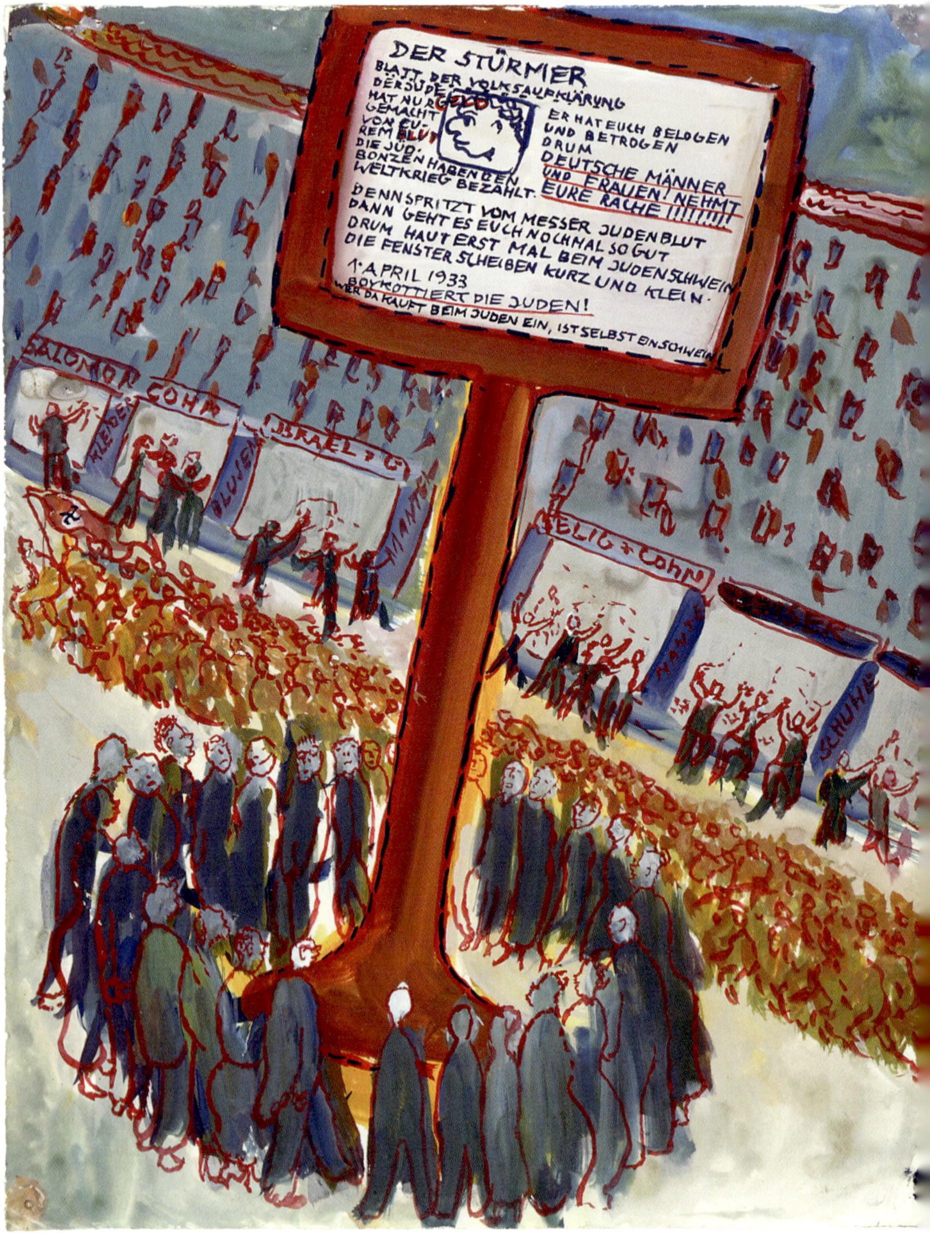
DER STÜRMER
BLATT DER VOLKSAUFKLÄRUNG
DER JUDE HAT NUR GELD GEMACHT VON EUREM BLUT
DIE JÜD. BONZEN HABEN DEN WELTKRIEG BEZAHLT.
ER HAT EUCH BELOGEN UND BETROGEN DRUM
DEUTSCHE MÄNNER UND FRAUEN! NEHMT EURE RACHE !!!!!!!!
DENN SPRITZT VOM MESSER JUDENBLUT
DANN GEHT ES EUCH NOCHMAL SO GUT
DRUM HAUT ERST MAL BEIM JUDENSCHWEIN
DIE FENSTERSCHEIBEN KURZ UND KLEIN.
1. APRIL 1933
BOYKOTTIERT DIE JUDEN!
WER DA KAUFT BEIM JUDEN EIN, IST SELBST EIN SCHWEIN
SALOMON
COHN
KLEIDER
BLUSEN
SELIG & COHN
SCHUHE

Der Stürmer:
Newspaper of Popular Enlightenment

The Jew has only made money from your blood.
The Jewish big shots paid for the world war.

The Jew has deceived and betrayed you, so German men and women! Take your revenge!!!

If Jewish blood spurts from the knife, you'll be much better off. That's why first of all smash the window-panes of the Jewish swines to bits.

1 April 1933
Boycott the Jews!
Whoever buys from a Jew is also a swine.

(bottom)

Melody: Gentlemen, here you see a serious gastric ulcer, but by using the new method I have invented we can save the case

PROFESSOR KANN
"Out – get out."

(opposite)

Melody: If we have to leave the university, we still have the Jewish hospital

Melody: But by using the new method he has invented we can save the case...

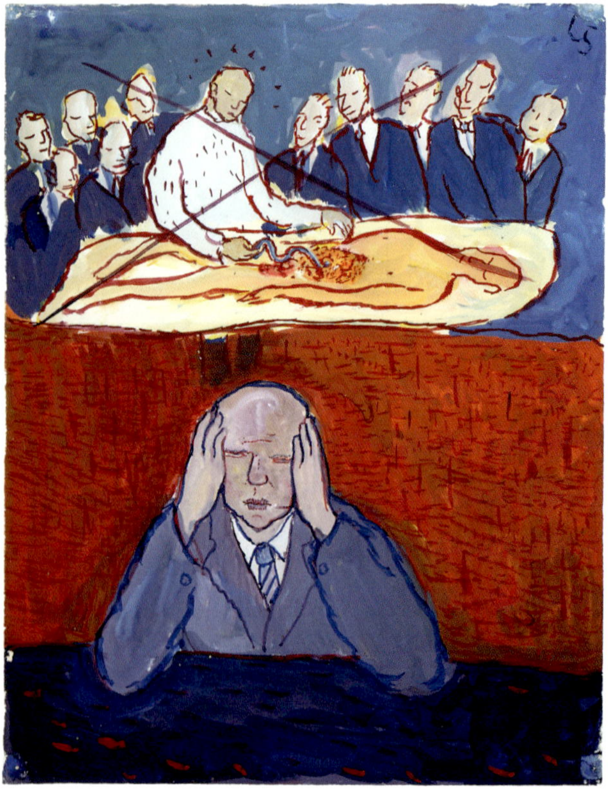

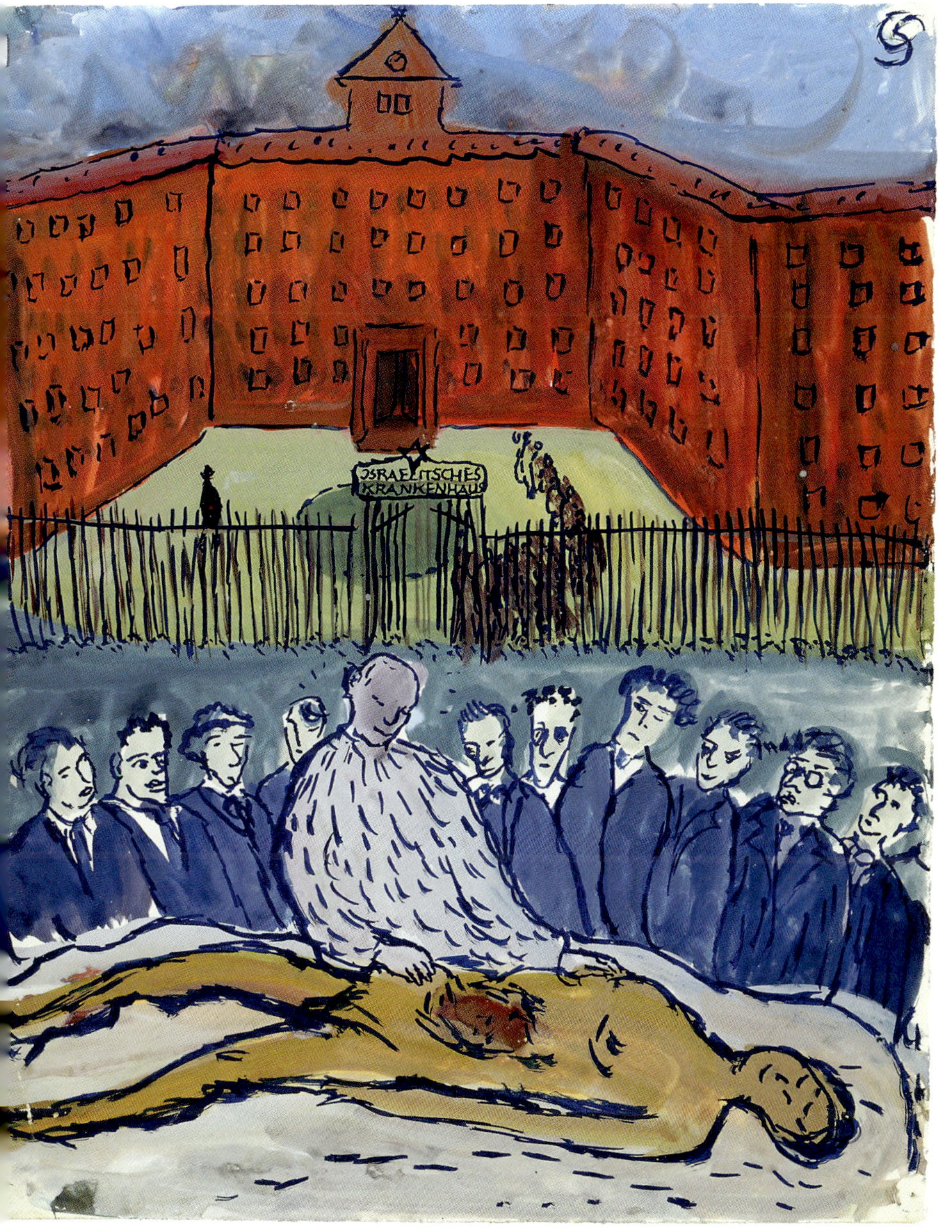
ISRAELITSCHES
KRANKENHAUS

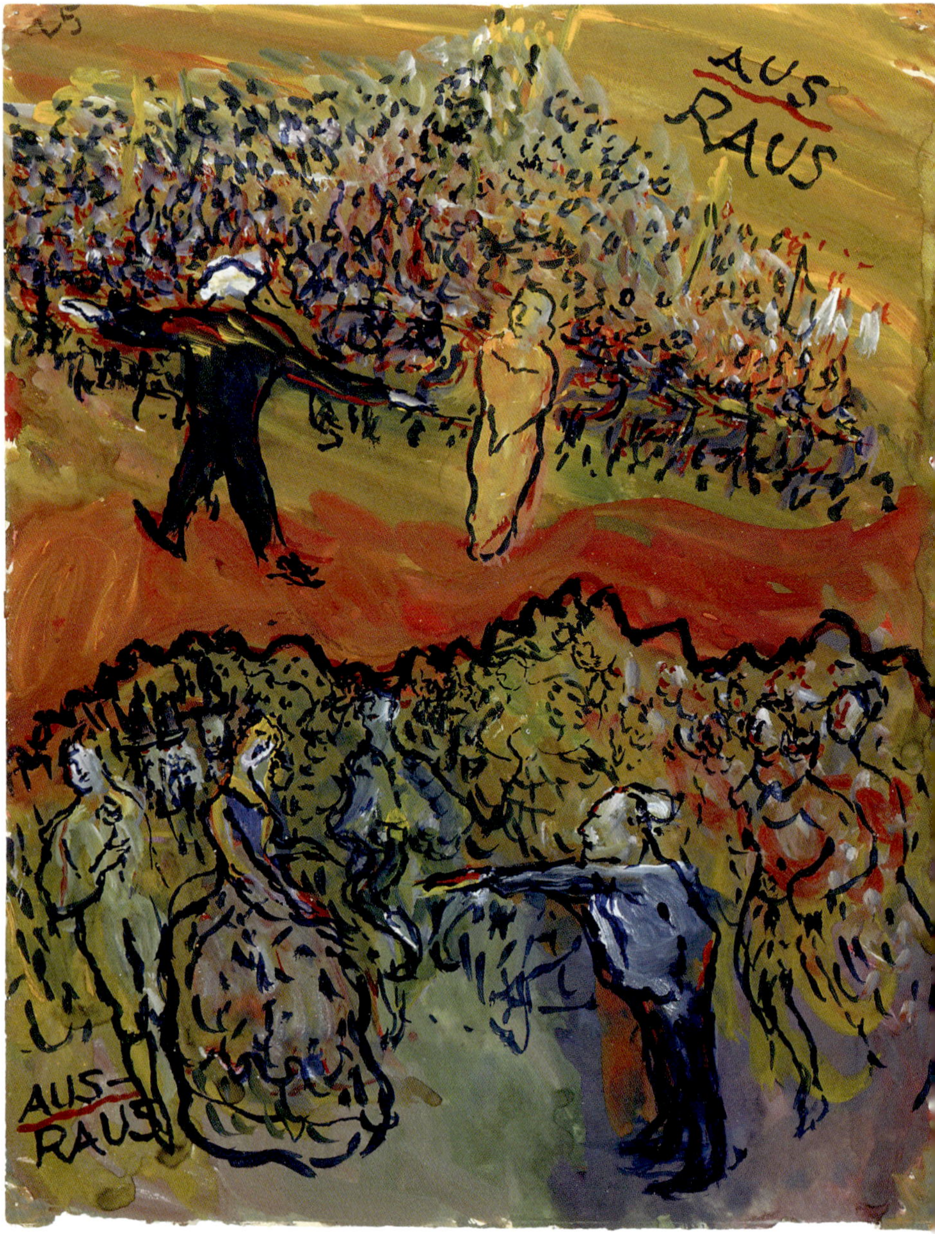
AUS
RAUS
AUS-
RAUS

(opposite)

Melody: Der du von dem Himmel bist... [Thou who art from Heaven...] Weary am I of my days – wherefore all this pain, this pleasure... Sweet peace, come, oh come into my breast... At last there approaches – where I shall wait for you, O my beloved.

NAZIS IN THE AUDIENCE
"OUT – GET OUT"

Dr Singsang

(bottom)

DR SINGSANG
"One might establish a Jewish theatre – that would be a big help to all the artists."

Melody: First movement of Kleine Nachtmusik – Mozart

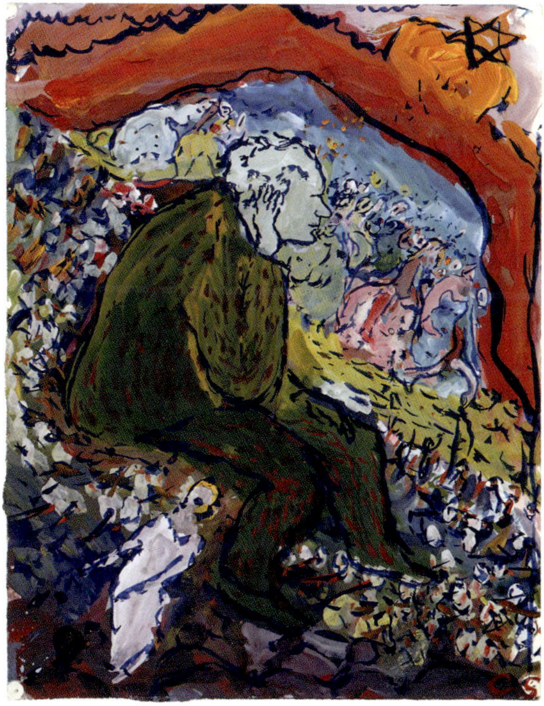

DR SINGSANG
"I'll write down the statutes and take them with me to the Ministry!"

The same melody

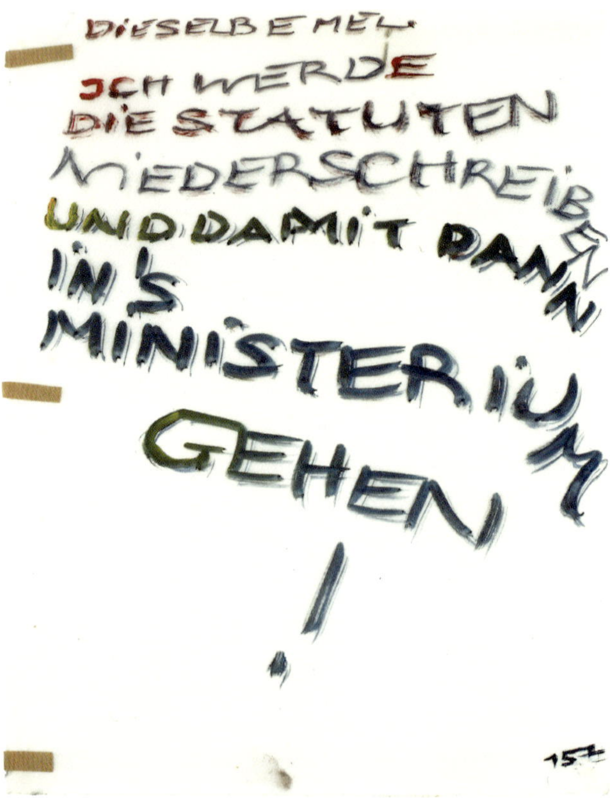

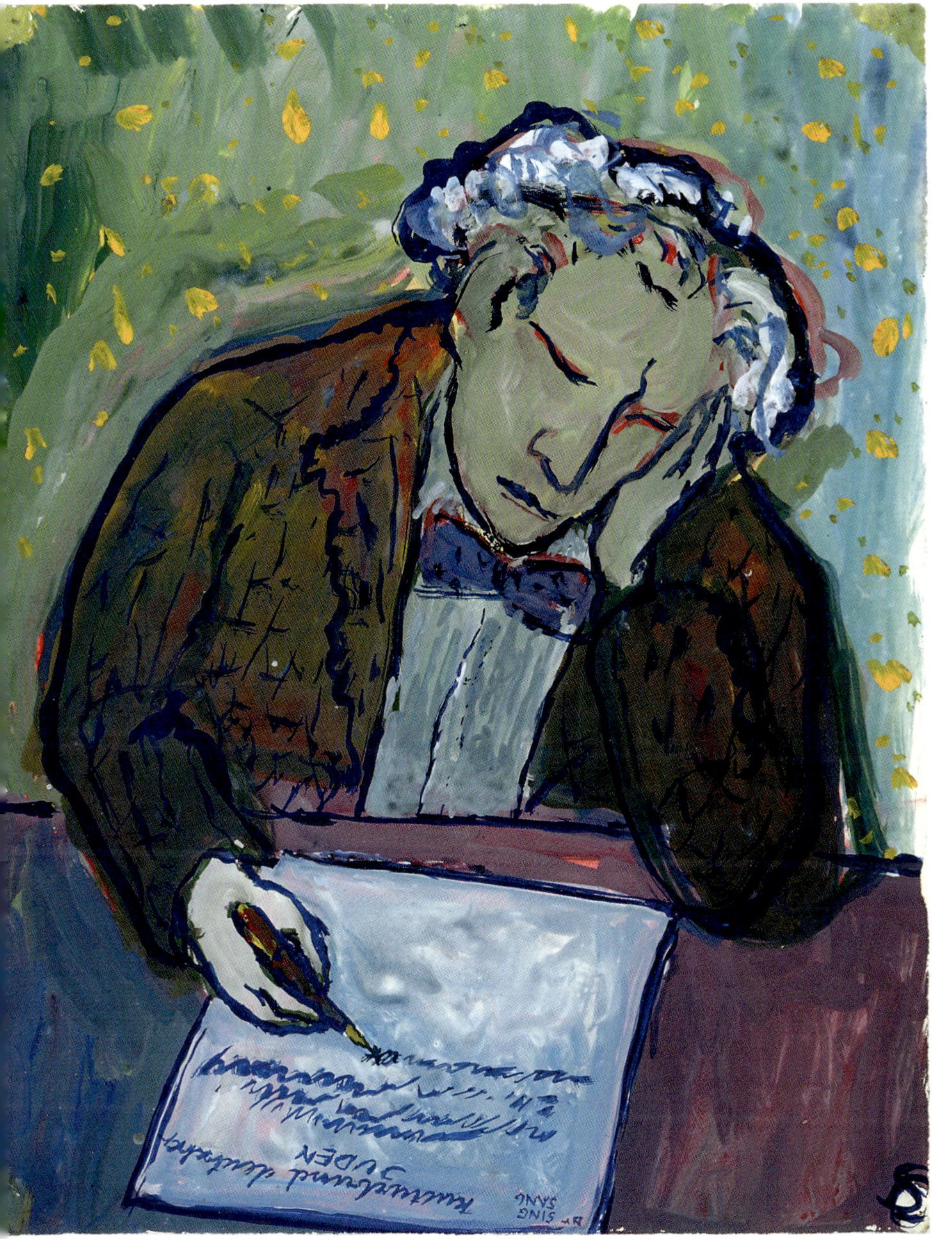

(bottom)

MINISTER
“I am the Minista for Propaganda! I’m busy night and day, no time for rest or play. Come in, come in!” (to himself) “Yes, this is a good project, probably he would be my man. Just a pity he’s a Jew – must see if I cannot make him an honorary Aryan.”

(opposite)

MINISTER
“Your request has been approved. Have a cigarette.”

Melody: <u>I</u> <u>am</u> <u>the</u> <u>Minista</u> <u>for</u> <u>Propaganda!</u> <u>I’m</u> <u>busy</u> <u>night</u> <u>and</u> <u>day</u>, <u>no</u> <u>time</u> <u>for</u> <u>rest</u> <u>or</u> <u>play</u>

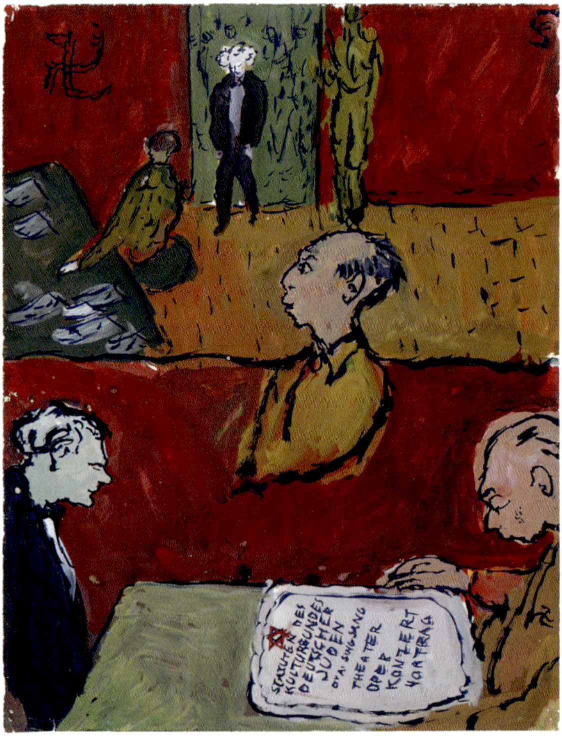

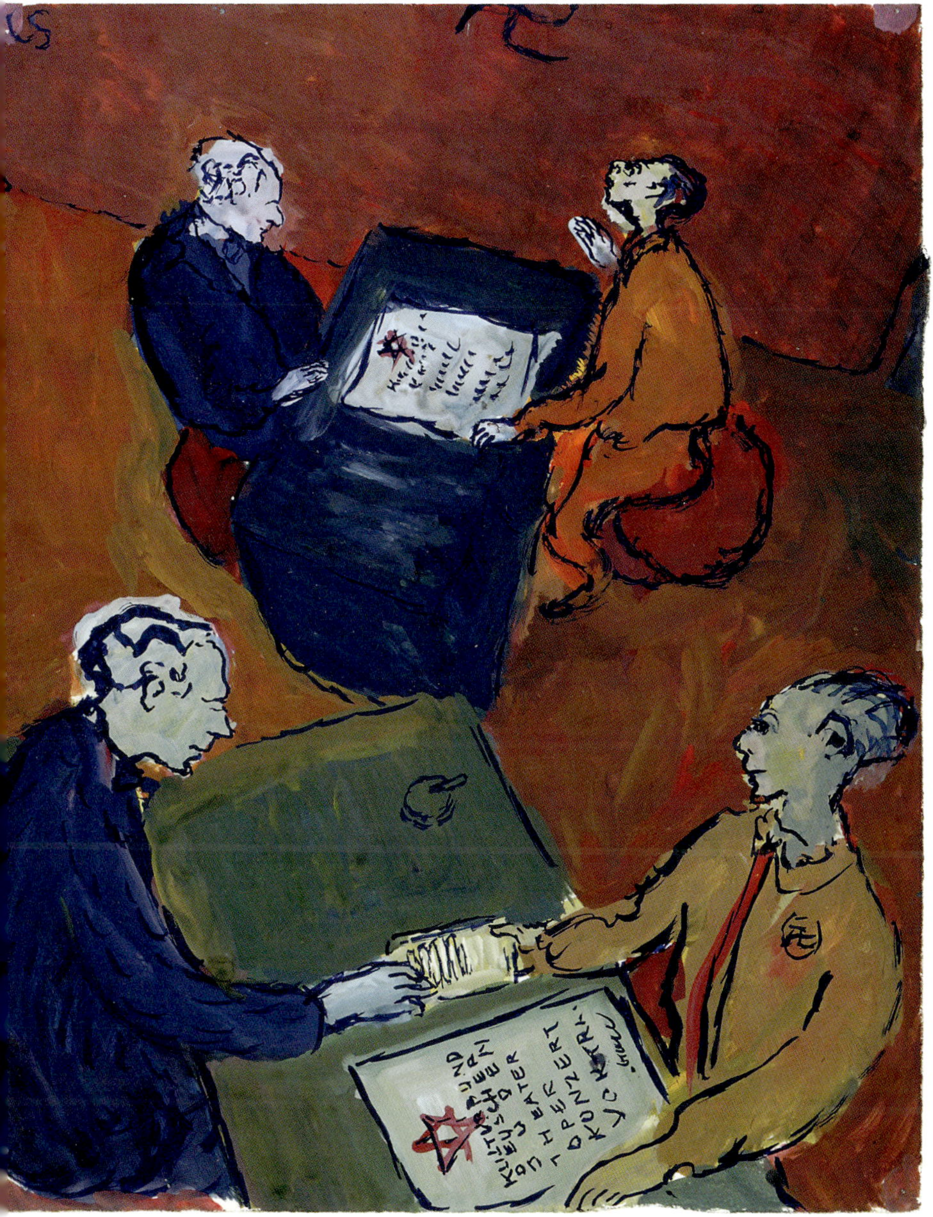

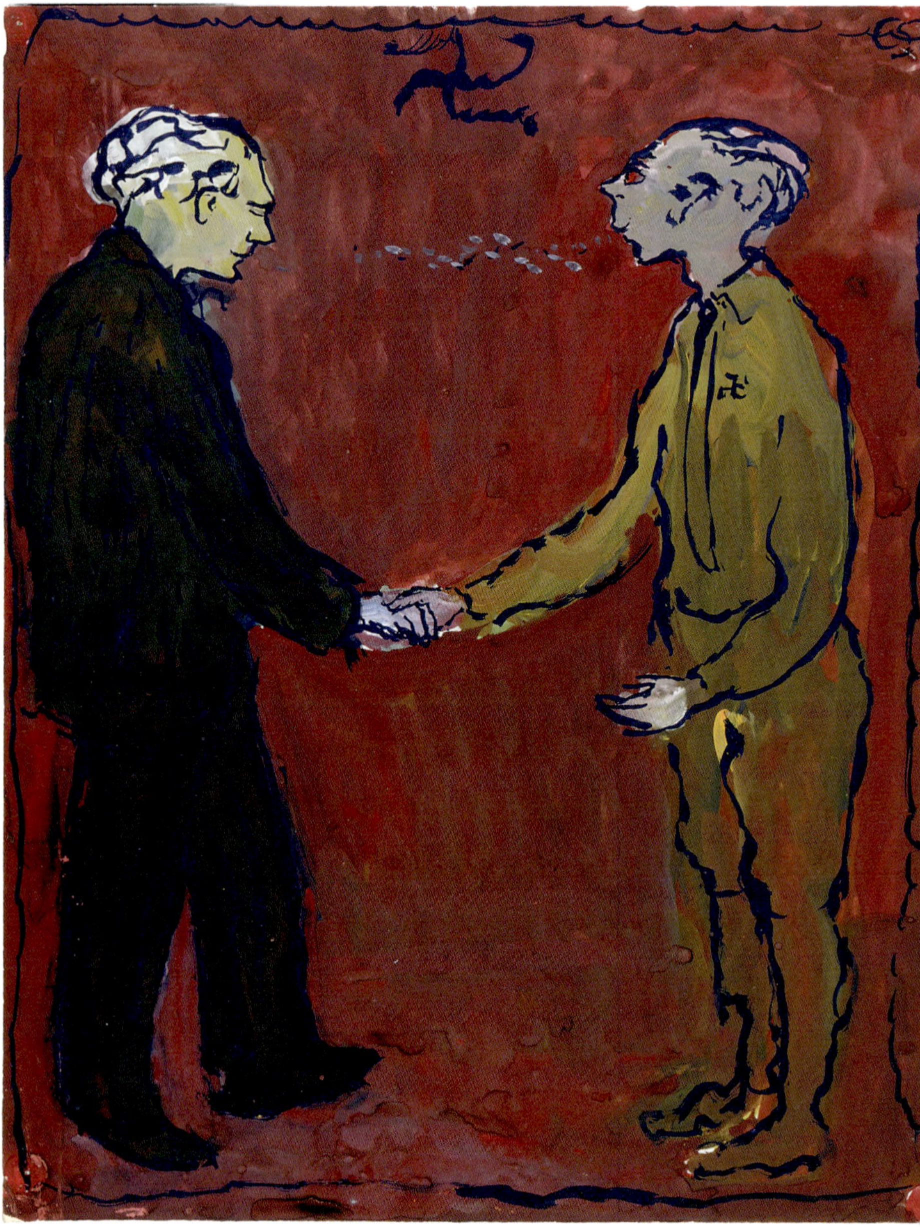

MINISTER
“It’s been a pleasure, you would have been just the man. A pity I can’t use you here for me. But if you should need me, don’t hesitate to call on me.”

DR SINGSANG
“The honour would be mine.”
(to himself) “You swine.”

Same melody

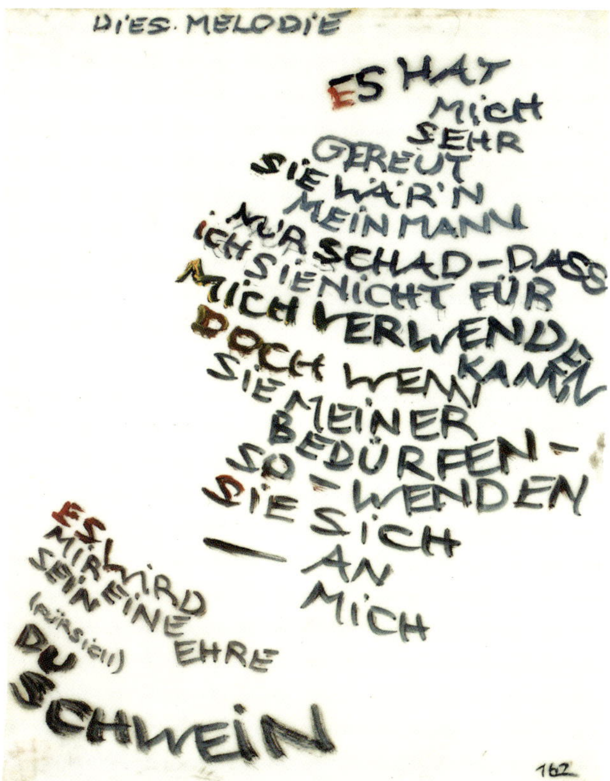

Melody: Dopo tante tante peine

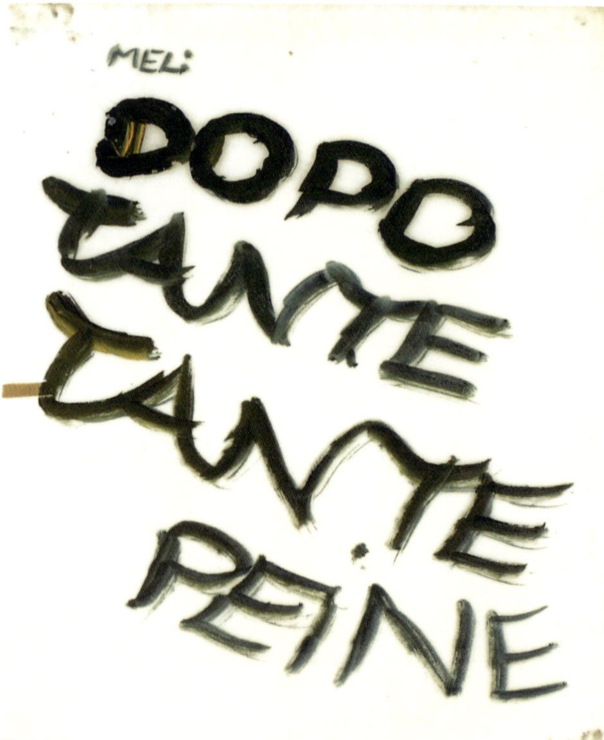

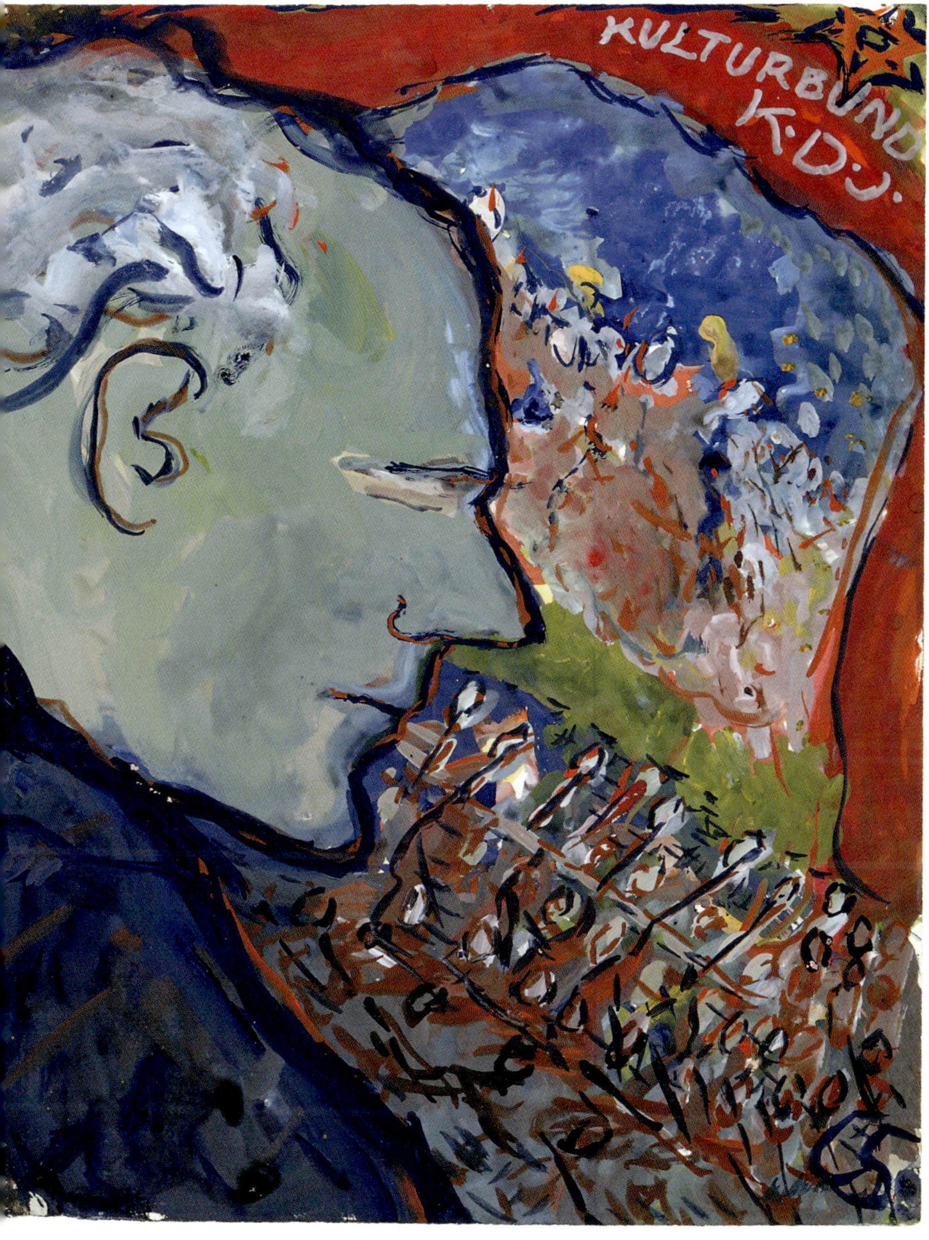
KULTURBUND
K·D·J.

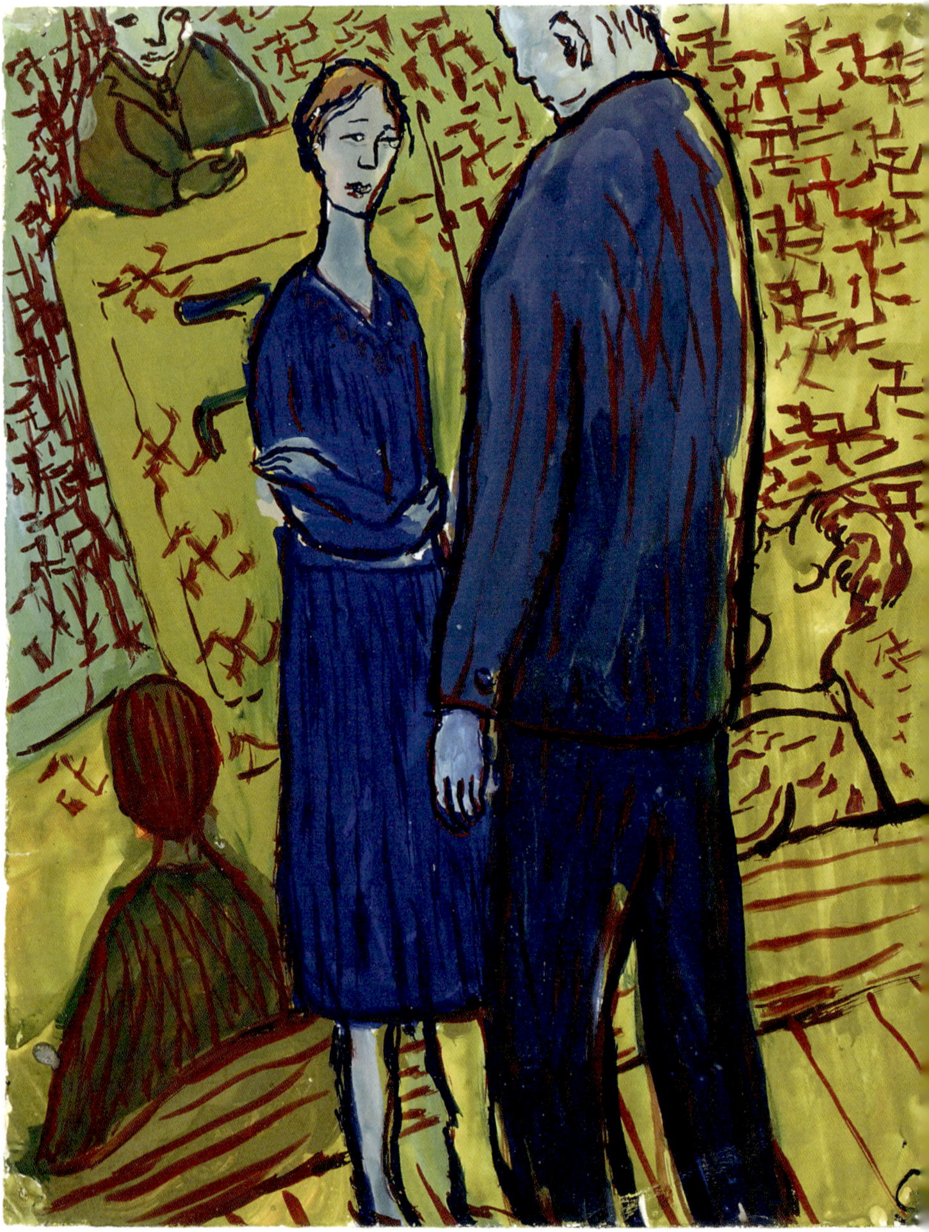

CHARLOTTE KANN – OVER AND OVER AGAIN:
“I won’t go back to school again. You can do what you want with me. I won’t go back to school. It’s no fun for me.”

ALBERT KANN
“I only wanted that you, at the very least, do your finals.”

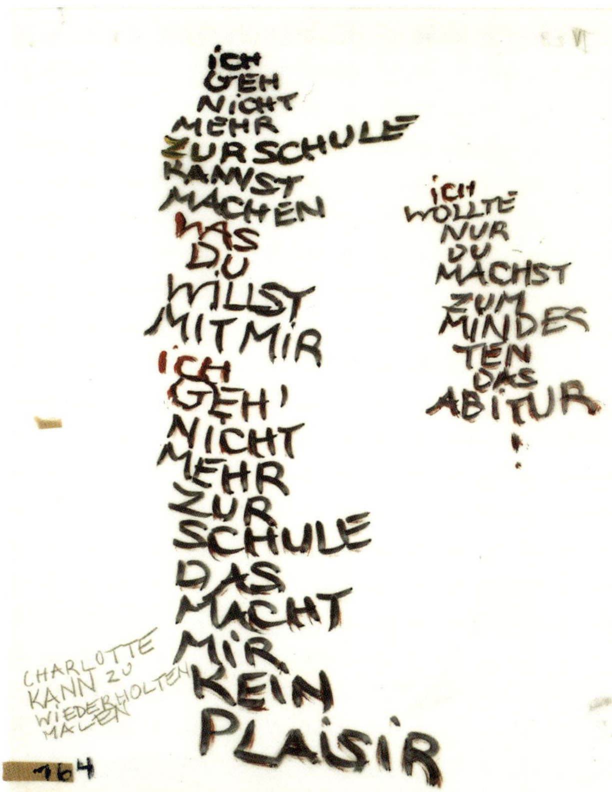

(bottom)

CHARLOTTE
"Perhaps – if I could learn to draw – that might be something. Perhaps – I could learn to draw... that is a lot of fun for me."

Melody: Ich hört' ein Bächlein rauschen
[I heard a brooklet rushing]

(opposite)

Roma aeterna città divina. Oh, in my redemption's pain,
I can feel Thy might again – – Roma aeterna città divina.

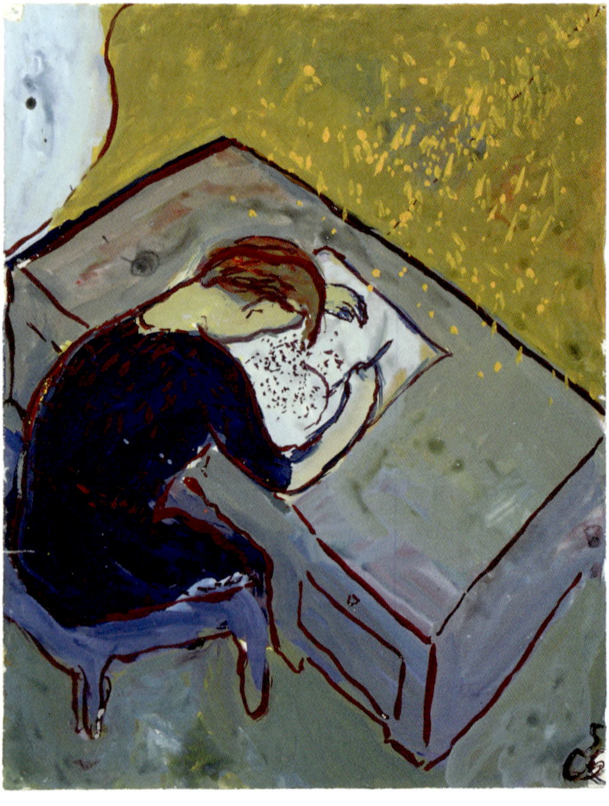

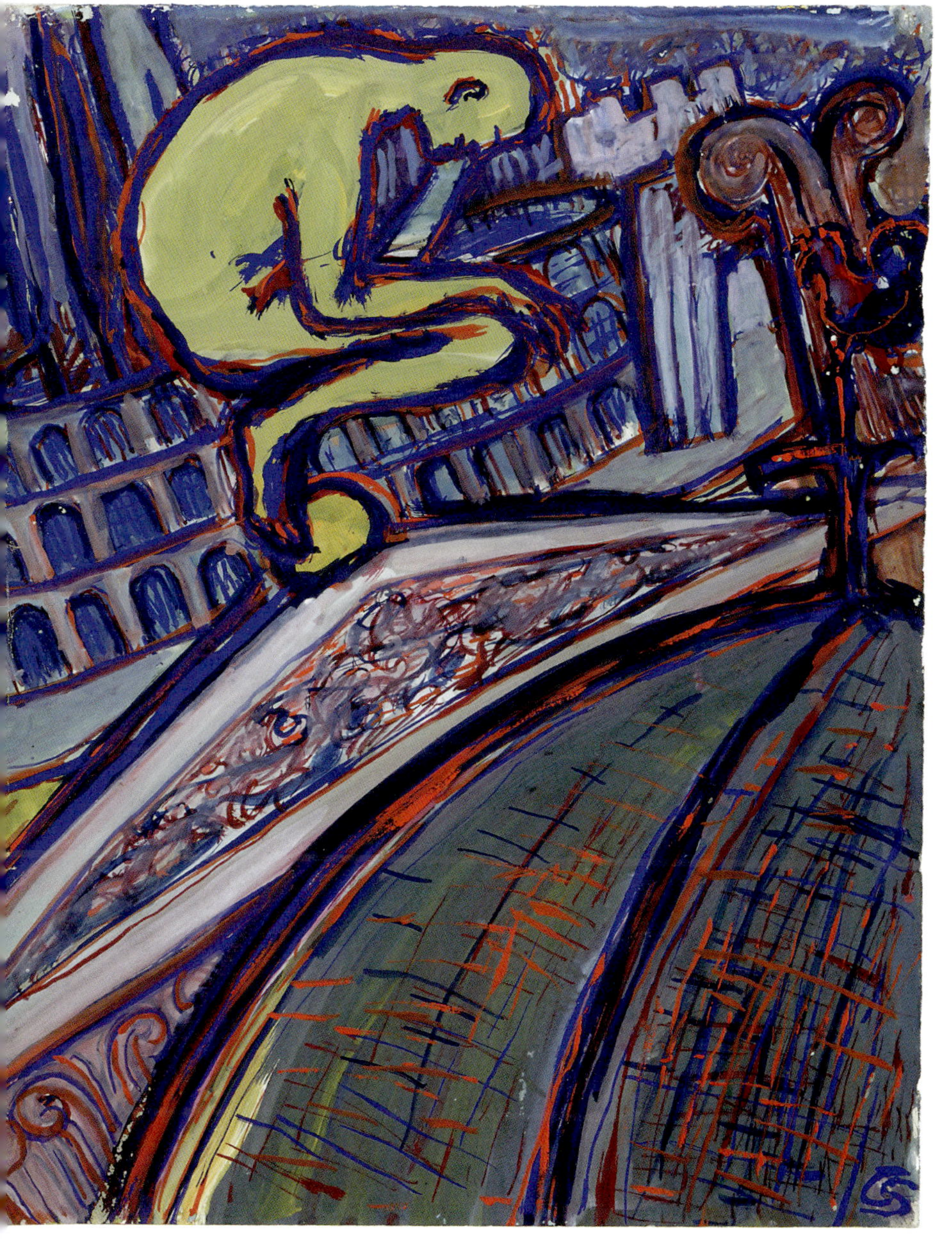

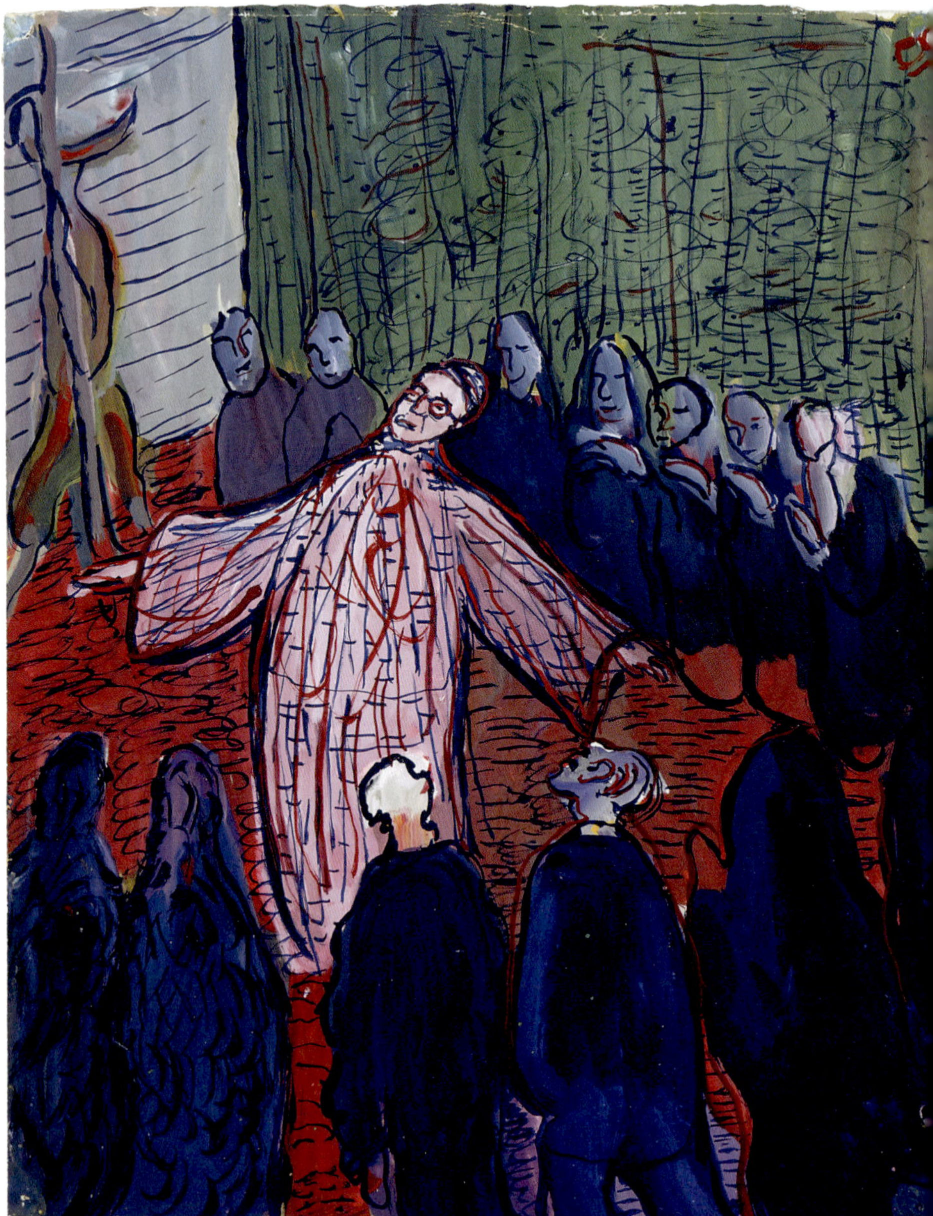

(opposite)

POPE
"I am Pius XI, God's Vicar on earth.
Tiens, tiens, tiens. What are those little
Jews doing here?"

The same melody

(bottom)

And then: this Michelangelo, I find him extremely magnificent – there really is a sovereign power in them. One must, however, twist one's neck a lot to see anything at all. He hovers too high in God's Highness, however, ça vaut la peine!

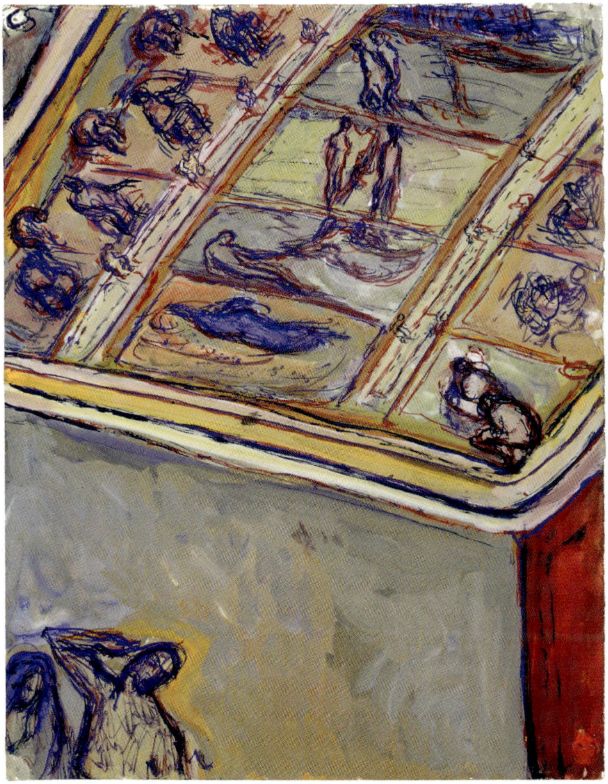

Michelangelo's <u>Last Judgement</u>.
"I prefer the <u>School of Athens</u>."
"I think I find it grandiose."
"It's excellent."

Melody: <u>Like a great body of bodies,</u>
<u>man surges forward</u>

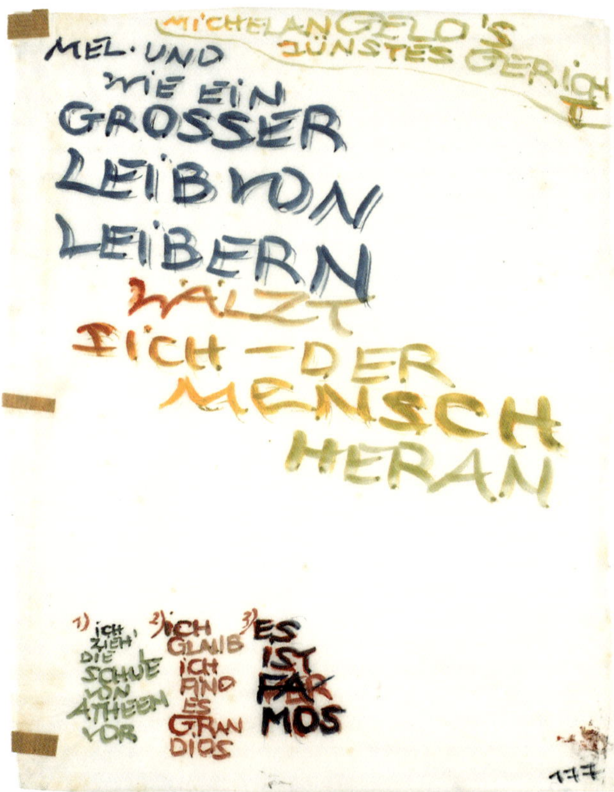

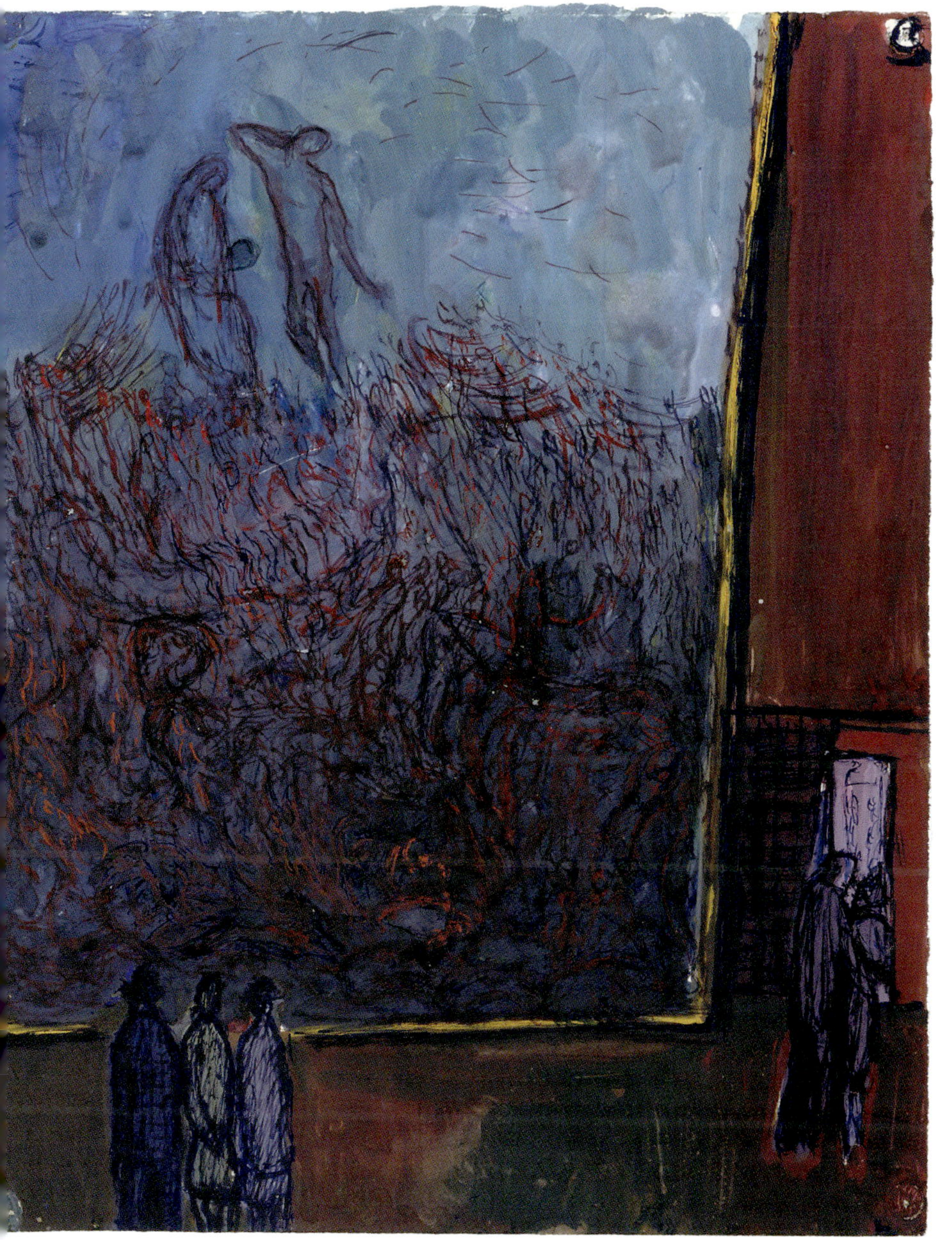

(bottom)

“And this Pietà.
I love it a lot.”

(opposite)

Roma divina città aeterna. And in the ray of redemption – I can feel your might again. And away from your blue into nordic grey – Away from our happiness, must we return.

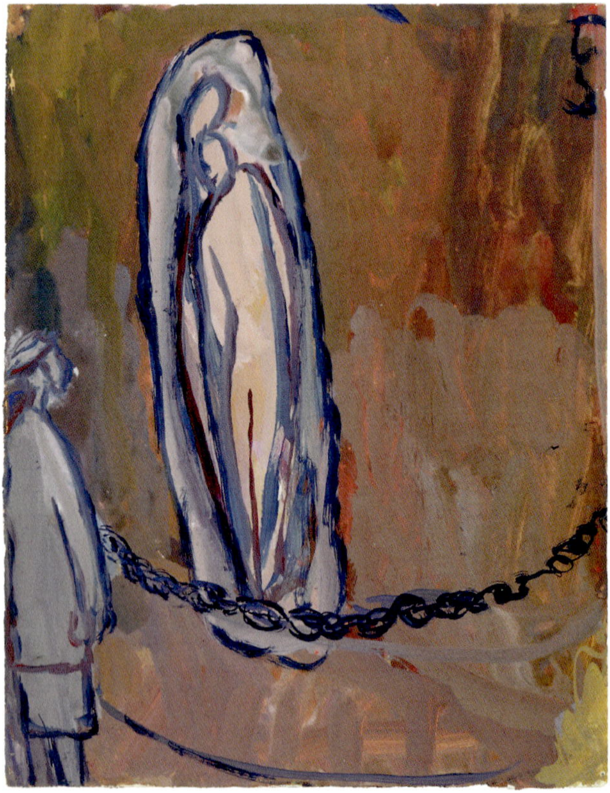

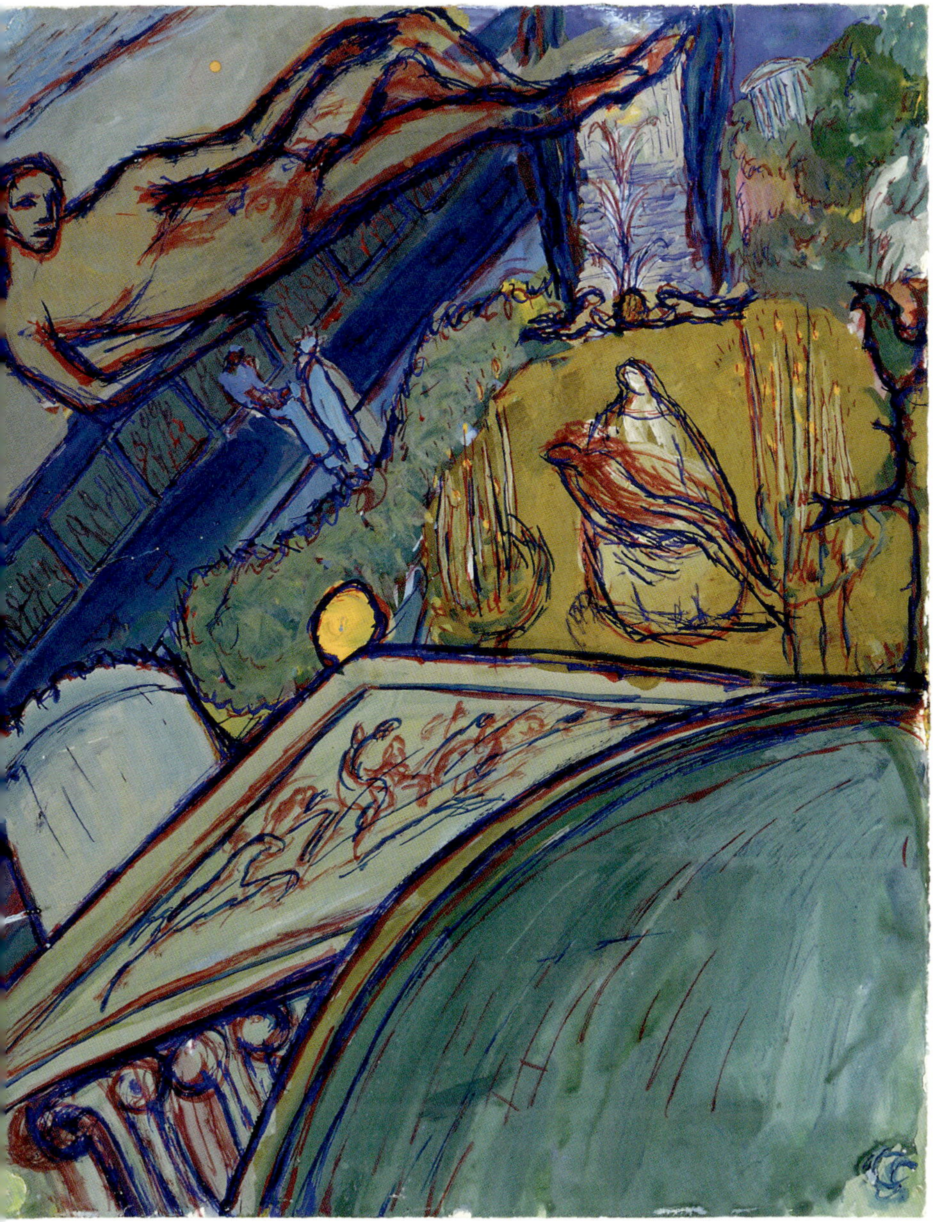

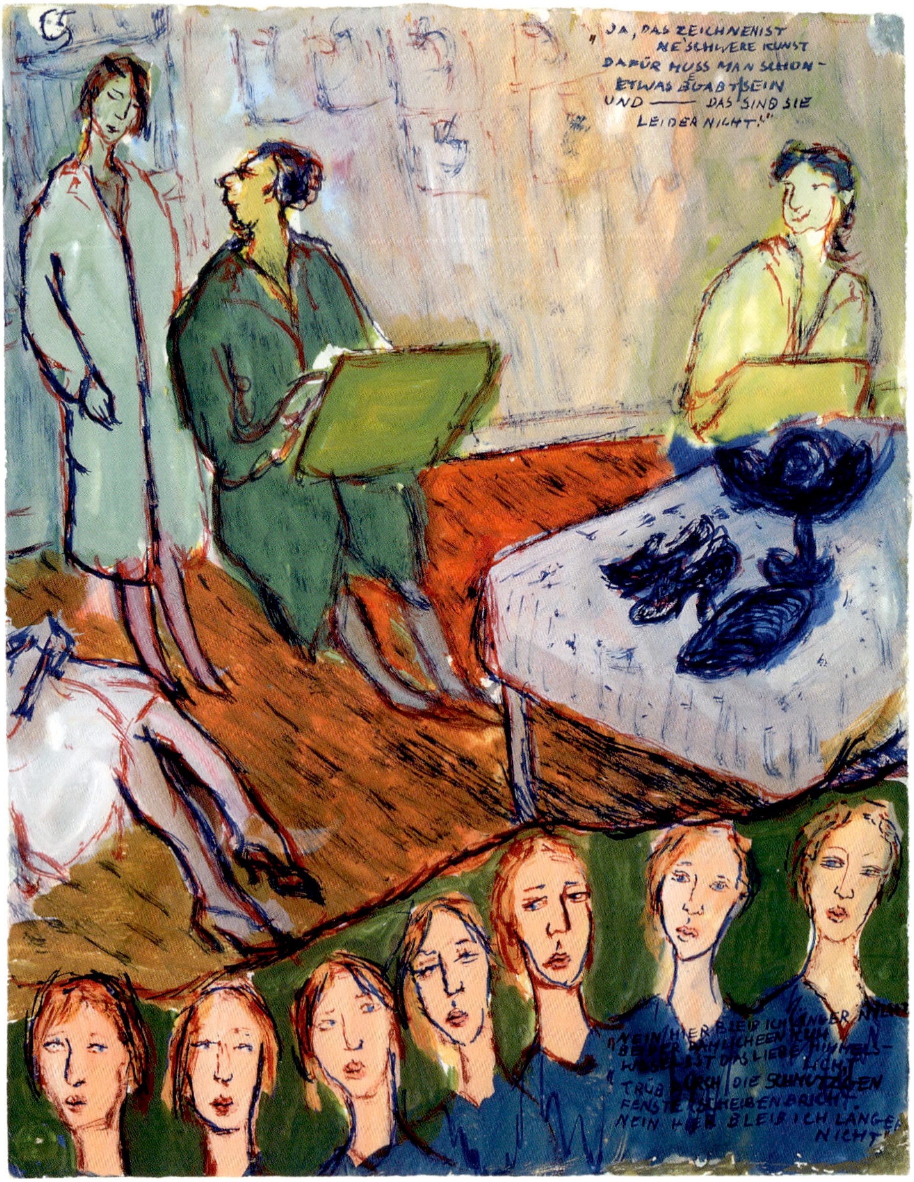
„JA, DAS ZEICHNEN IST
NE SCHWERE KUNST
DAFÜR MUSS MAN SCHON
ETWAS BEGABT SEIN
UND —— DAS SIND SIE
LEIDER NICHT!"
„NEIN HIER BLEIB ICH
TRÜB DIE
NEIN BLEIB ICH
NICHT"

(opposite)

FASHION DRAWING TEACHER
"Yes, drawing is a difficult art.
One must be somewhat gifted at it
– and unfortunately you are not."

CHARLOTTE
"No, I will not stay here any longer with this stupid cow, where even the dear heavenly light breaks murkily through the dirty window panes. No, I will not stay here any longer."

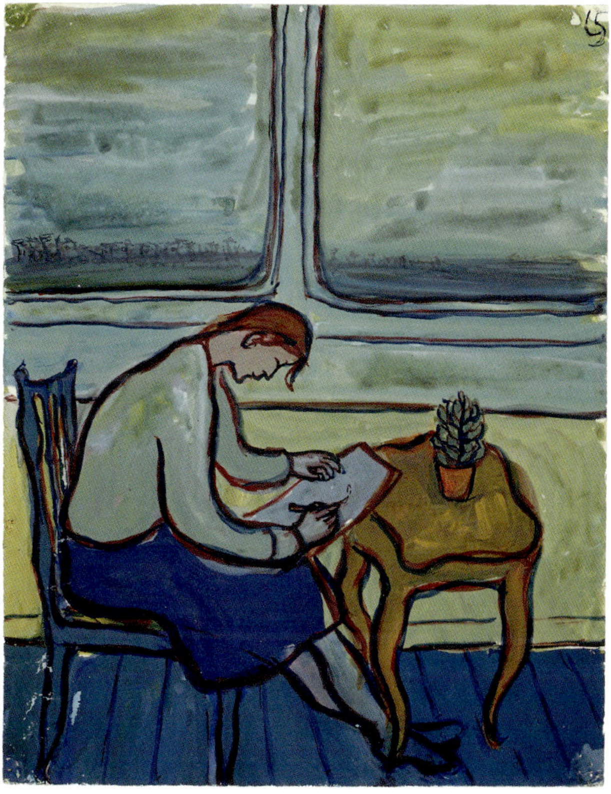

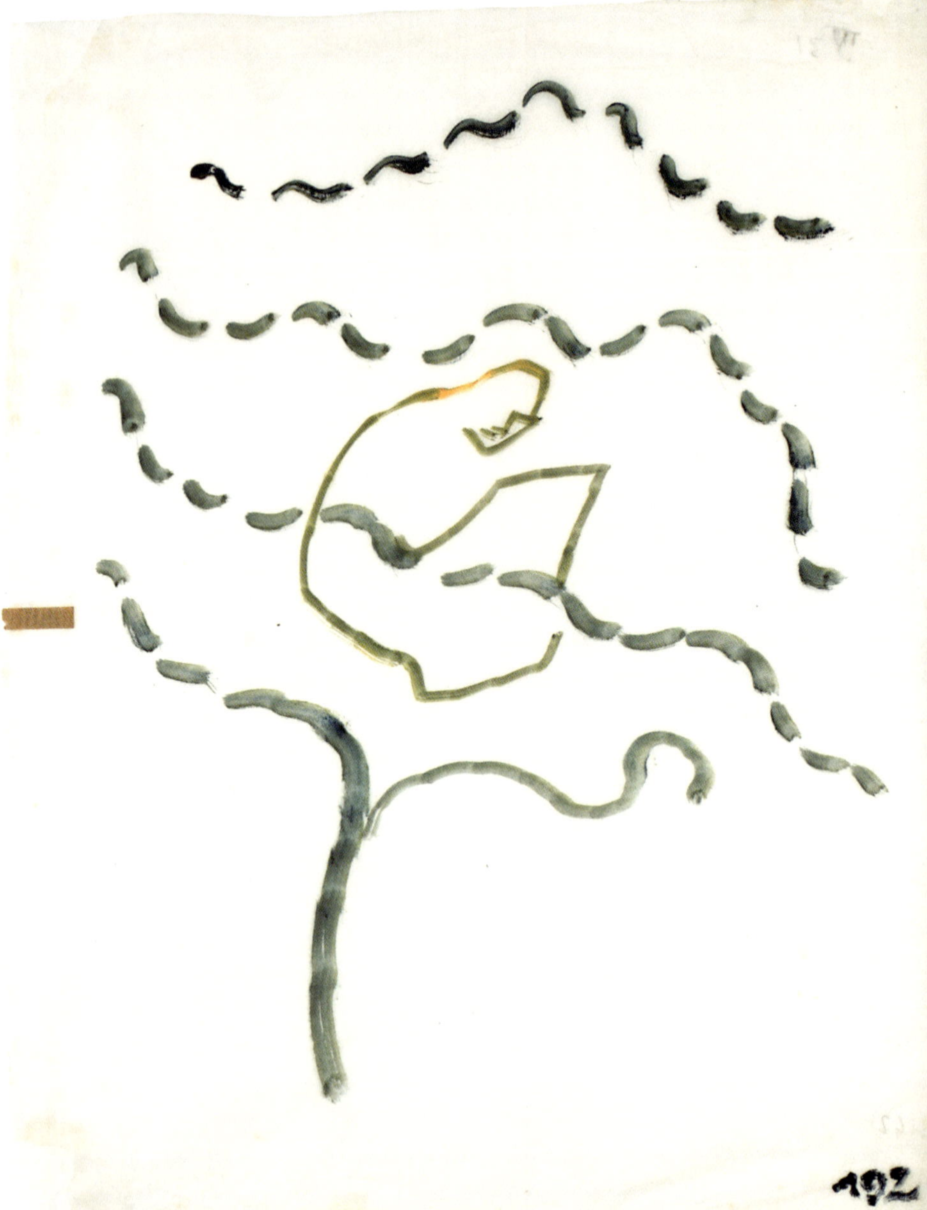

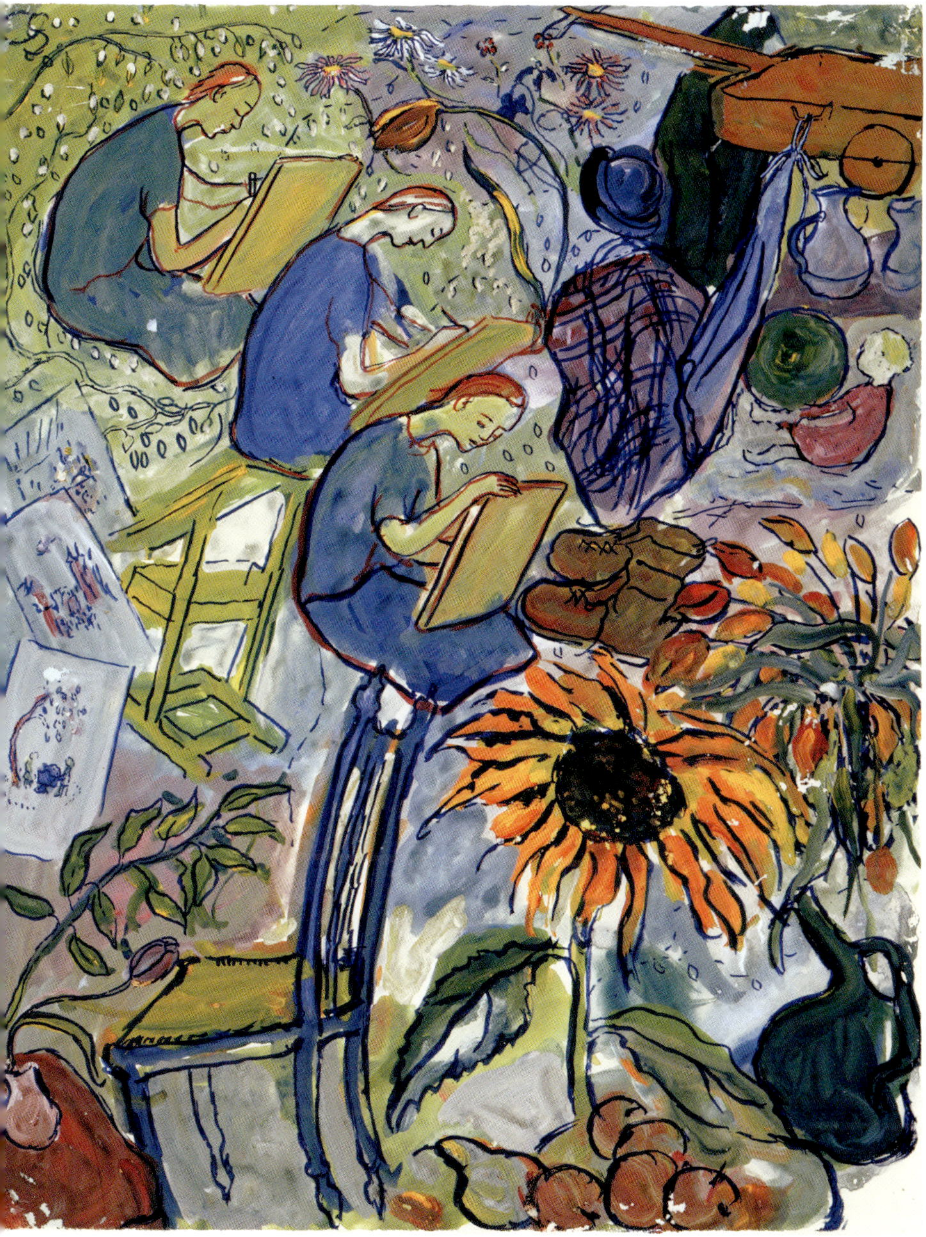

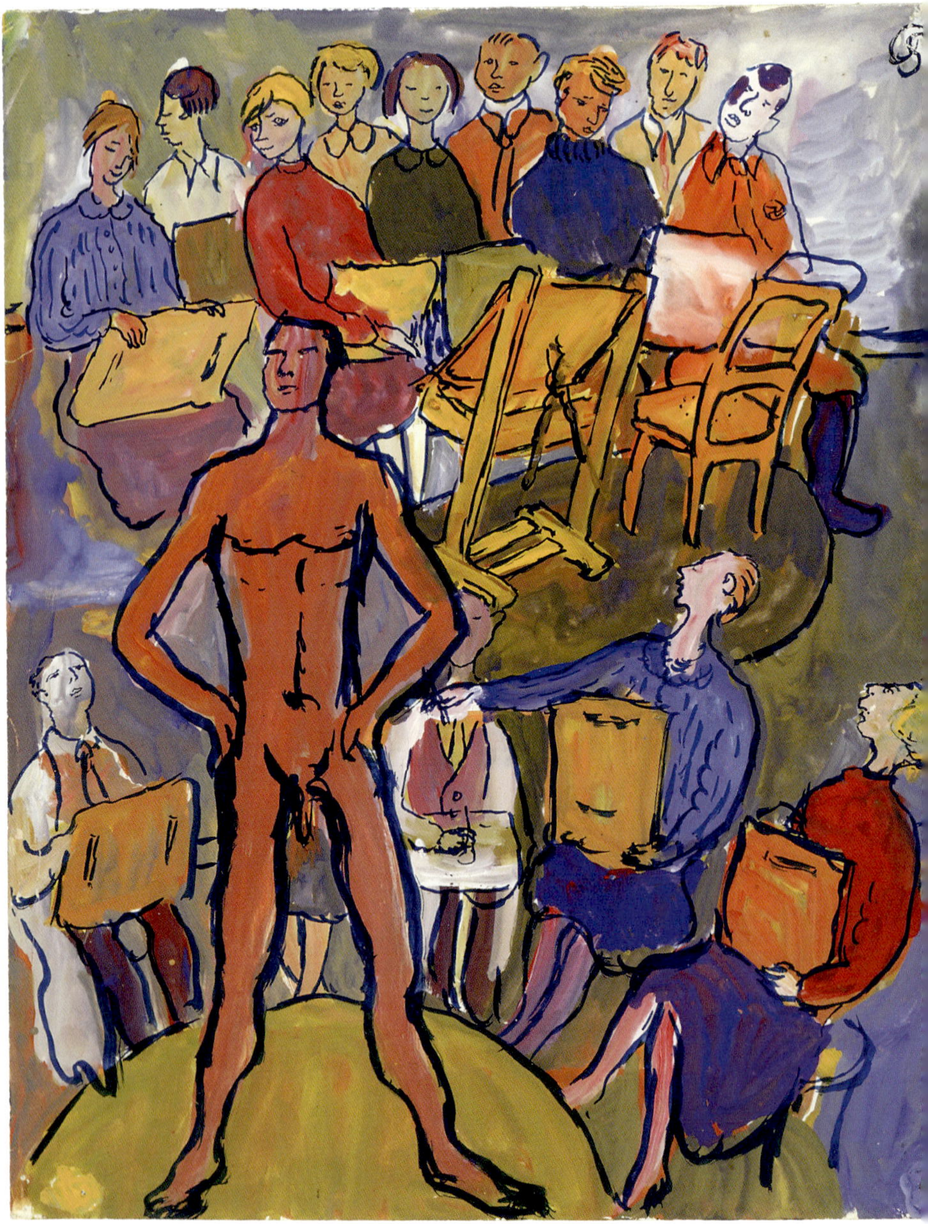

(opposite)

“Yes, this time it works.”

To the melody: <u>Allons enfants de la patrie</u>

(bottom)

PROFESSOR
<u>Üb immer Treu und Redlichkeit bis an dein kühles Grab</u>
– <u>und weiche keinen Fingerbreit von Gottes Wegen ab</u>
[Always be faithful and true up to your cool grave
– and do not stray a finger’s width from God’s ways].

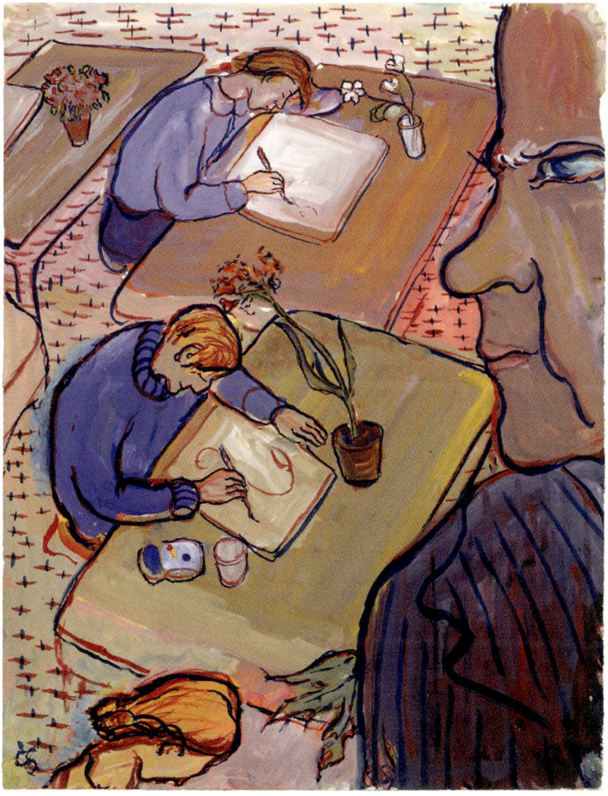

(bottom)

BARBARA
"I am Barbara, very much loved by all, but
I only love the one – my own."

(opposite)

Out there in the forest there he stands – there dwells many a beautiful king's child – in the forest – there we want to listen. Sleep gently, Sleeping Beauty, you pretty picture!

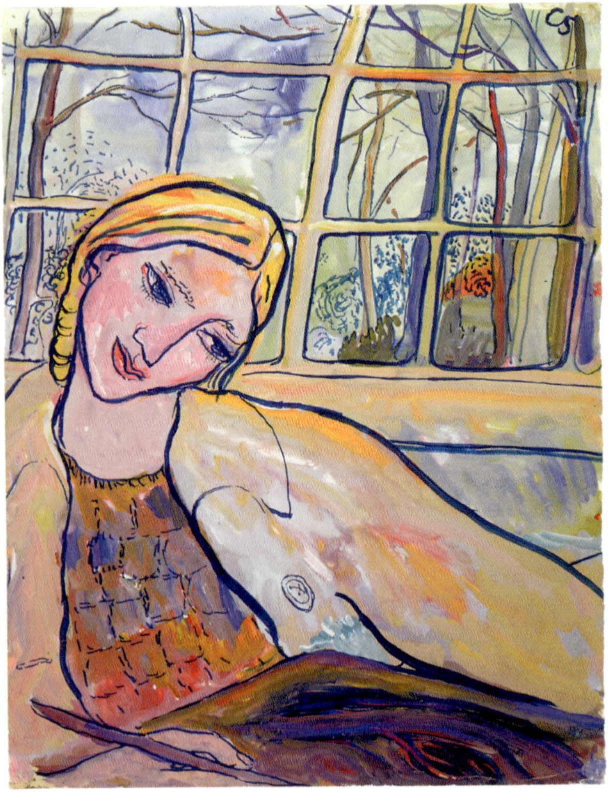

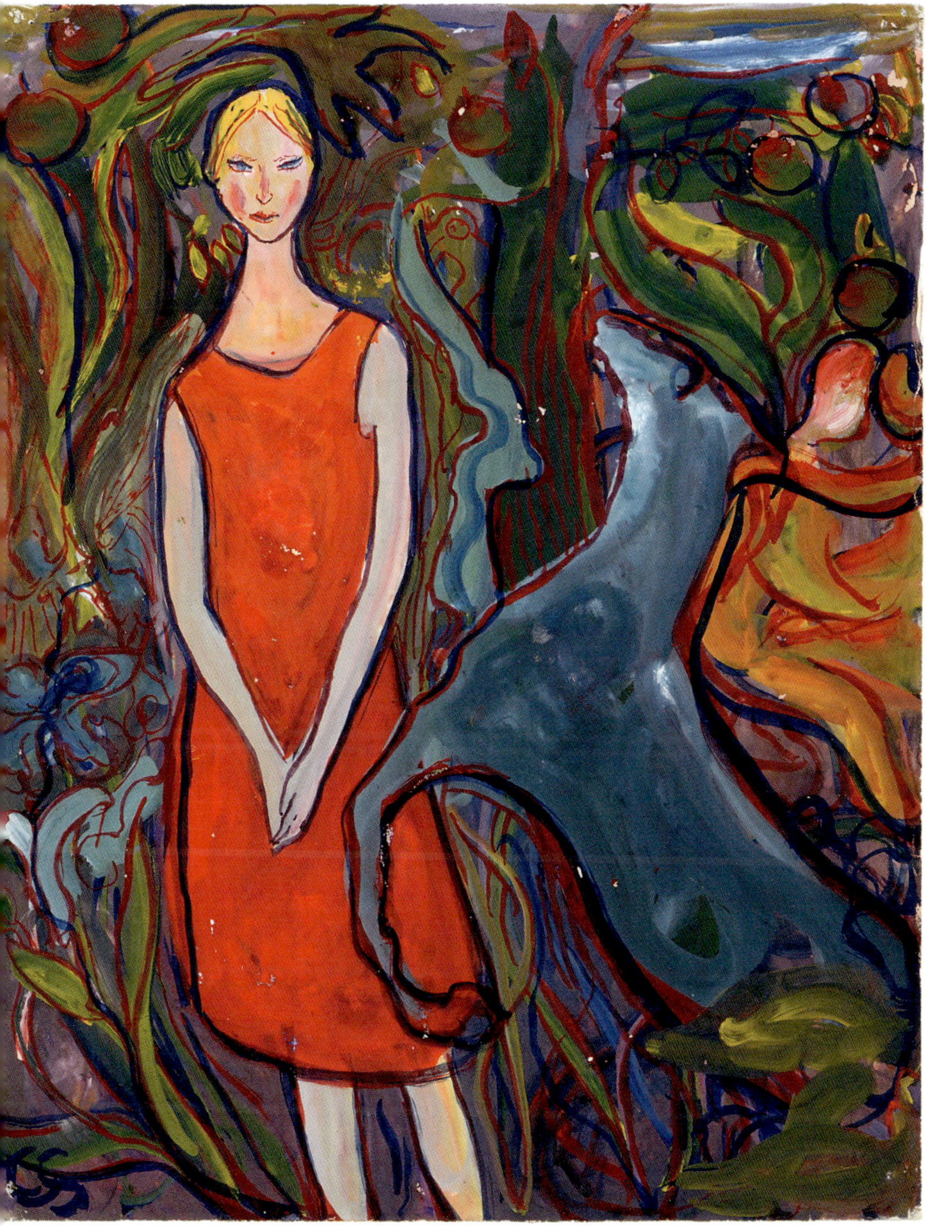

And Charlotte made progress in
her studies, and she even made
friends with Barbara.

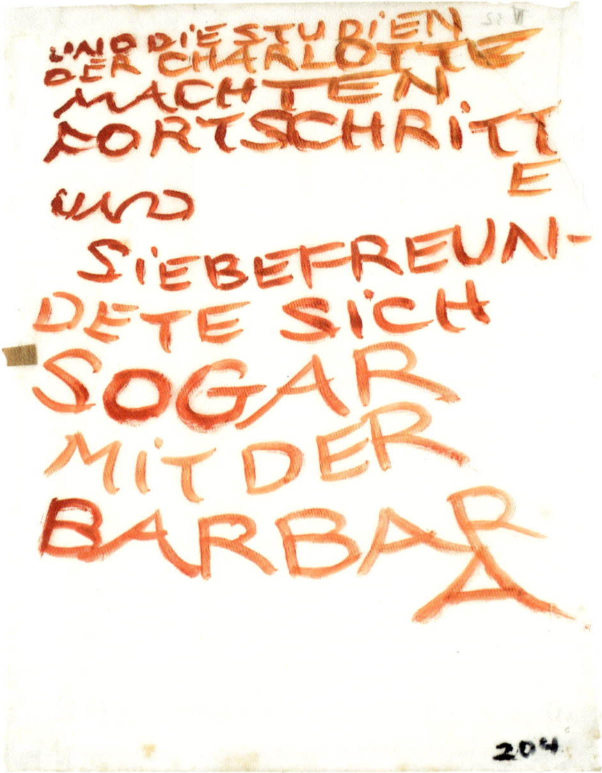

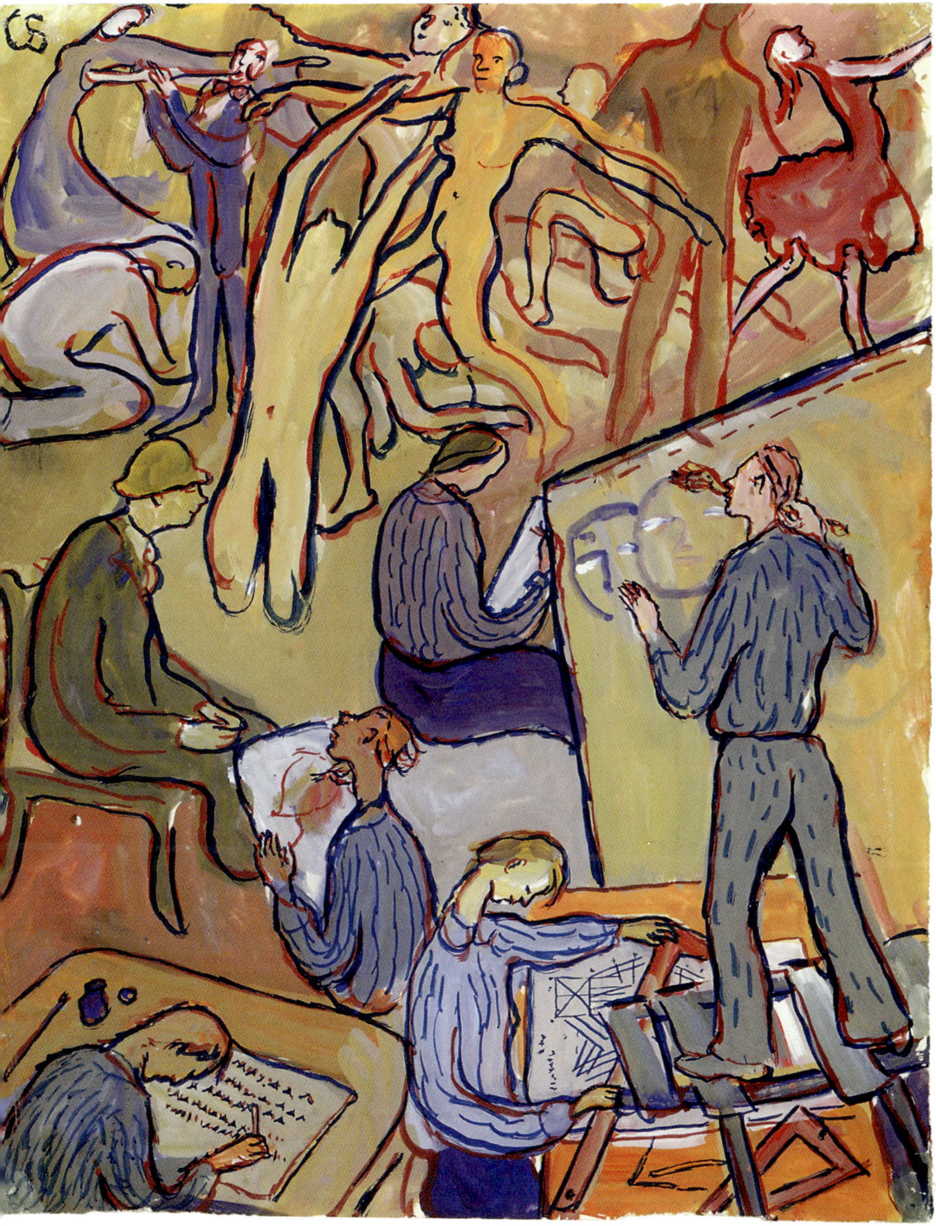
CS

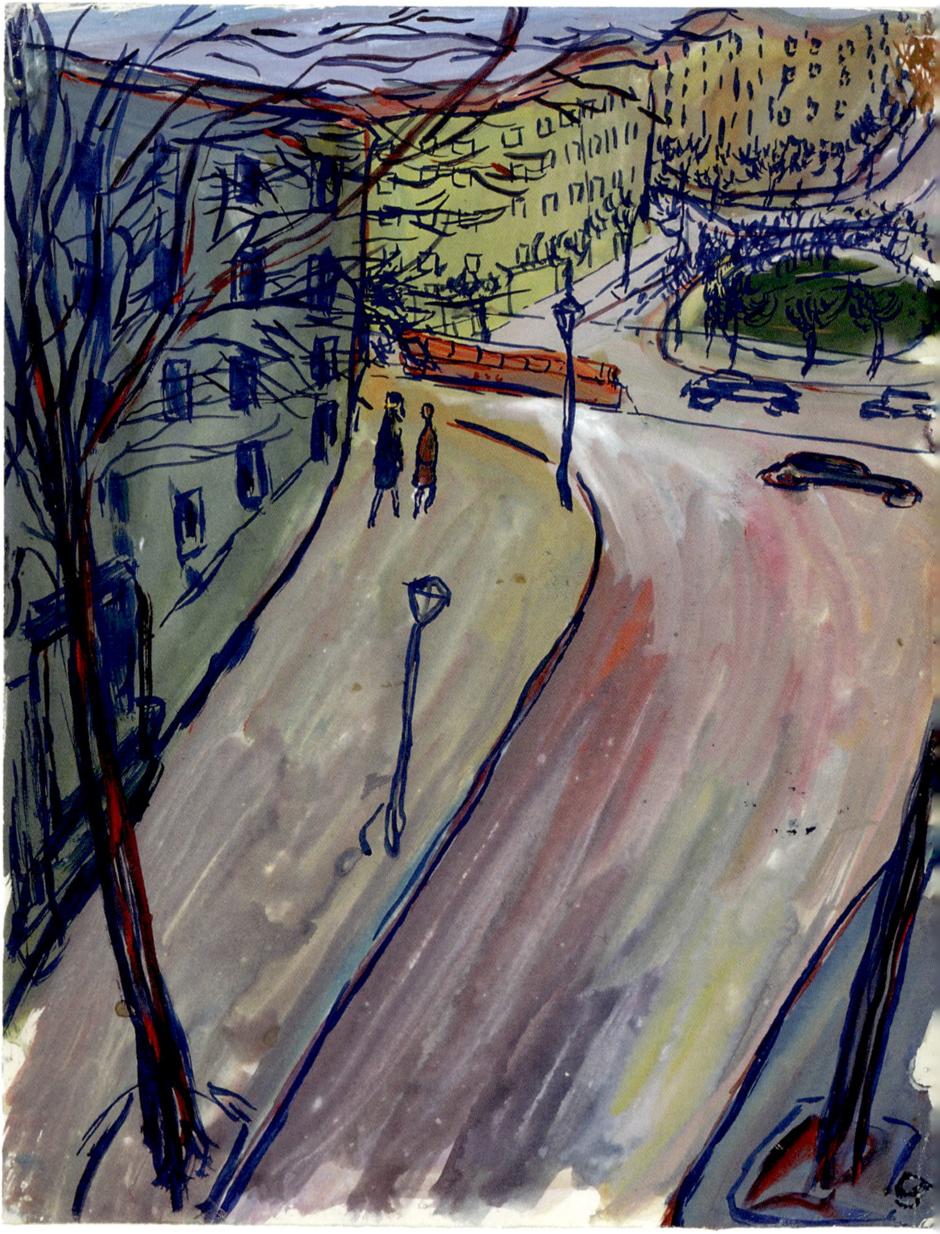

(opposite)

And they walked home together, absorbed in silent communication.

(following pages)

... noticed by anyone, for Dr Singsang, who had meanwhile been promoted to a god by his circle, was under the same pressure with his many duties as she [Paulinka] was – her glorious voice no longer possessed the same warm, expressive tone as in Professor Klingklang's day. Needless to say, she noticed nothing of this herself. She still thought of her beloved Klingklang, whom she also had promoted to a god, when she sang.

And if anyone would have come and dared to cast the least doubt about her life or her singing, she would have certainly laughed at it.

So convinced was she of her own glory.

Süßer Freund, du blickest mich verwundert an
[Sweet friend, you look at me with surprise].

END OF PRELUDE

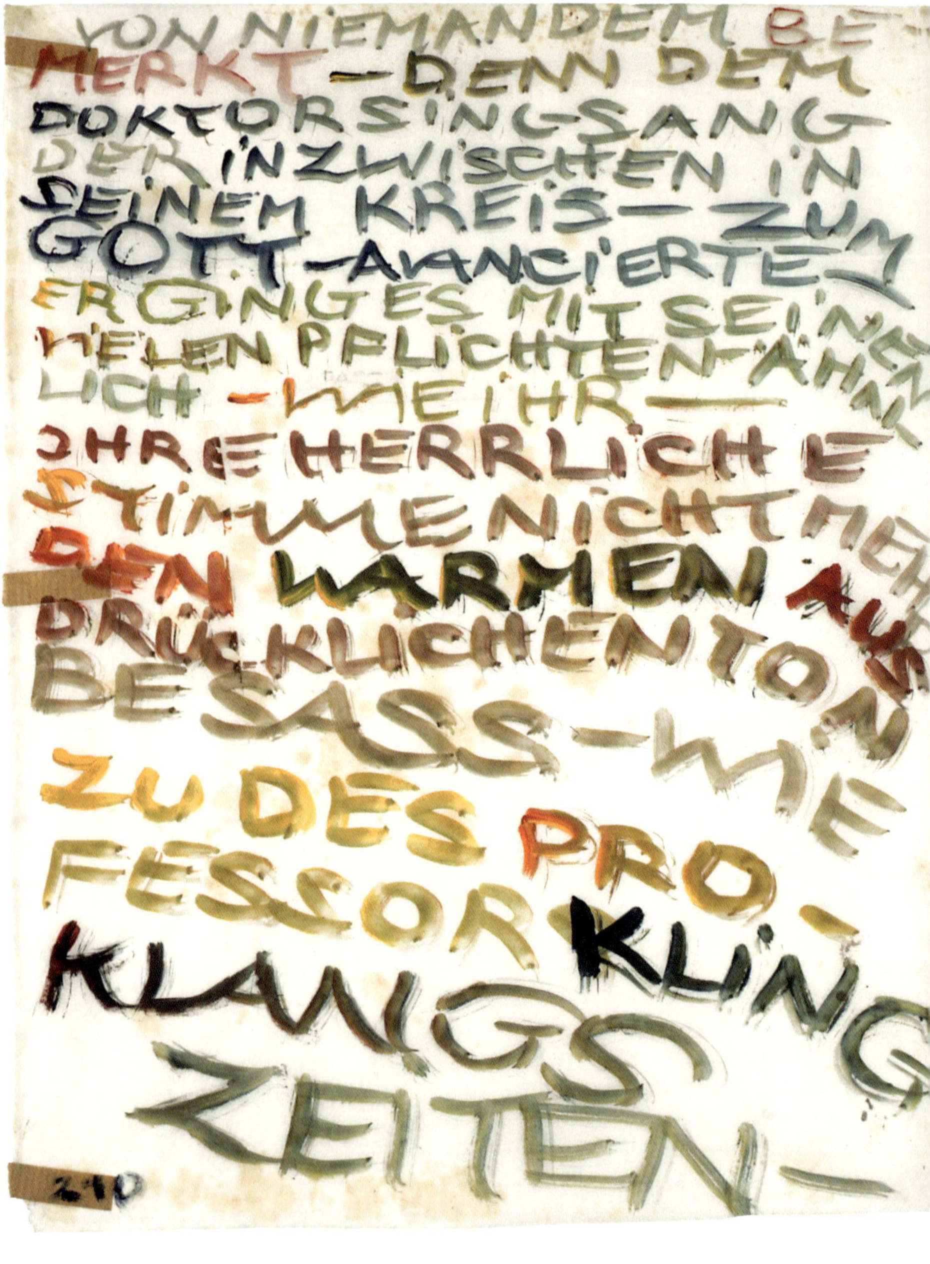
VON NIEMANDEM BE-
MERKT — DENN DEM
DOKTORSINGSANG
DER INZWISCHEN IN
SEINEM KREIS — ZUM
GOTT-AVANCIERTE
ERGINGES MIT SEINE
VIELEN PFLICHTEN ÄHN
LICH — WIE IHR —
IHREHERRLICHE
STIMMENICHT MEH
DEN WARMEN AUS
DRÜCKLICHEN TON
BESASS — WIE
ZU DES PRO-
FESSOR KLIN-
KLANGS
ZEITEN —
210

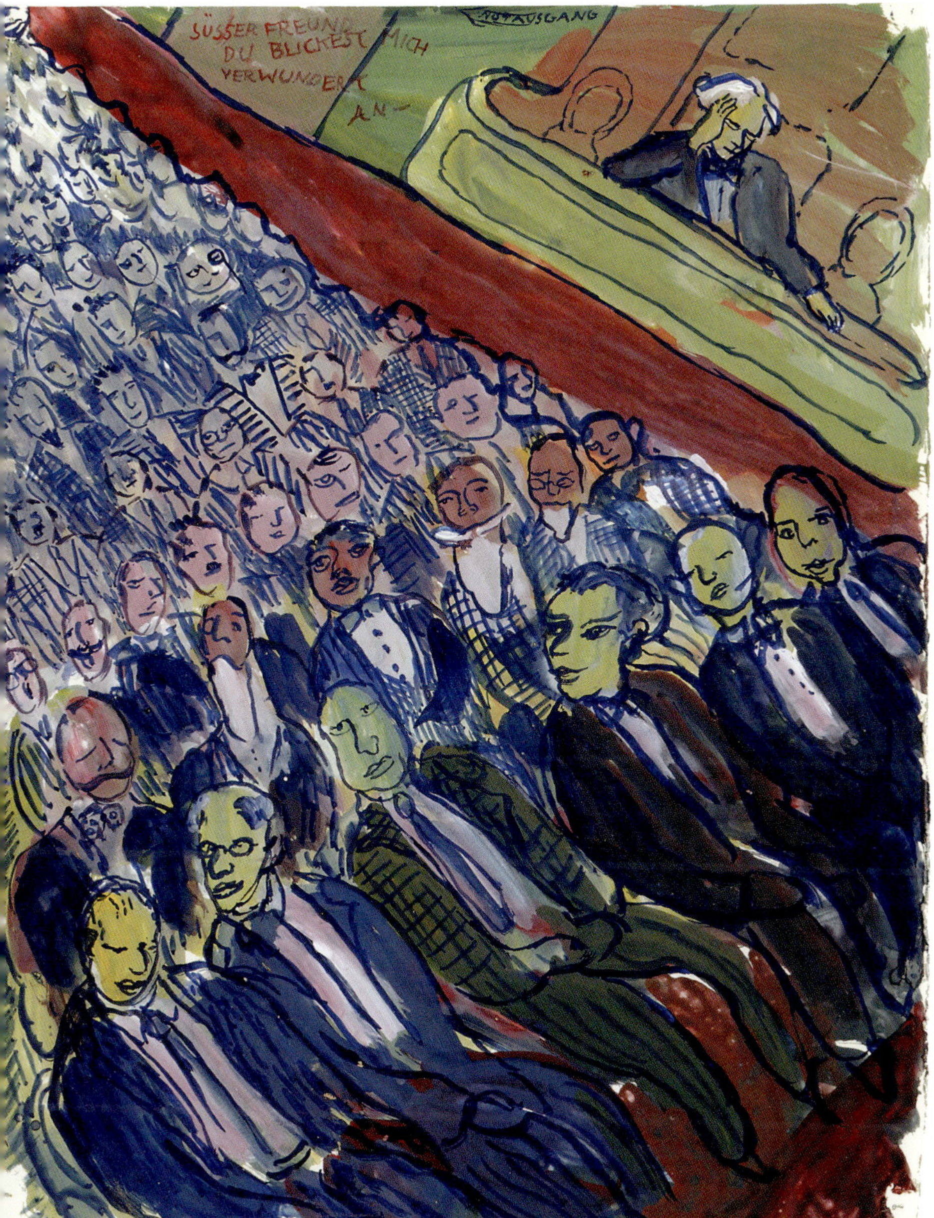
SÜSSER FREUN
DU BLICKEST MICH
VERWUNDERT
AN
NOTAUSGANG

MAIN SECTION

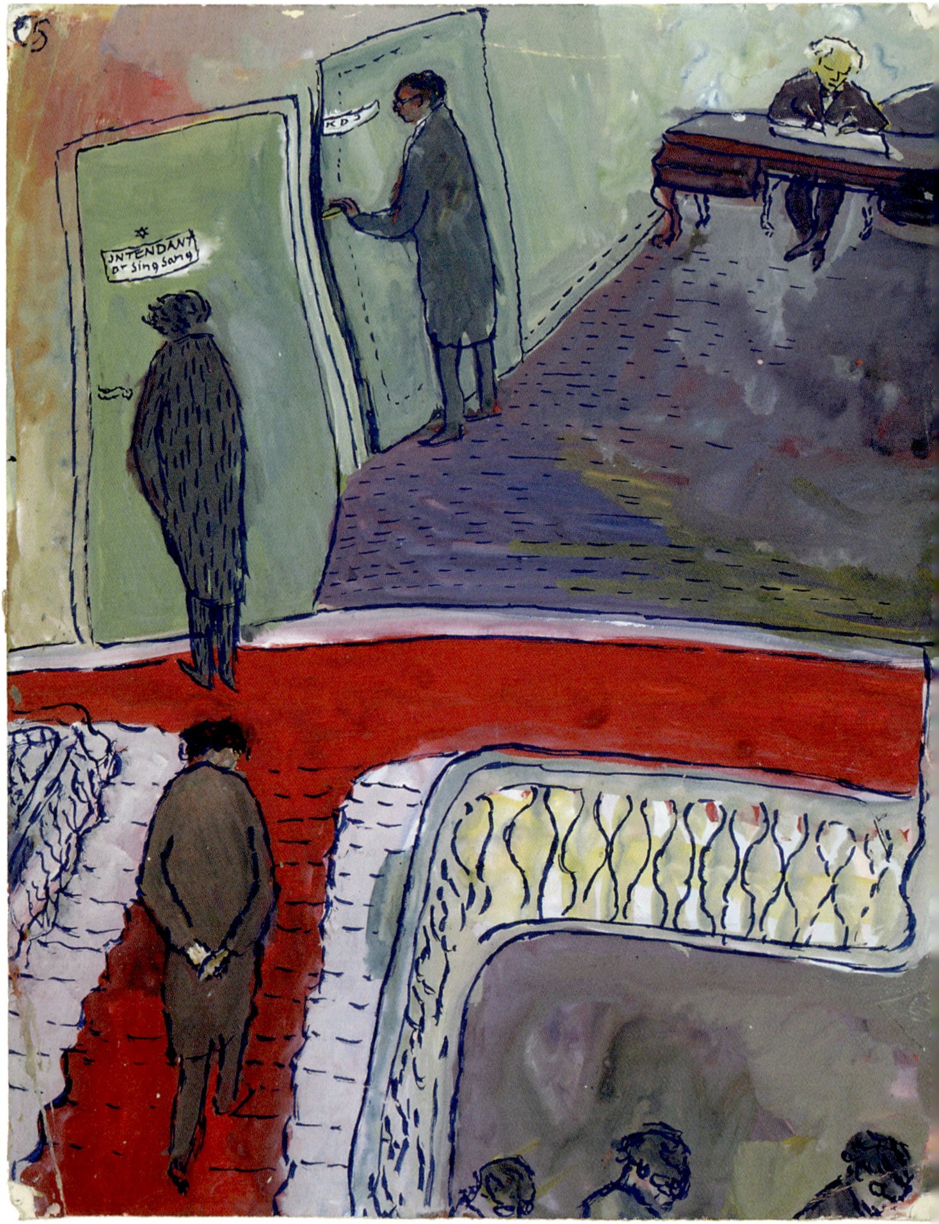

INTENDANT
Dr Singsang
KDJ

BEGINNING
OF MAIN SECTION I

Amadeus Daberlohn, prophet of song,
enters to the melody of the Toreador's Song
Courage in his heart, victorious.

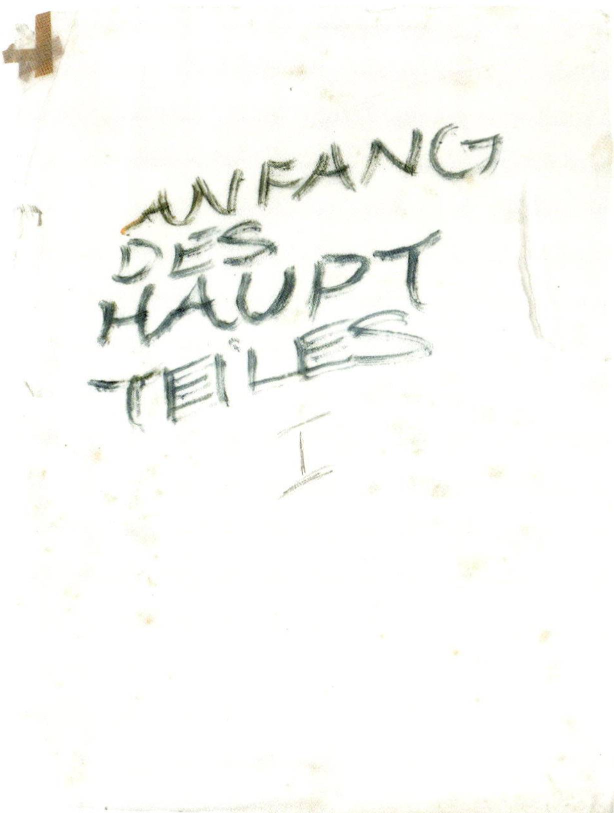

Thus he comes to Dr Singsang for, alas,
he lacks permission to teach, and Singsang
is authorised to give it to him.

DR SINGSANG
"Have a seat."

To the melody: <u>I'm busy night and day, not time for rest or play</u>

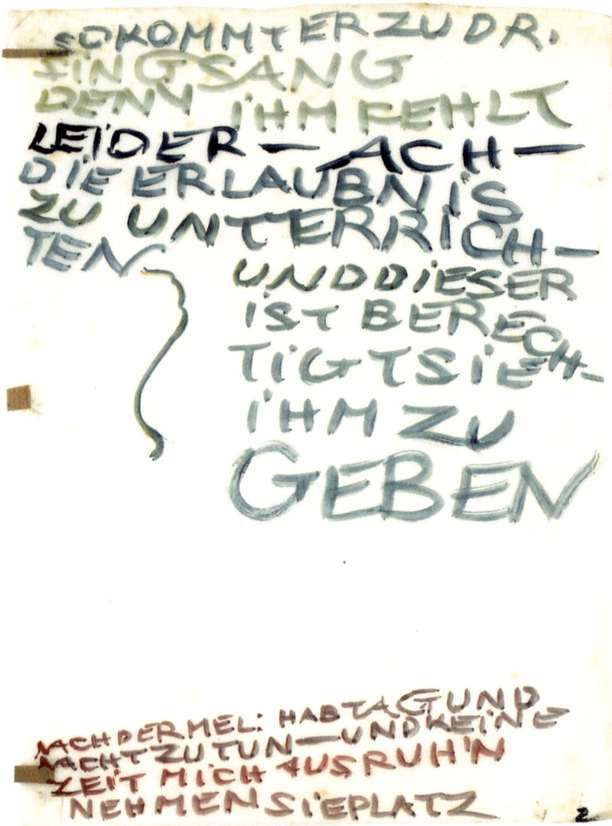

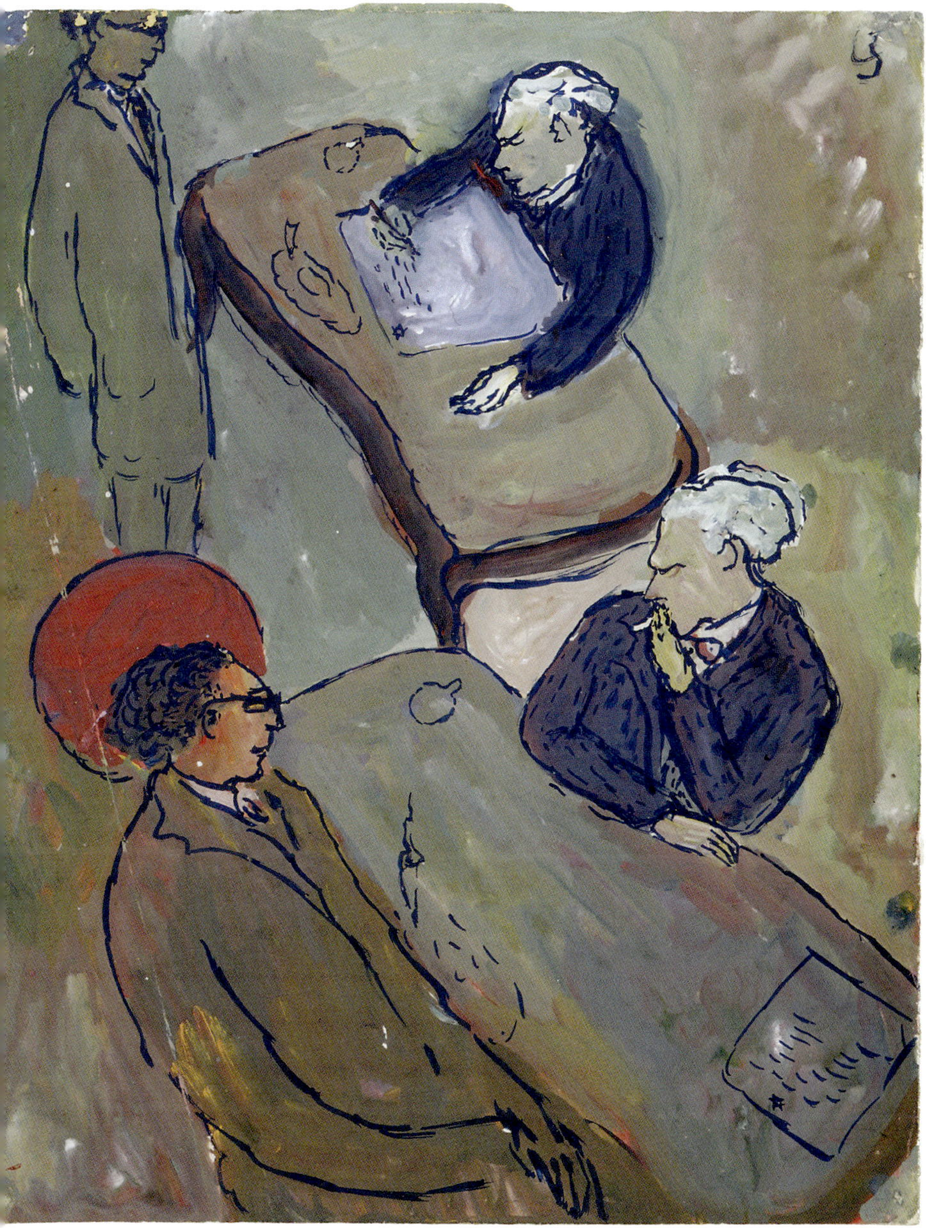

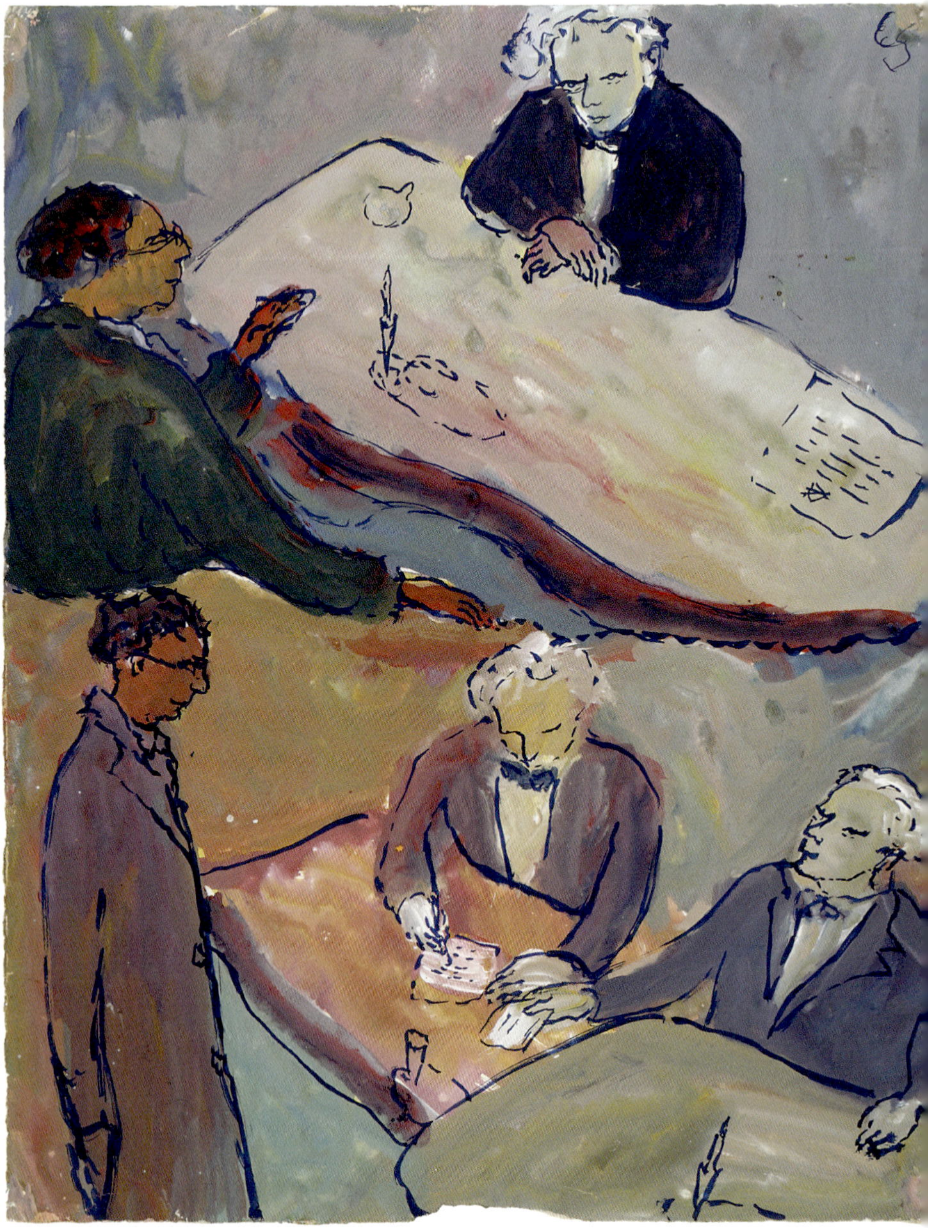

To the melody: What you are telling me sounds very interesting – however, I have no time to listen to you. Let me recommend you to a very great singer; she can test "your knowledge" and report back to me.

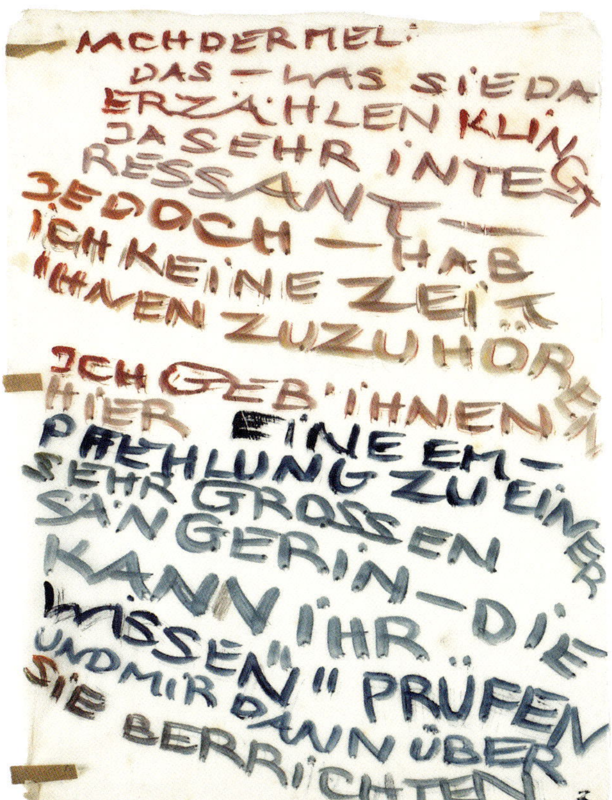

And that's how the new man enters the Bimbam-Kann home. And has a look around.

Melody: Strange, my feelings. This blue-red room always tells me a whole, whole lot.

And now our play begins!

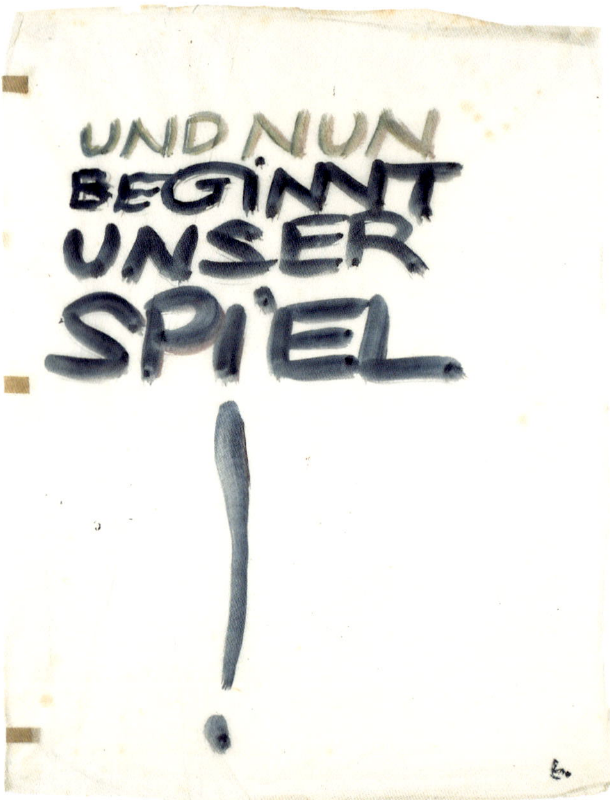

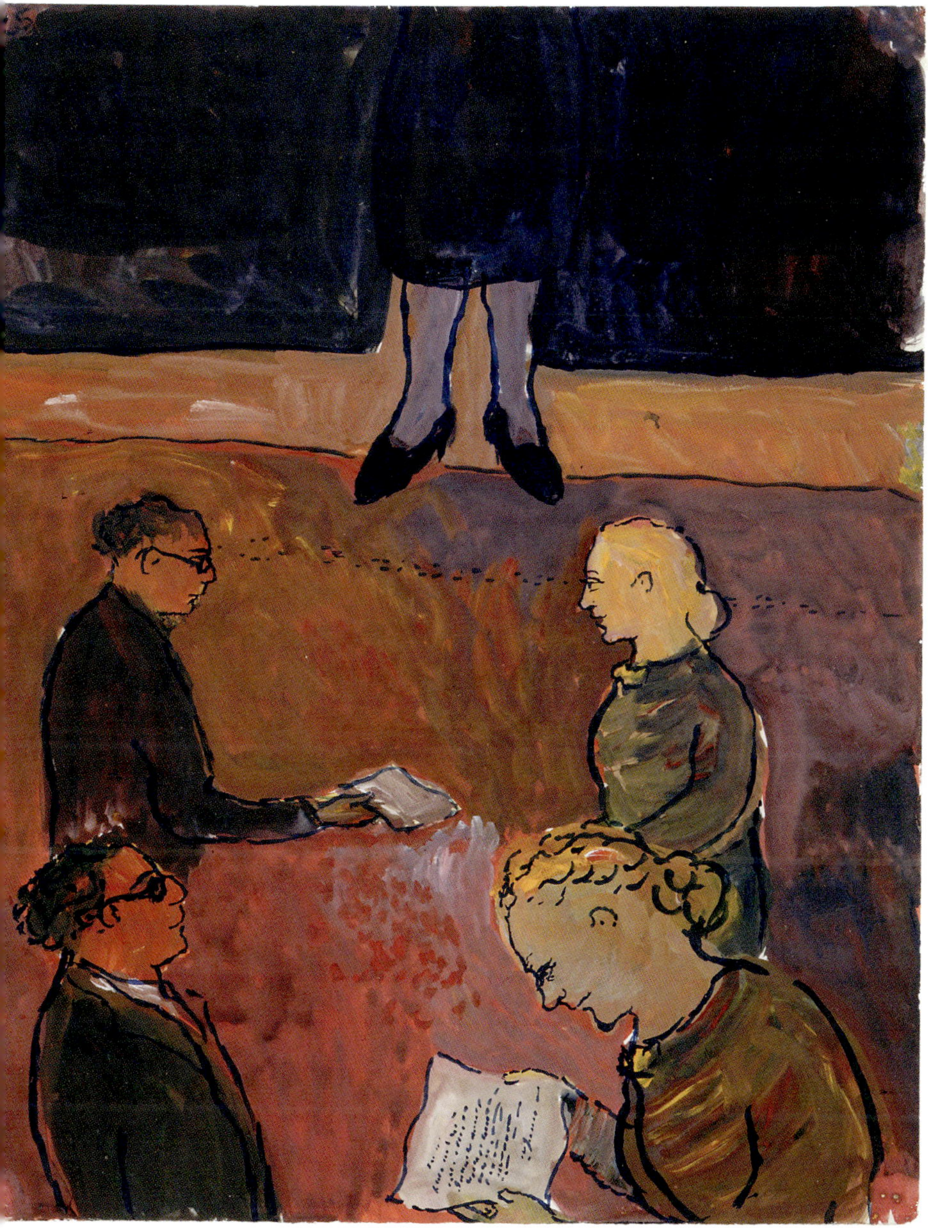

(bottom)

PAULINKA
"So we should work together."

(opposite)

DABERLOHN
"Torment myself from early morning to late
at night. If I would at least earn something.
But no one, no one, believes in me.
Only me, isn't that really ridiculous."

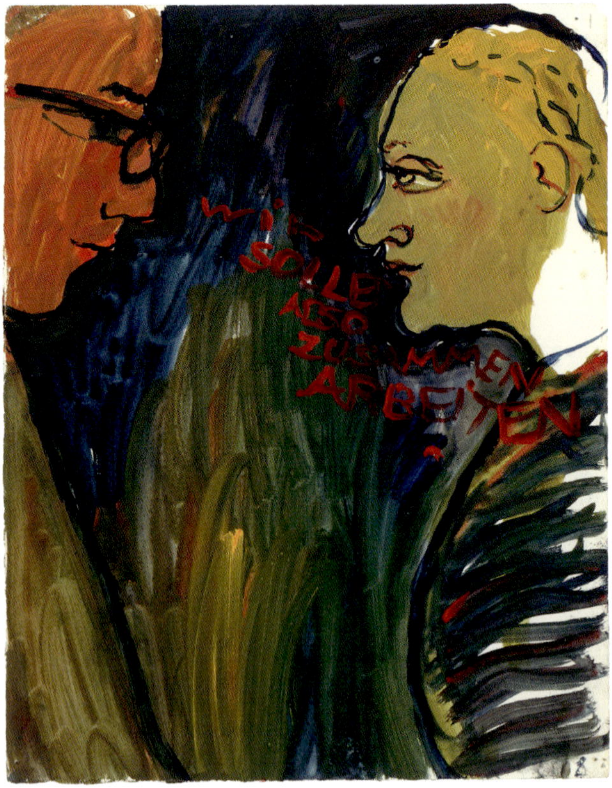

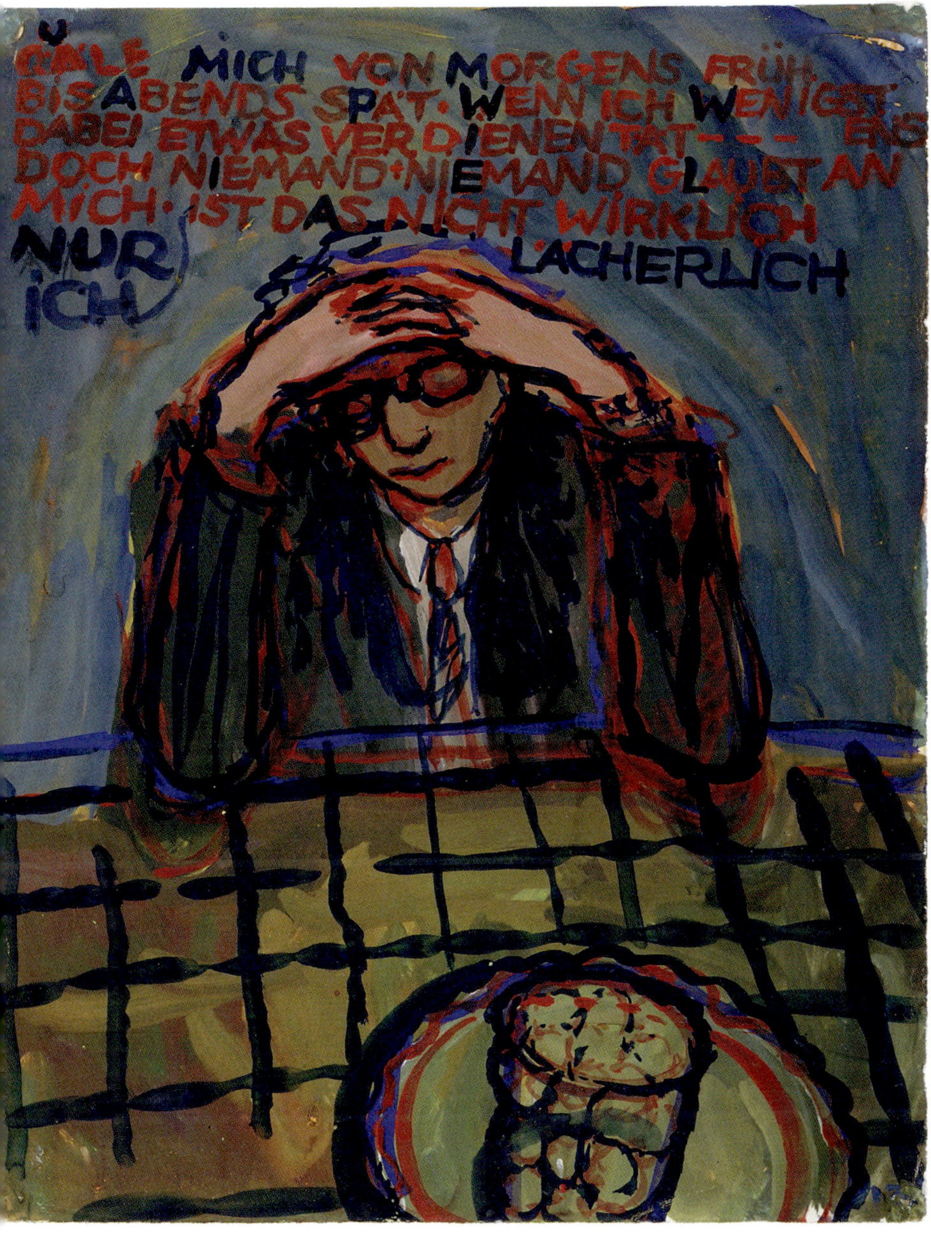
U
QÄLE MICH VON MORGENS FRÜH
BIS ABENDS SPÄT. WENN ICH WENIGST-
DABEI ETWAS VERDIENEN TÄT - - - ENS
DOCH NIEMAND + NIEMAND GLAUBT AN
MICH. IST DAS NICHT WIRKLICH
NUR ICH
LÄCHERLICH

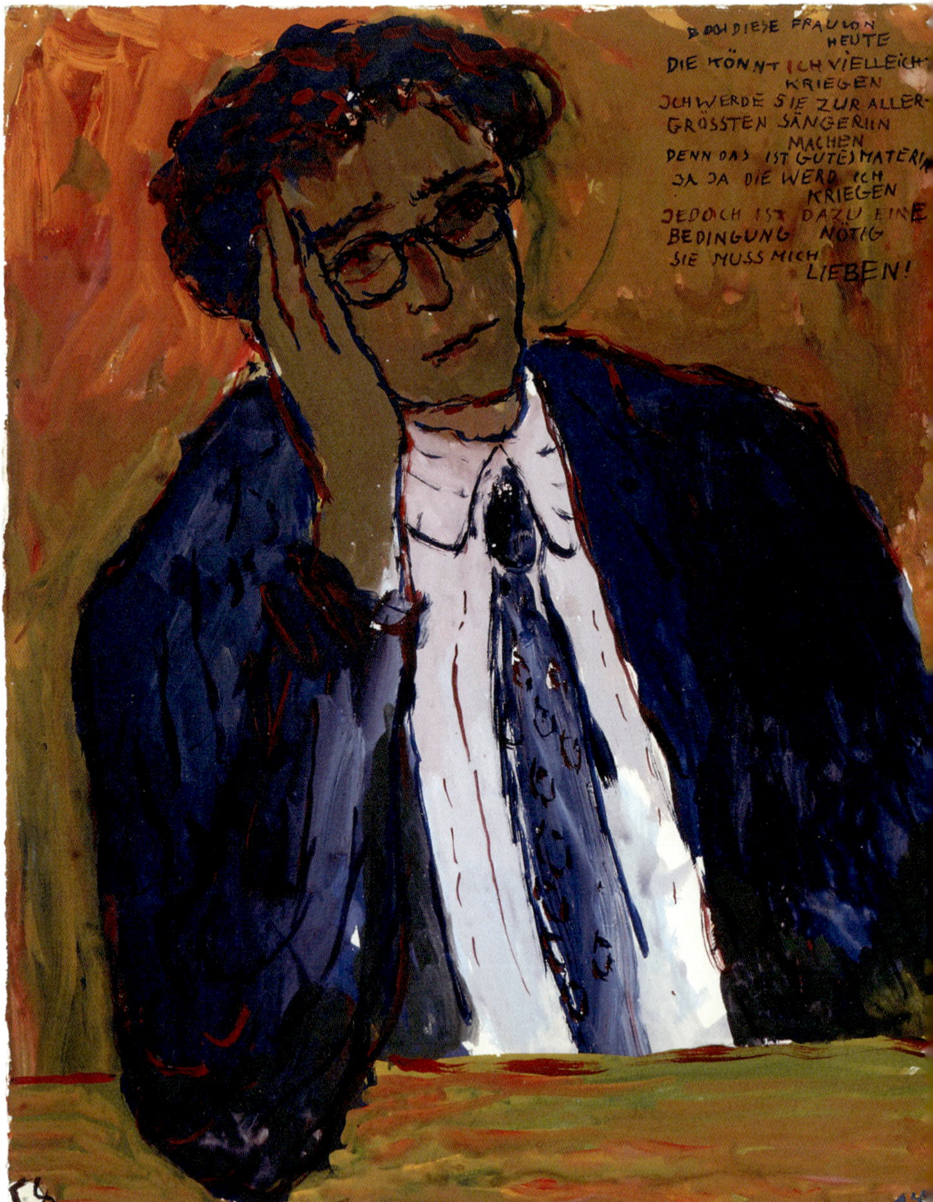
DOCH DIESE FRAU VON HEUTE
DIE KÖNNT ICH VIELLEICHT KRIEGEN
ICH WERDE SIE ZUR ALLER-GRÖSSTEN SÄNGERIN MACHEN
DENN DAS IST GUTES MATERIA
JA JA DIE WERD ICH KRIEGEN
JEDOCH IST DAZU EINE BEDINGUNG NÖTIG
SIE MUSS MICH LIEBEN!

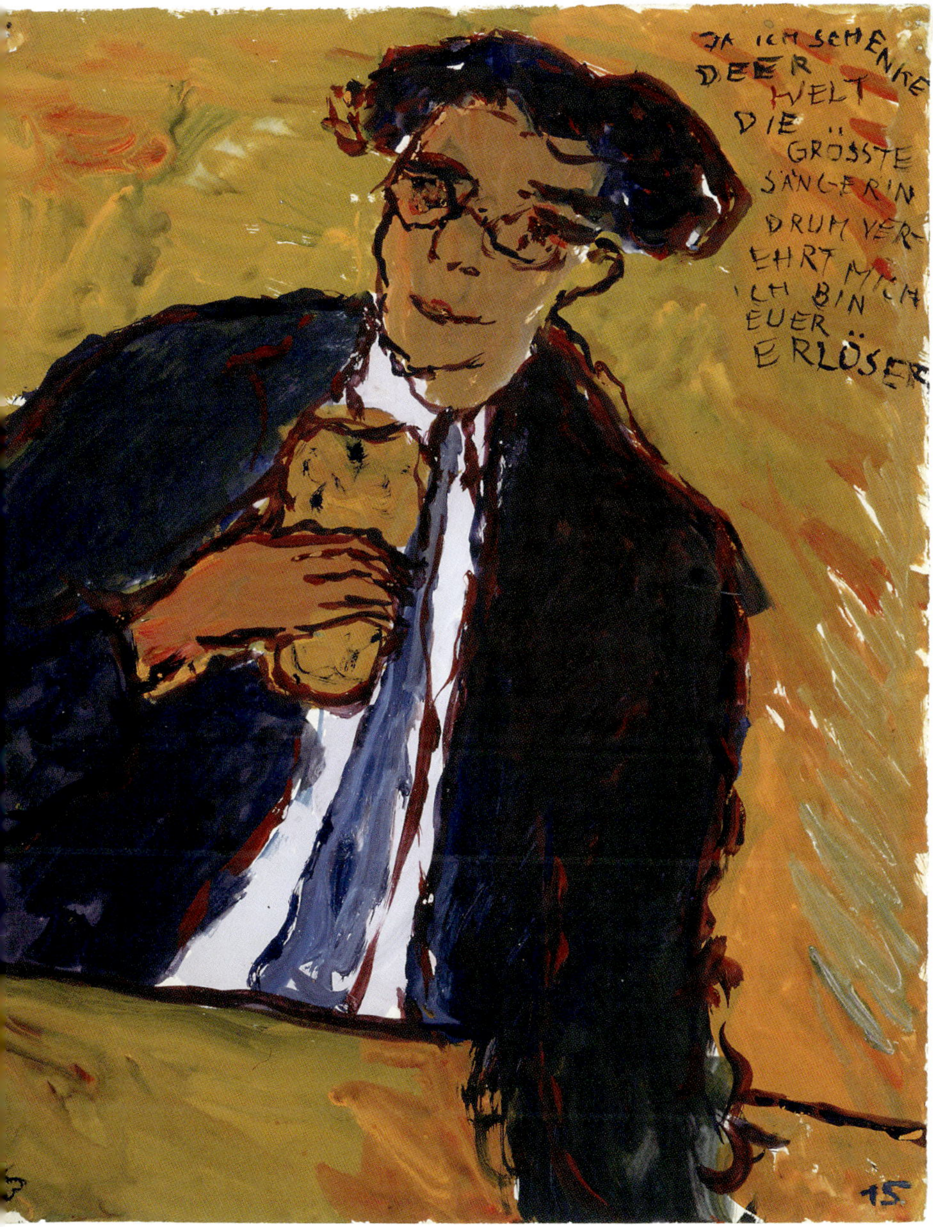
JA ICH SCHENKE
DEER
WELT
DIE
GRÖSSTE
SÄNGERIN
DRUM VER-
EHRT MICH
ICH BIN
EUER
ERLÖSER
15

(page 290)

"But this woman from today, maybe I could get her.
I will make her the greatest of all singers, since
this is good material. Yes, yes, I'll get her. But for
this there's one condition – she must love me!"

(page 291)

"Yes, I shall give to the world its greatest singer.
So you must revere me – I am your redeemer!"

(opposite)

"Now I must go. It is already past midnight.
But it stays that way. My singer will be made.
It is no magic, I will get her, she must love me."

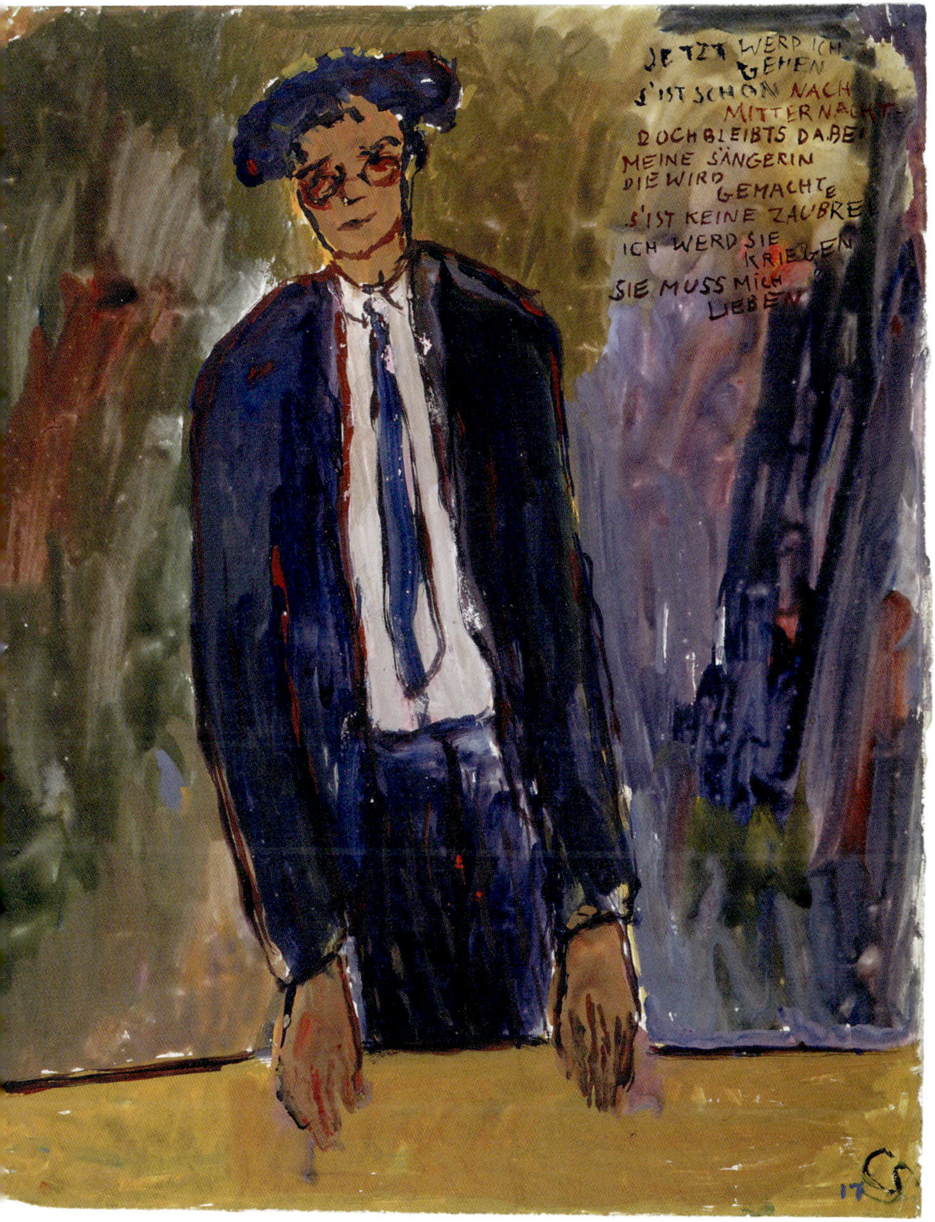
JETZT WERD ICH GEHEN
S'IST SCHON NACH MITTERNACHT
DOCHBLEIBTS DABEI
MEINE SÄNGERIN
DIE WIRD GEMACHTE
S'IST KEINE ZAUBRE
ICH WERD SIE KRIEGEN
SIE MUSS MICH LIEBEN

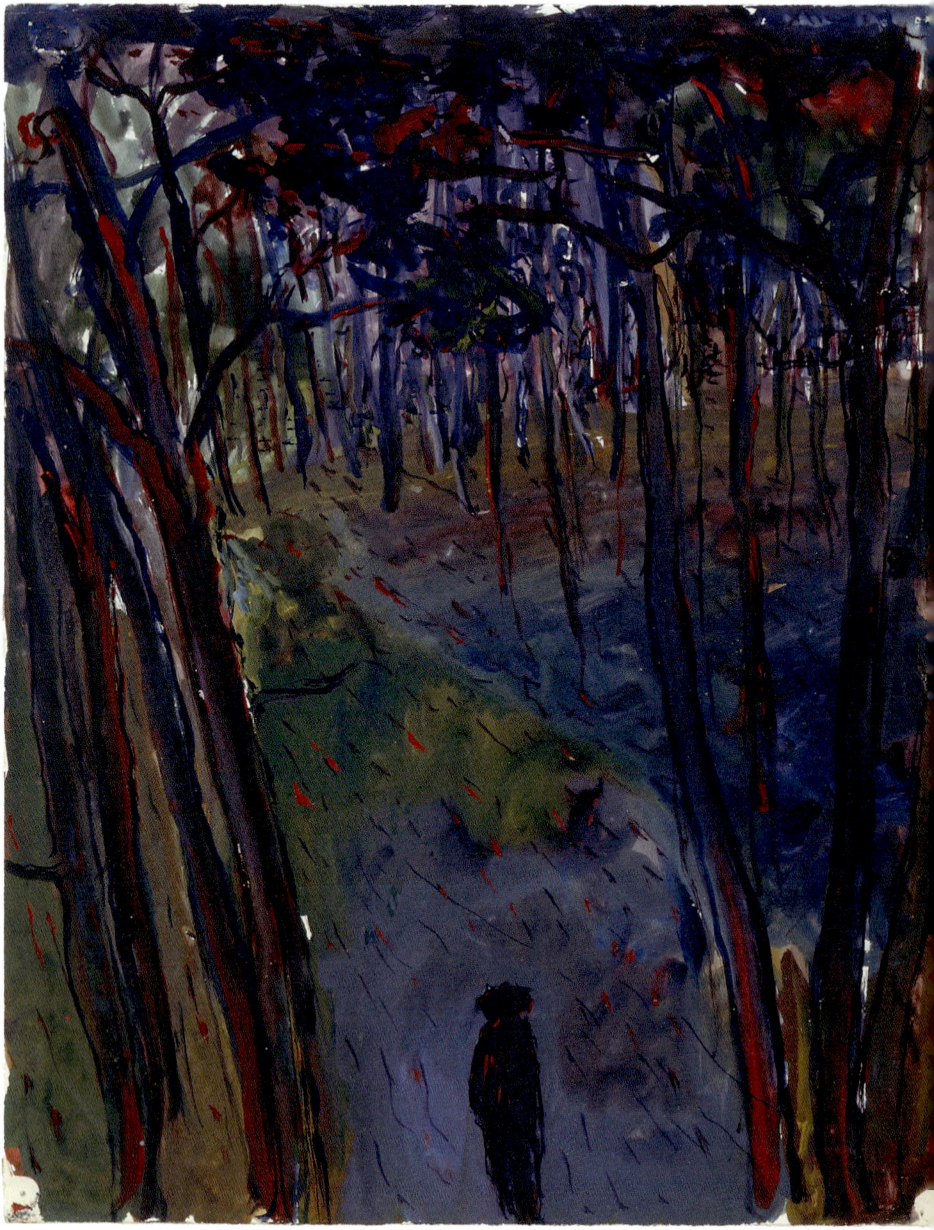

With these words
he goes home.

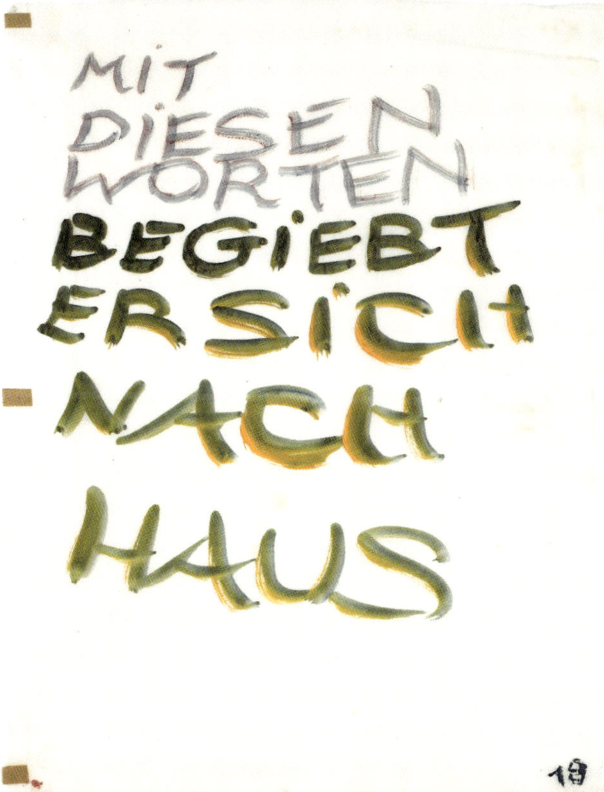

Here you see him standing, like many a woman,
at the window — so full of dreams —
so full of longing.

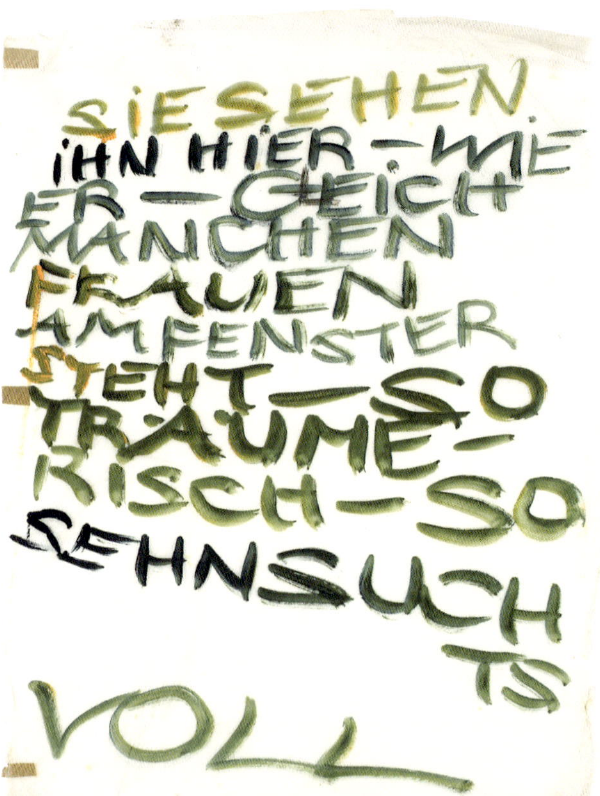

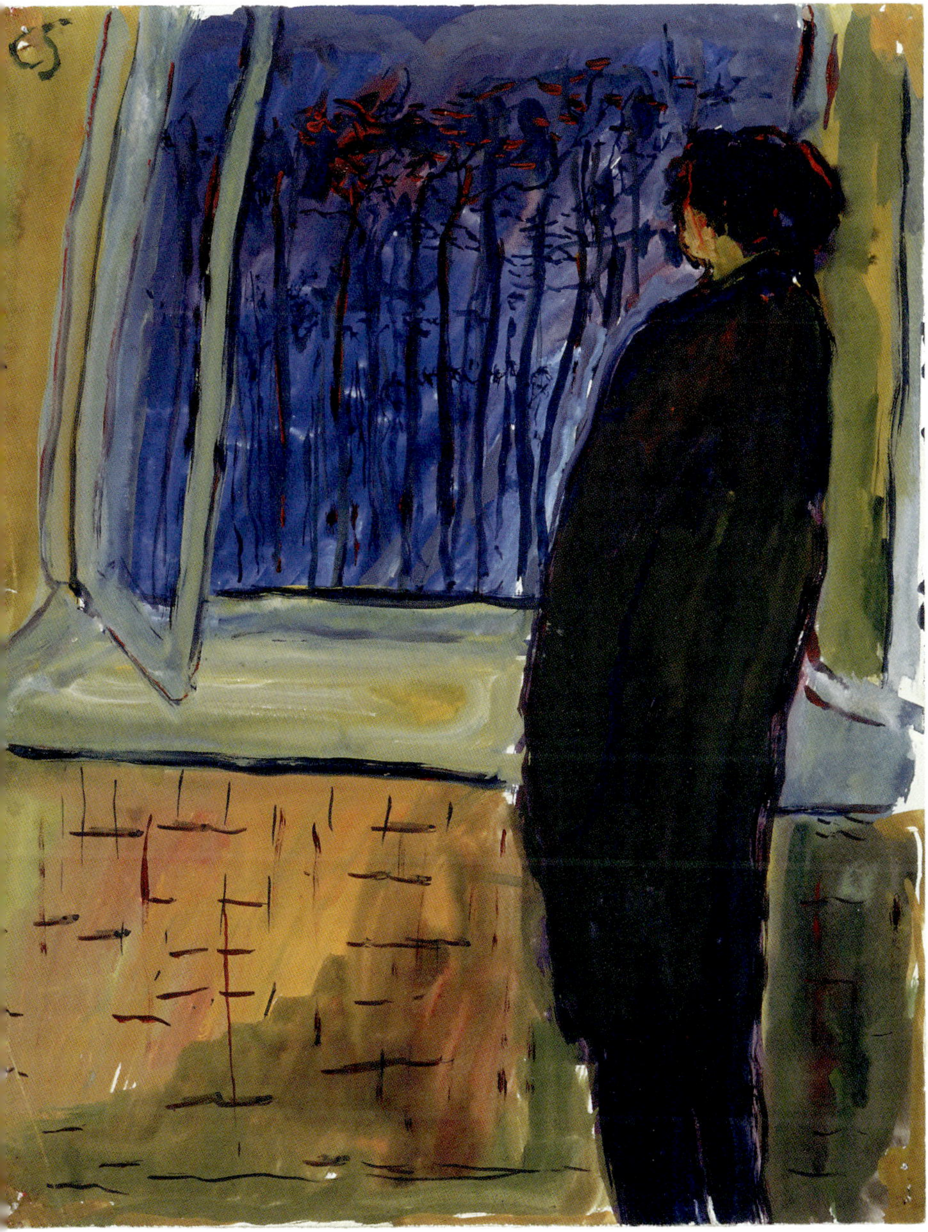

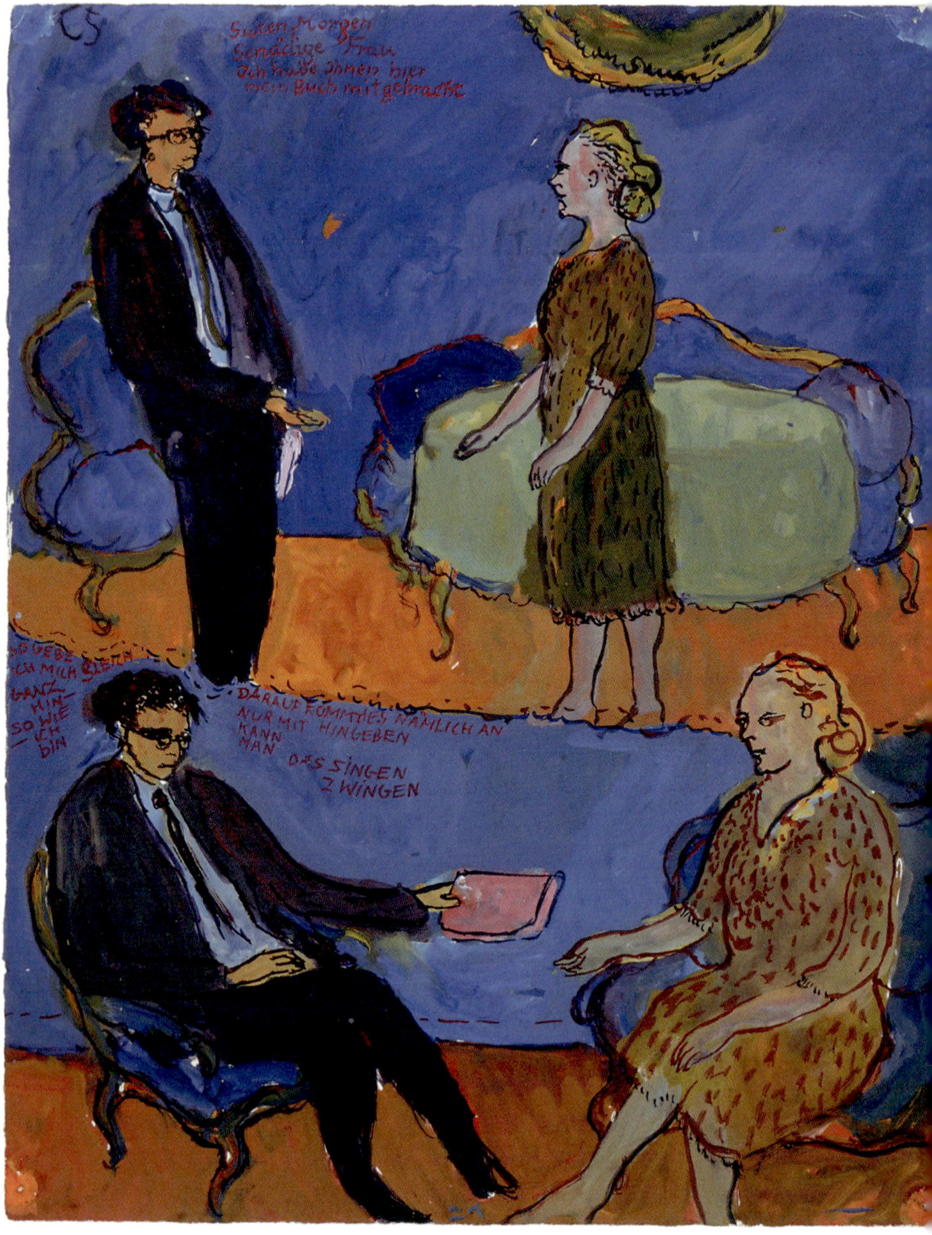
Guten Morgen
Gnädige Frau
Ich habe Ihnen hier
mein Buch mitgebracht
SO GEBE ICH MICH
GANZ HIN- SO WIE ICH BIN
DARAUF KOMMT ES NÄMLICH AN
NUR MIT HINGEBEN
KANN MAN DAS SINGEN
Z WINGEN

(opposite)

DABERLOHN
"Good morning, madam. I've brought you my book." ("So I throw myself at her feet, just as I am. For that's what it's about. Only by surrendering can one manage to sing.")

(right)

"Many of my theories will surprise you. However, I'm only going back to nature.

Take a baby. It cries because it is hungry, and many a singer would envy it for the power and endurance of its voice.

When you were a little girl, in Klingklang's times, you sang much more beautifully.
Now you have a husband whom, although you cherish him, you do not love. You have friends who admire you, but singing you only do for the public."

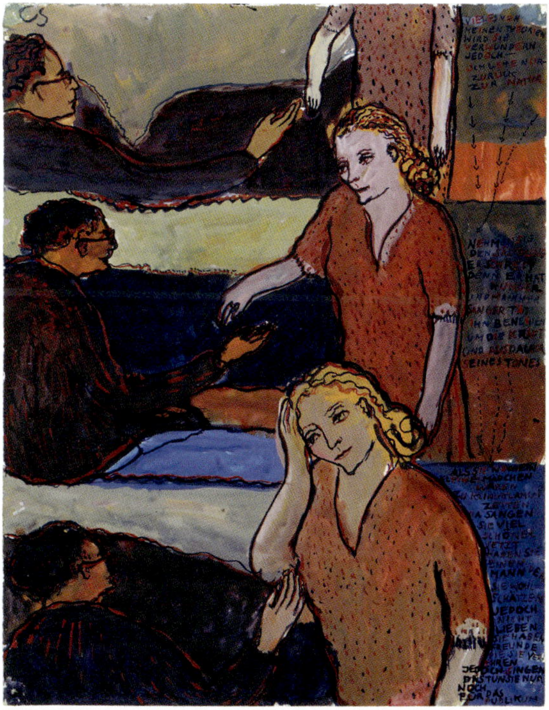

(bottom)

"Do you know these words of Nietzsche, 'Learn to sing, Oh my soul'?

What does that mean if not the urge to freedom?

And for me freedom is synonymous with singing.

But that's enough of theories."

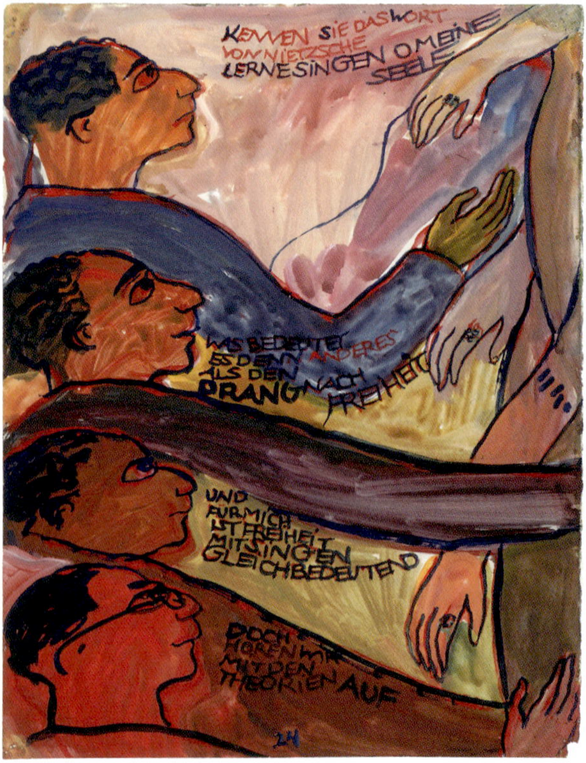

(opposite)

"Goodbye then, early tomorrow, at ten, at ten

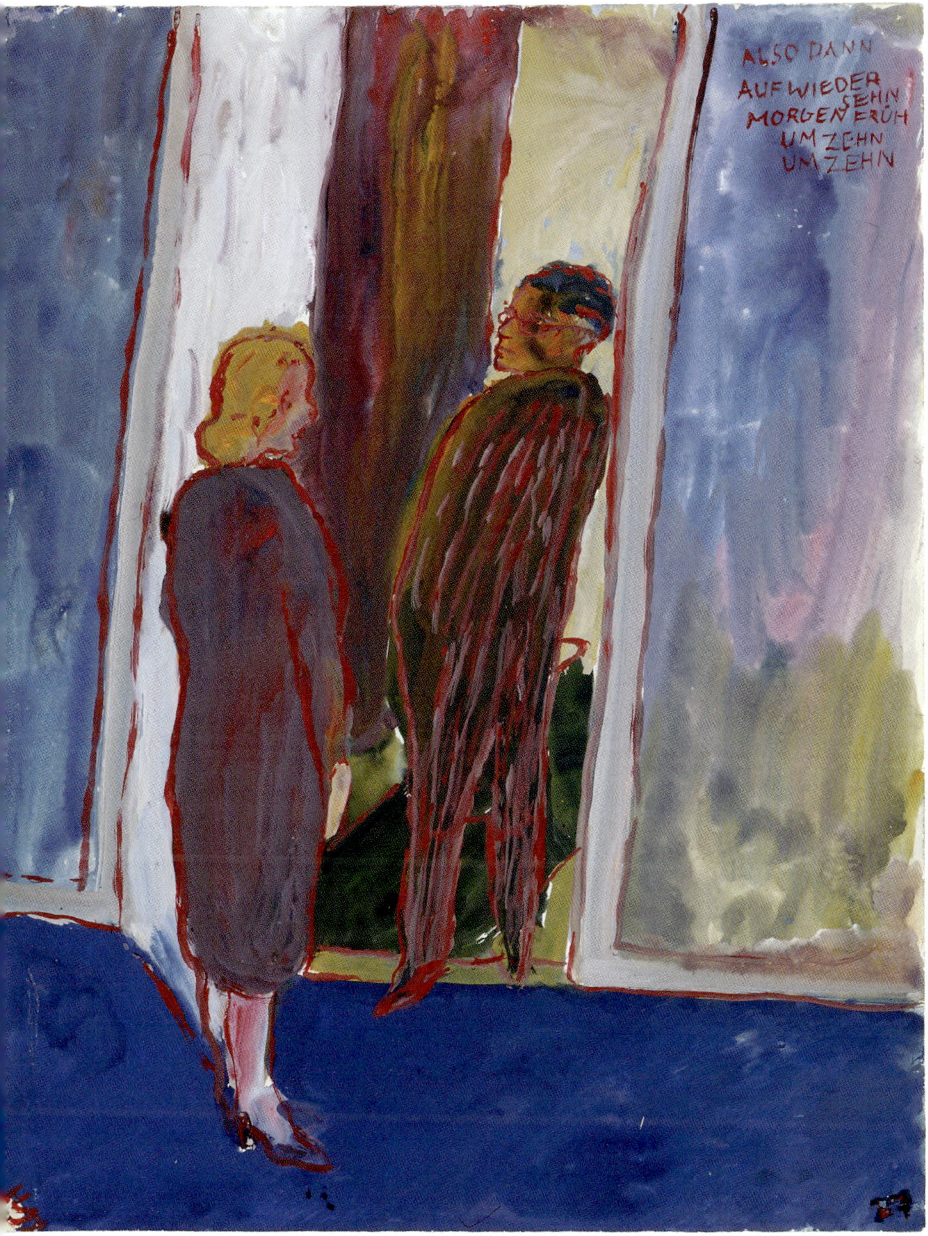
ALSO DANN
AUF WIEDER SEHN
MORGEN FRÜH
UM ZEHN
UM ZEHN

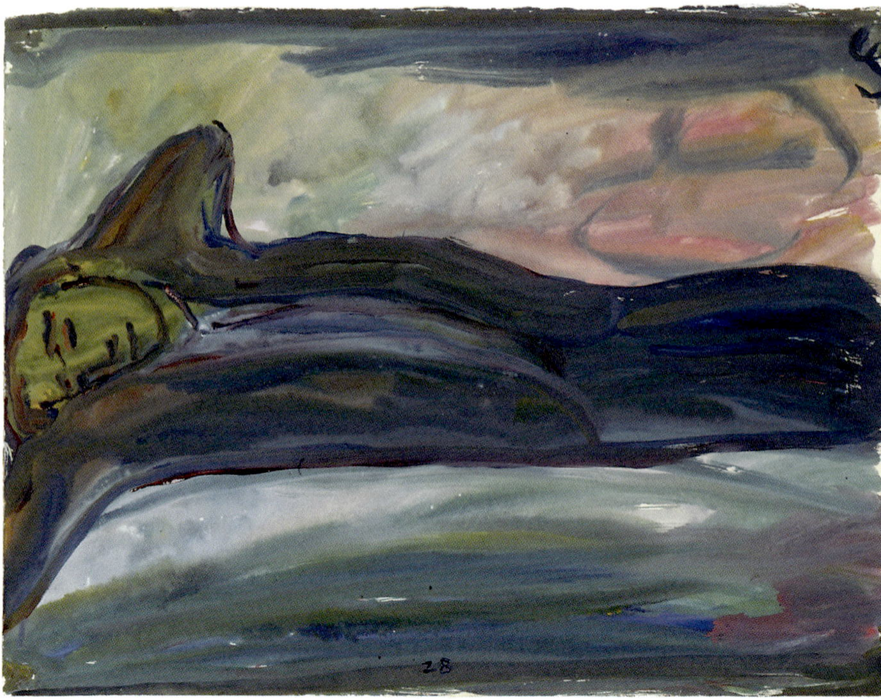

(top)

He falls asleep, and sees in his dream how Paulinka sings: Bist du bei mir, geh ich mit Freuden zum Sterben und zu meiner Ruh [When thou art near, I go with joy to my death and to my rest].

(opposite)

NEXT MORNING

PAULINKA
"Your book has shaken me profoundly. Have you really experienced all that???"

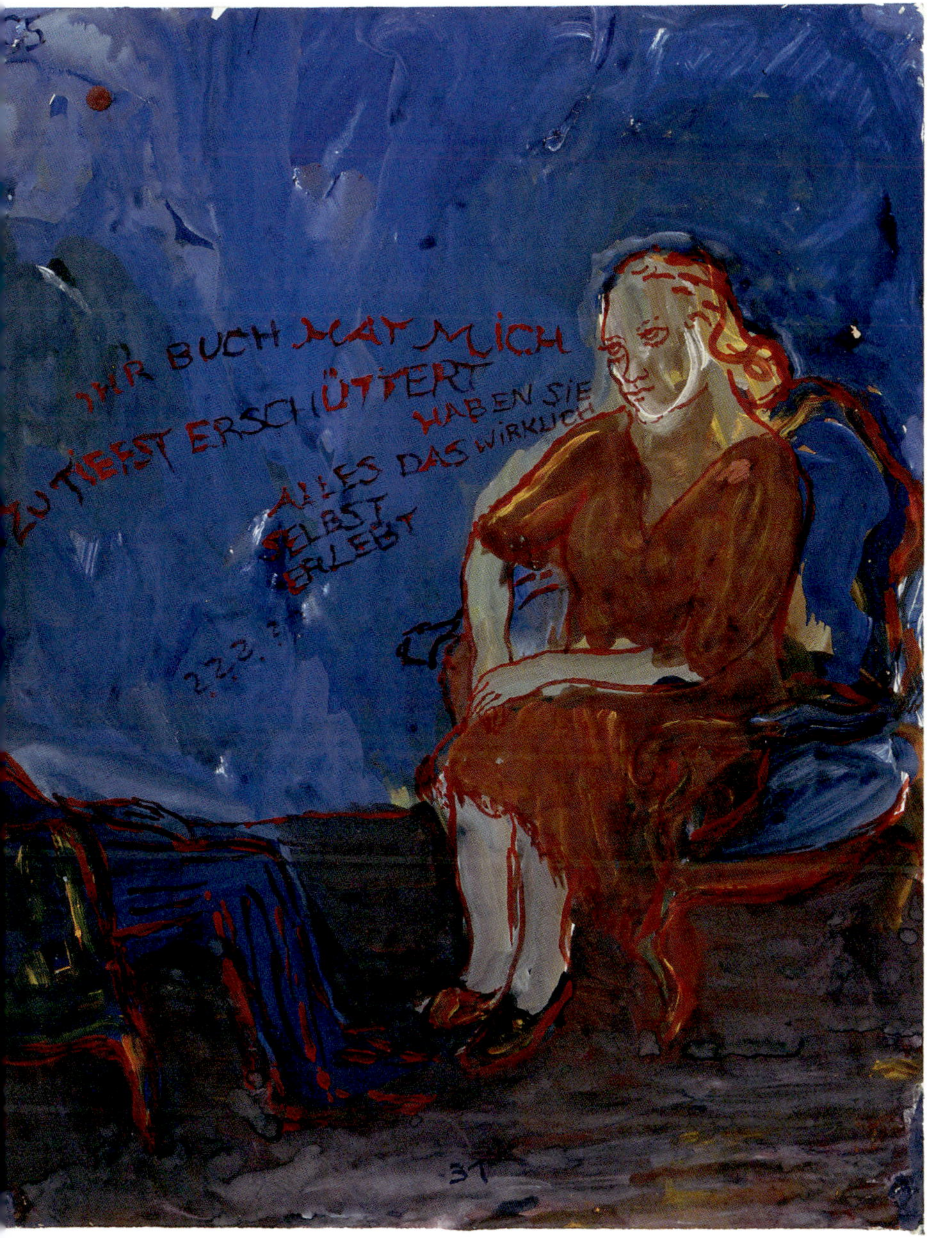
35
IHR BUCH HAT MICH
ZU TIEFST ERSCHÜTTERT
HABEN SIE
ALLES DAS WIRKLICH
SELBST
ERLEBT
2.2.3.
37

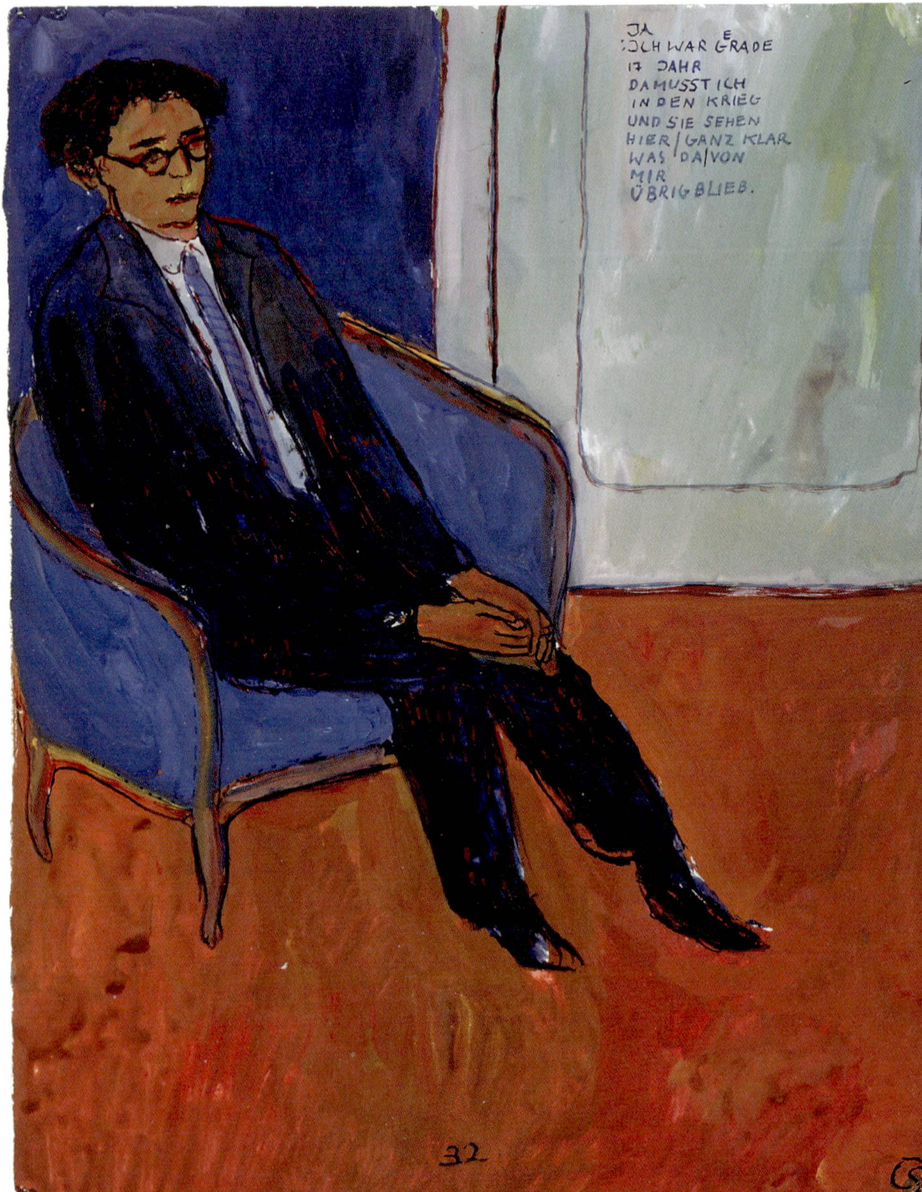
JA
ICH WAR GERADE
17 JAHR
DAMUSST ICH
IN DEN KRIEG
UND SIE SEHEN
HIER / GANZ KLAR
WAS DA/VON
MIR
ÜBRIGBLIEB.
32

(opposite)

DABERLOHN
"Yes, I was barely 17 when I had to go to war,
and here you clearly see what's left of me."

(bottom)

"For a long time I was buried. And I woke up among corpses. And when I then miraculously came home again, and when I then... I had partially lost my memory."

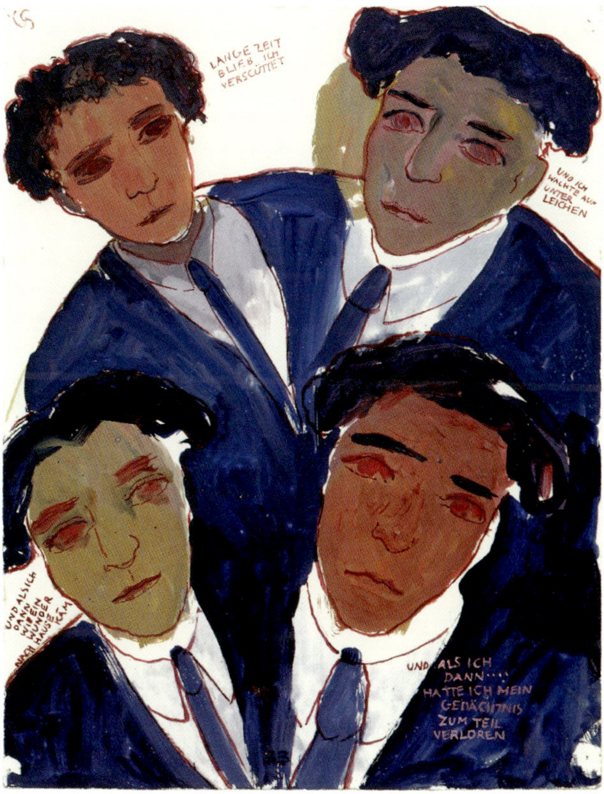

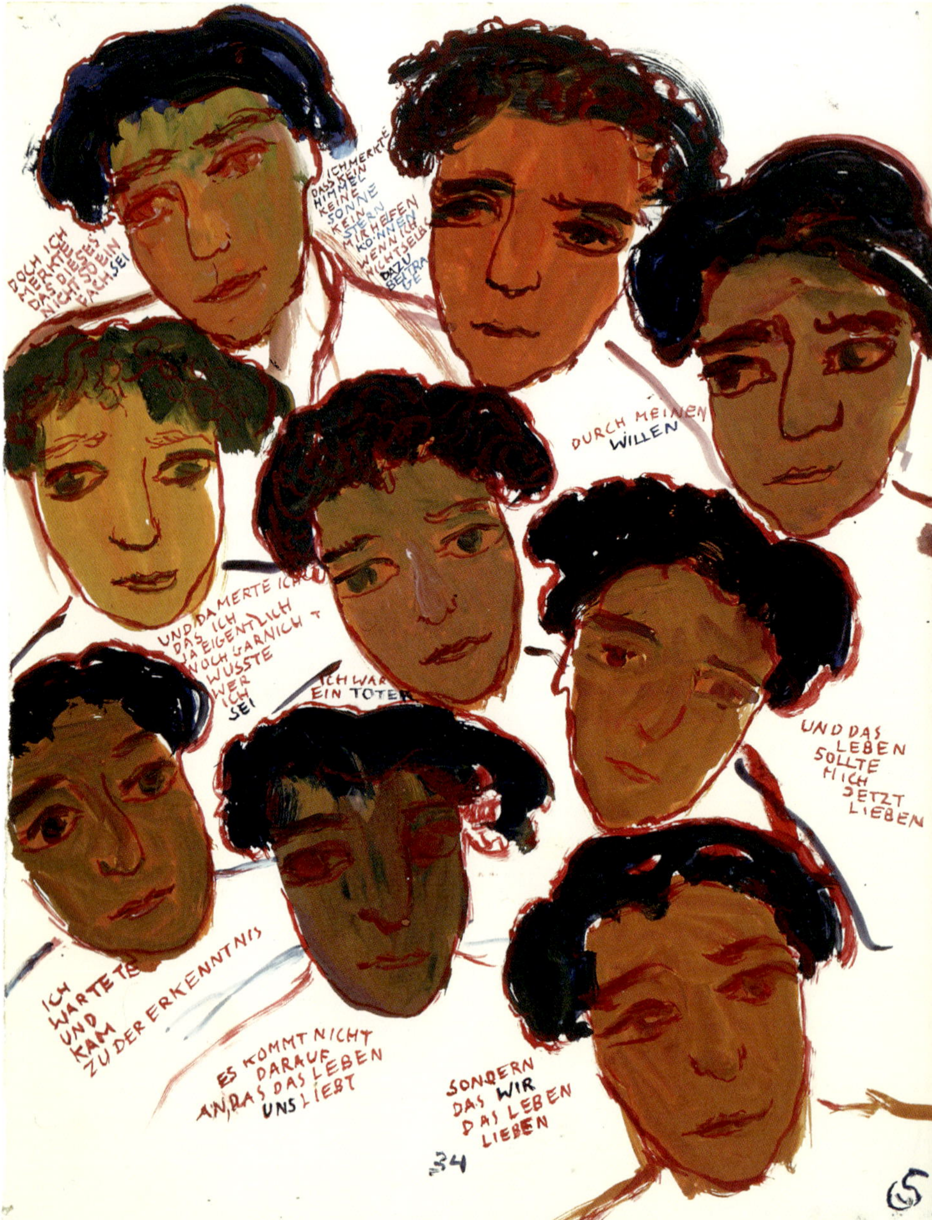
DOCH ICH MERKTE DAS DIESES NICHT SO EINFACH SEI
ICH MERKTE DASS KEIN HIMMEL KEINE SONNE KEIN STERN MIR HELFEN KÖNNEN WENN ICH NICHTSELBS DAZU BEITRAGE
DURCH MEINEN WILLEN
UND DA MERKTE ICH DAS ICH DA EIGENTLICH NOCH GARNICH WUSSTE WER ICH SEI
ICH WAR EIN TOTER
UND DAS LEBEN SOLLTE MICH JETZT LIEBEN
ICH WARTETE UND KAM ZU DER ERKENNTNIS
ES KOMMT NICHT DARAUF AN, DAS DAS LEBEN UNS LIEBT
SONDERN DAS WIR DAS LEBEN LIEBEN
34
65

(opposite)

“But then I realised that this was not so easy.
I realised that no heaven, no sun, no star could
help me if I did not contribute through my own will.

And then I realised that actually I still had no idea
who I was.

I was a corpse. And life was supposed to love me now.

I waited and came to the realisation: it does not
matter whether life loves us, but that we love life.”

(page 308)

“And I was more of a dead person than living one, and
I kept hearing the cries for help of a comrade whom
I could have saved. But I did not do it because I knew
it would cost me my life.

Then when my memory was restored I often experienced
terrible seizures. As I sometimes still do.

I was sent to a neurologist. And he sent me to Italy.
So that for me too, so that for me too, is the sky blue
again.”

(page 309)

“And I began to study myself. And became aware that
there are two sides to everything: day and night, sun
and shadow, death and life.

One of those sides, death, I was now familiar with,
because, you see, I had risen from the dead. There
remained only for me that I become familiar with the
other side, with life, to be this perfect creature...
whom you see before you.”

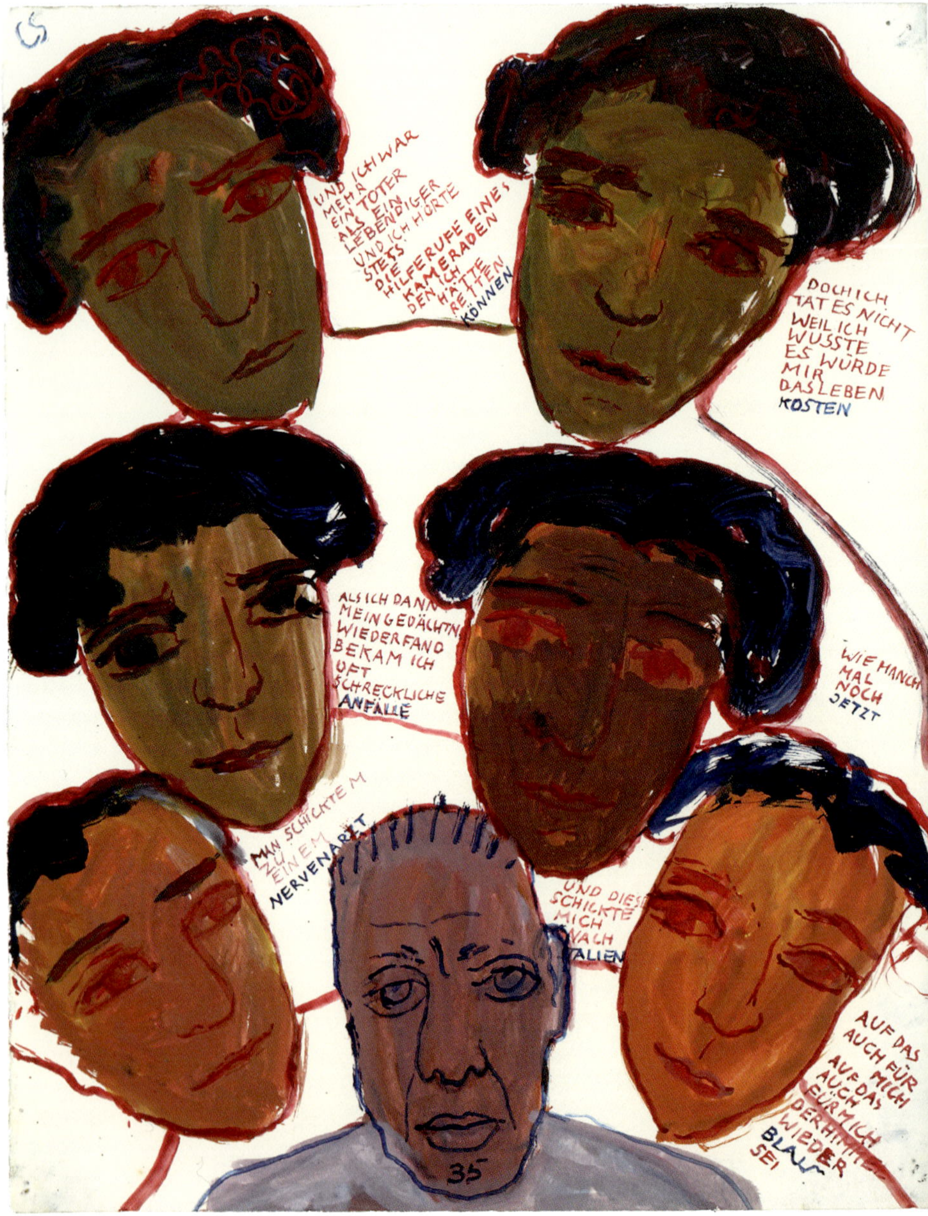
CS
UND ICH WAR MEHR EIN TOTER ALS EIN LEBENDIGER UND ICH HÖRTE STETS DIE HILFERUFE EINES KAMERADEN DEN ICH HÄTTE RETTEN KÖNNEN
DOCH ICH TAT ES NICHT WEIL ICH WUSSTE ES WÜRDE MIR DAS LEBEN KOSTEN
ALS ICH DANN MEIN GEDÄCHTNIS WIEDERFAND BEKAM ICH OFT SCHRECKLICHE ANFÄLLE
WIE MANCHMAL NOCH JETZT
MAN SCHICKTE MICH ZU EINEM NERVENARZT
UND DIESER SCHICKTE MICH NACH ITALIEN
AUF DAS AUCH FÜR MICH AUF DAS AUCH FÜR MICH DER HIMM WIEDER BLAU SEI
35

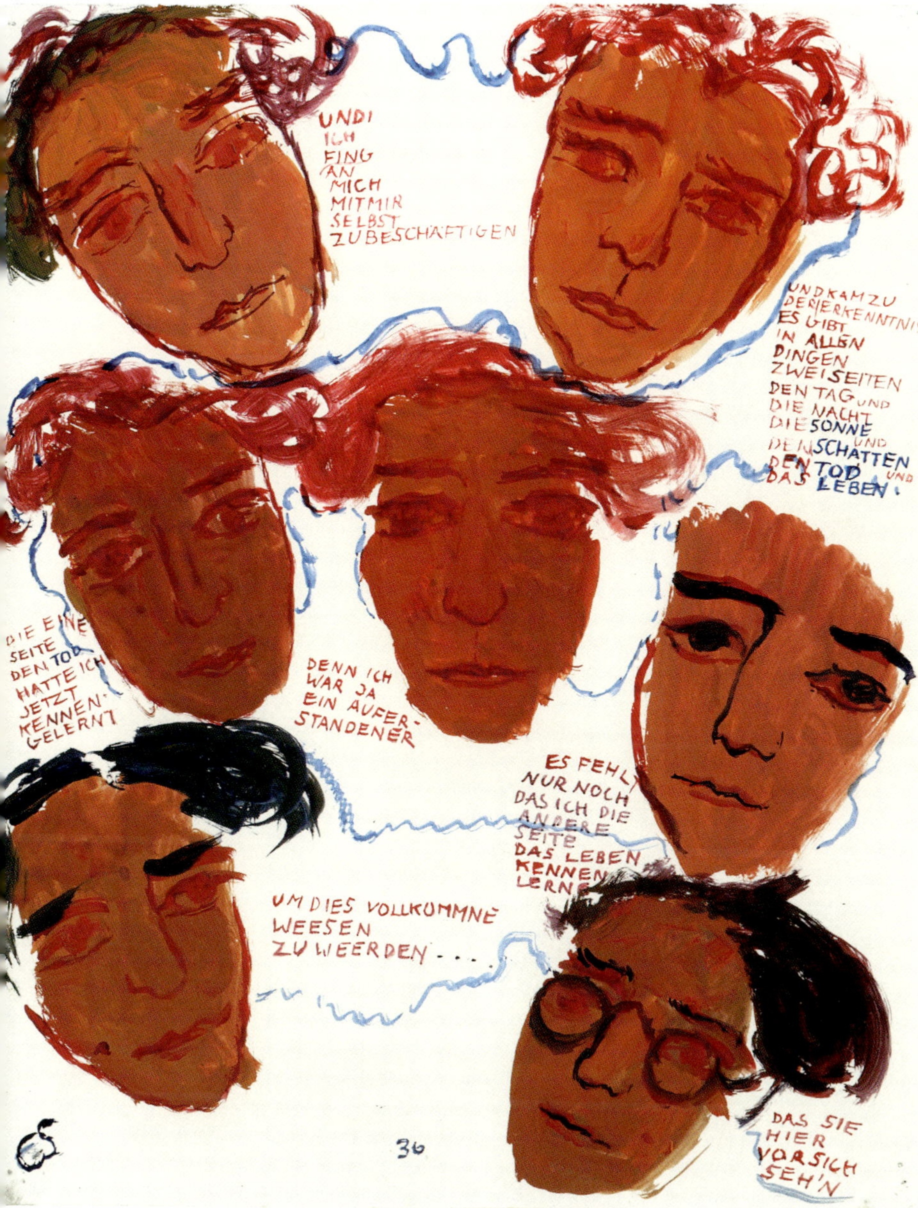
UNDI
ICH
FING
AN
MICH
MITMIR
SELBST
ZUBESCHÄFTIGEN
UNDKAMZU
DER ERKENNTNIS
ES GIBT
IN ALLEN
DINGEN
ZWEISEITEN
DEN TAG UND
DIE NACHT
DIE SONNE
UND
DEN SCHATTEN
DEN TOD UND
DAS LEBEN.
DIE EINE
SEITE
DEN TOD
HATTE ICH
JETZT
KENNEN-
GELERNT
DENN ICH
WAR JA
EIN AUFER-
STANDENER
ES FEHLT
NUR NOCH
DAS ICH DIE
ANDERE
SEITE
DAS LEBEN
KENNEN
LERN
UM DIES VOLLKOMMNE
WEESEN
ZU WEERDEN ....
DAS SIE
HIER
VORSICH
SEH'N
36

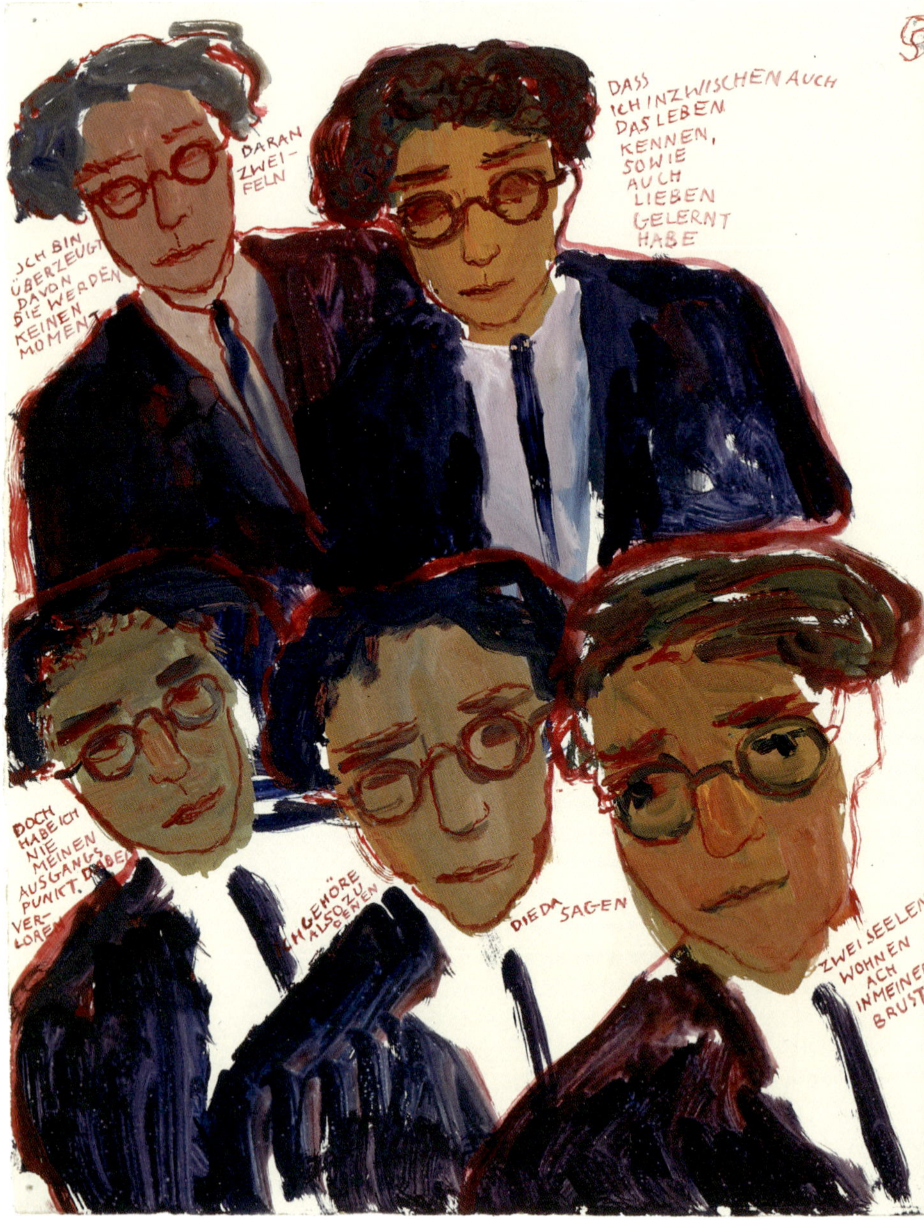
DARAN ZWEI-FELN
JCH BIN ÜBERZEUGT DAVON DIE WERDEN KEINEN MOMENT
DASS ICH INZWISCHEN AUCH DAS LEBEN KENNEN, SOWIE AUCH LIEBEN GELERNT HABE
DOCH HABE ICH NIE MEINEN AUSGANGSPUNKT. DABEI VERLOREN
ICH GEHÖRE ALSO ZU DENEN
DIE DA SAGEN
ZWEI SEELEN WOHNEN ACH IN MEINER BRUST

(opposite)

"I am convinced you will not doubt for a moment that
I have known and learned to love life in the meantime.

But I have never lost my point of departure.

I belong thus to those who say: 'Two souls dwell
in my breast.'"

(bottom)

DABERLOHN
"I've got to go now. Goodbye."

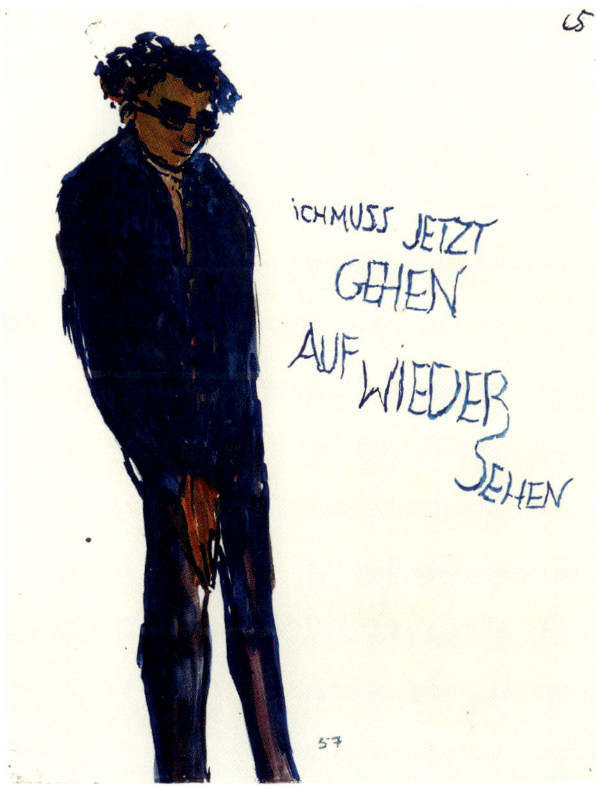

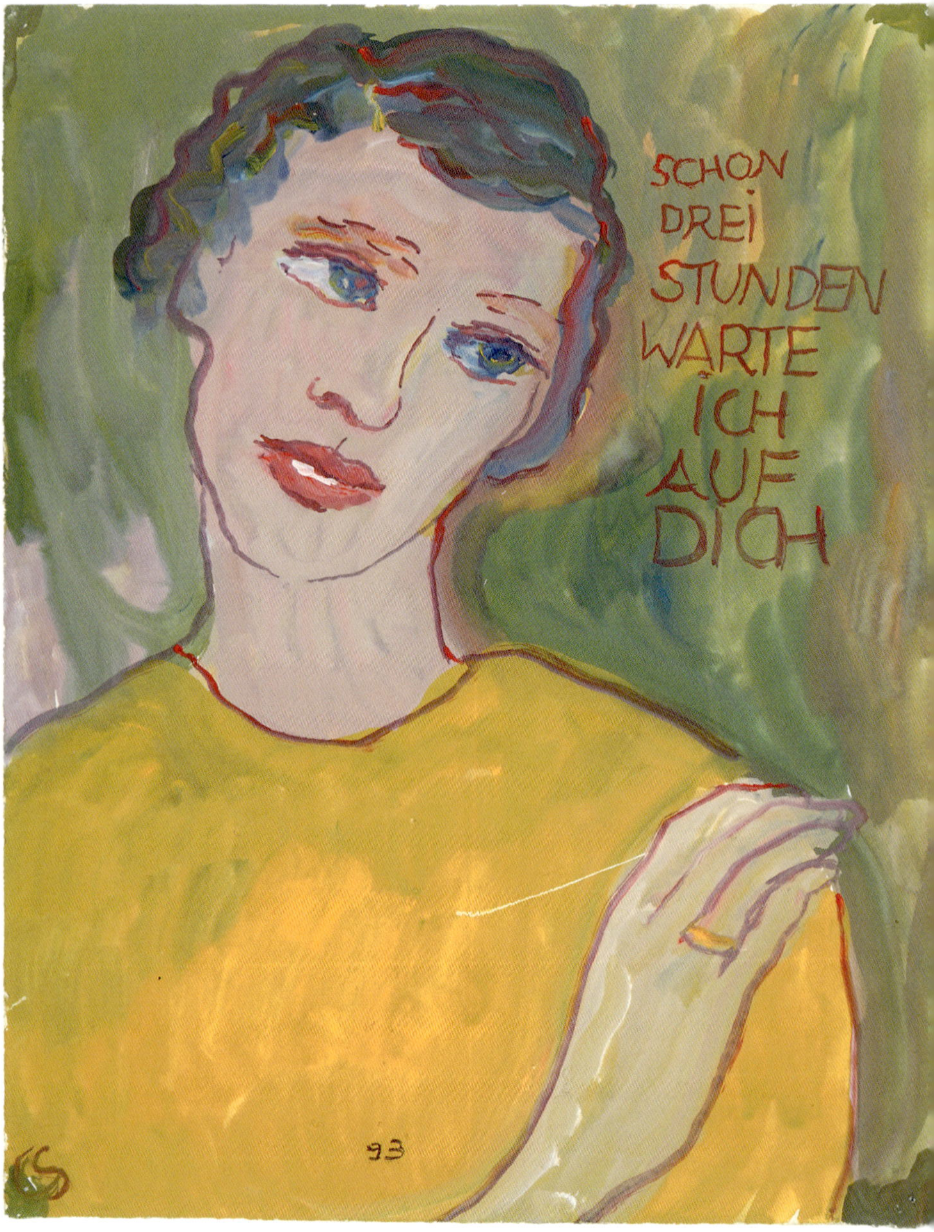
SCHON
DREI
STUNDEN
WARTE
ICH
AUF
DICH
93

(opposite)

DABERLOHN'S FIANCÉE
"I've been waiting for you for three hours!"

(bottom)

DABERLOHN
"Yes, my child, I couldn't possibly
get here any earlier."

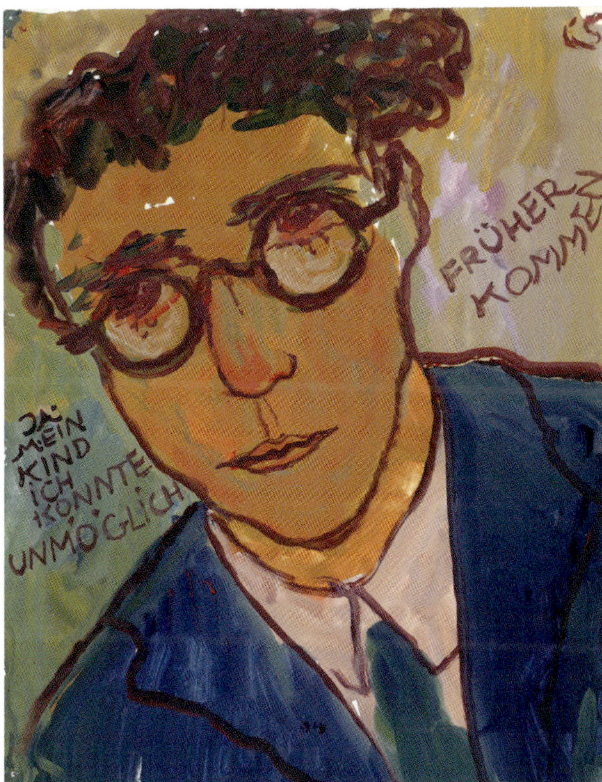

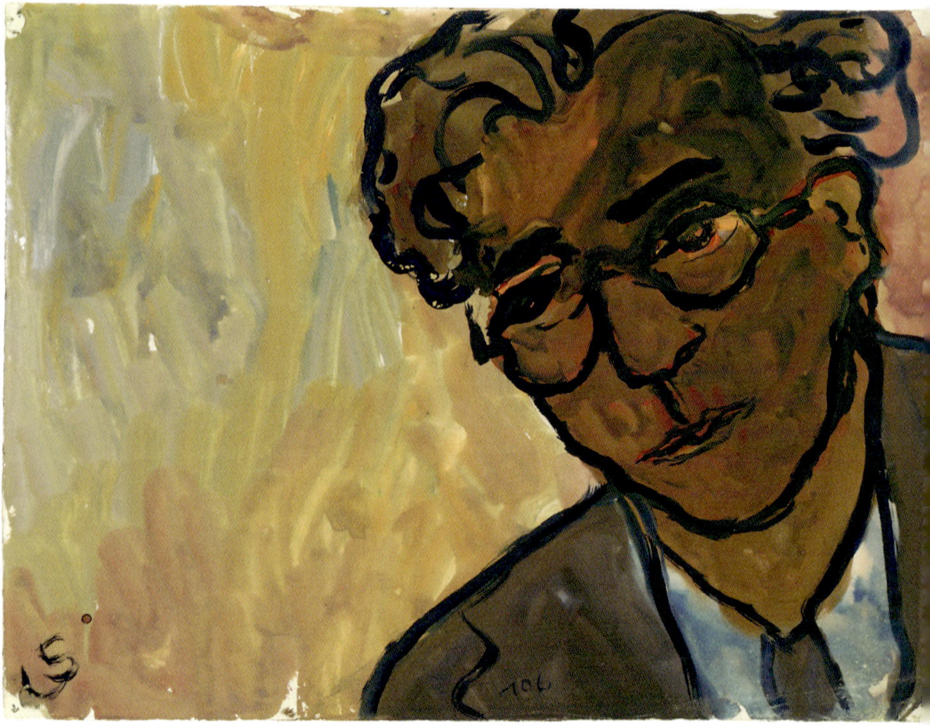

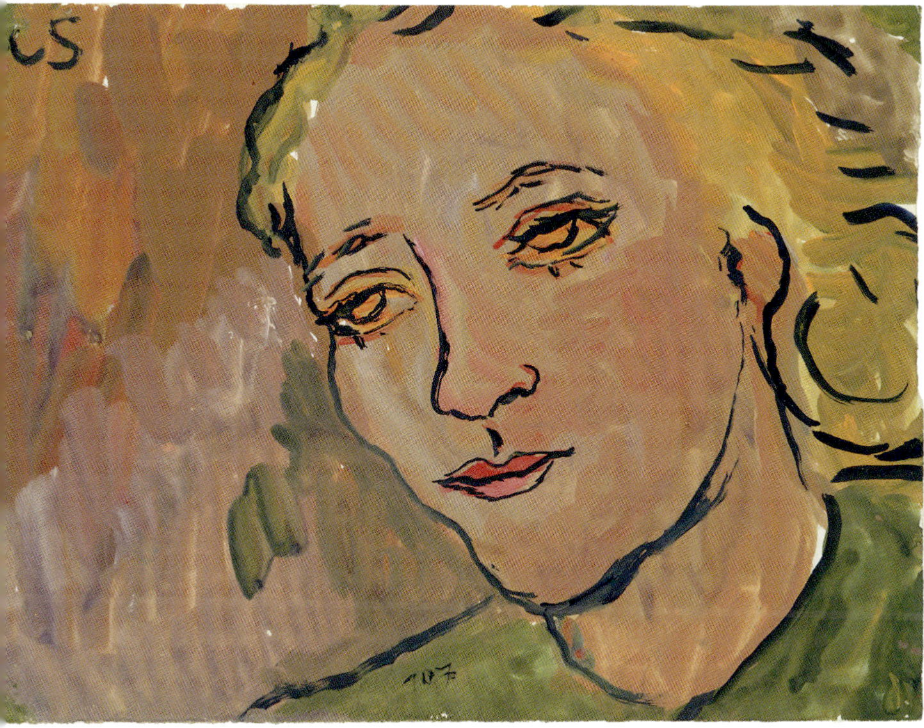
CS

CHAPTER FOUR
CHRISTMAS!

It is in Daberlohn's nature to firmly believe in things he has said once. Unconsciously he suggests them to himself for so long until they have become irrefutable, one could almost say, laws. This process takes place in him within a minute, and people who understand his nature instinctively feel strange by this unique firmness and self-conviction with which he knows how to put things.

DABERLOHN
"Don't laugh at me. I believe in the dice.
Anyone who throws three sixes in a row can
expect something important to happen to him."

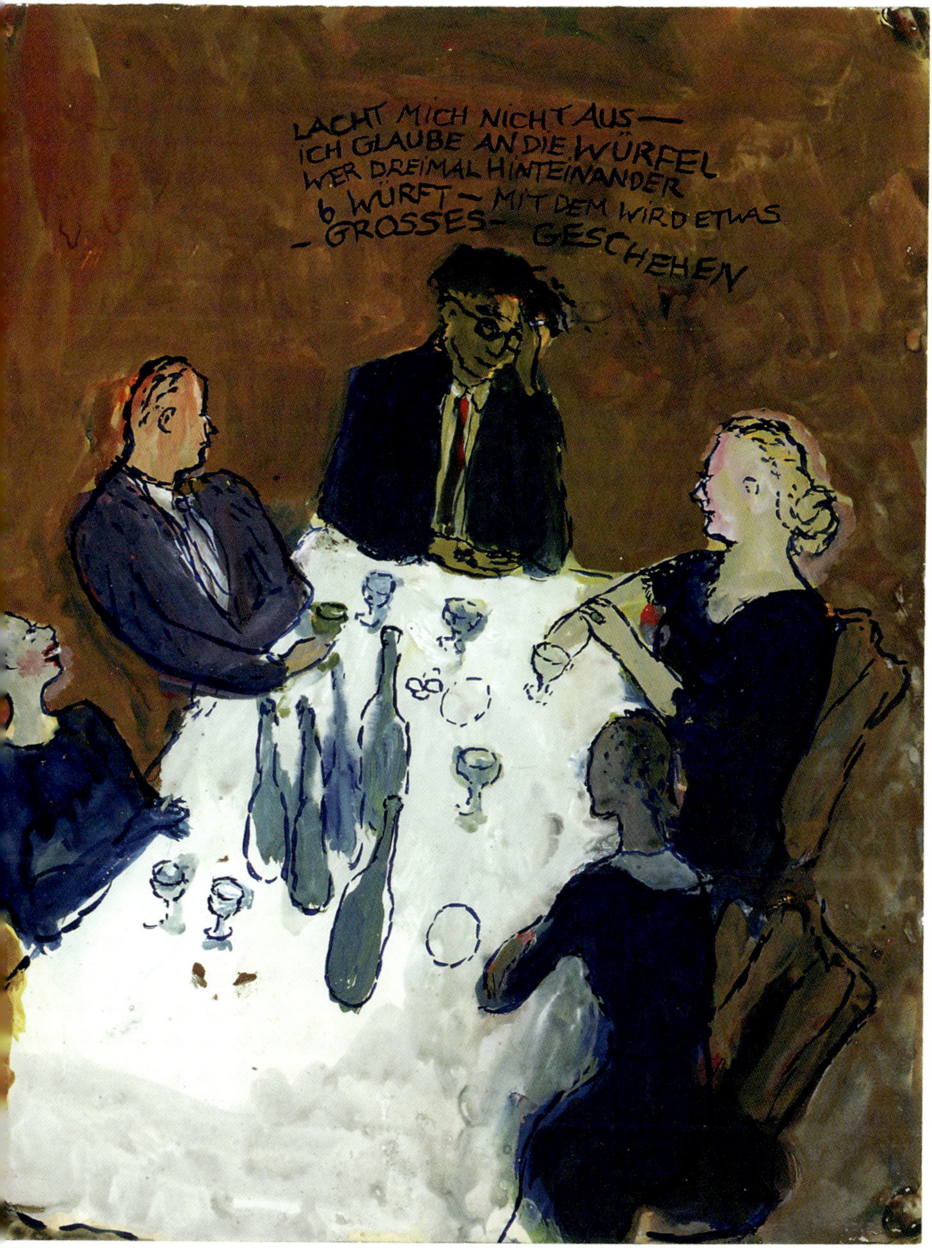
LACHT MICH NICHT AUS—
ICH GLAUBE AN DIE WÜRFEL
WER DREIMAL HINTEINANDER
6 WÜRFT — MIT DEM WIRD ETWAS
— GROSSES— GESCHEHEN

(bottom)

In the following sheets the author further attempts to depict the processes of his artistic vision.

He, Daberlohn, sees in all things only the expression. And the expression of the expression is the tricoloured line that is built up very slowly and with much deliberation.

He is truly disappointed that Paulinka did not throw three sixes in a row so that she would become the greatest singer on earth.

DABERLOHN
"Madonna, you disappoint me."

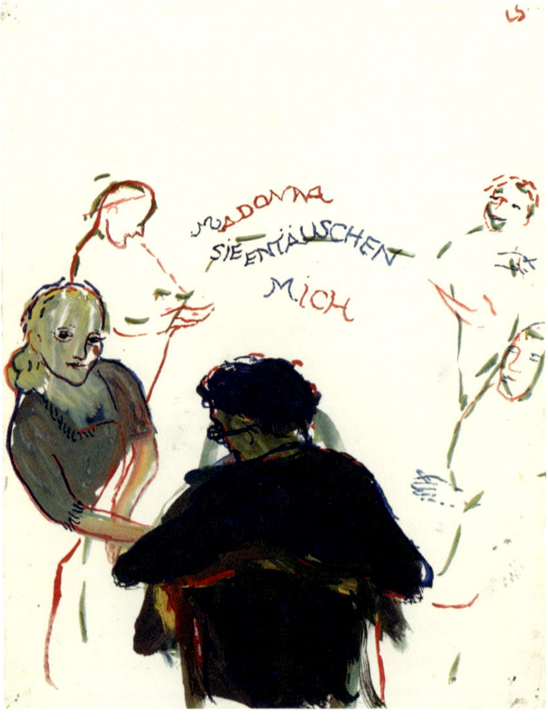

(opposite)

"I am infinitely sorry to say that none of those present will reach the desired goal.

However, should there be one among you – who is dissatisfied with this unsatisfactory outcome – I shall be happy to continue – the game in the next room!"

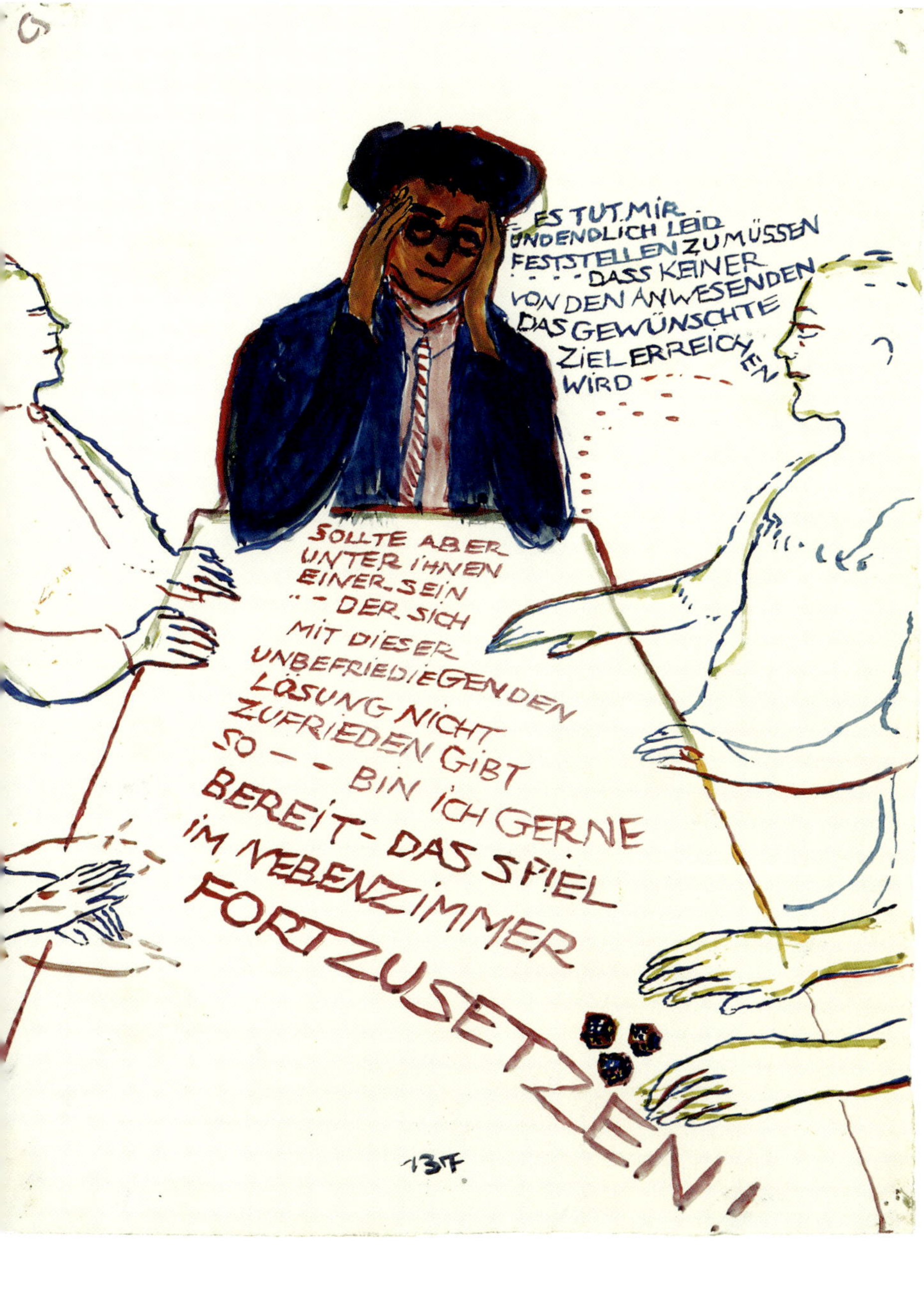
ES TUT MIR UNDENDLICH LEID FESTSTELLEN ZU MÜSSEN - - - DASS KEINER VON DEN ANWESENDEN DAS GEWÜNSCHTE ZIEL ERREICHEN WIRD
SOLLTE ABER UNTER IHNEN EINER SEIN - - DER SICH MIT DIESER UNBEFRIEDIEGENDEN LÖSUNG NICHT ZUFRIEDEN GIBT SO - - BIN ICH GERNE BEREIT - DAS SPIEL IM NEBENZIMMER FORTZUSETZEN.
13F

He is, after all, generous enough to give other people beside “his” singer an opportunity to lay claim to his prophecies.

At the moment his whole attention is directed towards Charlotte, who is shown here trying to throw three sixes in a row.

DABERLOHN
“You will get very far later, for – young
lady – because you have, my little lady,
very much ambition, my little lady.”

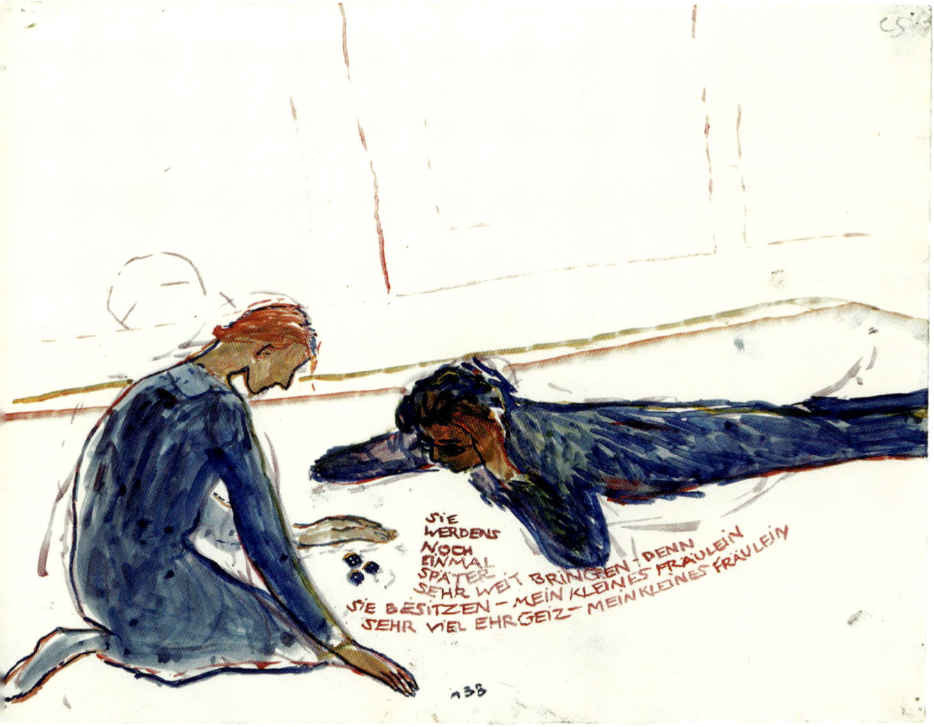

ER IST IMMERHIN GROSSZÜGIG GENUG
DAZU VERANLAGT AUCH NOCH
ANDEREN MENSCHEN AUSSER
SEINER "SÄNGERIN" GELEGENHEIT
„ZU GEBEN SEINE PROPHEZEIHUNG
FÜR SICH IN ANSPRUCH ZU NEHMEN EN

IM AUGENBLICK IST SEINE
EINSTELLUNG VOLLKOMMEN
AUF DIE SICH HIER BEMÜHEN-
DE DREI MAL HINTEREINANDER
SECHS ZU WÜRFELNDE
CHARLOTTE GERICHTET.

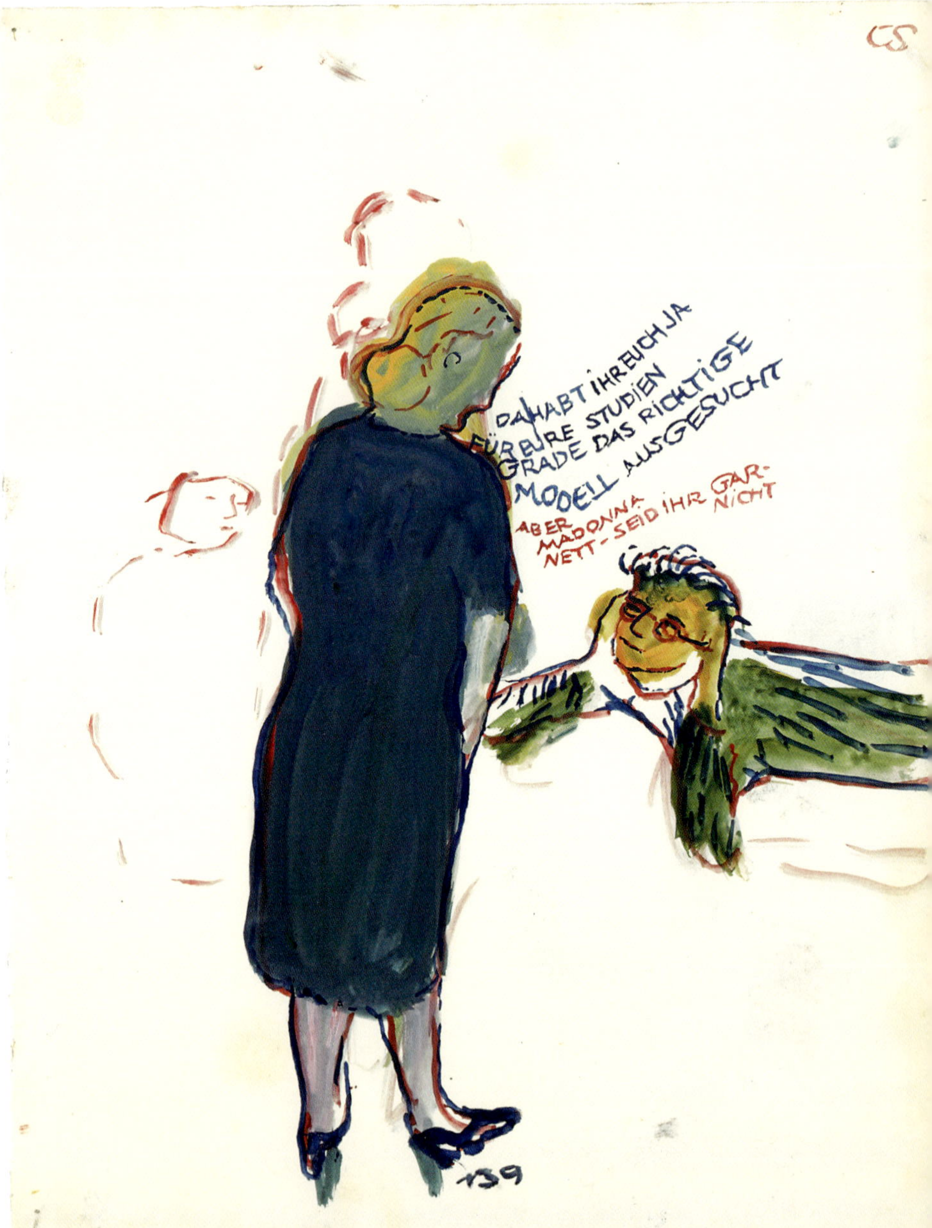
CS
DA HABT IHR EUCH JA
FÜR EURE STUDIEN
GRADE DAS RICHTIGE
MODELL AUSGESUCHT
ABER MADONNA NETT-SEID IHR GAR-NICHT
139

(opposite)

PAULINKA
"You have chosen just the right model
for your studies."

DABERLOHN
"But Madonna, that's not nice of you at all."

(bottom)

DABERLOHN
"Will you sing something for us now?"

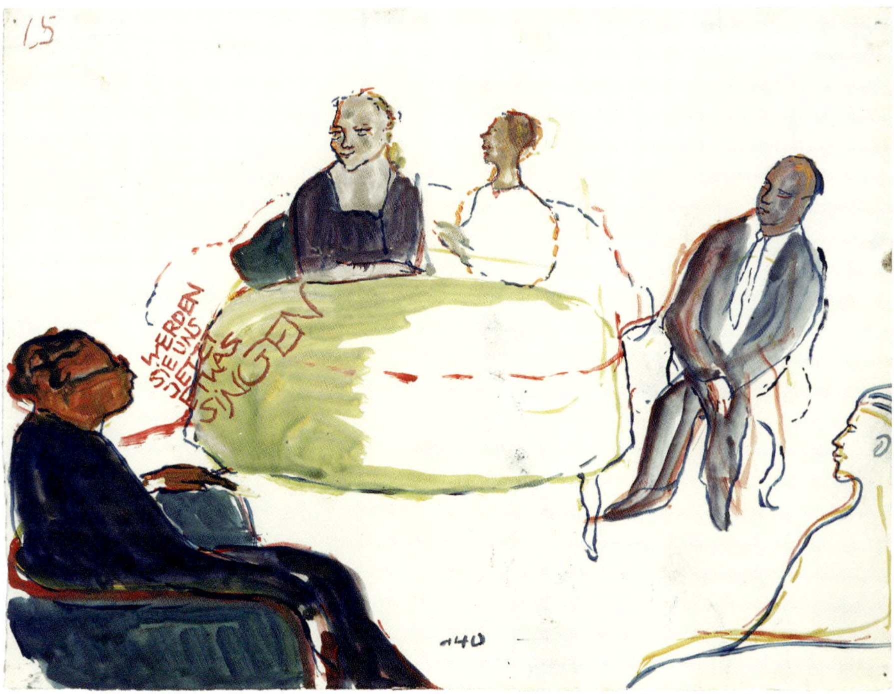

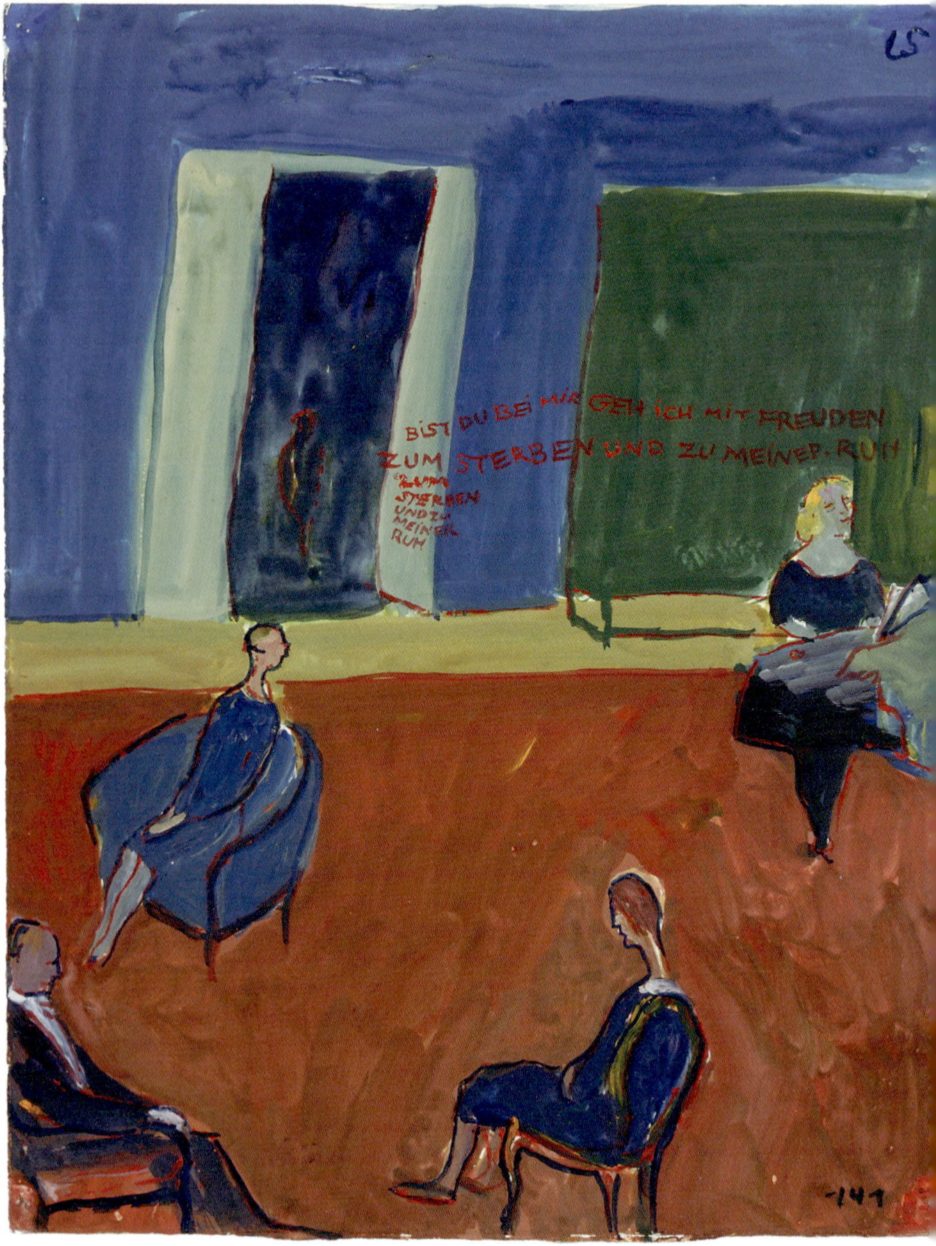
65
BIST DU BEI MIR GEH ICH MIT FREUDEN
ZUM STERBEN UND ZU MEINER RUH
STERBEN
UND ZU
MEINER
RUH
-147

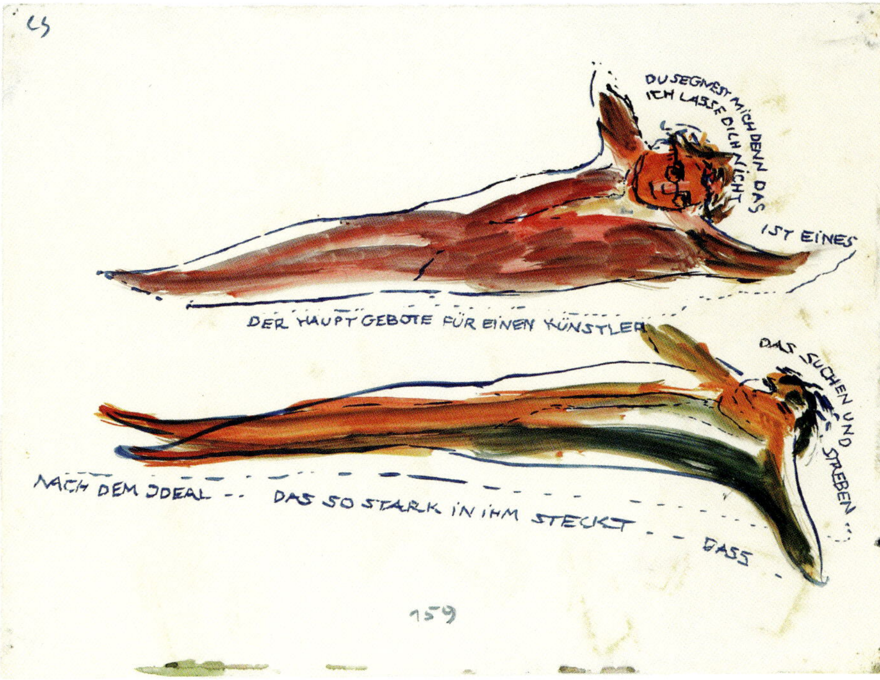

(opposite)

PAULINKA
When thou art near, I go with joy to my death and to my rest, to my death and to my rest.

(top)

DABERLOHN
"'I will not let thee go, except thou bless me,' that is one of the main commandments for an artist. The searching and striving for the ideal that is so strong in him that..."

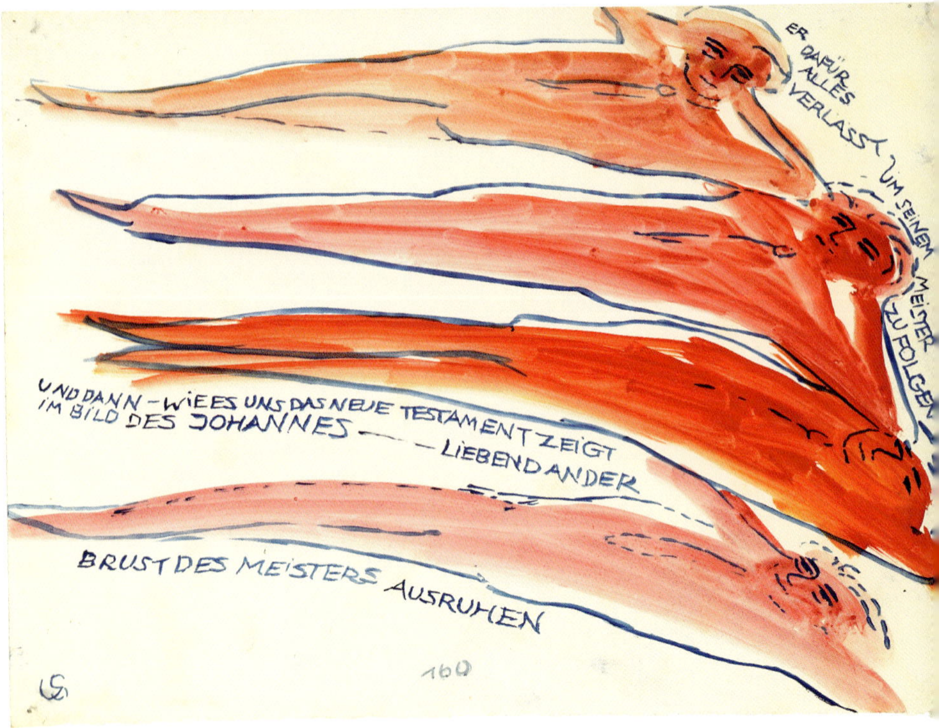

"... he'll leave everything to follow his Master and then,
as we see in the New Testament in the image of John,
to lean lovingly against the Master's breast resting."

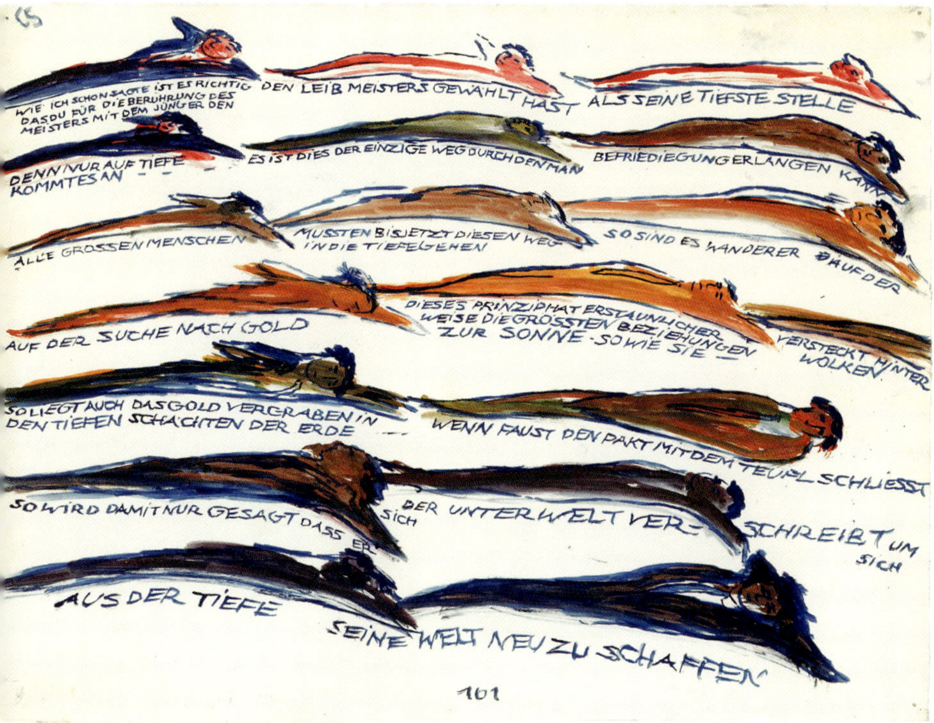

"As I already said, it is right that you choose the Master's body as its deepest point for the contact between Master and disciple, depth being all that matters. It is the only way by which one can achieve contentment. Until now all great men had to take this path into the depths. Thus they are wanderers in search of gold.

Astoundingly enough, this principle has the greatest relations to the sun. Like the sun hidden behind clouds, gold, too, lies buried in the deep shafts of the earth.

When Faust concluded his pact with the Devil, it is only said that he commits himself to the underworld in order to create his world anew from the depths."

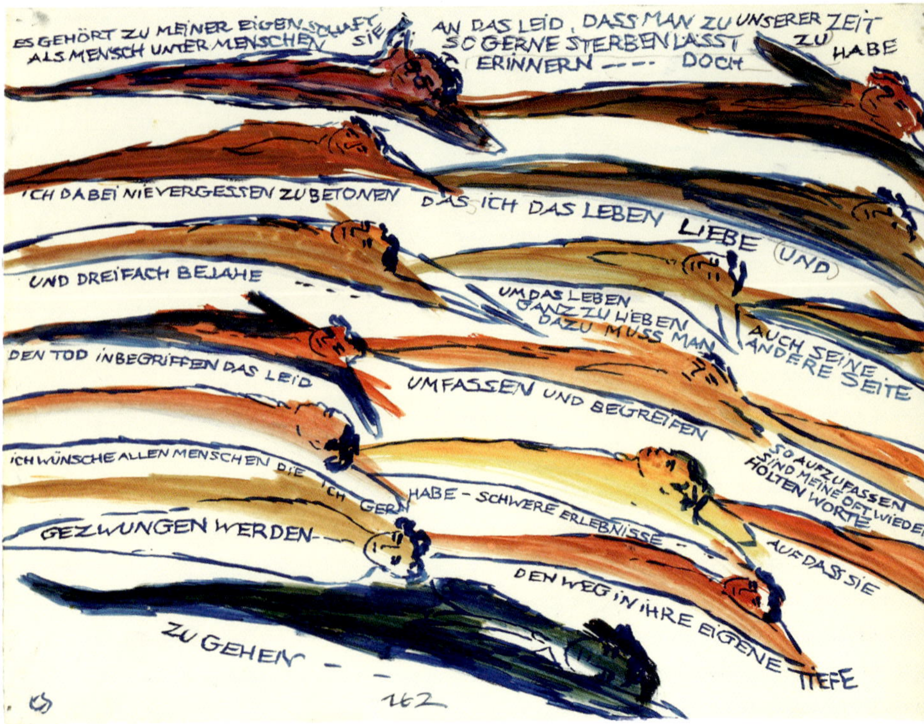

"It is part of my nature as a human being among human beings to remind them of the suffering, which in our day we like to let die.

Yet I have never forgotten to emphasise that I love life and affirm it threefold. To love life completely one must also embrace and comprehend its other side: death, including suffering.

This is how my oft-repeated words must be understood: I wish to all those whom I love to undergo hard experiences so that they will be forced to follow the path into their own depths."

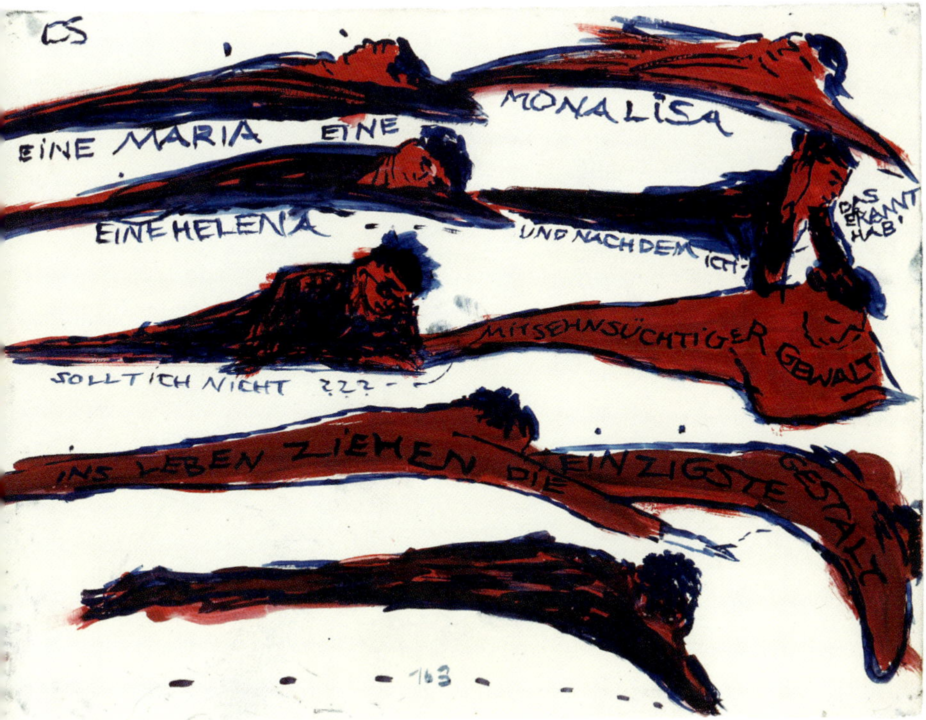

"A Mary – a Mona Lisa – a Helen, and now having recognised this, should I not ??? with yearning force bring this unique form to life?"

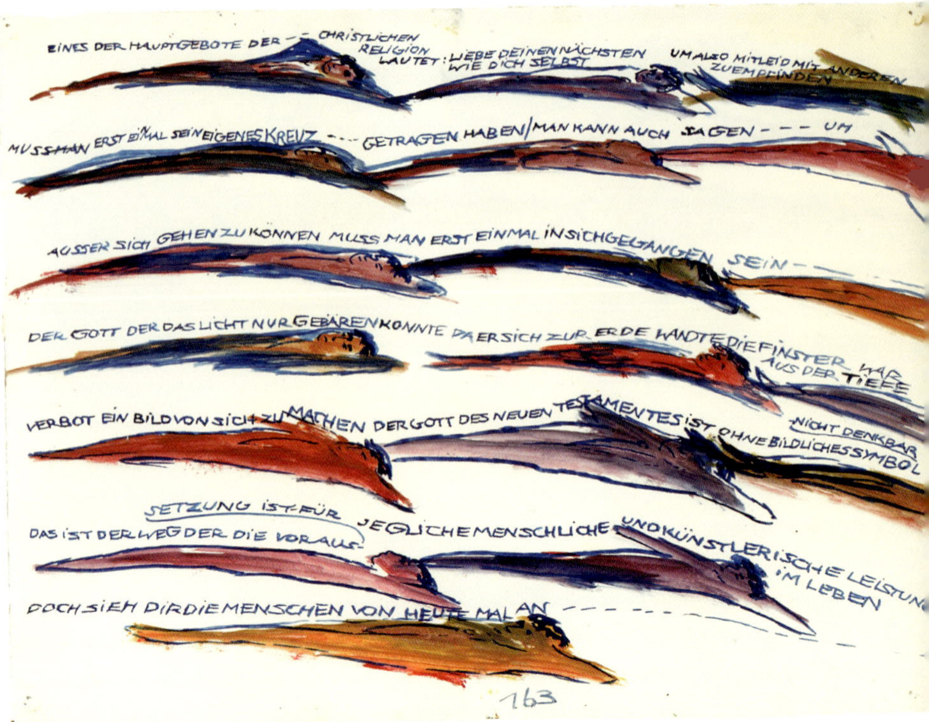

"One of the chief commandments of the Christian religion is: 'Love thy neighbour as thyself.' Thus to be compassionate towards others, one must first have borne one's own cross.

One can also say: in order to go out of oneself one must first have gone into oneself. The God who could only give birth to light when he turned to the Earth, which was dark from the depths, forbade the making of an image of Himself.

The God of the New Testament is unimaginable without a pictorial symbol. This path is the prerequisite for every human and artistic endeavour in life.

But just look at the people of today..."

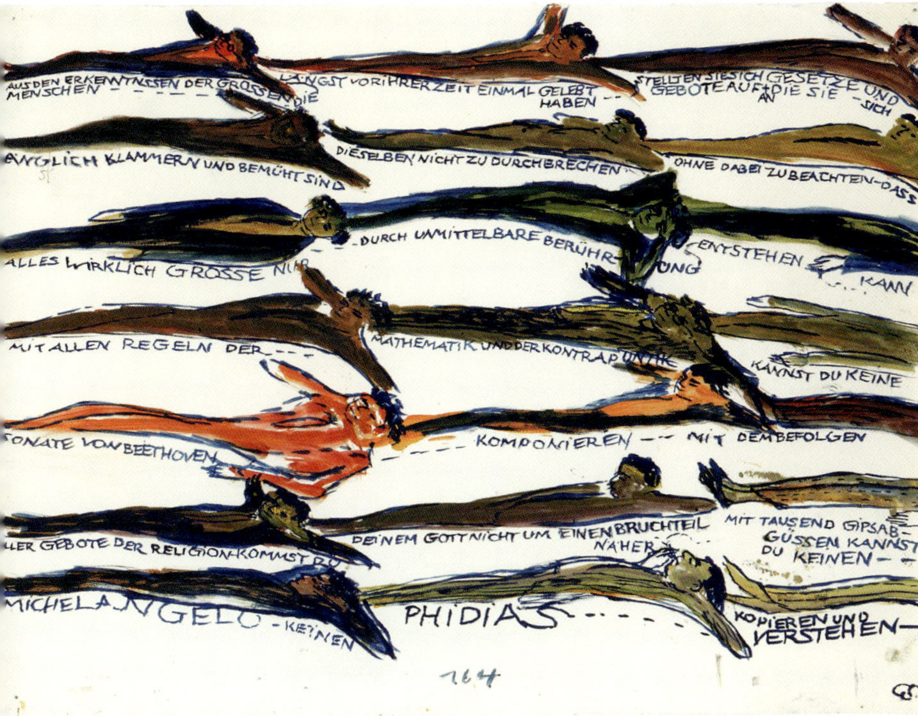

"Using the perceptions of great men who lived long before their time, they drew up laws and commandments to which they anxiously clung, striving not to transgress them, unaware that all truly great achievements can arise only through direct contact.

With all the rules of mathematics and counterpoint, you cannot compose a Beethoven sonata. By following all religious commandments, you do not come closer to your God by so much as a fraction. With a thousand plaster casts, you cannot copy or understand a Michelangelo or a Phidias."

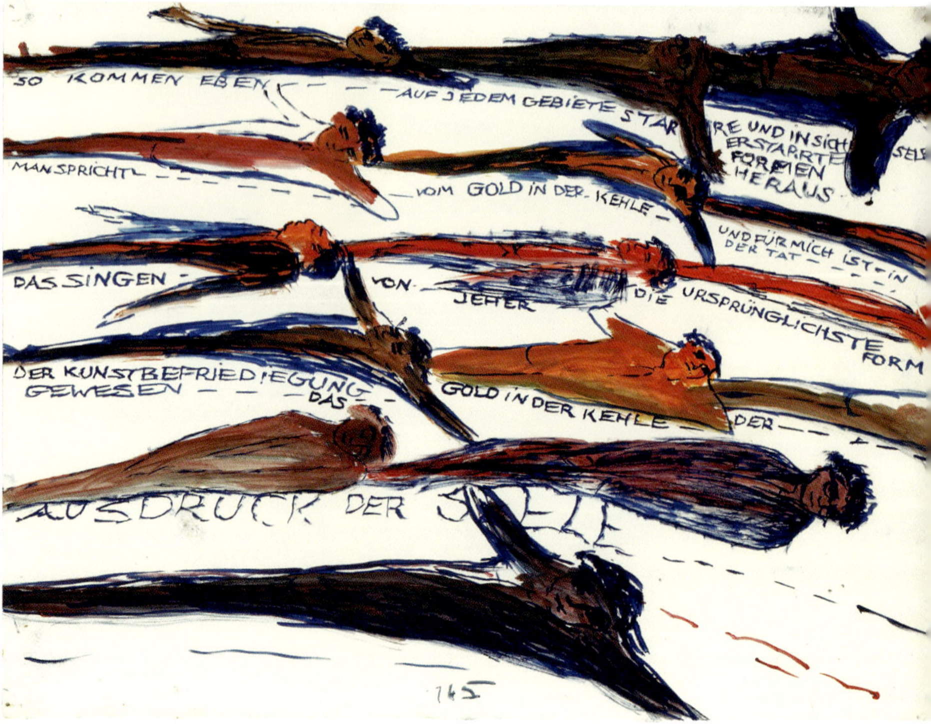

"So in every field rigid and self-rigidified forms emerge. One speaks of a golden throat, and indeed for me singing has always been the most pristine form of artistic satisfaction.

The throat of gold – the expression of the soul – "

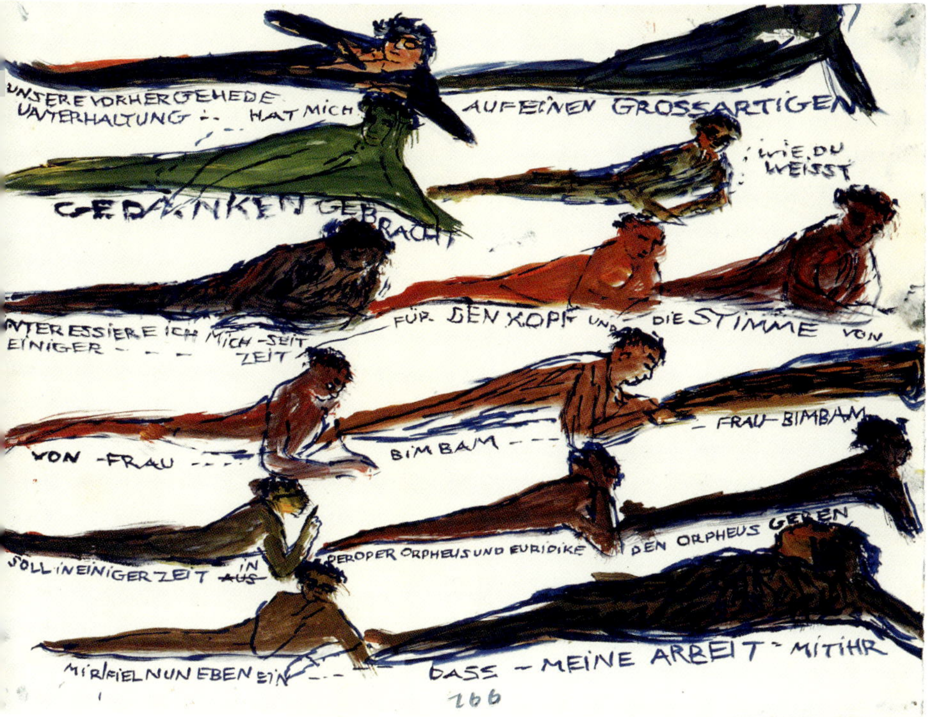

"Our previous conversation has given me a marvellous idea. As you know, I have been interested for some time in the head and voice of Mrs Bimbam.

Mrs Bimbam is said to be providing Orpheus in the opera Orpheus and Eurydice in the future. It has just occurred to me that my work with her..."

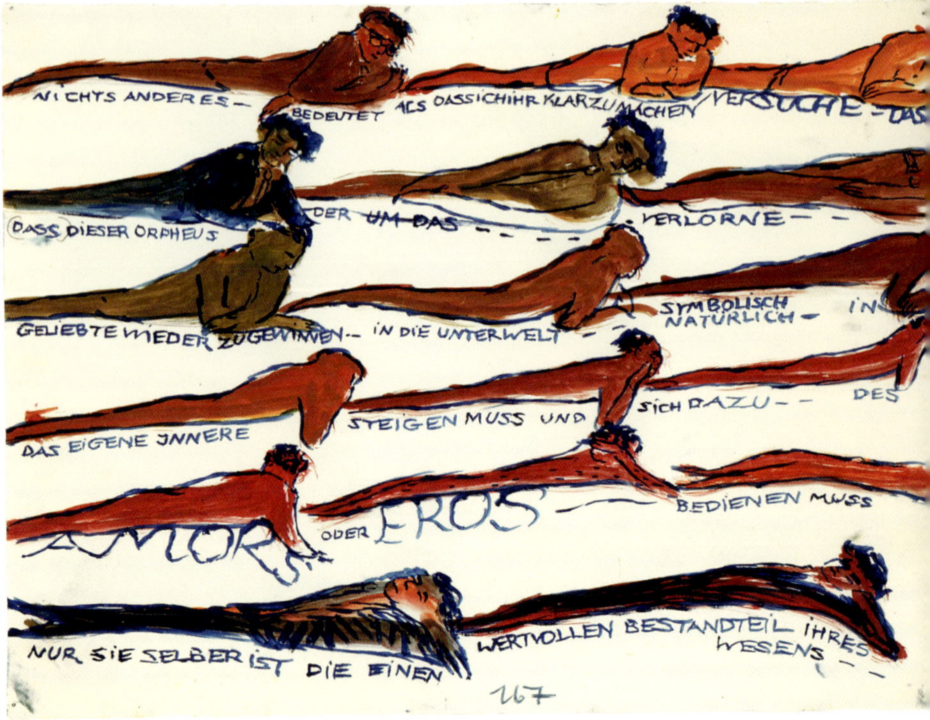

"... means nothing less than my endeavour to make her understand that this Orpheus, in order to regain his lost beloved, must descend – symbolically, of course – into the underworld, into his own depths, for which he needs the help of Cupid or Eros.

It is only she herself who has lost a valuable part of her being..."

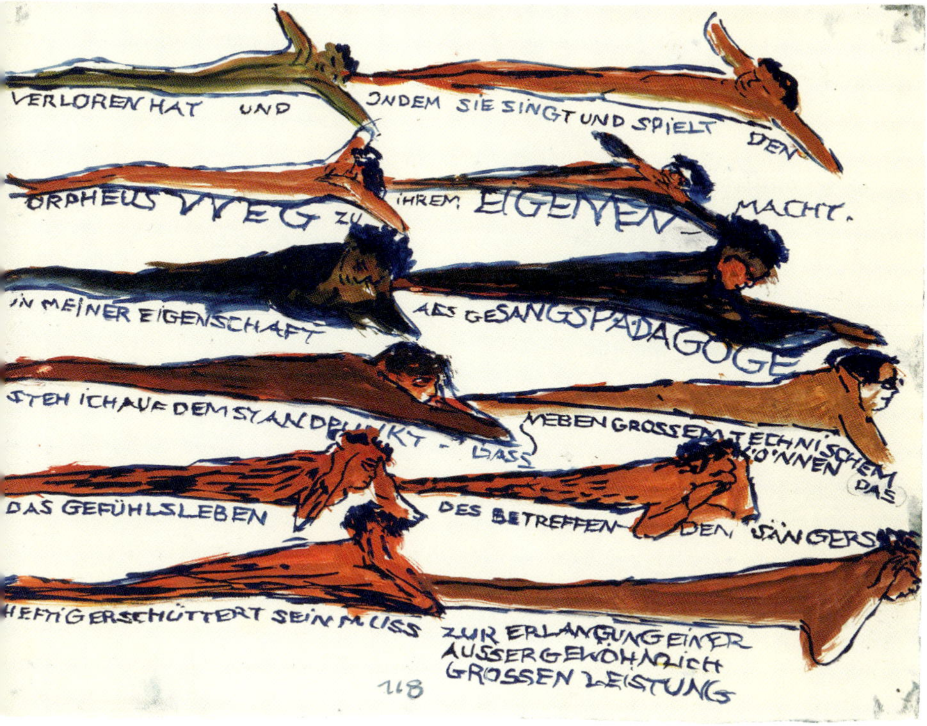

"... and in singing and acting makes Orpheus's path her own.

In my capacity of singing teacher I maintain that, apart from great technical ability, the emotional life of the singer must suffer a great upheaval to enable that singer to achieve exceptional results."

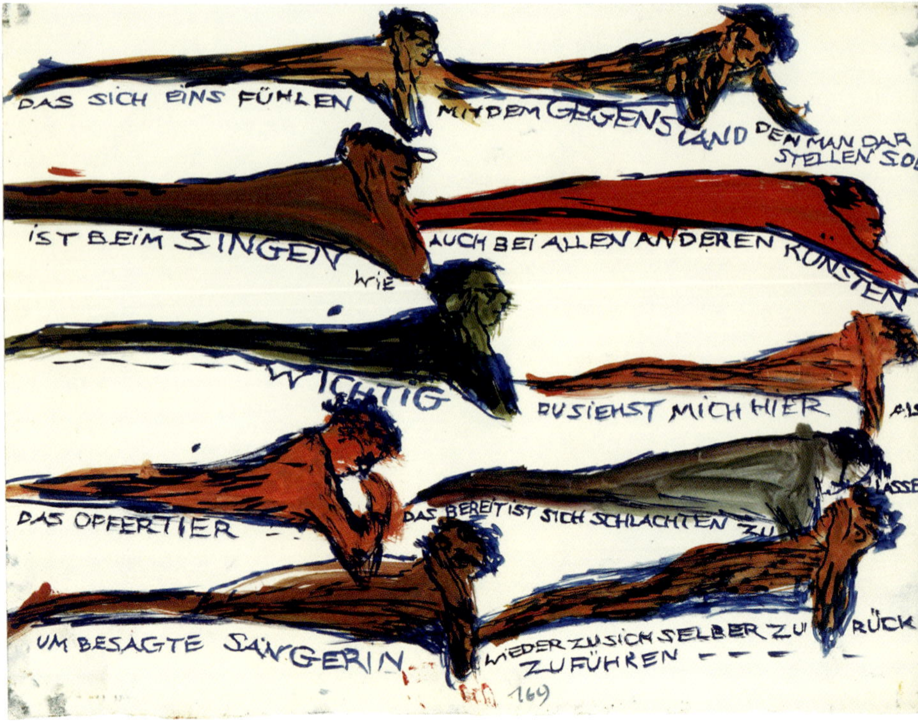

“The feeling of total oneness with the object that is to be represented is as important in singing as in every other art.

So you see me here, the sacrificial animal, prepared to let itself be slaughtered to lead this aforementioned singer back to herself.”

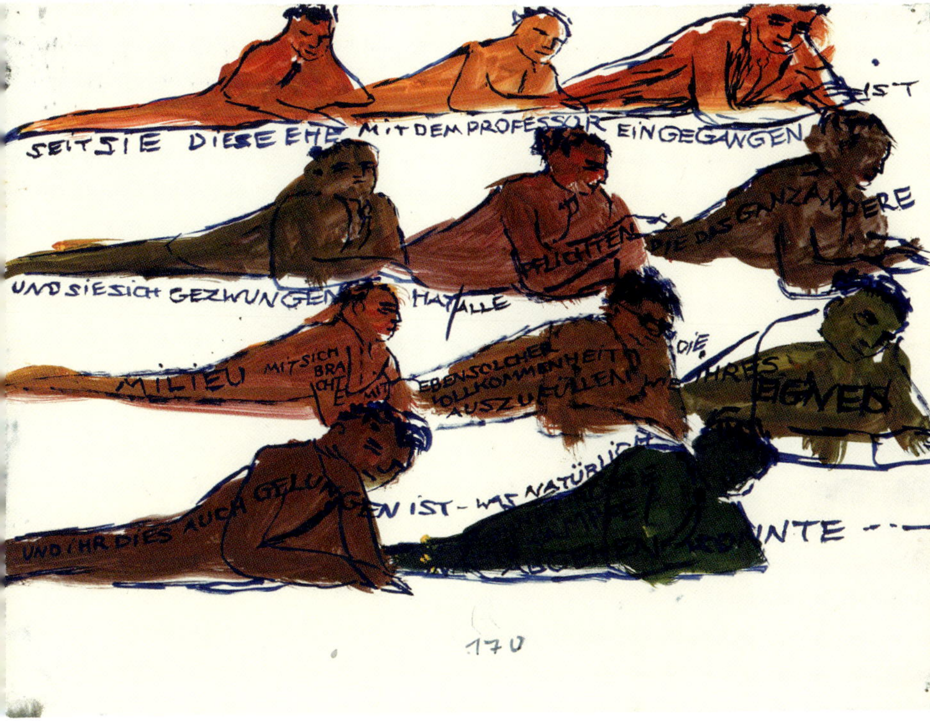

"Since she married the professor and forced herself to carry out all the duties entailed by that quite different milieu as consummately as she does those of her own milieu, and since she succeeded in this too – which, of course, could not happen without great inner conflicts..."

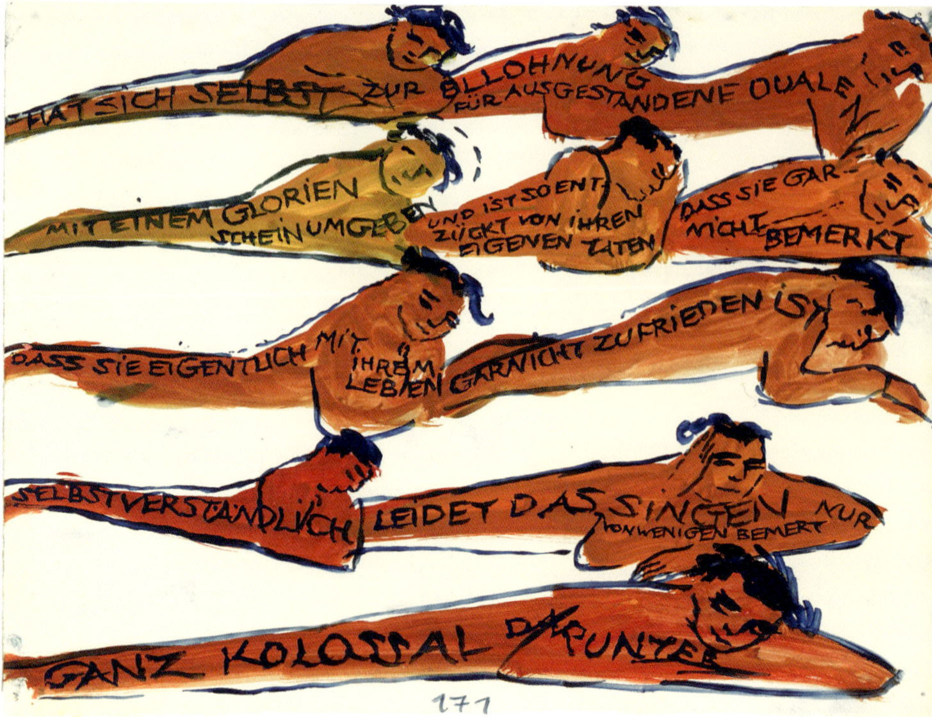

"... she has, as a reward for the torments endured, invested herself with a halo and is so enchanted by her own deeds that she fails to notice that actually she is far from satisfied with her life. Needless to say, her singing – although, only a few have noticed – suffers colossally from this."

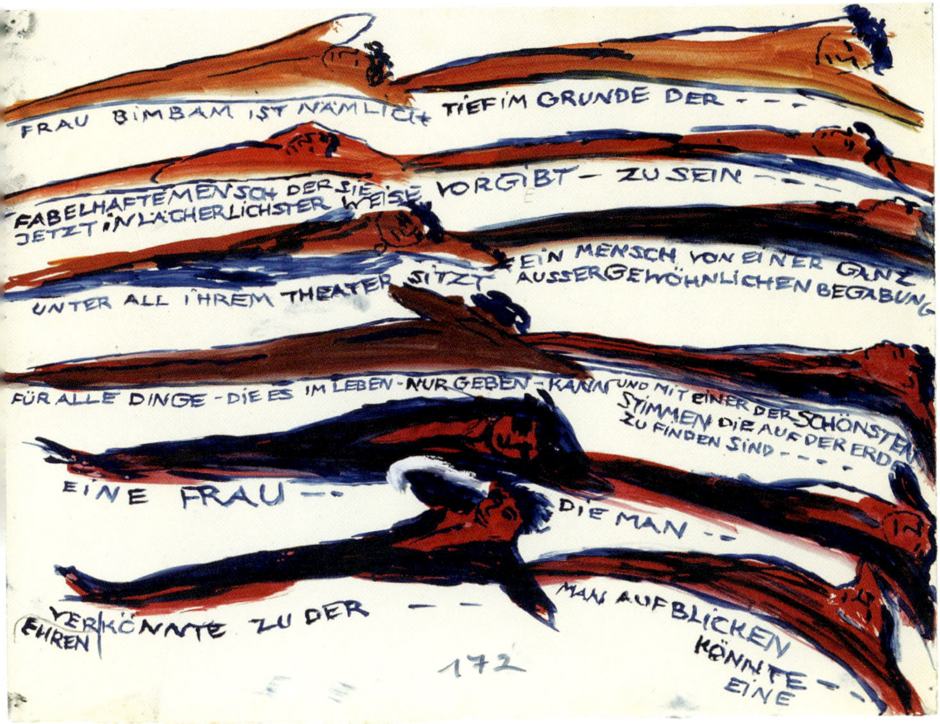

"Mrs Bimbam is, at heart, essentially the marvellous person she is now pretending to be, in the most ridiculous way. Beneath all her theatricality is a person of quite extraordinary talents for all things that only life can give, and with one of the most beautiful voices to be found anywhere on earth.

A woman whom one could adore,
to whom one could look up – a..."

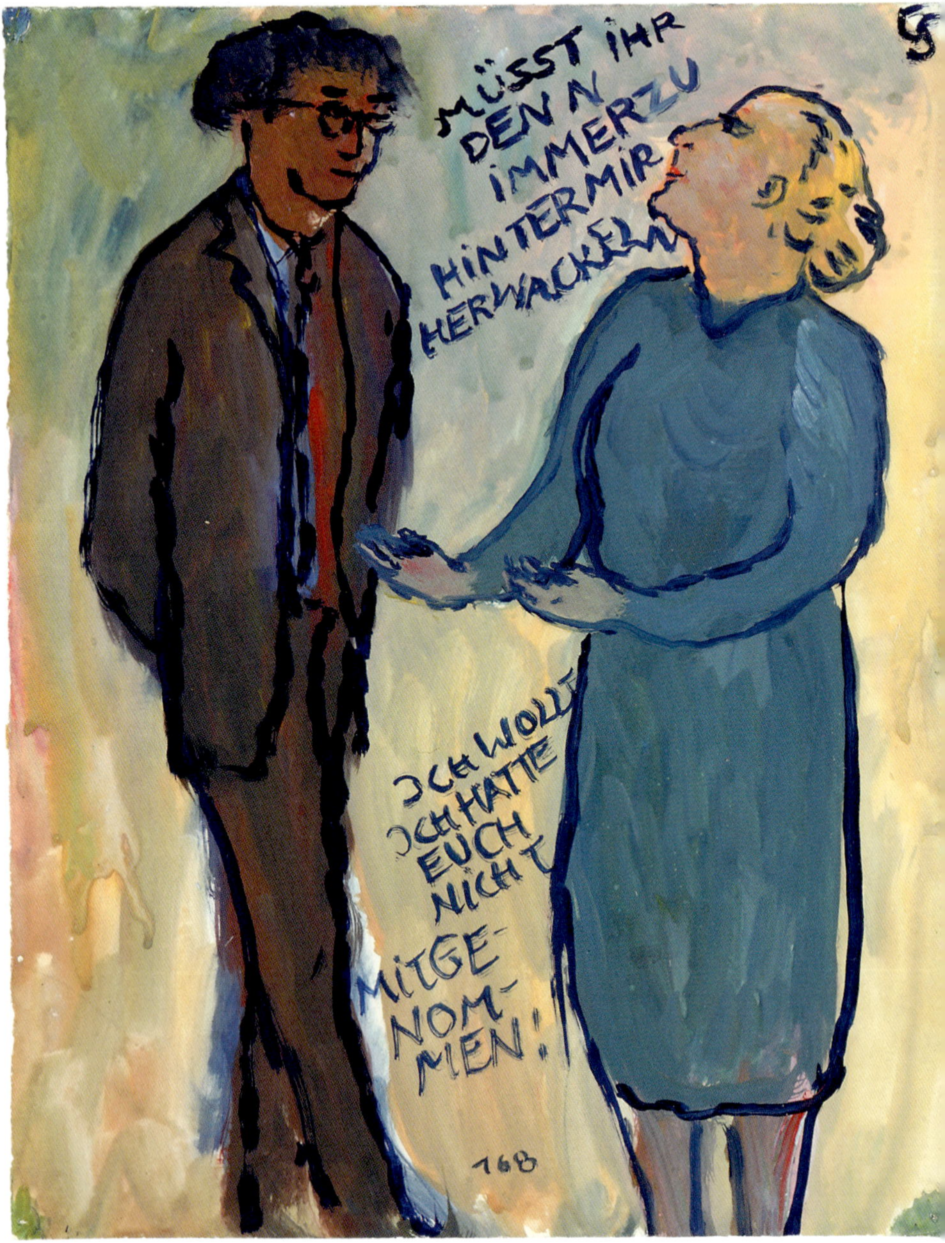
MÜSST IHR
DENN
IMMERZU
HINTERMIR
HERWACKELN
ICH WOLLT
ICH HATTE
EUCH
NICHT
MITGE-
NOM-
MEN!
168

(opposite)

CHAPTER SIX
ORPHEUS, OR THE WAY TO A DEATH MASK

Again the game with Paulinka's head begins – but here he constructs nothing. It appears to him in absolute clarity and resoluteness like a panoptical distortion.

PAULINKA
"Must you always keep tottering after me?
I wish I hadn't brought you along!"

(bottom)

"Are you here again? No, it's almost more than I can take from you."

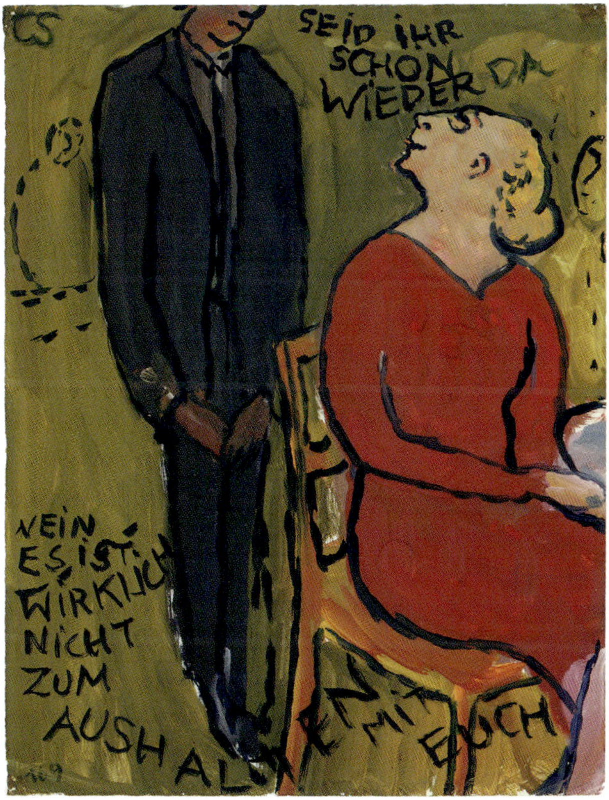

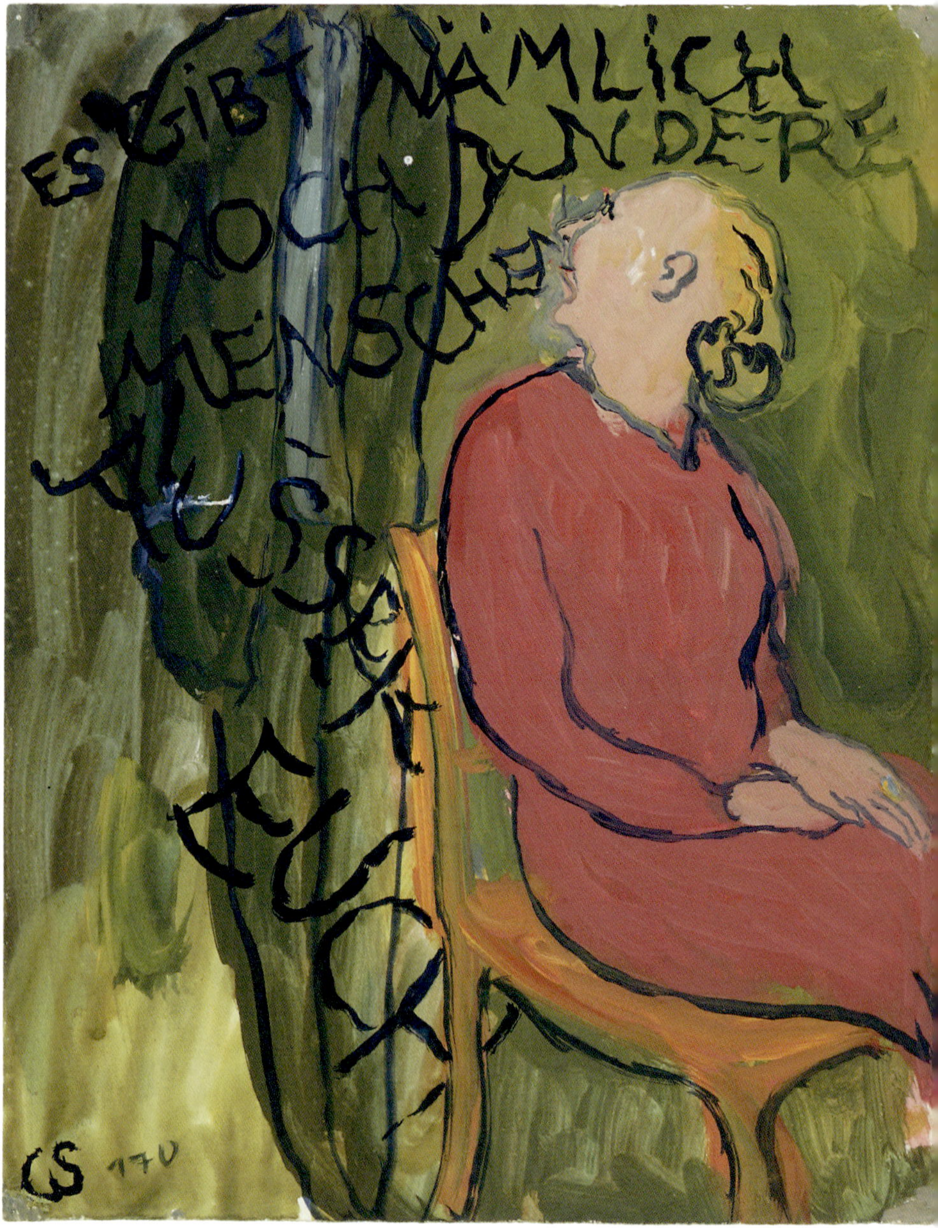
ES GIBT NÄMLICH
NOCH ANDERE
MENSCHEN
AUSSER
EUCH
CS

(opposite)

“There are other people
beside you, you see...”

(bottom)

“You’re spoiling the entire Orpheus
for me with your continuous presence.”

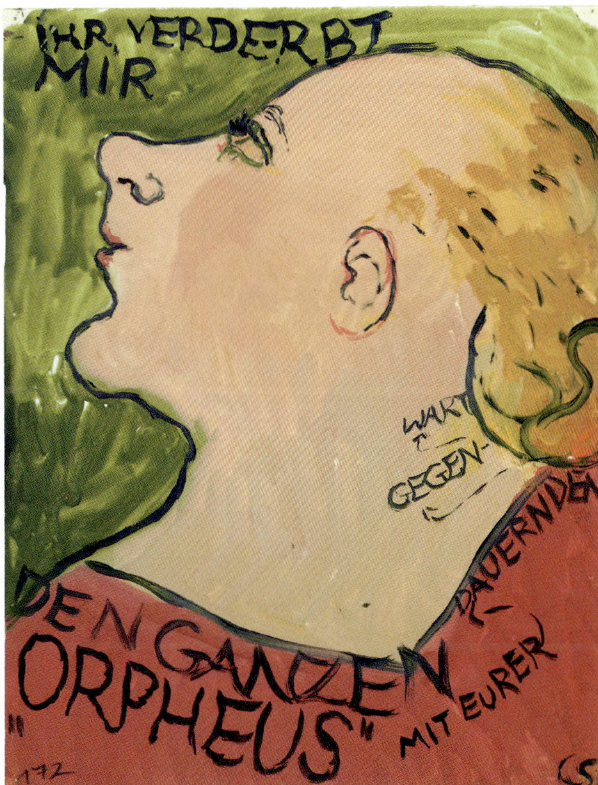

(bottom)

Upon arrival on the street he reflects upon the general blindness of people.

DABERLOHN
"How ugly she suddenly looked."

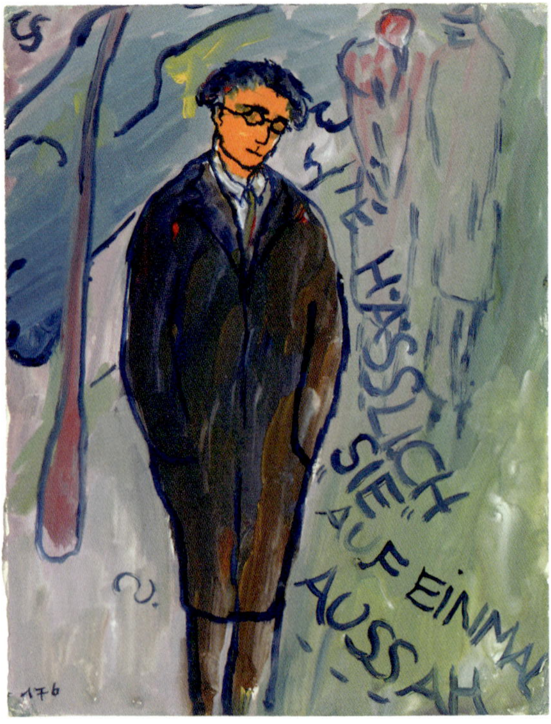

(opposite)

"And I also regret, on top of it, that I'm not a performing artist but only a theoretician. Can one be more of a practical artist than I am? Out of deadened human material I create living worlds. Everything I say is not theory but actually experienced. Who can understand what that means: really experienced? Most people simply vegetate."

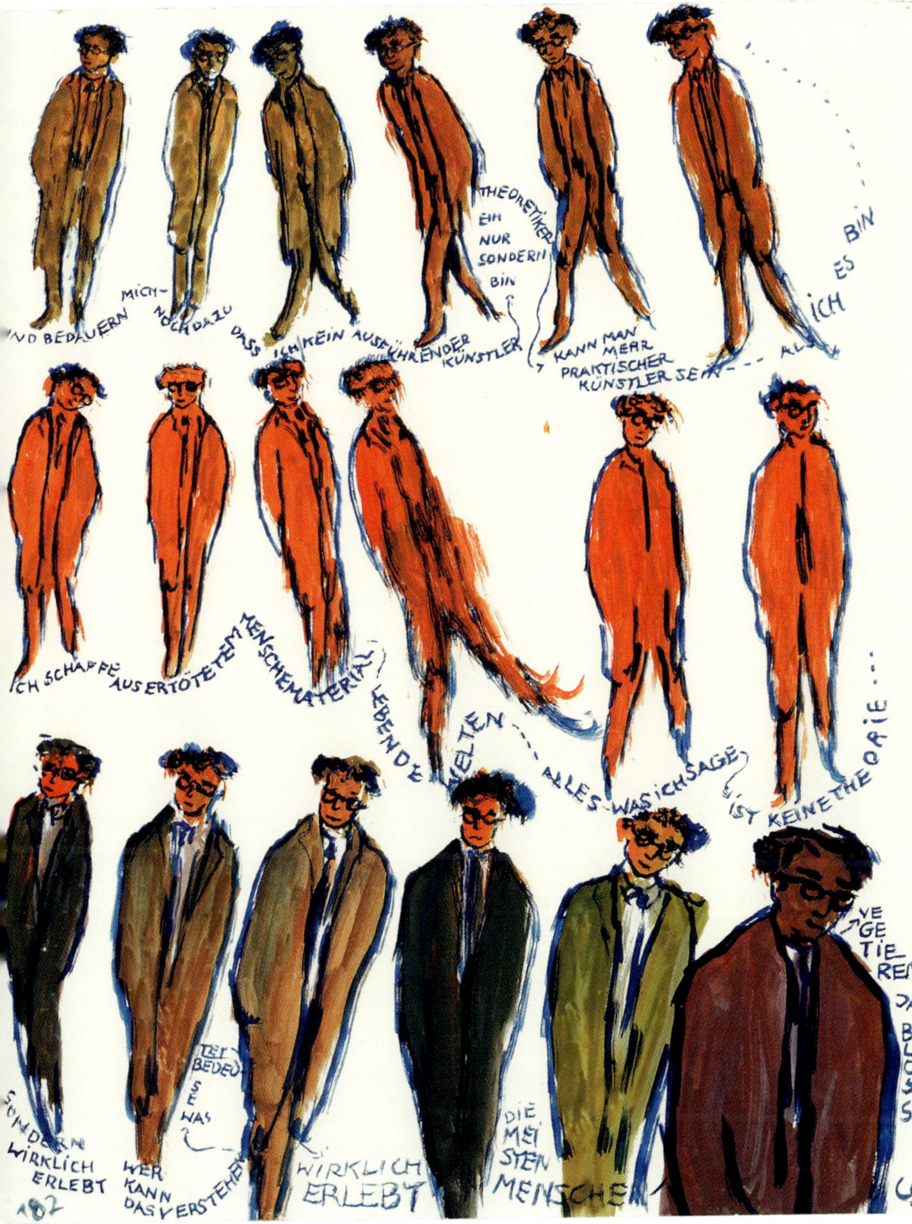
UND BEDAUERN MICH- NOCH DAZU DASS ICH KEIN AUSFÜHRENDER KÜNSTLER
THEORETIKER EIN NUR SONDERN BIN
KANN MAN MEHR PRAKTISCHER KÜNSTLER SEIN --- ALS ICH ES BIN
ICH SCHAFFE AUS ERTÖTETEM MENSCHEMATERIAL LEBENDE WELTEN .... ALLES WAS ICH SAGE IST KEINE THEORIE ...
SONDERN WIRKLICH ERLEBT
182
WER KANN DAS VERSTEHEN
TET BEDEU SE WAS
WIRKLICH ERLEBT
DIE MEI STEN MENSCHE
VE GE TIE REN
JA BLOSS
CS

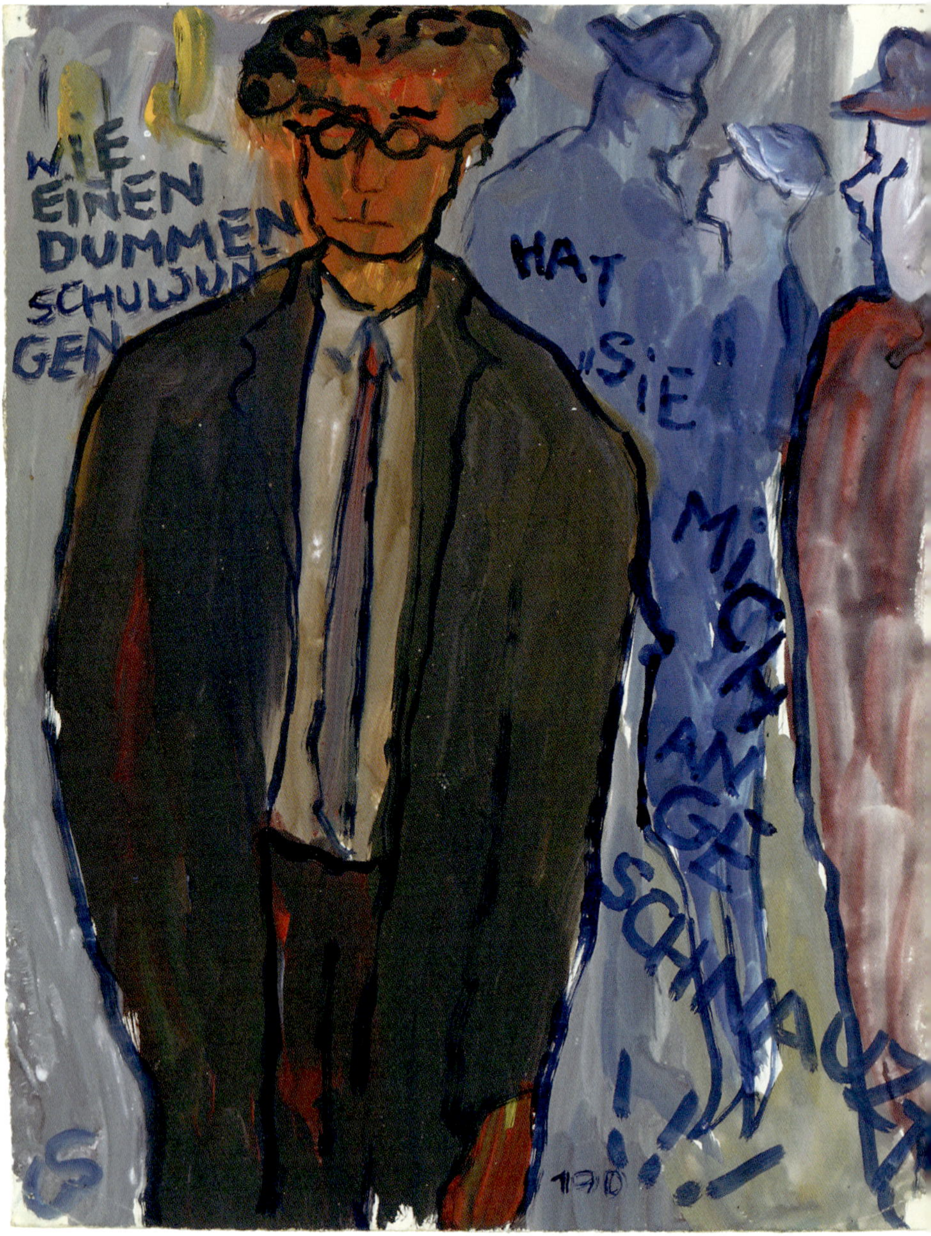
WIE
EINEN
DUMMEN
SCHULJUN
GEN
HAT
"SIE"
MICH
ANGE
SCHMA

(opposite)

"'She' scolded me like
a dumb schoolboy!"

(bottom)

"I have lost all desire
to go to the performance."

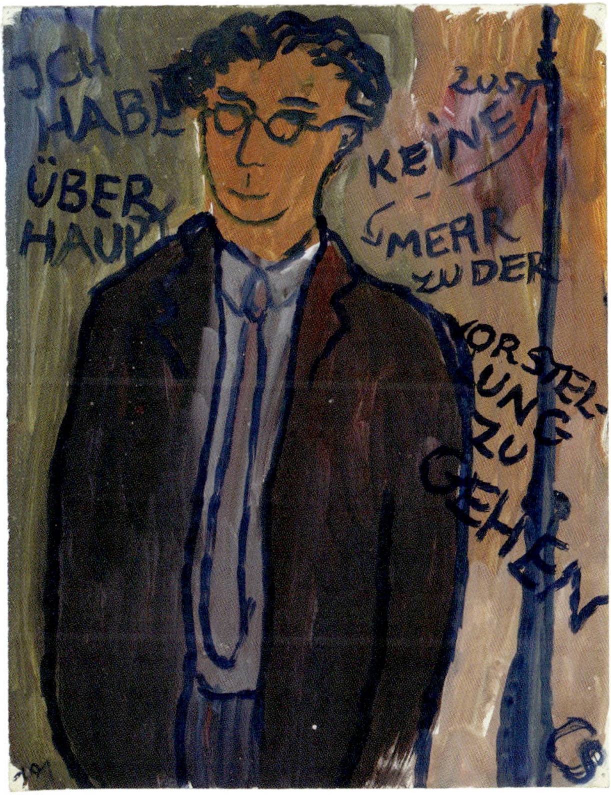

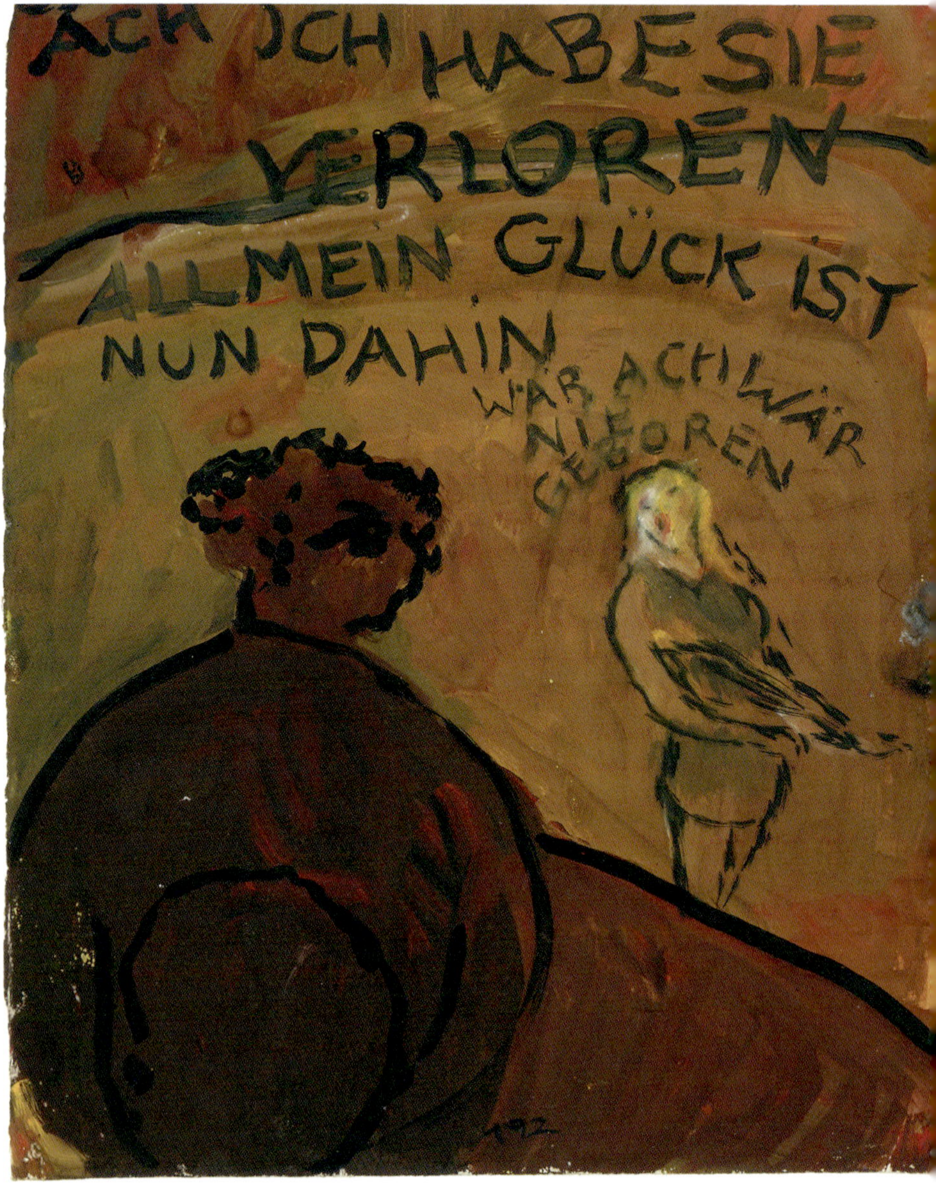
ACH ICH HABESIE
VERLOREN
ALLMEIN GLÜCK IST
NUN DAHIN
WÄR ACH WÄR
NIE
GEBOREN

(opposite)

An hour later, however, he is sitting in the theatre.

PAULINKA SINGS
Ach, ich habe sie verloren, all mein Glück ist nun dahin. Wär, ach wär ich nie geboren
[Oh, I have lost her, all my happiness is now gone. How I wish that never was I born].

(bottom)

Kehre wieder, Euridice [Come back to me, Eurydice].

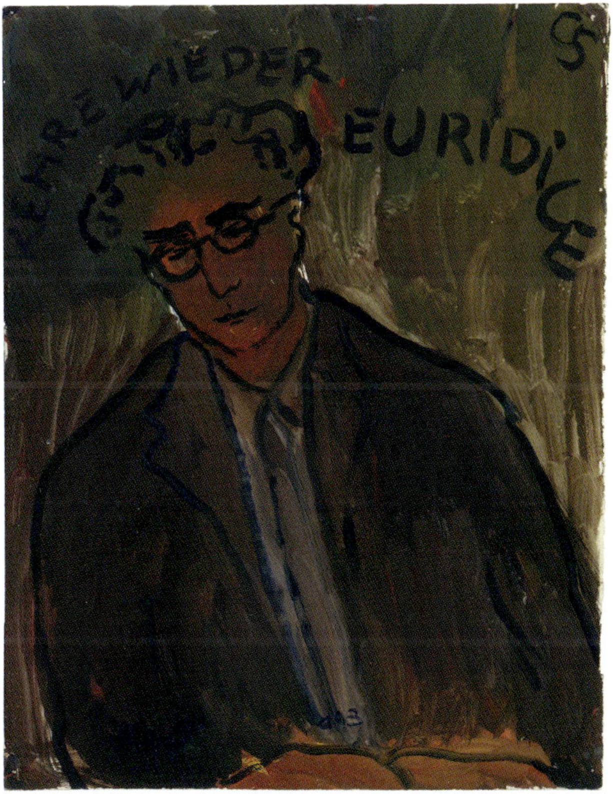

(bottom)

Paulinka sings as purely and beautifully as she rarely did since Professor Klingklang's times.

(opposite)

AUDIENCE
"Bravo, bravissimo."

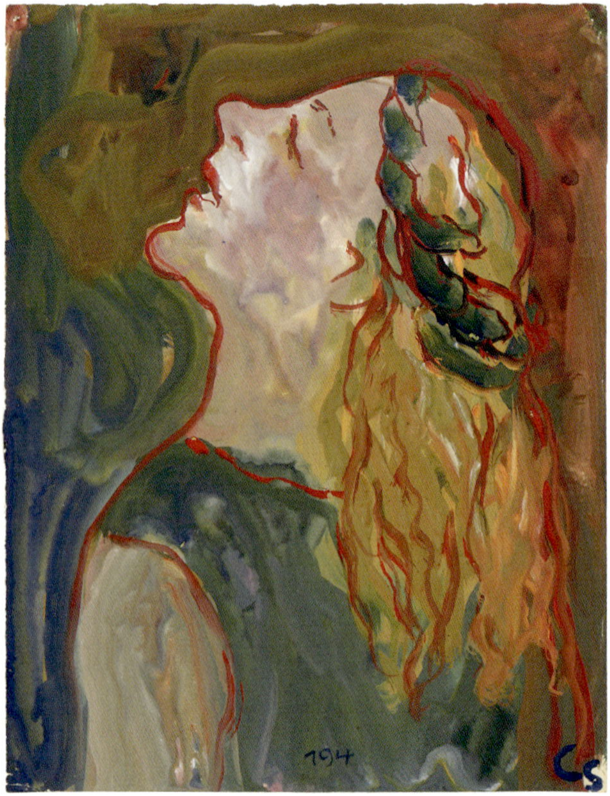

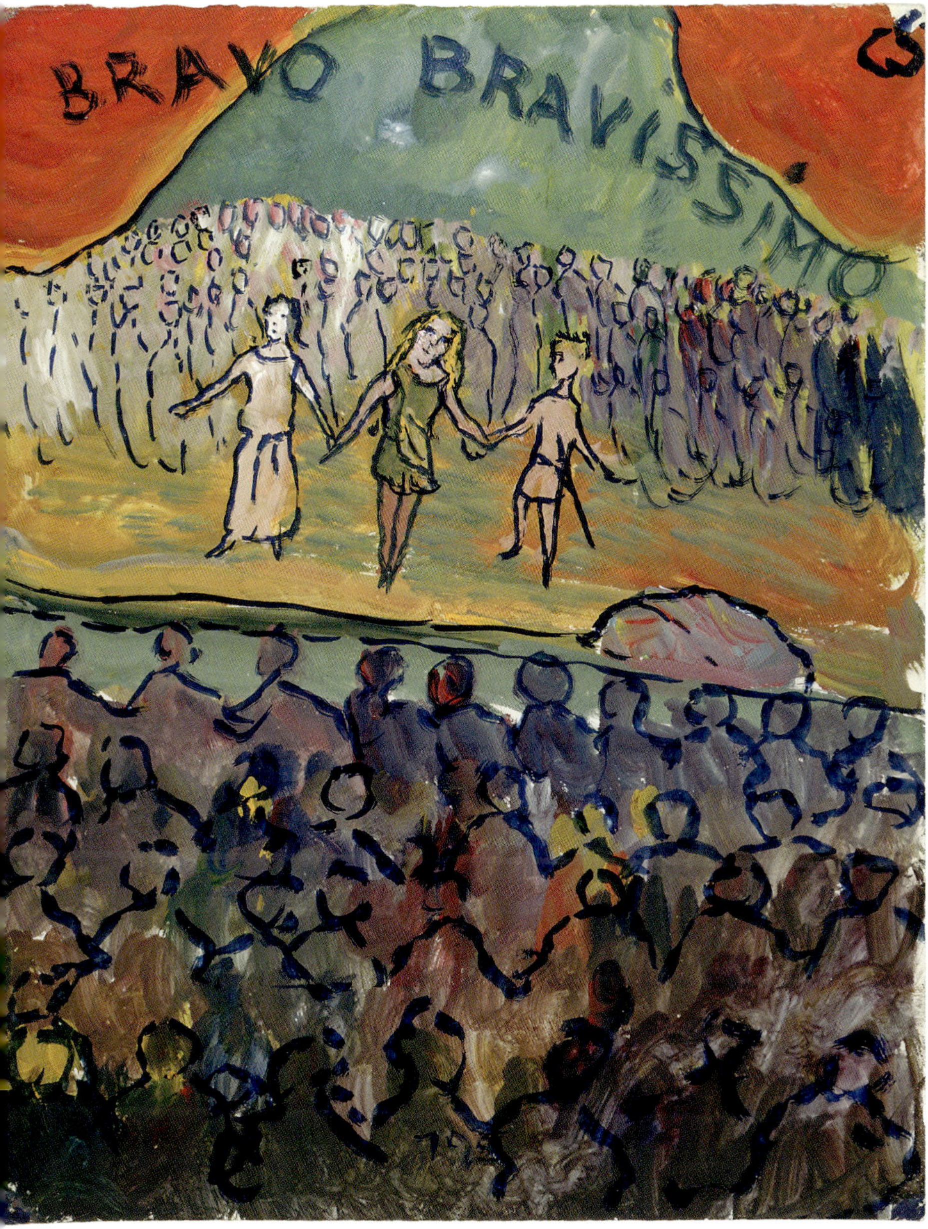
BRAVO BRAVISSIMO

(bottom)

DABERLOHN
“Bravo, bravissimo!”

(opposite)

CONDUCTOR
“This Orpheus you can be sure of singing on the world’s greatest stage with the greatest success!”

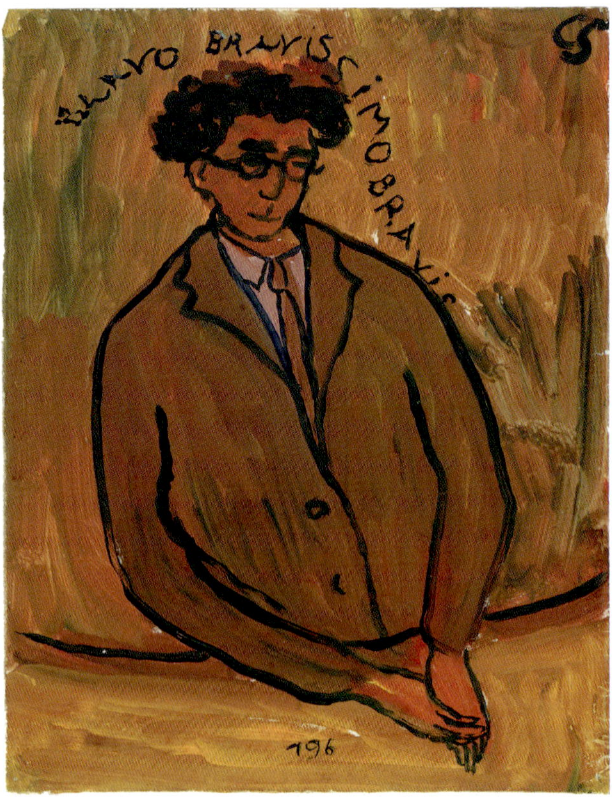

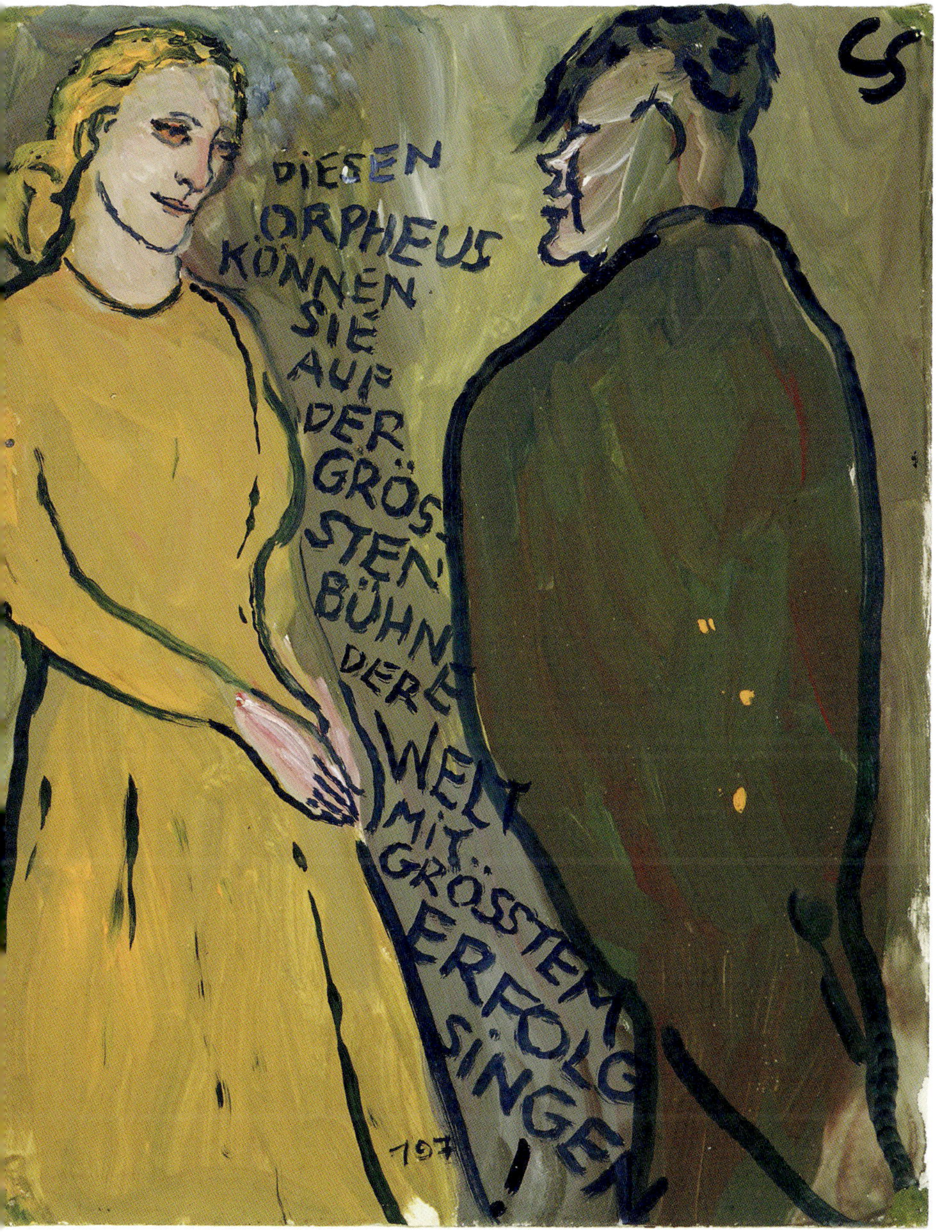
DIESEN
ORPHEUS
KÖNNEN
SIE
AUF
DER
GRÖSS-
TEN
BÜHNE
DER
WELT
MIT
GRÖSSTEM
ERFOLG
SINGEN!
CS
197

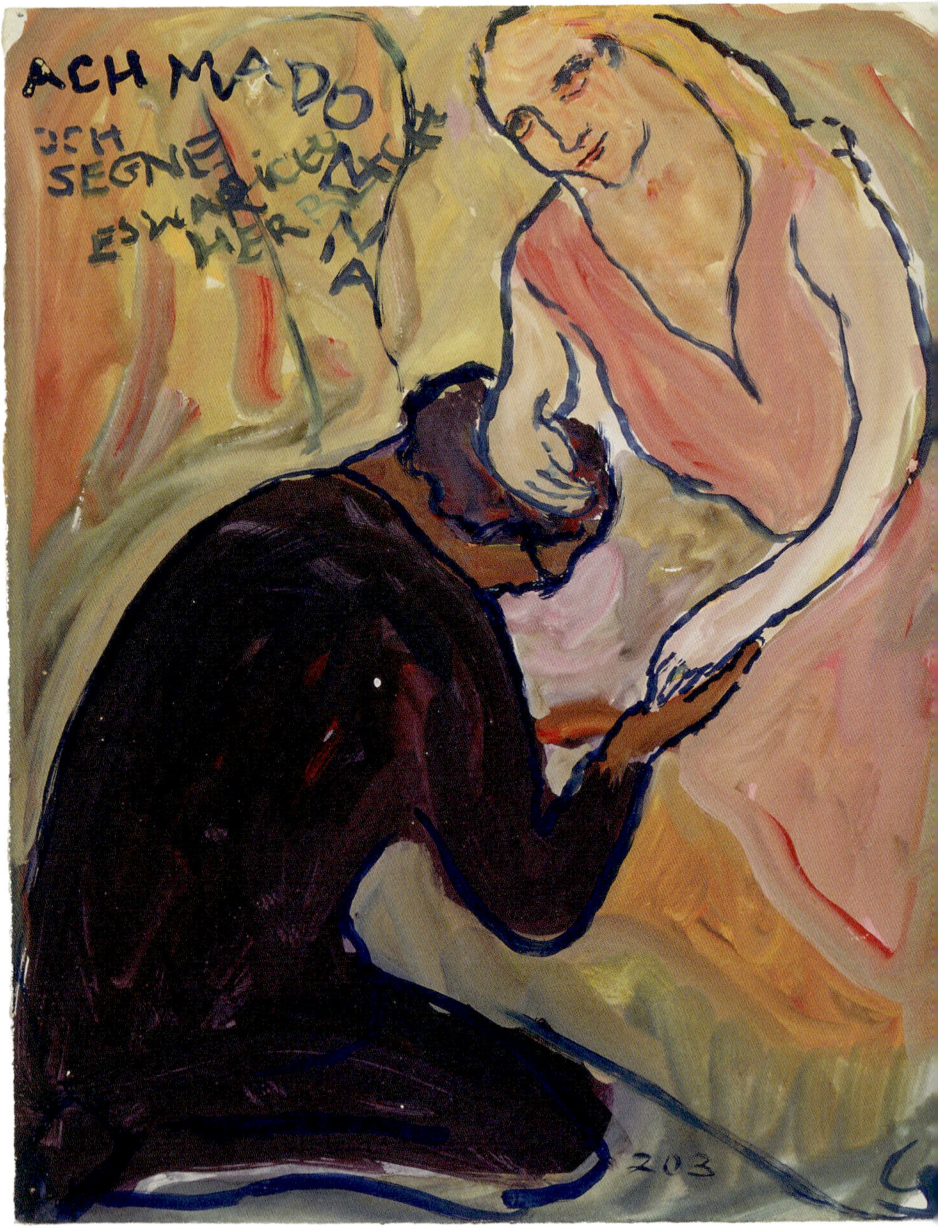
ACH MADO
203

(opposite)

DABERLOHN
“Oh Madonna, I bless you.
It was glorious.”

(bottom)

PAULINKA
“Please go now, goodnight.”

DABERLOHN
“Oh my sun, do not leave me.”

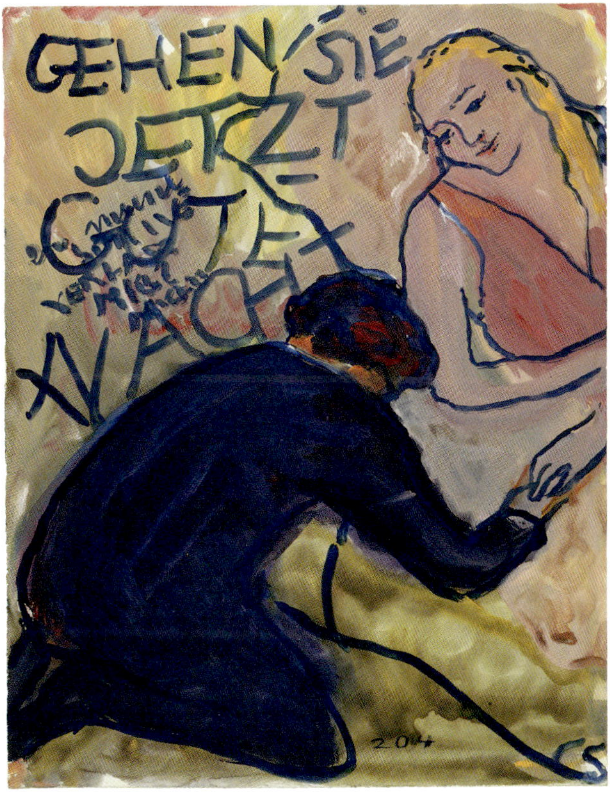

(bottom)

Fate mocks him. The small (small-minded) girl with the stuffy ideas appears to him as the image of the warm, glorious woman and Madonna.

(opposite)

Hot blood flows through his body.

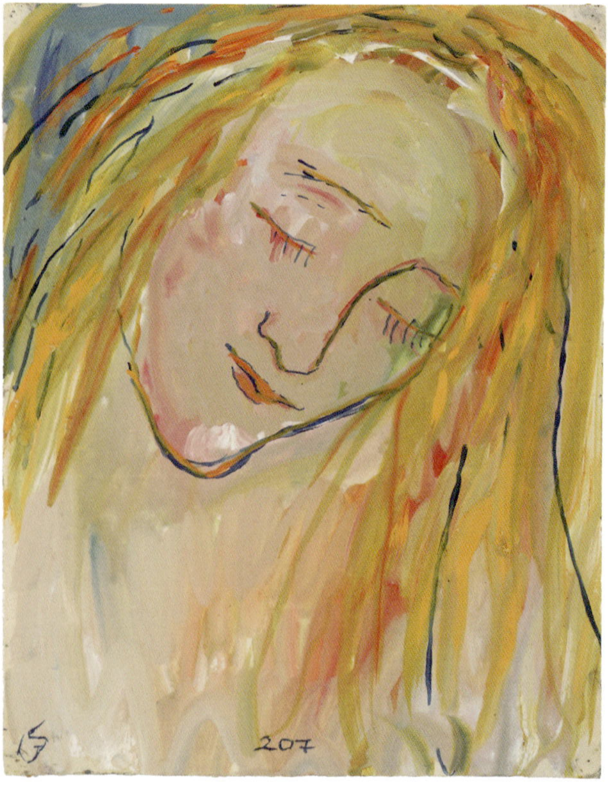

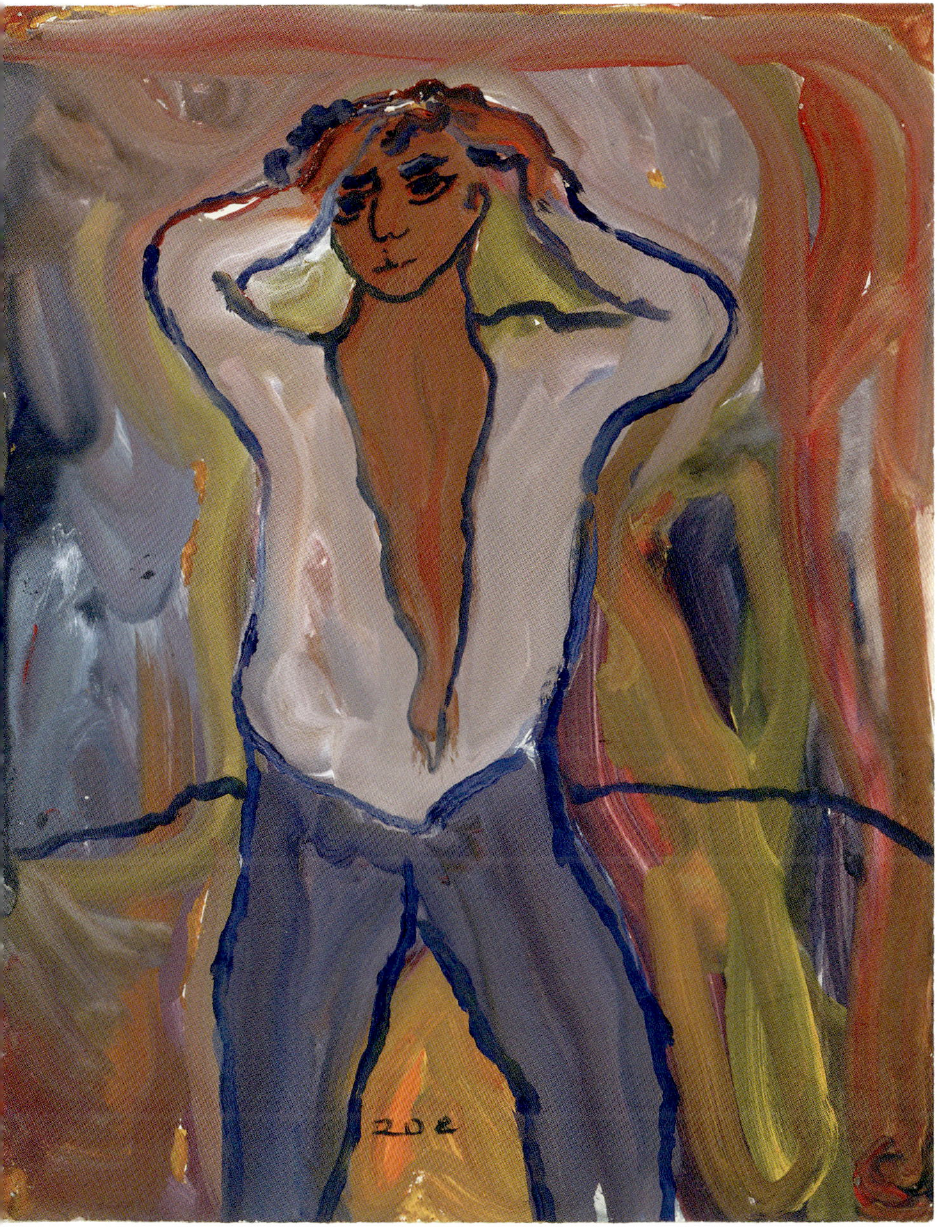

He recalls the conversation with his friend the sculptor and its culmination – to have his own death mask made in order to discover the nature of what determines the transition from life to death.

Having reached the highest point of both spiritual and physical despair, he feels exactly like someone suspended between death and life and consequently decides to have the experiment with the death mask carried out on himself.

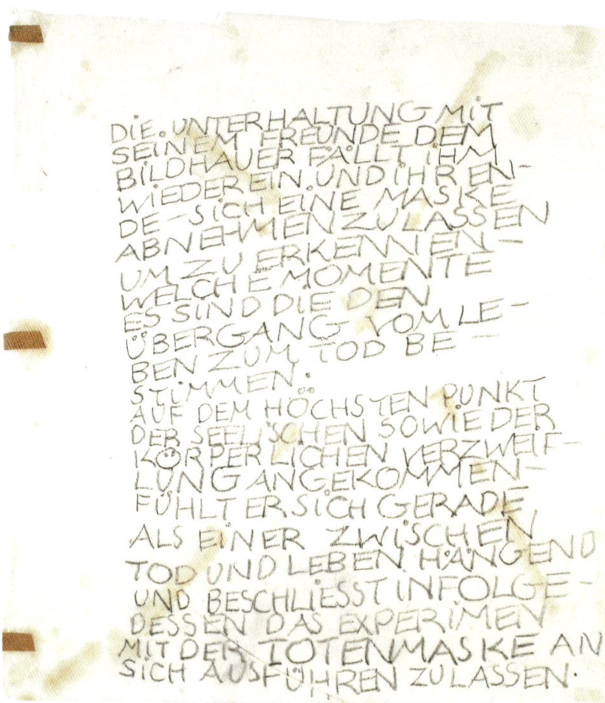
DIE. UNTERHALTUNG MIT
SEINEM FREUNDE DEM
BILDHAUER FÄLLT IHM
WIEDER EIN. UND IHR EN-
DE - SICH EINE MASKE
ABNEHMEN ZU LASSEN
UM ZU ERKENNEN -
WELCHE MOMENTE
ES SIND DIE DEN
ÜBERGANG VOM LE-
BEN ZUM TOD BE-
STIMMEN.
AUF DEM HÖCHSTEN PUNKT
DER SEELISCHEN SOWIE DER
KÖRPERLICHEN VERZWEIF-
LUNG ANGEKOMMEN-
FÜHLT ER SICH GERADE
ALS EINER ZWISCHEN
TOD UND LEBEN HÄNGEND
UND BESCHLIESST INFOLGE-
DESSEN DAS EXPERIMENT
MIT DER TOTENMASKE AN
SICH AUSFÜHREN ZU LASSEN.

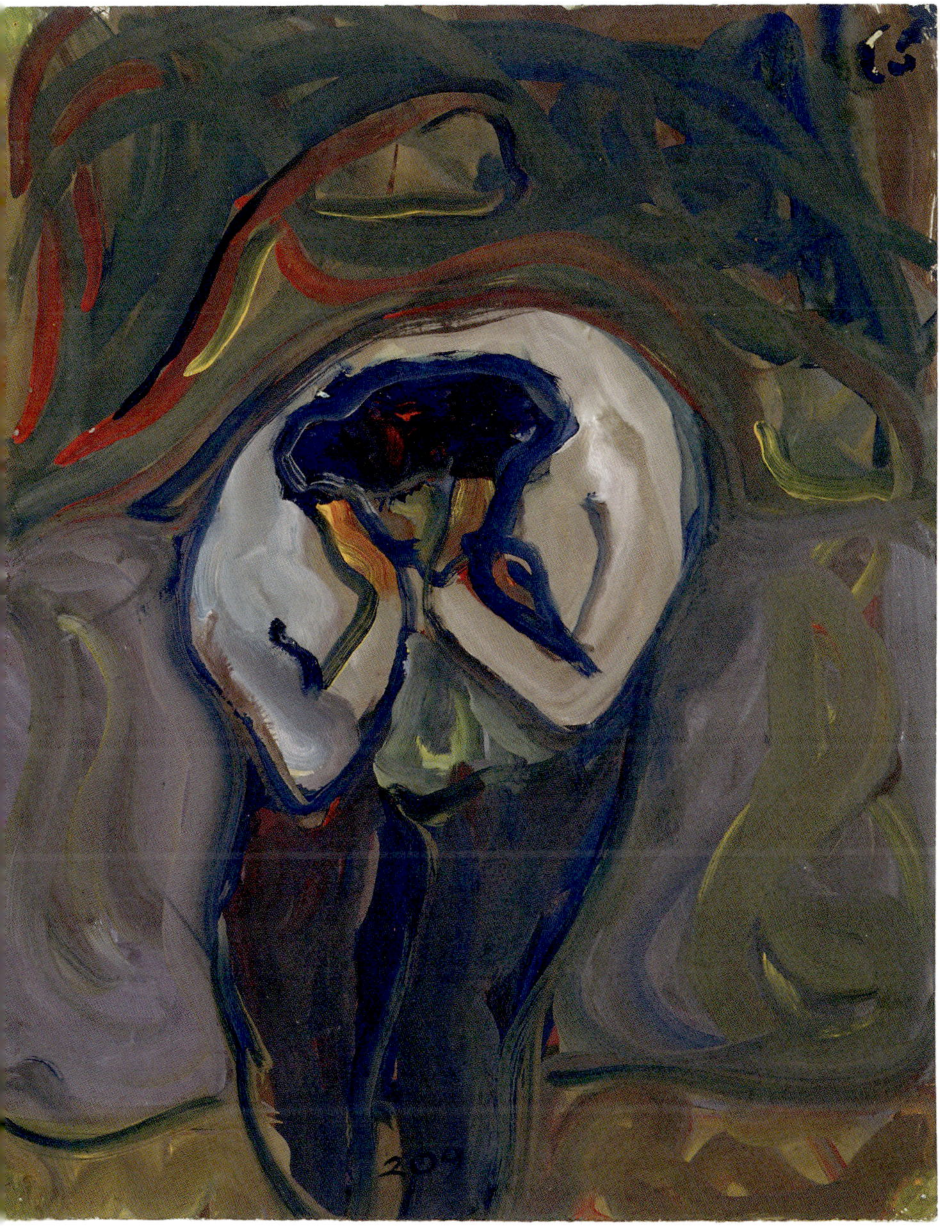

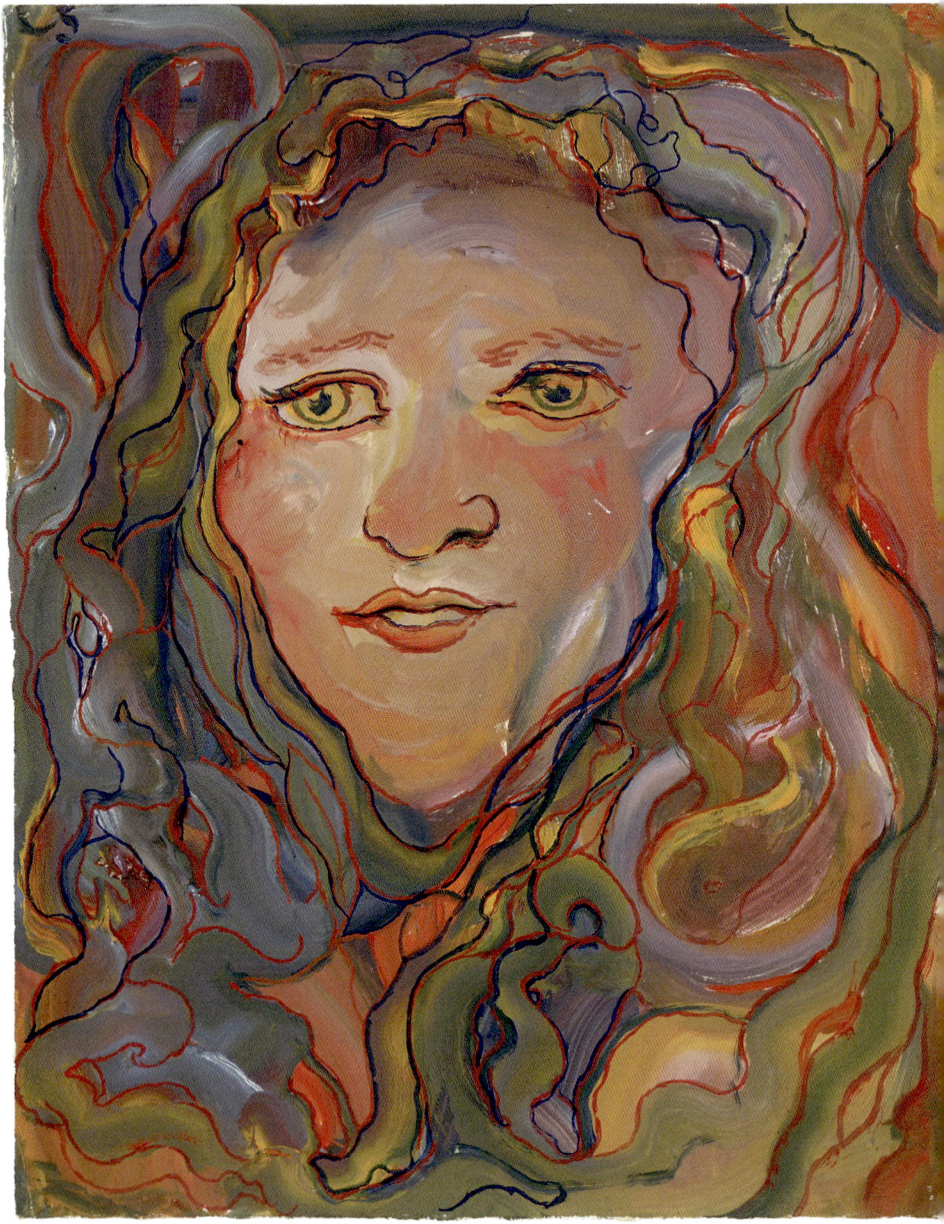

(opposite)

While his face is being worked on, the following is taking place in his mind: It is a quite colourful, musical mood that dominates him. From confused lines and threads, a theatrical mask of Paulinka takes shape.

(bottom)

Inside he is still enveloped by the profound, musical, “theatre-mask-like” mood.

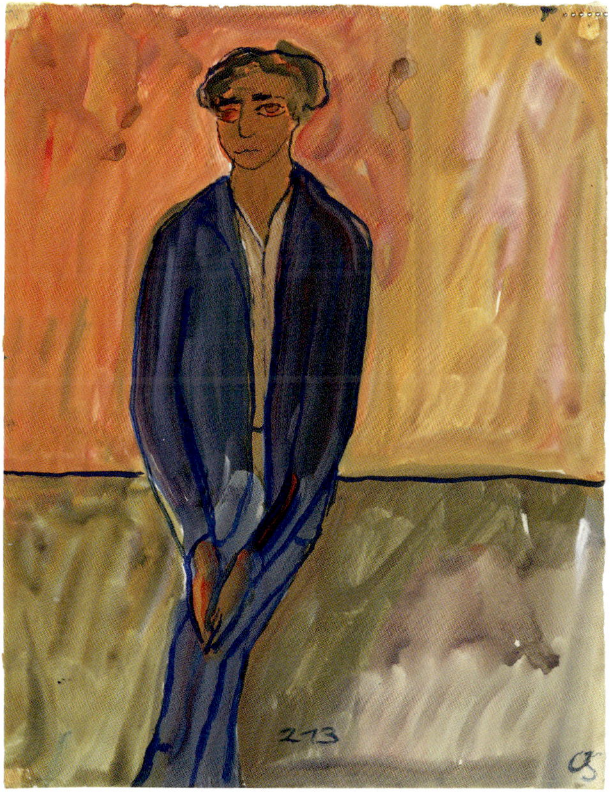

Learn to sing,
oh my soul.

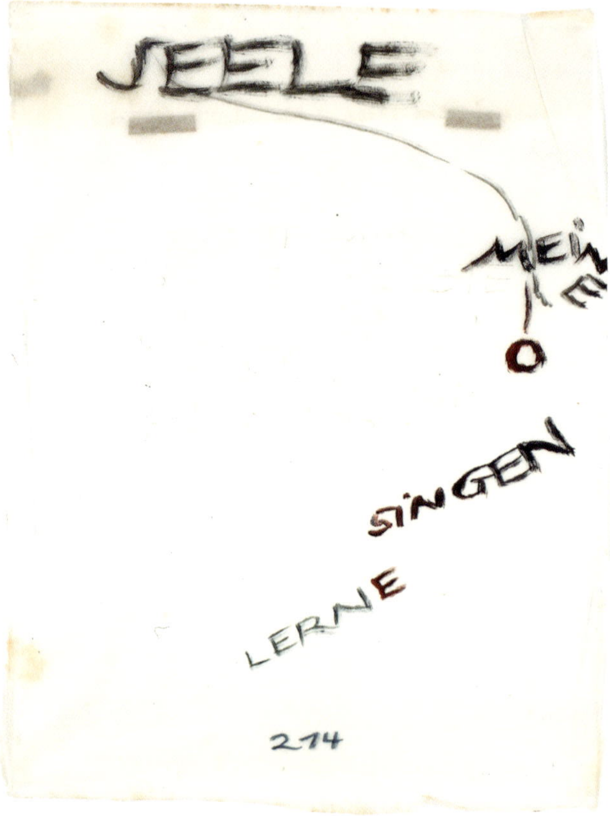

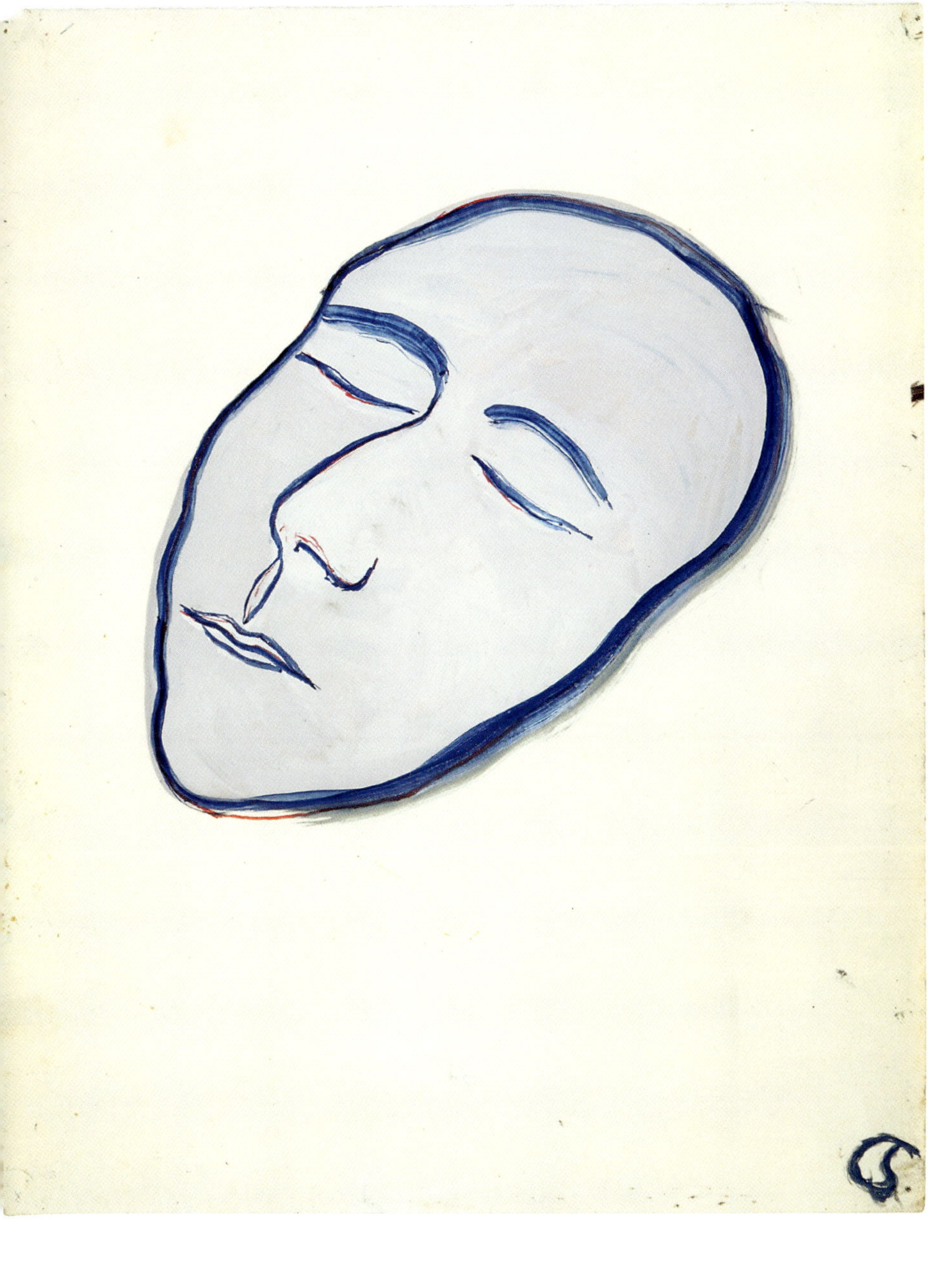

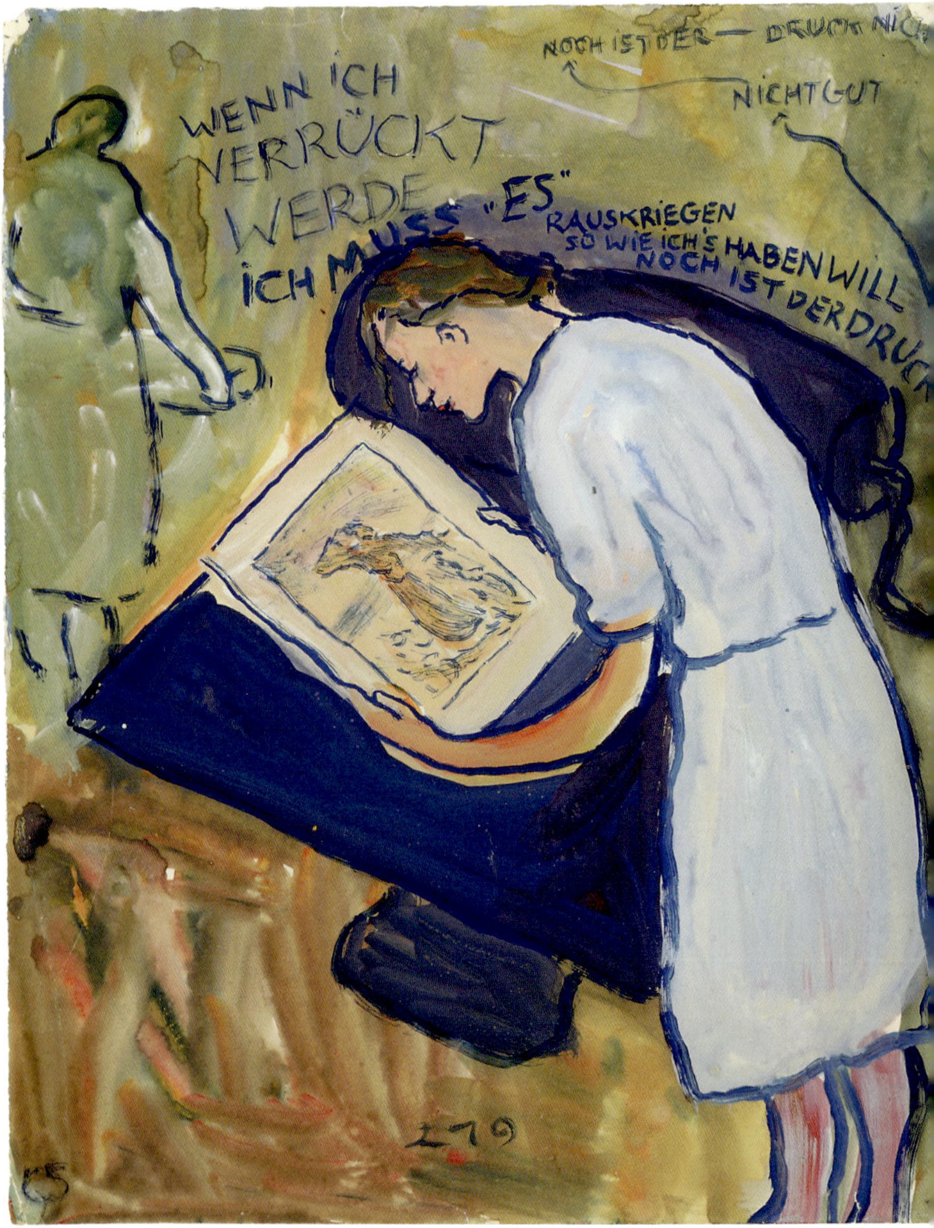
NOCH IST DER — DRUCK
NICHT GUT
WENN ICH VERRÜCKT WERDE
ICH MUSS „ES" RAUSKRIEGEN SO WIE ICH'S HABEN WILL
NOCH IST DER DRUCK

Meanwhile Charlotte is intensively absorbed in her efforts to express in an etching what subconsciously binds her so much to Daberlohn. There is a man by the sea, surrounded by a group of young people. He is speaking to them, and they are listening. In the background a youth of medium height points to his forehead. He wants to say, that those people there are truly haywire and crazy.

CHARLOTTE
"Even if it makes me crazy – I must get 'it'
the way I want it. It still isn't good.
The print still isn't..."

Daberlohn's diagnosis contains encouragement for Charlotte. The etching has no particular artistic worth and betrays no above-average talent – but concept and execution reveals a touching effort – which does not escape him.

DABERLOHN
"In my opinion you are destined to create something above average."

DABERLOHNS DIAGNOSE ENTHÄLT
AUFMUNTERNDES FÜR CHARLOTTE

DIE RADIERUNG HAT KEINEN BESON-
DEREN KÜNSTLERISCHEN WERT UND VER-
RÄT KEIN SEHR ÜBERDURCHSCHNITTLICHES
TALENT — DOCH LIEGT IN AUFFASSUNG
UND AUSFÜHRUNG EIN RÜHRENDES
BEMÜHEN — DAS IHM NICHT ENTGEHT.

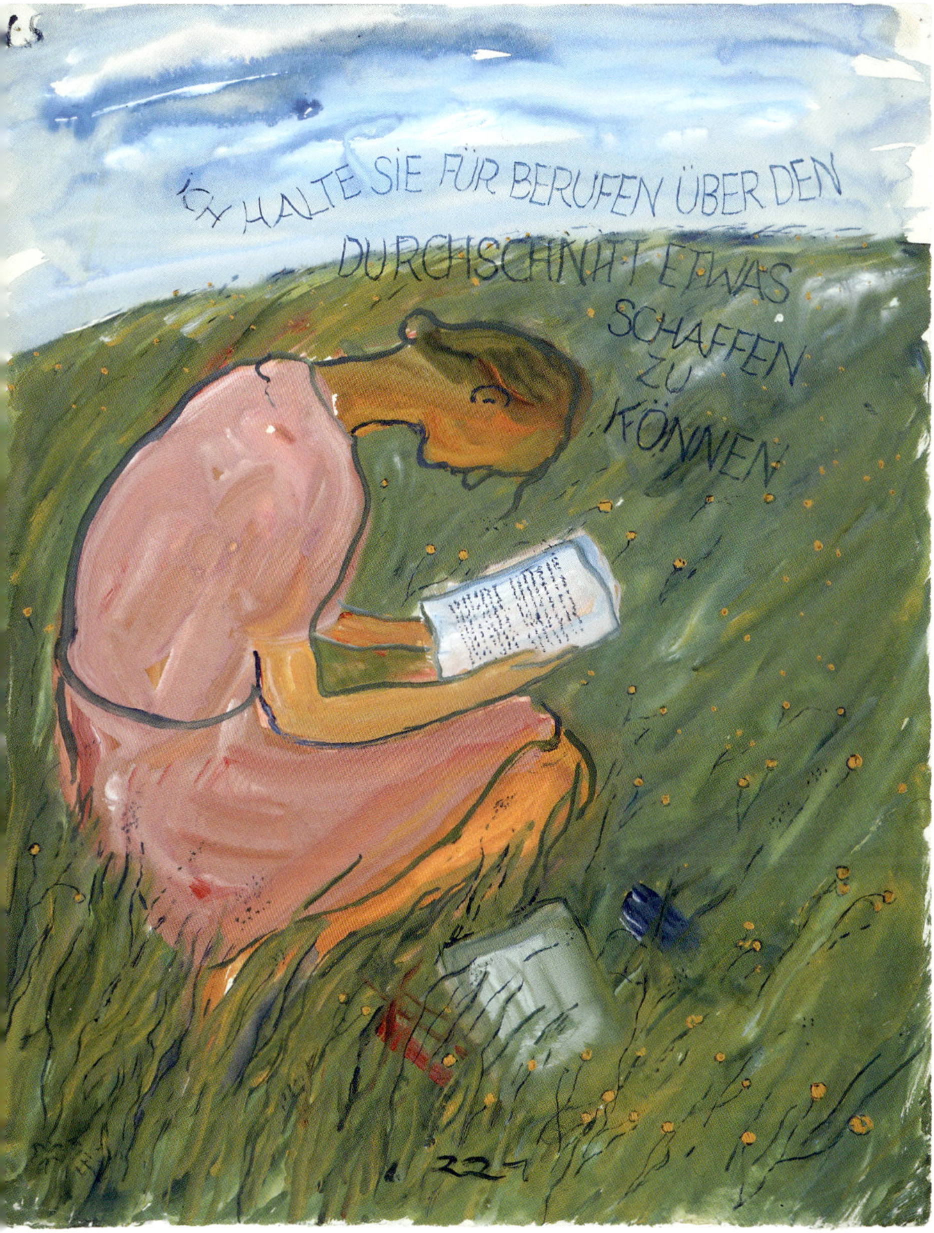
ICH HALTE SIE FÜR BERUFEN ÜBER DEN
DURCHSCHNITT ETWAS
SCHAFFEN
ZU
KÖNNEN
224

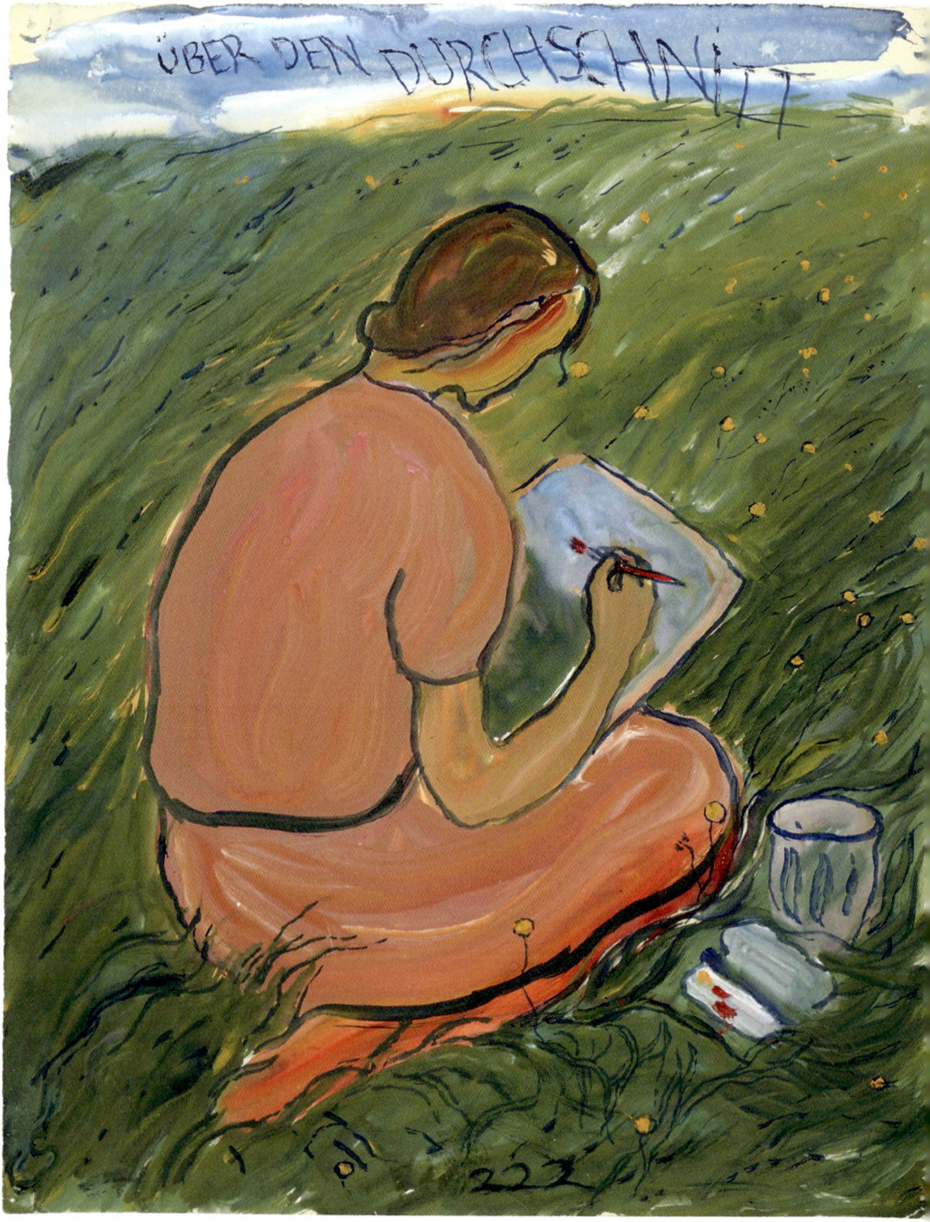
ÜBER DEN DURCHSCHNITT

“Above the average”

She is very encouraged by his letter and really feels quite proud that someone finds it worth wasting his thoughts on her.

While beginning to paint the buttercup-strewn meadow where she happens to be sitting, she decides to make his prophecy come true and actually create something “that goes above average”.

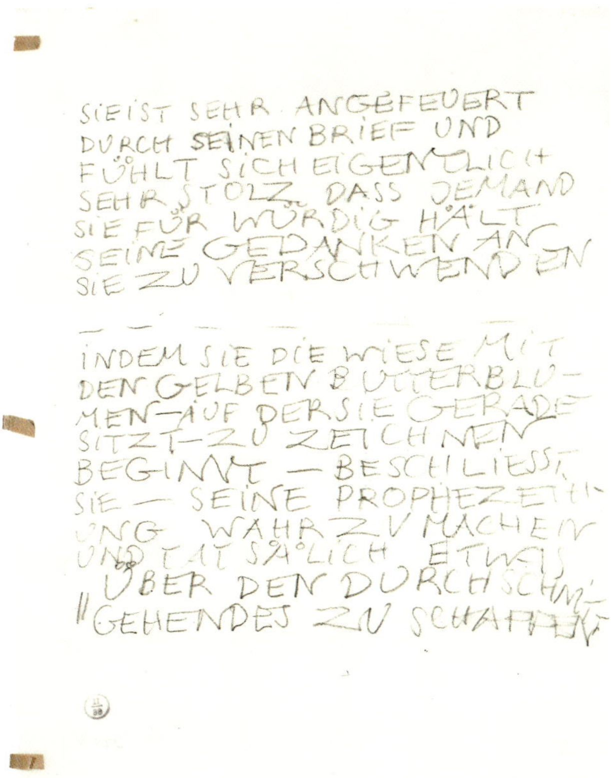
SIE IST SEHR ANGEFEUERT
DURCH SEINEN BRIEF UND
FÜHLT SICH EIGENTLICH
SEHR STOLZ, DASS JEMAND
SIE FÜR WÜRDIG HÄLT
SEINE GEDANKEN AN
SIE ZU VERSCHWENDEN

INDEM SIE DIE WIESE MIT
DEN GELBEN BUTTERBLU-
MEN – AUF DER SIE GERADE
SITZT – ZU ZEICHNEN
BEGINNT – BESCHLIESST
SIE – SEINE PROPHEZEIH-
UNG WAHR ZU MACHEN
UND TATSÄCHLICH ETWAS
„ÜBER DEN DURCHSCHNITT
GEHENDES ZU SCHAFFEN“

(bottom)

CHARLOTTE
"I picked 'it' for 'him'.
One says, it brings luck."

(opposite)

CHARLOTTE
"Which sheet would you like?"

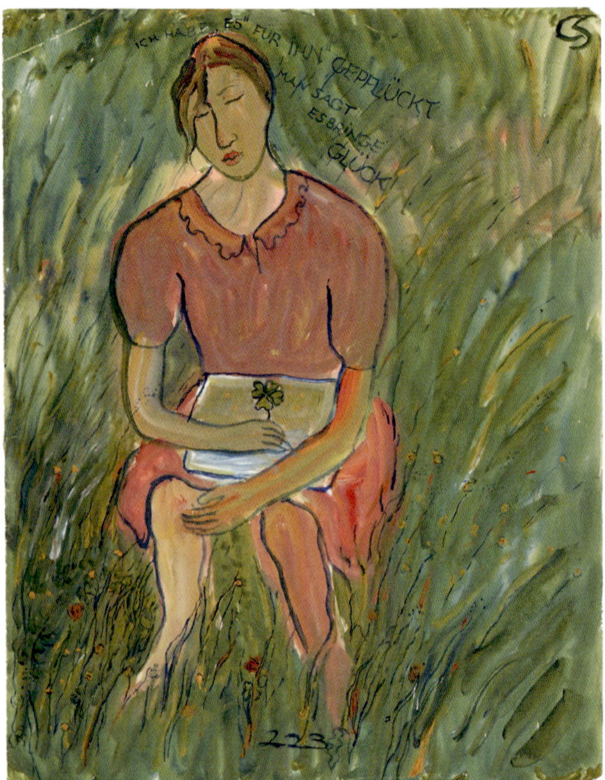

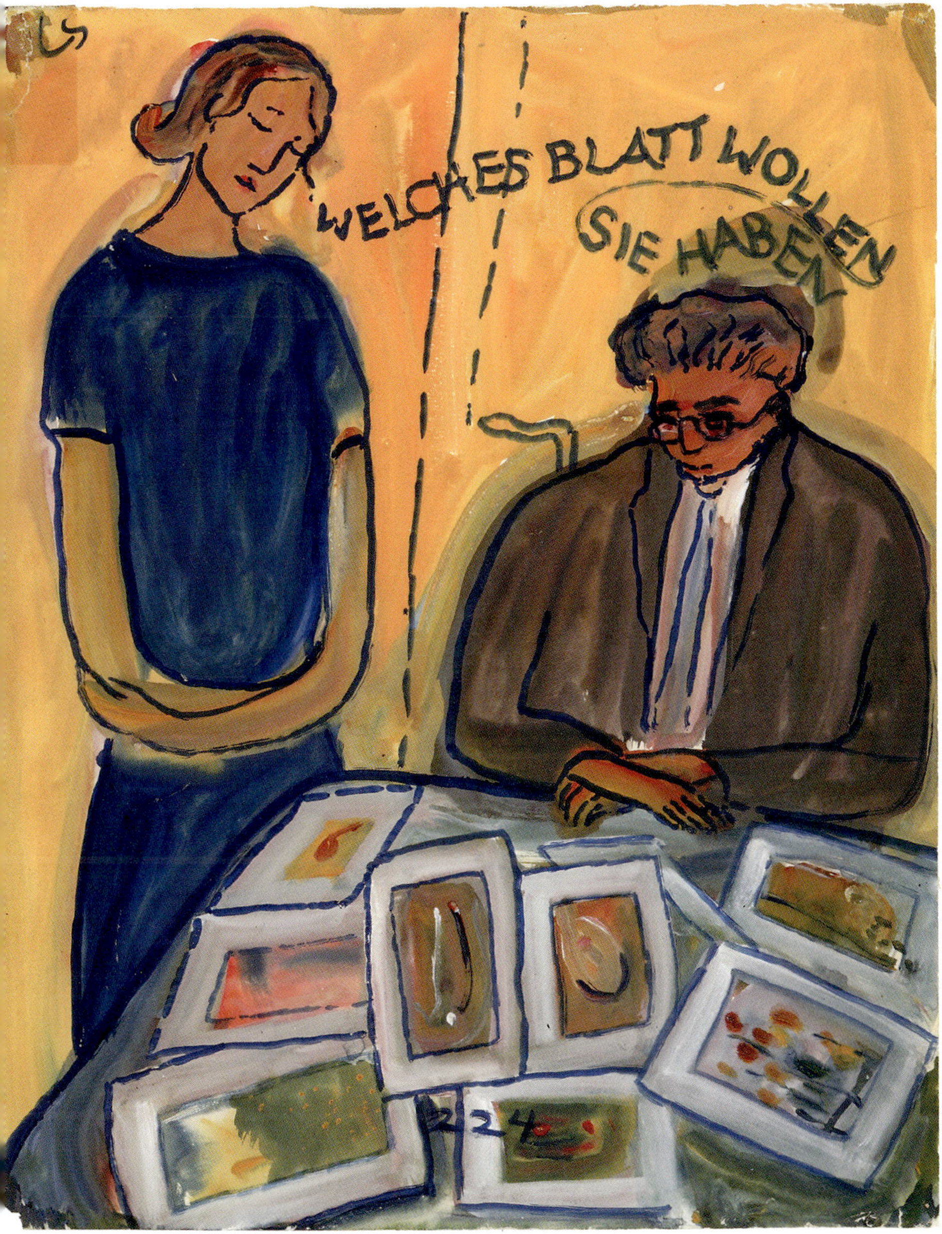
WELCHES BLATT WOLLEN
SIE HABEN

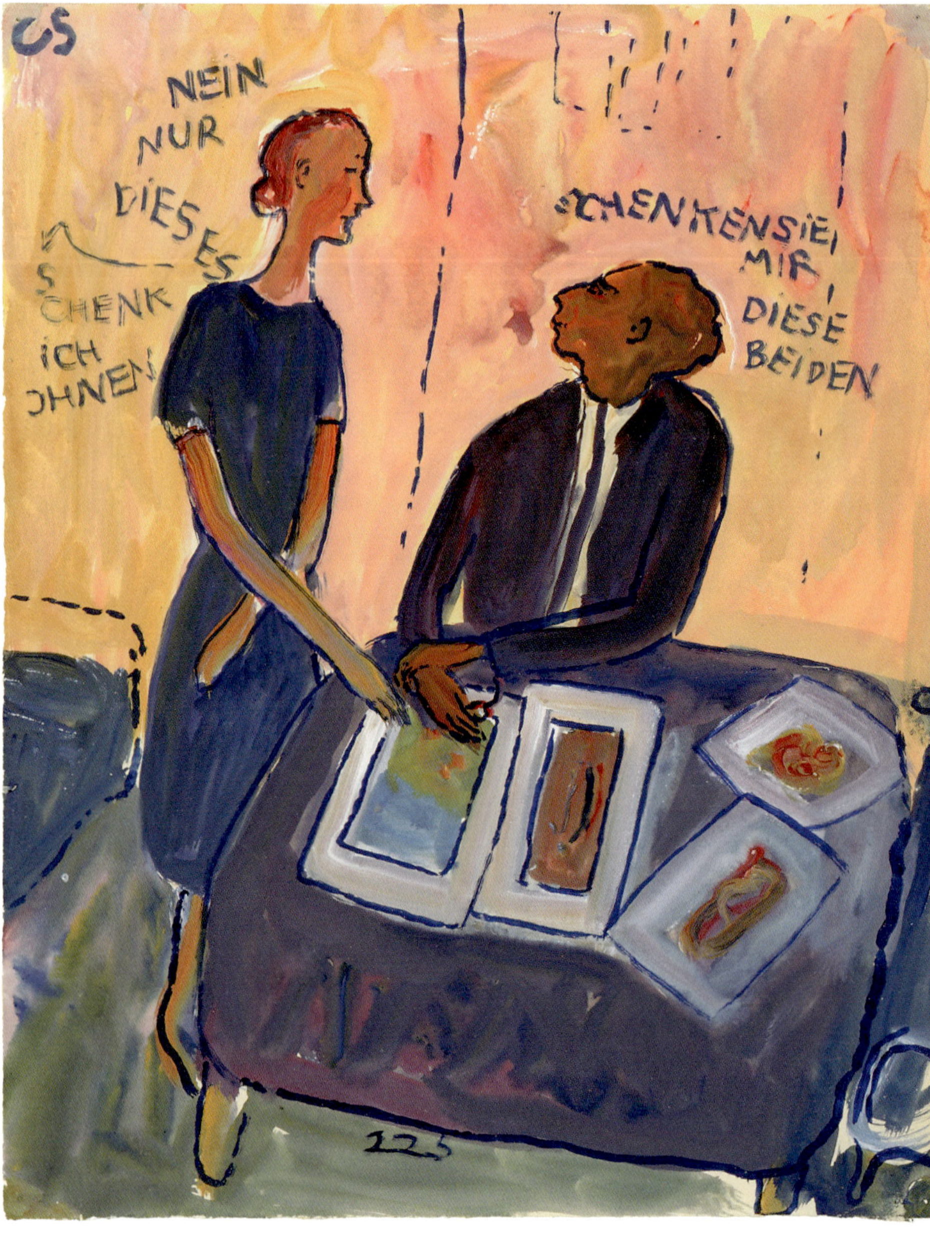
CS
NEIN NUR DIESES SCHENK ICH IHNEN
SCHENKENSIE MIR DIESE BEIDEN
225

Back from her trip, Charlotte shows him her drawings, and after a brief but highly concentrated inspection he chooses The Meadow with the Yellow Buttercups, and another sheet entitled Death and the Maiden, and asks her to give him both.

DABERLOHN
"Give me these two."

CHARLOTTE
"No, I'll only give you this one."

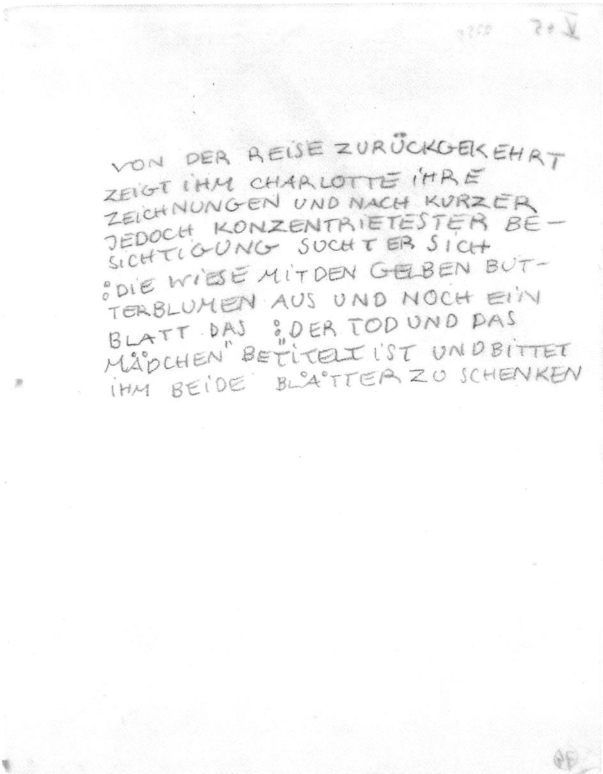
VON DER REISE ZURÜCKGEKEHRT
ZEIGT IHM CHARLOTTE IHRE
ZEICHNUNGEN UND NACH KURZER
JEDOCH KONZENTRIETESTER BE-
SICHTIGUNG SUCHT ER SICH
„DIE WIESE MIT DEN GELBEN BUT-
TERBLUMEN AUS UND NOCH EIN
BLATT DAS „DER TOD UND DAS
MÄDCHEN" BETITELT IST UND BITTET
IHM BEIDE BLÄTTER ZU SCHENKEN

(bottom)

DABERLOHN
"I'd like to have Death and the Maiden, too. 'That's' the two of us."

(opposite)

Having arrived at Paulinka in the familiar blue-and-red room, he reflects on Charlotte's drawings. In so doing he almost becomes a delicate young girl himself.

DABERLOHN
"Just take a look at these two drawings."

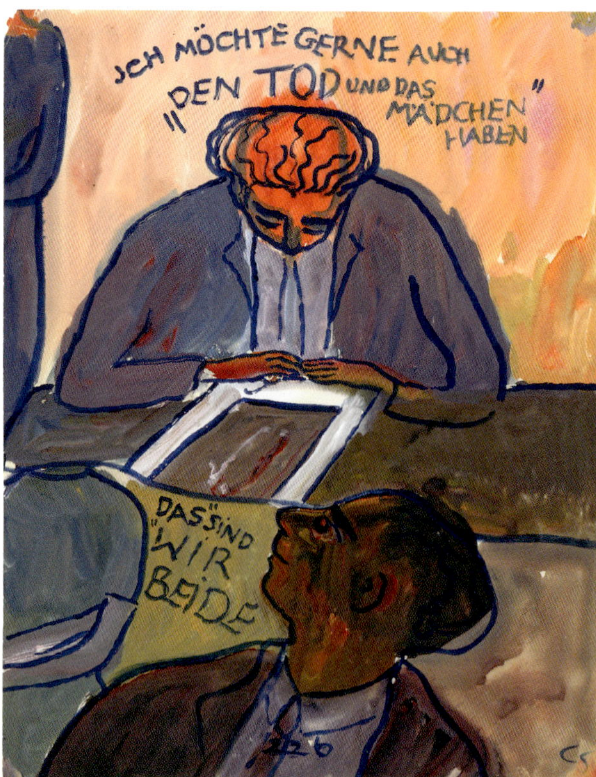

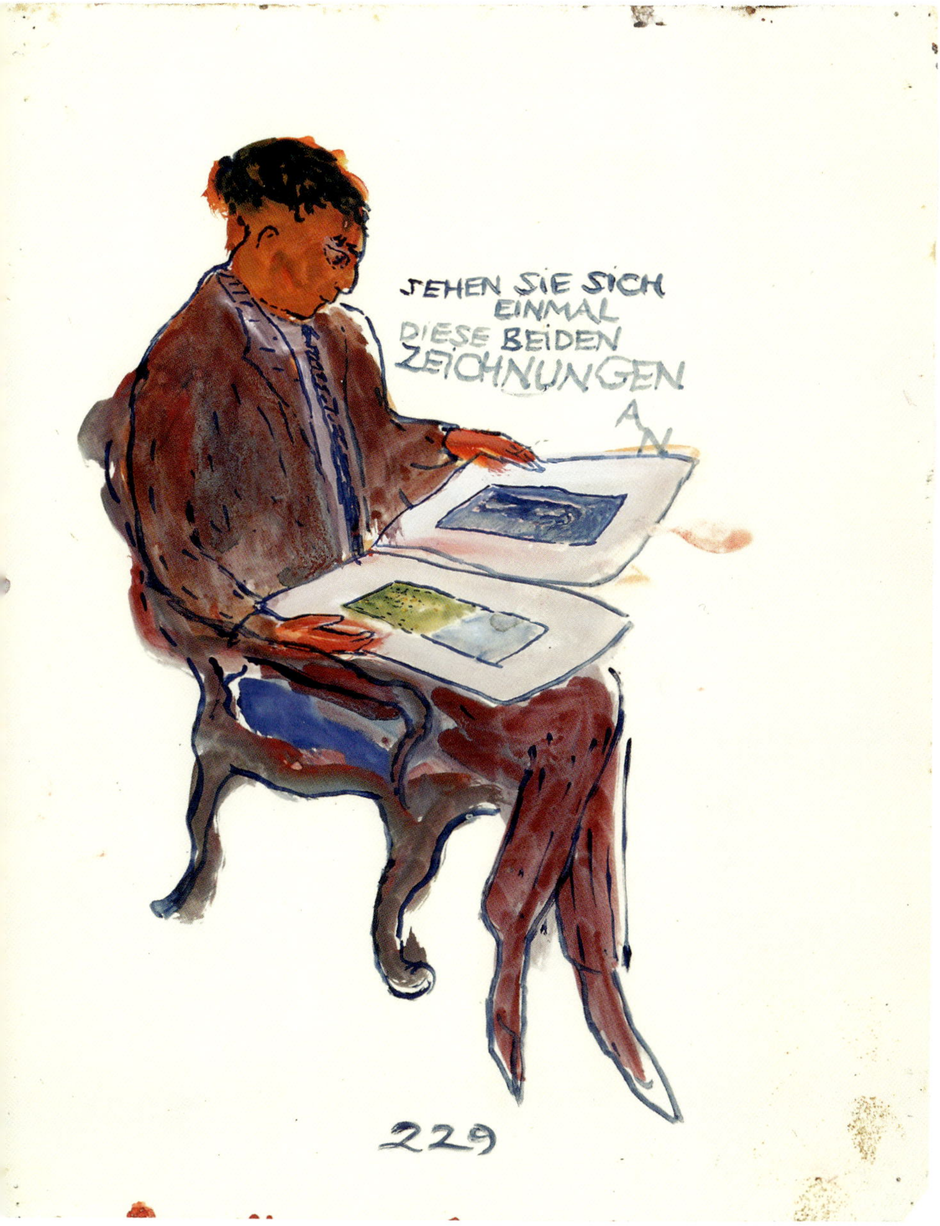
SEHEN SIE SICH EINMAL DIESE BEIDEN ZEICHNUNGEN AN
229

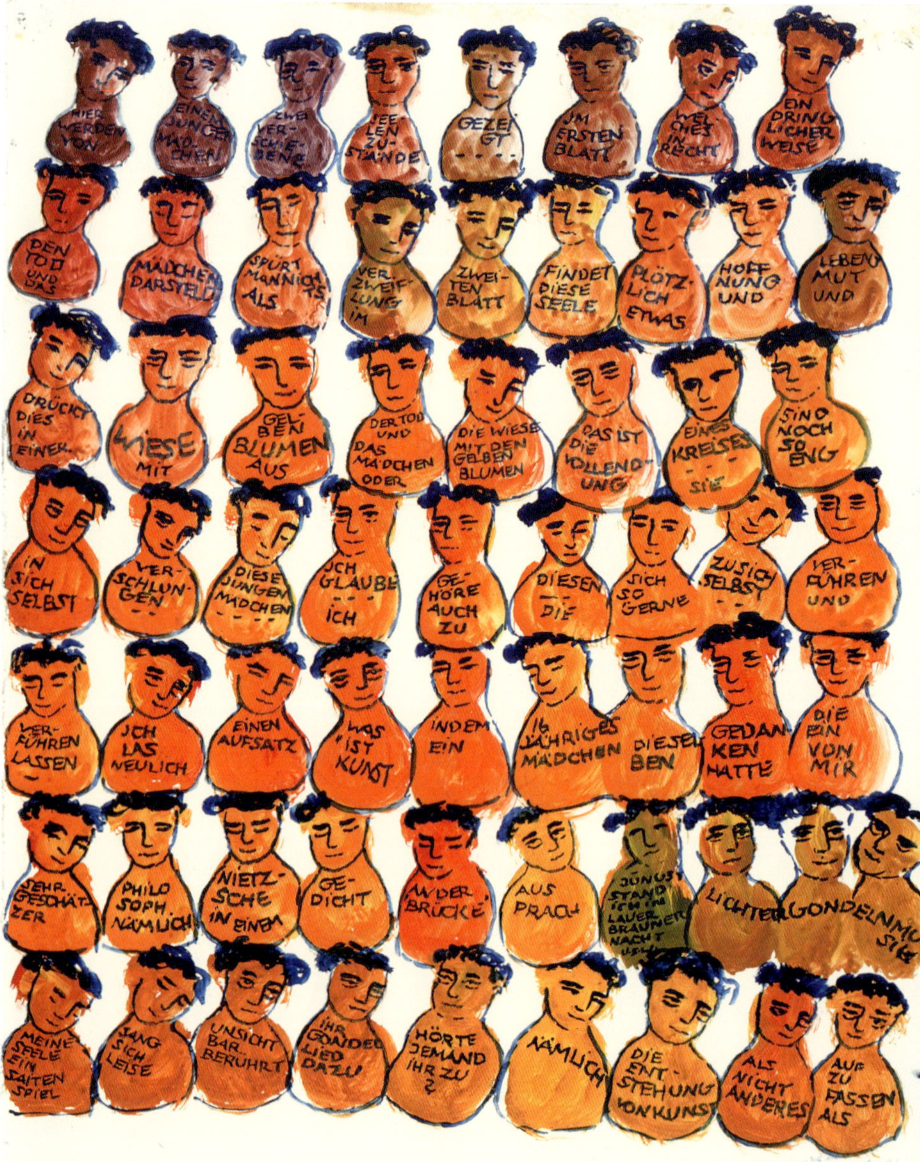

HIER WERDEN VON
EINEN JUNGEN MÄD-CHEN
ZWEI VER-SCHIE-DENE
SEE-LEN ZU-STÄNDE
GEZEI-GT - - - -
IM ERSTEN BLATT
WEL-CHES IN RECHT
EIN DRING LICHER WEISE
DEN TOD UND DAS
MÄDCHEN DARSTELLT
SPÜRT MAN NICHTS ALS
VER-ZWEIF-LUNG IM
ZWEI-TEN BLATT
FINDET DIESE SEELE
PLÖTZ-LICH ETWAS
HOFF NUNG UND
LEBENS MUT UND
DRÜCKT DIES IN EINER
WIESE MIT
GEL-BEN BLUMEN AUS
DER TOD UND DAS MÄDCHEN ODER
DIE WIESE MIT DEN GELBEN BLUMEN
DAS IST DIE VOLLEND-UNG
EINES KREISES - - SIE
SIND NOCH SO ENG
IN SICH SELBST
VER-SCHLUN-GEN
DIESE JUNGEN MÄDCHEN - - - -
ICH GLAUBE - - - ICH
GE-HÖRE AUCH ZU
DIESEN - - DIE
SICH SO GERNE
ZU SICH SELBST
VER-FÜHREN UND
VER-FÜHREN LASSEN
ICH LAS NEULICH
EINEN AUFSATZ
WAS IST KUNST
INDEM EIN
16 JÄHRIGES MÄDCHEN
DIESEL-BEN
GEDAN-KEN HATTE
DIE EIN VON MIR
SEHR GESCHÄT-ZER
PHILO SOPH NÄMLICH
NIETZ-SCHE IN EINEM
GE-DICHT
AN DER BRÜCKE
AUS PRACH
JÜNGST STAND ICH IN LAUER BRAUNER NACHT USW.
LICHTER GONDELN MU-SIK
MEINE SEELE EIN SAITEN SPIEL
SANG SICH LEISE
UNSICHT BAR BERÜHRT
IHR GONDEL LIED DAZU
HÖRTE JEMAND IHR ZU ?
NÄMLICH
DIE ENT-STEHUNG VON KUNST
ALS NICHT ANDERES
AUF ZU FASSEN ALS
230

“Here we see two different spiritual states of a young girl...

In the first sheet, which strikingly depicts Death and the Maiden, one doesn’t feel anything but despair. In the second sheet this soul suddenly finds some hope and courage to face life and expresses this in a meadow with yellow flowers. Death and the Maiden or The Meadow with Yellow Flowers: that is the completion of a circle.

They are still so closely intertwined with each other, these young girls...

I believe I, too, belong to those who so readily seduce themselves, and let themselves be seduced.

I recently read an essay, What is Art?, in which a 16-year-old girl had the same thoughts as those expressed by a philosopher I greatly admire, I mean Nietzsche, in a poem called Venice.

‘Not long ago I stood in warm, brown night,’ etc. ‘Lights, gondolas, music. My soul, a string music, was singing silently, invisibly touched, accompanied by its gondola song. Did someone listen to it?’

Namely, to conceive of the creation of art as nothing...”

(opposite)

"... less than touching something external with the creator's soul.

And again, when I saw these two drawings, I was reminded of the essay by that other young girl in which she makes it very clear that when she is happy and begins to draw, bright colours and red and yellow dots come from her brush, and when her mood is dull her colours also turn blackish grey.

And it should of course be noted that this is true regardless of the subject matter the artist wishes to depict.

What comes now, as if by chance, are these sheets placed before us, the spiritual mood at the moment of creation, with the themes in accord, Death and the Maiden, the despair-filled theme, together with Meadow with Yellow Flowers – with a hopeful one – so here, in small, of course, are works of art, and my perception of the similarity with the products of young girls and certain geniuses is completely justified. Like young girls..."

(page 380)

"... certain great men, such as the aforementioned Nietzsche, have a boundless yearning to surrender themselves to a particular object. And this yearning for beauty is clothed in such a tender emotion that the natural satisfaction seems to them, like at first also to most young girls, more often than not something to be avoided. The almost impossible execution of this insight then begets the indefatigably creative genius. Man seeks in art that which he believes nature denies him. Michelangelo, for example, and many of the ancient Greeks, belonged to them. More or less men who..."

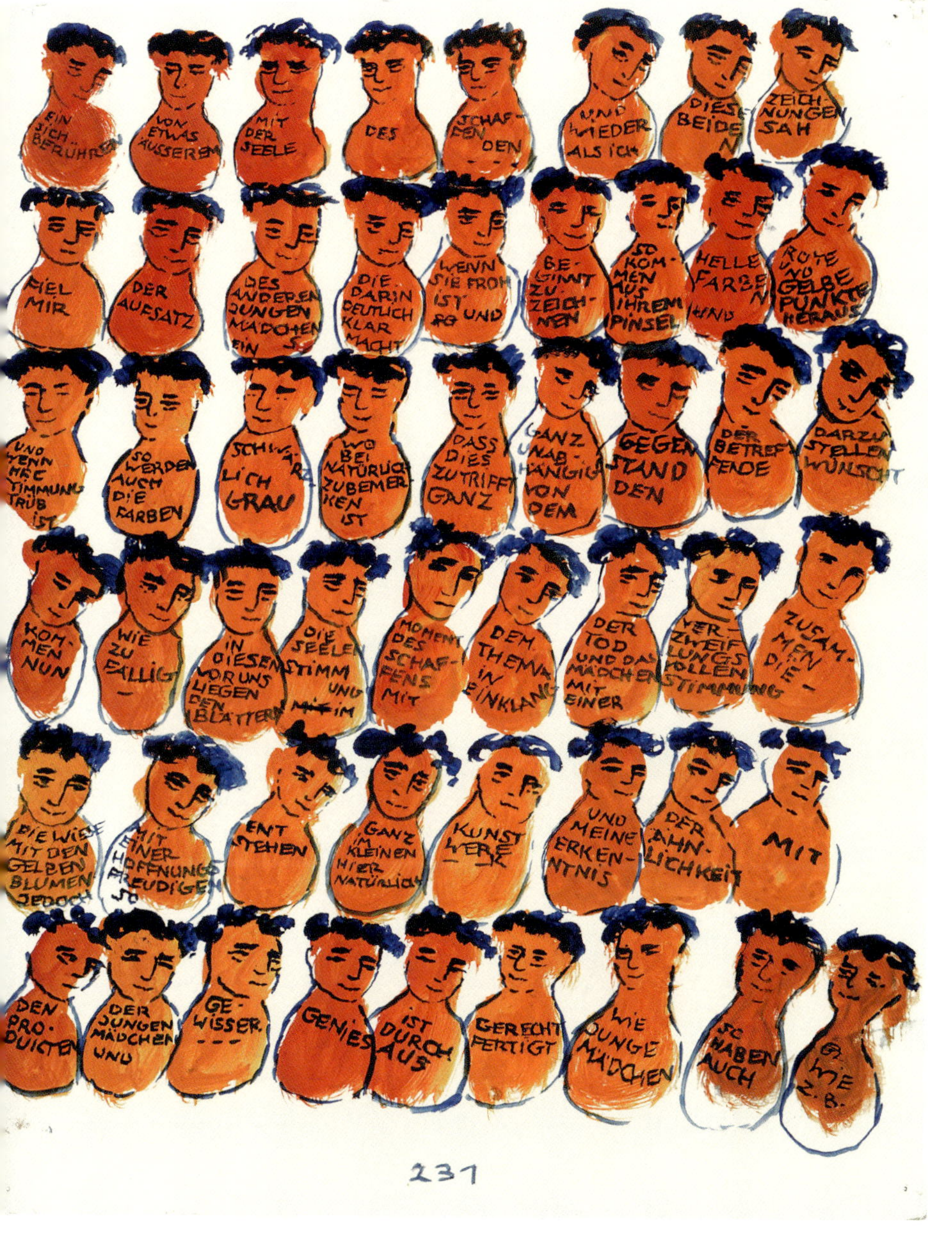
EIN SICH BERÜHREN
VON ETWAS ÄUSSEREM
MIT DER SEELE
DES
SCHAFFEN DEN
UND WIEDER ALS ICH
DIESE BEIDEN
ZEICHNUNGEN SAH
FIEL MIR
DER AUFSATZ
DES ANDEREN JUNGEN MÄDCHENS EIN
DIE DARIN DEUTLICH KLAR MACHT
WENN SIE FROH IST UND
BEGINNT ZU ZEICHNEN
SO KOMMEN AUS IHREM PINSEL
HELLE FARBEN UND
ROTE UND GELBE PUNKTE HERAUS
UND WENN IHRE STIMMUNG TRÜB IST
SO WERDEN AUCH DIE FARBEN
SCHWÄRZLICH GRAU
WOBEI NATÜRLICH ZU BEMERKEN IST
DASS DIES ZUTRIFFT GANZ
GANZ UNABHÄNGIG VON DEM
GEGENSTAND DEN
DER BETREFFENDE
DARZUSTELLEN WÜNSCHT
KOMMEN NUN
WIE ZUFÄLLIG
IN DIESEN VOR UNS LIEGENDEN BLÄTTERN
DIE SEELENSTIMMUNG ~~MIT~~ IM
MOMENT DES SCHAFFENS MIT
DEM THEMA IN EINKLANG
DER TOD UND DAS MÄDCHEN MIT EINER
VERZWEIFLUNGSVOLLEN STIMMUNG
ZUSAMMEN DIE
DIE WIESE MIT DEN GELBEN BLUMEN JEDOCH
MIT EINER HOFFNUNGSFREUDIGEN
ENTSTEHEN
GANZ IM KLEINEN HIER NATÜRLICH
KUNSTWERKE
UND MEINE ERKENNTNIS
DER ÄHNLICHKEIT
MIT
DEN PRODUKTEN
DER JUNGEN MÄDCHEN UND
GEWISSER ---
GENIES
IST DURCHAUS
GERECHTFERTIGT
WIE JUNGE MÄDCHEN
SO HABEN AUCH
WIE Z.B.
237

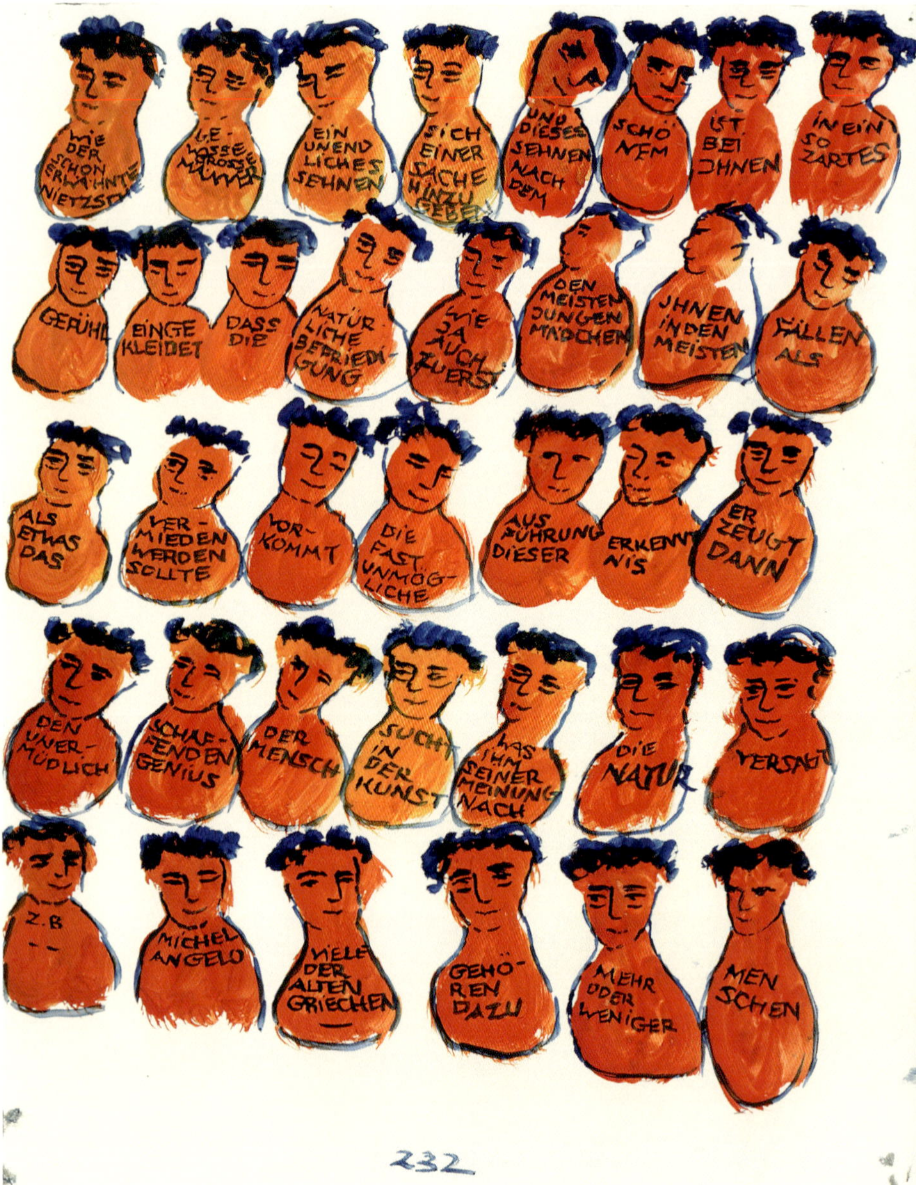
WIE DER SCHON ERWÄHNTE NIETZSC
EIN UNEND LICHES SEHNEN
SICH EINER SACHE HINZU GEBEN
UND DIESES SEHNEN NACH DEM
SCHÖ NEM
IST BEI JHNEN
IN EIN SO ZARTES
GEFÜHL
EINGE KLEIDET
DASS DIE
NATÜR LICHE BEFRIEDI GUNG
WIE JA AUCH ZUERST
DEN MEISTEN JUNGEN MÄDCHEN
JHNEN IN DEN MEISTEN
FÄLLEN ALS
ALS ETWAS DAS
VER-MIEDEN WERDEN SOLLTE
VOR-KOMMT
DIE FAST UNMÖG-LICHE
AUS FÜHRUNG DIESER
ERKENNT NIS
ER ZEUGT DANN
DEN UNER-MÜDLICH
SCHAF-FENDEN GENIUS
DER MENSCH
SUCHT IN DER KUNST
WAS IHM SEINER MEINUNG NACH
DIE NATUR
VERSAGT
Z.B
MICHEL ANGELO
VIELE DER ALTEN GRIECHEN
GEHÖ-REN DAZU
MEHR ODER WENIGER
MEN SCHEN
232

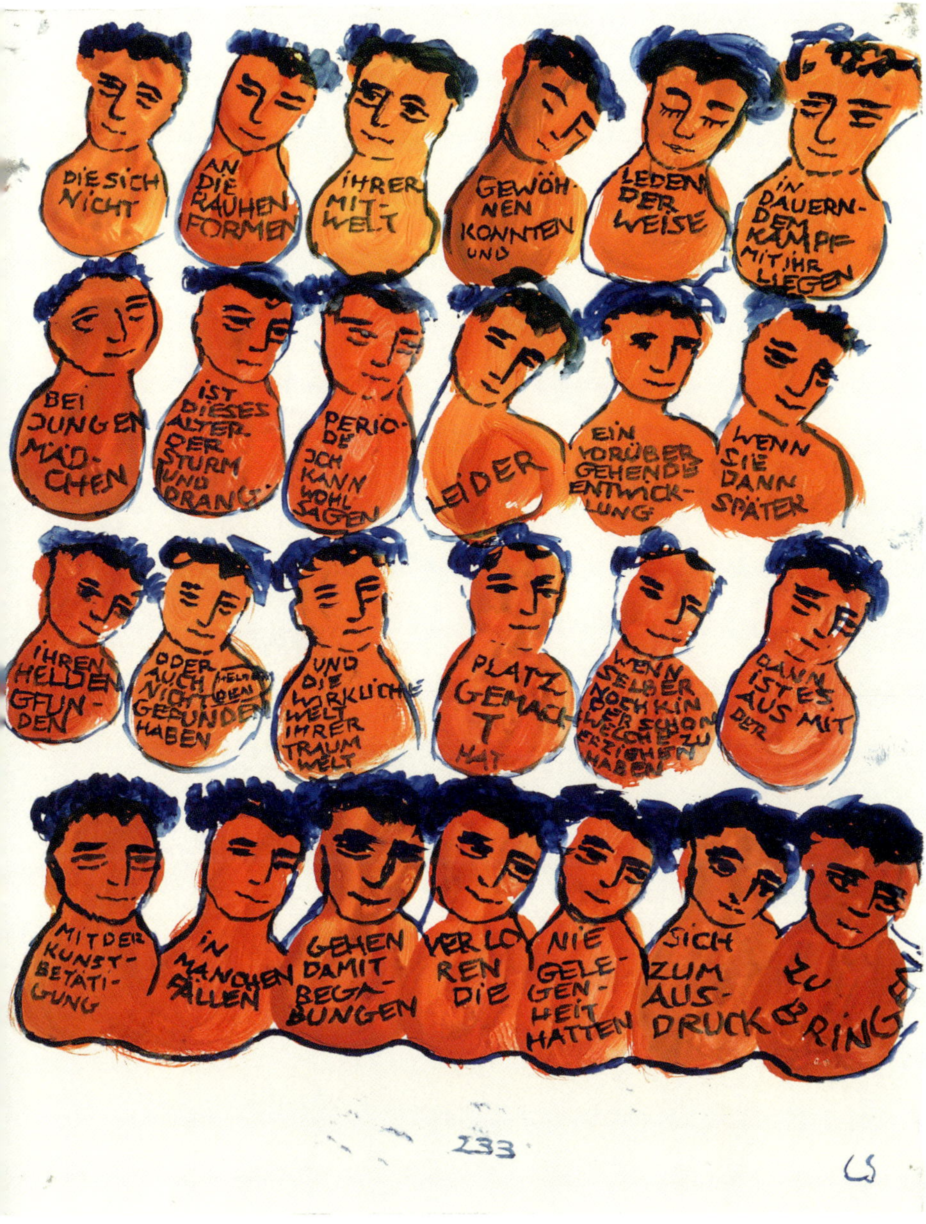
DIE SICH NICHT
AN DIE RAUHEN FORMEN
IHRER MIT-WELT
GEWÖH-NEN KONNTEN UND
LEIDEN-DER WEISE
IN DAUERN-DEM KAMPF MIT IHR LIEGEN
BEI JUNGEN MÄD-CHEN
IST DIESES ALTER DER STURM UND DRANG
PERIO-DE ICH KANN WOHL SAGEN
LEIDER
EIN VORÜBER GEHENDE ENTWICK-LUNG
WENN SIE DANN SPÄTER
IHREN HELDEN GFUN-DEN
ODER AUCH NICHT GEFUNDEN HABEN
UND DIE WIRKLICHE WELT IHRER TRAUM WELT
PLATZ GEMACH T HAT
WENN SELBER NOCH KIN DER SCHON WELCHE ZU ERZIEHEN HABEN
DANN IST ES AUS MIT DER
MIT DER KUNST-BETÄTI-GUNG
IN MANCHEN FÄLLEN
GEHEN DAMIT BEGA-BUNGEN
VERLO-REN DIE
NIE GELE-GEN-HEIT HATTEN
SICH ZUM AUS-DRUCK
ZU BRINGEN
233
CS

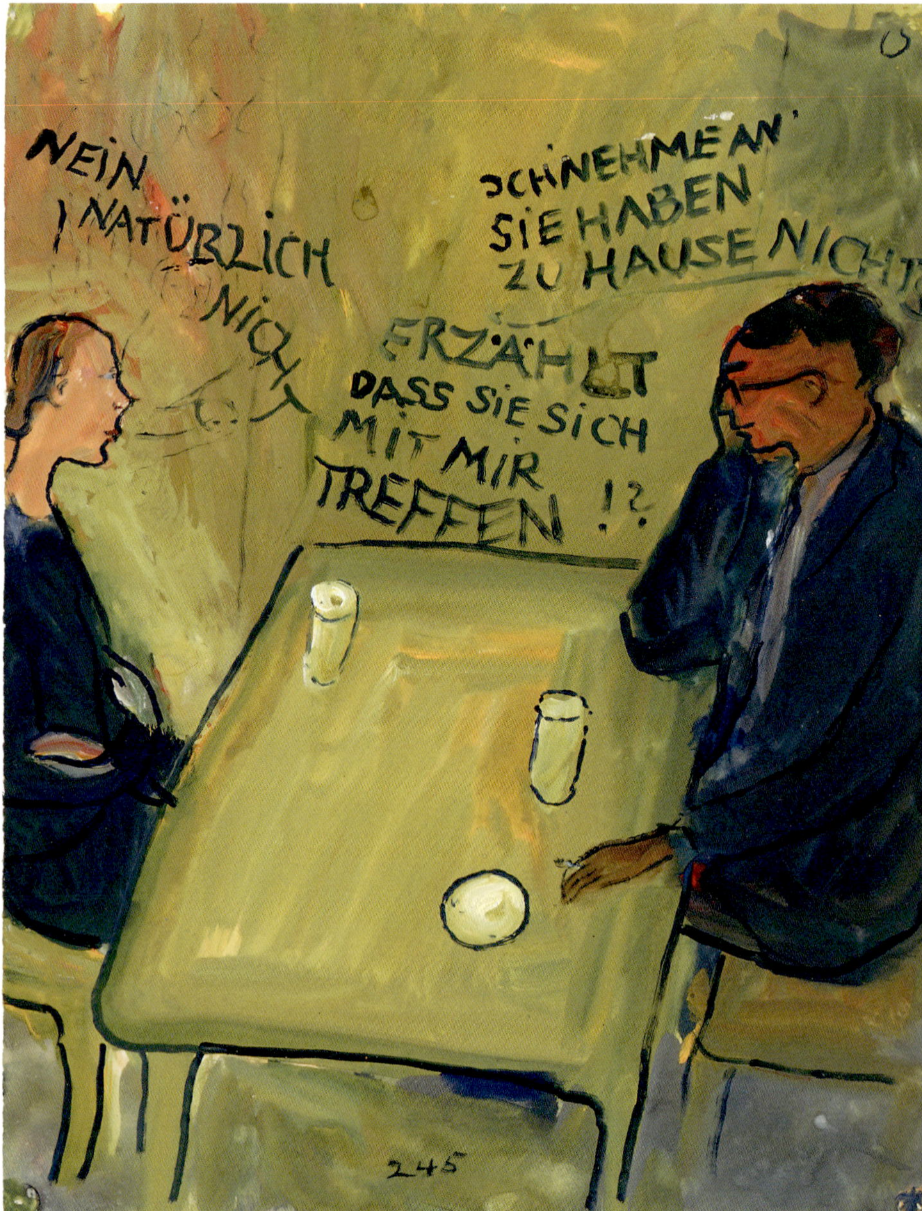
NEIN NATÜRLICH NICHT
ICH NEHME AN SIE HABEN ZU HAUSE NICHTS ERZÄHLT DASS SIE SICH MIT MIR TREFFEN !?
245

(page 381)

"... cannot adapt to the rough forms of the world around them and suffer as they perpetually struggle against it.

In the case of young girls, this age of 'Sturm und Drang' is – alas – a passing development. When later on they have, or have not, found their hero, and their dream world has given way to the real world, when – still children themselves – they already have children to bring up, that puts an end to their artistic activities. In some cases, talents are lost that never had a chance to express themselves."

(opposite)

DABERLOHN
"I take it that you haven't said anything at home about meeting me?"

CHARLOTTE
"No, of course not!"

DABERLOHN

"Well, you do show a certain amount of courage. Perhaps you're not nearly as shy as you make out, perhaps you're quite a 'dangerous' girl! Only, you're still so terribly tense: Good grief, spread your arms, what you need is a good kick in a certain part of the body."

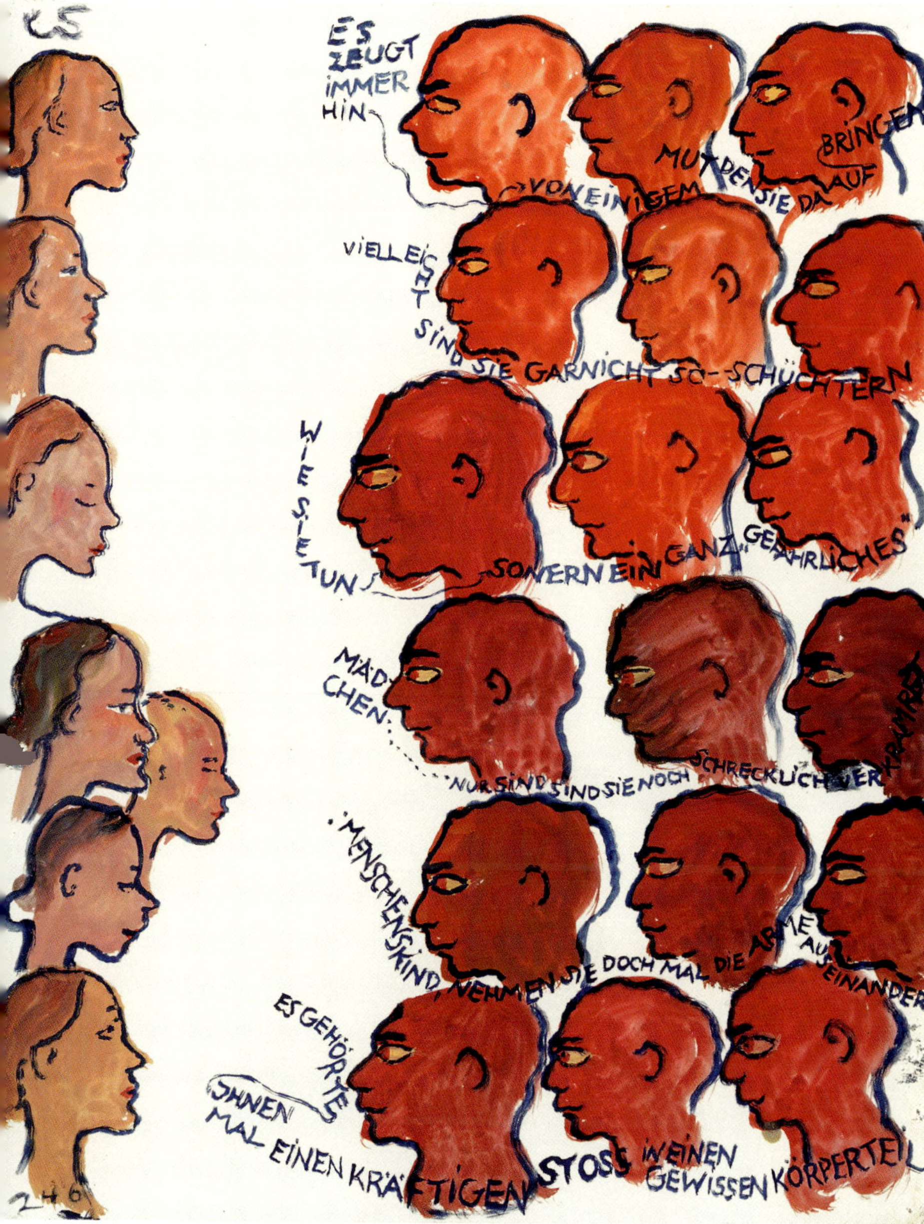
CS
ES ZEUGT IMMERHIN VON EINIGEM MUT DEN SIE DA AUFBRINGEN
VIELLEICHT SIND SIE GARNICHT SO--SCHÜCHTERN
WIE SIE TUN SONDERN EIN GANZ „GEFÄHRLICHES"
MÄDCHEN NUR SIND SIND SIE NOCH SCHRECKLICH VERKRAMPFT
„MENSCHENSKIND, NEHMEN SIE DOCH MAL DIE ARME AUSEINANDER
ES GEHÖRTE IHNEN MAL EINEN KRÄFTIGEN STOSS IN EINEN GEWISSEN KÖRPERTEIL
246

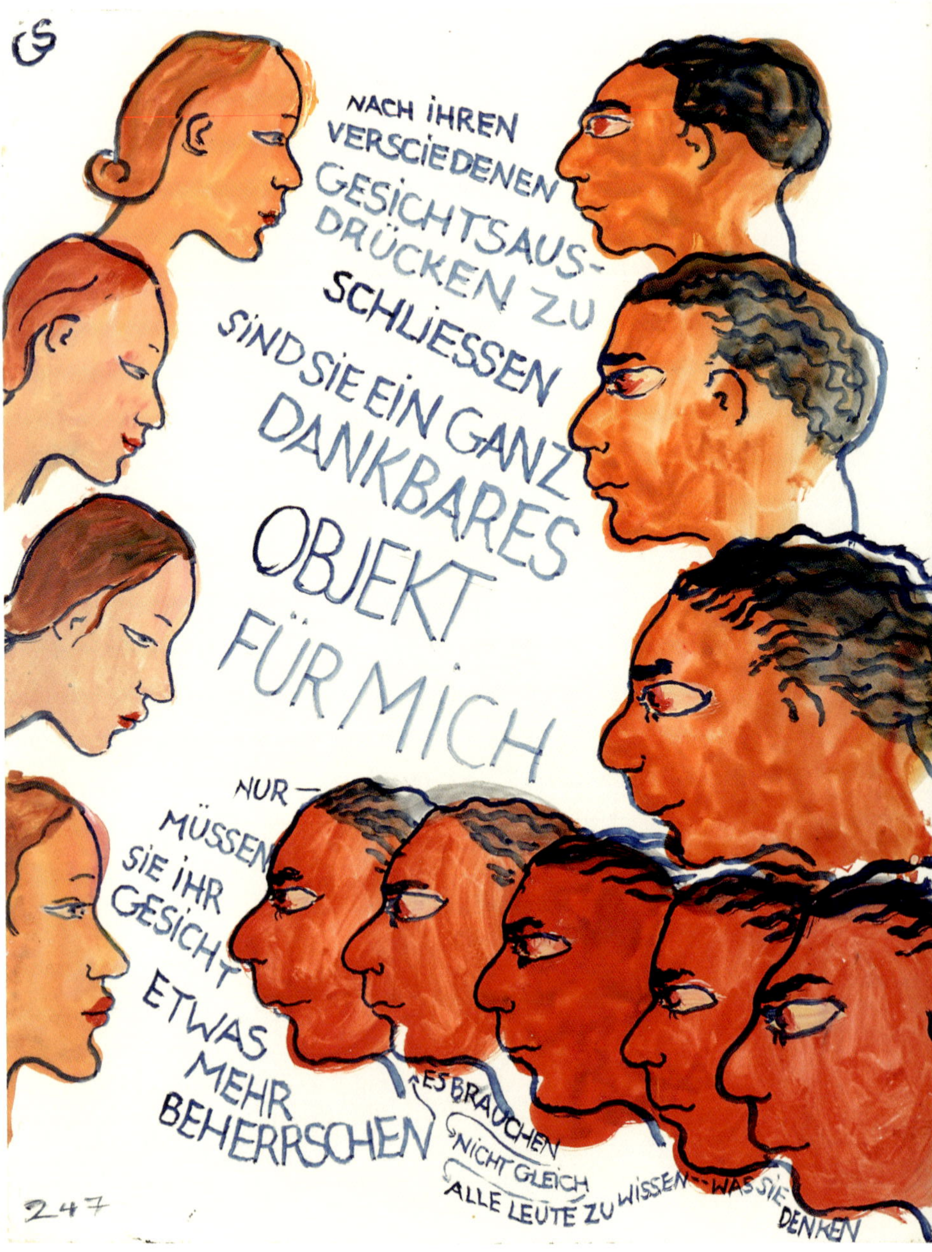
GS
NACH IHREN
VERSCIEDENEN
GESICHTSAUS-
DRÜCKEN ZU
SCHLIESSEN
SIND SIE EIN GANZ
DANKBARES
OBJEKT
FÜR MICH
NUR —
MÜSSEN
SIE IHR
GESICHT
ETWAS
MEHR
BEHERRSCHEN
ES BRAUCHEN
NICHT GLEICH
ALLE LEUTE ZU WISSEN — WAS SIE
DENKEN
247

(opposite)

He suddenly finds Charlotte significant for his future theories.

DABERLOHN
"To judge by the various expressions on your face, you are quite a grateful object for me. Only you must control your face a bit more – it's not necessary for all the people to know what you're thinking."

(bottom)

"Do you actually love me?"

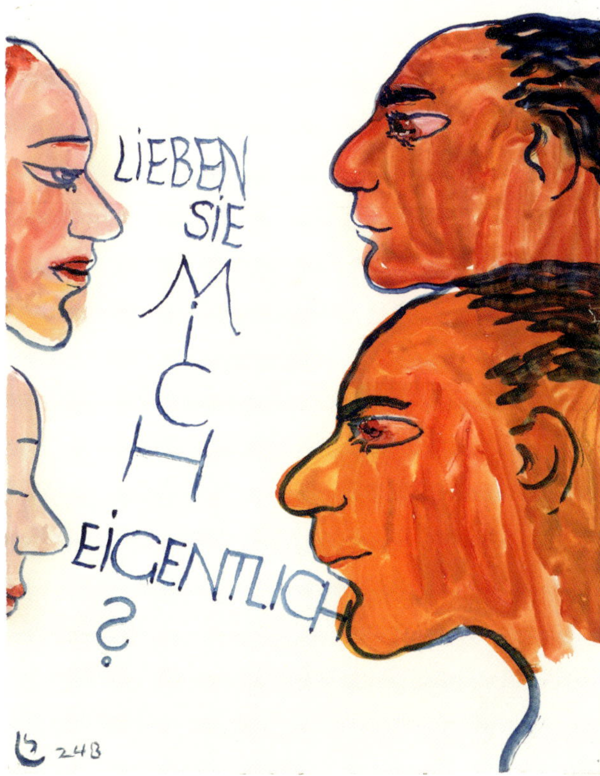

(bottom)

“Now we go home again, otherwise your mother will scold you if you come so late.”

(opposite)

“Okay then, goodbye, see you tomorrow at ten.”

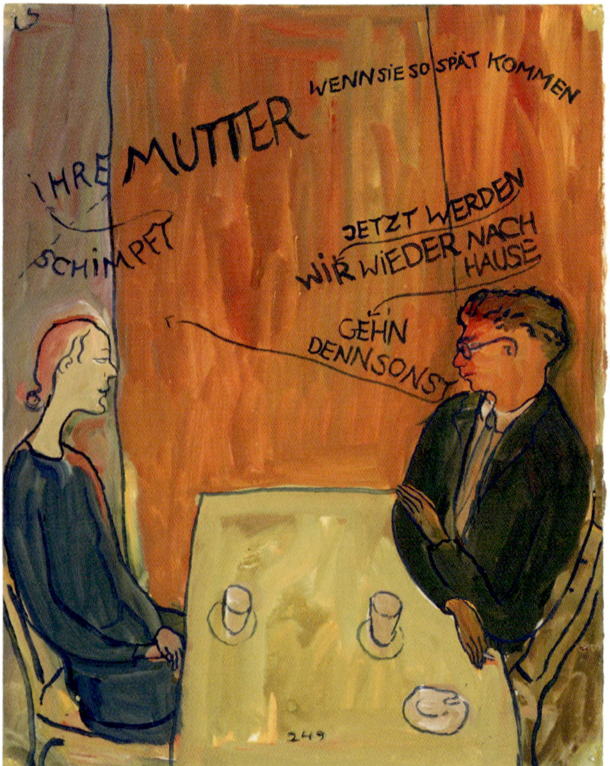

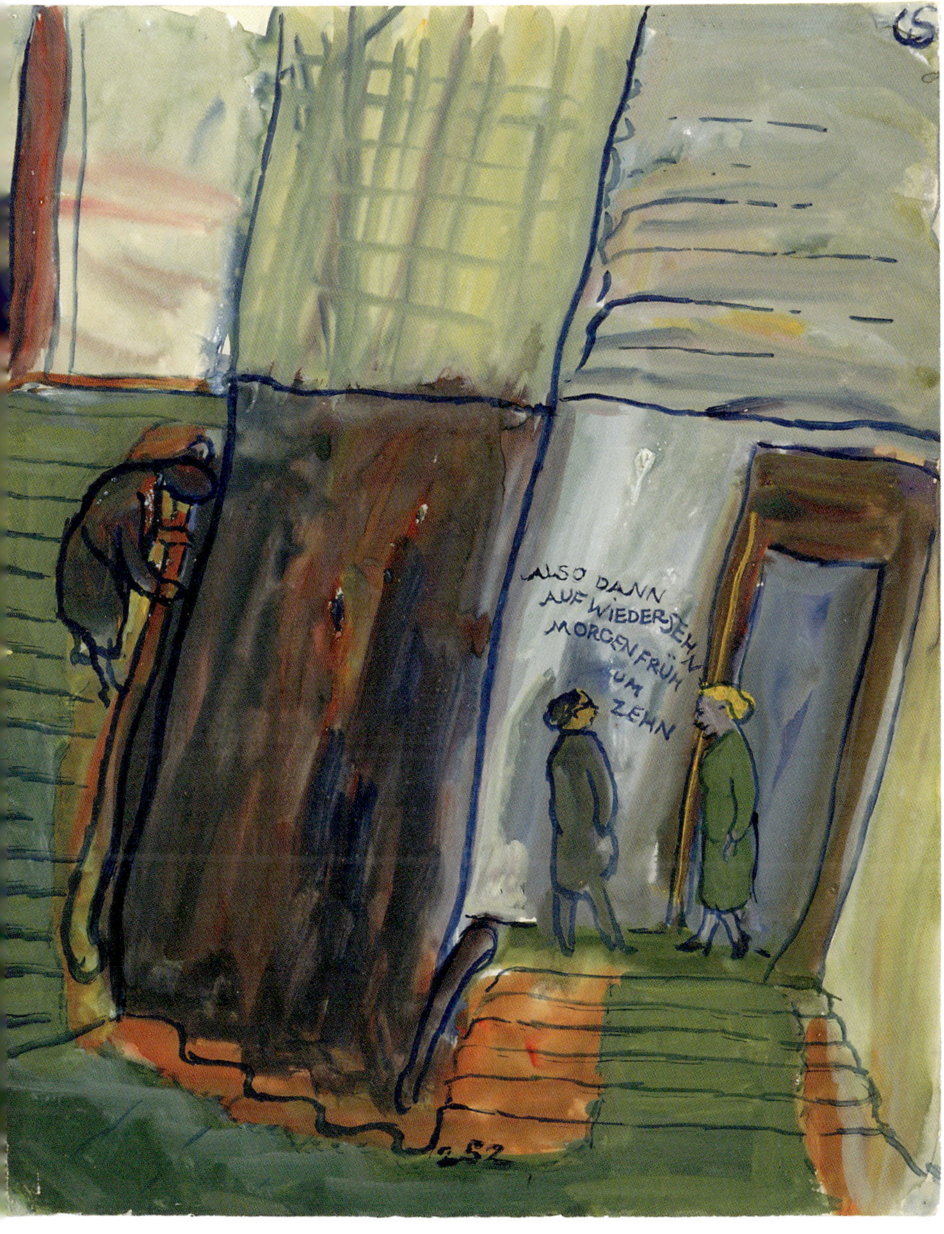

ALSO DANN
AUF WIEDERSEHN
MORGEN FRÜH
UM
ZEHN
CS
2.52

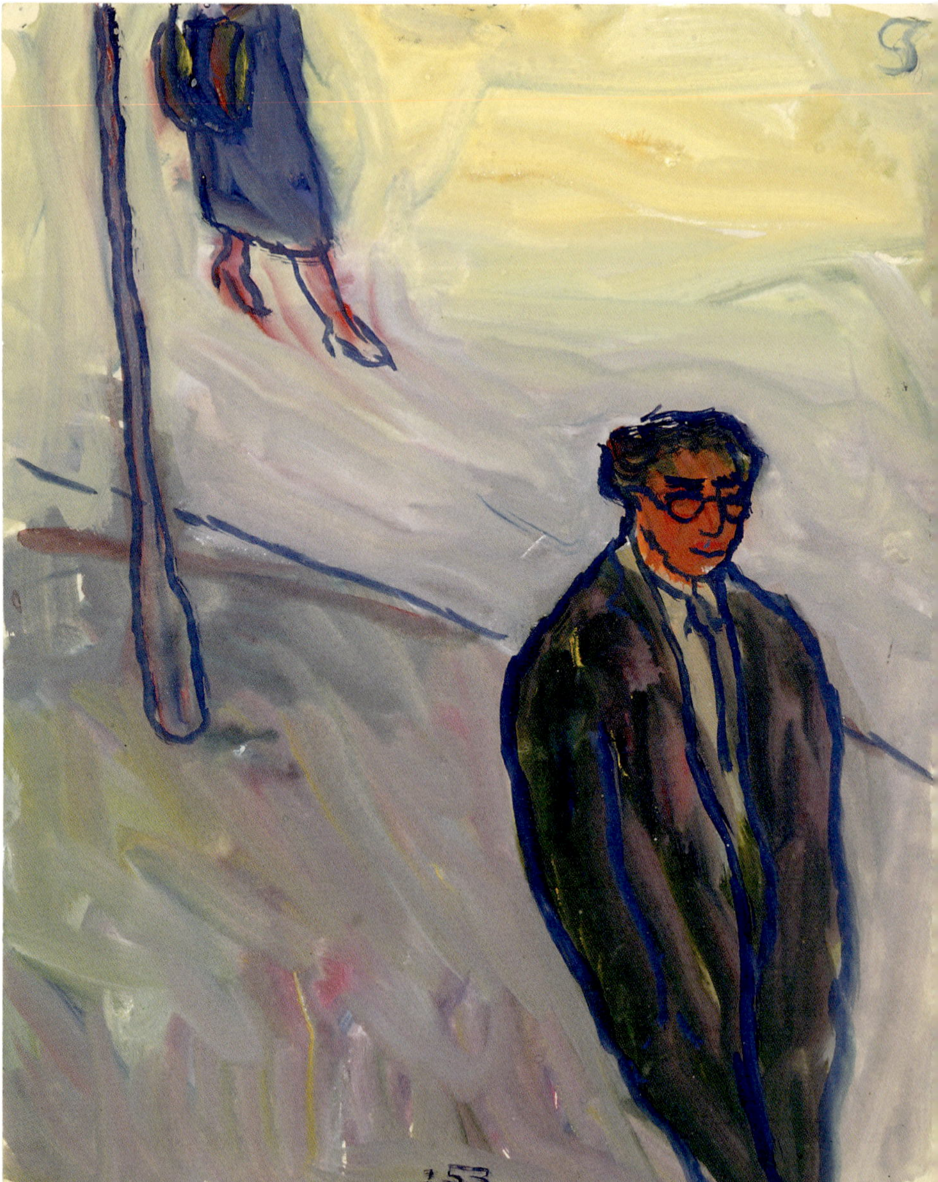

(bottom)

DABERLOHN
"Oh, Madonna!"

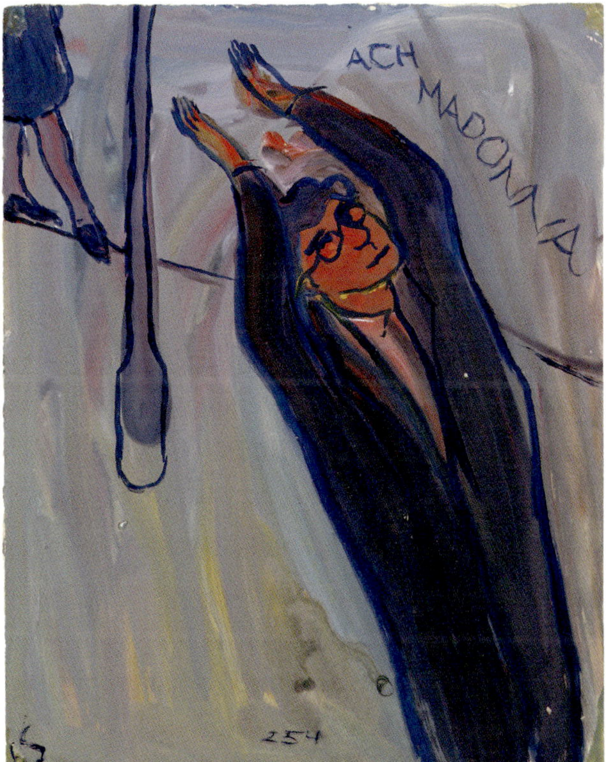

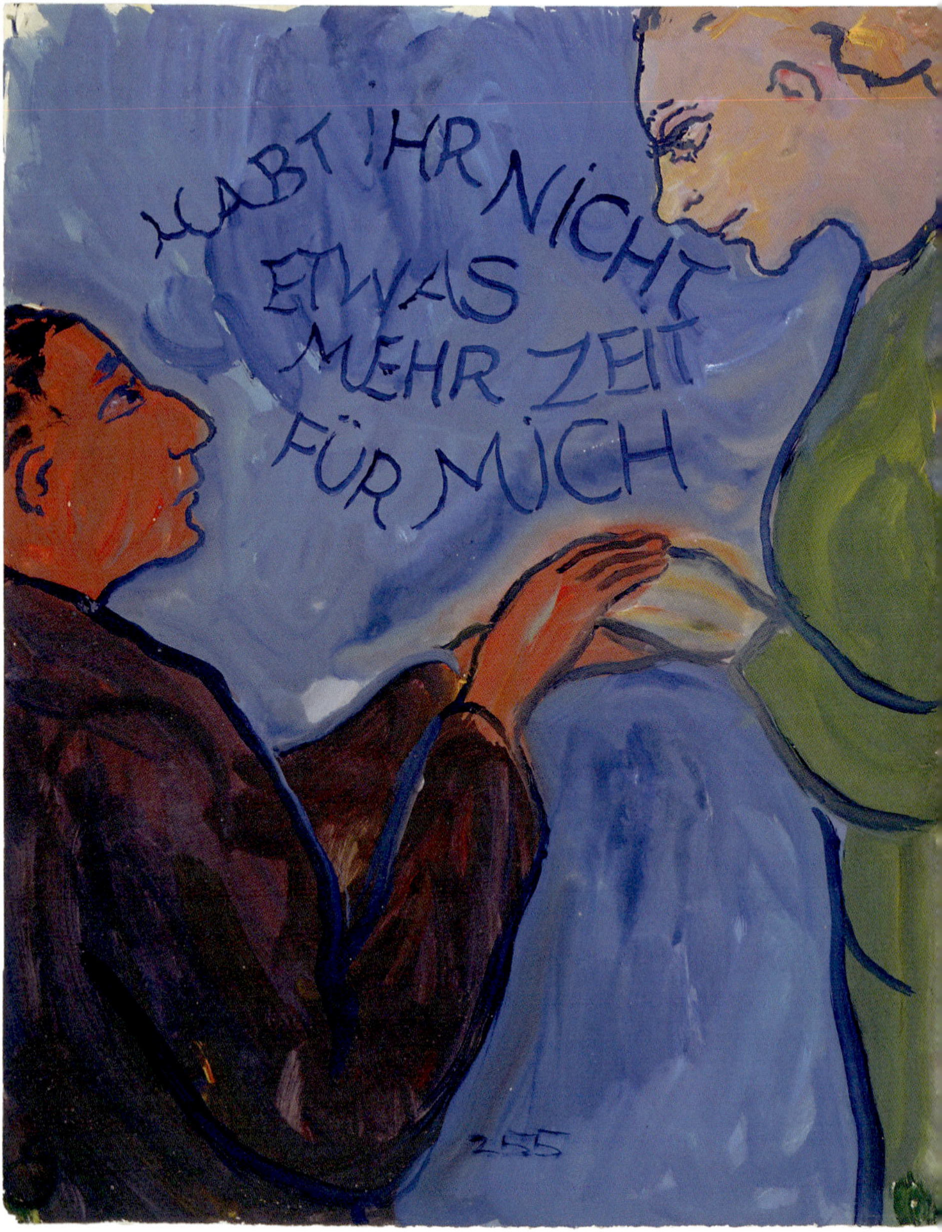
HABT IHR NICHT
ETWAS
MEHR ZEIT
FÜR MICH
255

(opposite)

DABERLOHN
"Don't you have a bit more
time for me?"

(bottom)

PAULINKA
"But, my friend, you're here everyday,
sometimes also two times – isn't that enough?"

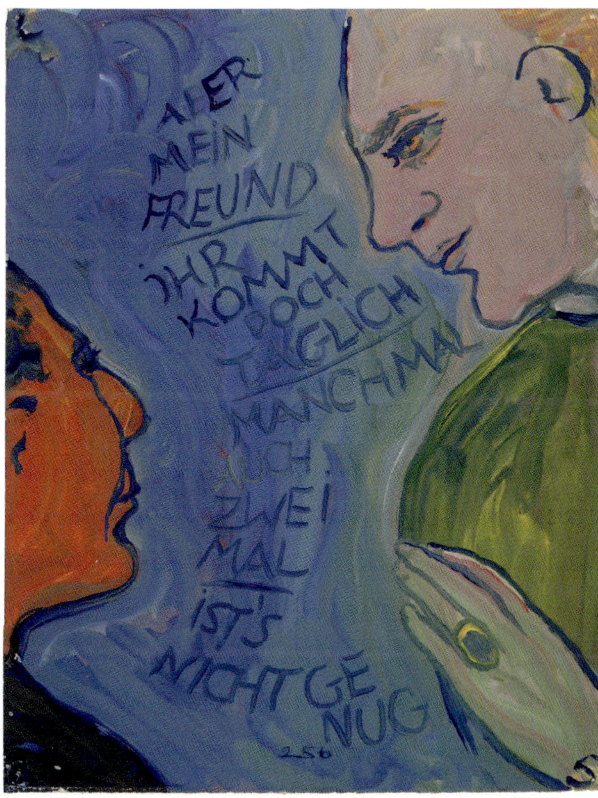

(bottom)

"One of the most beautiful Rembrandt paintings: Saul and David, separated by a curtain. Saul is weeping because he feels he has lost God. Since David has made him aware of this by his singing, he hates him; just as Tolstoy in his Kreutzer Sonata hates women, Beethoven, music. Just as Nietzsche hates God and Christ. If the power of our sensuality allows for no other way out, we must beat it to death..."

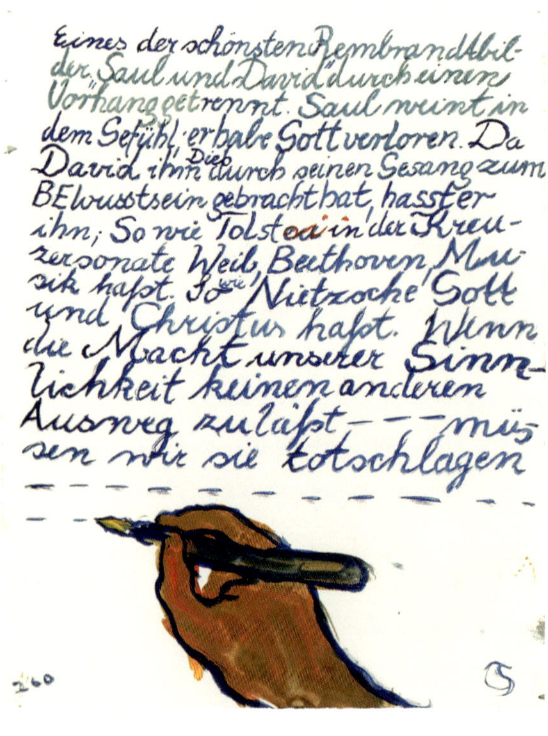

(opposite)

Charlotte is not sure of her emotions. Is it jealousy or something else developing in her where love is concerned?

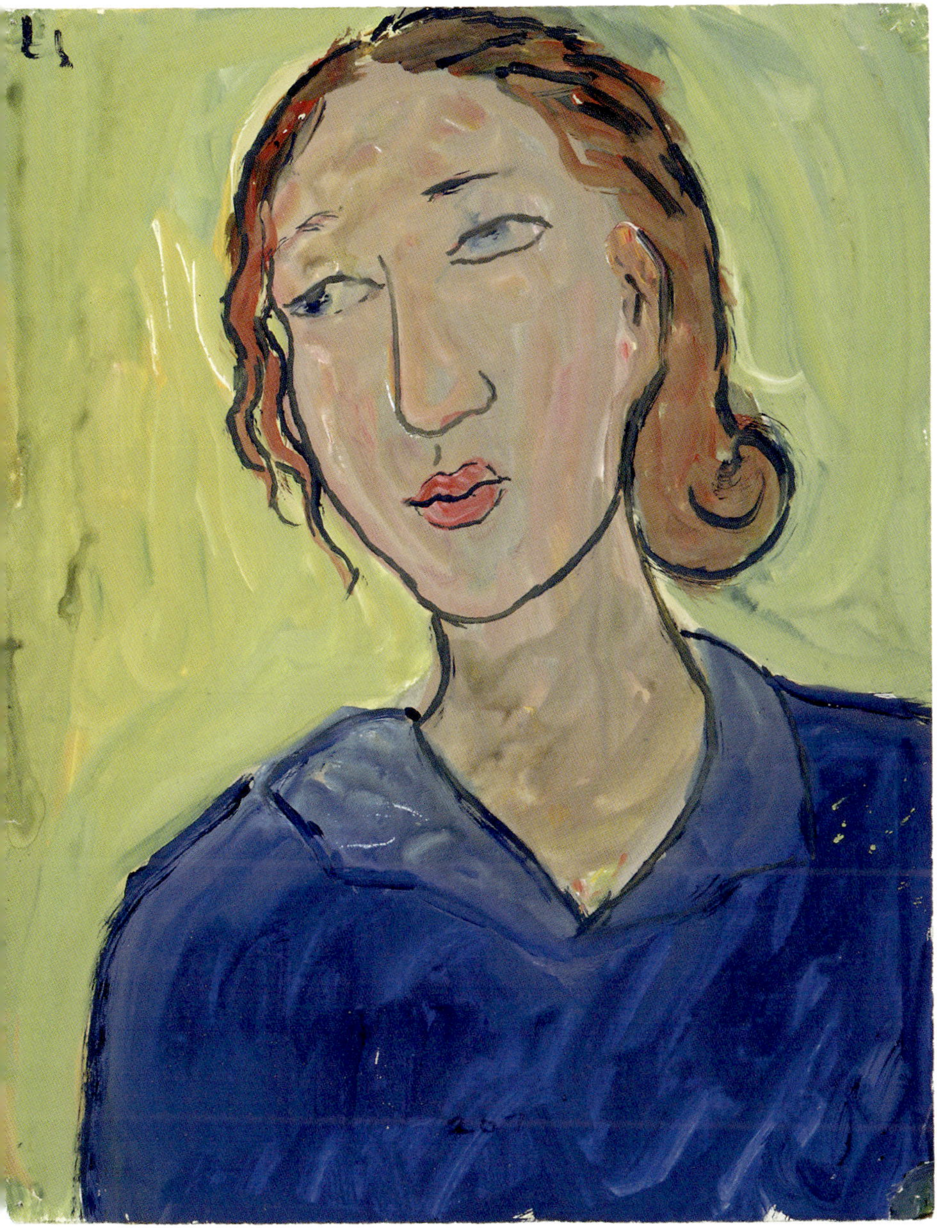

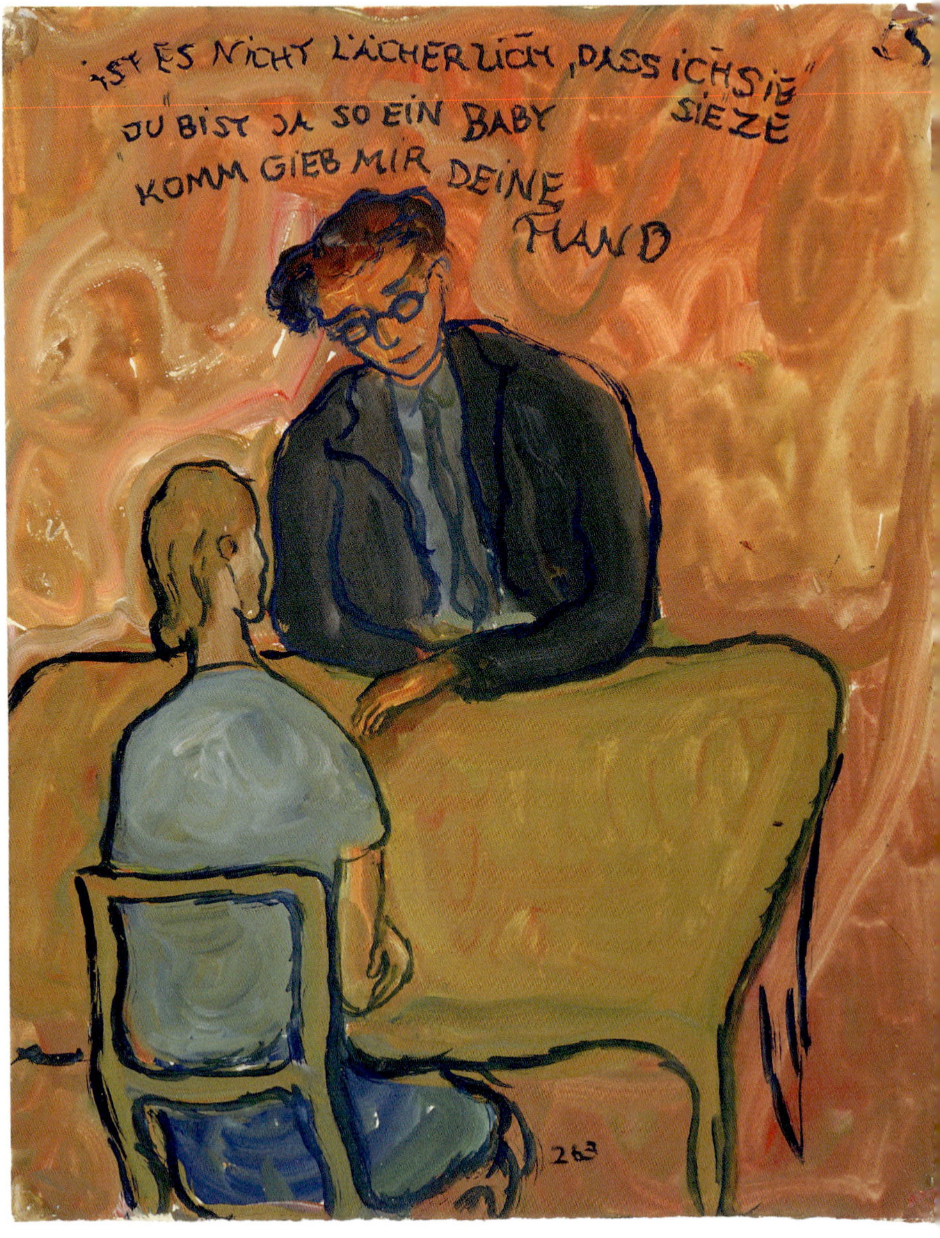
"IST ES NICHT LÄCHERLICH, DASS ICH SIE SIEZE"
"DU BIST JA SO EIN BABY
KOMM GIEB MIR DEINE HAND

(opposite)

DABERLOHN
“Isn’t it absurd that I address ‘you’ so formally? ‘You’re’ such a baby, come give me your hand.”

(bottom)

DABERLOHN
“Real painter’s hands.”

CHARLOTTE
“To me they’re just ugly.”

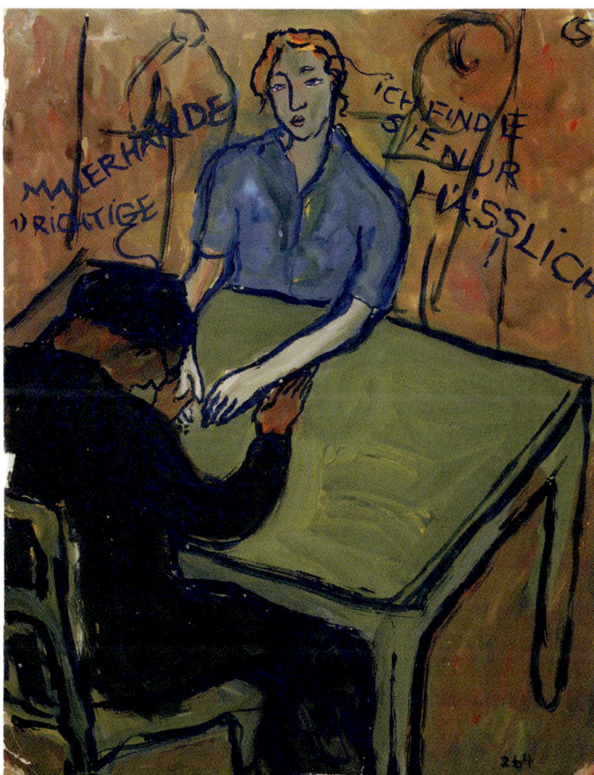

CHARLOTTE
“You would be beautiful to paint – ”

DABERLOHN (to himself)
“Little girl, if you only knew what one has to go through to be able to paint.”

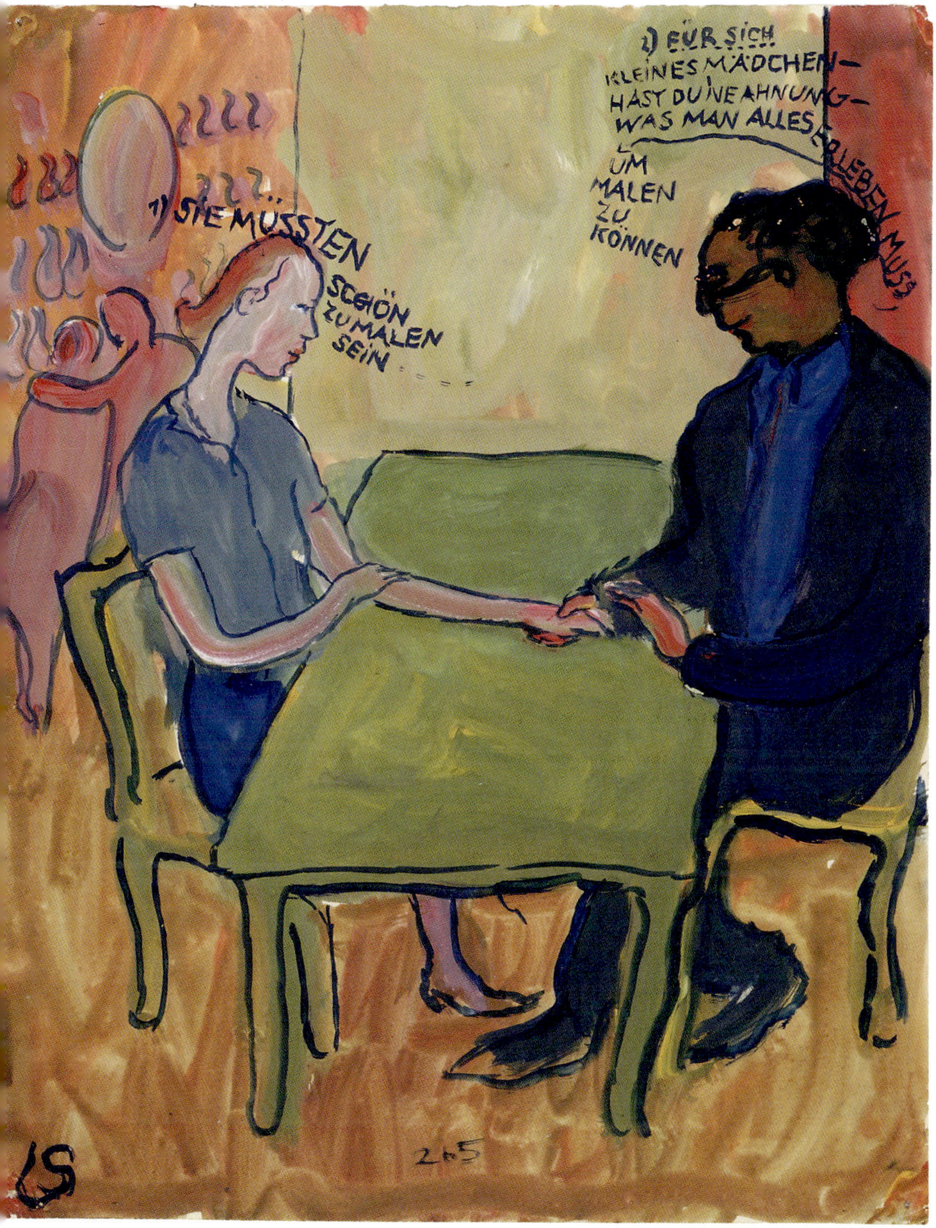
1) SIE MÜSSTEN
SCHÖN
ZU MALEN
SEIN - - - -
2) FÜR SICH
KLEINES MÄDCHEN —
HAST DU NE AHNUNG —
WAS MAN ALLES
ERLEBEN MUSS
UM
MALEN
ZU
KÖNNEN

(opposite)

DABERLOHN
"Aren't you afraid of me? After all,
I'm a total stranger to you."

CHARLOTTE
"I love you."

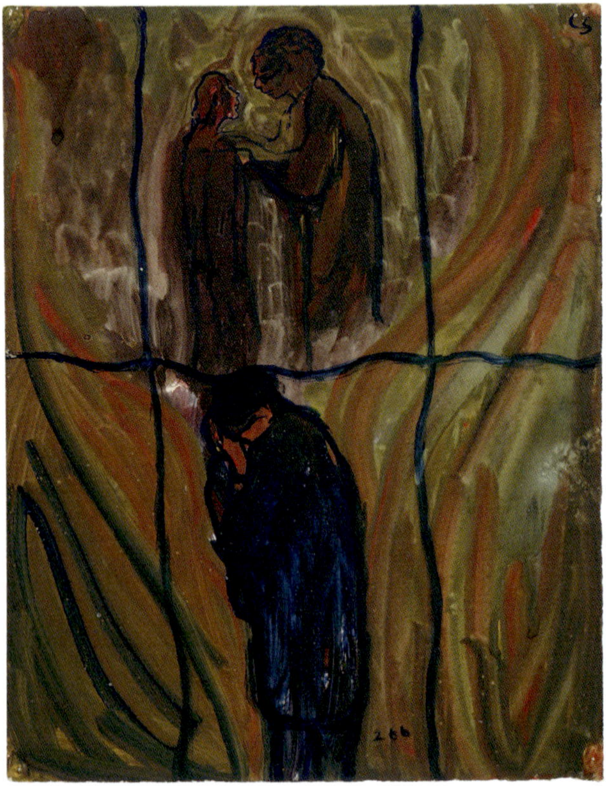

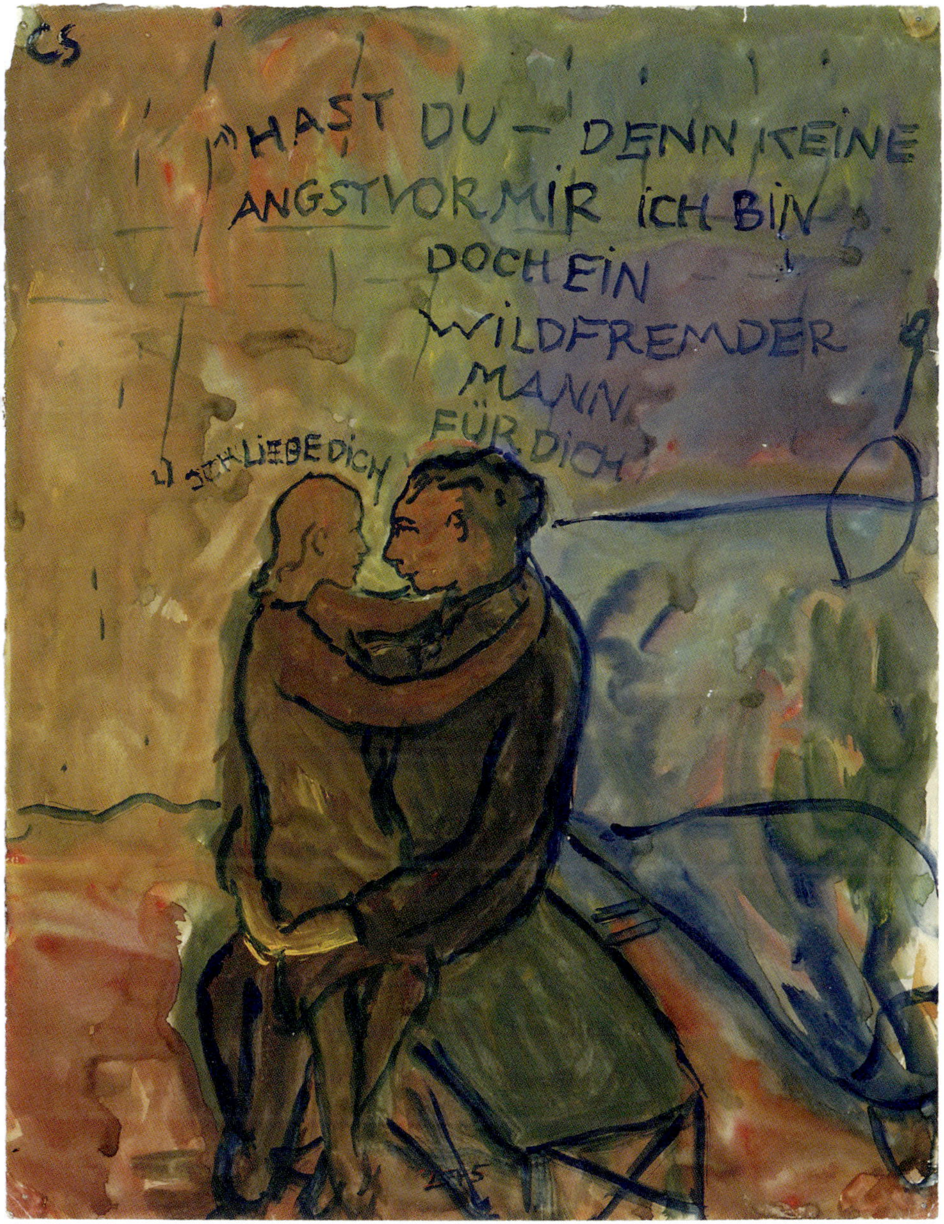
CS
»HAST DU – DENN KEINE
ANGST VOR MIR ICH BIN
DOCH EIN
WILDFREMDER
MANN
FÜR DICH
ICH LIEBE DICH

(bottom)

CHARLOTTE
"Oh, please stay –
you shouldn't go."

DABERLOHN
"No, let me go.
I 'must' leave now."

(opposite)

DABERLOHN
"Goodbye."

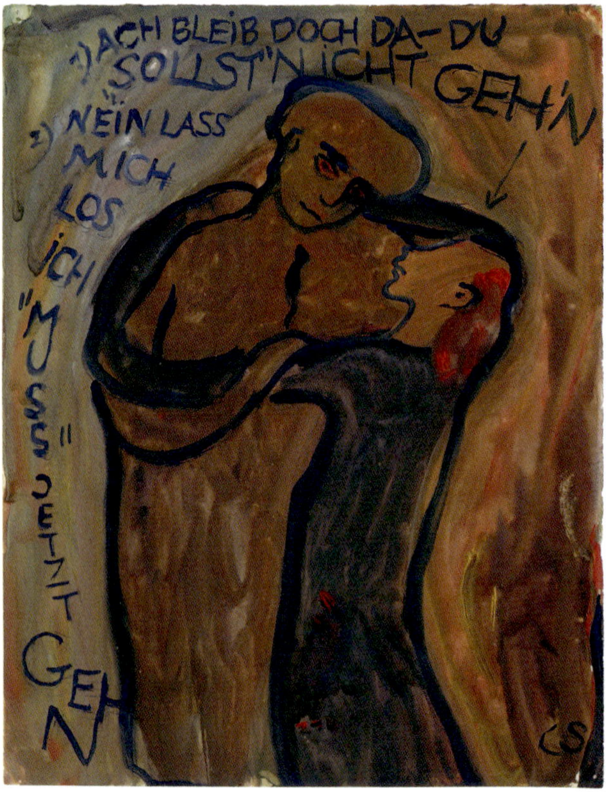

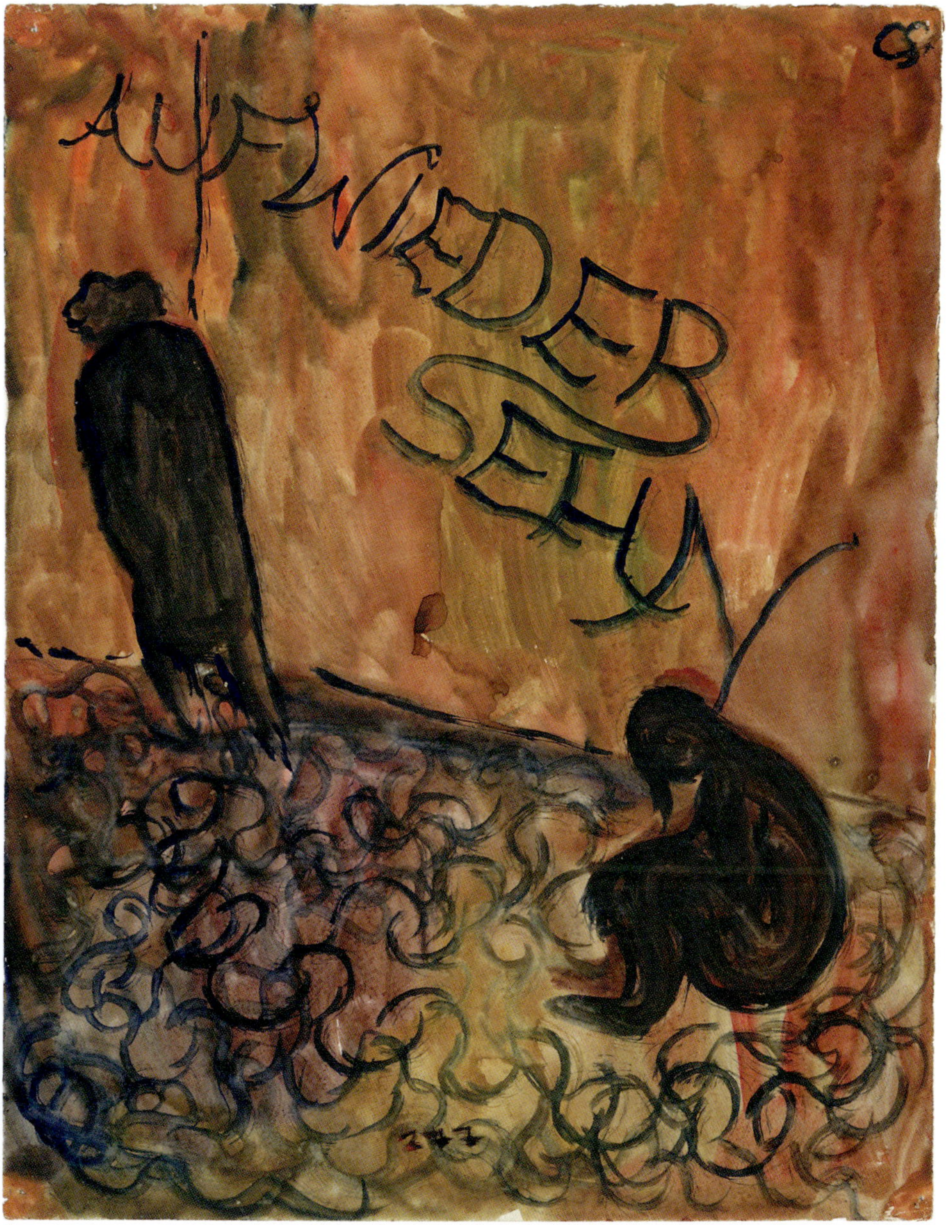
AUF
WIEDER
SEHN

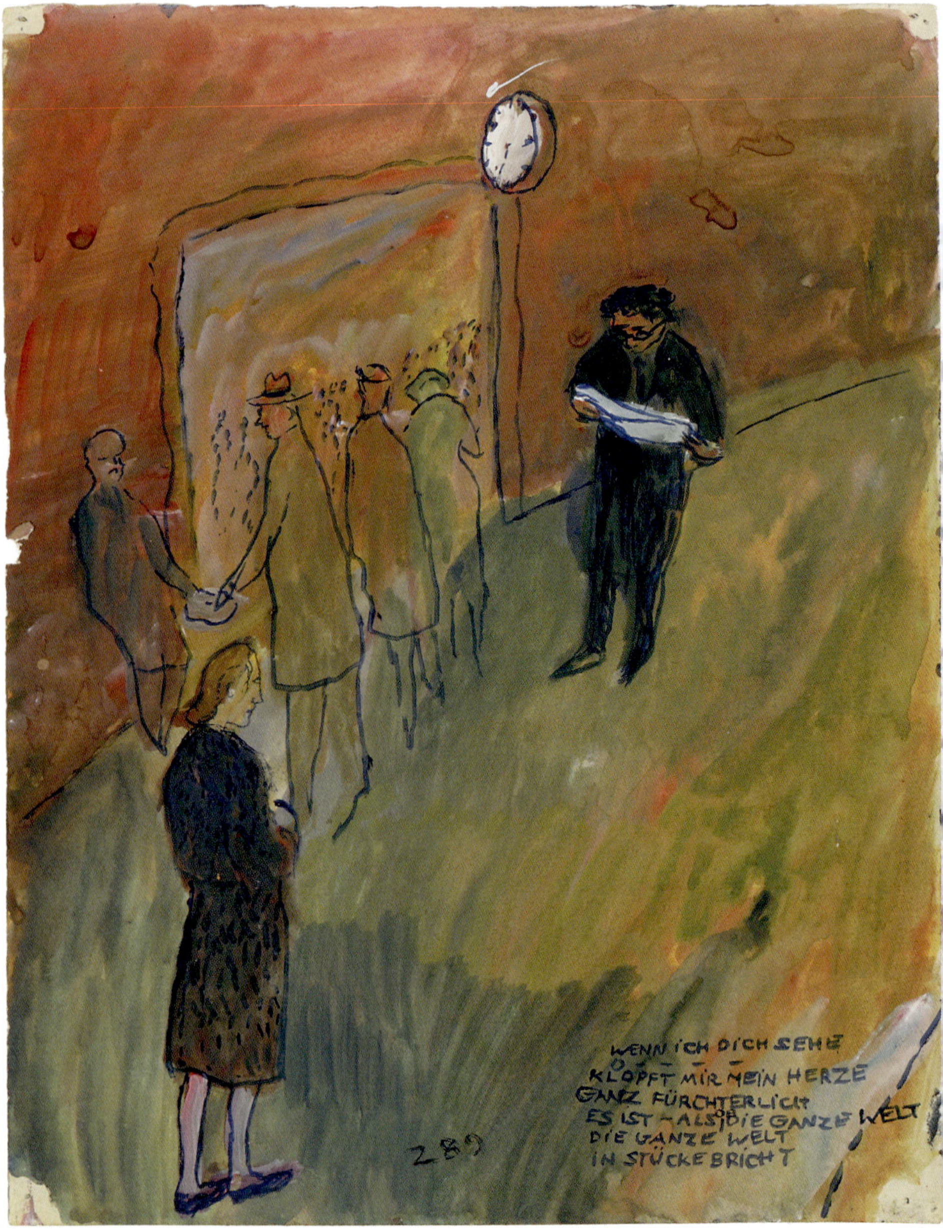
WENN ICH DICH SEHE
KLOPFT MIR MEIN HERZE
GANZ FÜRCHTERLICH
ES IST – ALS OB DIE GANZE WELT
DIE GANZE WELT
IN STÜCKE BRICHT
289

CHARLOTTE
“When I see thee,
Oh – – –
My heart doth
beat terribly.
It is – as if the whole world,
the whole world,
the whole world,
breaks into pieces.”

(bottom)

CHARLOTTE
"When I see thee,
Oh – – –
I feel as if I am
in Paradise.
I believe that on earth,
Oh – – –
No other man
compares to you."

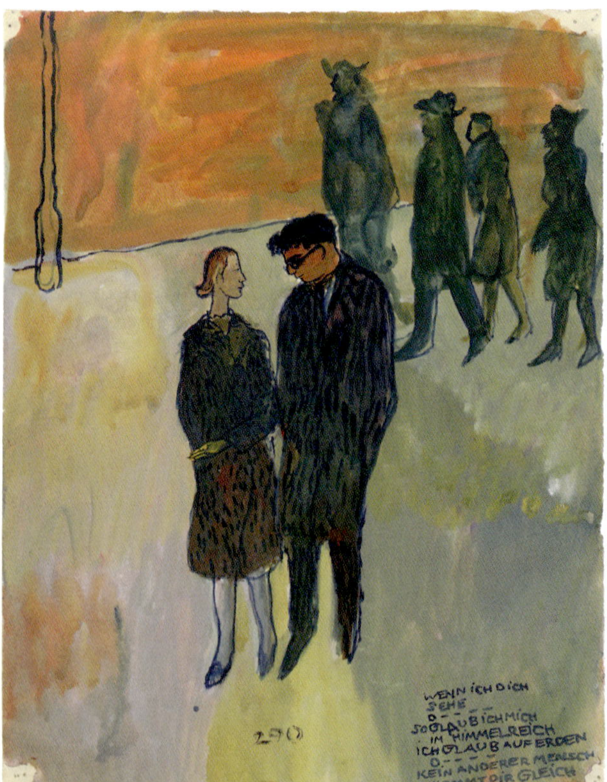

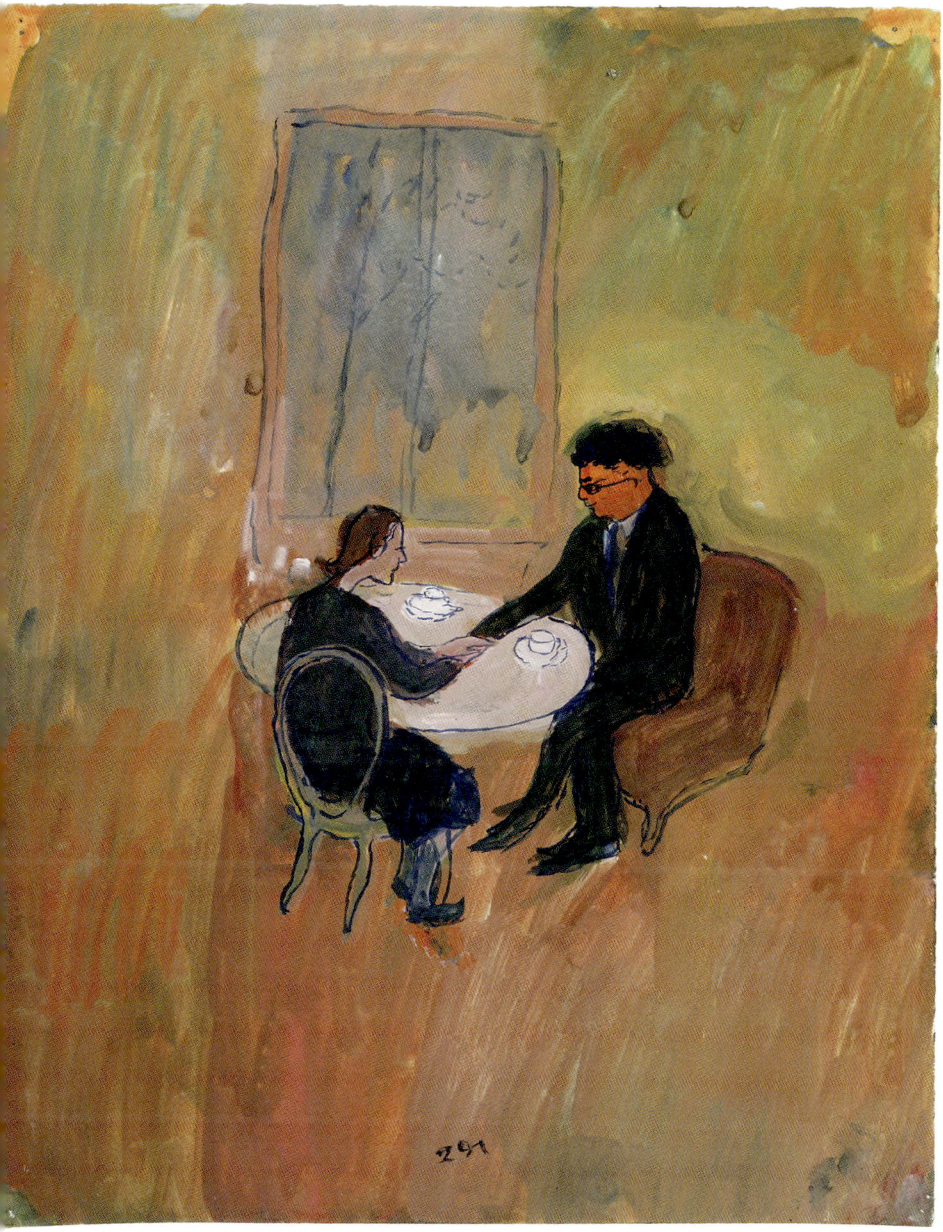

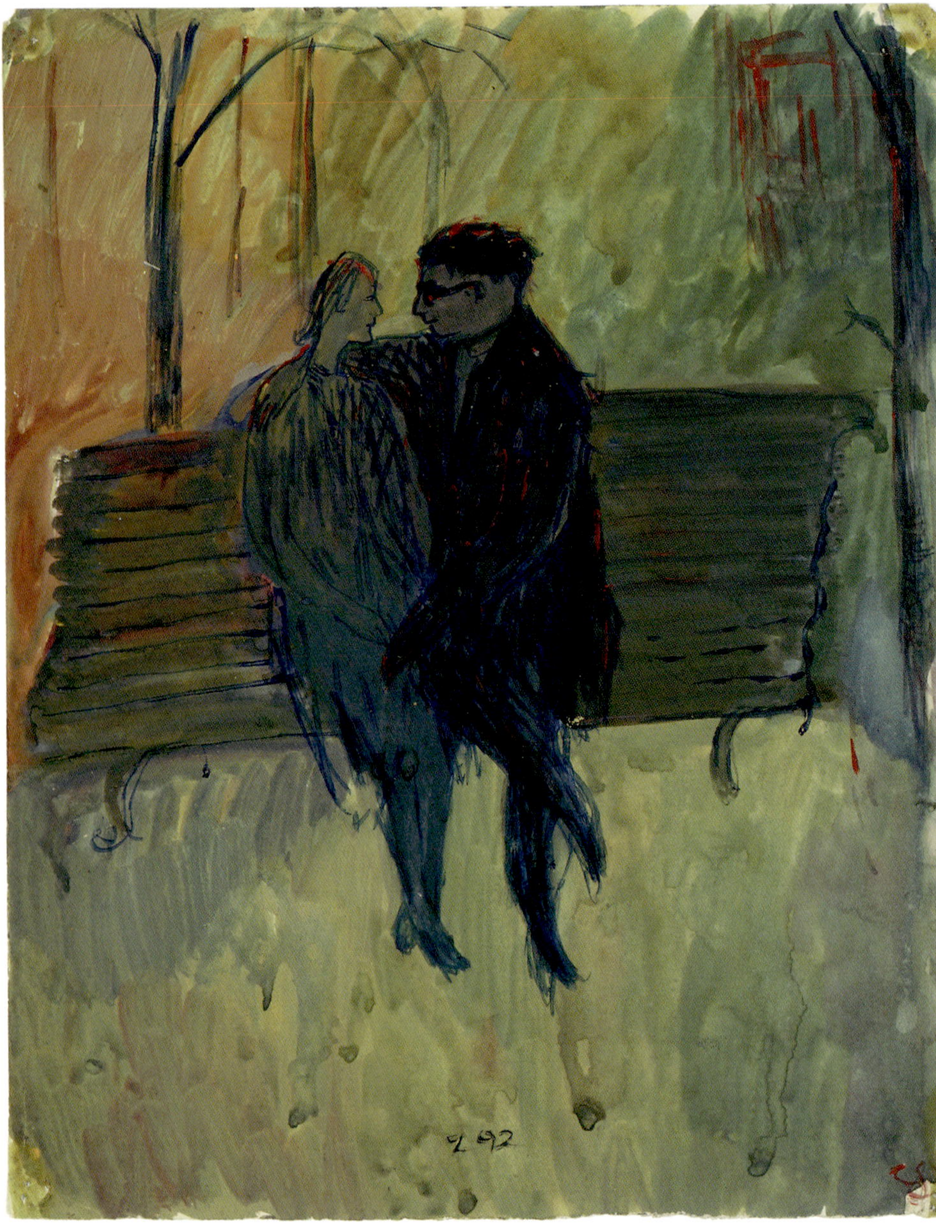

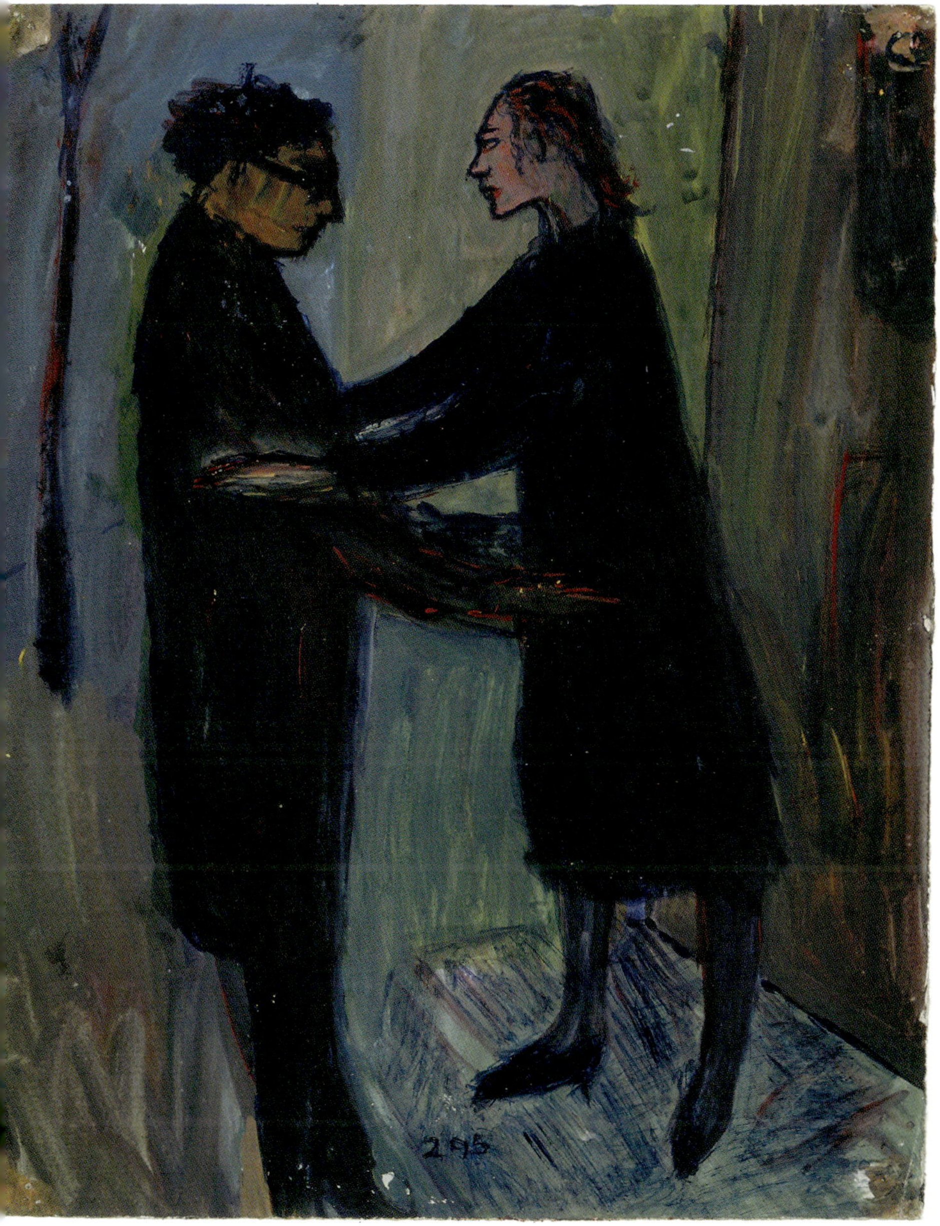

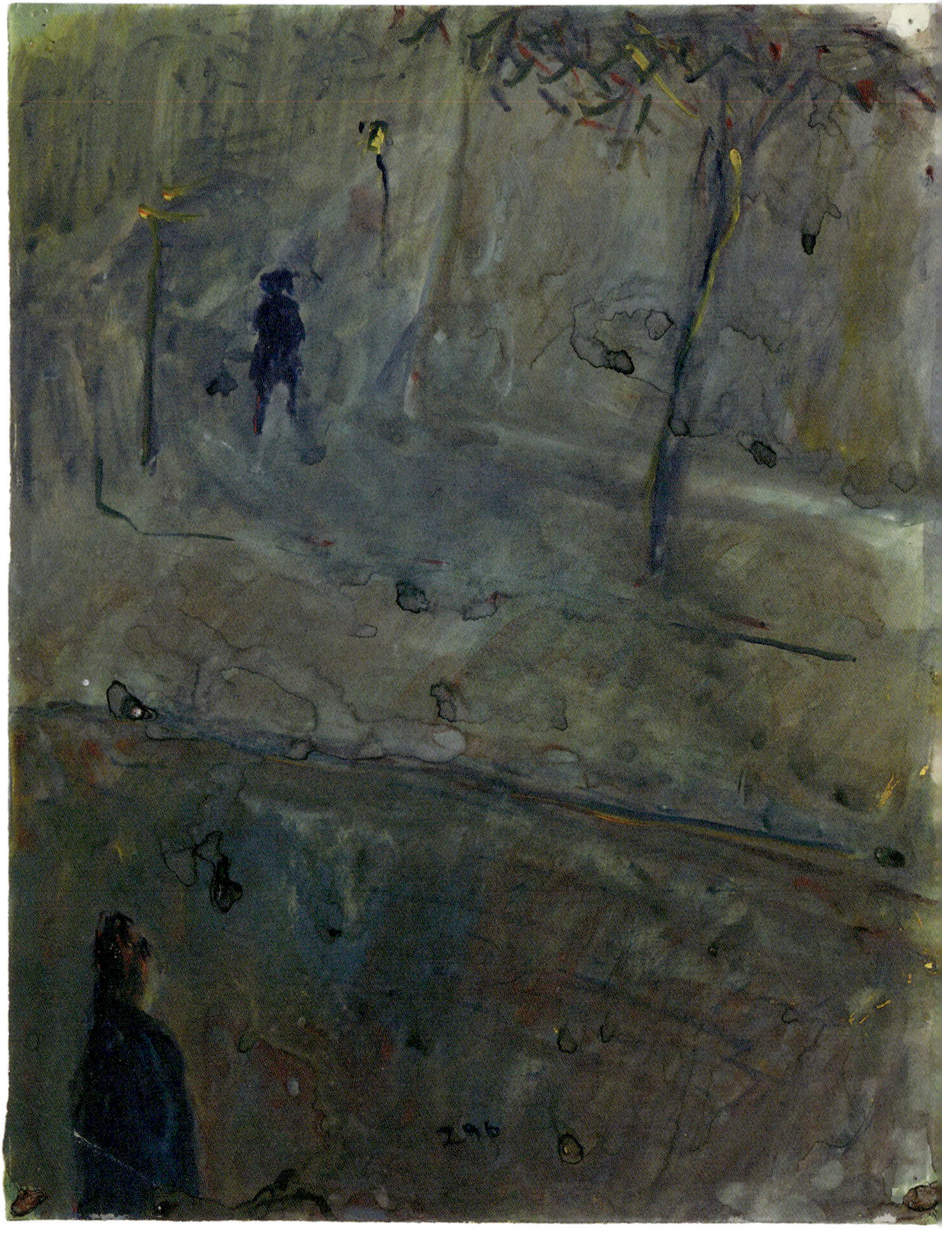

(bottom)

Here we see him, sitting at his desk waiting for inspiration for the book he intends to write.

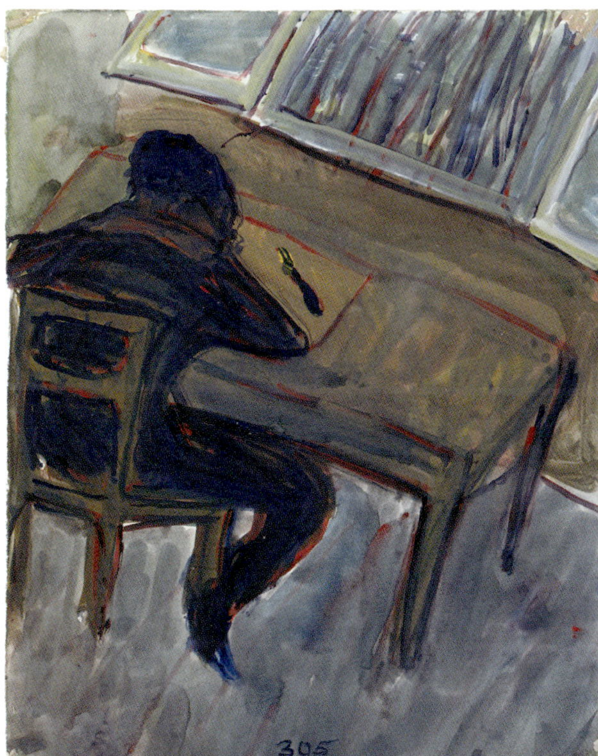

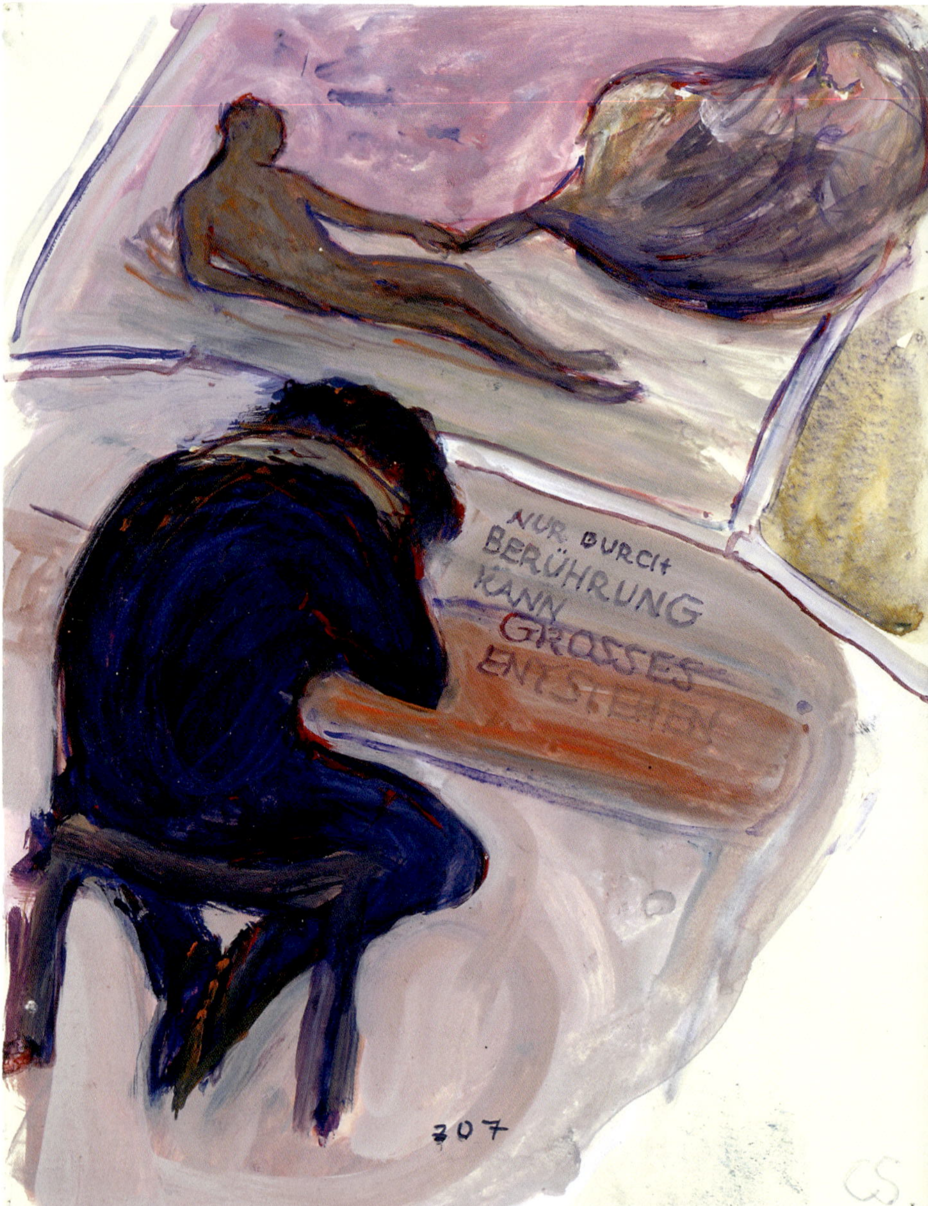
NUR DURCH
BERÜHRUNG
KANN
GROSSES
ENTSTEHEN
307

The following sheets are those that to the author seem the strangest.

Without doubt they have their origin in the Michelangelo Rome series of the Main Section that was sung with the loudest and most penetrating voice of this entire “opus”.

(Creation of Adam)
(from Michelangelo)

DABERLOHN
“Only by touching
can greatness be achieved.”

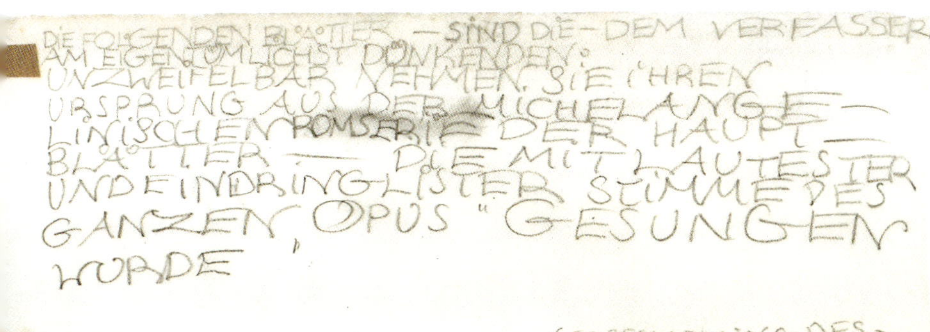
DIE FOLGENDEN BLÄTTER — SIND DIE — DEM VERFASSER
AM EIGENTÜMLICHST DÜNKENDEN.
UNZWEIFELBAR NEHMEN SIE IHREN
URSPRUNG AUS DER MICHELANGE—
LINISCHEN ROMSERIE DER HAUPT—
BLÄTTER — DIE MIT LAUTESTER
UND EINDRINGLISTER STIMME DES
GANZEN „OPUS" GESUNGEN
WURDE

(ERSCHAFFUNG DES ADAM)
(VON MICHELANGELO)

CHAPTER TEN

DABERLOHN
"Don't laugh at me, I believe in the dice.
Only by touching can greatness be achieved."

To the melody: Roma divina città aeterna.
Great is Michelangelo.

Softly, as Night, also by Michelangelo – appears, resonates the odd familiar melody:

Roma divina città aeterna – and in our redemption's pain we can feel Thy might again.

Incidentally, the same tune engendered the sheet:
"Don't laugh at me – I believe in the dice.
Anyone who throws three sixes in a row can..."

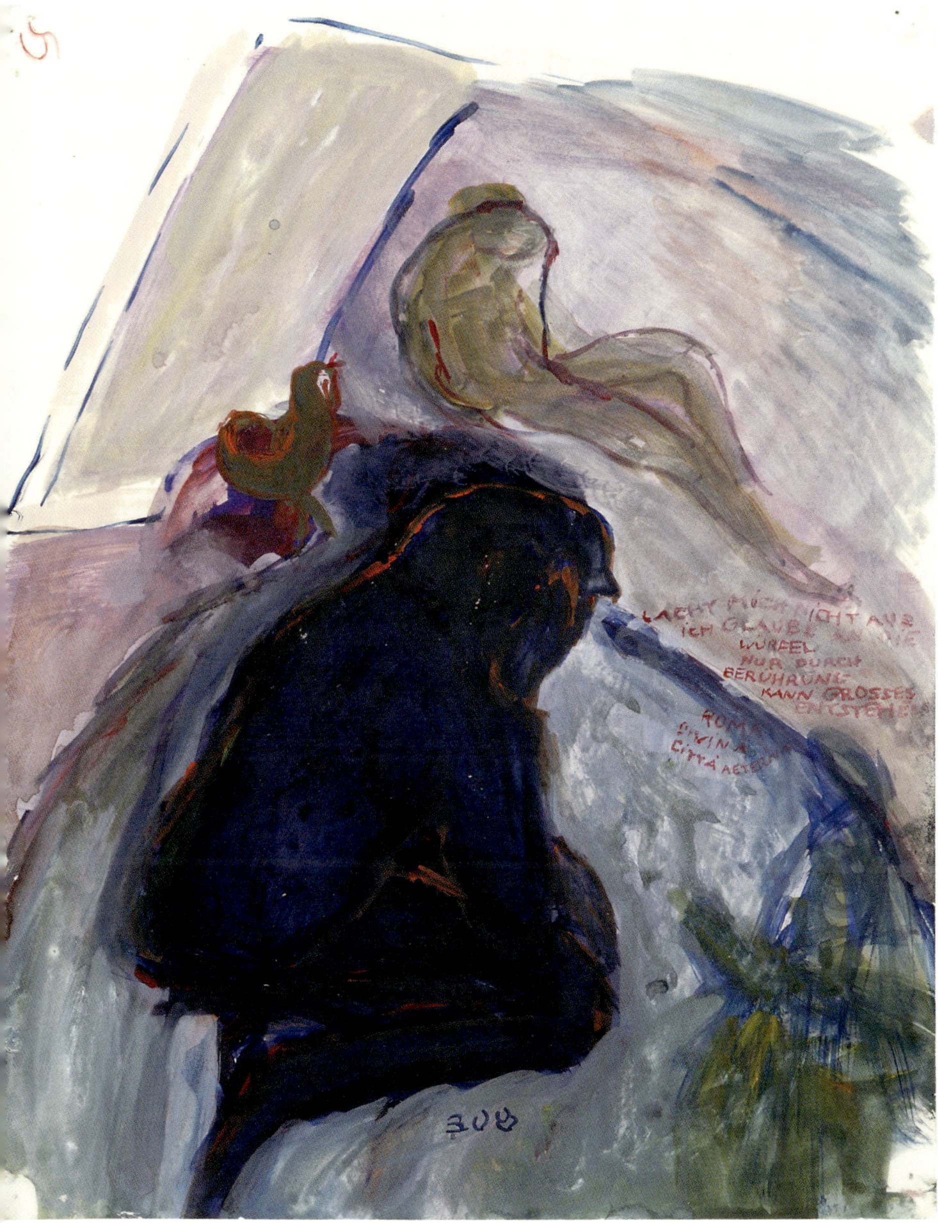
LACHT MICH NICHT AUS
ICH GLAUBE AN DIE
WÜRFEL
NUR DURCH
BERÜHRUNG
KANN GROSSES
ENTSTEHEN
ROMA
DIVINA
308

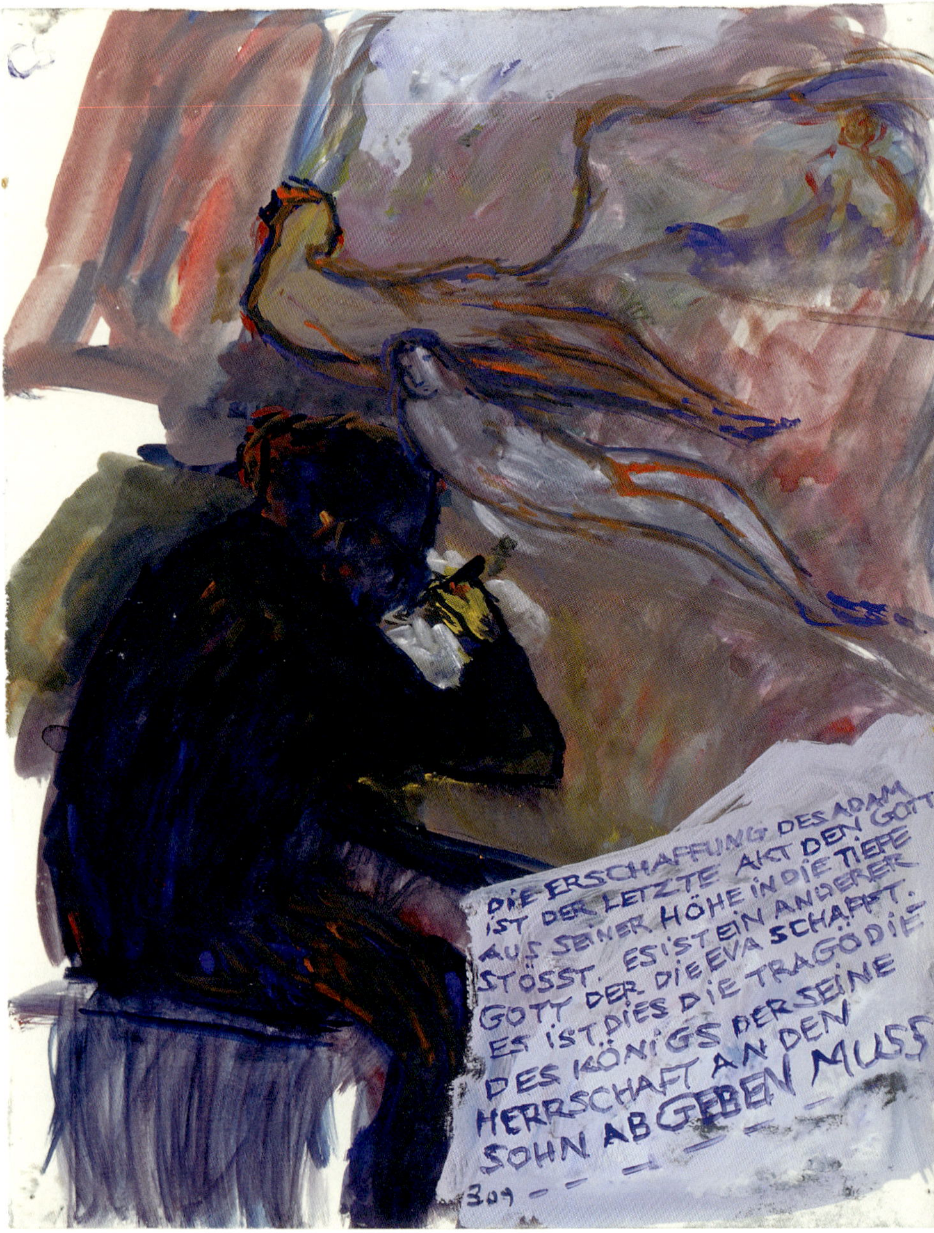
DIE ERSCHAFFUNG DES ADAM
IST DER LETZTE AKT DEN GOTT
AUS SEINER HÖHE IN DIE TIEFE
STÖSST. ES IST EIN ANDERER
GOTT DER DIE EVA SCHAFFT.
ES IST DIES DIE TRAGÖDIE
DES KÖNIGS DER SEINE
HERRSCHAFT AN DEN
SOHN AB GEBEN MUSS
309

(opposite)

It is Daberlohn's own story – the experience of a modern man in the year 1938 – that finds expression in the greatest of all human achievements, the Bible, as depicted by one of the mightiest geniuses of all time, Michelangelo.

DABERLOHN
"The creation of Adam is God's final act which He hurls from His heights into the depths. It is another God who creates Eve. This is the tragedy of the king who must hand over His dominion to his son – "

(page 418)

"In the Last Judgement, God the Father is missing. His dominion has passed over to His Son."

(page 419)

"Adam arisen in Christ – now the conqueror of the underworld!"

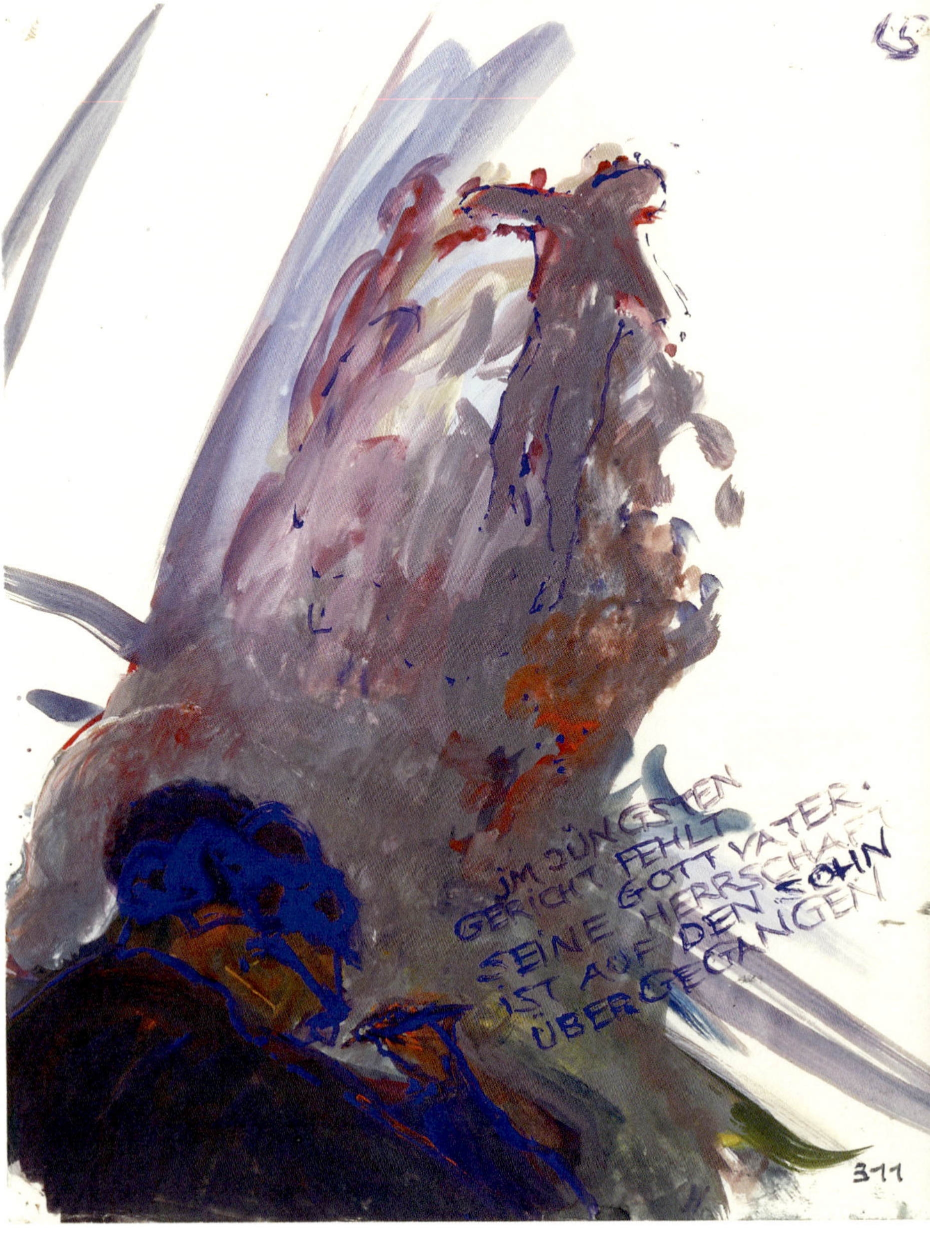
65
IM JÜNGSTEN
GERICHT FEHLT
GOTT VATER.
SEINE HERRSCHAFT
IST AUF DEN SOHN
ÜBERGEGANGEN
311

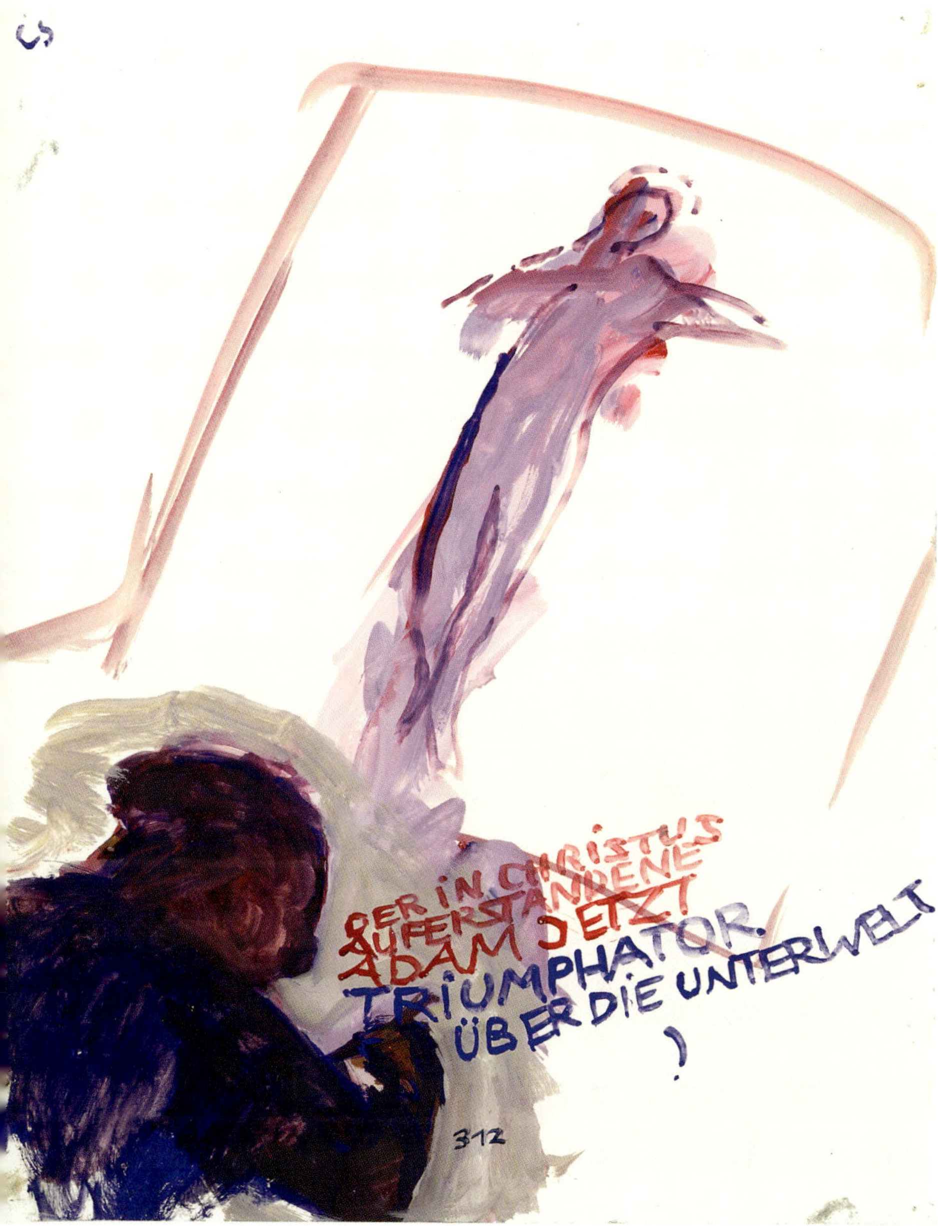
DER IN CHRISTUS
AUFERSTANDENE
ADAM JETZT
TRIUMPHATOR.
ÜBER DIE UNTERWELT
?
312

At the movies, he feels, on an equal level with the hero passing before his eyes, equal of his ideal. At the movies he follows his path to the heights, to his refuge, the dream world that is to help him ignore the grey blackish harshness of daily life.

His dream – to be like this hero – almost like gods – flying up in the air dancing, rising up dancing in front of skyscrapers – isn't that the same as the old woman praying in the cathedral and thinking of the imminent bliss of heavenly joys – and...

DABERLOHN
"People dancing in front of skyscrapers, old woman praying in the cathedral – for me they are the same, that is my vision."

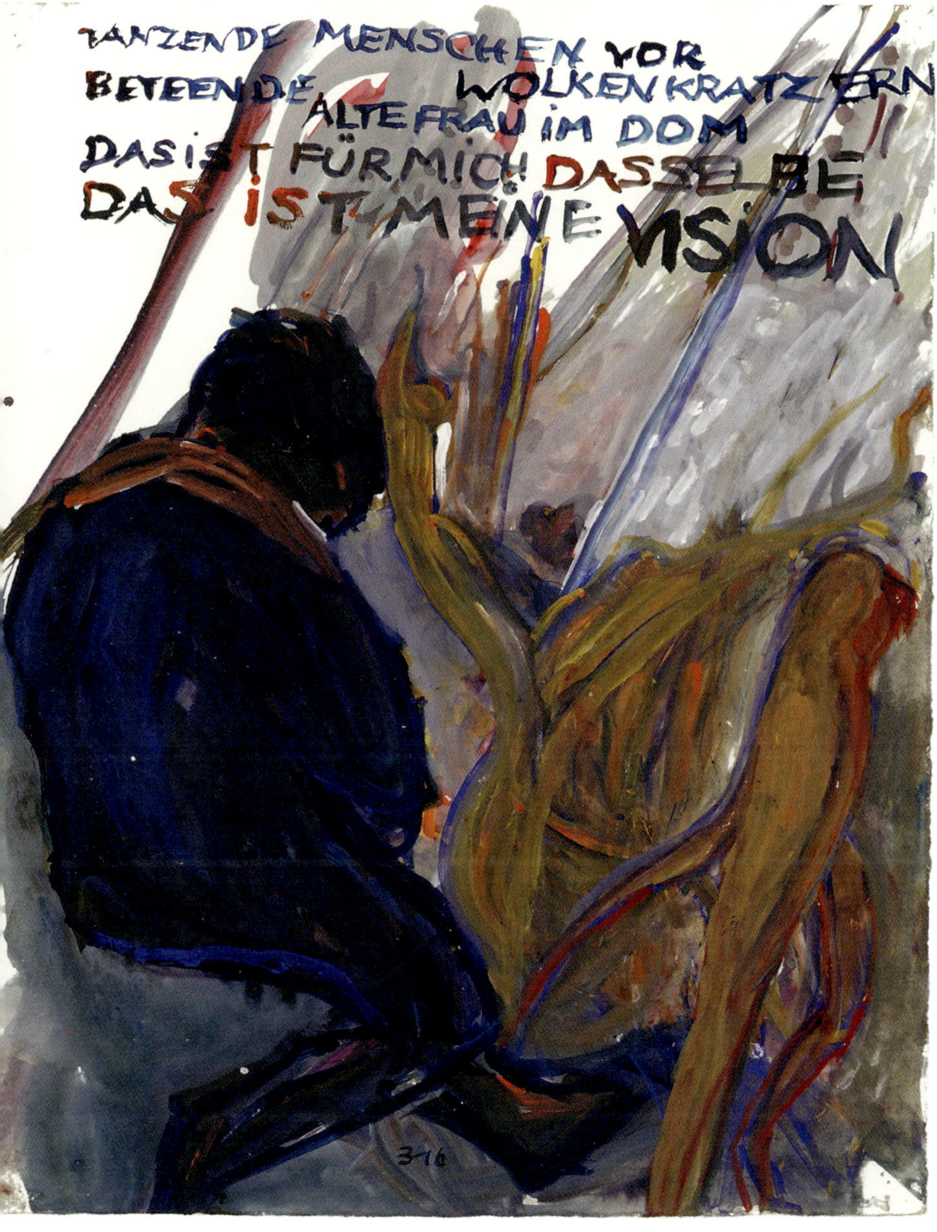
TANZENDE MENSCHEN VOR
BETEENDE WOLKENKRATZERN
ALTE FRAU IM DOM
DAS IST FÜR MICH DASSELBE
DAS IST MEINE VISION

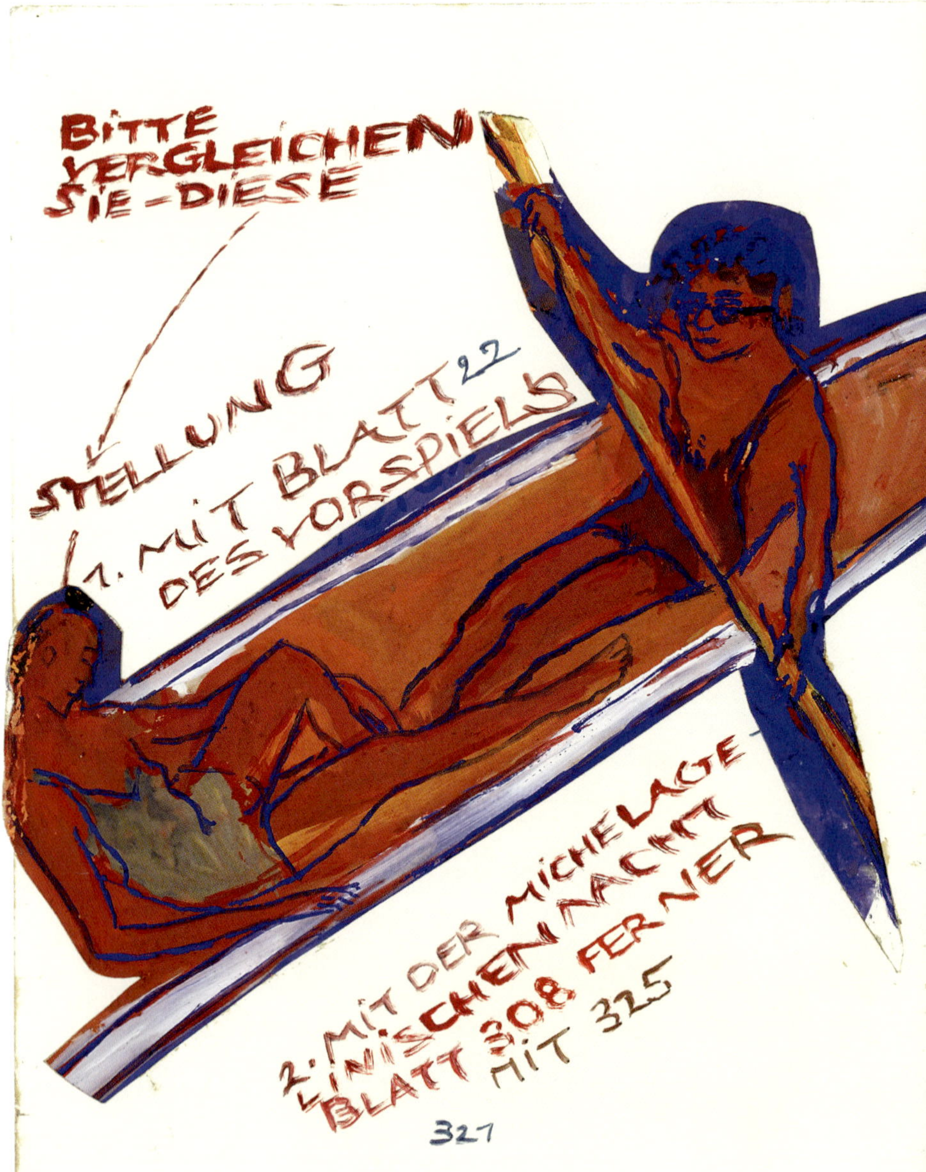
BITTE VERGLEICHEN SIE-DIESE
STELLUNG
1. MIT BLATT 22 DES VORSPIELS
2. MIT DER MICHELAGELINISCHEN NACHT BLATT 308 FERNER MIT 325
327

With their boat, which bears the name of Daberlohn's fiancée, they have arrived at a sandy-reedy bay, where they pause to rest.

Please compare this pose.
1. with no. 22 of the Prelude,
2. with Michelangelo's <u>Night</u>, sheet no. 308,
also with no. 325.

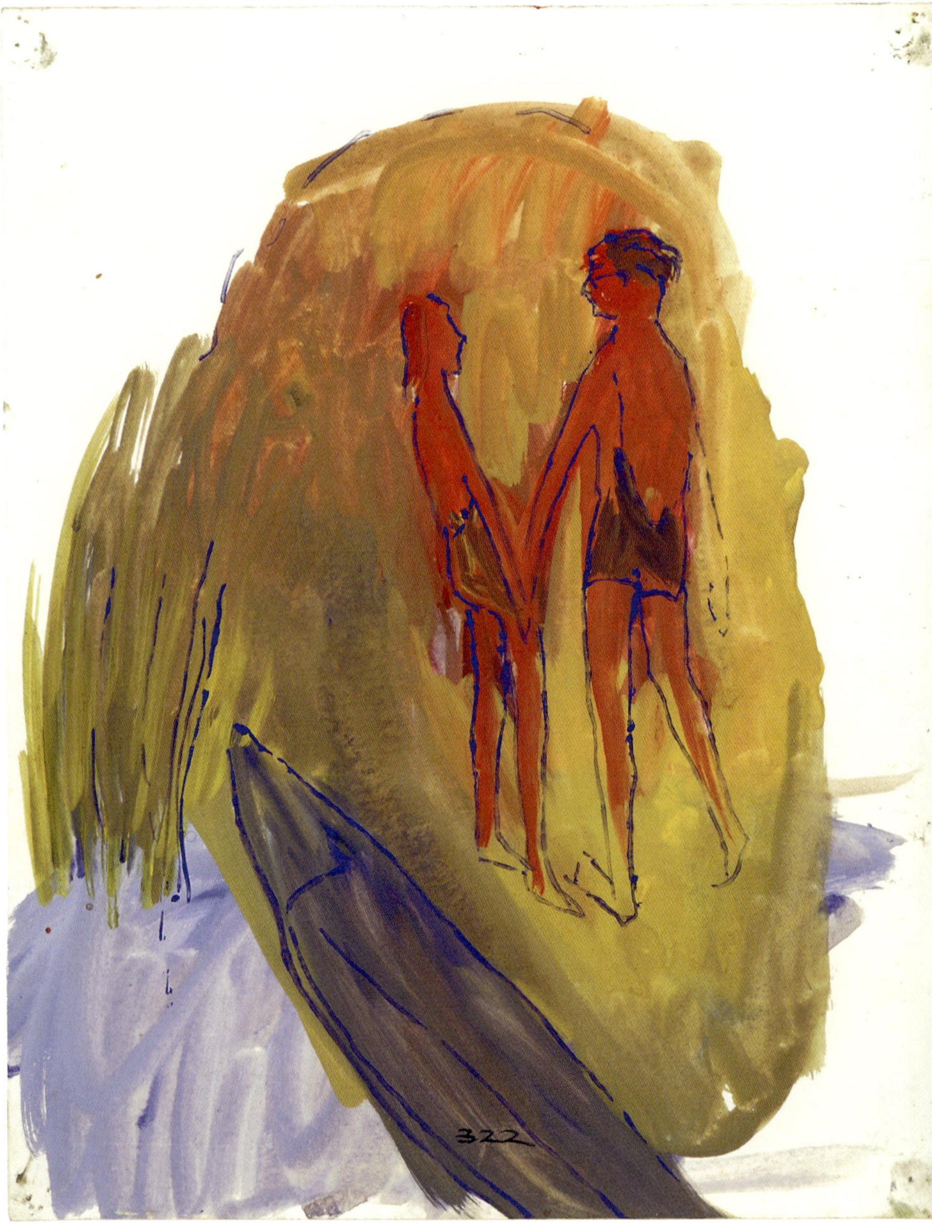
322

(bottom)

He continues “his experiments,” which, as always, are very interesting to him.

Charlotte stays immobile – that has never occurred to him in years of practice. He has the feeling of something cold and dead-like and is astonishingly interested.

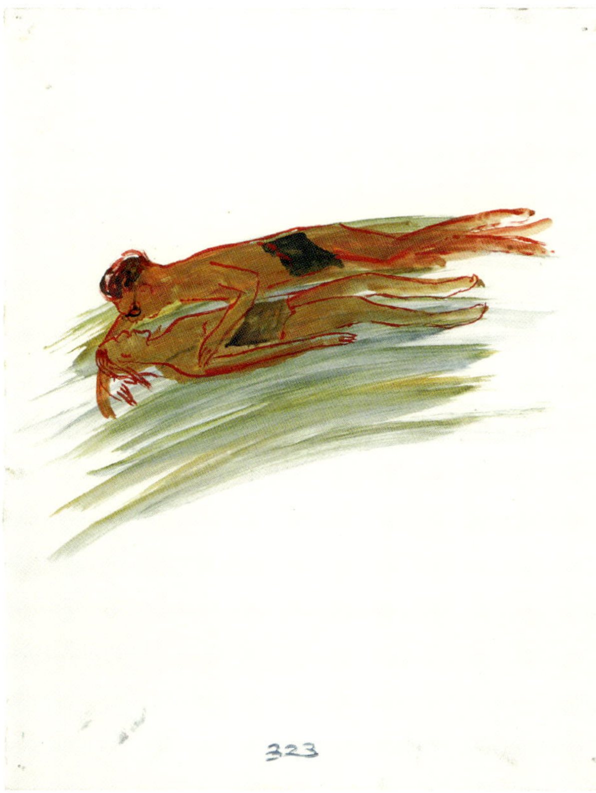

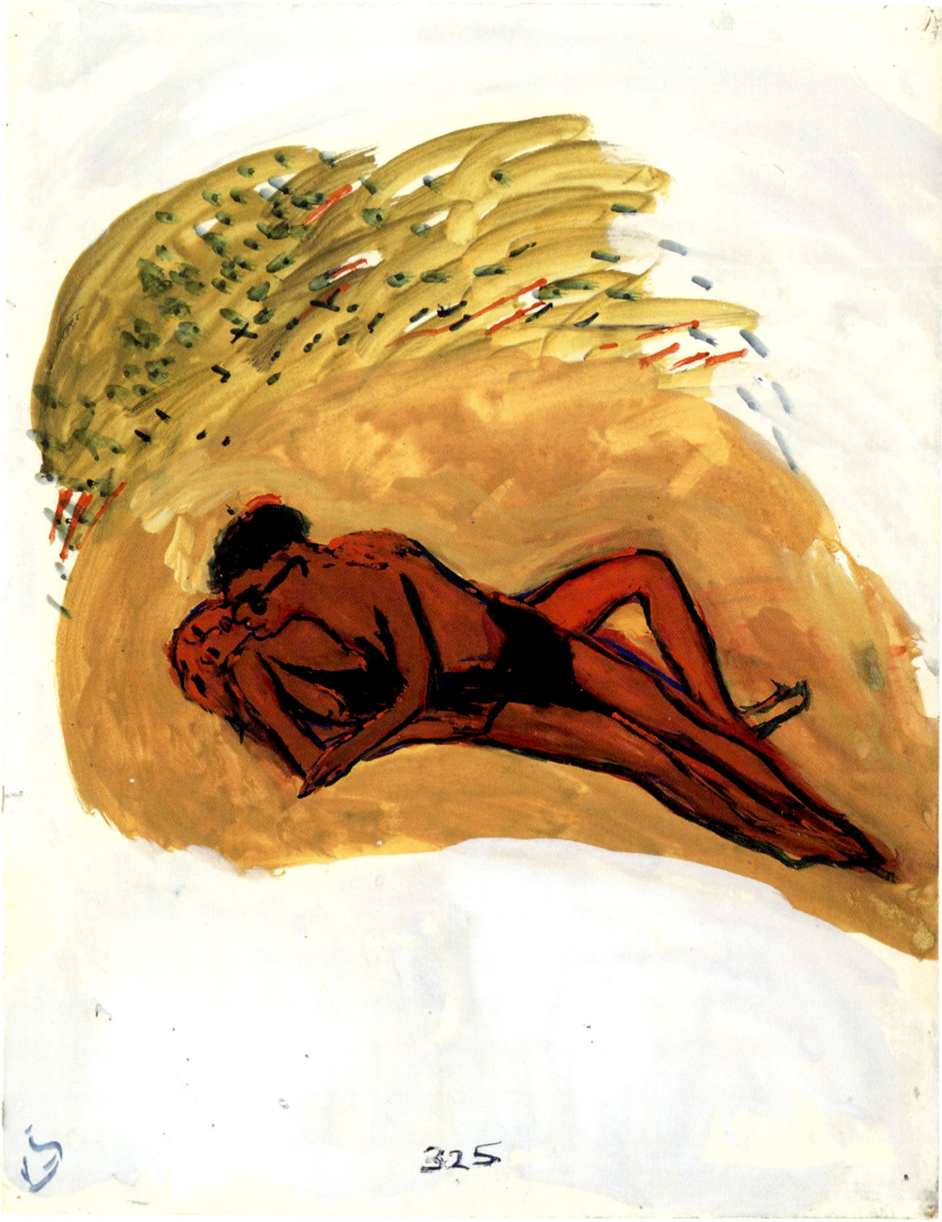
325

(opposite)

But suddenly his hypersensitive nerves are touched by a firelike current... which is only natural – considering that this sheet was created to the tune of: Wie ich dich liebe – so hat noch nie – noch nie ein Mensch geliebt [How I love you – this is how, never – never has a human being loved so before].

(bottom)

It was only a second. Charlotte lies there as if it were not her who had brought about this fiery stream. Perhaps if Daberlohn had known old Mrs Knarre, he would once again have closed in on a family resemblance – just as you can after reading the Epilogue.

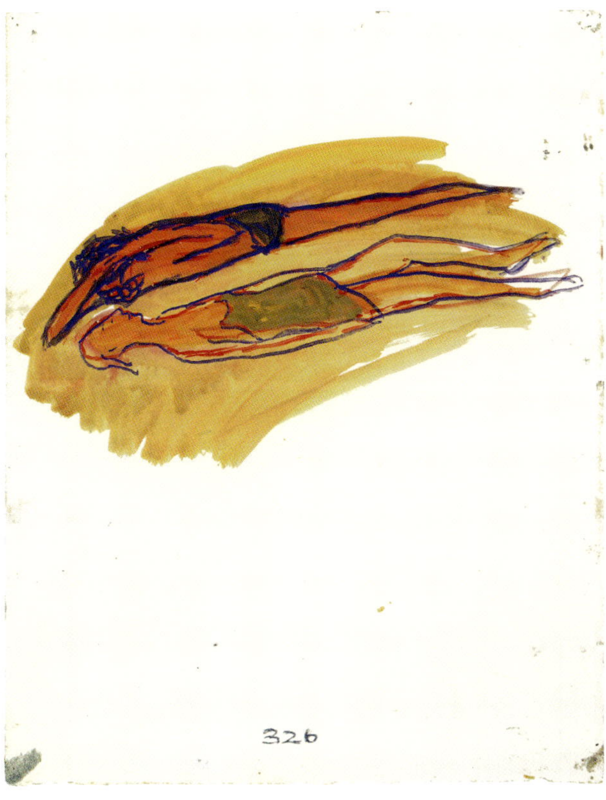

For the time being he is entirely absorbed in his vision of the new religion that is to usher in the "earthly" resurrection of suffering humanity.

DABERLOHN
"Now there's going to be a thunderstorm."

CHARLOTTE
"I love thunderstorms. Come on, let's go into the water."

DABERLOHN
"That is the new religion."

The thunderstorm increases the urgency of his thoughts.

DABERLOHN
"Do you see how it flashes, do you hear how it thunders? That's my new religion."

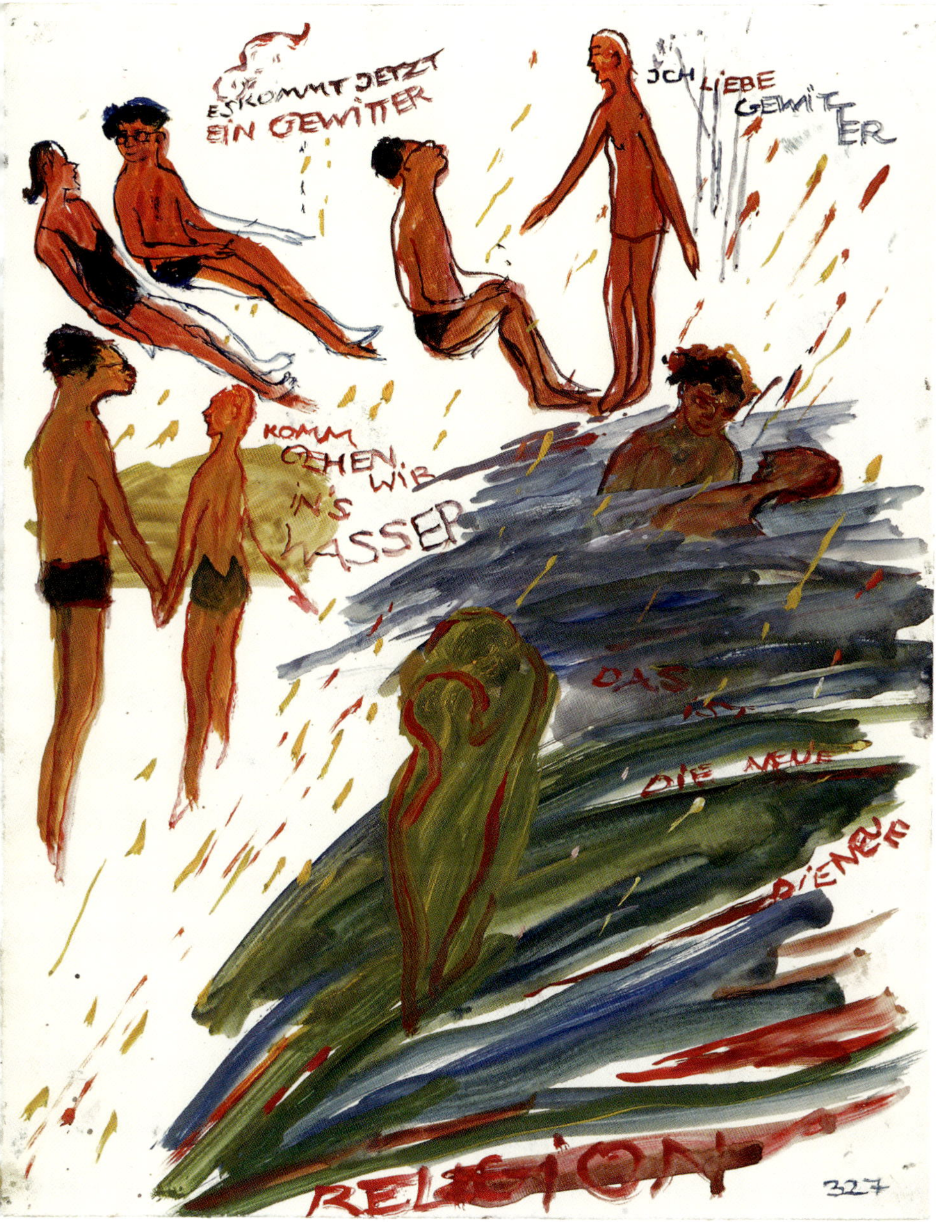
ES KOMMT JETZT EIN GEWITTER
JCH LIEBE GEWITTER
KOMM GEHEN WIR IN'S WASSER
DAS IST DIE NEUE
DIE NEUE
RELIGION
327

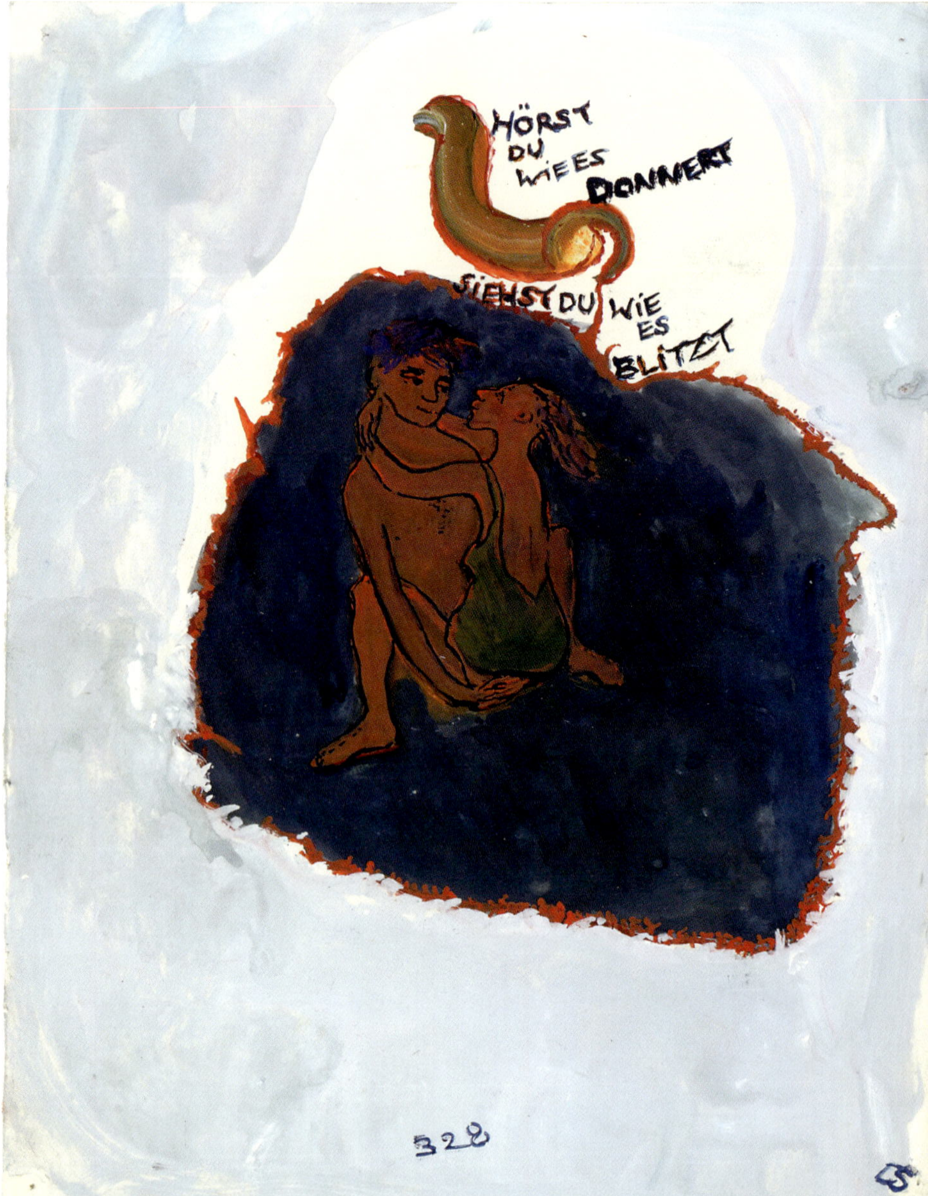
HÖRST DU WIEES DONNERT
SIEHST DU WIE ES BLITZT
328

(opposite)

"Do you hear the thunder;
can you see the lightning?"

(bottom)

He endeavours to implant
something of himself into her...

DABERLOHN
"So far, thunder and lightning
have always cleansed the world best."

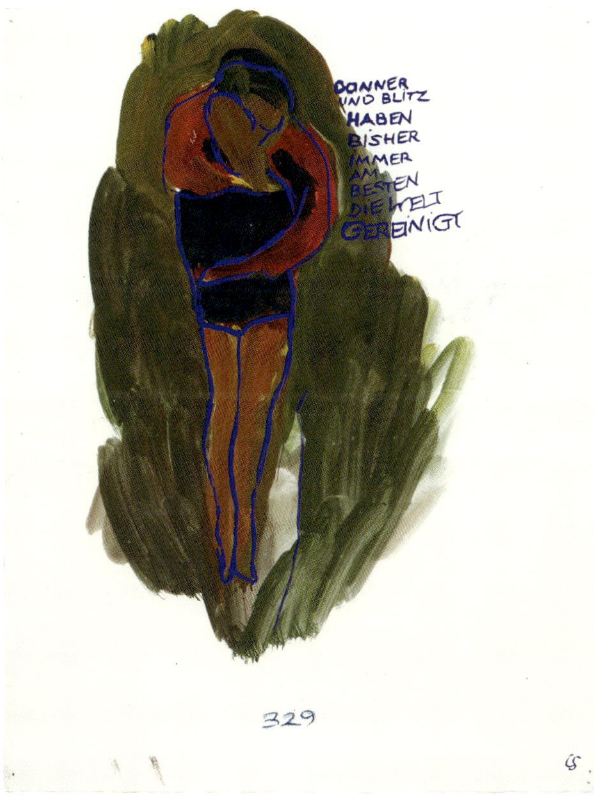

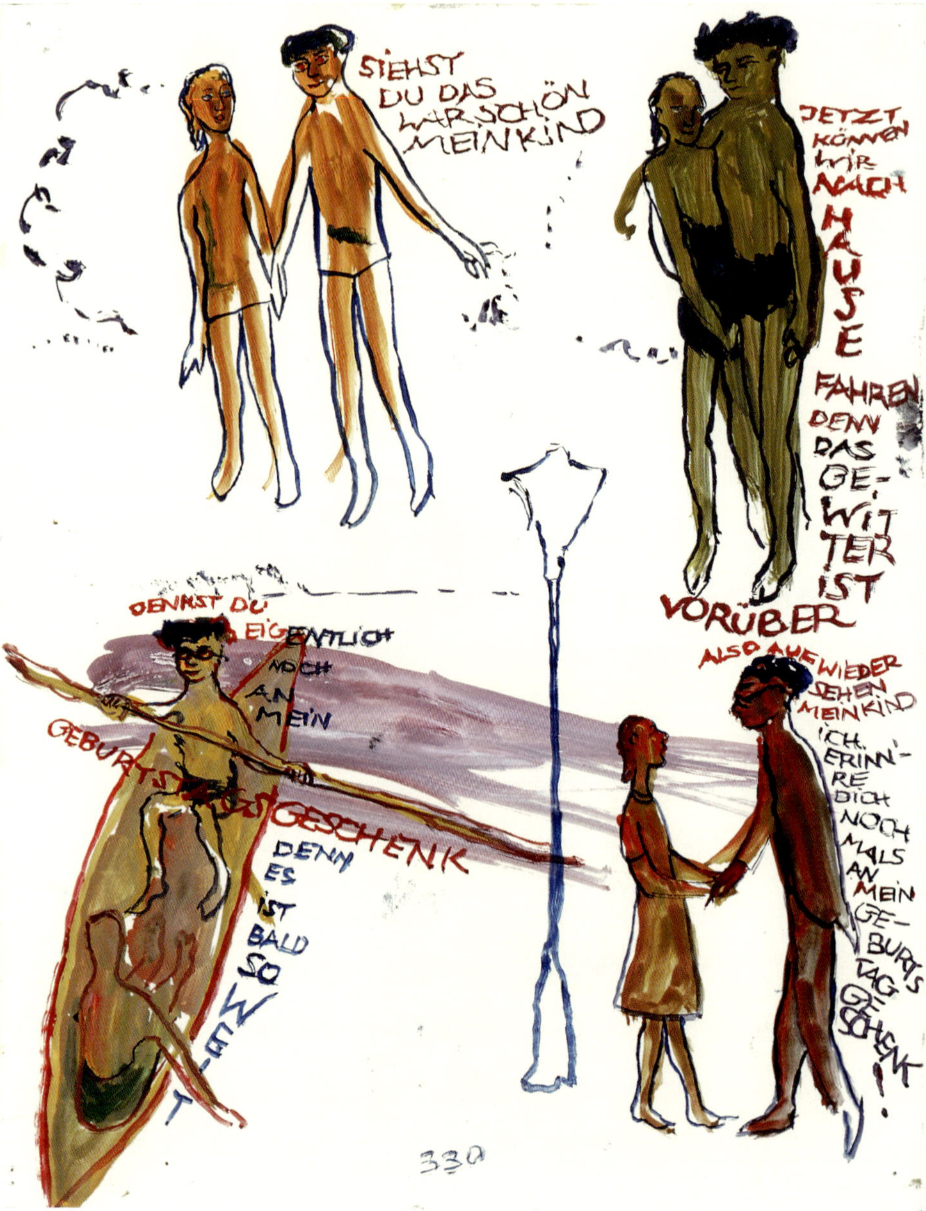
SIEHST DU DAS WAR SCHÖN MEIN KIND
JETZT KÖNNEN WIR NACH HAUSE FAHREN DENN DAS GE-WITTER IST VORÜBER
DENKST DU EIGENTLICH NOCH AN MEIN GEBURTSTAGSGESCHENK
DENN ES IST BALD SO WEIT
ALSO AUF WIEDER SEHEN MEIN KIND
ICH ERINN-RE DICH NOCH MALS AN MEIN GE-BURTS TAG GE-SCHENK!
330

... and even feels a sense of satisfaction after exertion.

DABERLOHN
"Do you see, that was lovely, my child. That was lovely! Now we can go home, the thunderstorm is over. By the way, are you remembering my birthday present? It's not far off now. Well then, goodbye, my child. May I remind you again of my birthday present!"

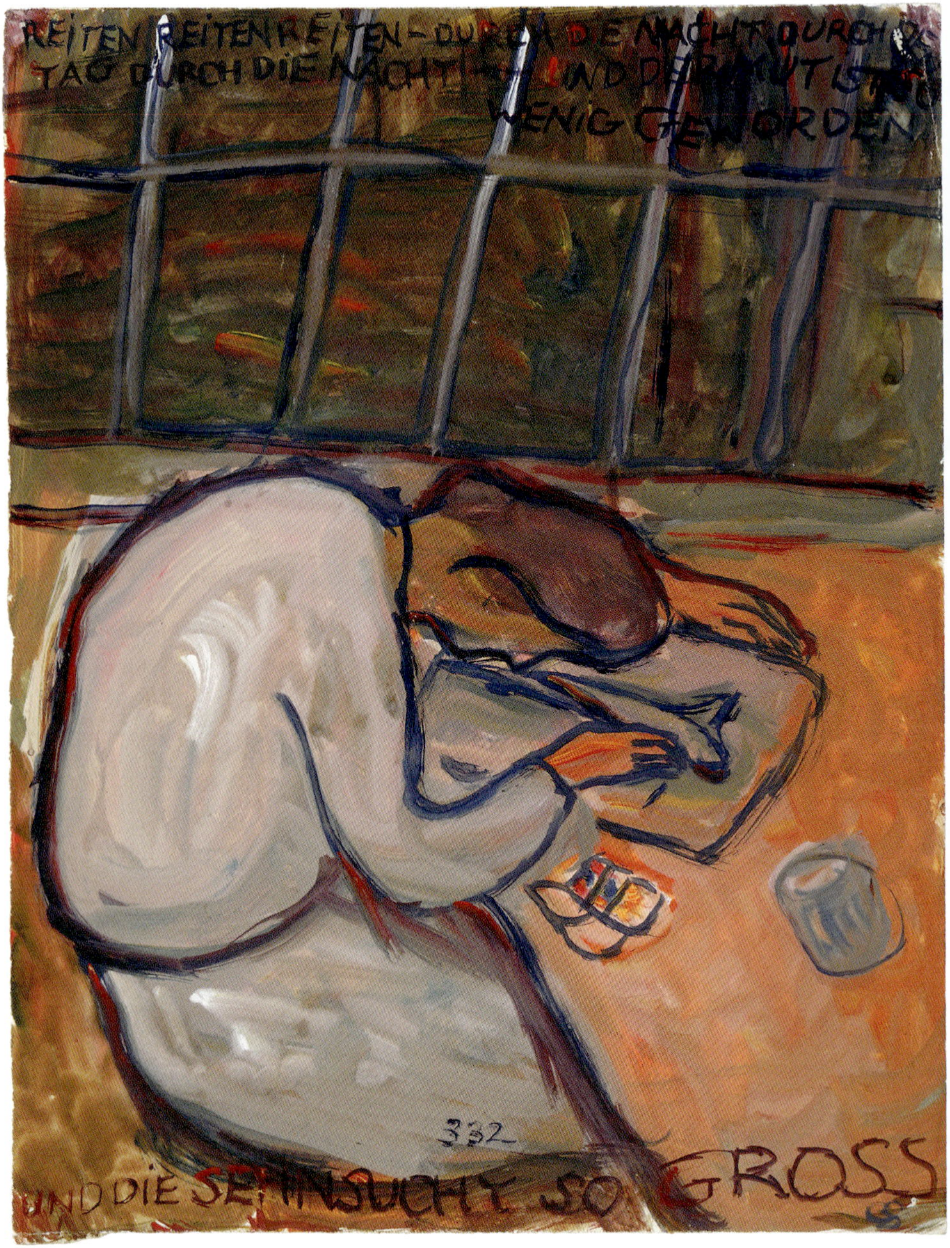
REITEN REITEN REITEN – DURCH DIE NACHT DURCH
TAG DURCH DIE NACHT UND DER MUT IST SO
WENIG GEWORDEN
332
UND DIE SEHNSUCHT SO GROSS

(opposite)

She becomes utterly engrossed in accomplishing the work of illustration.

“Ride, ride, ride – through the night, through the day, through the night – and courage has become so small, and yearning so great.”

(bottom)

“Quietly whooshing, the hour slowly trickles into the dream of night.”

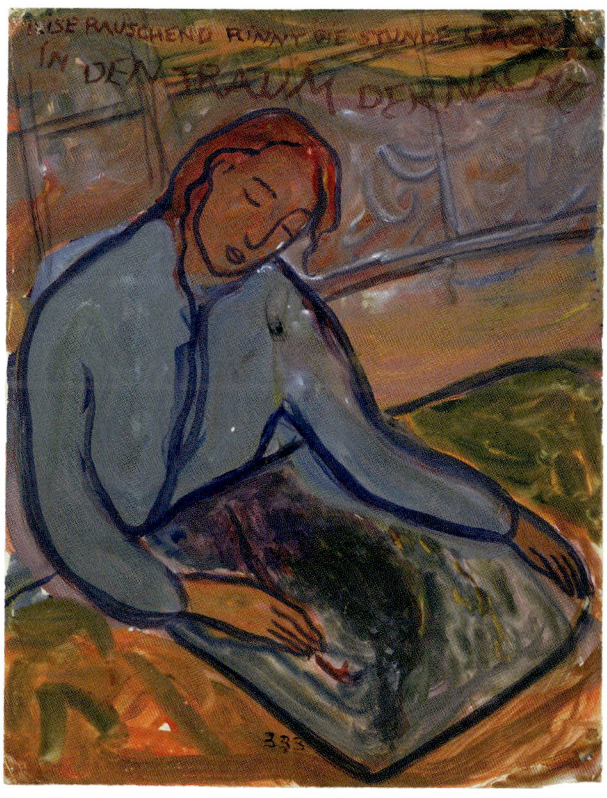

(bottom)

“And he threw his horse into
the midst of the enemies...”

(opposite)

“... and died under the slowly
dying flames of the blazing flag.”

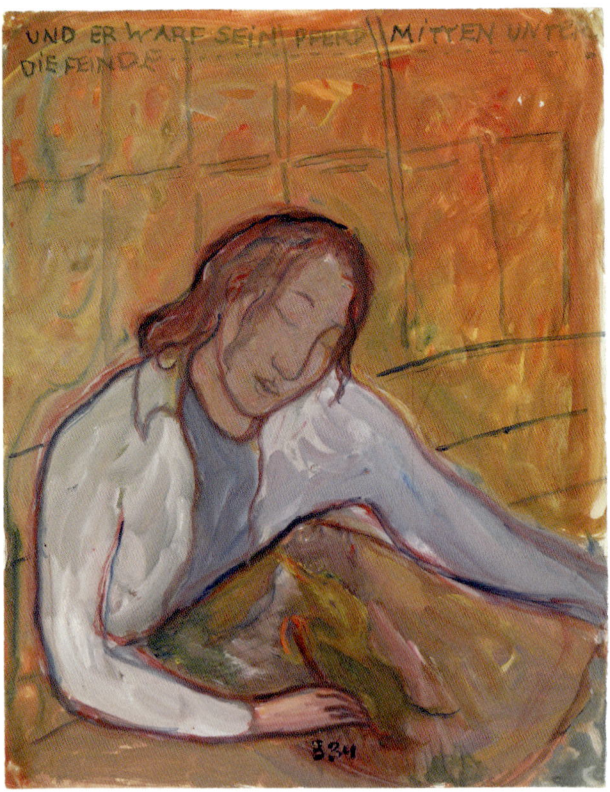

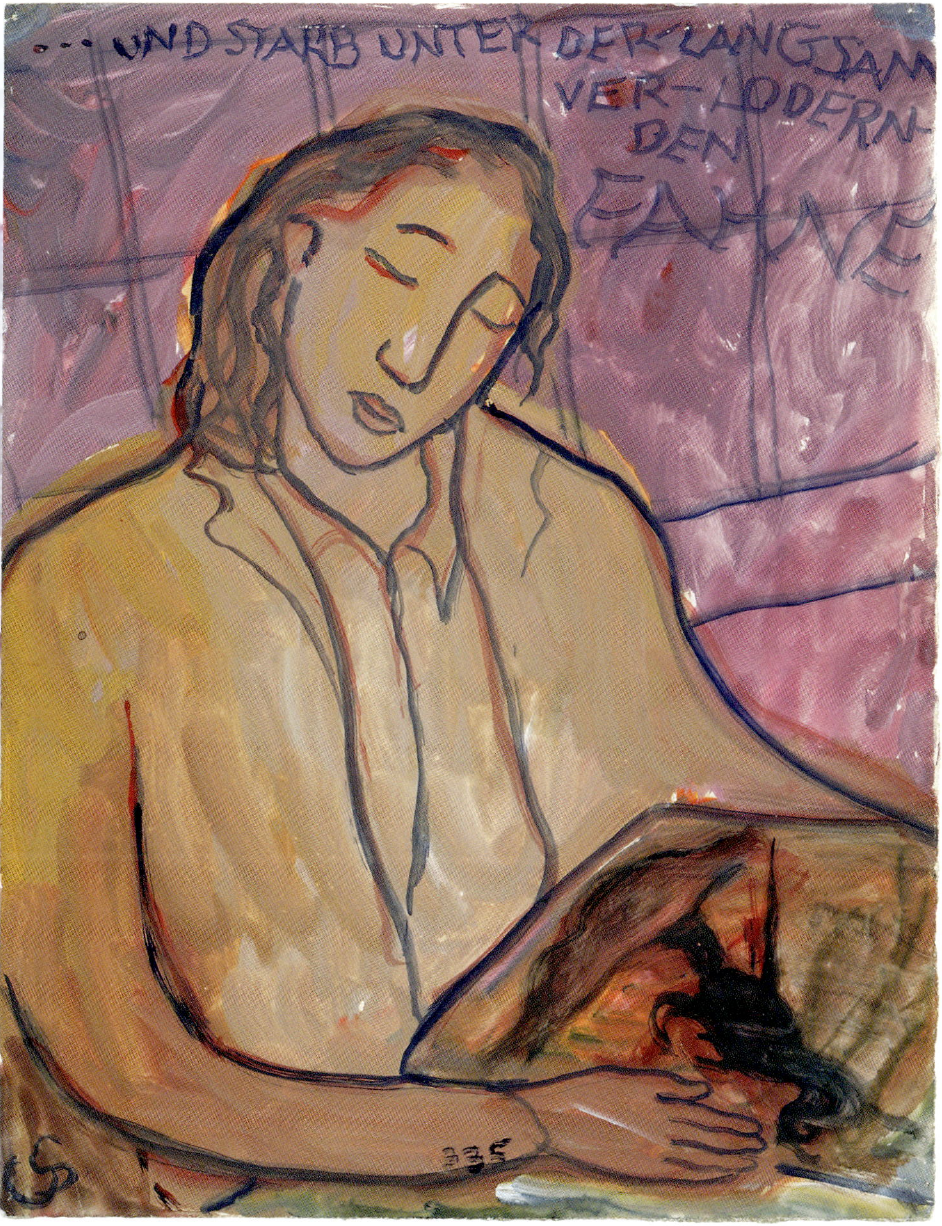
... UND STARB UNTER DER LANGSAM
VER-LODERN-
DEN
FAHNE

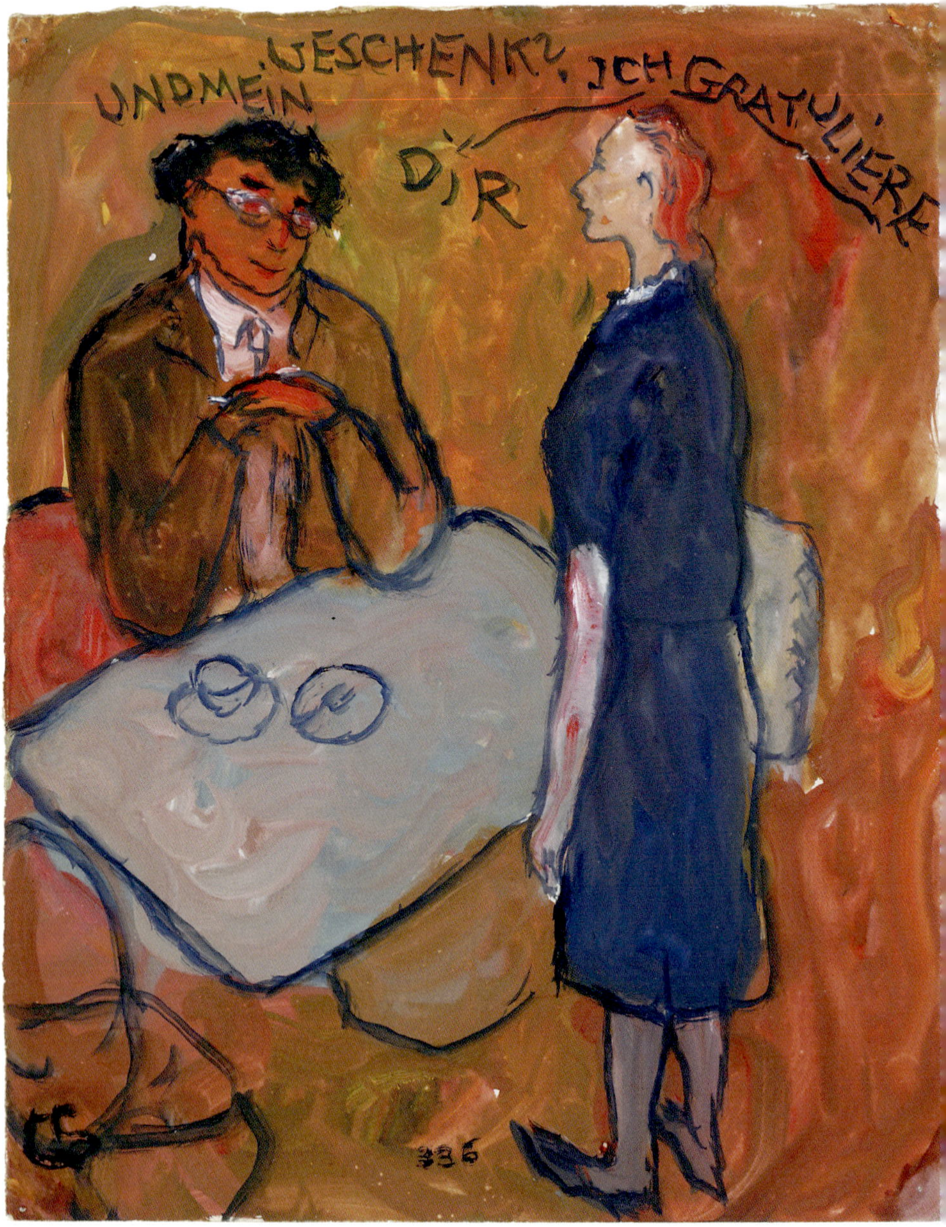
UND MEIN GESCHENK?
ICH GRATULIERE DIR
336

(opposite)

And on the day of the birthday she appears in the small café – highly contended that, after her long efforts, the illustrations have turned out surprisingly well.

CHARLOTTE
"I congratulate you."

DABERLOHN
"And my present?"

(right)

Friend Daberlohn seems to have a very busy day ahead of him. Charlotte is very disappointed – so much so that everything in front of her eyes turns into indistinct forms.

DABERLOHN
"Yes – I'll have a look at it later, at home, since today I have terribly little time."

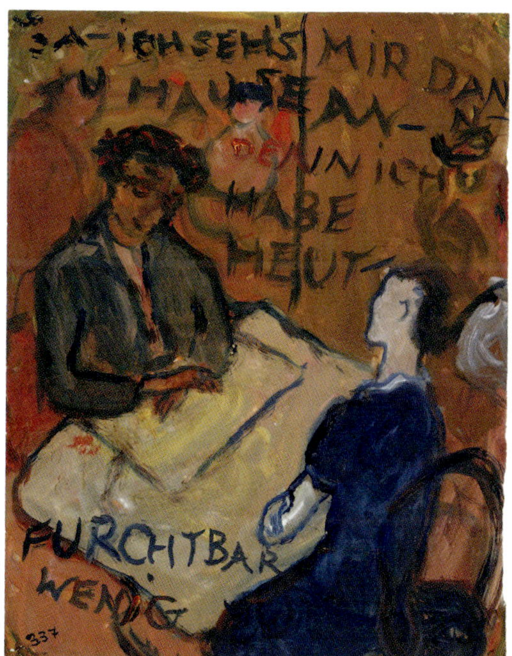

(bottom)

DABERLOHN
"So, when shall we
meet again?"

CHARLOTTE
"For the time being, not at all!"

DABERLOHN
"Just as you wish,
young lady."

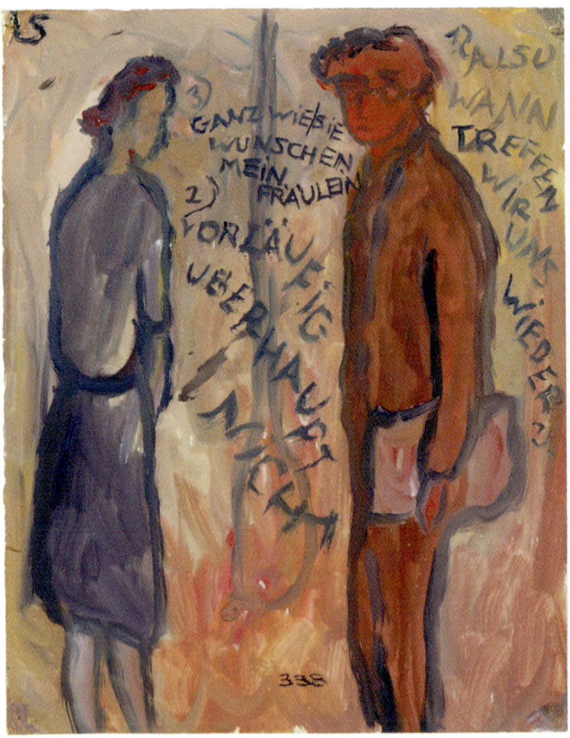

(opposite)

"Since today I have
horribly little time."

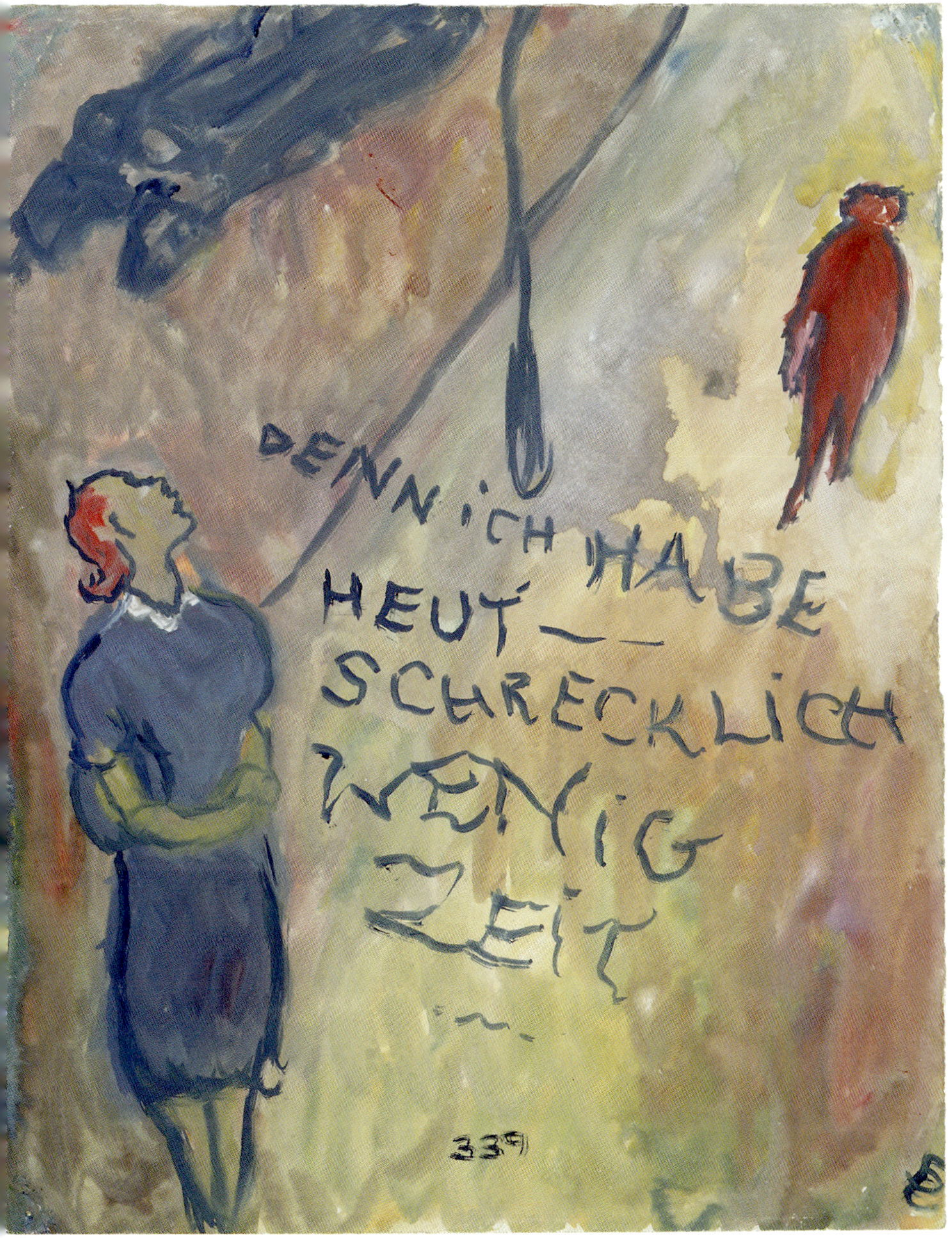
DENN ICH HABE
HEUT
SCHRECKLICH
WENIG
ZEIT
339

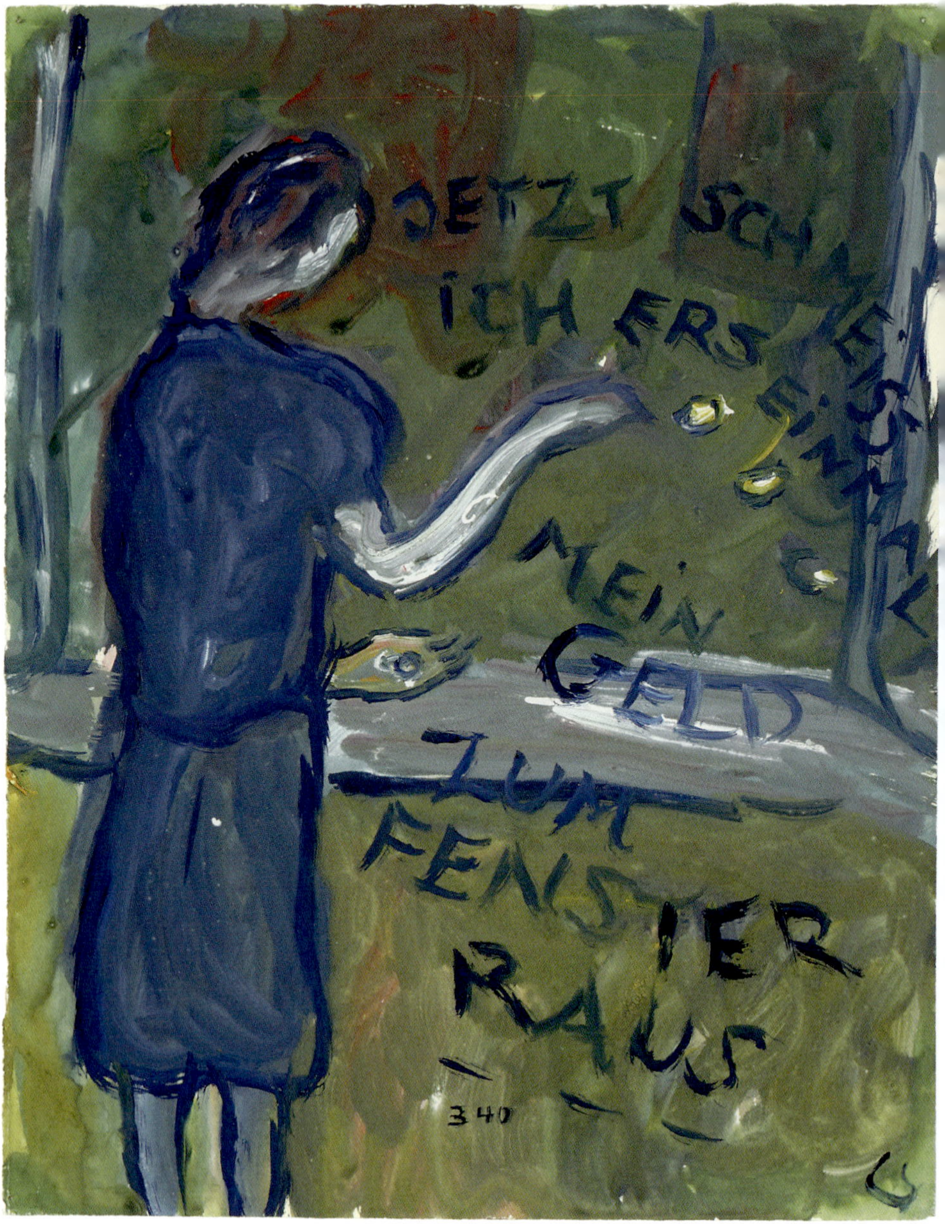
JETZT SCHMEISS
ICH ERST EINMAL
MEIN GELD
ZUM FENSTER
RAUS
340

(opposite)

She is filled with grief
mingled with rage.

CHARLOTTE
"First of all, I'll throw
my money out of the window."

(bottom)

"Best I'll throw myself
out right after."

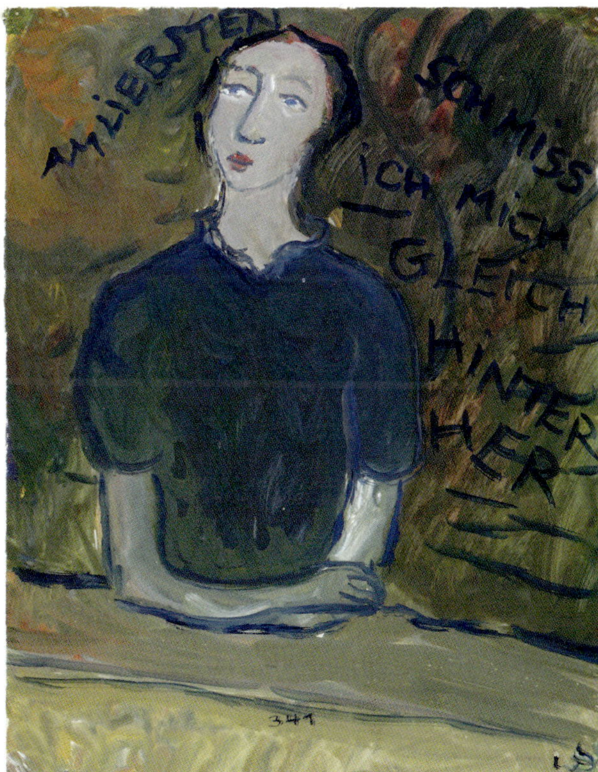

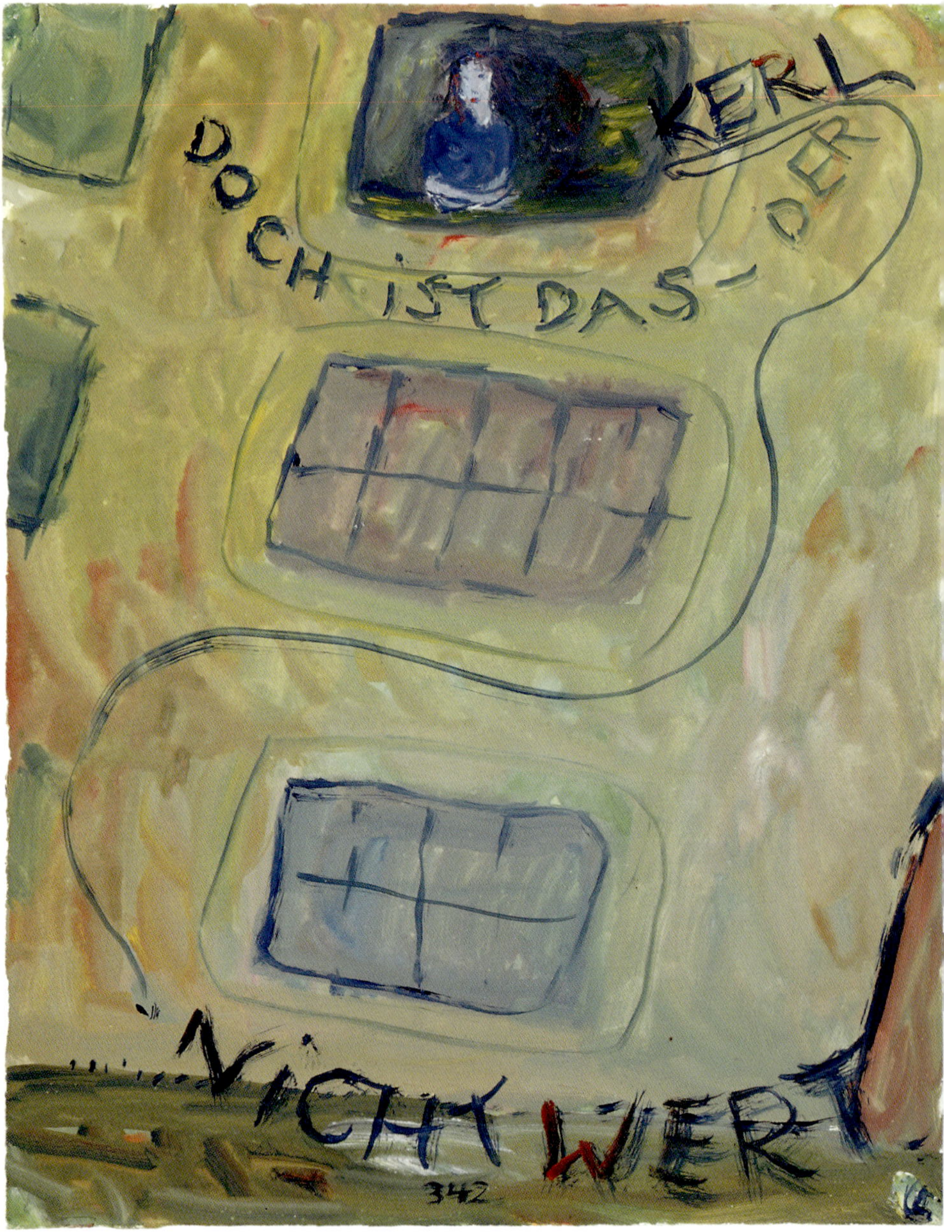
KERL
DOCH IST DAS - DER
NICHT WERT
342

(opposite)

"But the fellow's not worth it."

(bottom)

"Besides, someday I'll find out how he liked the drawings."

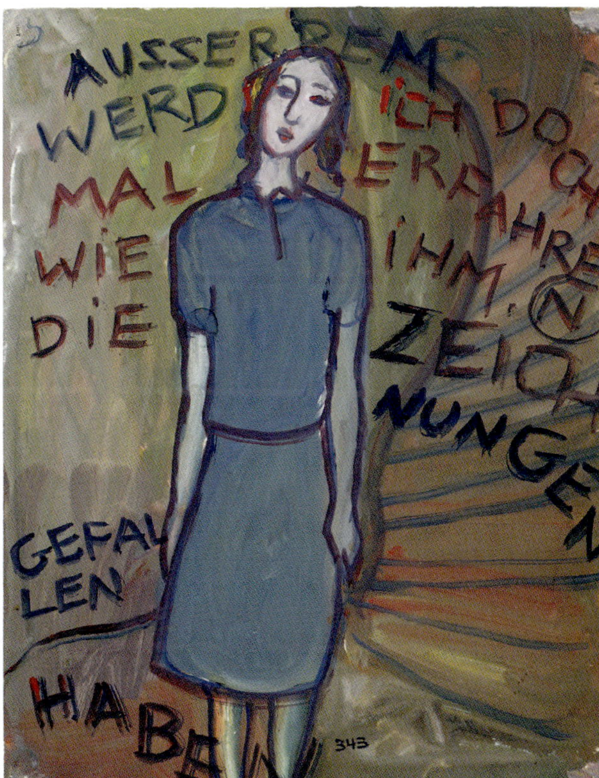

(opposite)

"Orpheus, or The Way to a Mask.
Learn to sing, Oh my soul! (Nietzsche)"

(page 448)

"Why aren't you the image in which I have invented you?

This is the explanation why men have fought each other at all times, why even God is wrathful at His creatures. In Adam He created His most beautiful dream. He wanted the child to be liberated from the knowledge of good and evil. To know the meaning of good and evil meant, for Adam, knowing Eve. That is why the path led from Adam to Christ, so that finally the words would be expressed – Woman, what have I to do with thee? One must first go into oneself to be able to go out of oneself. In the Last Judgement, God the Father is missing. His dominion has passed over to His Son. Adam arisen in Christ – now the conqueror of the u..."

(page 449)

"God appeared as the most tormented person on this earth. The Old Testament forbids any image of God, whereas the New Testament is unthinkable without the symbol of the Crucified One. Where Judaism has been able to use music as a counterbalance, Christianity uses the image of the Madonna by His side.

Love thy neighbour as thyself. In order to follow this commandment it is necessary first to love – to know – oneself. One must first go into oneself to be able to go out of oneself. All men of genius have gone this path. One means of going out of oneself is, for me – the movies –
modern man's machine for producing himself.

Old woman praying in the cathedral, or people dancing in front of skyscrapers – nothing goes as far as the human imagination. Leonardo da Vinci invented submarines as well as flying contraptions, conjur..."

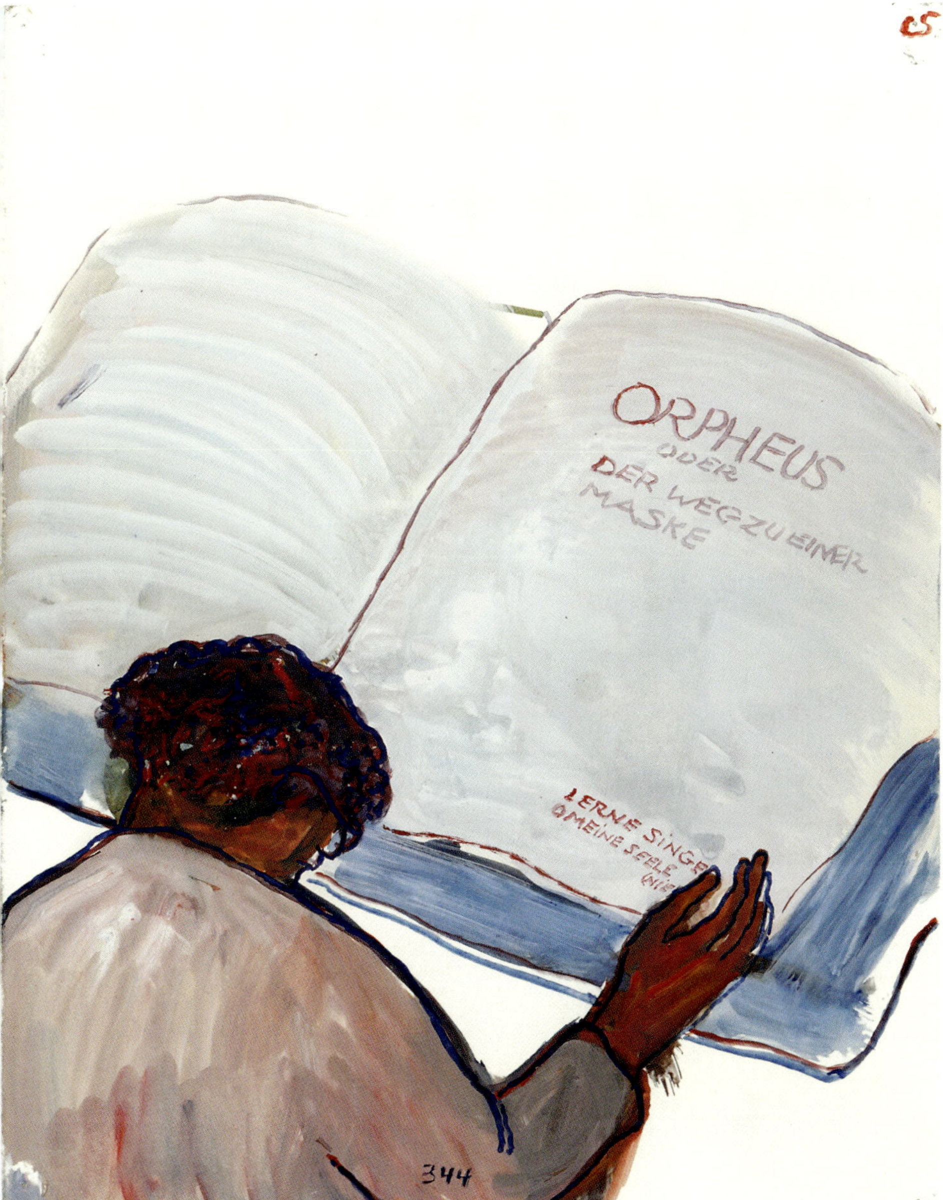
cS
ORPHEUS
ODER
DER WEG ZU EINER
MASKE
LERNE SINGE
O MEINE SEELE
344

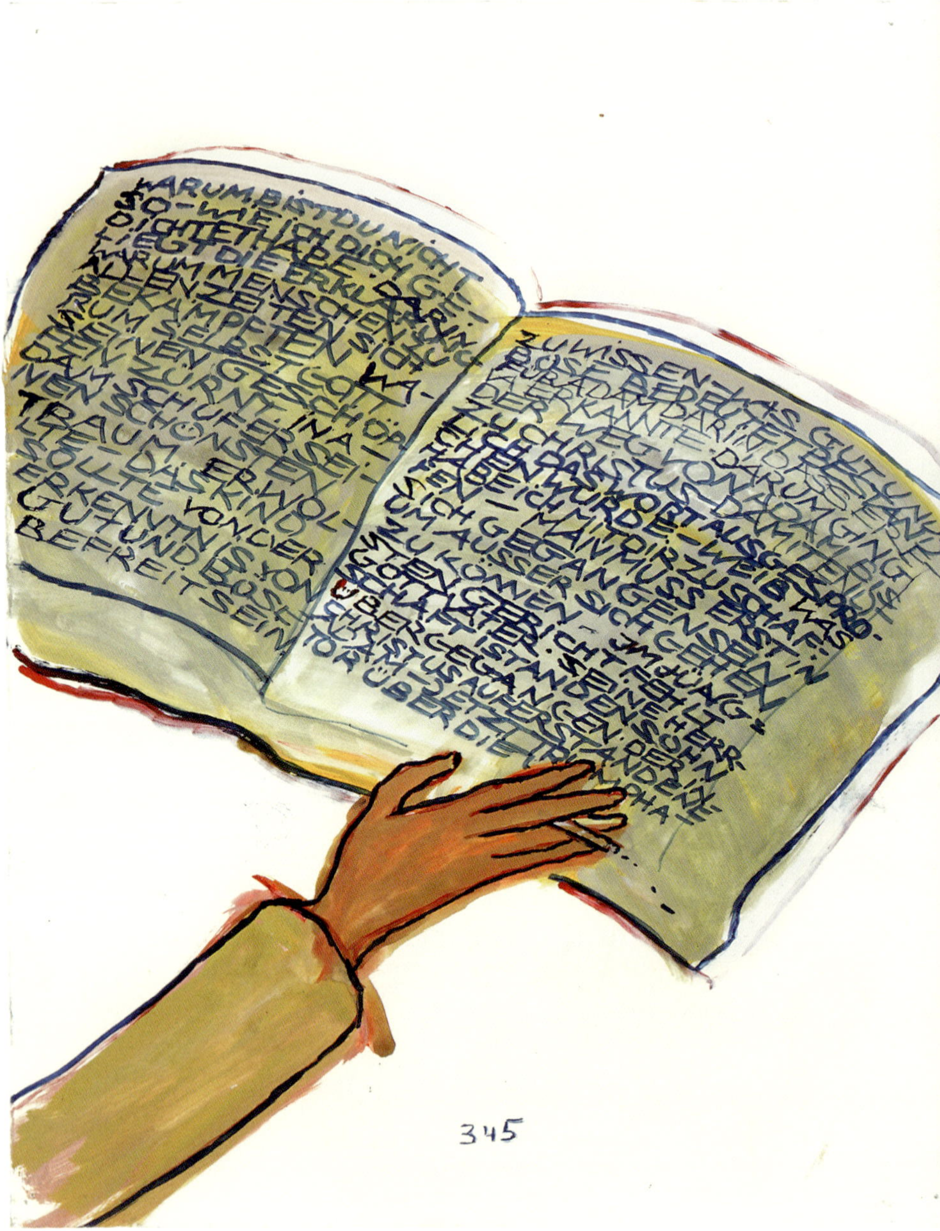
345

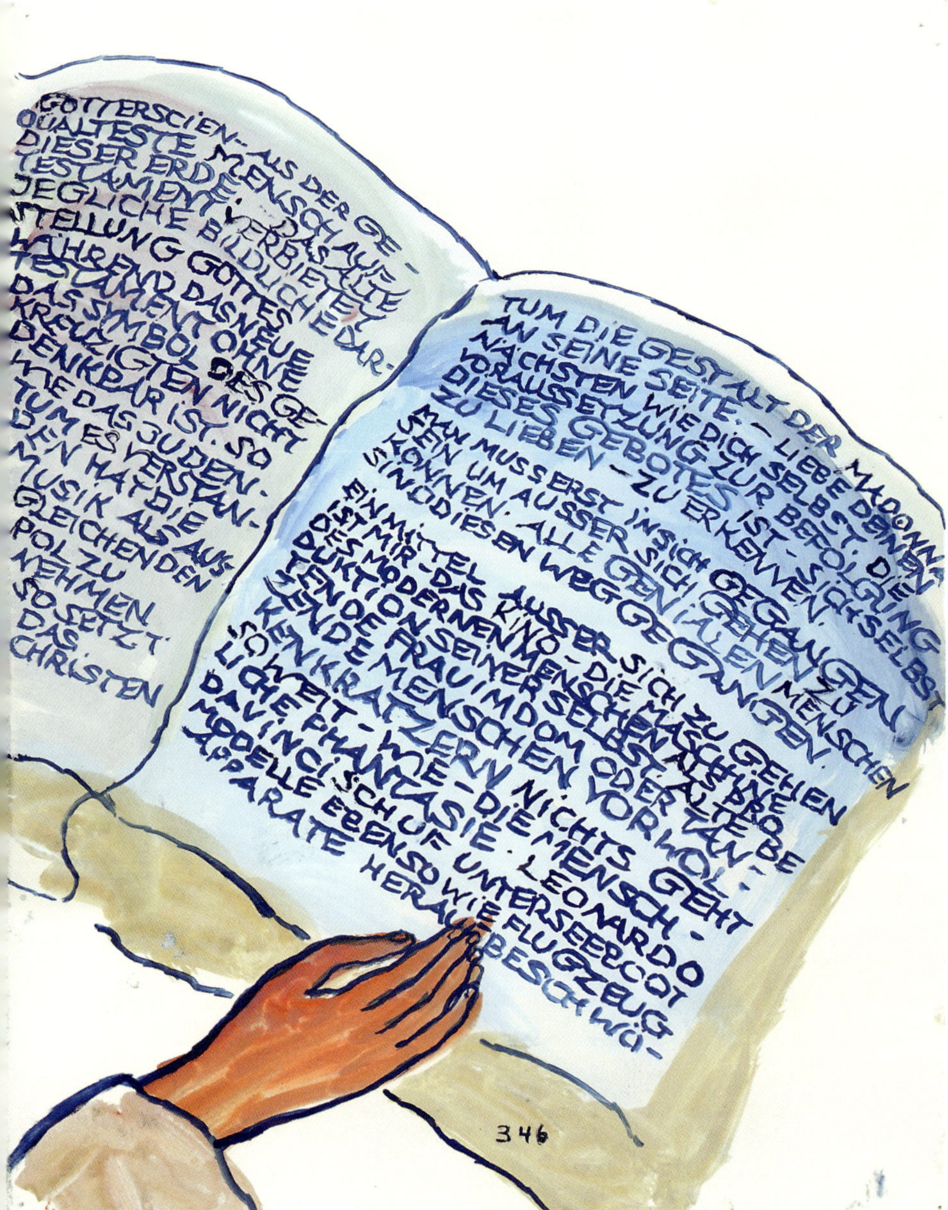
GOTTERSCIEN- AUS DER GE-
QUÄLTESTE MENSCH AUF
DIESER ERDE. DAS ALTE
TESTAMENT VERBIETET
JEGLICHE BILDLICHE DAR-
STELLUNG GOTTES
WÄHREND DAS NEUE
TESTAMENT OHNE
DAS SYMBOL DES GE-
KREUZIGTEN NICHT
DENKBAR IST. SO
WIE DAS JUDEN-
TUM ES VERSTAN-
DEN HAT DIE
MUSIK ALS AUS
GLEICHENDEN
POL ZU
NEHMEN.
SO SETZT
DAS
CHRISTEN
TUM DIE GESTALT DER MADONNA
AN SEINE SEITE. - LIEBE DEINEN
NÄCHSTEN WIE DICH SELBST. DIE
VORAUSSETZUNG ZUR BEFOLGUNG
DIESES GEBOTES IST - SICH SELBST
ZU LIEBEN - ZU ERKENNEN.
MAN MUSS ERST IN SICH GEGANGEN
SEIN UM AUSSER SICH GEHEN ZU
KÖNNEN. ALLE GENIALEN MENSCHEN
SIND DIESEN WEG GEGANGEN.
EIN MITTEL AUSSER SICH ZU GEHEN
IST MIR - DAS KINO - DIE MASCHINE
DES MODERNEN MENSCHEN. ALS PRO-
DUKTION SEINER SELBST ALTE BE-
STEHENDE FRAUIMDOM ODER TAN-
ZENDE MENSCHEN VOR WOL-
KENKRATZERN NICHTS GEHT
SO WEIT - WIE - DIE MENSCH-
LICHE PHANTASIE. LEONARDO
DA VINCI SCHUF UNTERSEEBOOT
MODELLE EBENSO WIE FLUGZEUG
APPARATE HERAUFBESCHWÖ-
346

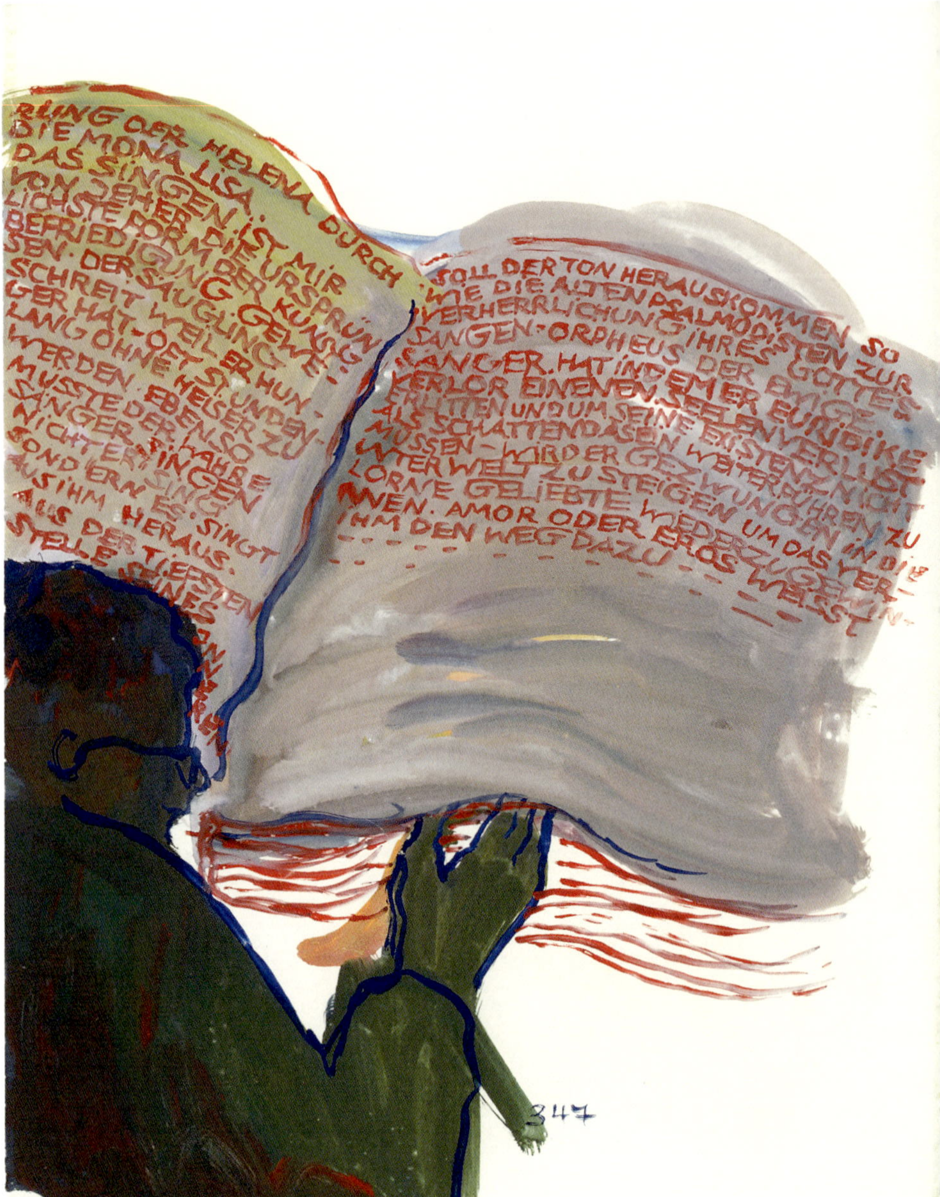
RUNG ODER HELENA DURCH
DIE MONA LISA.
DAS SINGEN. IST MIR
VON JEHER DIE URSPRÜN
LICHSTE FORM DER KUNST
BEFRIEDIGUNG GEWE-
SEN. DER SÄUGLING
SCHREIT WEIL ER HUN-
GER HAT-OFT ST. UNDEN
LANG OHNE HEISER ZU
WERDEN. EBENSO
MUSSTE DER WAHRE
SÄNGER SINGEN
NICHT ER SINGT
SONDERN ES SINGT
AUS IHM HERAUS.
AUS DER TIEFSTEN
STELLE SEINES
INNEREN.
SOLL DER TON HERAUSKOMMEN SO
WIE DIE ALTEN PSALMODISTEN ZUR
VERHERRLICHUNG IHRES GOTTES
SANGEN - ORPHEUS DER EWIGE
SÄNGER. HAT INDEM ER EURIDIKE
VERLOR EINEN SEELENVERLUST
ERLITTEN UND UM SEINE EXISTENZ NICHT
ALS SCHATTENDASEIN WEITERFÜHREN ZU
MÜSSEN - WIRD ER GEZWUNGEN IN DIE
UNTERWELT ZU STEIGEN UM DAS VER-
LORNE GELIEBTE WIEDERZUGEWIN-
NEN. AMOR ODER EROS WEISST
IHM DEN WEG DAZU
347

"...ing up Helen by means of the Mona Lisa.

For me, singing has always been the most primordial form of artistic satisfaction. The infant cries because it is hungry – sometimes for hours without becoming hoarse. The true singer should sing in the same way. It is not he who sings but it sings out of him. The sound should emerge from the deepest place within him, the way the old psalmists sang to the glory of their God.

Orpheus, the timeless singer, in losing Eurydice suffered a spiritual loss, and in order not to have to continue his existence as a shadow creature he is forced to descend into the underworld to regain the lost beloved. Cupid or Eros shows him the way."

(opposite)

“Art can only be created by touching. ‘It was as if the sky had silently kissed the earth,’ this poem was found by the composer, and the melody was created. The singer, touched by word and melody, now contributes the third element, his instrument, the voice. And this human voice, it seems to me, reverberates from even greater depths than the voice of the poet, who needs words, or of the painter, who cannot do without brush and paints. Pure and solitary coming from the depths of the body, the voice of the perfect singer reaches our ear. A throat of gold – becomes the expression of the soul.

If the contemporary sculptor cannot work without the phonograph sounding in his ears ‘for inspiration of his soul,’ – this to me is proof that most artists of our time have lost the primordial sense of experience.”

(page 454)

“They hasten from one gratification to the next, without realising that all their urge to create turns them into apes and parrots.

Our entire culture is sick because it tries to regain its health from the past, and wherever we look we see either exaggerated sensuality, repulsive excesses of its lusts, or dusty bookworms only capable of criticising. All this, combined with the tragic turn that politics seem to be taking exemplifies the human race. And we should ask ourselves whether, as a result, we are not doomed to extinction, in order that mankind – having abandoned its optimistic, pampered view of the world – be reminded again of truly great, tragic world events.

One would think that the sufferings of the war – for which I take the image of Christ as a symbol – were sufficient a factor to put mankind back on its path, that the cross which everyone had to bear in the war years were heavy enough to enable people to take to heart the implication of my words – love thy neighbour as thyself.”

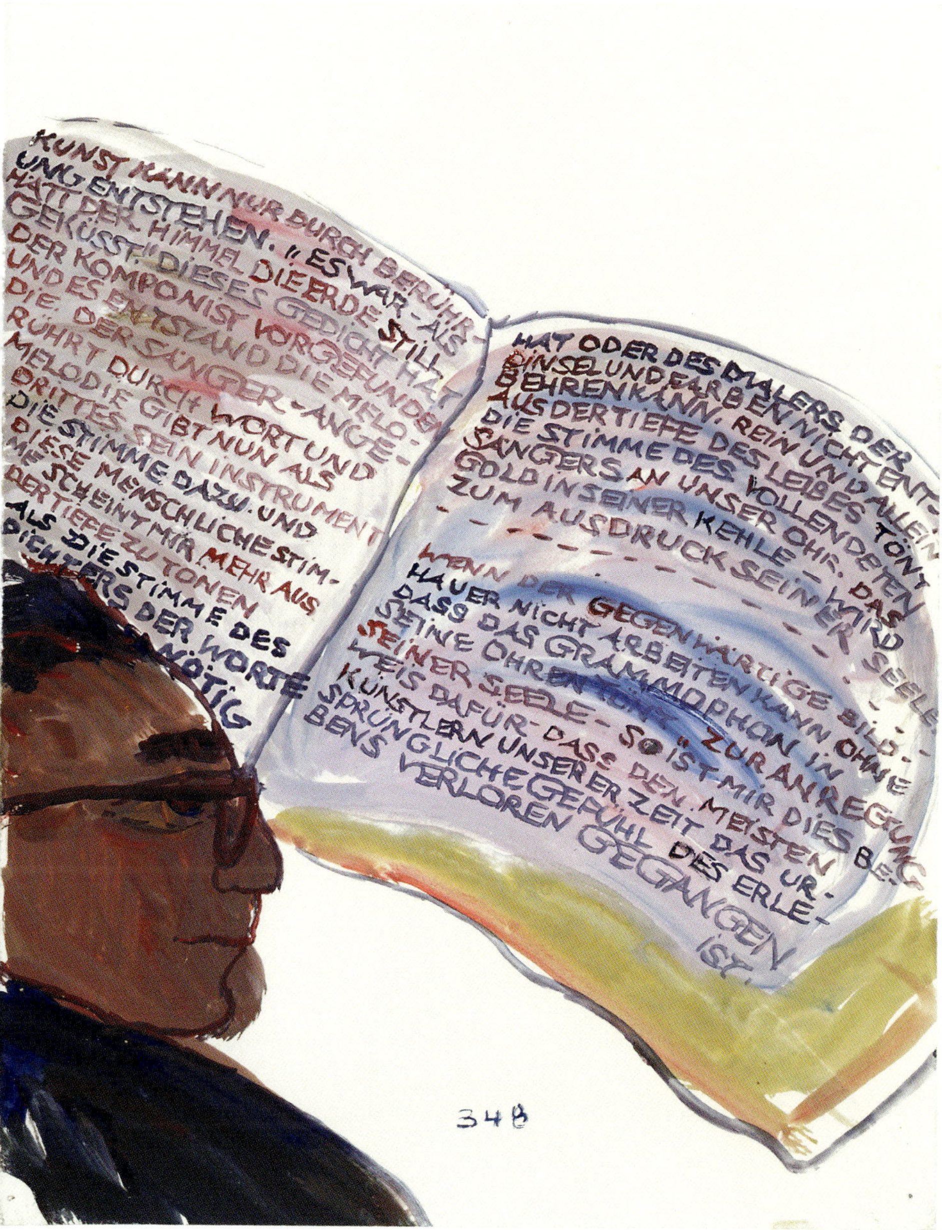
KUNST KANN NUR DURCH BERÜHR-
UNG ENTSTEHEN. "ES WAR - ALS
HÄTT DER HIMMEL DIE ERDE STILL
GEKÜSST." DIESES GEDICHT HAT
DER KOMPONIST VORGEFUNDEN
UND ES ENTSTAND DIE MELO-
DIE. DER SÄNGER - ANGE-
RÜHRT DURCH WORT UND
MELODIE GIBT NUN ALS
DRITTES SEIN INSTRUMENT
DIE STIMME DAZU. UND
DIESE MENSCHLICHE STIM-
ME SCHEINT MIR MEHR AUS
DER TIEFE ZU TONEN
ALS DIE STIMME DES
DICHTERS DER WORTE
NÖTIG
HAT ODER DES MALERS DER
PINSEL UND FARBEN NICHT ENT-
BEHREN KANN. REIN UND ALLEIN
AUS DER TIEFE DES LEIBES TÖNT
DIE STIMME DES VOLLENDETEN
SÄNGERS AN UNSER OHR. DAS
GOLD IN SEINER KEHLE - WIRD
ZUM AUSDRUCK SEINER SEELE.
WENN DER GEGENWÄRTIGE BILD-
HAUER NICHT ARBEITEN KANN OHNE
DASS DAS GRAMMOPHON IN
SEINE OHREN TÖNT "ZUR ANREGUNG
SEINER SEELE" - SO IST MIR DIES BE-
WEIS DAFÜR - DASS DEN MEISTEN
KÜNSTLERN UNSERER ZEIT DAS UR-
SPRÜNGLICHE GEFÜHL DES ERLE-
BENS VERLOREN GEGANGEN
IST.
348

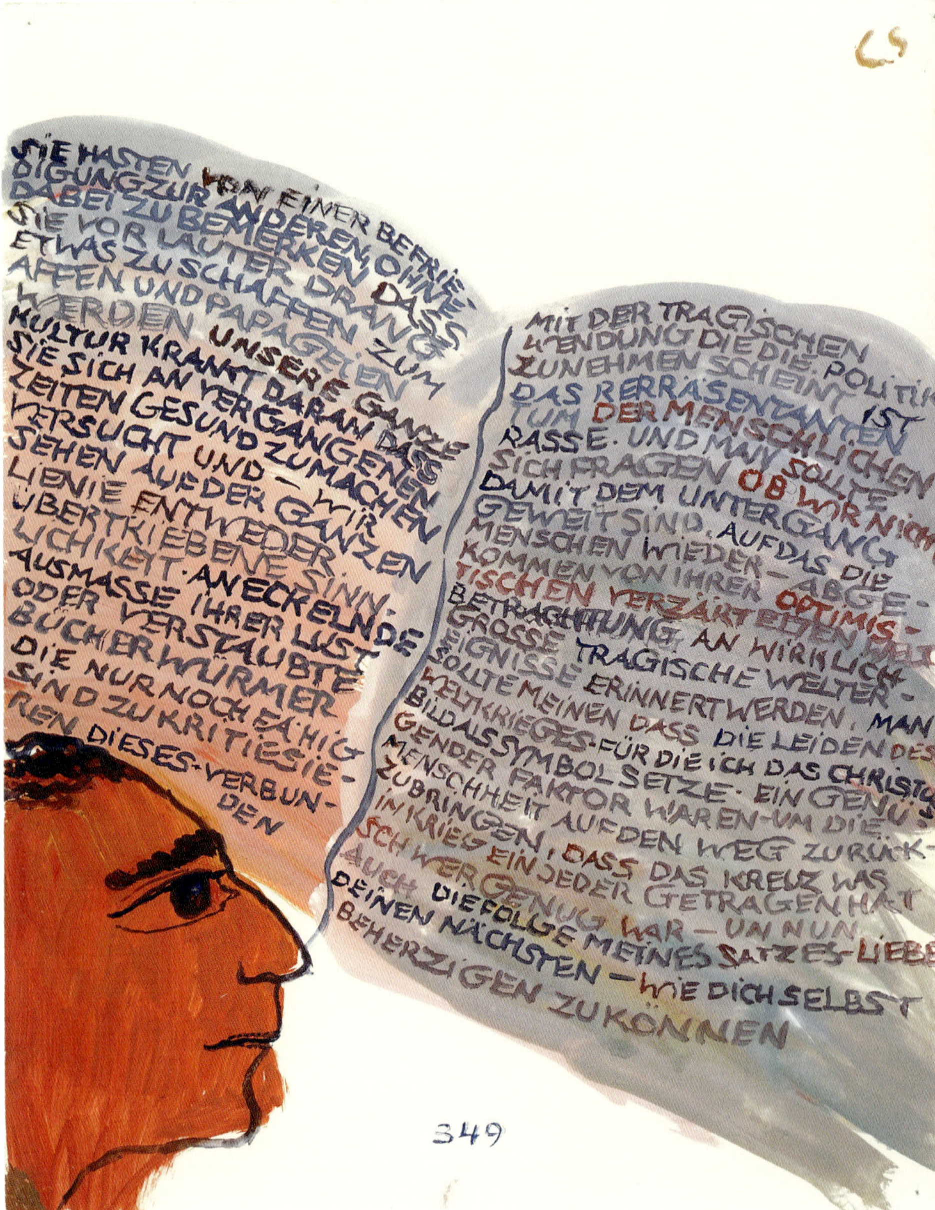
SIE HASTEN VON EINER BEFRIE-
DIGUNG ZUR ANDEREN, OHNE
DABEI ZU BEMERKEN DASS
SIE VOR LAUTER DRANG
ETWAS ZU SCHAFFEN ZUM
AFFEN UND PAPAGEIEN
WERDEN UNSERE GANZE
KULTUR KRANKT DARAN DASS
SIE SICH AN VERGANGENEN
ZEITEN GESUND ZU MACHEN
VERSUCHT UND - WIR
SEHEN AUF DER GANZEN
LIENIE ENTWEDER
ÜBERTRIEBENE SINN-
LICHKEIT. ANECKELNDE
AUSMASSE IHRER LUST
ODER VERSTAUBTE
BÜCHERWÜRMER
DIE NUR NOCH FÄHIG
SIND ZU KRITIESIE-
REN DIESES VERBUN-
DEN
MIT DER TRAGISCHEN
WENDUNG DIE DIE POLITIK
ZUNEHMEN SCHEINT IST
DAS RERRÄSENTANTEN
TUM DER MENSCHLICHEN
RASSE. UND MAN SOLLTE
SICH FRAGEN OB WIR NICHT
DAMIT DEM UNTERGANG
GEWEIT SIND. AUF DAS DIE
MENSCHEN WIEDER - ABGE-
KOMMEN VON IHRER OPTIMIS-
TISCHEN VERZÄRTELTEN WELT
BETRACHTUNG. AN WIRKLICH-
GROSSE TRAGISCHE WELTER-
EIGNISSE ERINNERT WERDEN. MAN
SOLLTE MEINEN DASS DIE LEIDEN DES
WELTKRIEGES - FÜR DIE ICH DAS CHRISTUS-
BILD ALS SYMBOL SETZE - EIN GENÜ-
GENDER FAKTOR WAREN - UM DIE
MENSCHHEIT AUF DEN WEG ZURÜCK-
ZUBRINGEN. DASS DAS KREUZ WAS
IN KRIEG EIN JEDER GETRAGEN HAT
SCHWER GENUG WAR - UN NUN
AUCH DIE FOLGE MEINES SATZES - LIEBE
DEINEN NÄCHSTEN - WIE DICH SELBST
BEHERZIGEN ZU KÖNNEN
349

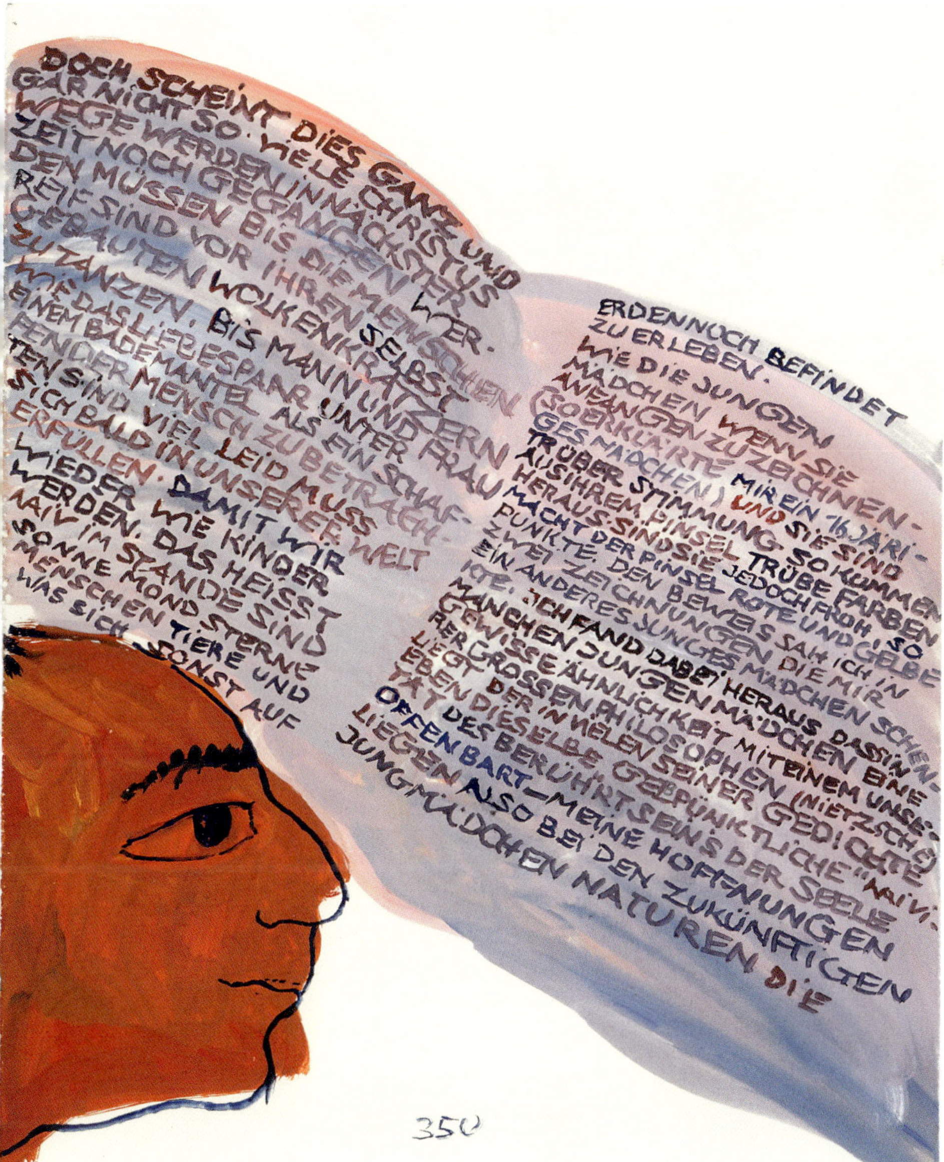
DOCH SCHEINT DIES GANZ UND
GAR NICHT SO. VIELE CHRISTUS
WEGE WERDEN IN NÄCHSTER
ZEIT NOCH GEGANGEN WER-
DEN MÜSSEN BIS DIE MENSCHEN
REIF SIND VOR IHREN SELBST
GEBAUTEN WOLKENKRATZERN
ZU TANZEN. BIS MANN UND FRAU
WIE DAS LIEBESPAAR UNTER
EINEM BADEMANTEL ALS EIN SCHAF-
FENDER MENSCH ZU BETRACH-
TEN SIND VIEL LEID MUSS
SICH BALD IN UNSERER WELT
ERFÜLLEN. DAMIT WIR
WIEDER WIE KINDER
WERDEN. DAS HEISST
NAIV IM STANDE SIND
SONNE MOND STERNE
MENSCHEN TIERE UND
WAS SICH SONST AUF
ERDEN NOCH BEFINDET
ZU ERLEBEN.
WIE DIE JUNGEN
MÄDCHEN WENN SIE
ANFANGEN ZU ZEICHNEN -
(SO ERKLÄRTE MIR EIN 16 JÄHRI-
GES MÄDCHEN) UND SIE SIND
TRÜBER STIMMUNG SO KOMMEN
AUS IHREM PINSEL TRÜBE FARBEN
HERAUS. SIND SIE JEDOCH FROH, SO
MACHT DER PINSEL ROTE UND GELBE
PUNKTE. DEN BEWEIS SAH ICH IN
ZWEI ZEICHNUNGEN DIE MIR
EIN ANDERES JUNGES MÄDCHEN SCHEN-
KTE. ICH FAND DABEI HERAUS DASS IN
MANCHEN JUNGEN MÄDCHEN EINE
GEWISSE ÄHNLICHKEIT MIT EINEM UNSE-
RER GROSSEN PHILOSOPHEN (NIETZSCHE)
LIEGT. DER IN VIELEN SEINER GEDICHTE
EBEN DIESELBE GEPÜNKTLICHE "NAIVI-
TÄT DES BERÜHRTSEINS DER SEELE
OFFENBART – MEINE HOFFNUNGEN
LIEGEN ALSO BEI DEN ZUKÜNFTIGEN
JUNGMÄDCHEN NATUREN DIE
350

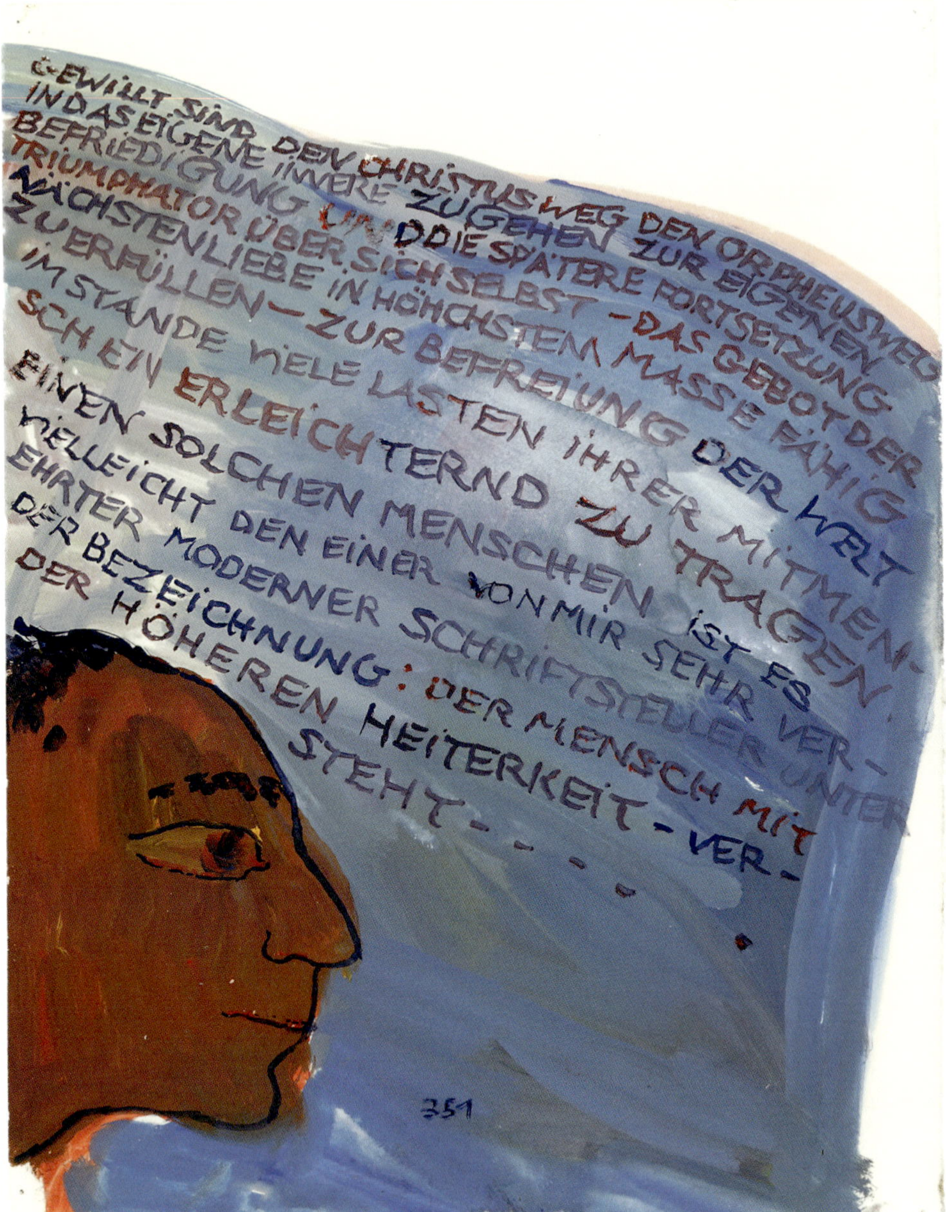
GEWILLT SIND DEN CHRISTUSWEG DEN ORPHEUSWEG
IN DAS EIGENE INNERE ZU GEHEN ZUR EIGENEN
BEFRIEDIGUNG UND DIE SPÄTERE FORTSETZUNG
TRIUMPHATOR ÜBER SICH SELBST – DAS GEBOT DER
NÄCHSTENLIEBE IN HÖCHSTEM MASSE FÄHIG
ZU ERFÜLLEN – ZUR BEFREIUNG DER WELT
IM STANDE VIELE LASTEN IHRER MITMEN-
SCHEN ERLEICHTERND ZU TRAGEN.
EINEN SOLCHEN MENSCHEN IST ES
VIELLEICHT DEN EINER VON MIR SEHR VER-
EHRTER MODERNER SCHRIFTSTELLER UNTER
DER BEZEICHNUNG: DER MENSCH MIT
DER HÖHEREN HEITERKEIT – VER-
STEHT – – – .
351

(page 455)

"Yet it absolutely doesn't seem that way. Many will have to follow in the footsteps of Christ in the time to come, until men are mature to dance in front of the skyscrapers they have built themselves. Until man and woman, like the couple under a bathrobe, may be regarded as one creative person. Much suffering must soon come to fulfil in our world that we may once again be as children. Which means naively be able to experience sun, moon, stars, men, beasts, and whatever else is to be found on earth.

Like young girls when they begin to draw (as the 16-year-old girl explained to me), if they are in a dull mood dark colours flow from their brush. But if they are happy, the brush makes red and yellow dots. I saw the proof in two pictures given to me by another young girl. There, I found out that in many young girls there is a certain resemblance to one of our great philosophers, Nietzsche, who in several of his poems reveals this same 'yellow-dotted' naivety of the soul that is touched. My hopes, therefore, lie with the future souls of young girls..."

(opposite)

"... who are willing to tread the path of Christ, the Orpheus path, into their own inner self for their own satisfaction as well as for the next stage: conquerors of themselves and able in the utmost degree to fulfil the commandment of loving thy neighbour; able to liberate the world by assuming many of their fellowman's burdens.

That is the kind of person, perhaps, who one of my greatly admired contemporary writers understands under the designation – the man with higher serenity."

(bottom)

CHARLOTTE
"It's two weeks now since I last spoke to him. Was I nothing but the object of his experiments?"

(opposite)

"But tonight I must speak to him, even if I have to stay all night on the street."

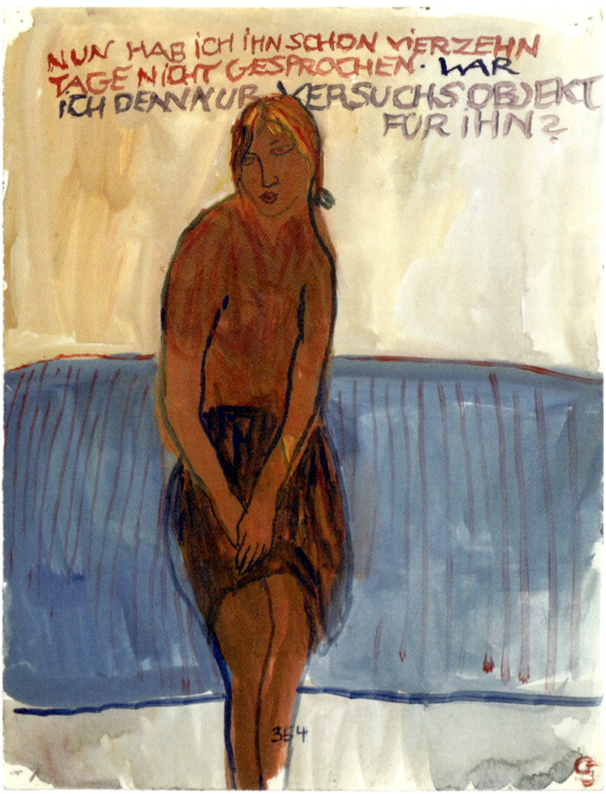

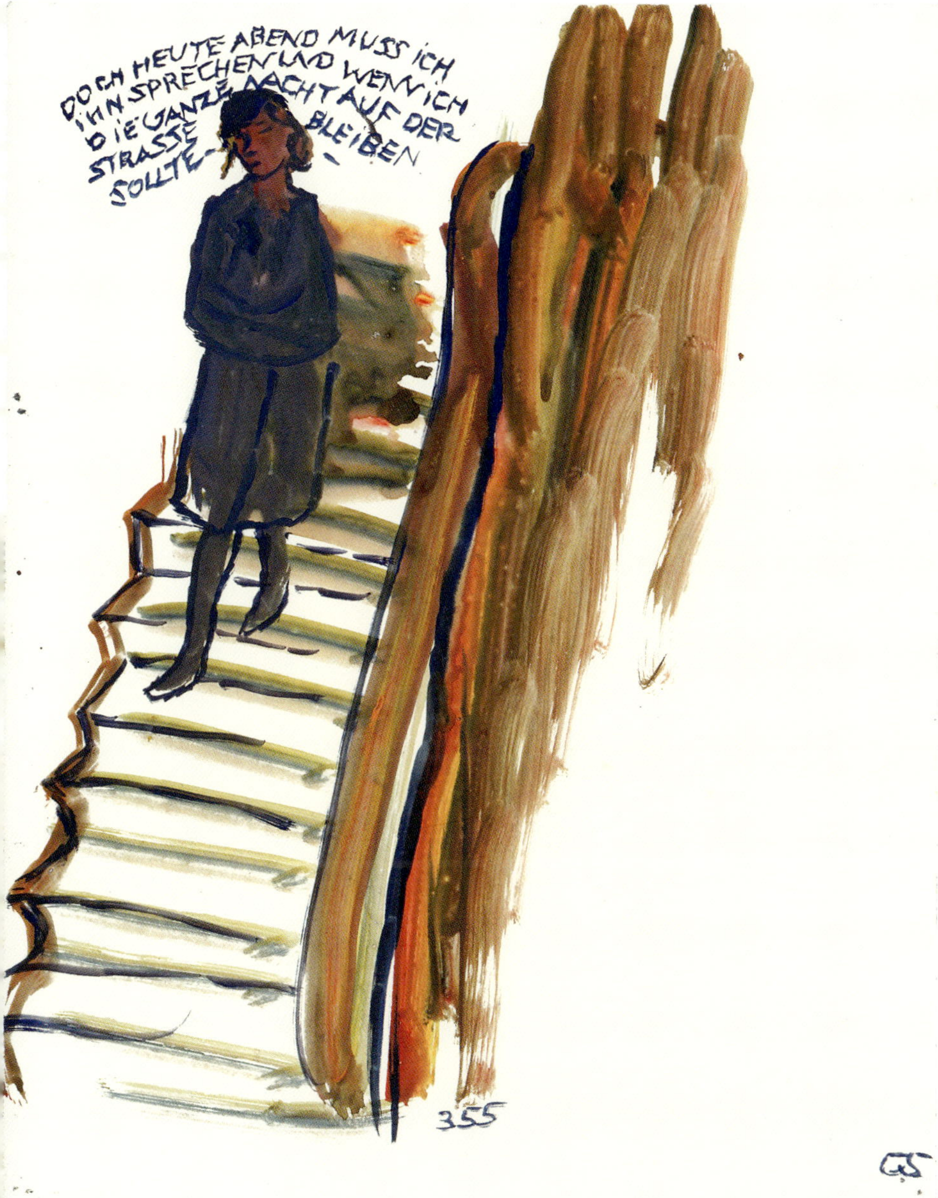
DOCH HEUTE ABEND MUSS ICH
IHN SPRECHEN UND WENN ICH
DIE GANZE NACHT AUF DER
STRASSE BLEIBEN
SOLLTE – –
355

(bottom)

“There goes my loved ones,
and no one cares about me.”

(opposite)

“Well, anyway, all three seem to be having
a good time. It’s already past one-thirty.”

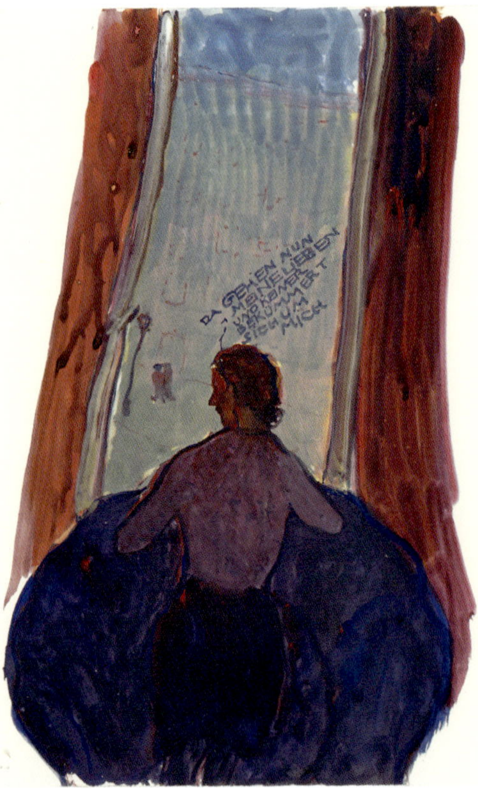

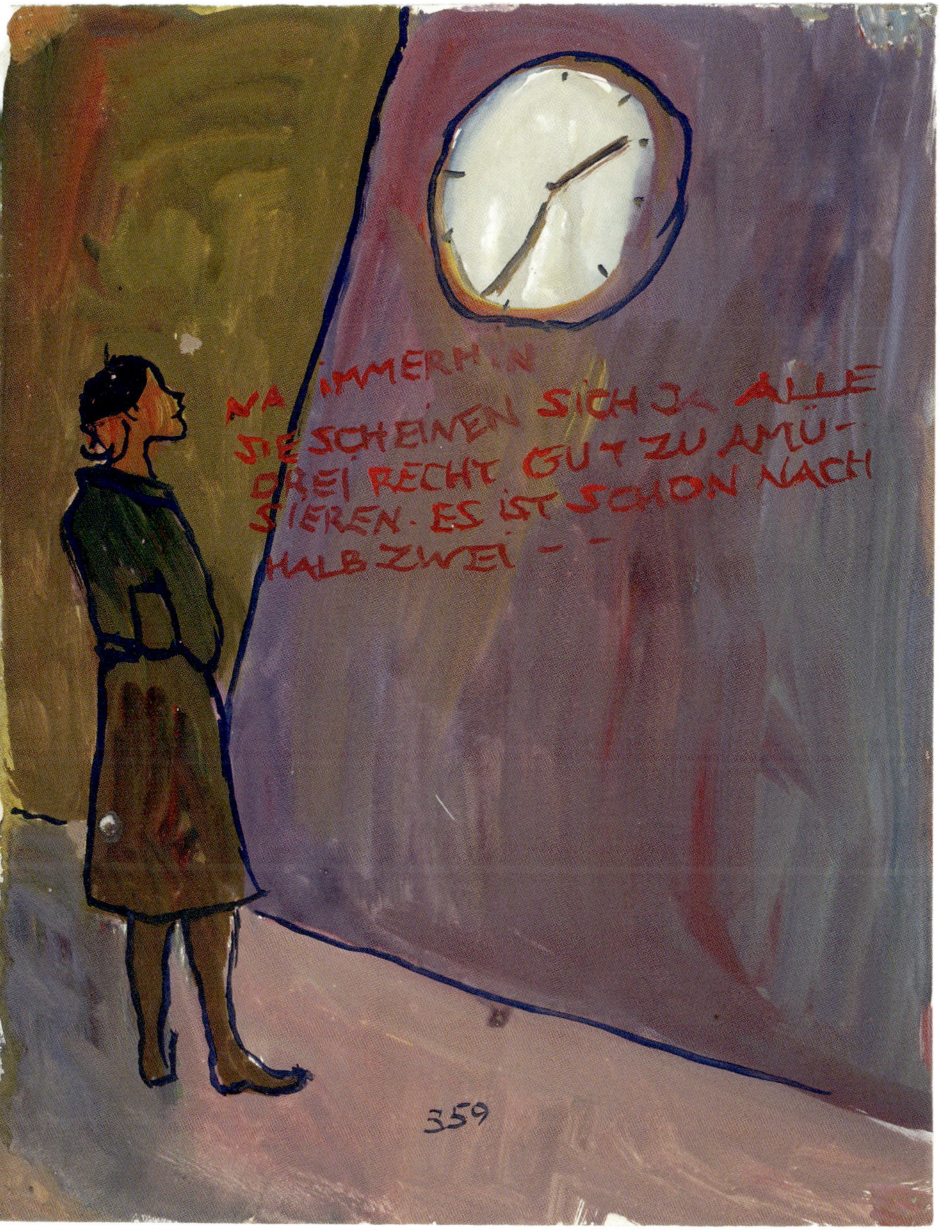
NA IMMERHIN
SIE SCHEINEN SICH JA ALLE
DREI RECHT GUT ZU AMÜ-
SIEREN. ES IST SCHON NACH
HALB ZWEI - -
359

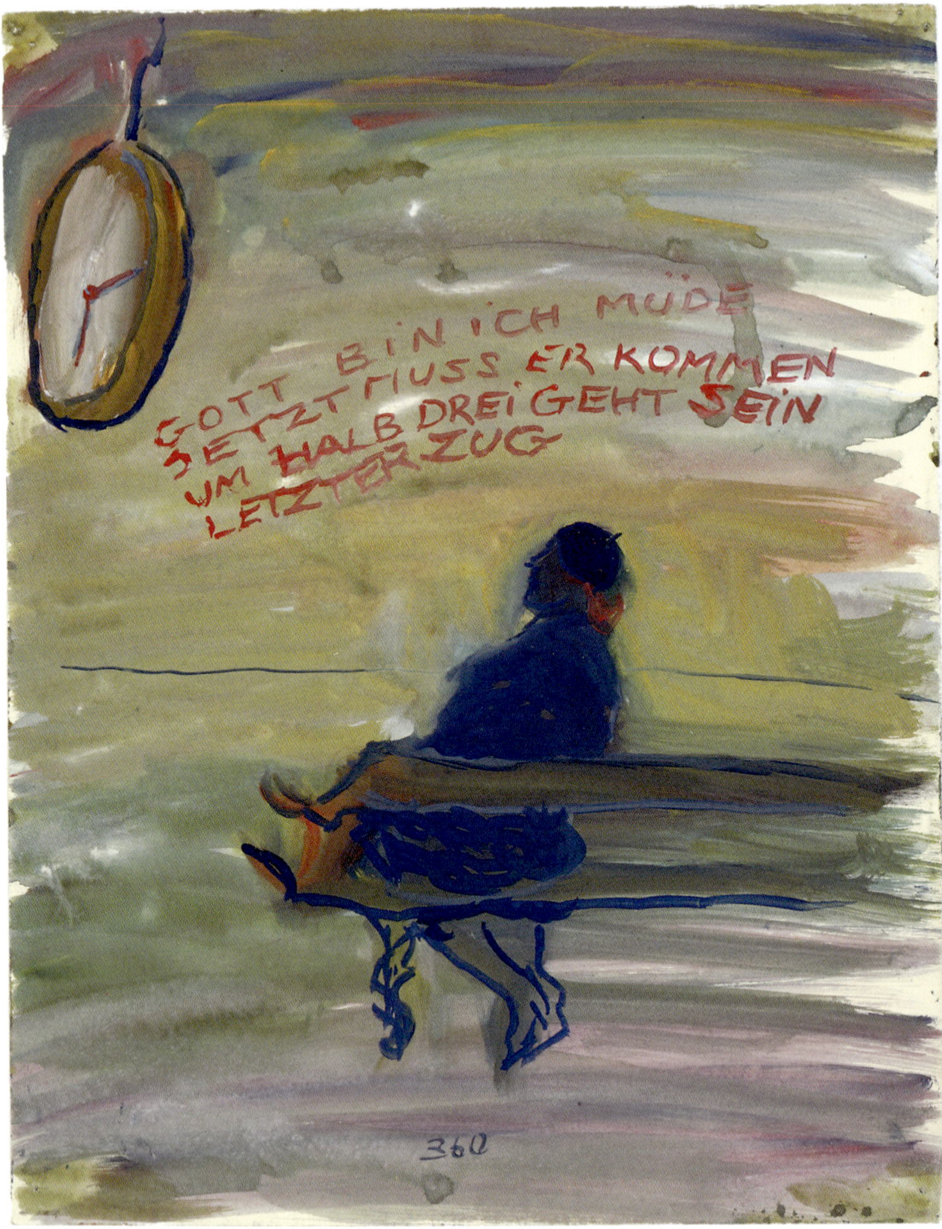
GOTT BIN ICH MÜDE
JETZT MUSS ER KOMMEN
UM HALB DREI GEHT SEIN
LETZTER ZUG
360

(opposite)

“God, am I tired! He must come now,
his last train leaves at two-thirty.”

(bottom)

DABERLOHN
“What are you doing here now,
young lady?”

CHARLOTTE
“I’m waiting for you.”

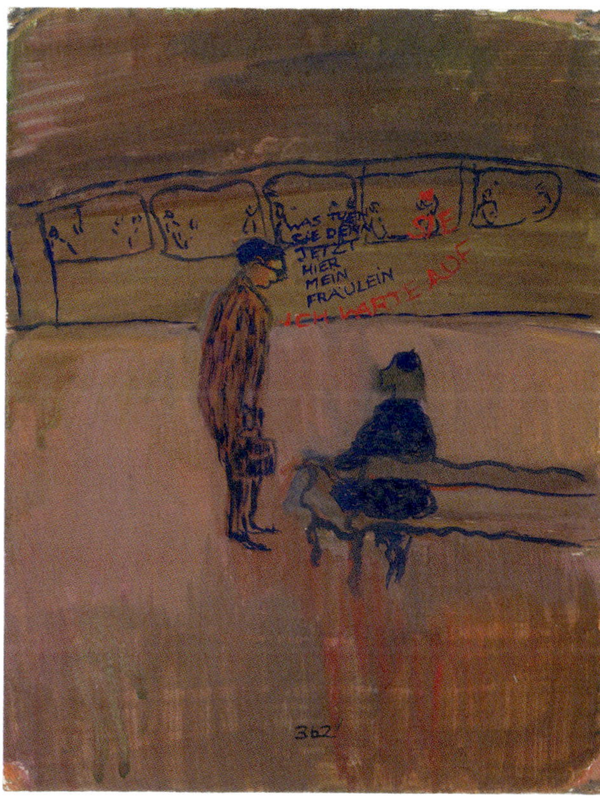

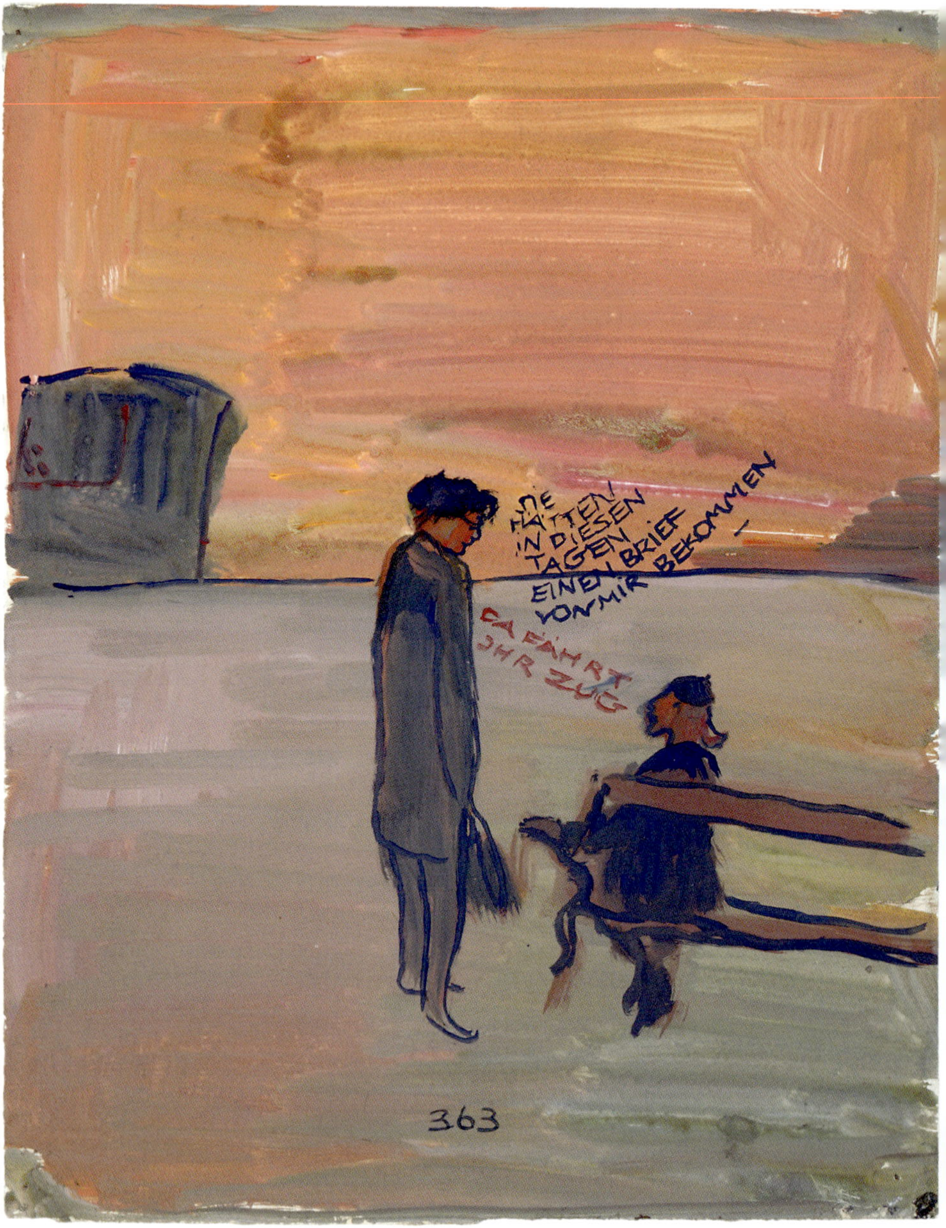
SIE HÄTTEN IN DIESEN TAGEN EINEN BRIEF VON MIR BEKOMMEN
DA FÄHRT IHR ZUG
363

(opposite)

DABERLOHN
"You would have received a letter
from me in the next few days."

CHARLOTTE
"There goes your train."

(bottom)

DABERLOHN
"Come, let's let it go,
let's let it go."

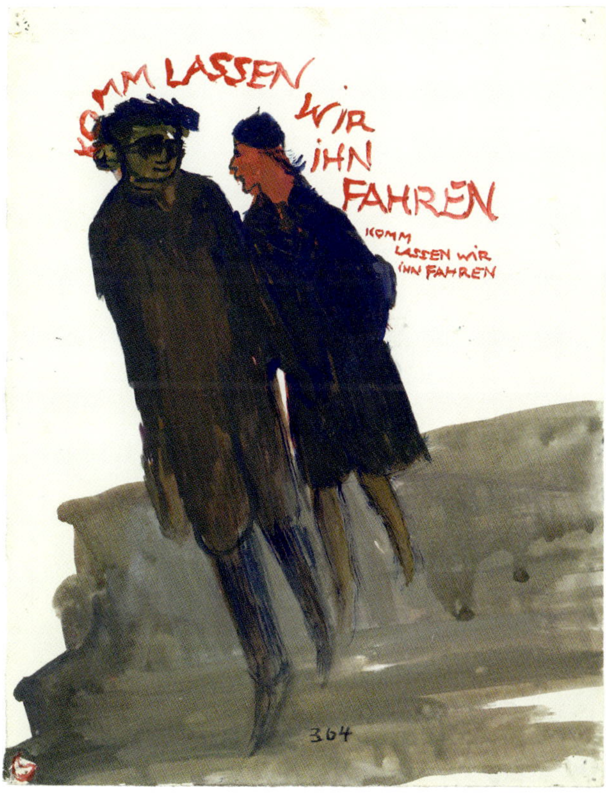

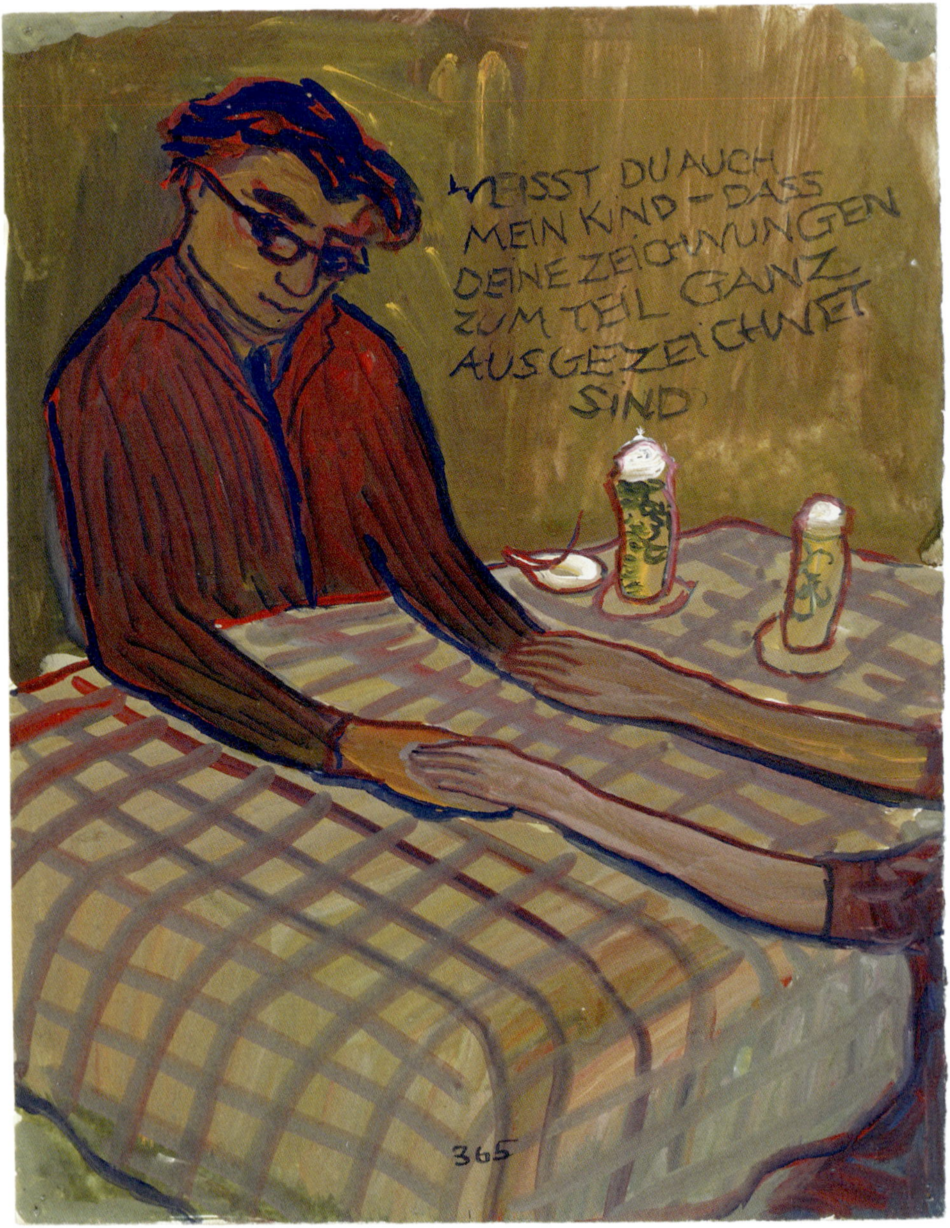
WEISST DU AUCH
MEIN KIND - DASS
DEINE ZEICHNUNGEN
ZUM TEIL GANZ
AUSGEZEICHNET
SIND
365

(opposite)

"Do you know, my child,
that some of your drawings
are quite excellent?"

(bottom)

"One day people will be
looking at us two."

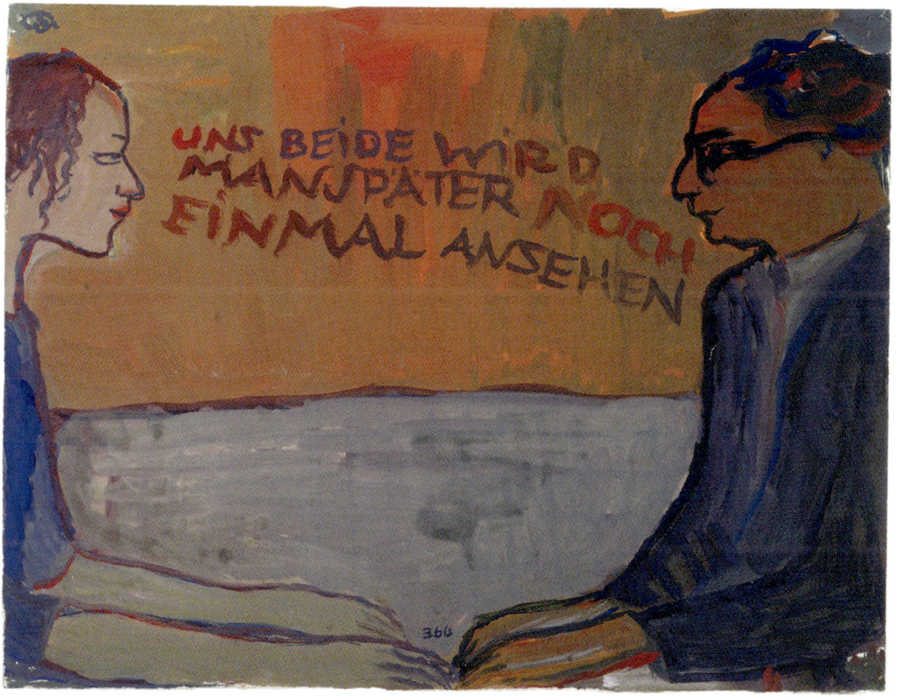

(bottom)

MR KRÜGER
"How long do you want to sit here?
I'm closing up now."

(opposite)

DABERLOHN
"It seems to me as if someone is playing
catch ball with the whole world."

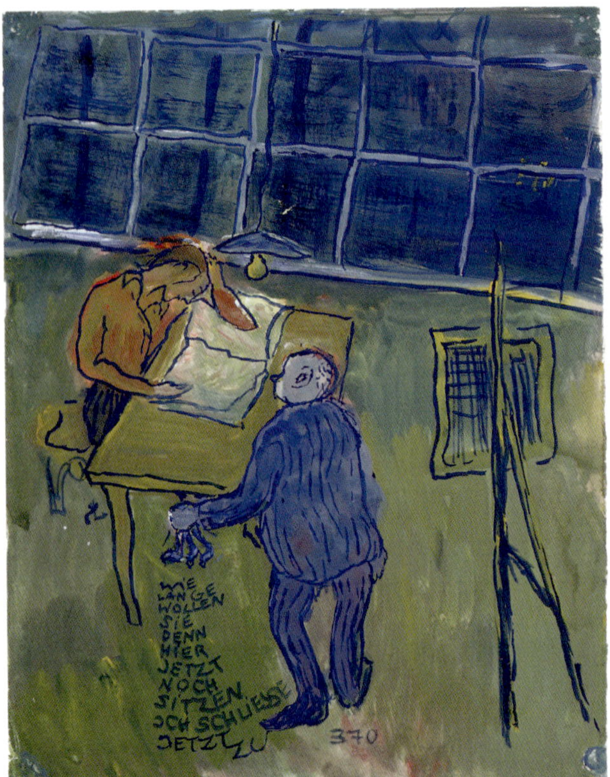

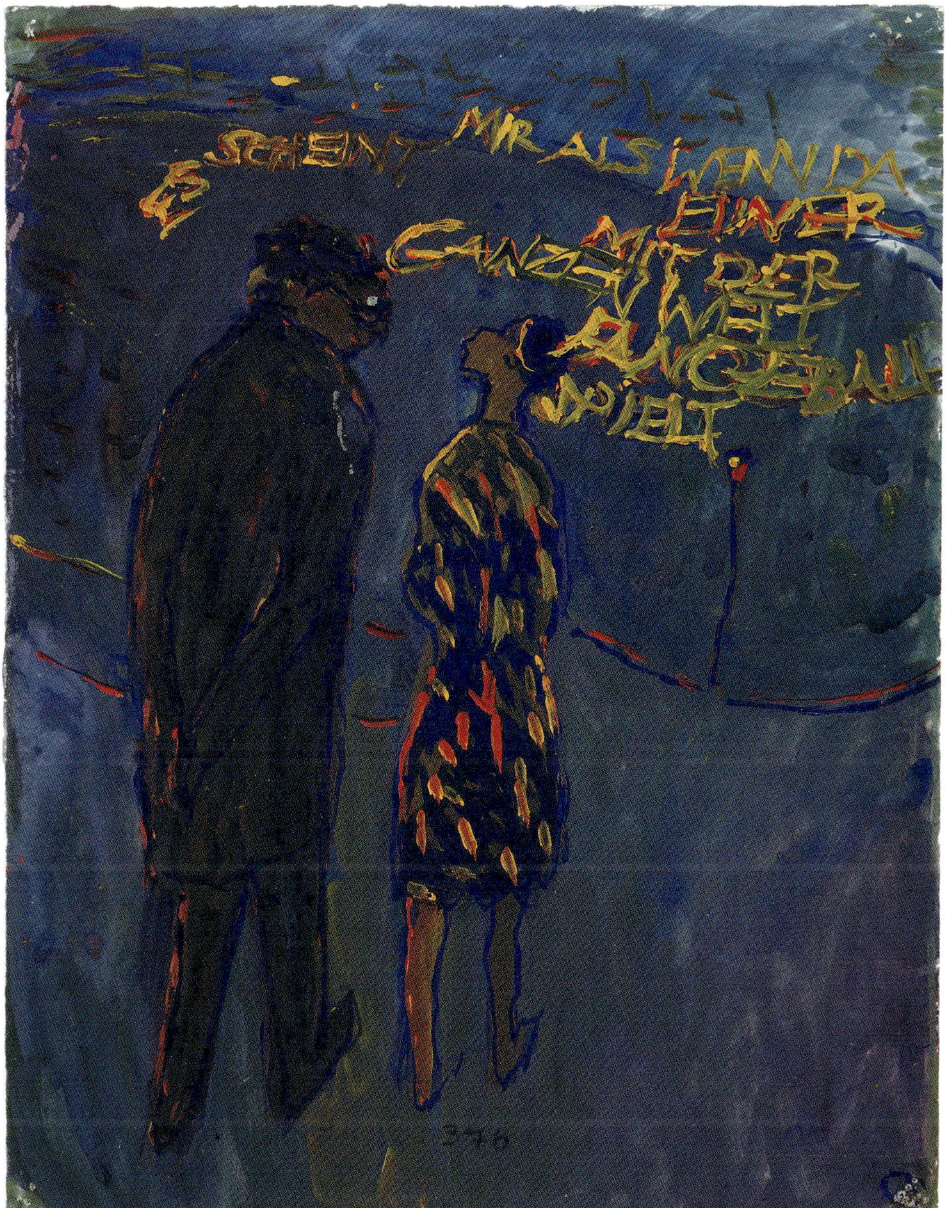
ES SCHEINT MIR ALS WENN DA
EINER
MIT DER
GANZEN WELT
FANGEBALL
SPIELT
376

DABERLOHN
"By a stroke of luck, at this same time a famous professor happens to be staying in our little town who, by virtue of his profession – namely psychoanalysis – is bound to be interested in this work. I'll show him my opus."

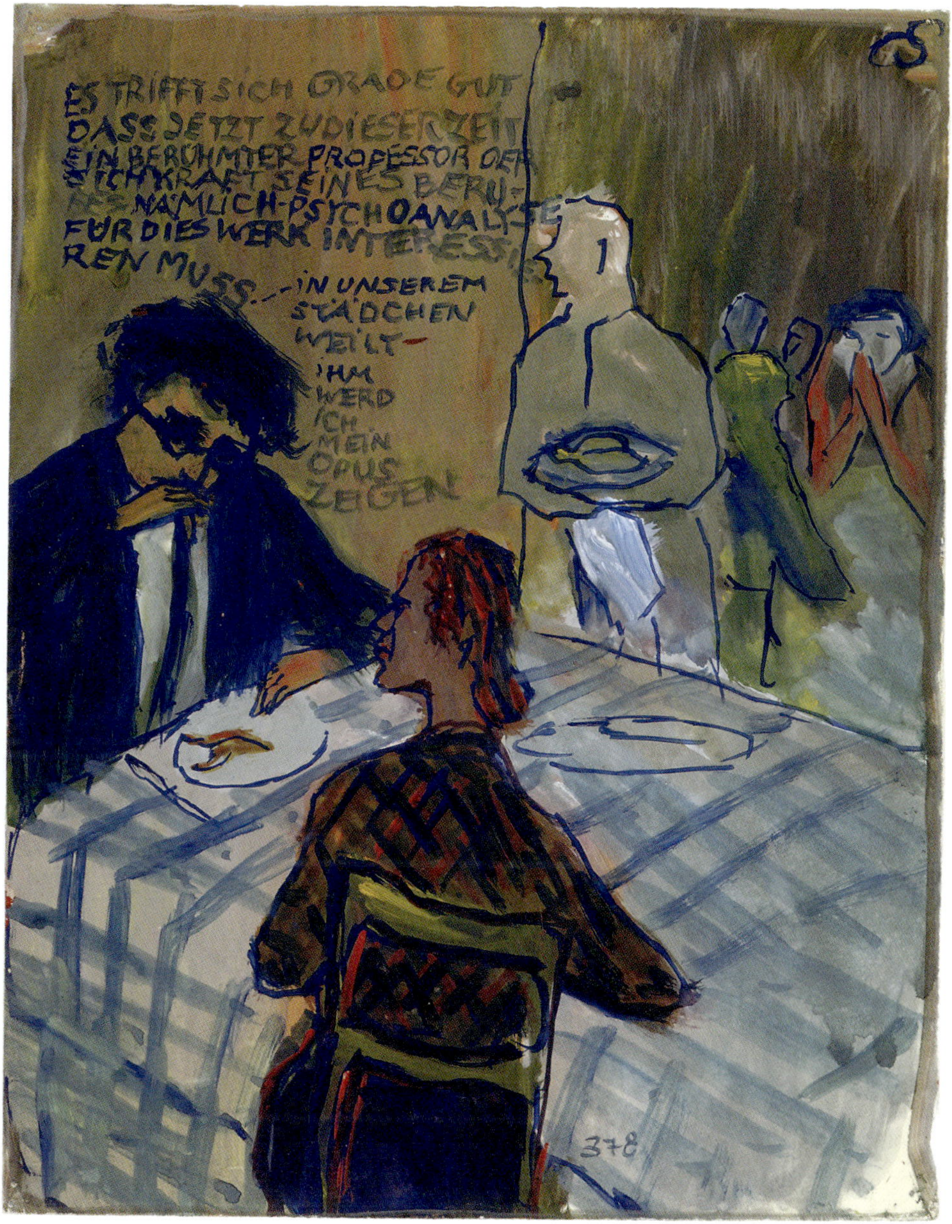
ES TRIFFT SICH GRADE GUT
DASS JETZT ZU DIESER ZEIT
EIN BERÜHMTER PROFESSOR DER
SICH KRAFT SEINES BERU-
FES NÄMLICH-PSYCHOANALYSE
FÜR DIES WERK INTERESSIE-
REN MUSS.--IN UNSEREM
STÄDCHEN
WEILT-
IHM
WERD
ICH
MEIN
OPUS
ZEIGEN
378

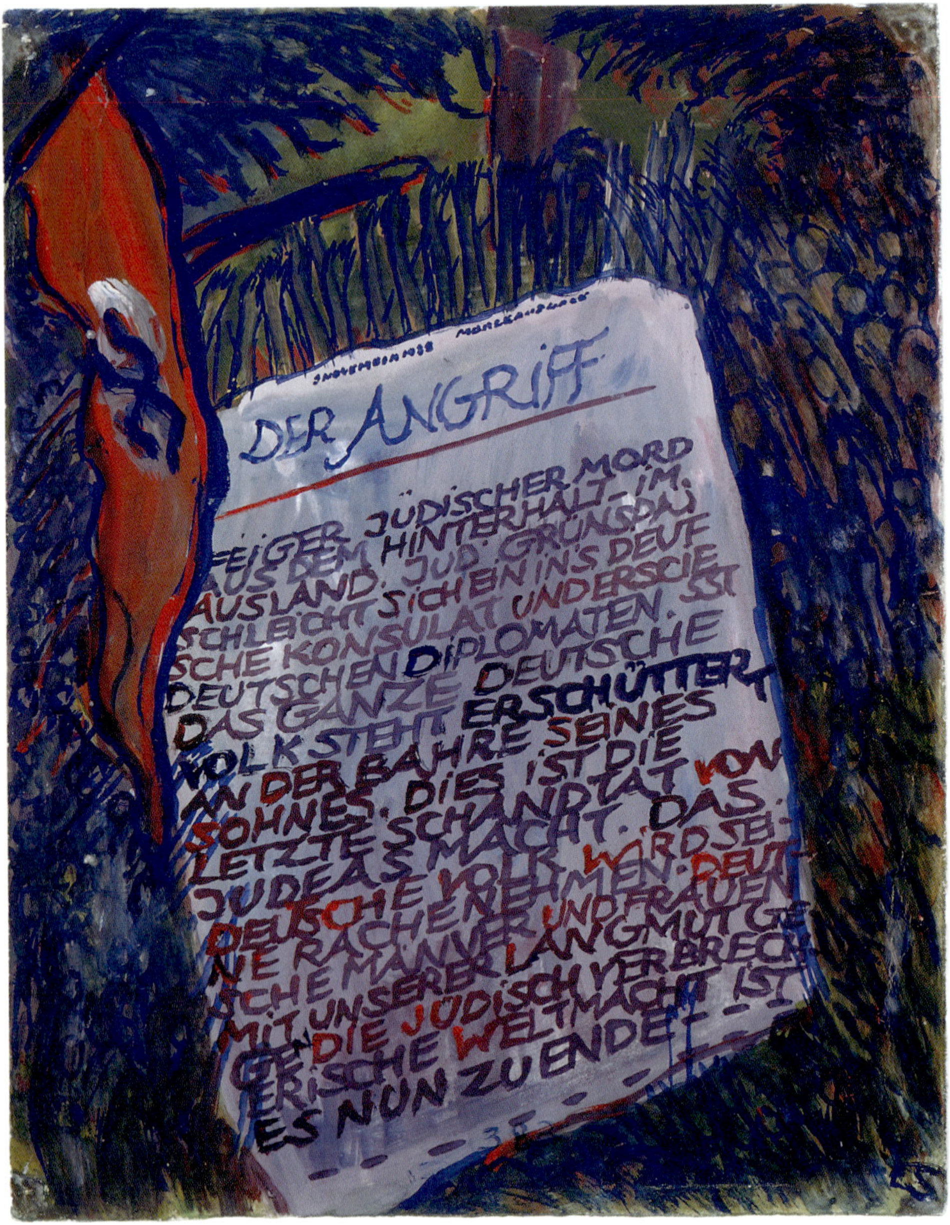
DER ANGRIFF
FEIGER JÜDISCHER MORD
AUS DEM HINTERHALT. IM
DAS GANZE DEUTSCHE
VOLK STEHT ERSCHÜTTERT
AN DER BAHRE SEINES
SOHNES. DIES IST DIE
LETZTE SCHANDTAT VON
JUDEAS MACHT. DAS
ES NUN ZU ENDE

(opposite)

NEW SECTION
CHAPTER ONE
AND TIME GOES ON

9 November 1938
The Attack.

Cowardly Jewish Murder from an ambush – abroad.
Jew Grünspan sneaks into the German Consulate and shoots German diplomat.

The entire German nation stands shocked at the bier of its son. This is the last disgraceful act of Judea's power. The German people will take their revenge. German men and women: Our forbearance against the criminal Jewish world-power has come to an end –

(bottom)

"Croak Judea!
Grab what you can!"

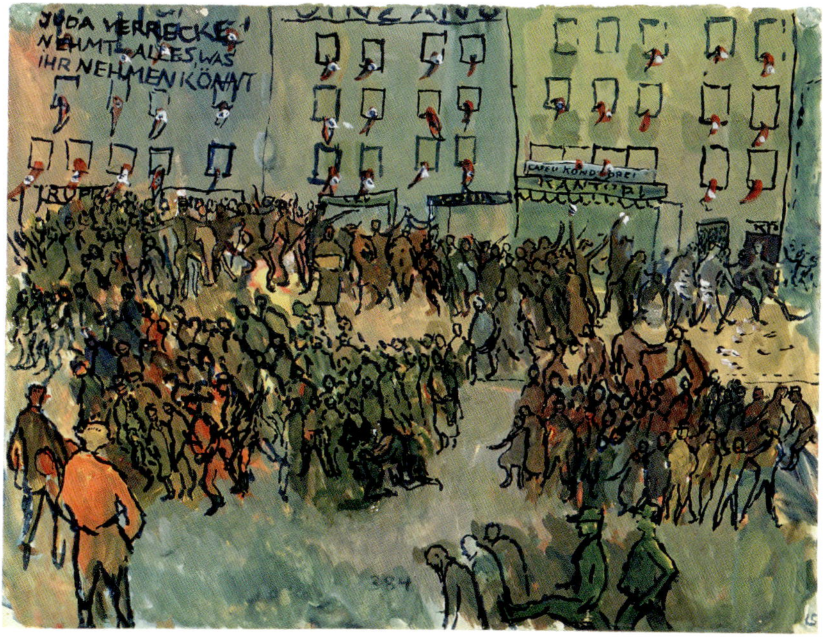

PAULINKA
"You must go to the hospital right away, my dear sniffle bunny, I'll run and get your little coat, I'll get your little hat."

MAID
"You must hide, professor. They've already picked up half the Jews in town."

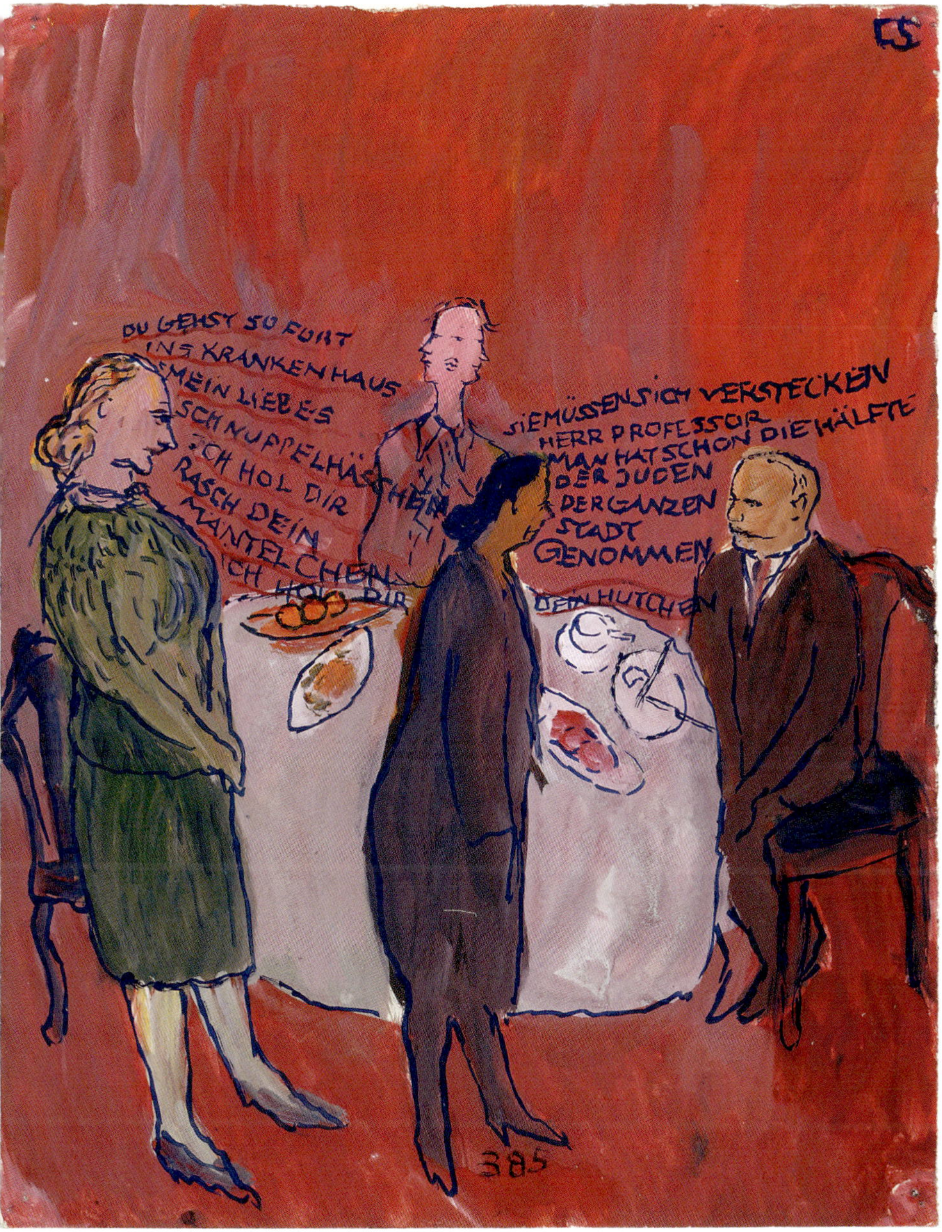
CS
DU GEHST SO FORT
INS KRANKENHAUS
MEIN LIEBES
SCHNUPPELHÄSCHEN
ICH HOL DIR
RASCH DEIN
MÄNTELCHEN
ICH HOL DIR
DEIN HUTCHEN
SIE MÜSSEN SICH VERSTECKEN
HERR PROFESSOR
MAN HAT SCHON DIE HÄLFTE
DER JUDEN
DER GANZEN
STADT
GENOMMEN
385

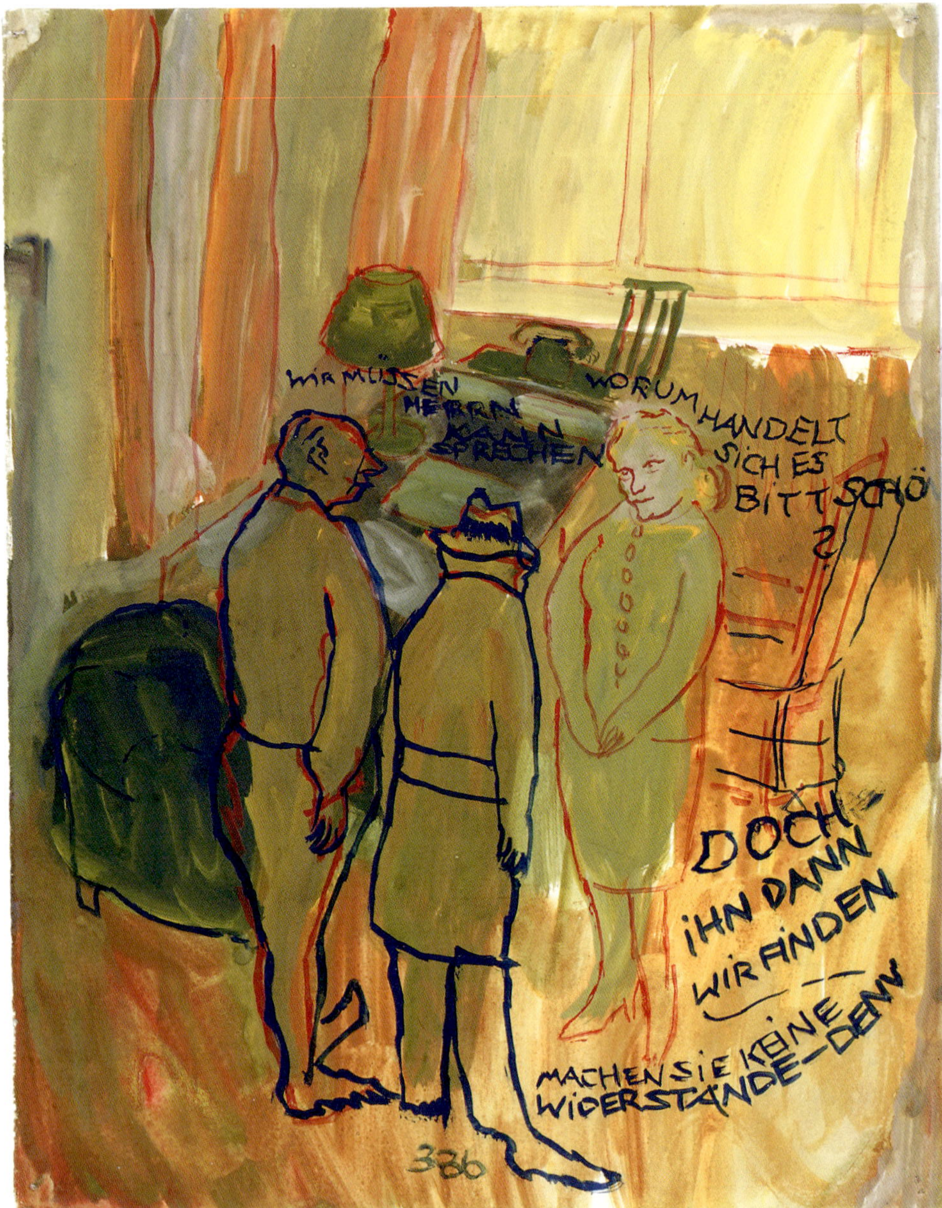
WIR MÜSSEN HERRN KAHN SPRECHEN
WORUM HANDELT SICH ES BITTSCHÖN ?
DOCH WIR FINDEN IHN DANN
MACHEN SIE KEINE WIDERSTÄNDE-DENN
336

(opposite)

POLICEMEN
"We have to speak to Mr Kann."

PAULINKA
"What is it about, please?"

POLICEMEN
"Don't be resistant –
in the end we'll find him anyway."

(bottom)

PAULINKA
"You must go to the police headquarters
and ask if you can bring your father
some warm things."

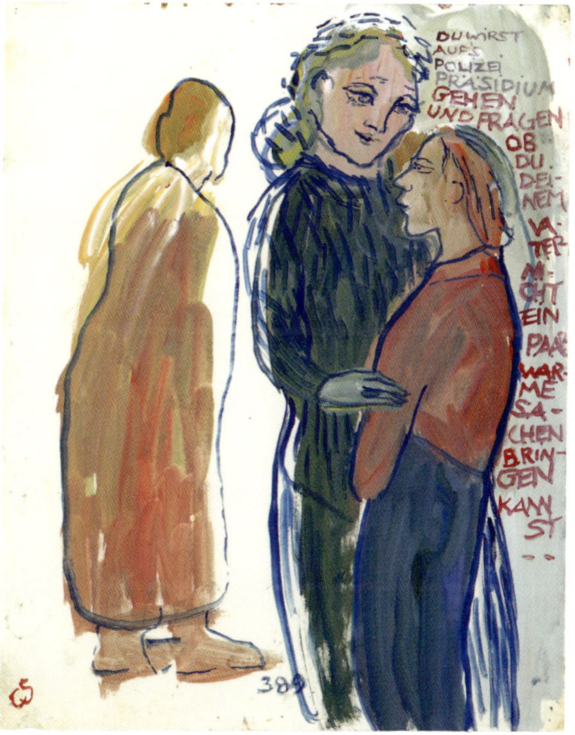

(bottom)

As for Paulinka, she'll tackle the situation more generously.

PAULINKA
"Meanwhile I'll pull every possible string to have him released."

(opposite)

PAULINKA
"There must be a way to get him released. I need a visa, I'll get it. Why do I have my charm if I can't win over any kind of person."

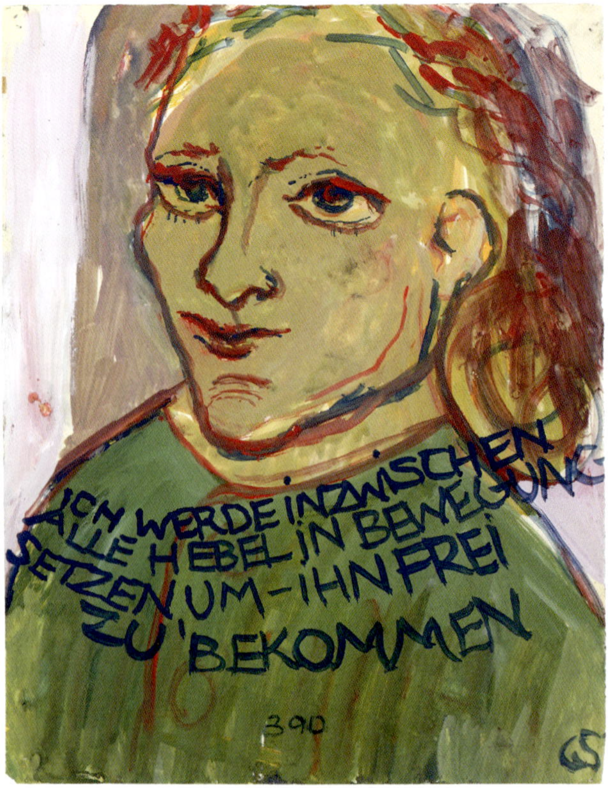

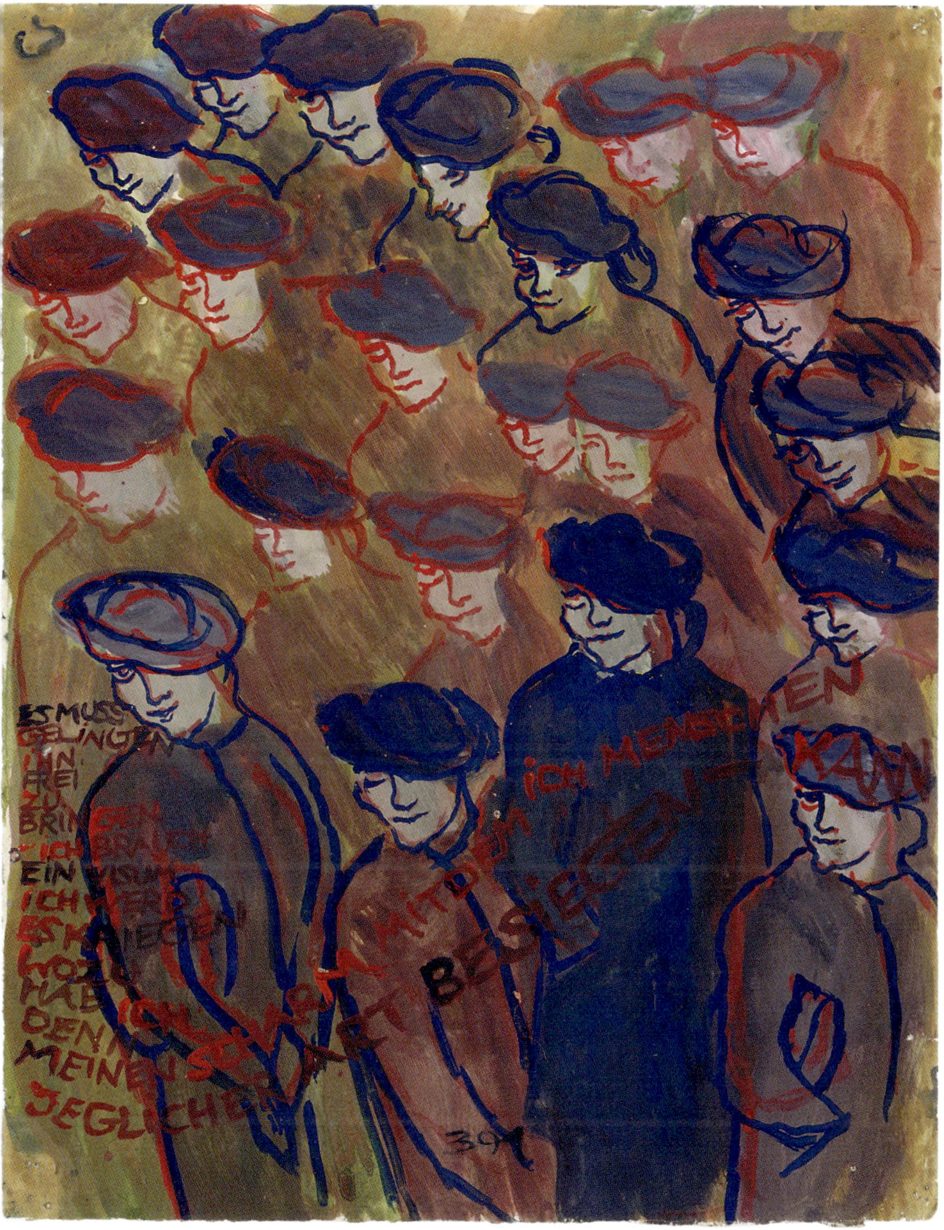
ES MUSS
GELINGEN
IHN
FREI
ZU
BRINGEN
EIN
MEINEN
JEGLICHEN
ICH MENSCHEN
KANN
394

Paulinka has suddenly remembered Charlotte's degenerate family on her mother's side, and a sense of dread – Charlotte might perhaps do something to herself – makes her go out onto the street and run after her because she had seen her from the window.

PAULINKA
"You stupid girl, why are you running away now? Your father is in the camp..."

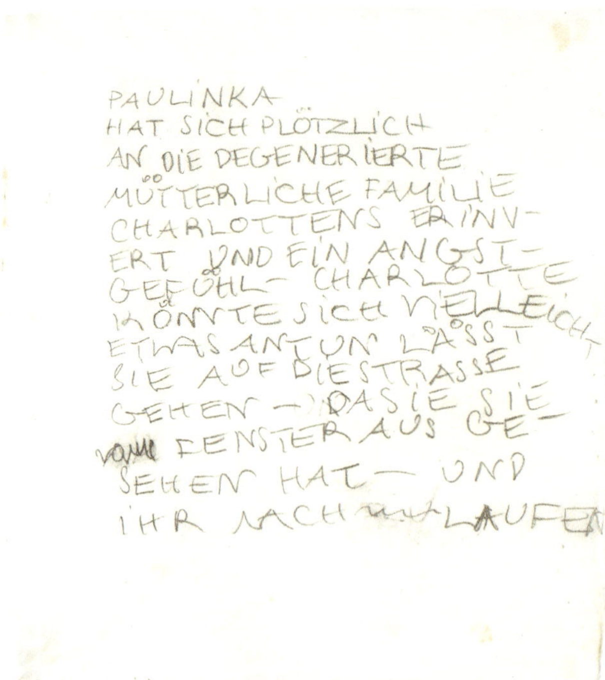

PAULINKA
HAT SICH PLÖTZLICH
AN DIE DEGENERIERTE
MÜTTERLICHE FAMILIE
CHARLOTTENS ERINN-
ERT UND EIN ANGST-
GEFÜHL – CHARLOTTE
KÖNNTE SICH VIELLEICHT
ETWAS ANTUN LÄSST
SIE AUF DIE STRASSE
GEHEN – DA SIE SIE
VOM FENSTER AUS GE-
SEHEN HAT – UND
IHR NACH LAUFEN

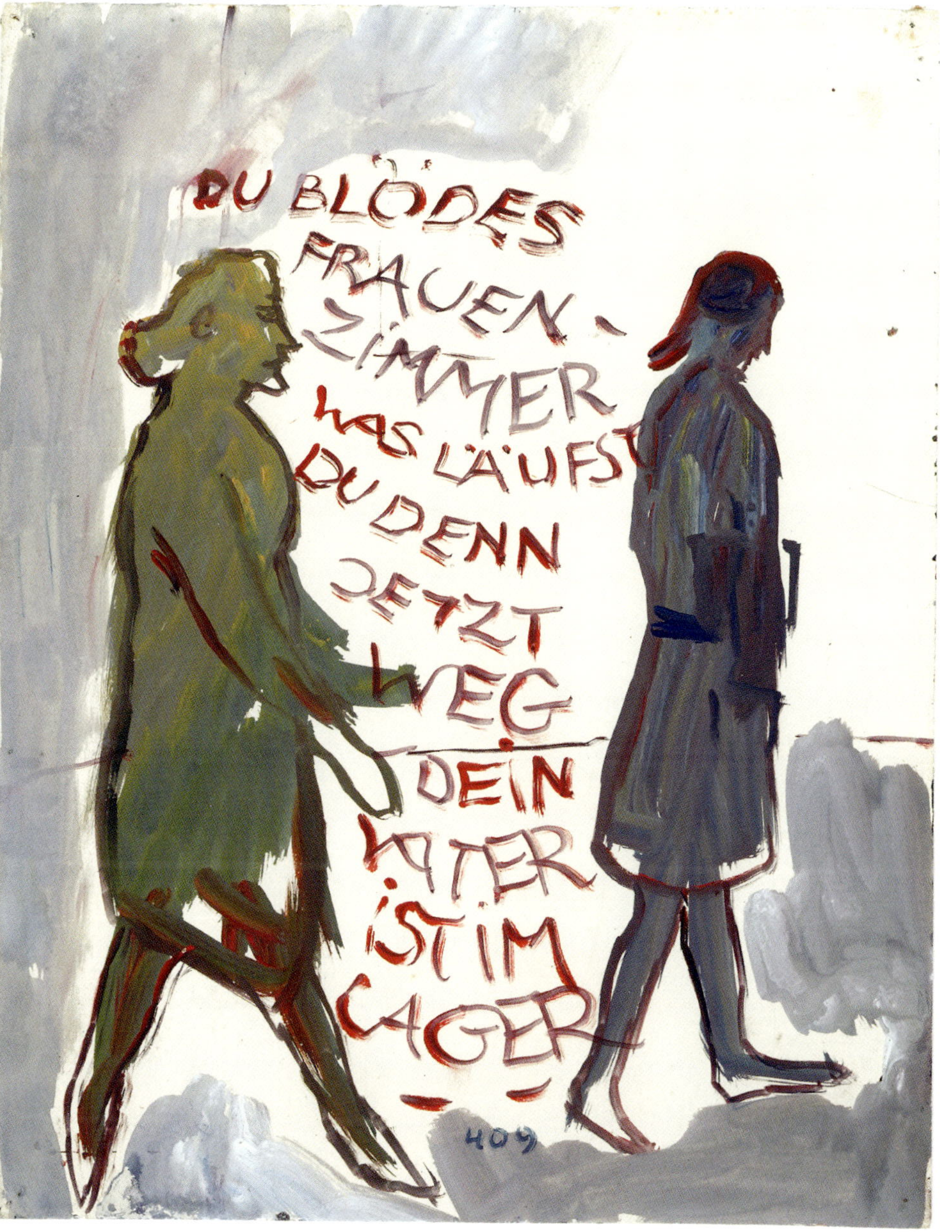
DU BLÖDES
FRAUEN-
ZIMMER
WAS LÄUFST
DU DENN
JETZT
WEG
DEIN
VATER
IST IM
LAGER
409

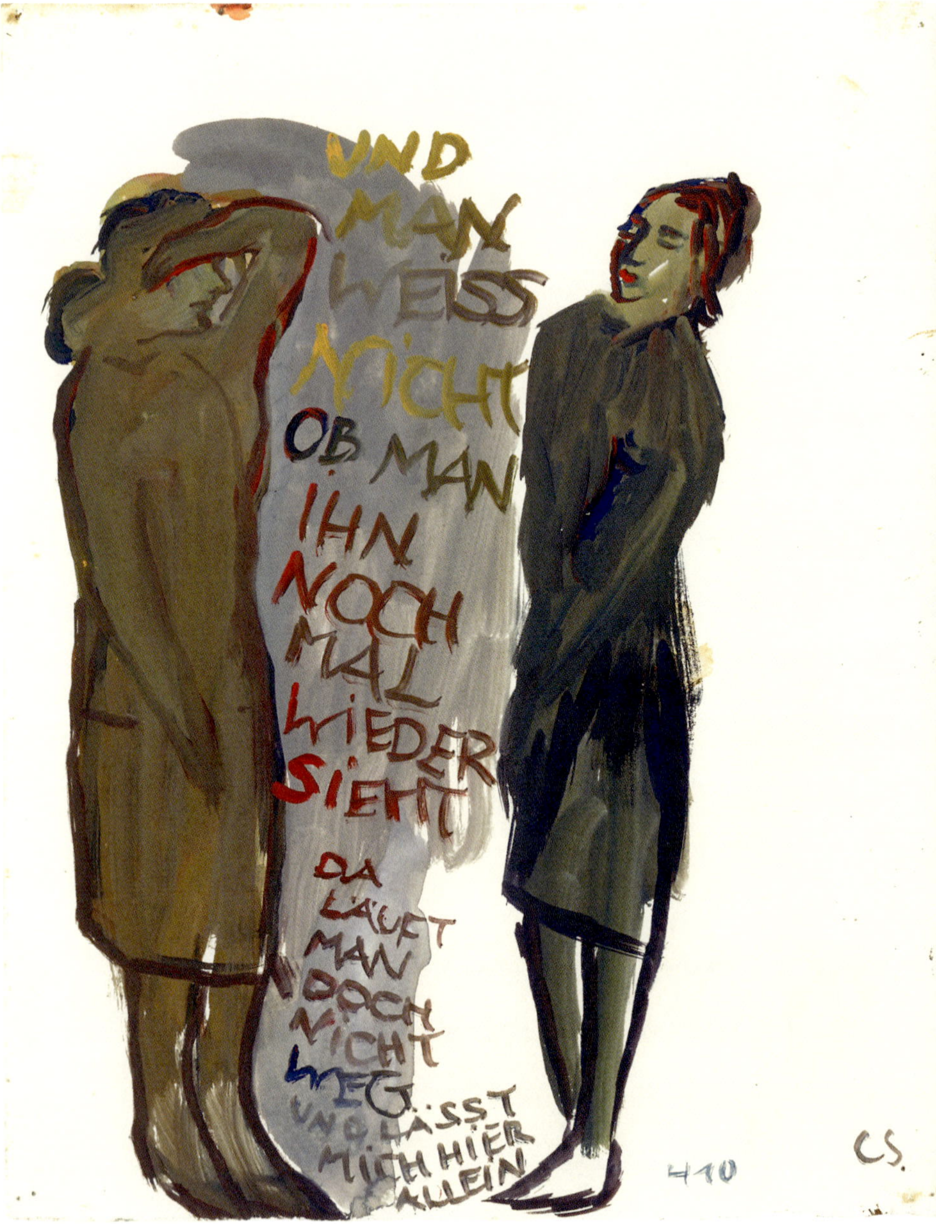
UND
MAN
WEISS
NICHT
OB MAN
IHN
NOCH
MAL
WIEDER
SIEHT
DA
LÄUFT
MAN
DOCH
NICHT
WEG
UND LÄSST
MICH HIER
ALLEIN
410
CS.

(opposite)

"... and one does not know if one will see him again. This is no time to run away and leave me here alone."

(bottom)

CHARLOTTE
"Oh, forgive me."

PAULINKA
"There's also no reason, either – "

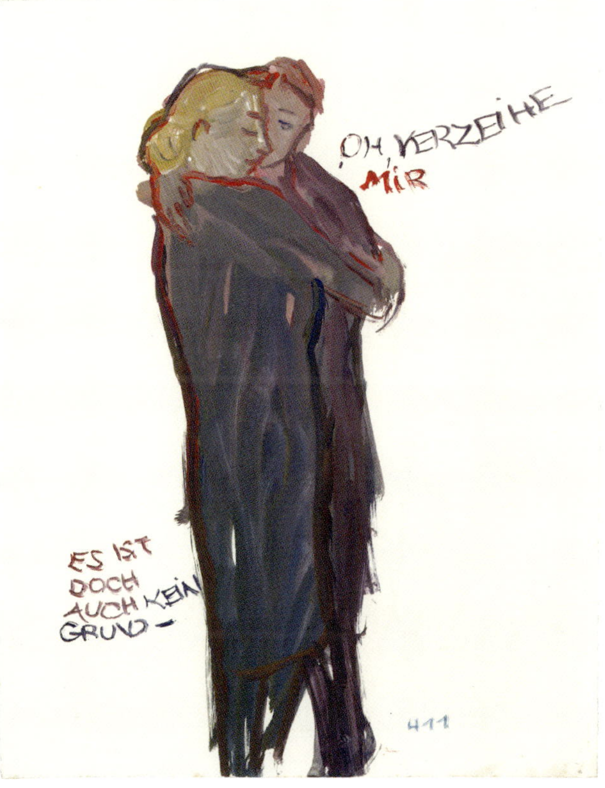

CHARLOTTE
“I have enough of this life.
I have enough of this time.”

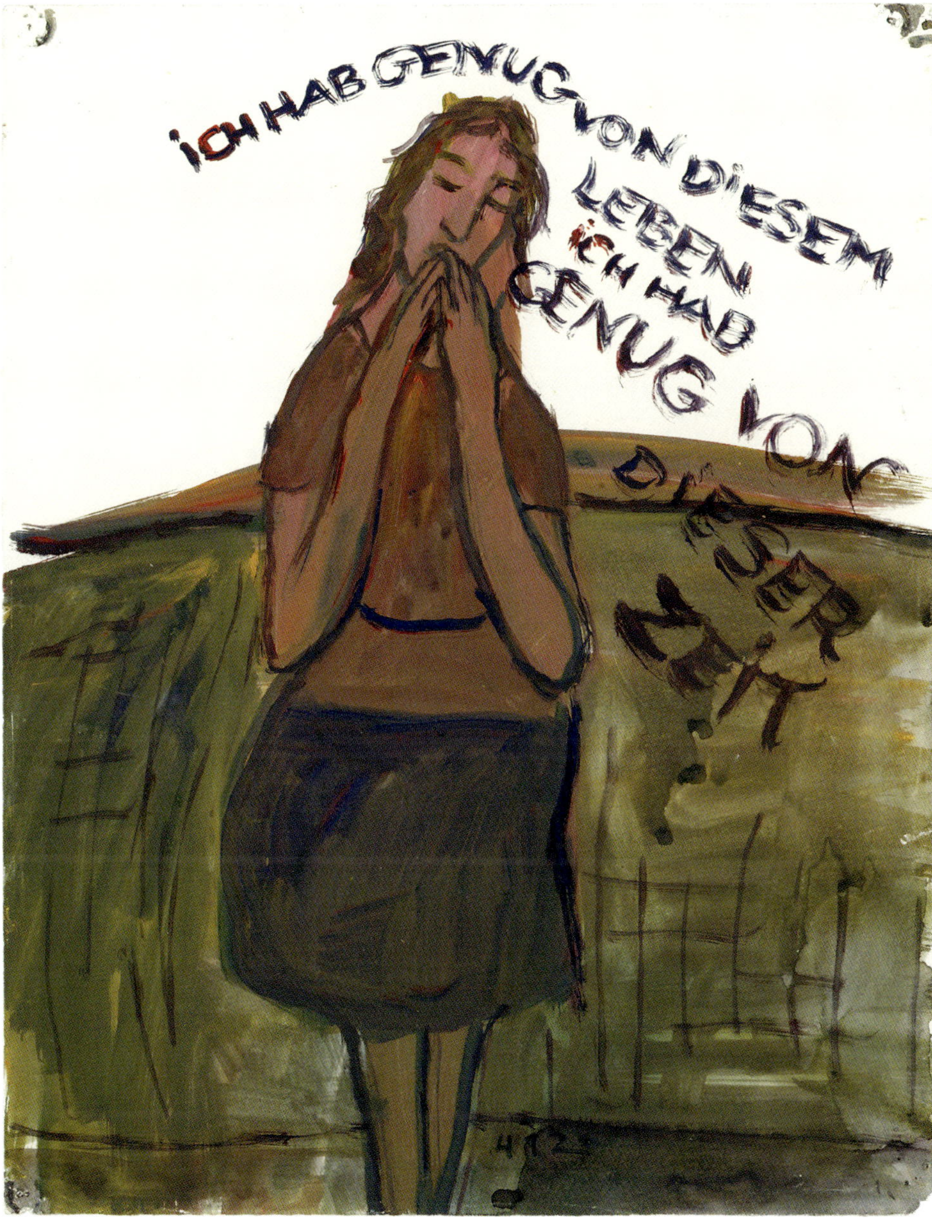
ICH HAB GENUG VON DIESEM
LEBEN
ICH HAB
GENUG VON
DIESER
ZEIT

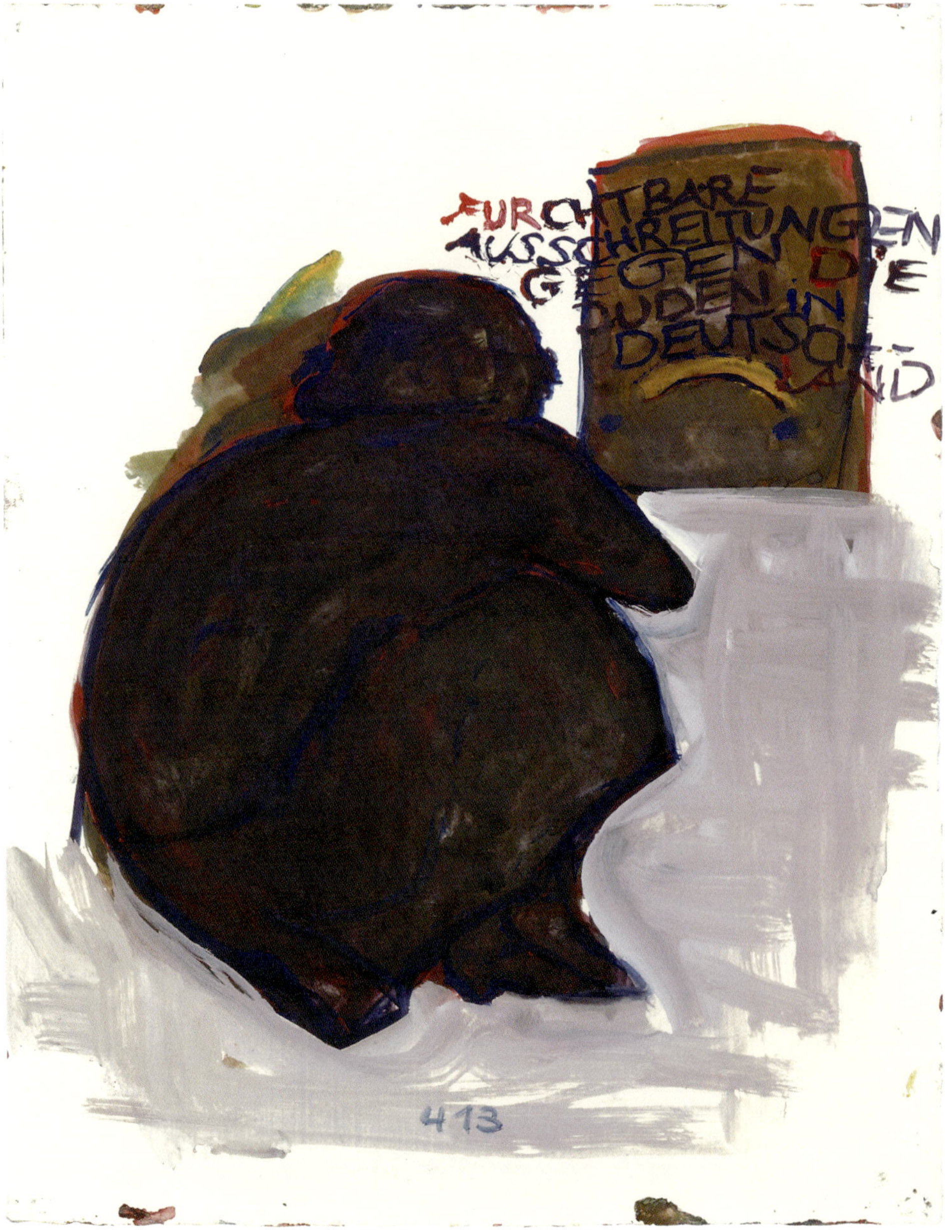
FURCHTBARE
AUSSCHREITUNGEN
GEGEN DIE
JUDEN IN
DEUTSCH-
LAND
413

CHAPTER TWO
THE GRANDMOTHER

Now we will make a small side-trip to the Knarre grandparents on the Côte d'Azur.

Mrs Knarre is constantly sitting by the radio.

"Terrible excesses against Jews in Germany."

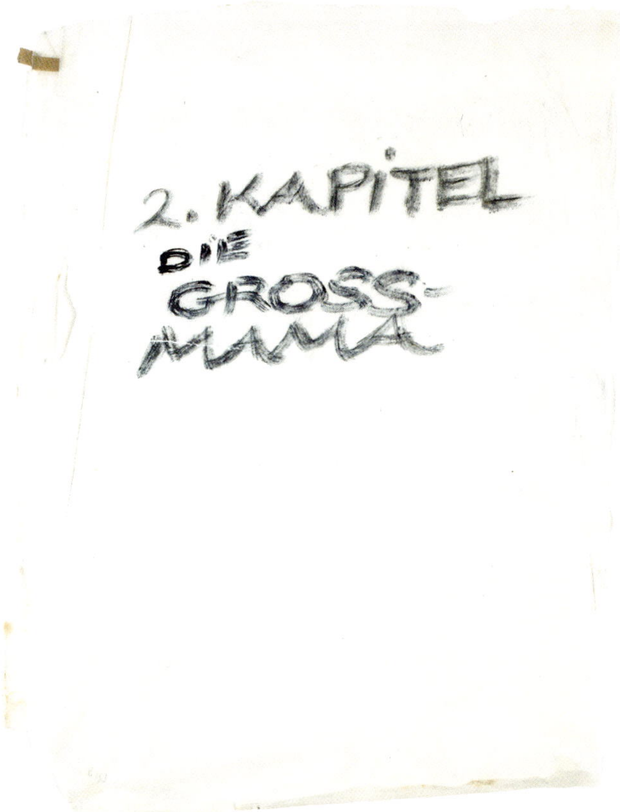

She will do everything to have Charlotte
with her as soon as possible!

GRANDMOTHER
"'She' must come here
as quickly as possible."

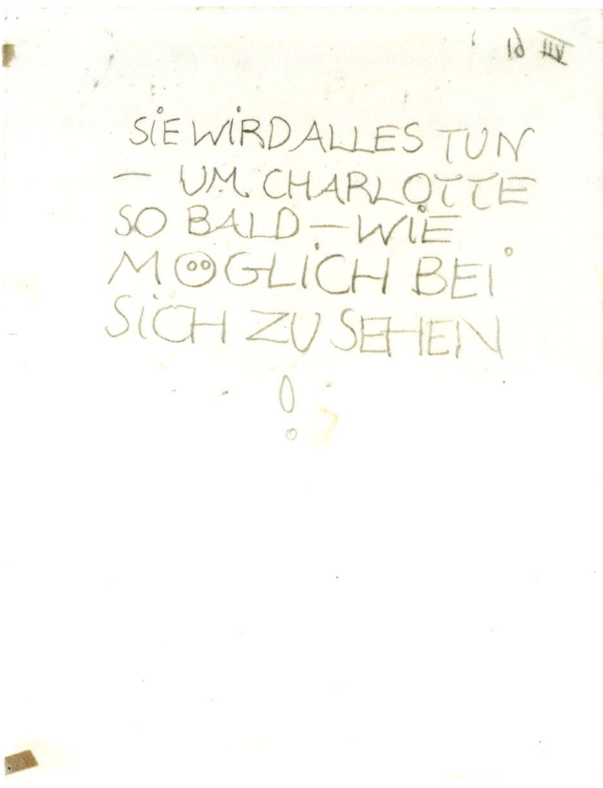

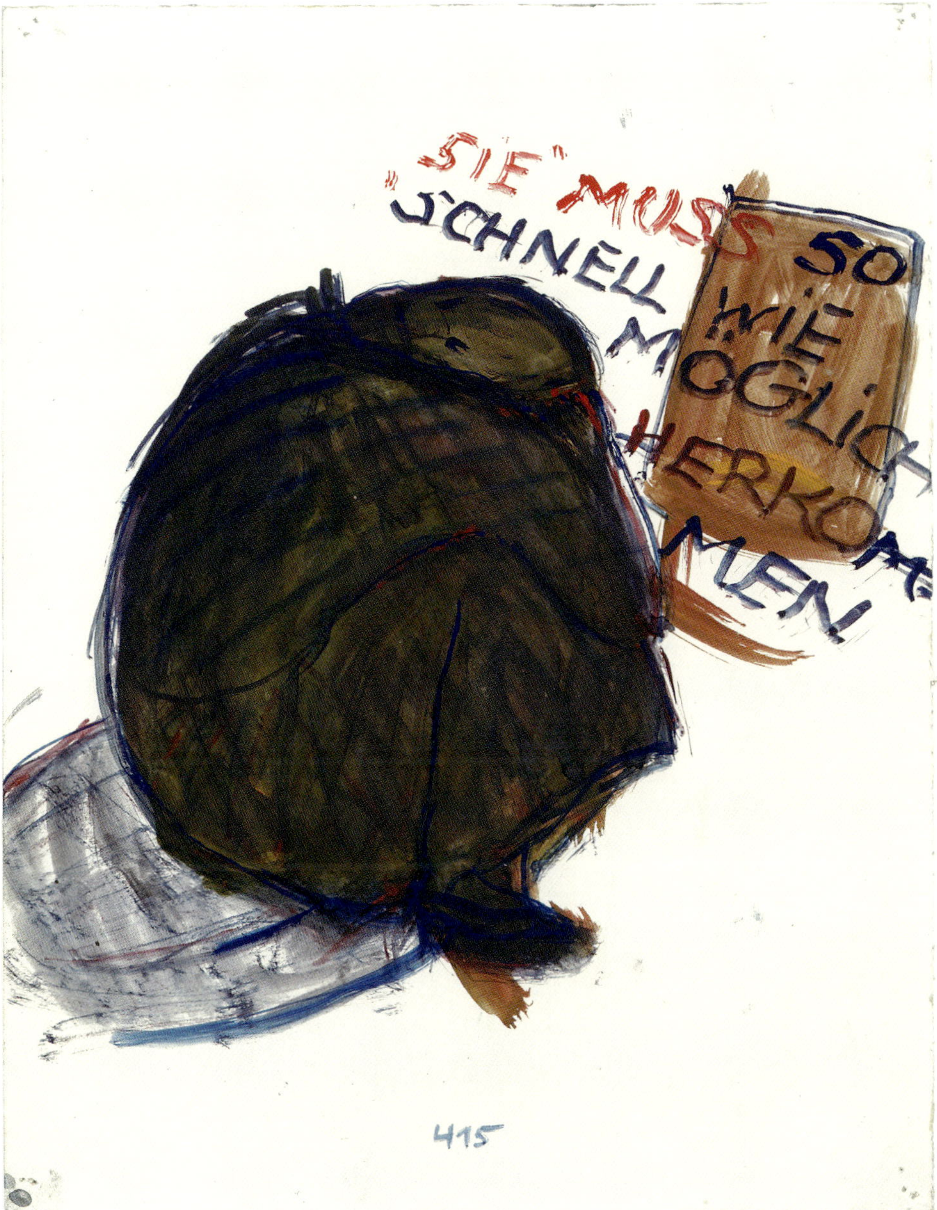
"SIE" MUSS
SCHNELL SO
WIE
MÖGLICH
HERKOM-
MEN.
415

VON SCHMERZ UND GRAUEN
IST DIE WELT ERFÜLLT.
NICHT HERRSCHEN SITTE NOCH
VERNUNFT
ZERSTÖRT SIND FREUNDSCH
AFT
UND VERTRAUEN.
STEHN WIR AM ABBRUCH
EINER NEUEN ZEIT?
ACH — WÄRE DOCH
DER FRIEDE NICHT
SO WEIT
DOCH — WIEDER MENSCHEN
SINNE SICH AUCH WANDLE —
ES BLEIBT NATUR — UN-
WANDELBAR UND SCHÖN.
DER VOGEL LIED ERSCH
ALLT
DIE BLUMEN BLÜH'N
UND RINGSUM HÜLLT DES
MONDES SILBERSCHEIN —
MEER — BERG UND TAL —
IN LICHTEM NEBEL EIN.
WOZU — DAS FRAGEN
NACH DEM SINN DER
SCHÖPFUNG
WOZU DAS FORSCHEN NACH
WOHER — WOHIN — SO
WIE NATUR — VERGEH-
END BLEIBT BESTEHEN
SO WIRD AUCH UNSRE
ASCHE NICHT
VERGEHEN!

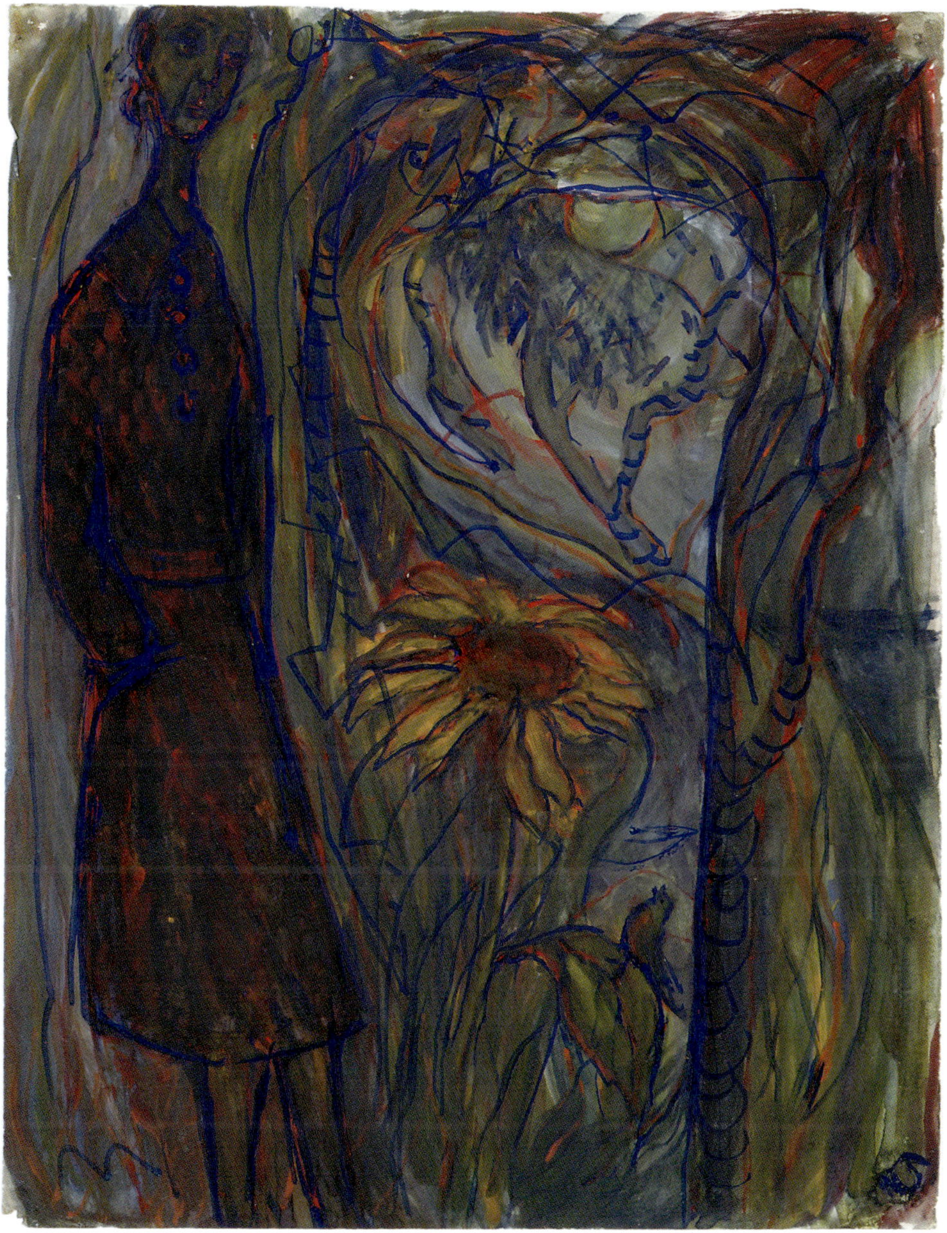

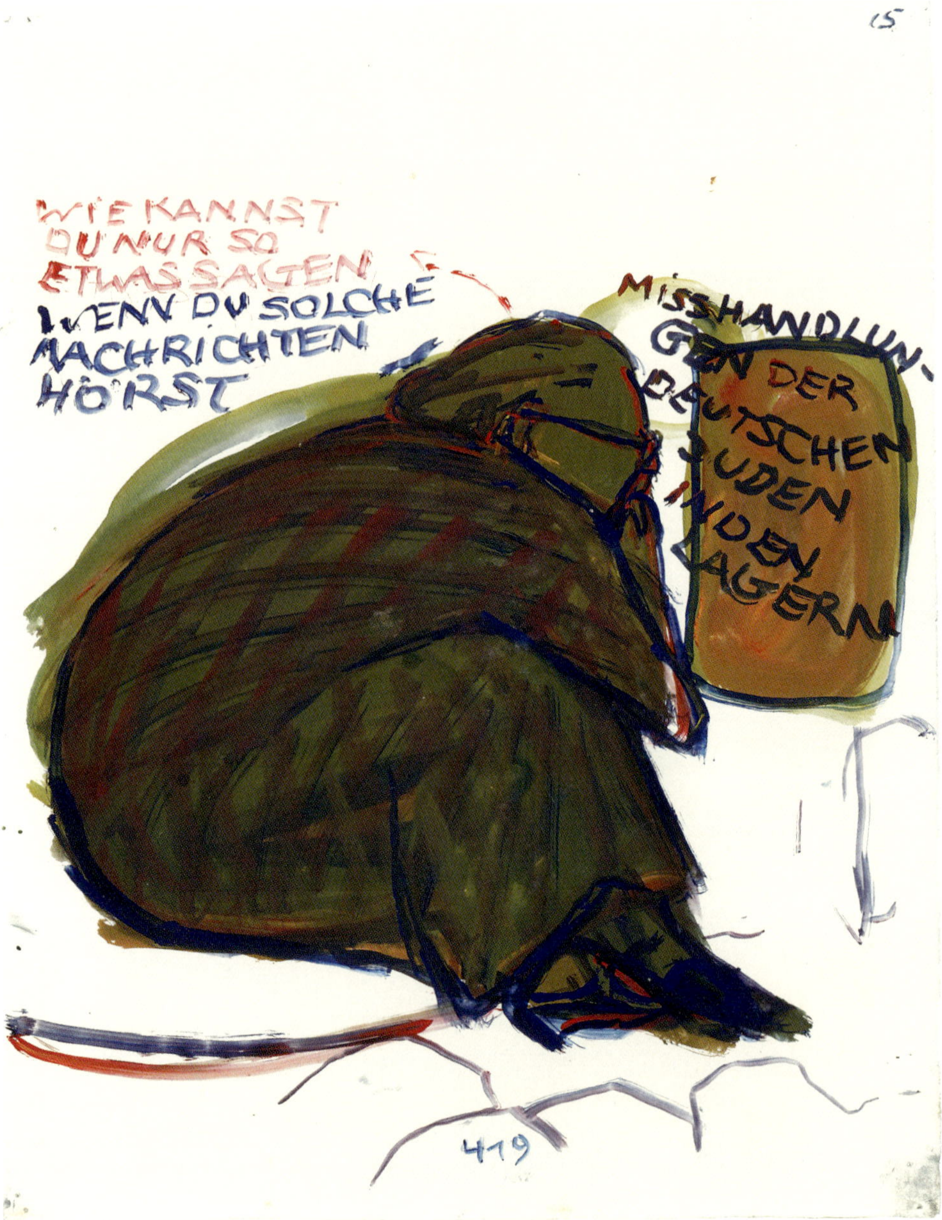
15
WIE KANNST
DU NUR SO
ETWAS SAGEN
WENN DU SOLCHE
NACHRICHTEN
HÖRST
MISSHANDLUN-
GEN DER
DEUTSCHEN
JUDEN
IN DEN
LAGERN
419

(previous pages)

One evening, while walking in the glorious nature, the following poem bursts forth from the torn inside of 70-year-old Mrs Knarre:

"The world is filled with suffering and horror.
Virtue and reason now prevail no more.
Friendship and trust are all destroyed.
Is this the threshold of a dawning age?
Ah me, if only peace were not so far.
Yet, changing hearts and souls of men withal –
Nature remains, unchangeable and fair.
Birdsong resounds, the trees and flowers bloom,
and all around the silv'ry moonlight swathes
mountain and dale in opalescent mist.
Why all this questing for creation's meaning,
why all this searching for the whence, the whither?
Just as, in fading, Nature has endured,
so is survival of our ash assured!"

(opposite)

GRANDMOTHER
"How can you say such a thing when you
hear news like that: 'Maltreatment
of the German Jews in the camps?'"

CHAPTER THREE
THE PAPA

Meanwhile, the former Professor Doctor of medicine is forced to do heavy manual labour.

CAMP COLONEL
“You have to work here,
there’ll be no loafing.”

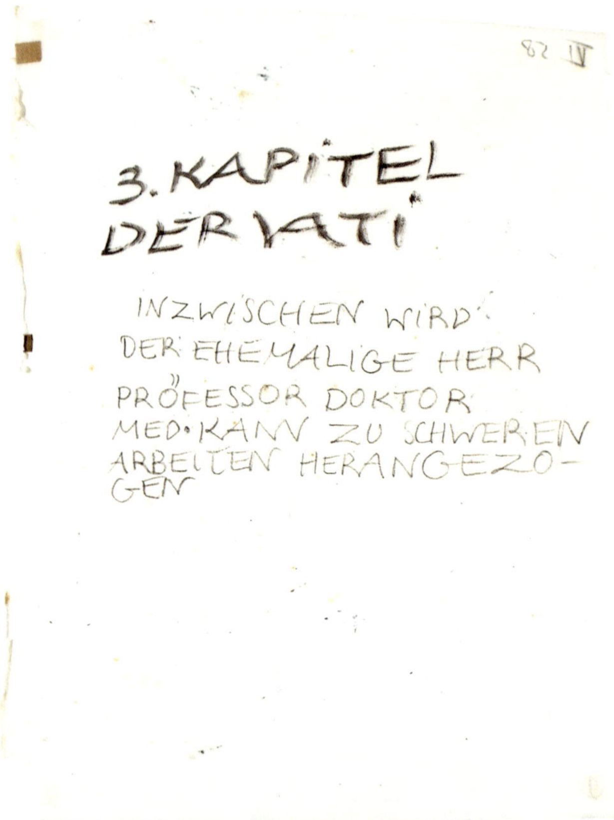

IV

3. KAPITEL
DER VATI

INZWISCHEN WIRD
DER EHEMALIGE HERR
PRÖFESSOR DOKTOR
MED. KANN ZU SCHWEREN
ARBEITEN HERANGEZO-
GEN

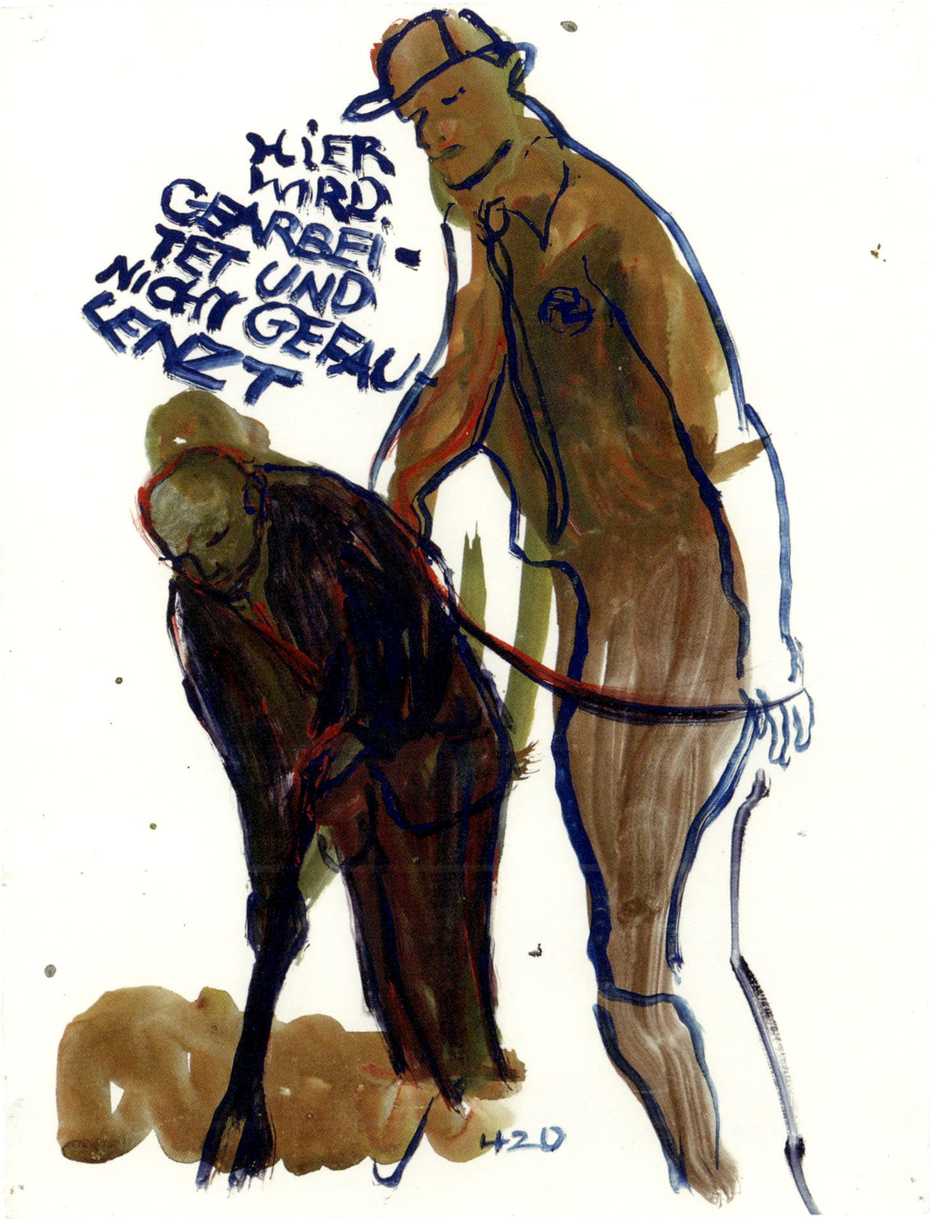
HiER
WIRD.
GEARBEI-
TET UND
NICHT GEFAU-
LENZT
420

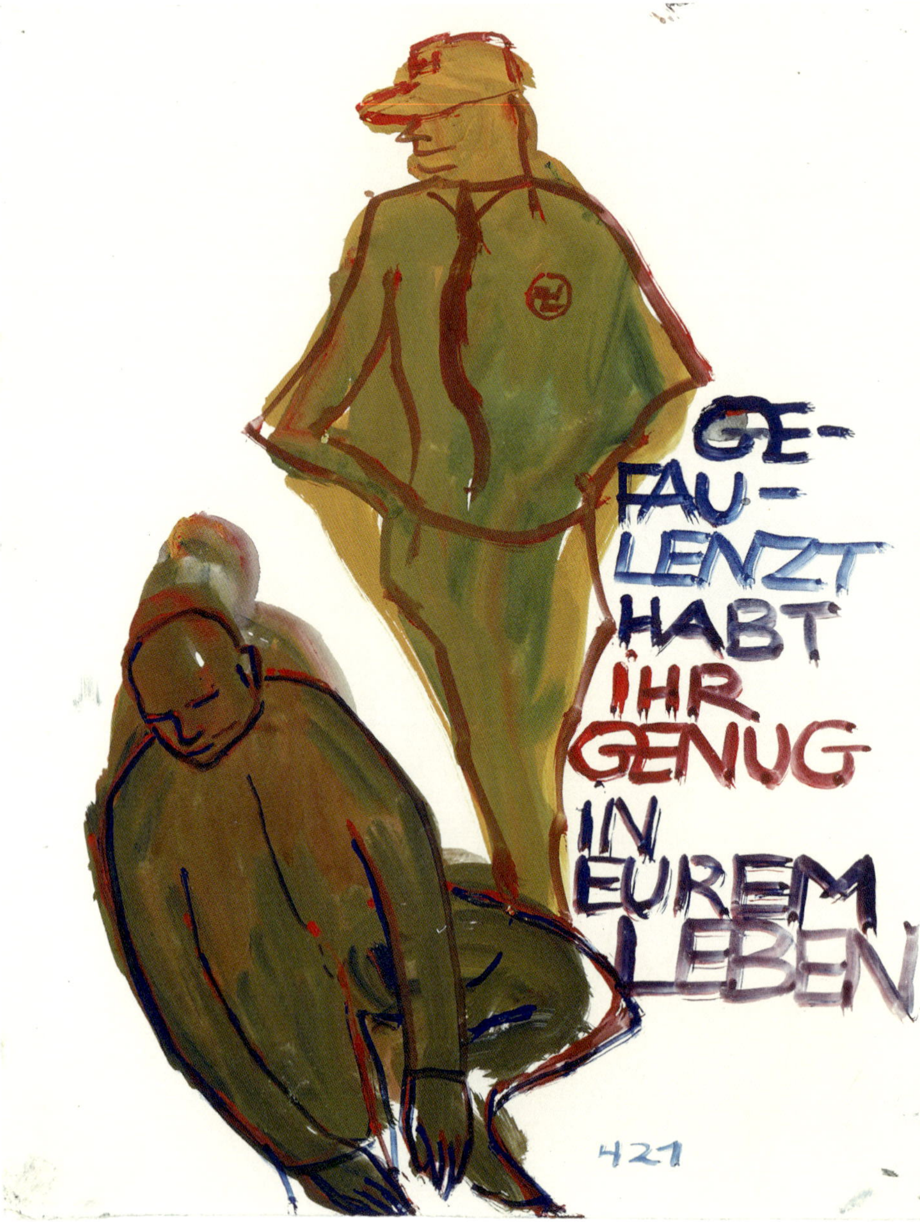
GE-
FAU-
LENZT
HABT
IHR
GENUG
IN
EUREM
LEBEN
427

(opposite)

CAMP COLONEL
"You've done enough loafing
in your lives."

(bottom)

Luckily for him, he has a wife who possesses, in addition to a magnanimously good heart, enough charm and intelligence to intervene successfully on his behalf.

PAULINKA
"It would mean – so much – to me if he could
be released quite soon."

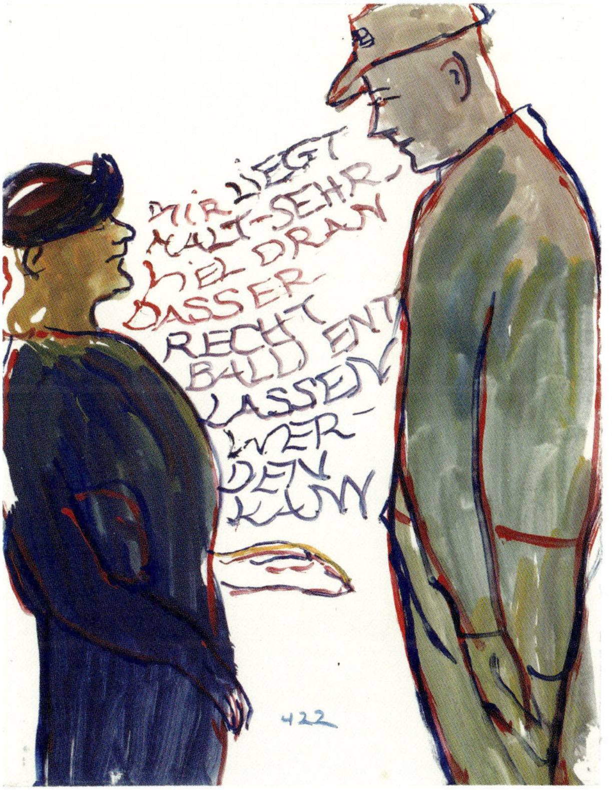

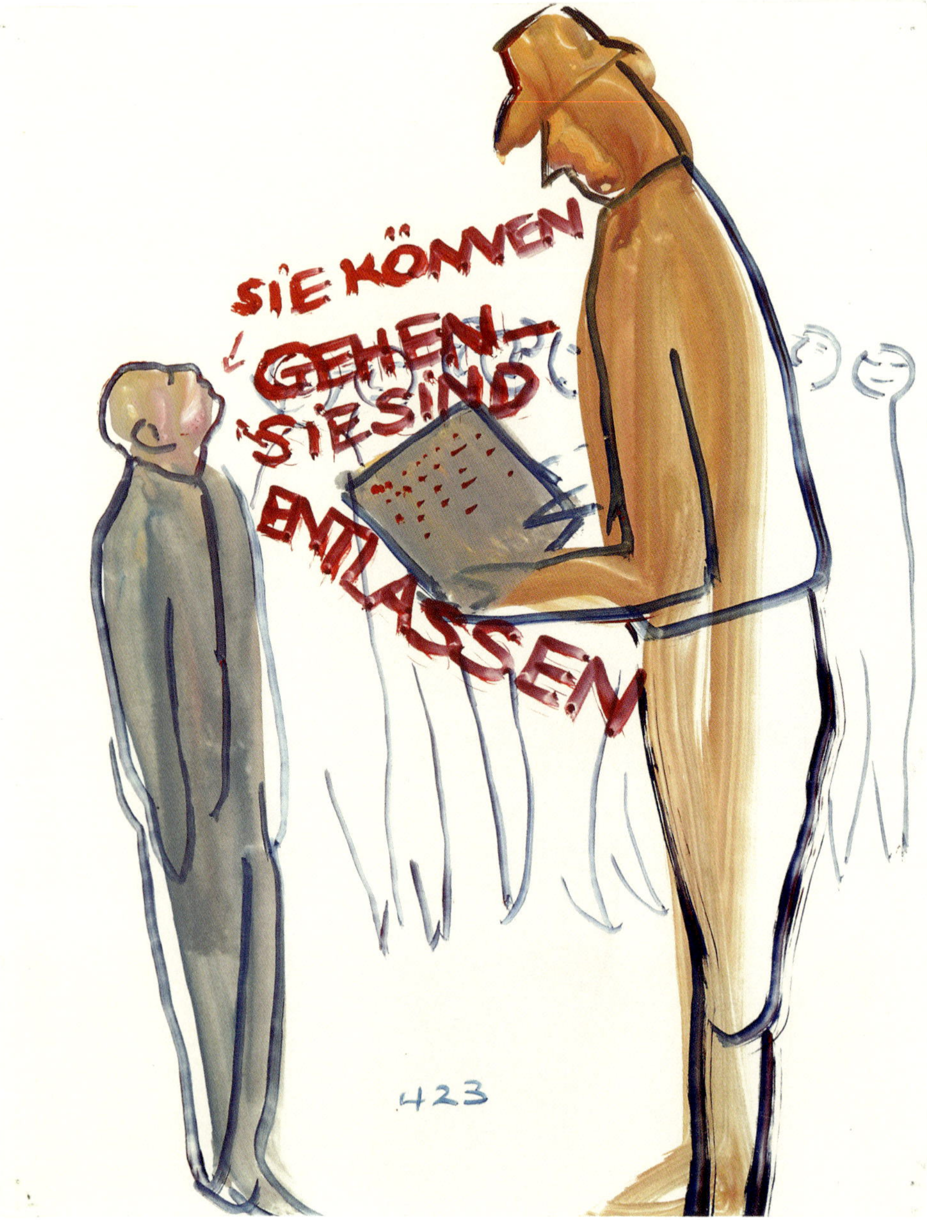
SIE KÖNNEN
GEHEN –
SIE SIND
ENTLASSEN
423

(opposite)

And, indeed, Paulinka's many efforts
do succeed in getting Albert released.

CAMP COLONEL
"You may go.
You're discharged."

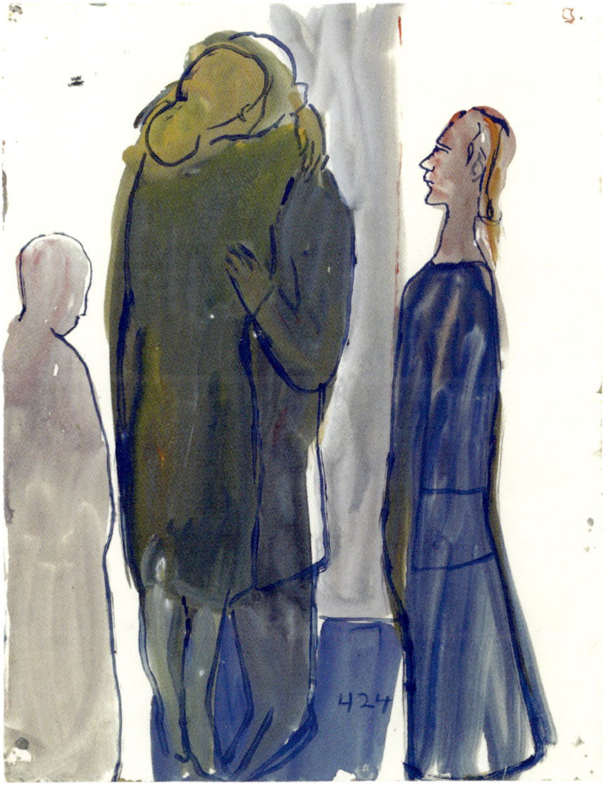

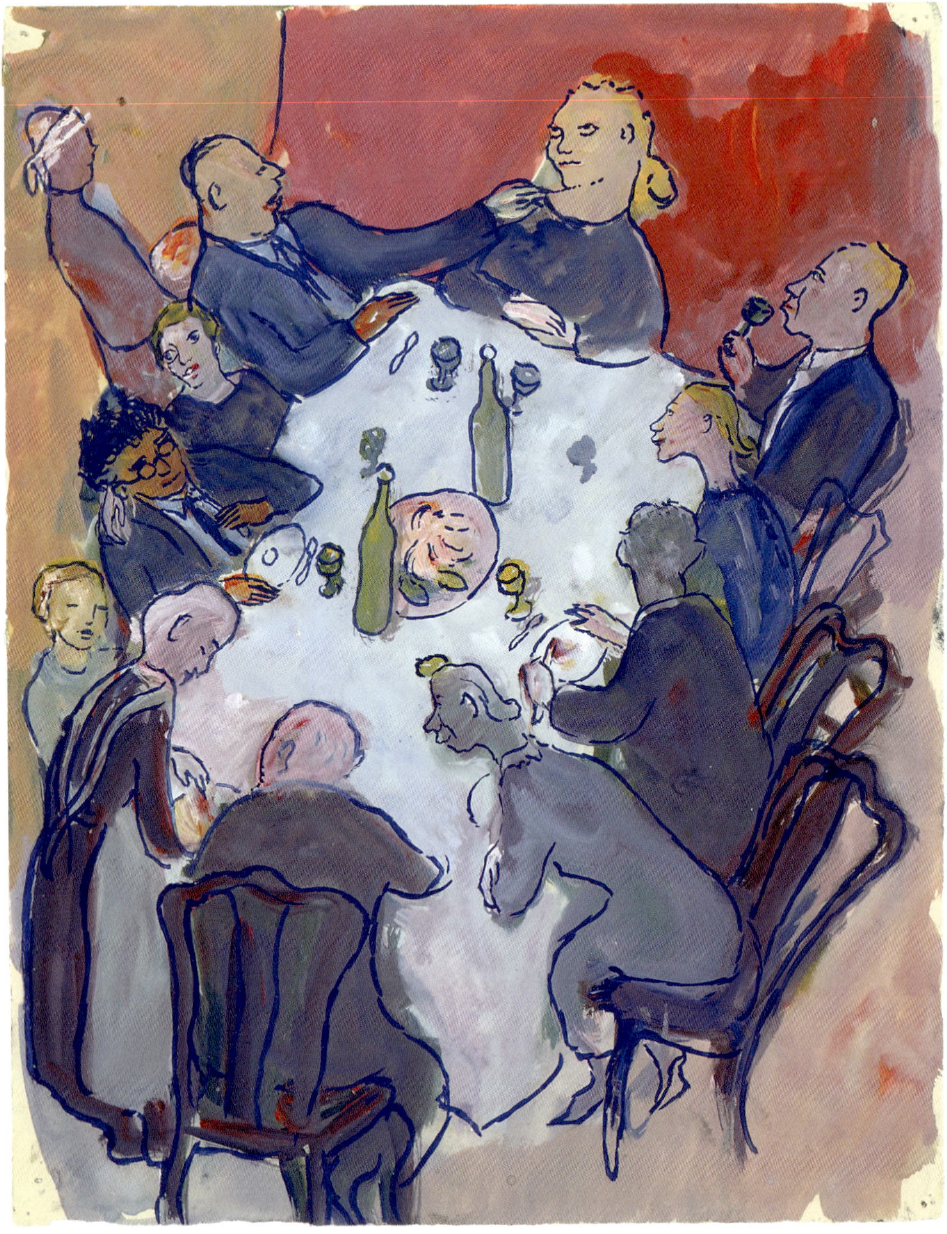

CHAPTER FOUR
THE GERMAN JEWS

The German Jews, of whom each one is so preoccupied with himself that, at a dinner party, a quiet observer feels as though he were in a goose pen.

ALBERT
"First of all I'm sending away
my daughter."

WOMAN TO HIS RIGHT
"And we're going to Australia!"

MAN BETWEEN WOMAN AND CHARLOTTE
"And what will you do?"

SCULPTOR
"And I'll go to the United States and become
the greatest sculptor in the world."

PAULINKA
"We'll be staying here for the time being."

MR BLÄHN
"And I'll go to the United States and there
I'll become the greatest singer in the world."

DABERLOHN'S FIANCÉE
"And we're going to America,
aren't we, Mucki..."

MAID
"Take this piece, Professor,
it's the best one."

(Unten)

MAN NEXT TO CHARLOTTE
"So you're going to America too?"

DABERLOHN
"To make your task easier for you
to look at my hand: here it is."

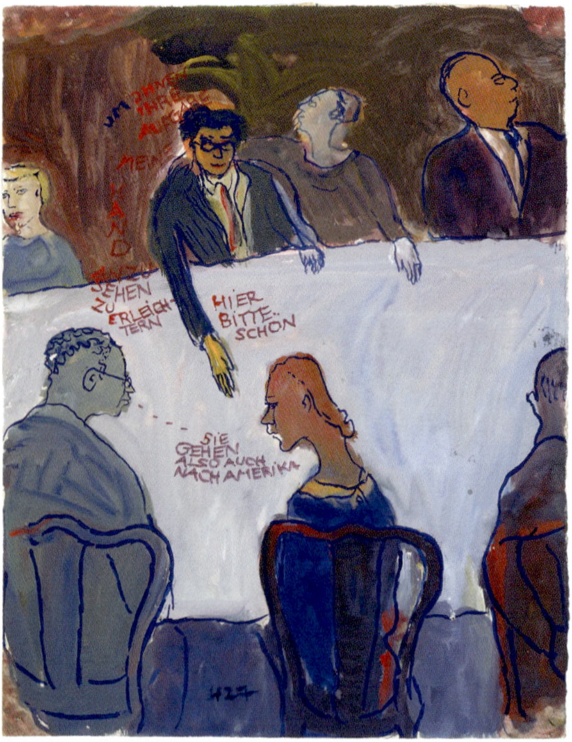

(opposite)

ALBERT
"So you're going to
America with your
fiancé."

DABERLOHN
"And you,
Madam, will
also be going to
Australia."

WOMAN
"Yes, we're
going to..."

PAULINKA
"Well, Blähn, you'll
be leaving us so
soon."

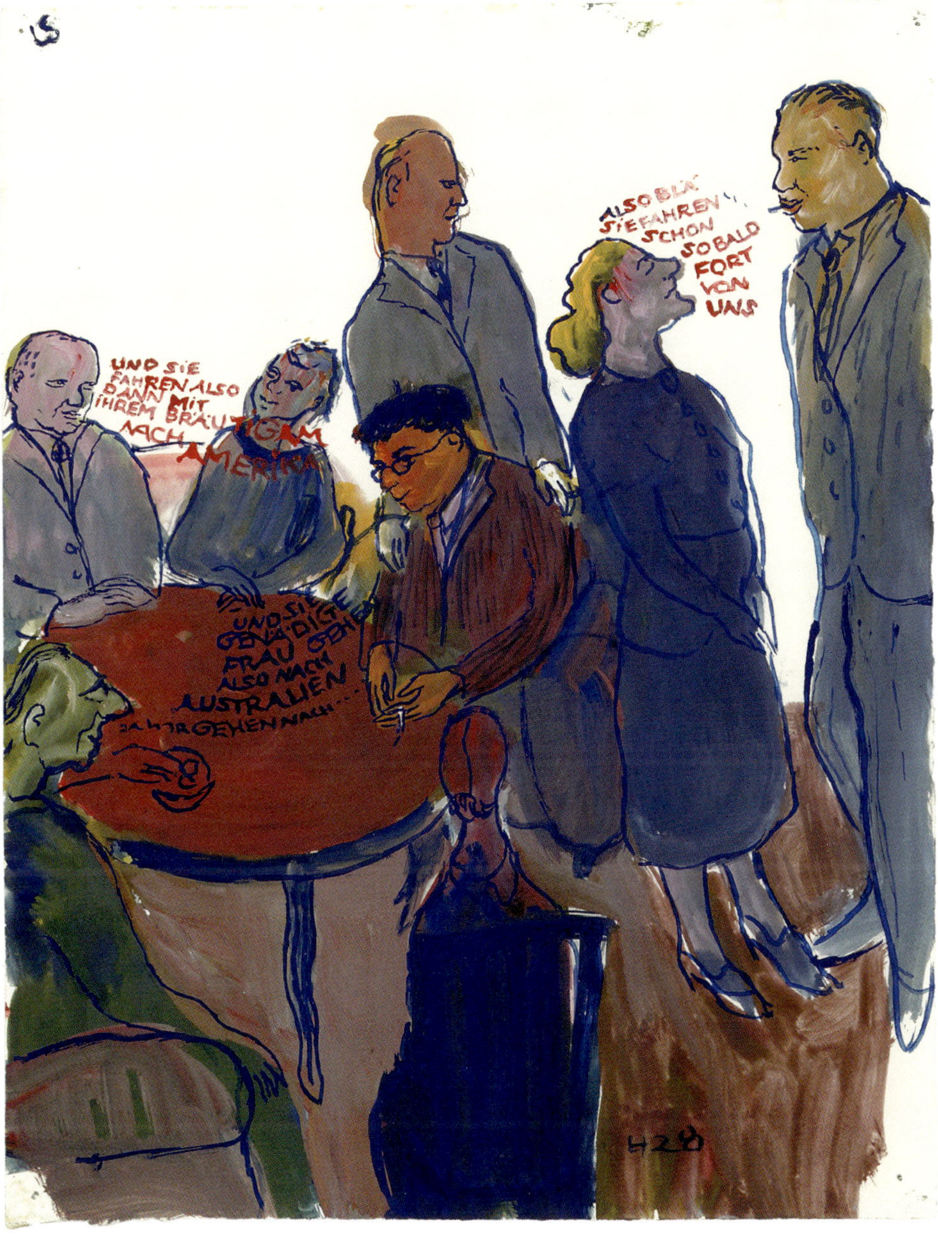
UND SIE FAHREN ALSO DANN MIT IHREM BRÄUTIGAM NACH AMERIKA
ALSO BLÄ SIE FAHREN SCHON SO BALD FORT VON UNS
UND SIE GENÄDIGE FRAU GEHEN ALSO NACH AUSTRALIEN...
WIR GEHEN NACH
428

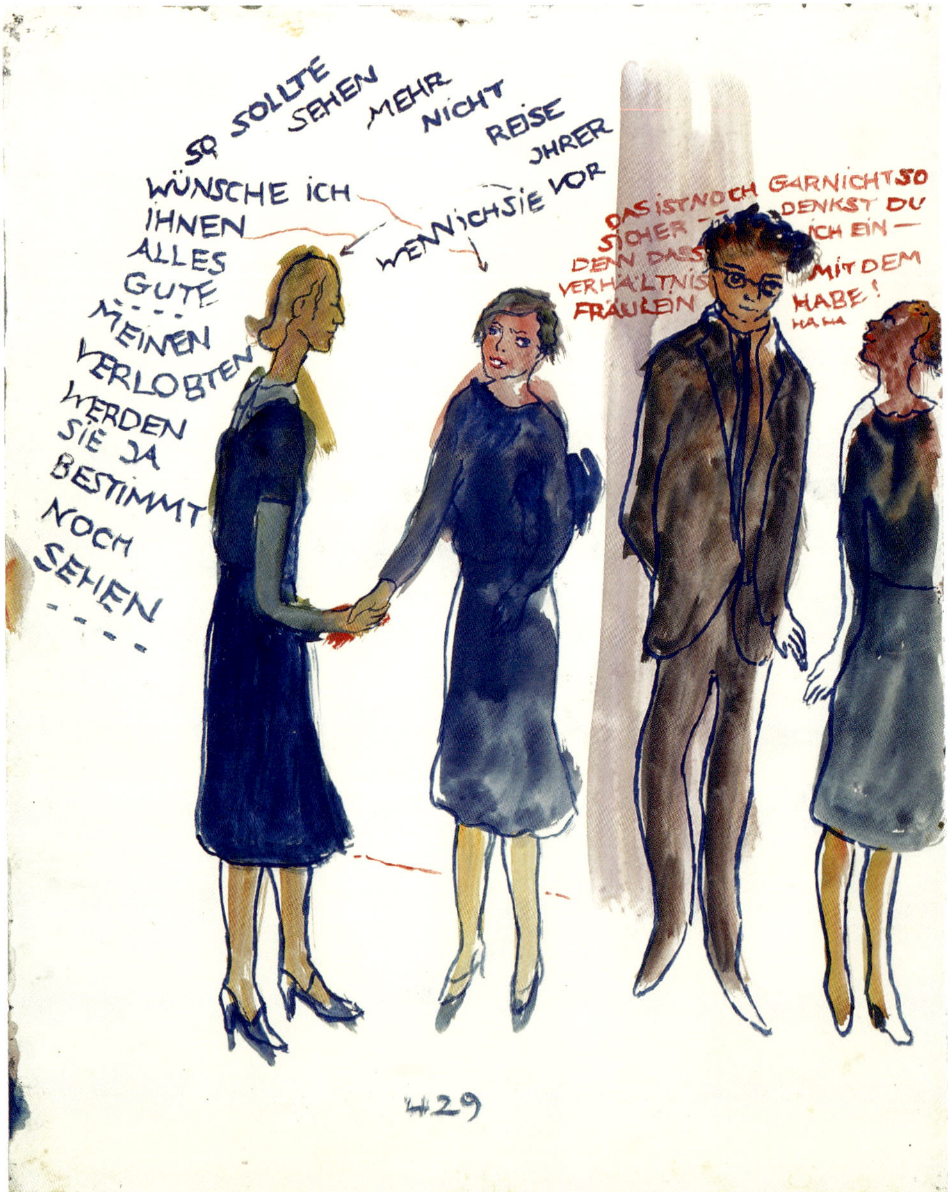
SO SOLLTE SEHEN MEHR NICHT REISE JHRER
WENN ICH SIE VOR
WÜNSCHE ICH IHNEN ALLES GUTE --- MEINEN VERLOBTEN WERDEN SIE JA BESTIMMT NOCH SEHEN ----
DAS IST NOCH GARNICHT SO SICHER -- DENKST DU DENN DASS ICH EIN — VERHÄLTNIS MIT DEM FRÄULEIN HABE! HAHA
429

(opposite)

DABERLOHN'S FIANCÉE
"If I shouldn't see you again before you leave, I wish you all the best – you'll surely see my fiancé again –"

DABERLOHN
"That's not so certain at all – do you think then that I'm having an affair with that young lady! Haha!"

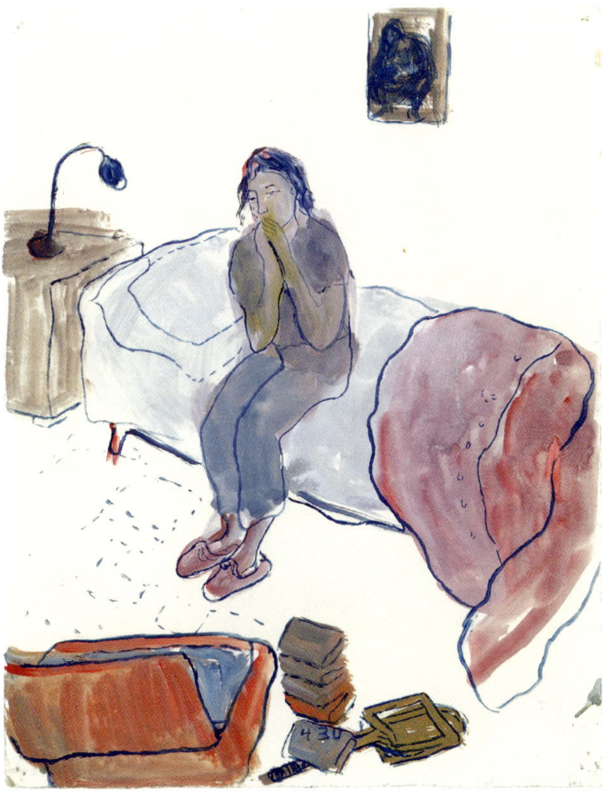

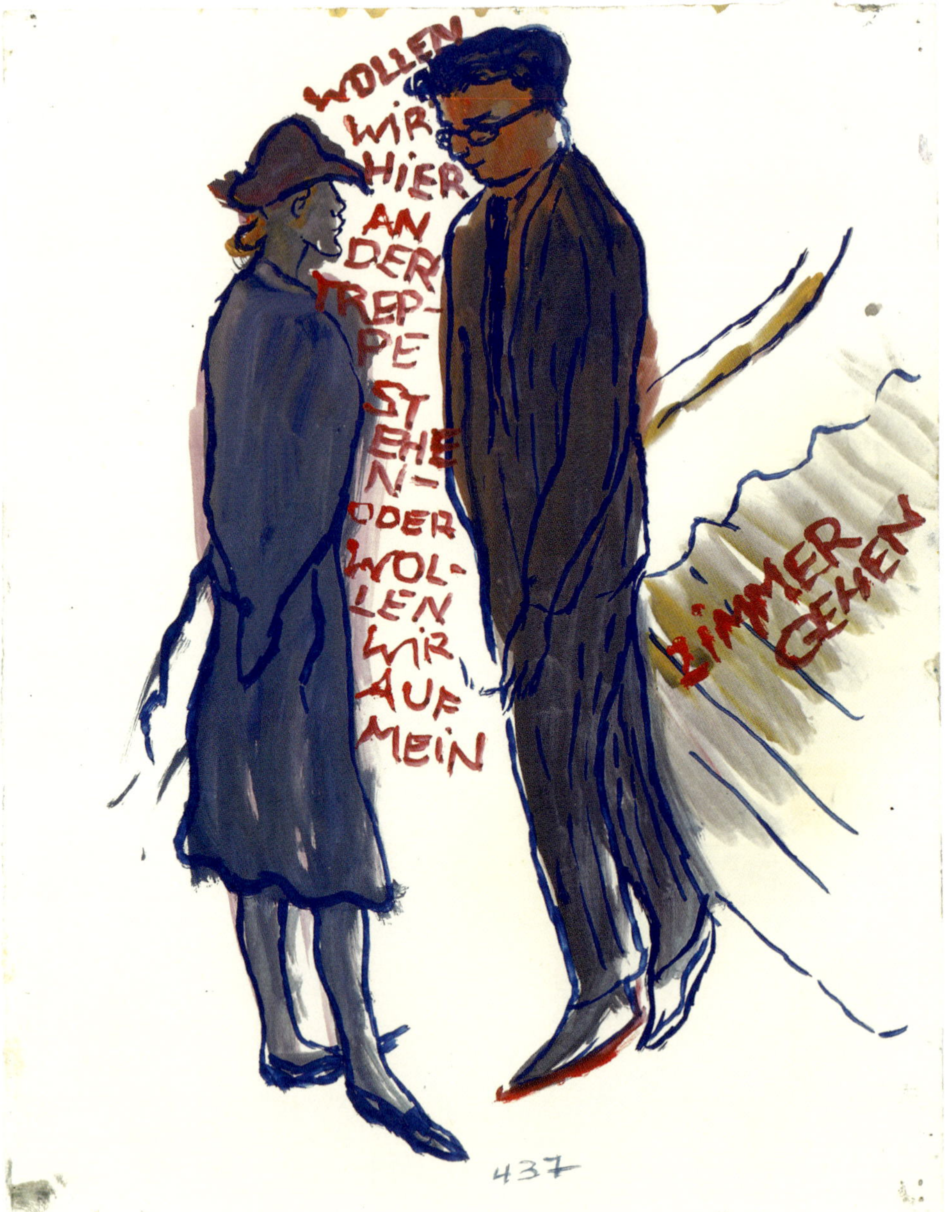
WOLLEN WIR HIER AN DER TREP-PE STEHEN- ODER WOL-LEN WIR AUF MEIN
ZIMMER GEHEN
437

(opposite)

DABERLOHN
"Shall we stand here by the stairs,
or shall we go up to my room?"

(bottom)

"Can you see that spot up there –
It represents Io and Jupiter."

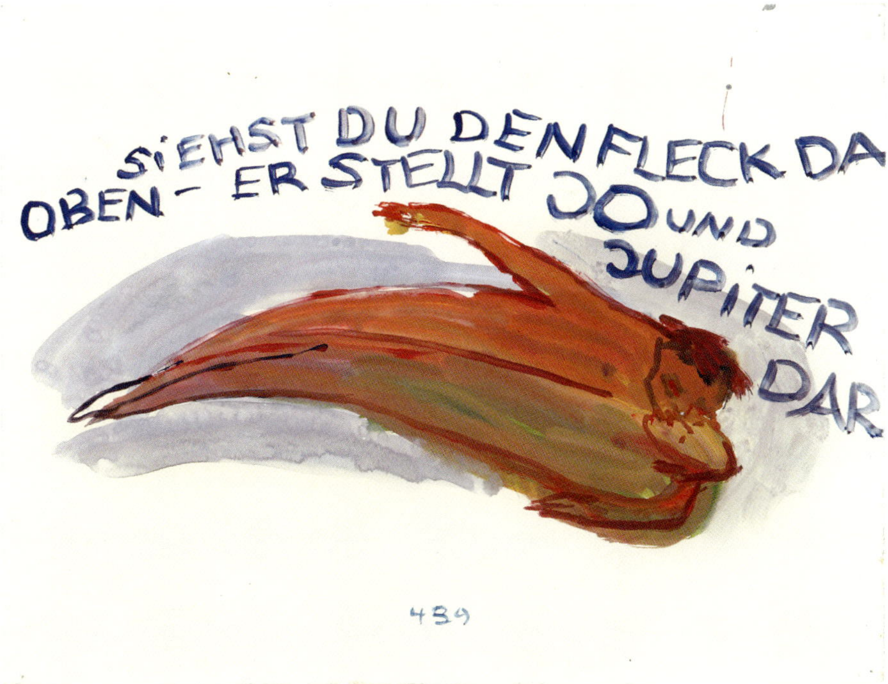

(bottom)

"And here is a farewell gift, a sheet – The Darkest Day – and I ask you not to forget that I love life and affirm it threefold. In order to love life completely, perhaps it is necessary to embrace and comprehend its other side: death."

(opposite)

"May you never forget that I believe in you."

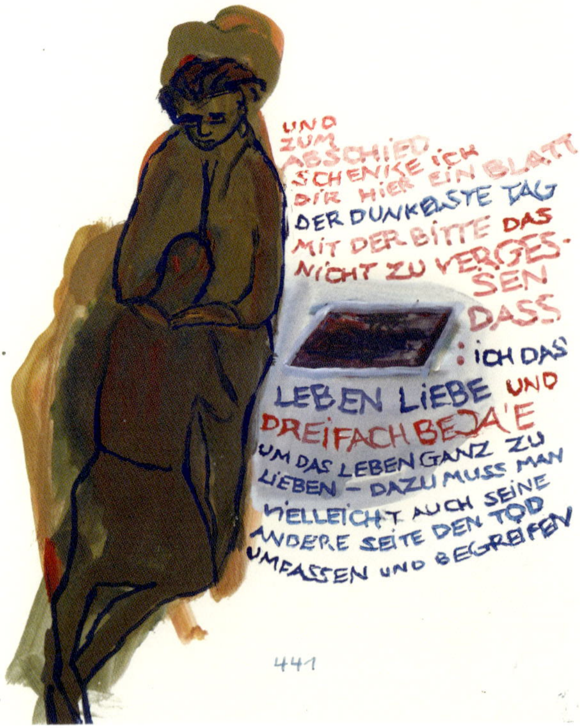

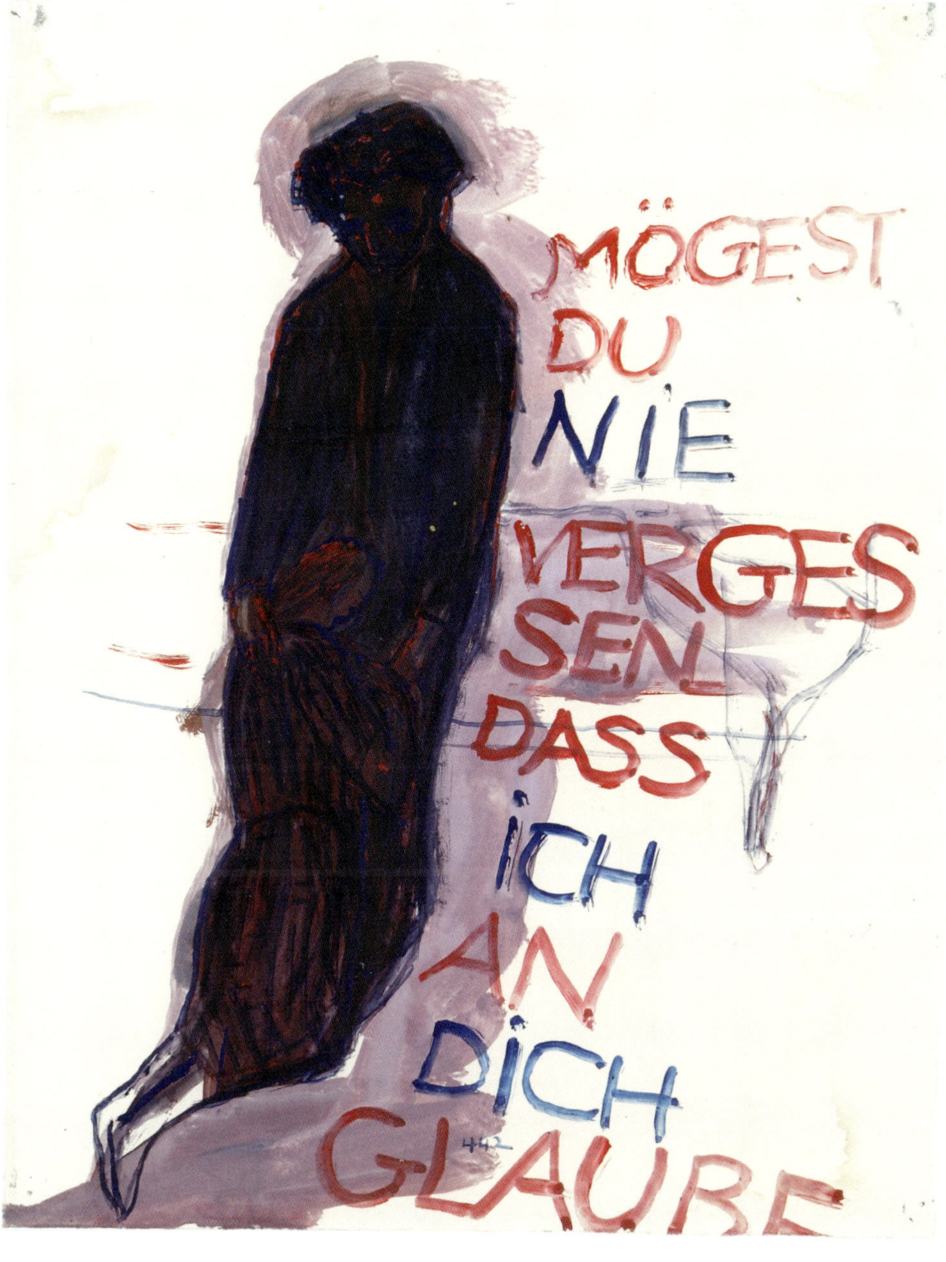
MÖGEST
DU
NIE
VERGES
SEN
DASS
ICH
AN
DICH
GLAUBE
442

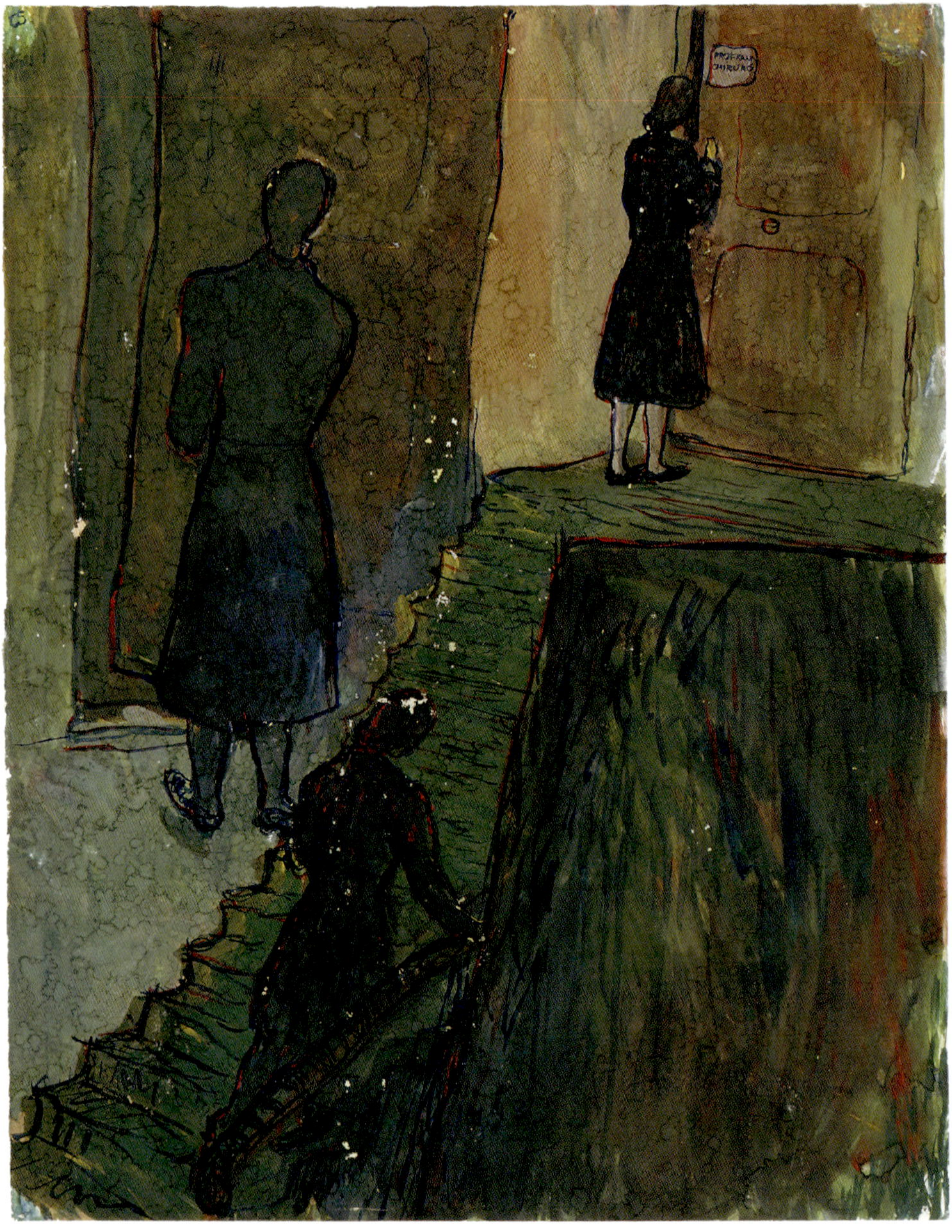

Here once again the visual concept changes.
It is Charlotte who once again begins to sing:
the song of farewell to her native land.

In these few pictures almost all the tunes from
Scenes 1 and 2 of the Prelude are repeated.

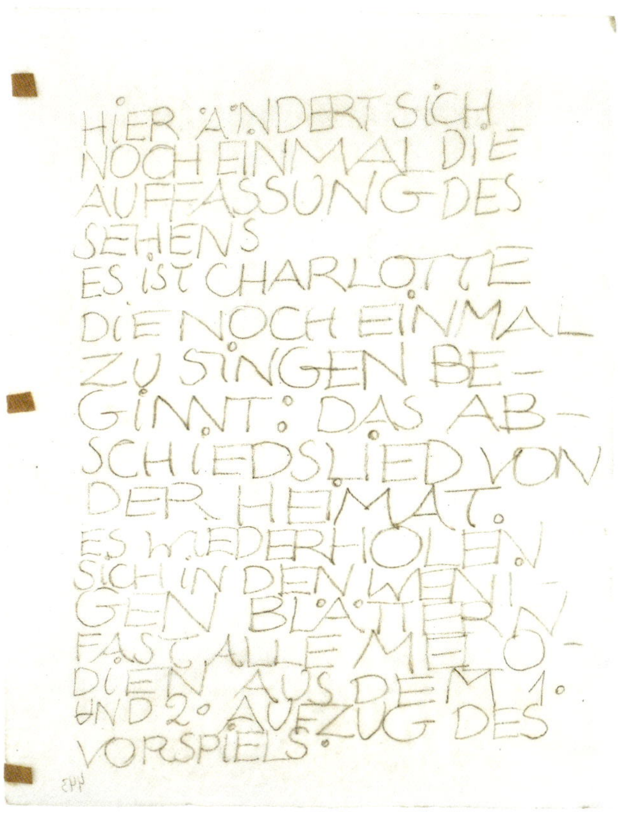

(bottom)

ALBERT
"And as a farewell gift,
I'm giving you my portrait."

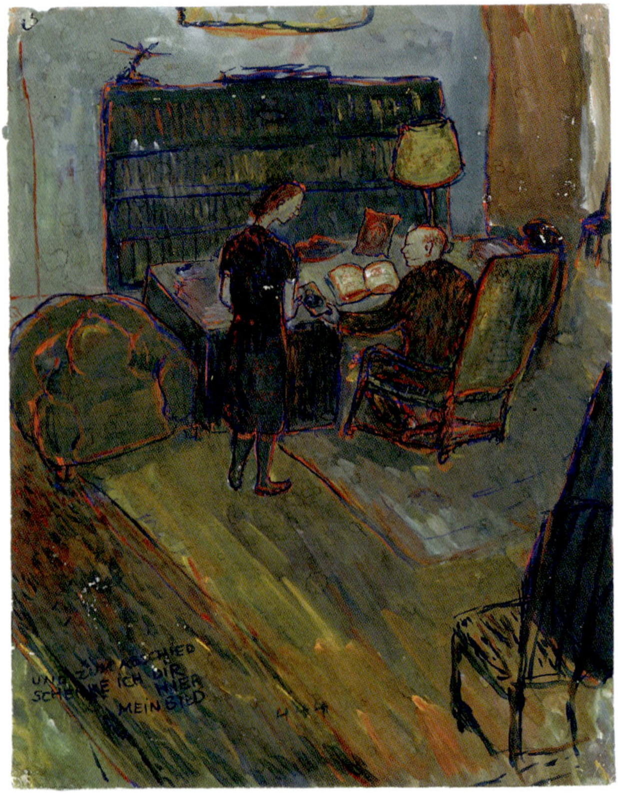

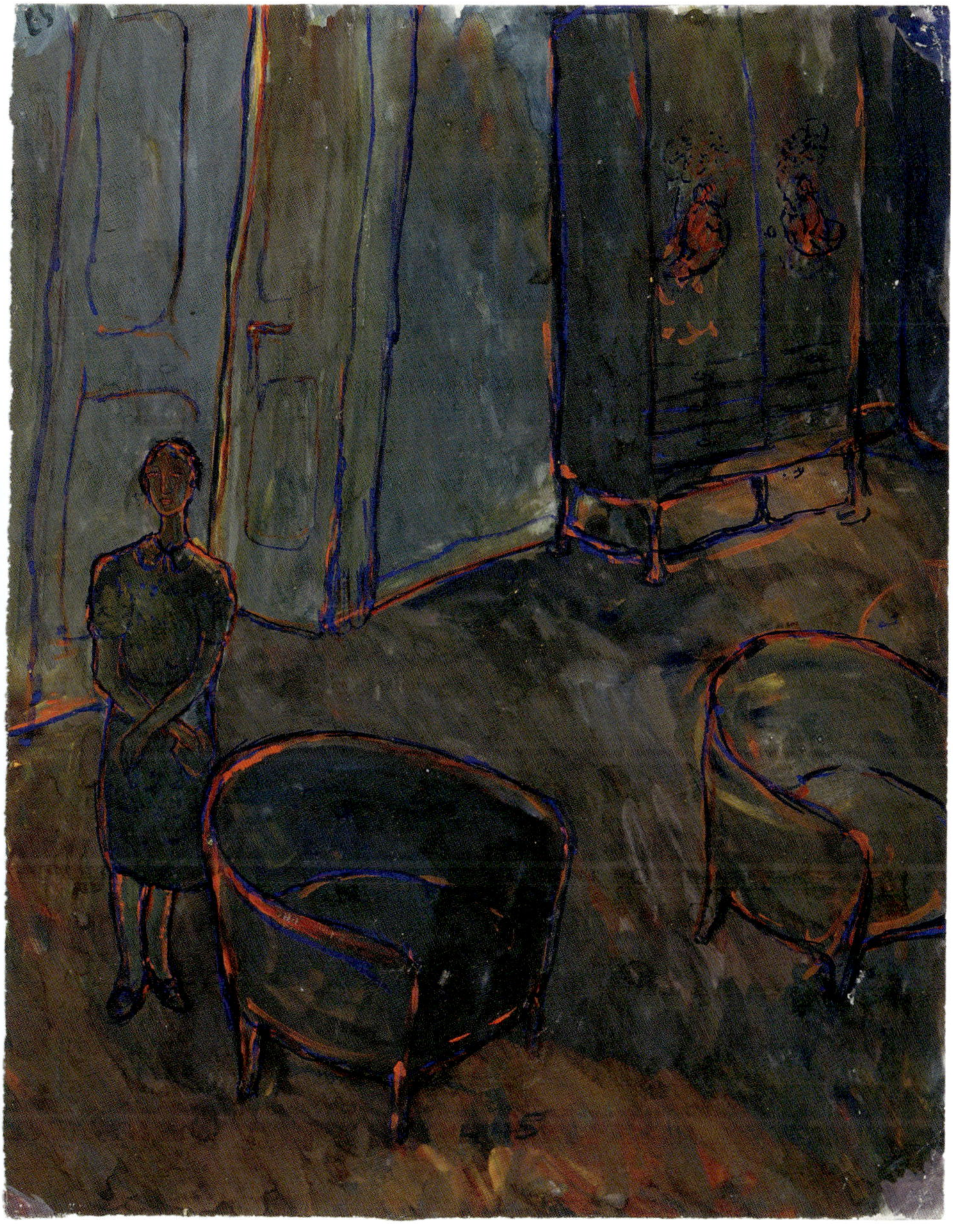

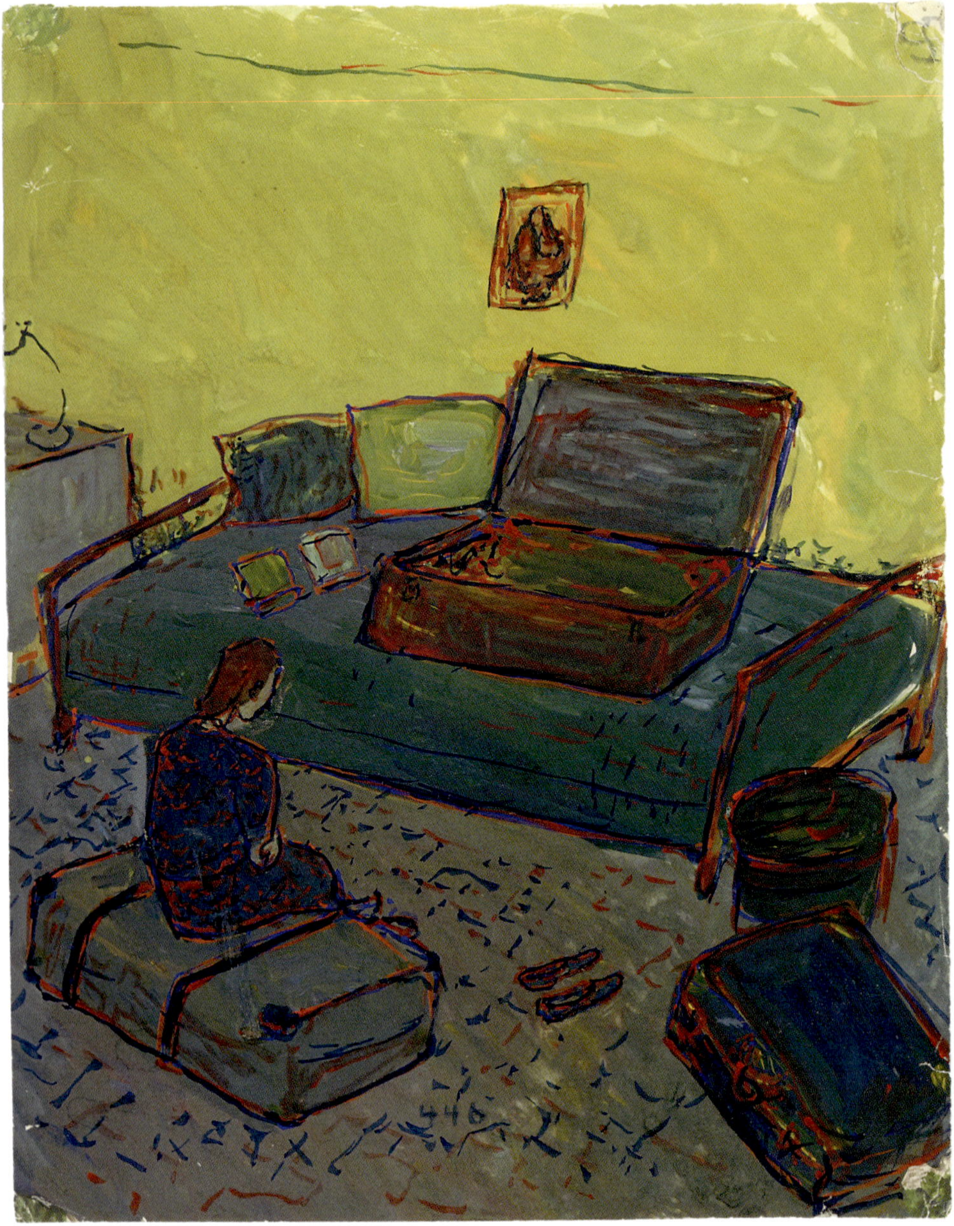

(bottom)

PARENTS
"Hurry up now. We have to leave, or we'll be late."

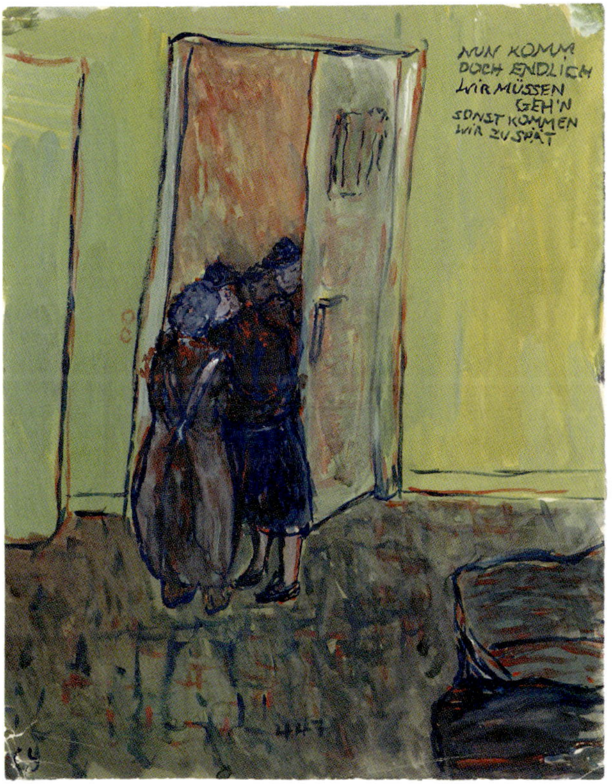

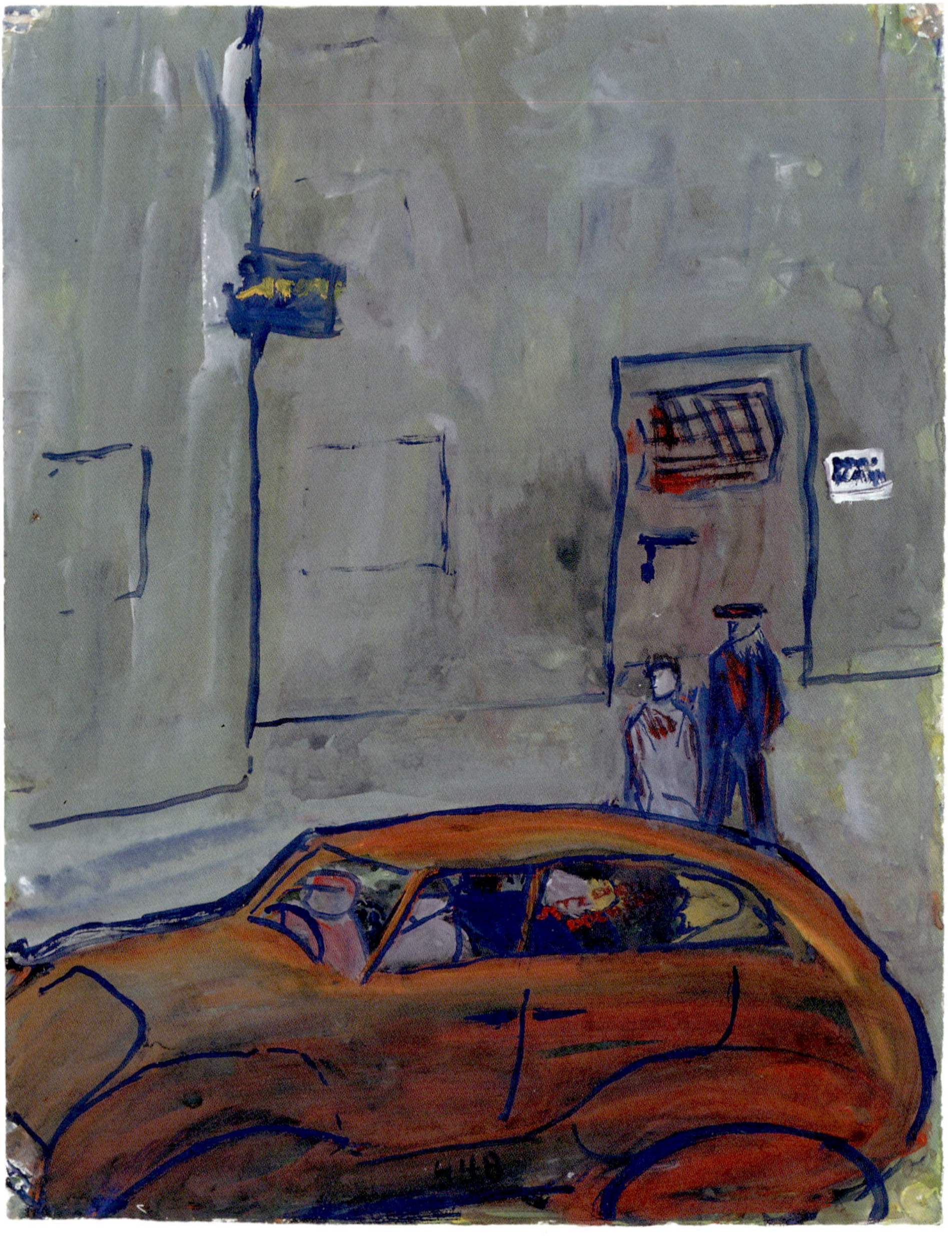

(opposite)

PAULINKA
"Please sit down now!"

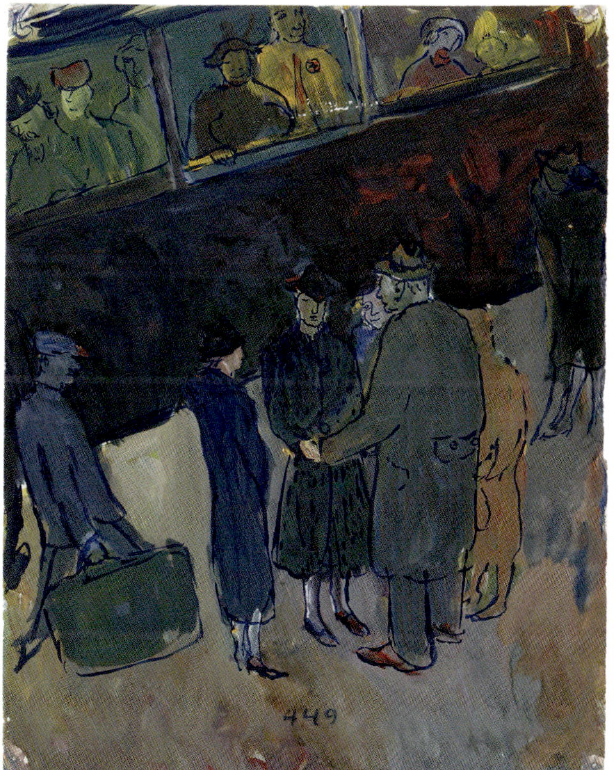

(opposite)

PARENTS
"You'd better get on the train now."

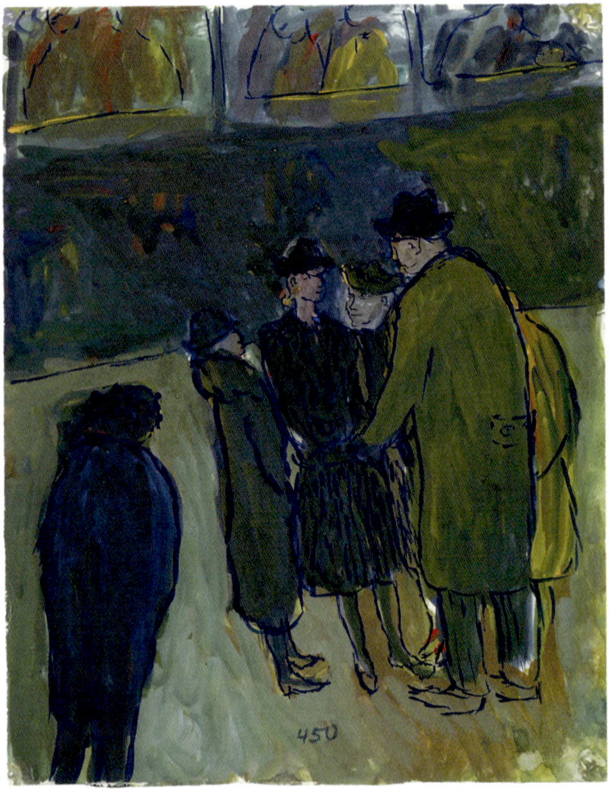

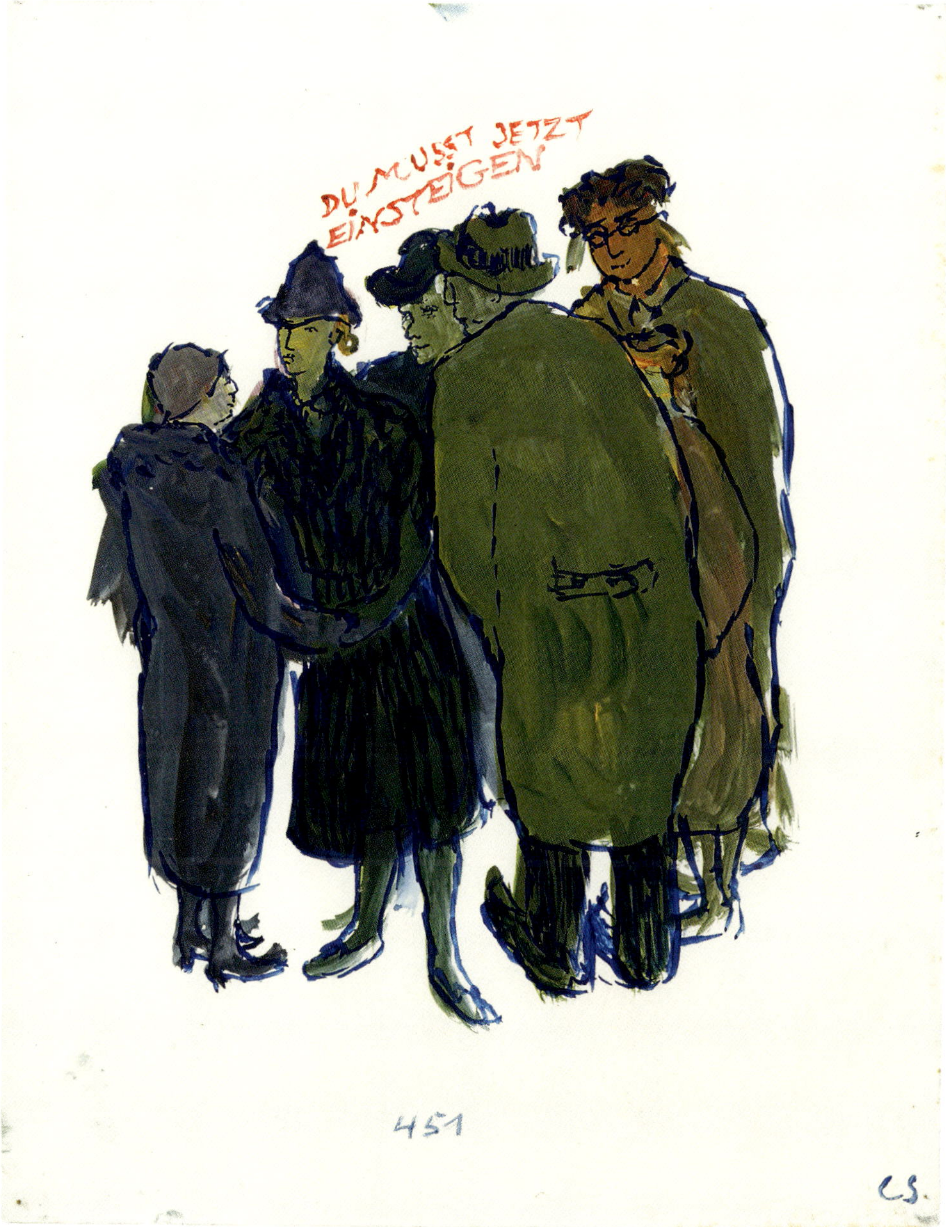
DU MUSST JETZT
EINSTEIGEN
451
CS.

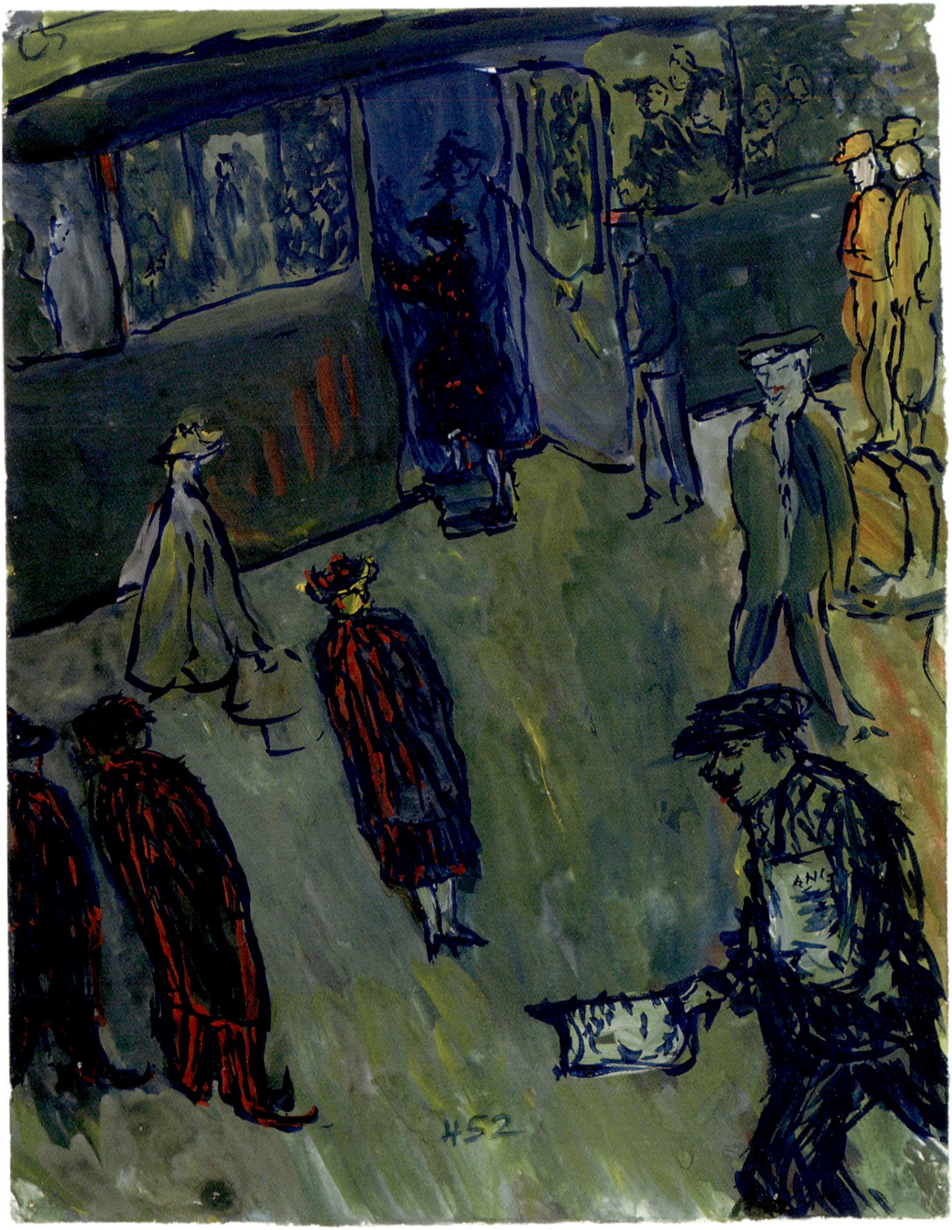

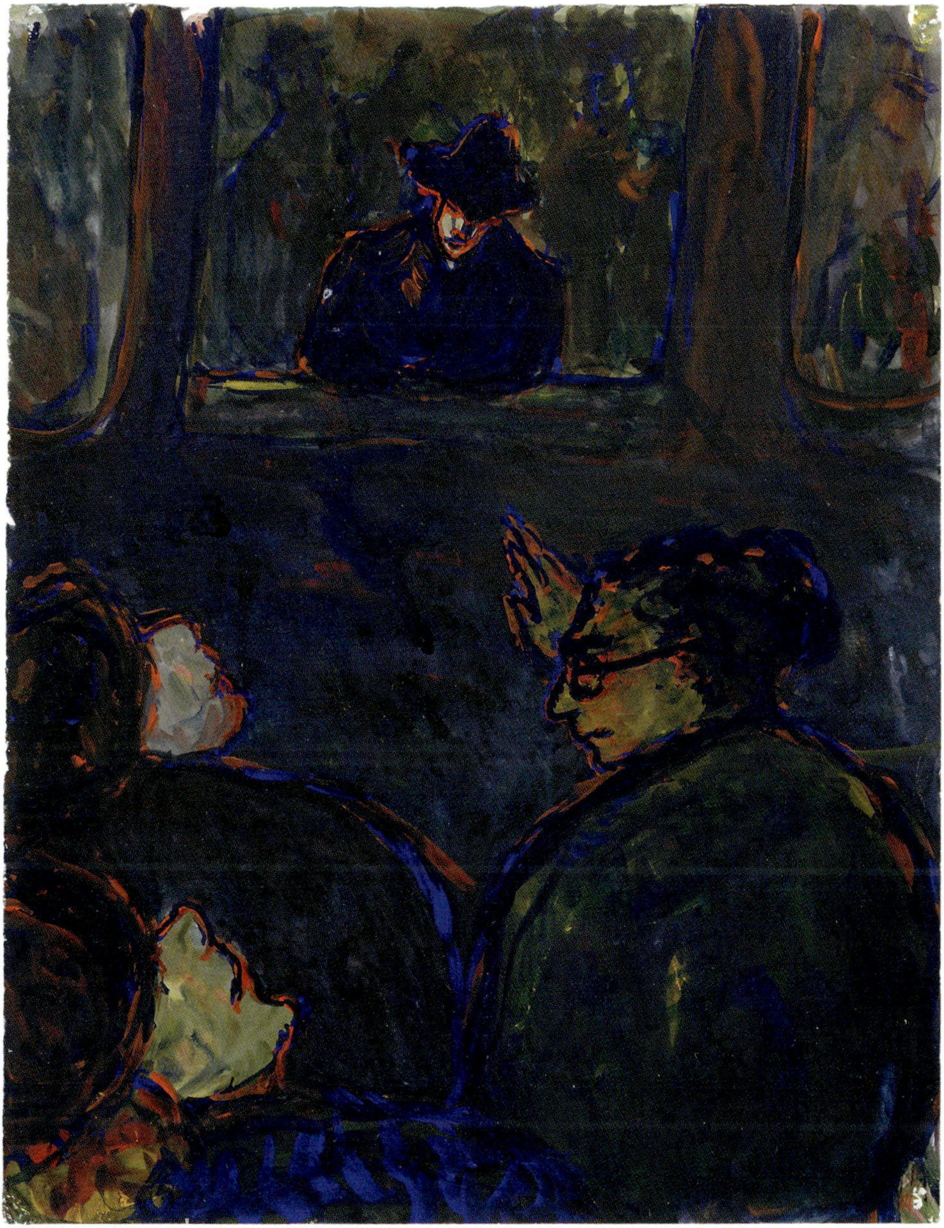

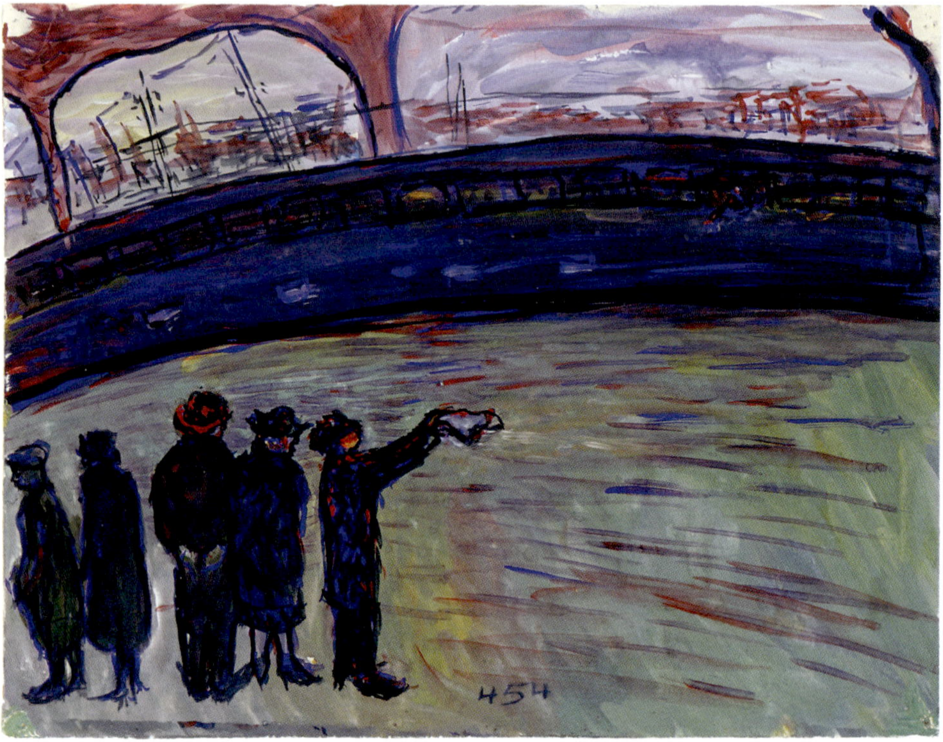
454

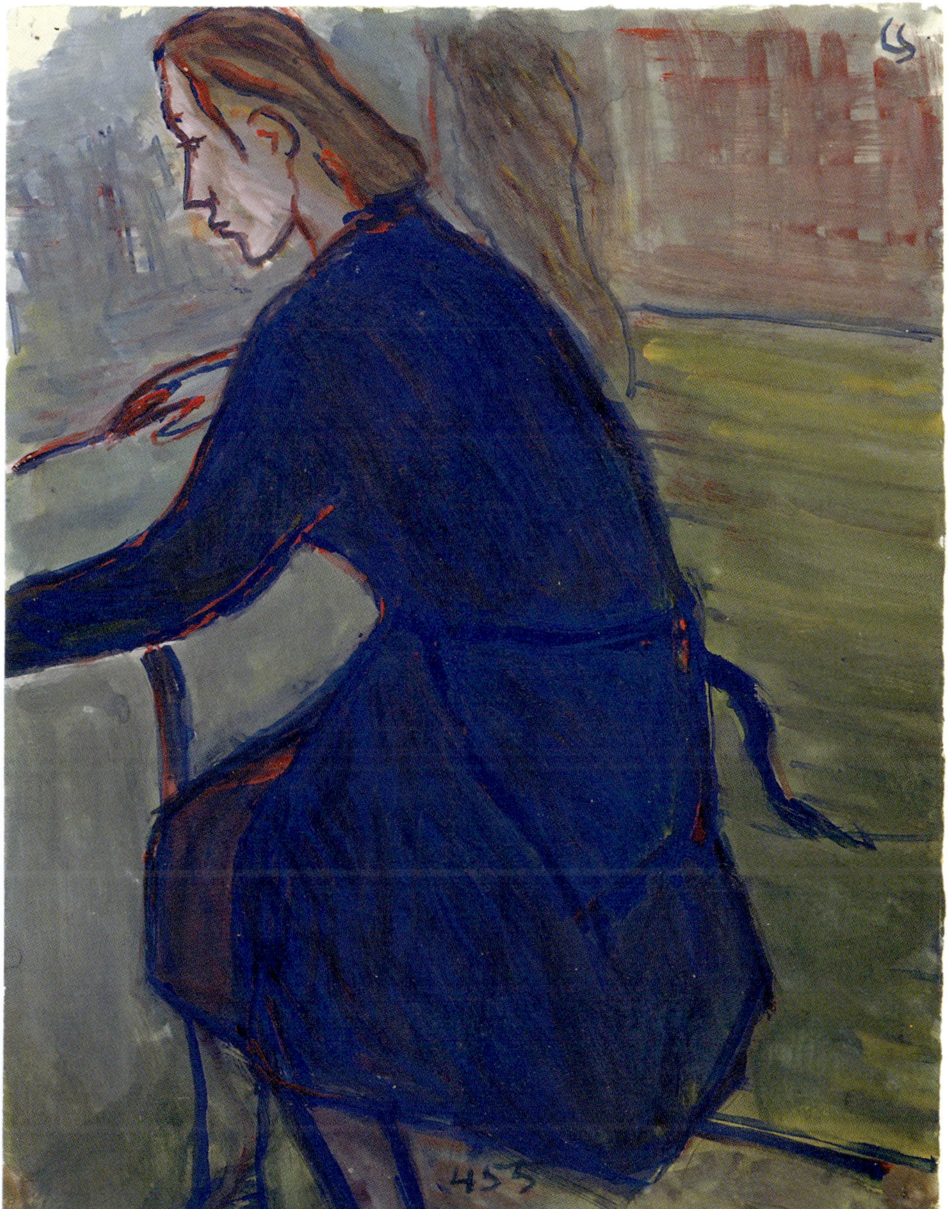
455

EPILOGUE

EPILOGUE

High on a cliff grow pepper trees — softly the wind stirs the small silvery leaves. Far below, foam dissolves — in the infinite span of the sea. Foams, dreams — my dreams on a blue surface. What makes you shape and reshape yourselves anew and brightly from so much pain and suffering. Who gave you the right?

Dream, speak to me — and whose servant are you? —
Why are you rescuing me?

High upon a cliff grow pepper trees.
Softly the wind stirs the small silvery leaves.

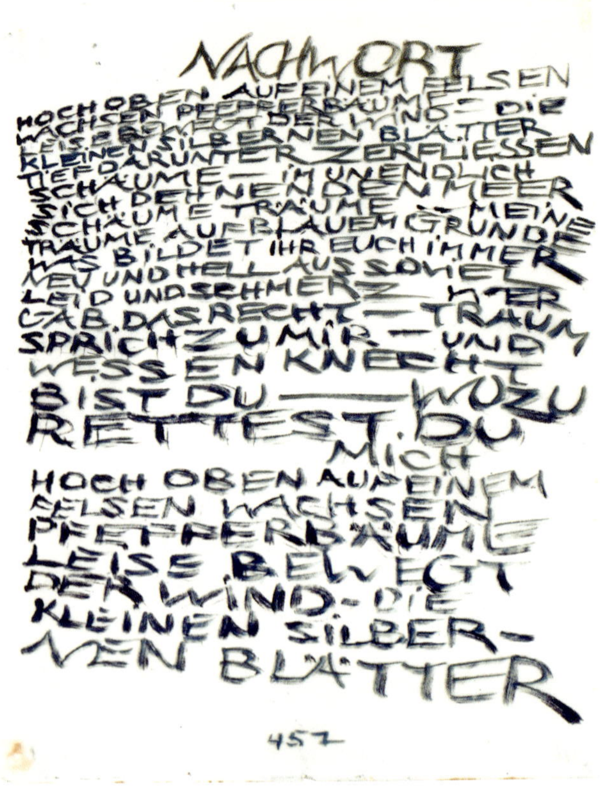

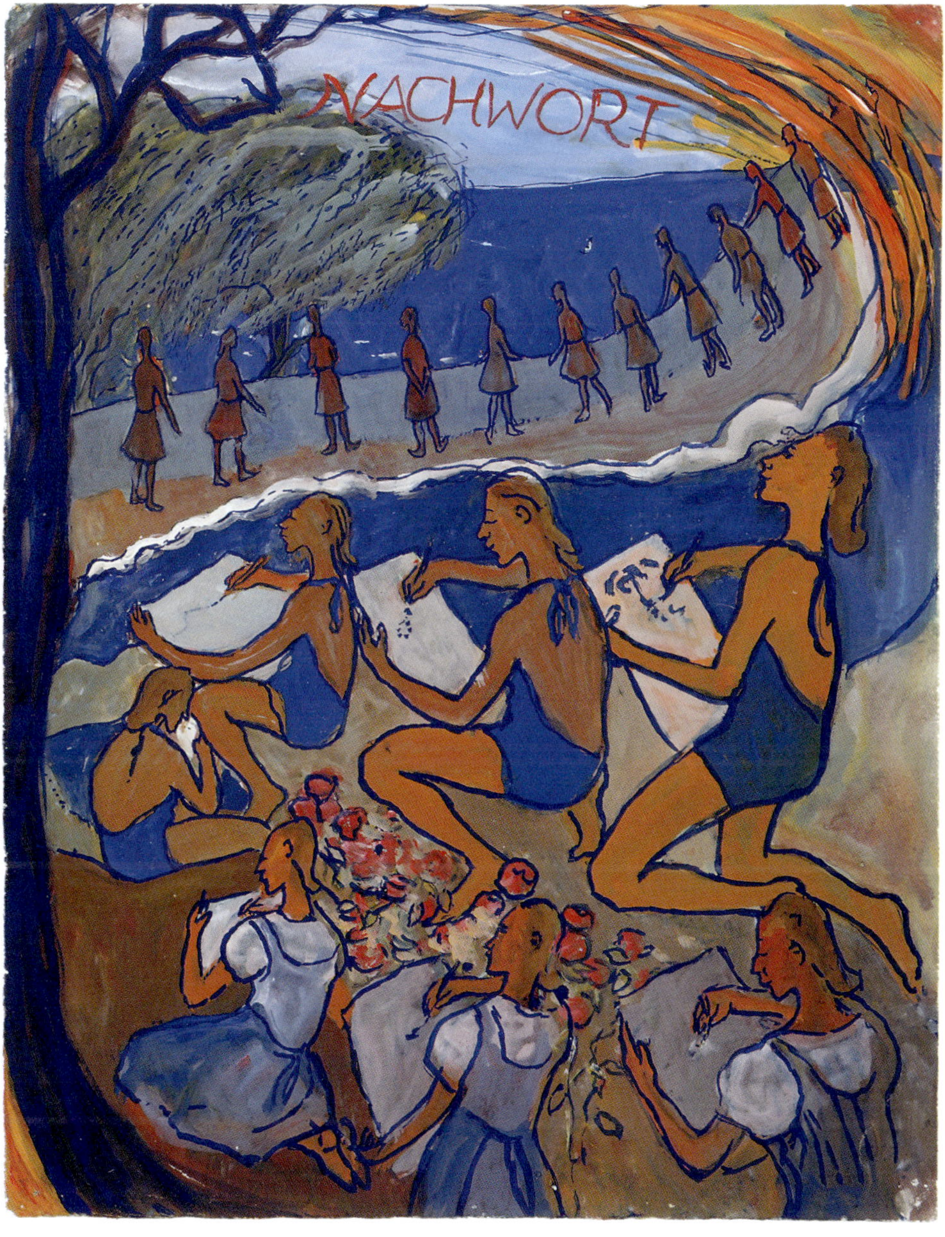
NACHWORT

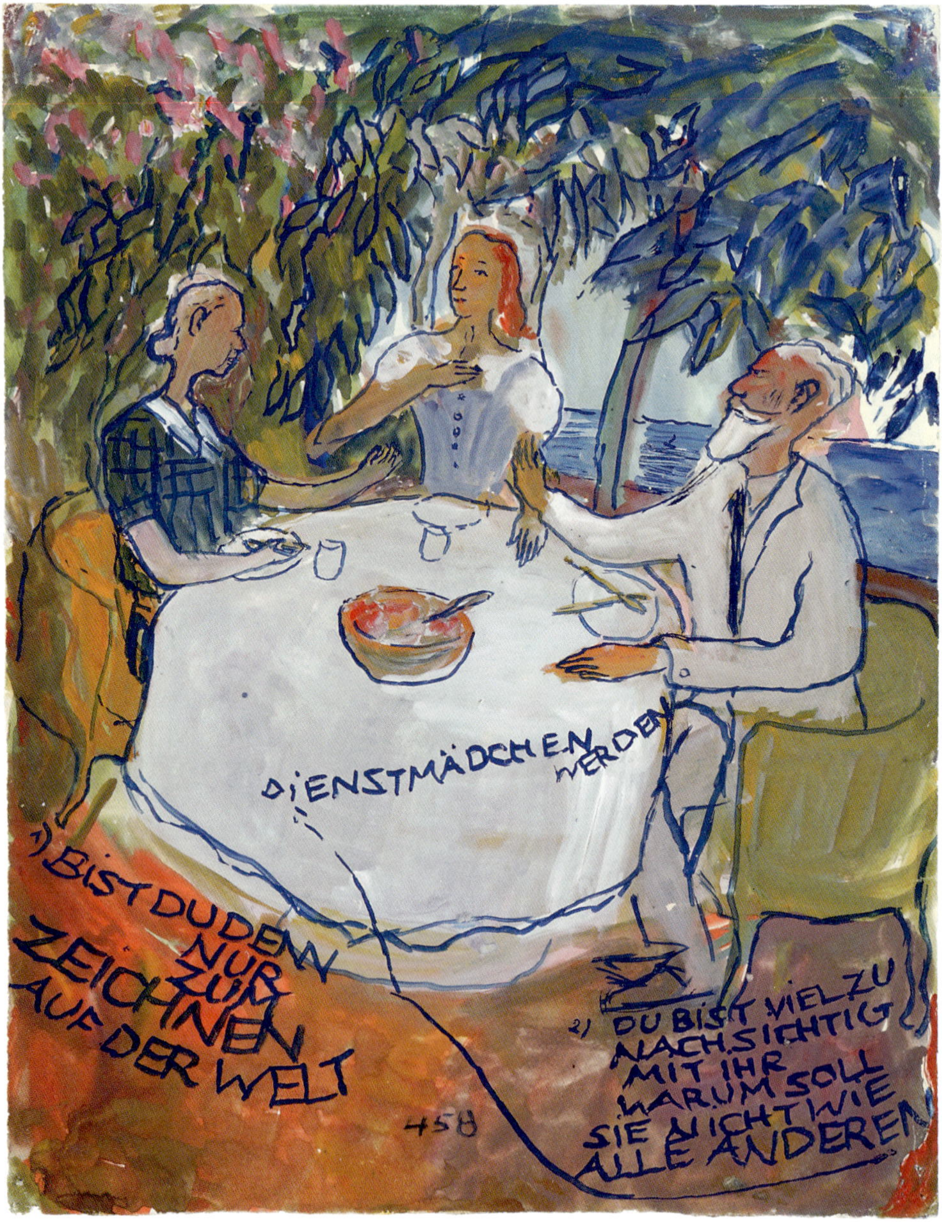
DIENSTMÄDCHEN WERDEN
1) BIST DU DENN NUR ZUM ZEICHNEN AUF DER WELT
2) DU BIST VIEL ZU NACHSICHTIG MIT IHR WARUM SOLL SIE NICHT WIE ALLE ANDEREN
458

(opposite)

GRANDMOTHER
"Are you here in the world only to draw?"

GRANDFATHER
"You are much too lenient with her.
Why shouldn't she become a maid like
all the others?"

(bottom)

"Just look at her. Is she not already
the personification of melancholy?"

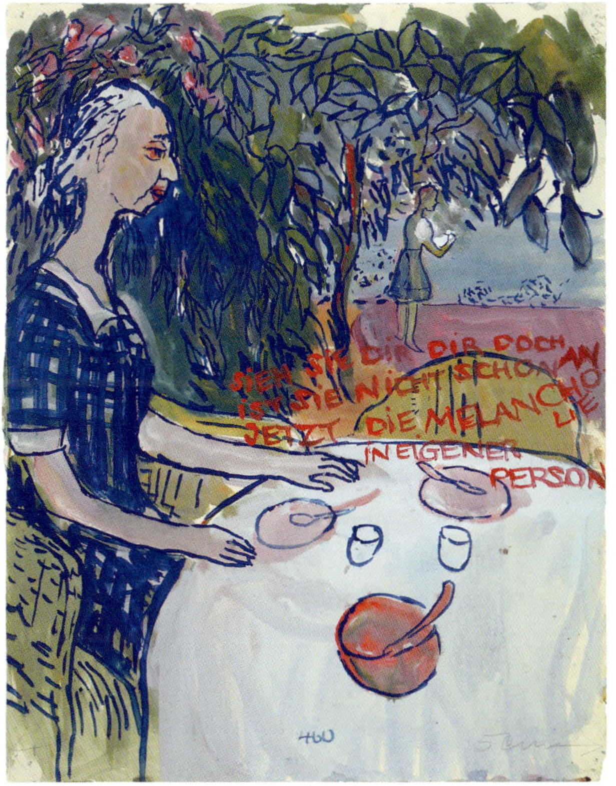

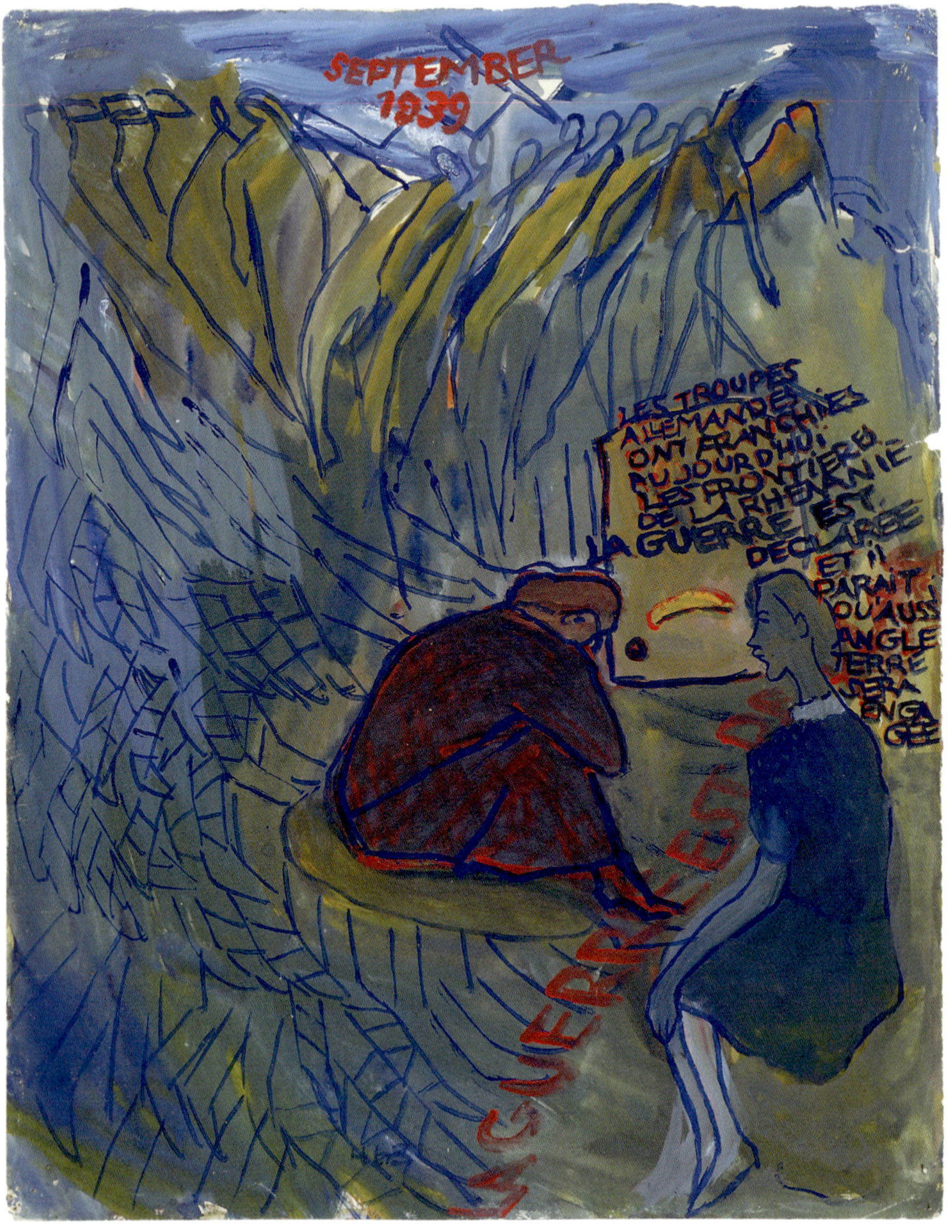
SEPTEMBER
1939
LES TROUPES
ALLEMANDES
ONT FRANCHIES
AUJOURDHUI
LES FRONTIERES
DE LA RHENANIE
LA GUERRE EST
DECLAREE
ET IL
PARAIT
QU'AUSS
ANGLE
TERRE
SERA
ENGA
GEE

(opposite)

SEPTEMBER 1939
LA GUERRE EST DÉCLARÉE

"Les troupes allemandes ont franchi aujourd'hui les frontières de la Rhénanie. La guerre est déclarée et il paraît qu'aussi Angleterre sera engagée."

(bottom)

Heute Nacht oder nie
[Tonight or never].

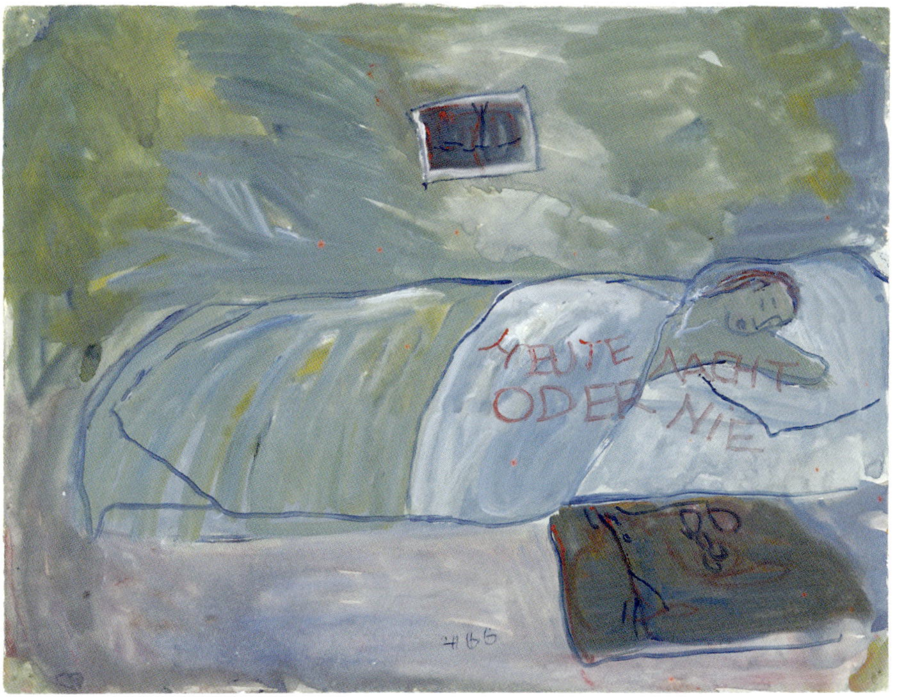

(bottom)

Old Mrs Knarre tries to hang herself in the bathroom. The awful pain that has pursued her throughout her life but had been kept somewhat in abeyance seems to have resurfaced into full consciousness as a result of the raging war, and she feels how her sharp intellect and her self-control, which had made her life worth living, is breaking up against a greater force. The fear of the onset of madness drives her to this decision.

(opposite)

"She is not dead, thank God."

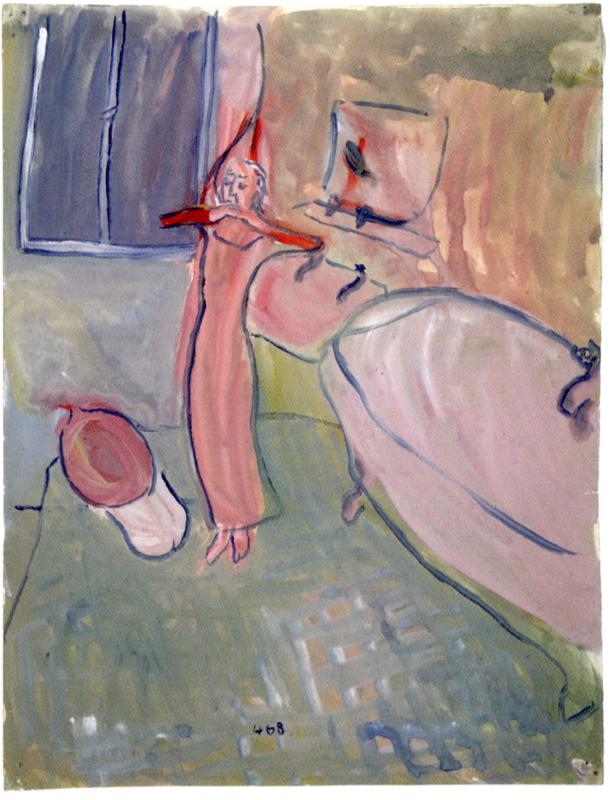

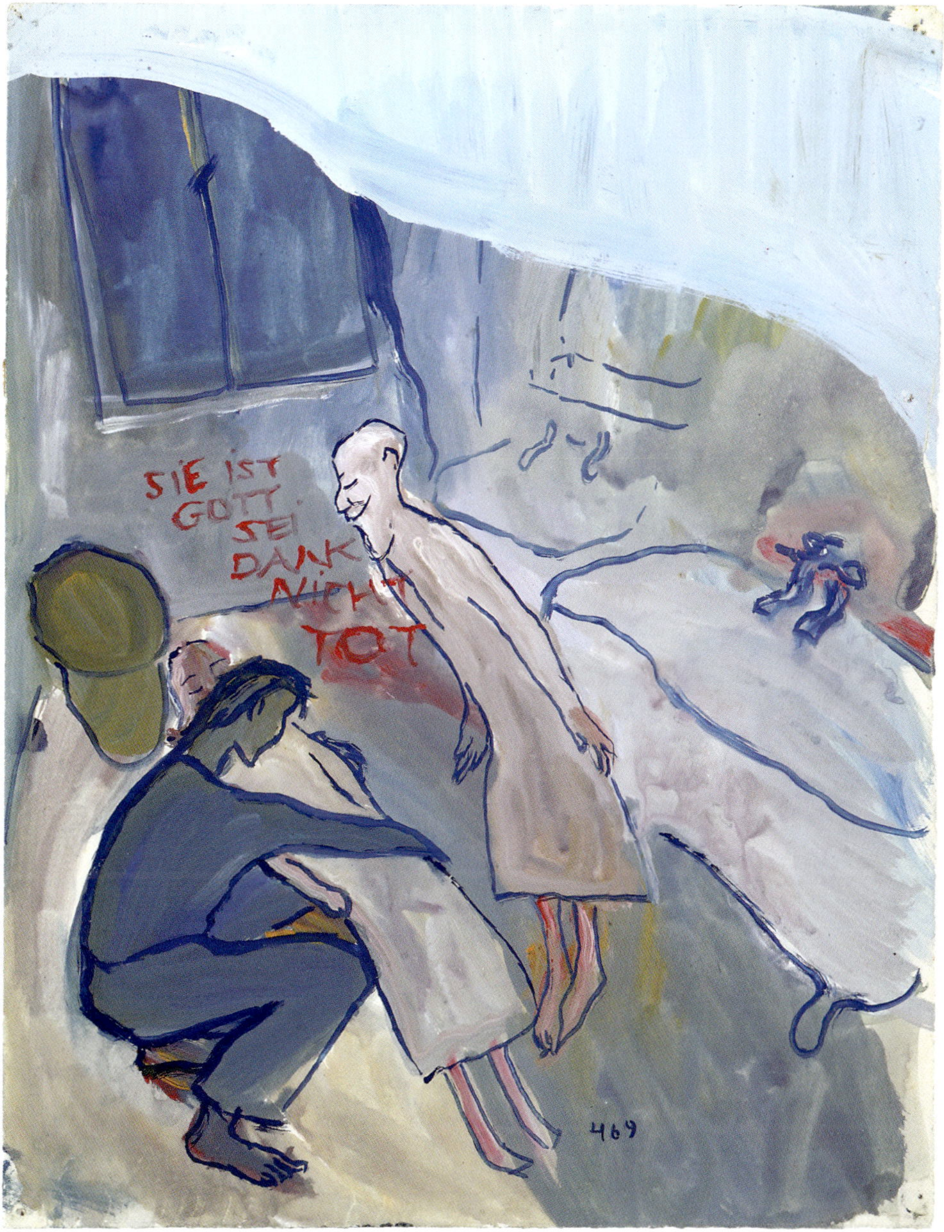
SIE IST GOTT SEI DANK NICHT TOT
469

Charlotte is altogether paralysed with shock and must first lie down stretched out.

CHARLOTTE
"After a life like that, to strangle one-self in the bathroom, it's too horrible. Oh God, I feel sick."

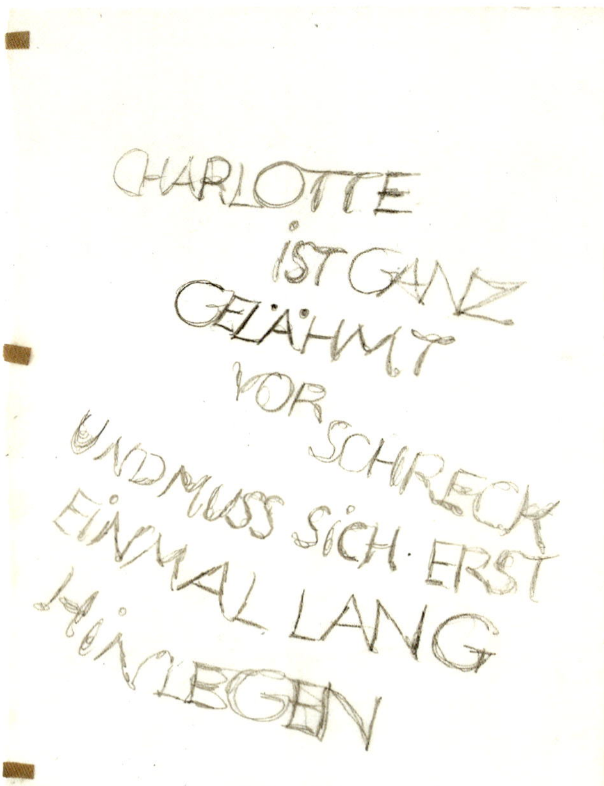

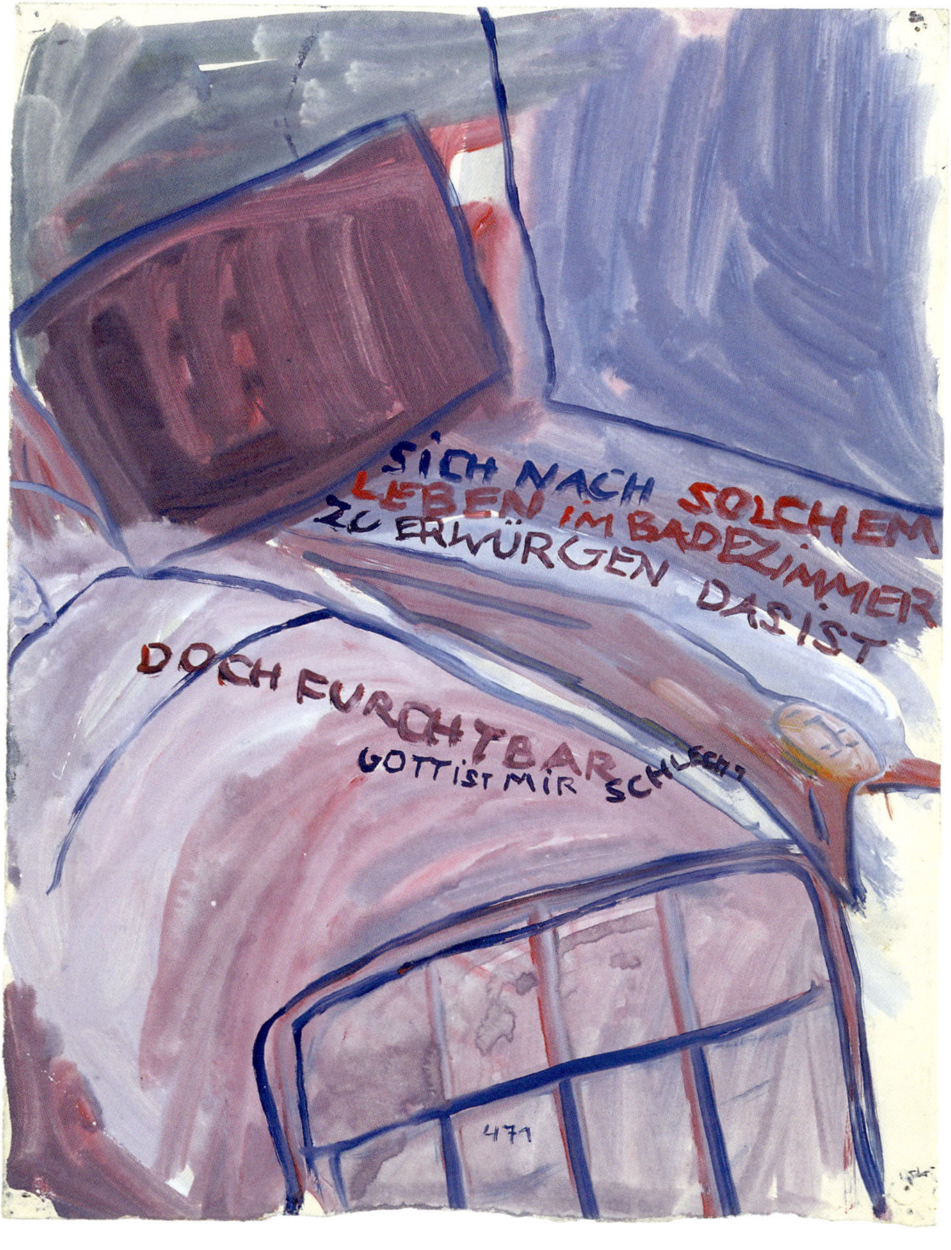
SICH NACH SOLCHEM
LEBEN IM BADEZIMMER
ZU ERWÜRGEN DAS IST
DOCH FURCHTBAR
GOTT IST MIR SCHLECHT
471

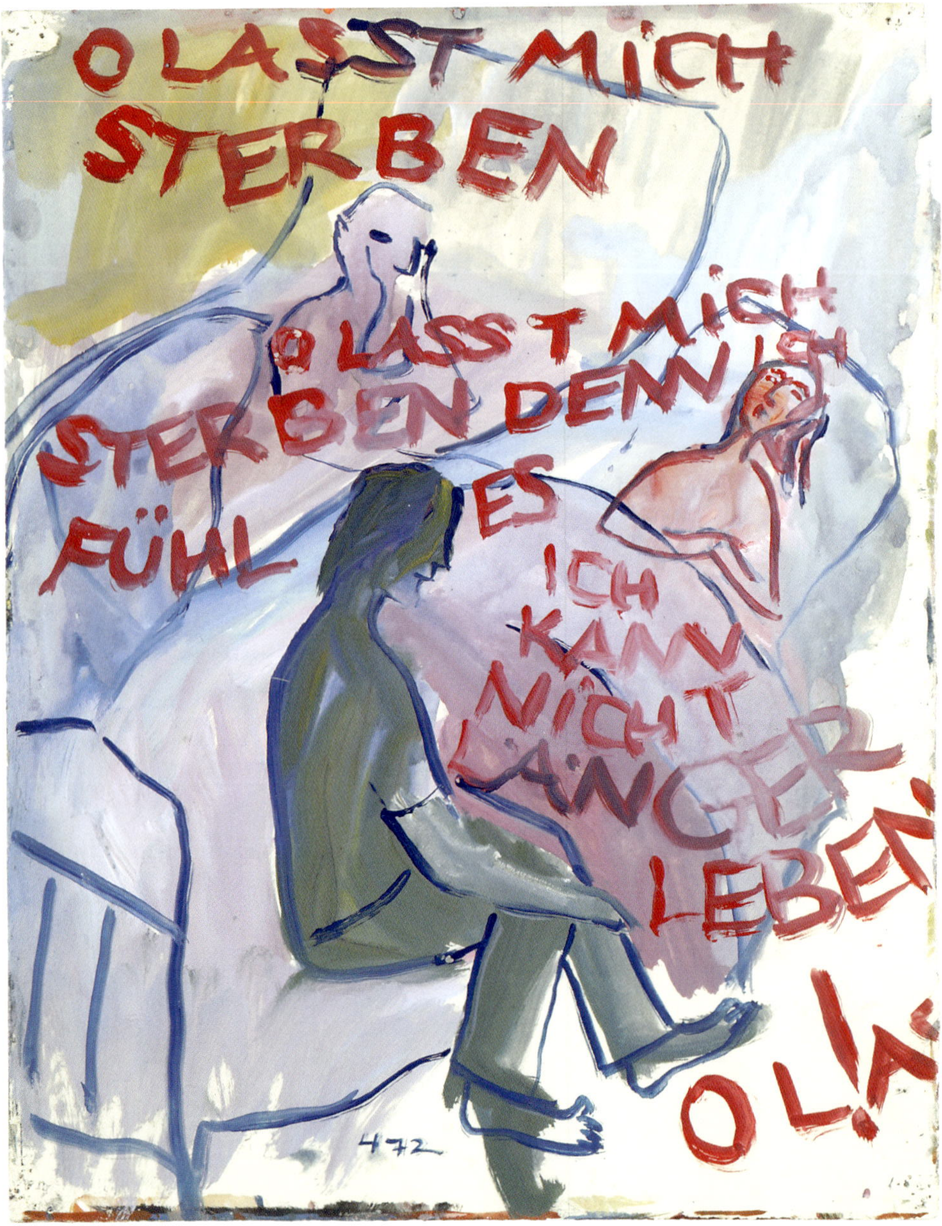
O LASST MICH
STERBEN
O LASST MICH
STERBEN DENN ICH
FÜHL ES
ICH
KANN
NICHT
LÄNGER
LEBEN
O!A
472

But now, following famous examples, she forces herself to go completely out of herself and to give all her attention to Grandma Knarre. Then she remembers Daberlohn and starts her therapy.

GRANDMOTHER
"Oh, let me die, let me die, since
I feel it, I can't go on living!"

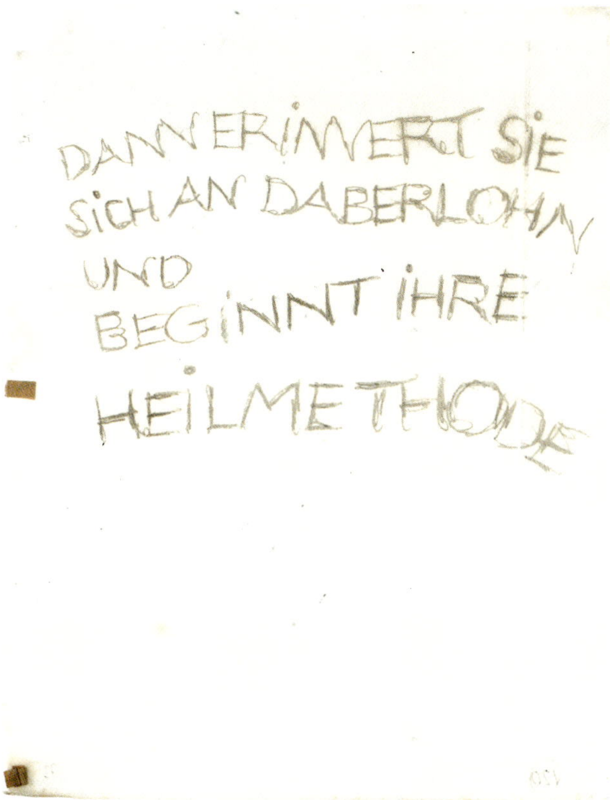

(bottom)

CHARLOTTE
"Grandma, look how the sun is shining."

GRANDMOTHER
"I see how the sun is shining."

(opposite)

CHARLOTTE
"Look at the flowers in the meadow. So much beauty, so much joy. Look at the mountains up there, so much sun, so much light."

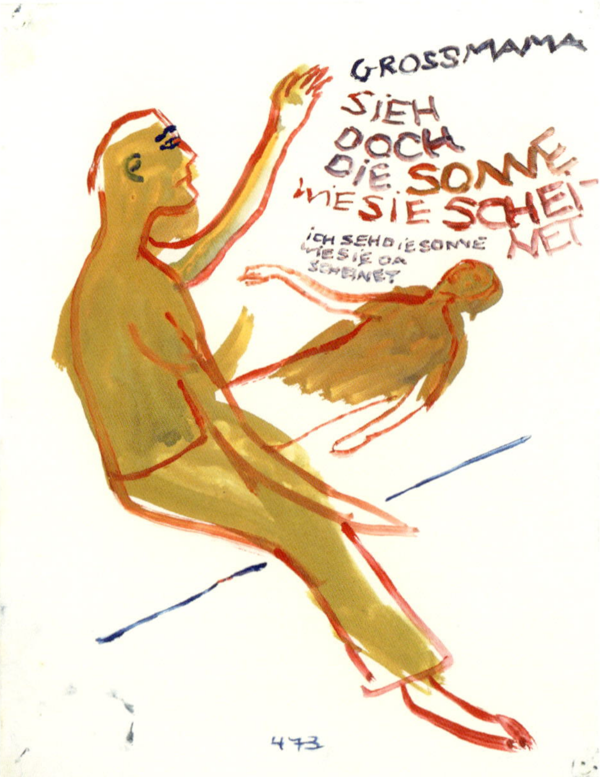

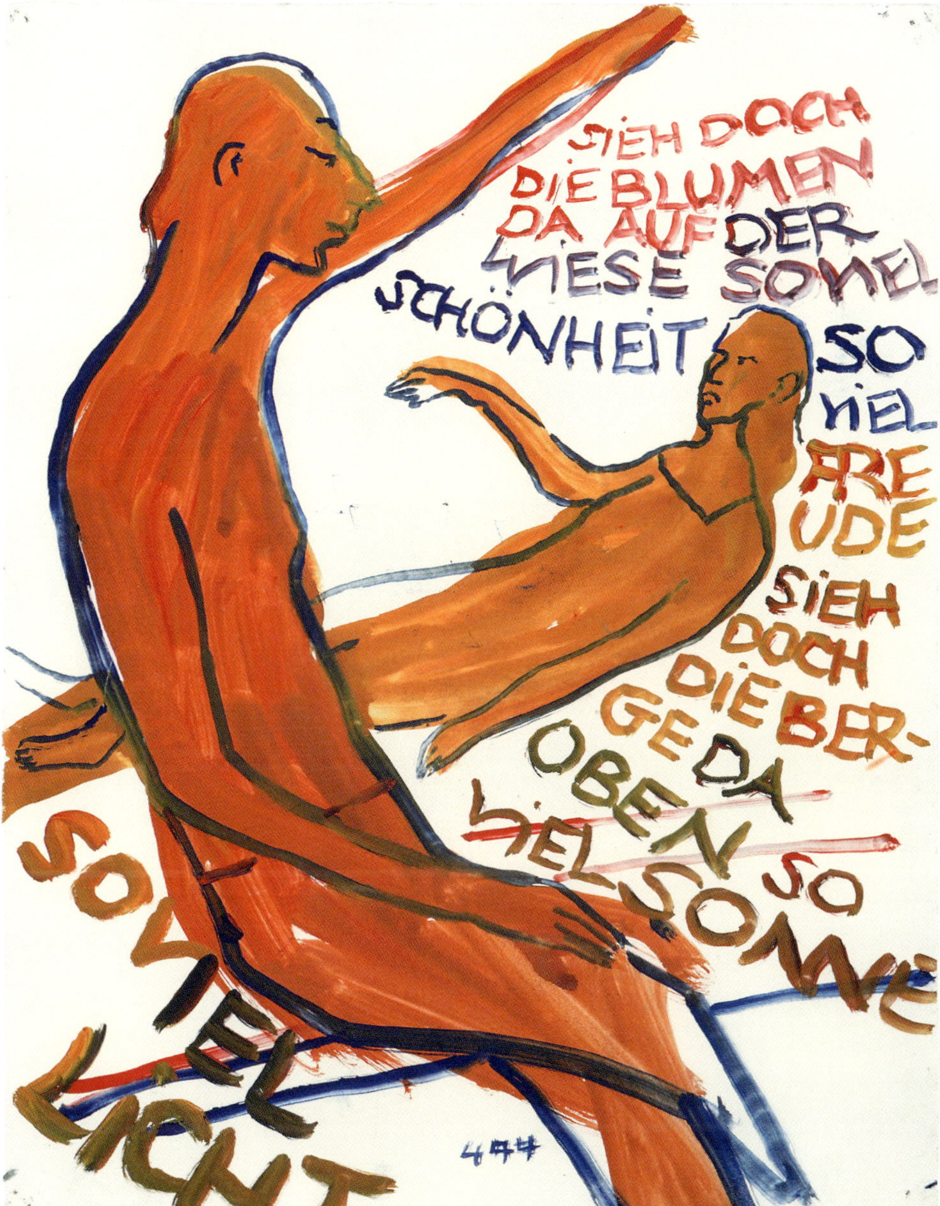
SIEH DOCH
DIE BLUMEN
DA AUF DER
WIESE SOVIEL
SCHÖNHEIT SO
VIEL
FREUDE
SIEH
DOCH
DIE BER-
GE DA
OBEN SO
VIEL SONNE
SO VIEL
LICHT
444

(bottom)

GRANDMOTHER
"I see the flowers blooming, so much beauty there in the meadow. I see the mountains up there, so much sun, so much light."

(opposite)

CHARLOTTE
"And our path leads us ever higher and ever purer. People dancing, can you hear them singing. Joy, joy everywhere."

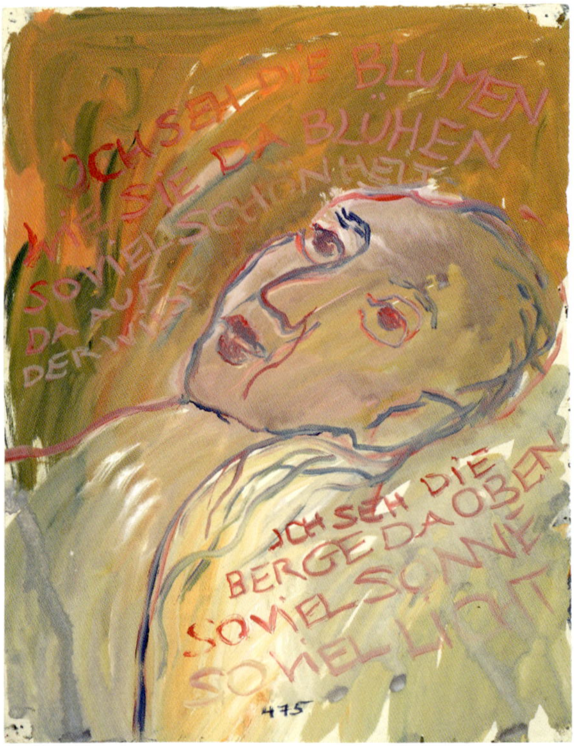

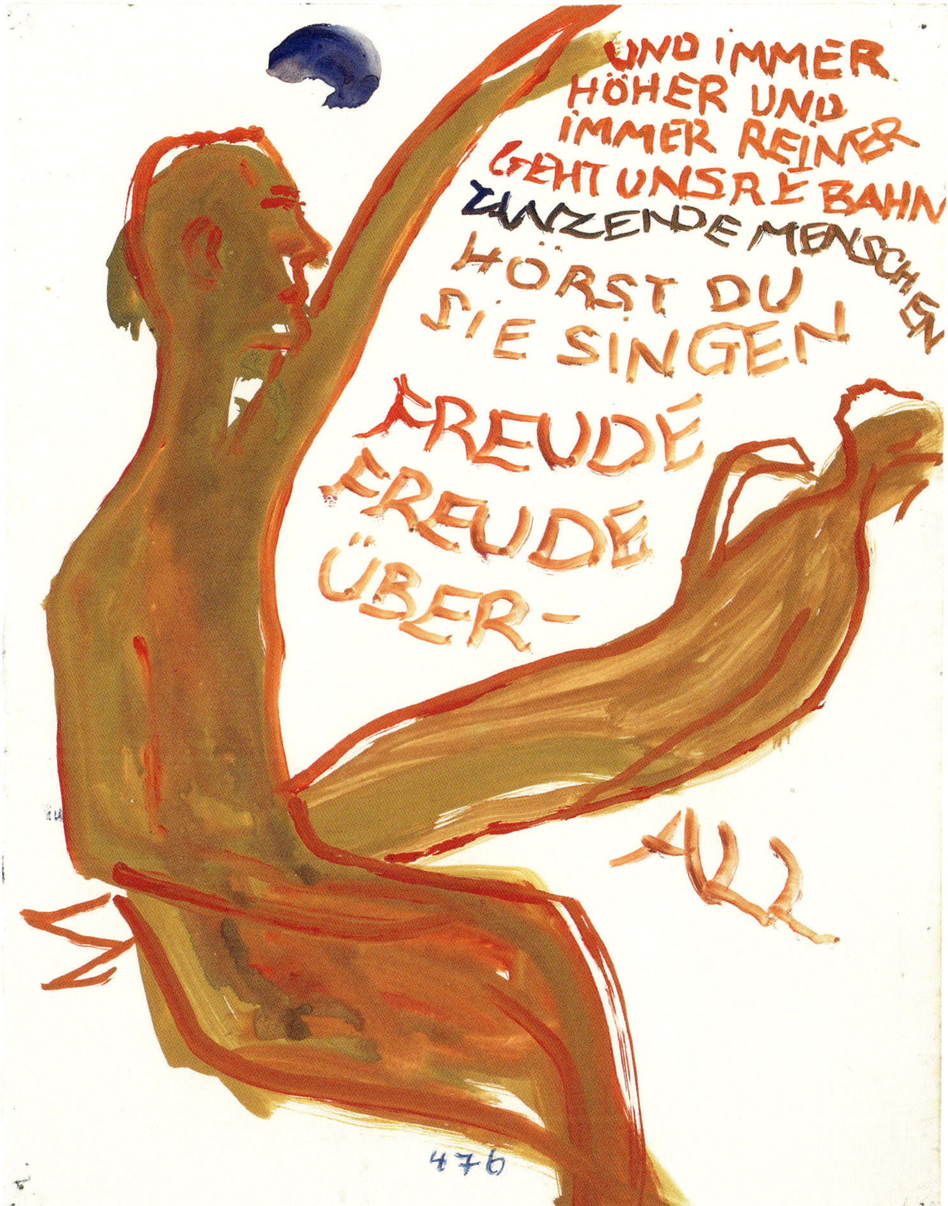
UND IMMER
HÖHER UND
IMMER REINER
GEHT UNSRE BAHN
TANZENDE MENSCHEN
HÖRST DU
SIE SINGEN
FREUDE
FREUDE
ÜBER-
ALL
476

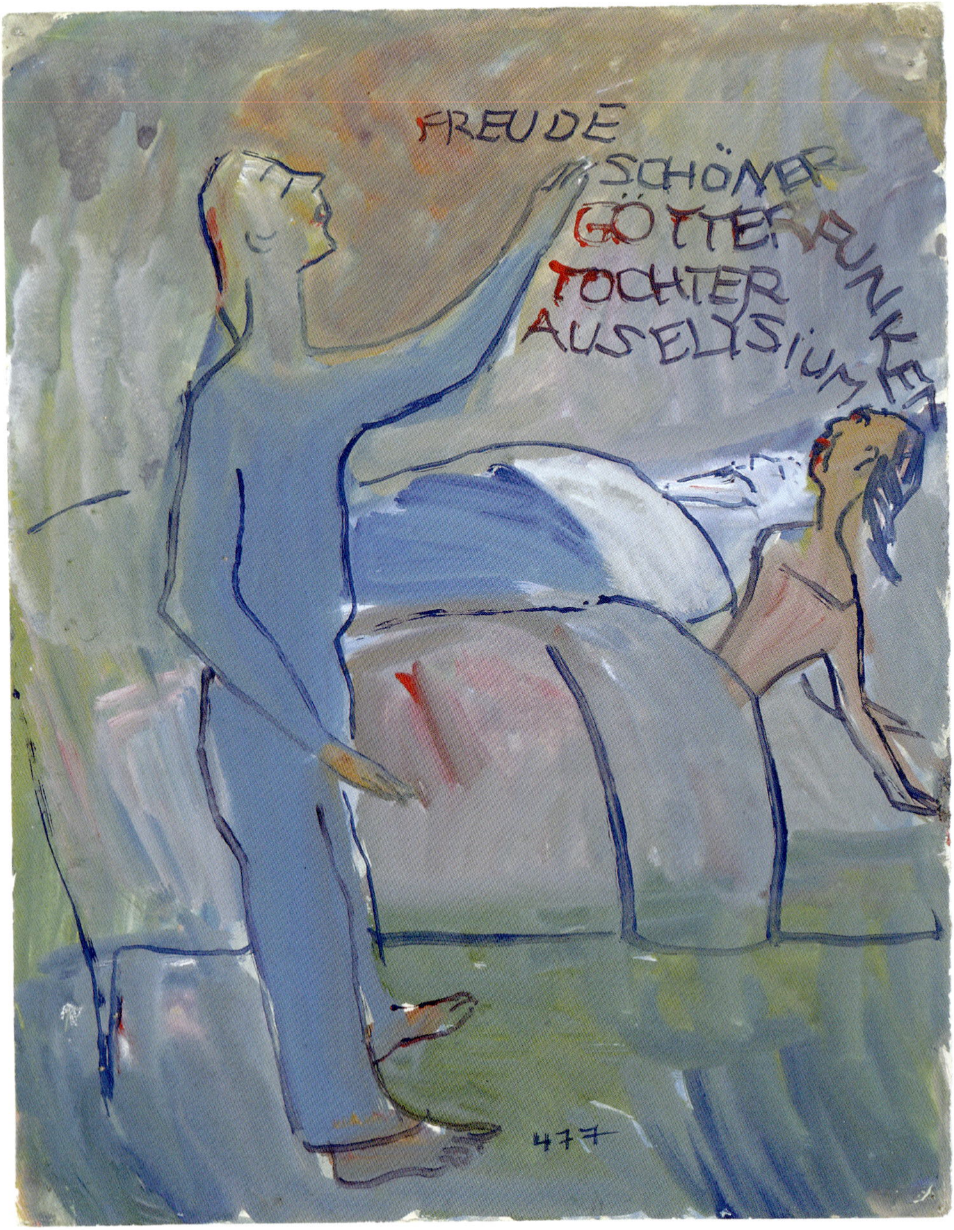
FREUDE
SCHÖNER
GÖTTERFUNKEN
TOCHTER
AUS ELYSIUM
477

(opposite)

CHARLOTTE
Freude, schöner Götterfunken,
Tochter aus Elysium
[Joy, beautiful sparks of the Gods,
daughter of Elysium].

(bottom)

GRANDFATHER
"Your mother first tried it with poison, then she threw herself out the window. Your Aunt Charlotte drowned herself, but the worst case was your Grandma's mother. For eight years she tried every day to escape the care of two nurses – in order to take her life – "

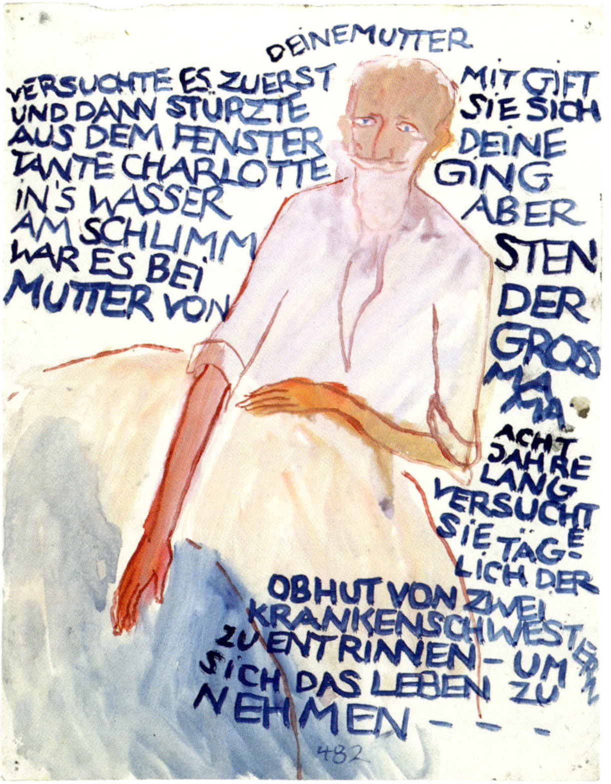

(opposite)

“It all began with her brother. He was a nice fellow, very talented, and was studying law when he began to show signs of beginning madness, expressed chiefly by unmotivated laughter. For a whole year he was kept completely isolated with a guard in your great grandmother’s garden house (as his doctor and brother-in-law I was his only visitor). In those days we had just been married, and you can imagine how it upset your grandmother was, who was very close to her brother. Then he recovered and could finish his studies. The doctors thought he should get married, and that was the beginning of the tragedy.”

(page 546)

“Your great grandmother who, although she was a very strict woman, attached great importance to class and wealth, forced him to marry a girl from a very rich family and he became very unhappy with her. He spent his married life more in our home than in his – until he finally drowned himself.

Needless to say, his mother reproached herself bitterly and came to the decision, which was accompanied by mental illness, to take her own life. We engaged two nurses who were forbidden to leave her alone for a single second, and we did succeed in seeing her die a natural death – from over-exertion. But the turbulence of those eight years – during which our children were born – was, especially for Grandma, almost beyond description.”

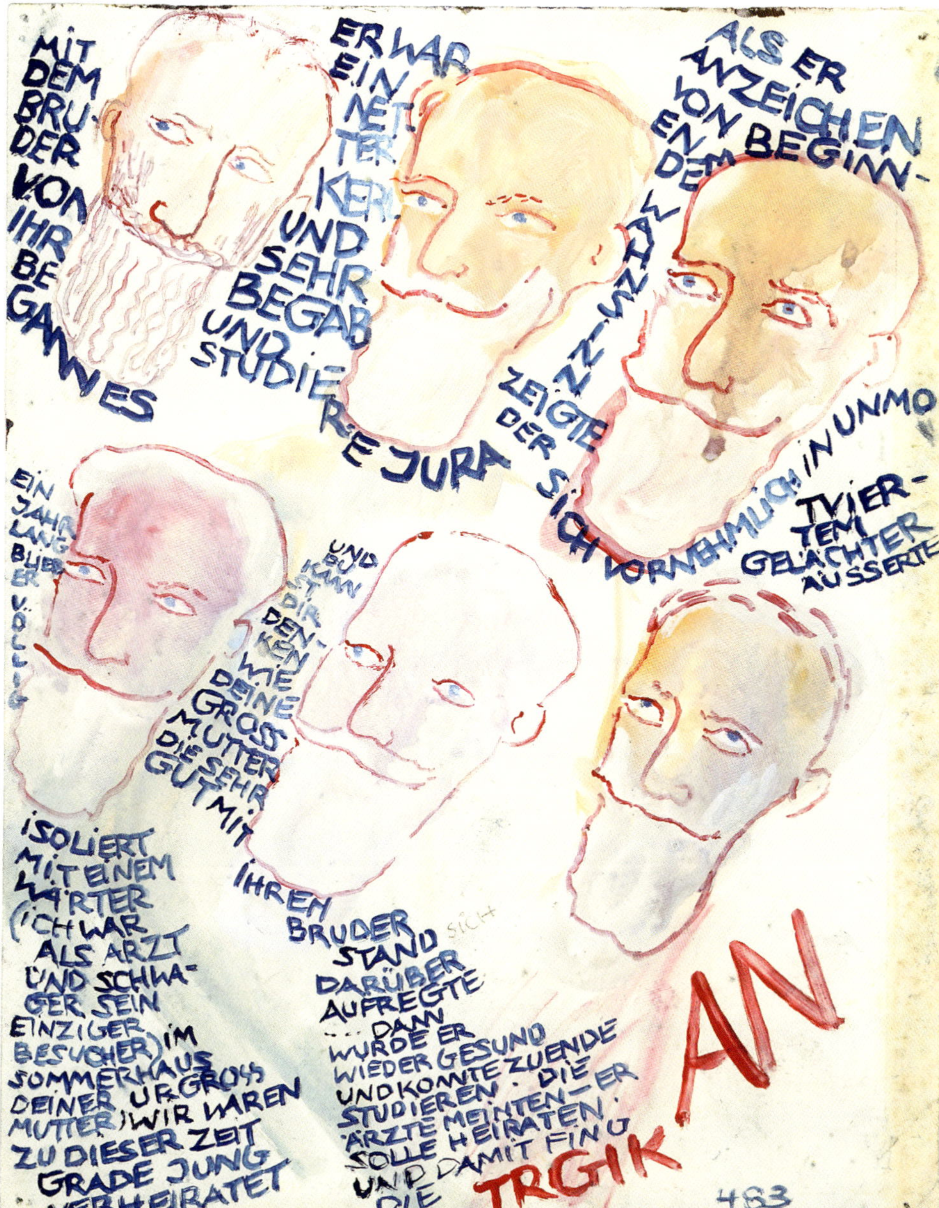
MIT DEM BRUDER VON IHR BEGANN ES
ER WAR EIN NETTER KERL UND SEHR BEGABT UND STUDIERTE JURA
ALS ER ANZEICHEN VON BEGINNENDEM WAHNSINN ZEIGTE DER SICH VORNEHMLICH IN UNMOTIVIERTEM GELÄCHTER ÄUSSERTE
EIN JAHR LANG BLIEB ER VÖLLIG
ISOLIERT MIT EINEM WÄRTER (ICH WAR ALS ARZT UND SCHWAGER SEIN EINZIGER BESUCHER) IM SOMMERHAUS DEINER URGROSSMUTTER, WIR WAREN ZU DIESER ZEIT GRADE JUNG VERHEIRATET
UND DU KANNST DIR DENKEN WIE DEINE GROSSMUTTER DIE SEHR GUT MIT IHREN BRUDER STAND SICH DARÜBER AUFREGTE ... DANN WURDE ER GESUND WIEDER UND KONNTE ZUENDE STUDIEREN. DIE ÄRZTE MEINTEN – ER SOLLE HEIRATEN. UND DAMIT FING DIE
TRGIK AN
483

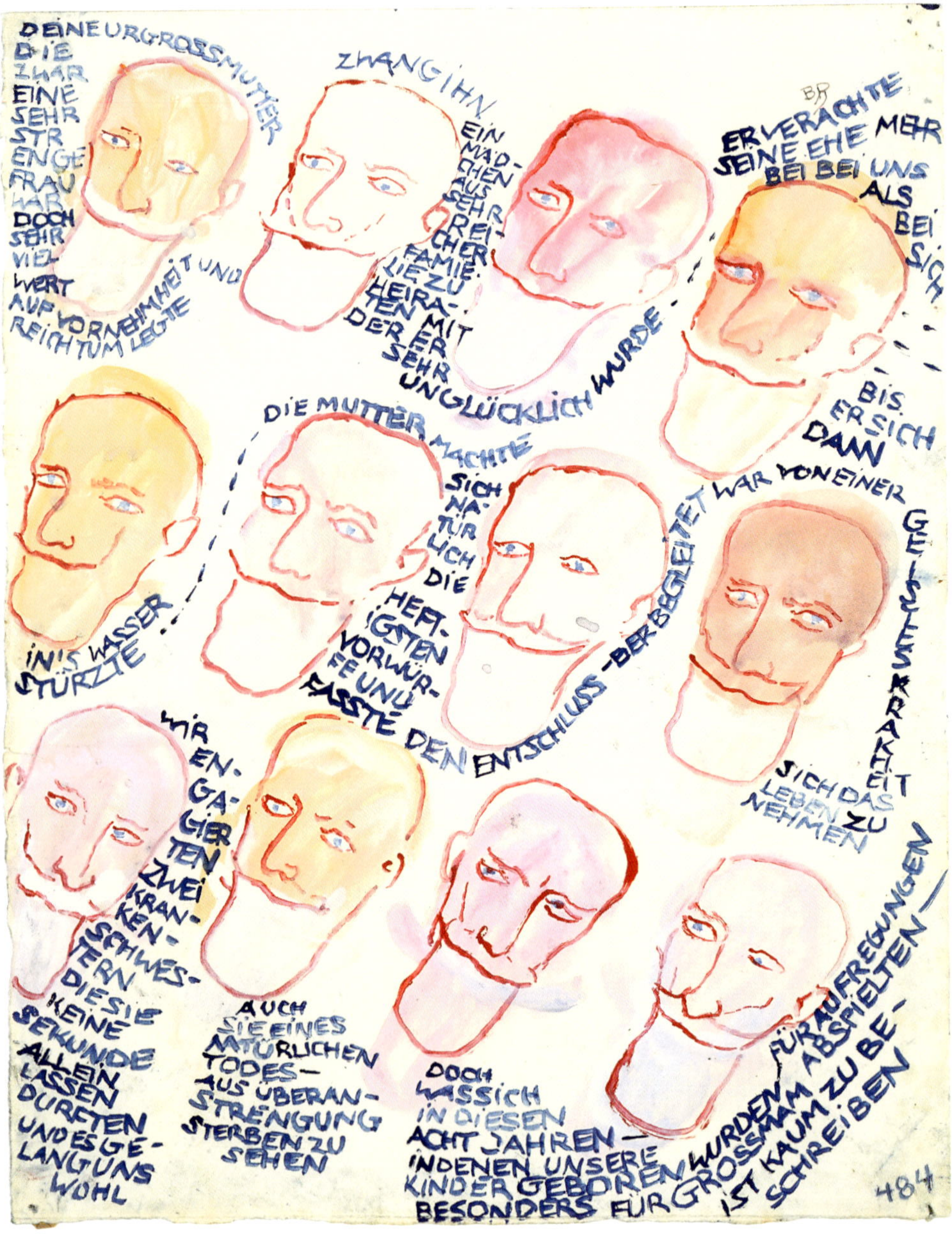
DEINE URGROSSMUTTER DIE ZWAR EINE SEHR STRENGE FRAU WAR DOCH SEHR VIEL WERT AUF VORNEHMHEIT UND REICHTUM LEGTE
ZWANG IHN EIN MÄDCHEN AUS SEHR REICHER FAMILIE ZU HEIRATEN MIT DER ER SEHR UNGLÜCKLICH WURDE
ER VERACHTETE SEINE EHE MEHR BEI BEI UNS ALS BEI SICH
BIS ER SICH DANN
IN'S WASSER STÜRZTE
DIE MUTTER MACHTE SICH NATÜRLICH DIE HEFTIGSTEN VORWÜRFE UND FASSTE DEN ENTSCHLUSS – DER BEGLEITET WAR VON EINER GEISTESKRAKHEIT
SICH DAS LEBEN ZU NEHMEN
WIR ENGAGIERTEN ZWEI KRANKENSCHWESTERN DIE SIE KEINE SEKUNDE ALLEIN LASSEN DURFTEN UND ES GELANG UNS WOHL
AUCH SIE EINES NATÜRLICHEN TODES – AUS ÜBERANSTRENGUNG STERBEN ZU SEHEN
DOCH WAS SICH IN DIESEN ACHT JAHREN – IN DENEN UNSERE KINDER GEBOREN WURDEN FÜR AUFREGUNGEN BESONDERS FÜR GROSSMAMA ABSPIELTEN – IST KAUM ZU BESCHREIBEN
BR
484

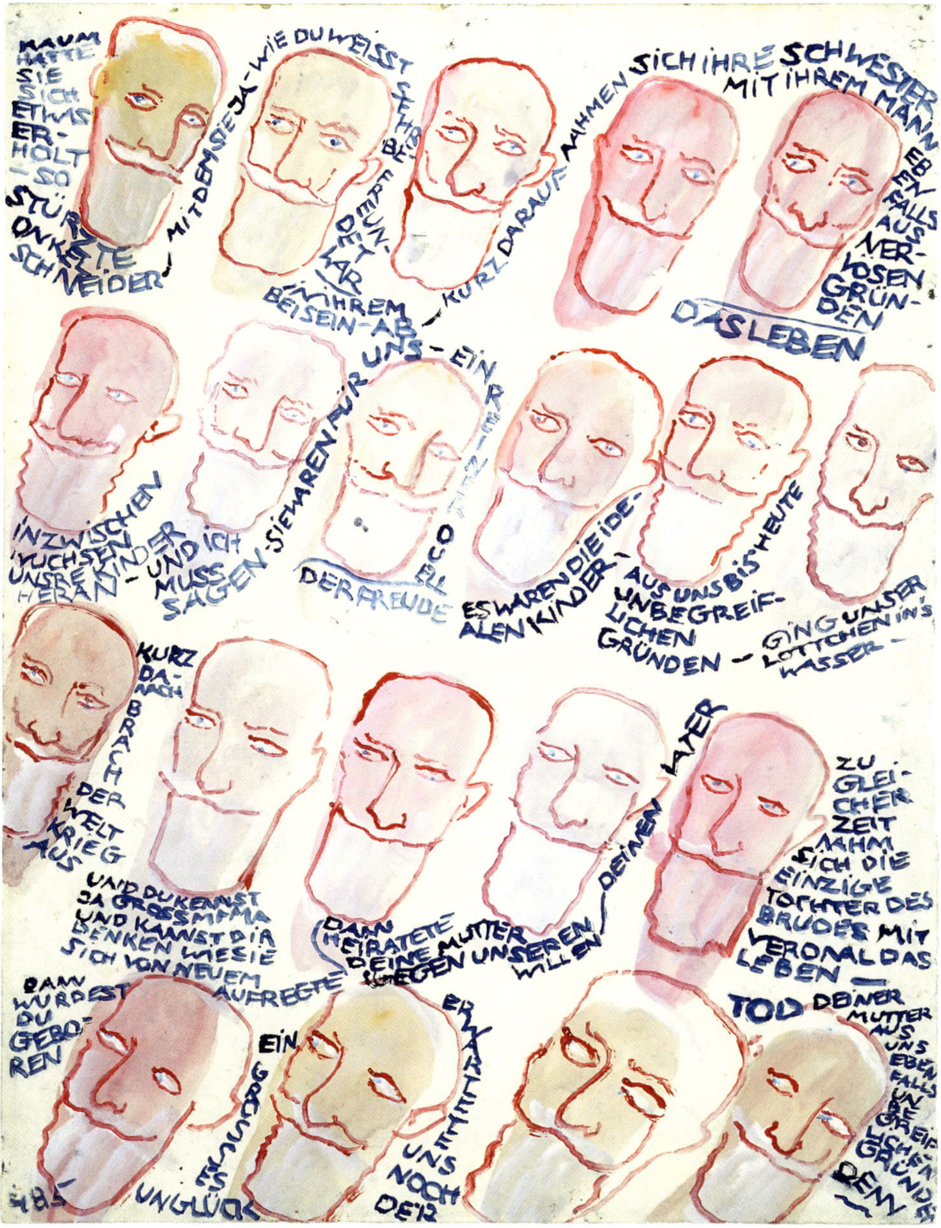
KAUM HATTE SIE SICH ETWAS ERHOLT – SO STÜRZTE ONKEL SCHNEIDER – MIT DEM SIE JA – WIE DU WEISST SEHR BEFREUNDET WAR – IN IHREM BEISEIN AB –
KURZ DARAUF NAHMEN SICH IHRE SCHWESTER MIT IHREM MANN EBENFALLS AUS NERVÖSEN GRÜNDEN DAS LEBEN
INZWISCHEN WUCHSEN UNSRE KINDER HERAN – UND ICH MUSS SAGEN – SIE WAREN FÜR UNS – EIN REINER QUELL DER FREUDE
ES WAREN DIE IDEALEN KINDER – AUS UNS BIS HEUTE UNBEGREIFLICHEN GRÜNDEN – GING UNSER LOTTCHEN INS WASSER –
KURZ DANACH BRACH DER WELTKRIEG AUS
UND DU KENNST JA GROSSMAMA UND KANNST DIR DENKEN WIE SIE SICH VON NEUEM AUFREGTE
DANN HEIRATETE DEINE MUTTER GEGEN UNSEREN WILLEN – DEINEN VATER
ZU GLEICHER ZEIT NAHM SICH DIE EINZIGE TOCHTER DES BRUDERS MIT VERONAL DAS LEBEN –
DANN WURDEST DU GEBOREN
EIN UNGLÜCK ERWARTETE UNS NOCH DER TOD DEINER MUTTER AUS UNS EBENFALLS UNBEGREIFLICHEN GRÜNDEN – DENN –
485

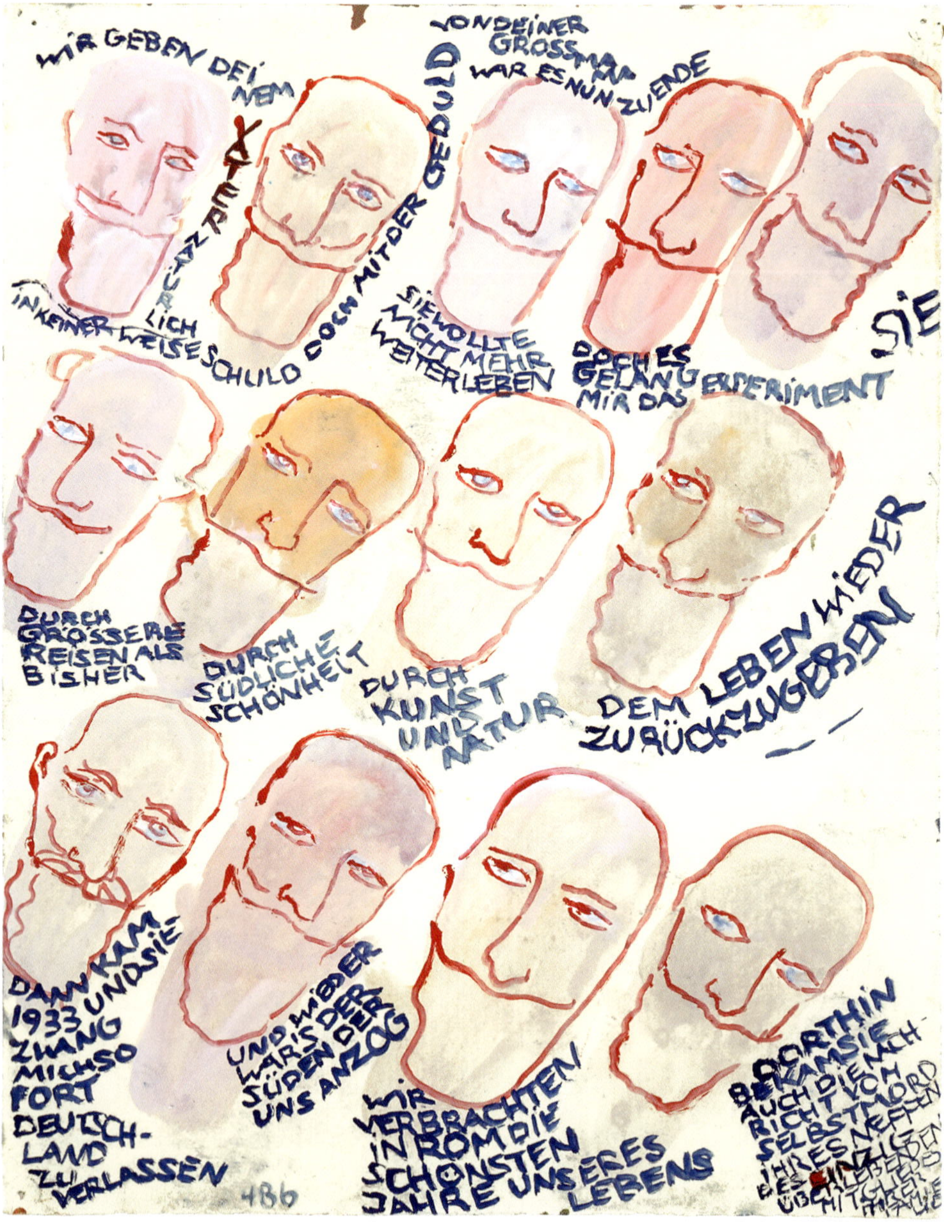
WIR GEBEN DEINEM VATER NATÜRLICH
IN KEINER WEISE SCHULD DOCH MIT DER GEDULD
VON DEINER GROSSMAMA WAR ES NUN ZU ENDE
SIE WOLLTE NICHT MEHR WEITERLEBEN
DOCH ES GELANG MIR DAS EXPERIMENT SIE
DURCH GRÖSSERE REISEN ALS BISHER
DURCH SÜDLICHE SCHÖNHEIT
DURCH KUNST UND NATUR
DEM LEBEN WIEDER ZURÜCKZUGEBEN
DANN KAM 1933 UND SIE ZWANG MICH SOFORT DEUTSCHLAND ZU VERLASSEN
UND WIEDER WAR'S DER SÜDEN DER UNS ANZOG
WIR VERBRACHTEN IN ROM DIE SCHÖNSTEN JAHRE UNSERES LEBENS
486

(page 547)

“Hardly had she recovered a bit – Uncle Schneider with whom, as you know, she was on very friendly terms – plunged to his death in her presence. Soon after that, her sister and her sister’s husband committed suicide, also due to a nervous malady.

Meanwhile our children were growing up – and I must say that they were a source of pure joy to us. They were ideal children – but for reasons we have never been able to fathom – our Lottie drowned herself.

Shortly after that, the war broke out, and you know what Grandma is like and you can imagine how that upset her all over again. Then, against our will, your mother married your father. At the same time her brother’s only daughter committed suicide with an overdose of Veronal.

Then you were born.

A great tragedy was still to come, the death of your mother, also for inexplicable reasons, for...”

(opposite)

“... of course we don’t attach any blame whatsoever to your father; but now your grandmother had come to the end of her tether. She didn’t want to go on living, but I succeeded in my experiment to restore her to life by means of more extended travels, by the beauty of the South, by art and nature.

Then came 1933, and she forced me to leave Germany immediately, and again it was the South that attracted us. In Rome we spent the happiest years of our lives. There, too, she received the news of the suicide of her nephew, the only surviving member of her family.”

Nobody had ever told Charlotte how some of her family had lost their lives.

CHARLOTTE
"I knew nothing of all that.
I always thought my mother had the
influenza and died of influenza."

MAN HATTE CHARLOTTE NIE-
MALS MITGETEILT AUF WELCHE
WEISE EIN TEIL IHRER FAMIELIE
UM'S LEBEN GEKOMMEN IST

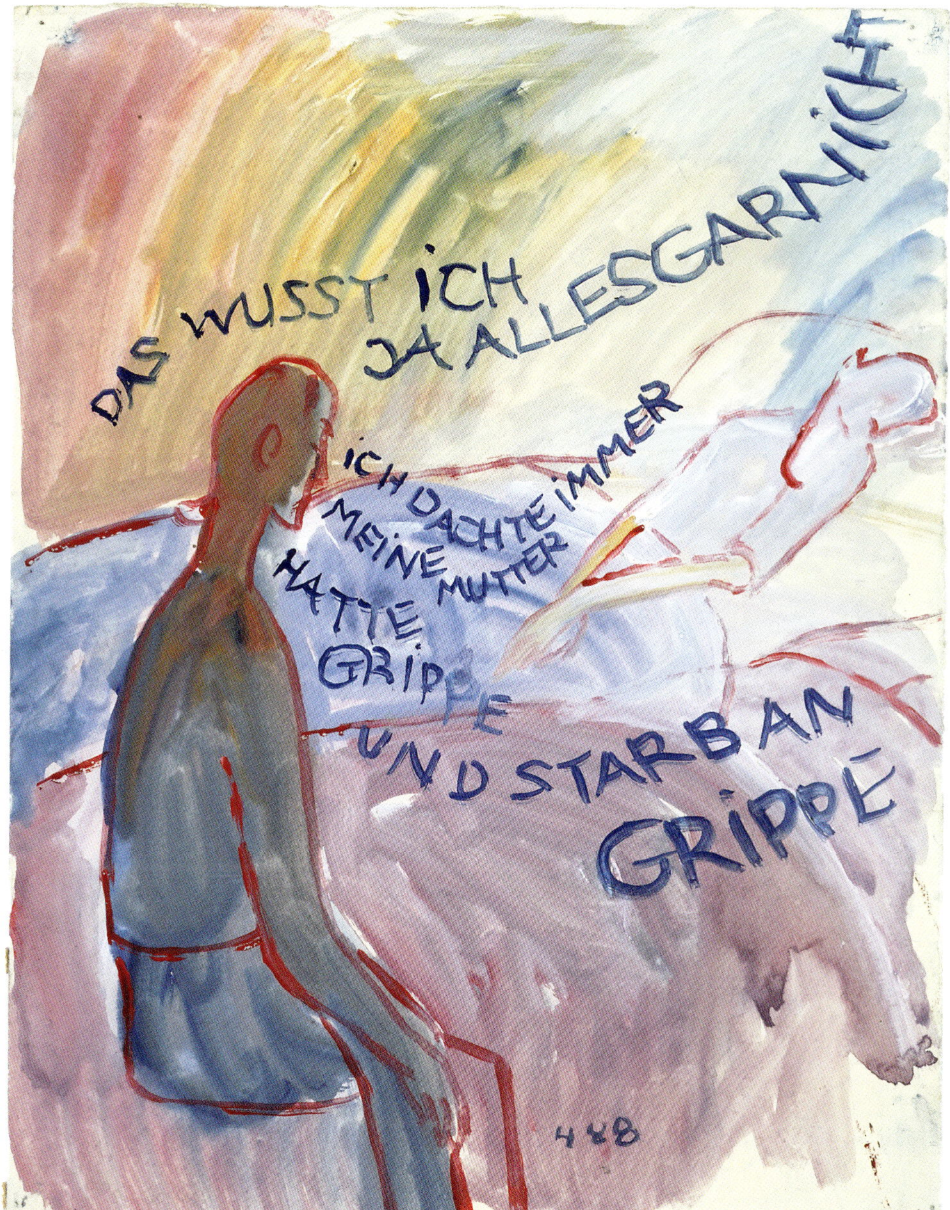
DAS WUSST ICH JA ALLESGARNICHT
ICH DACHTE IMMER
MEINE MUTTER
HATTE
GRIPPE
UND STARB AN
GRIPPE
488

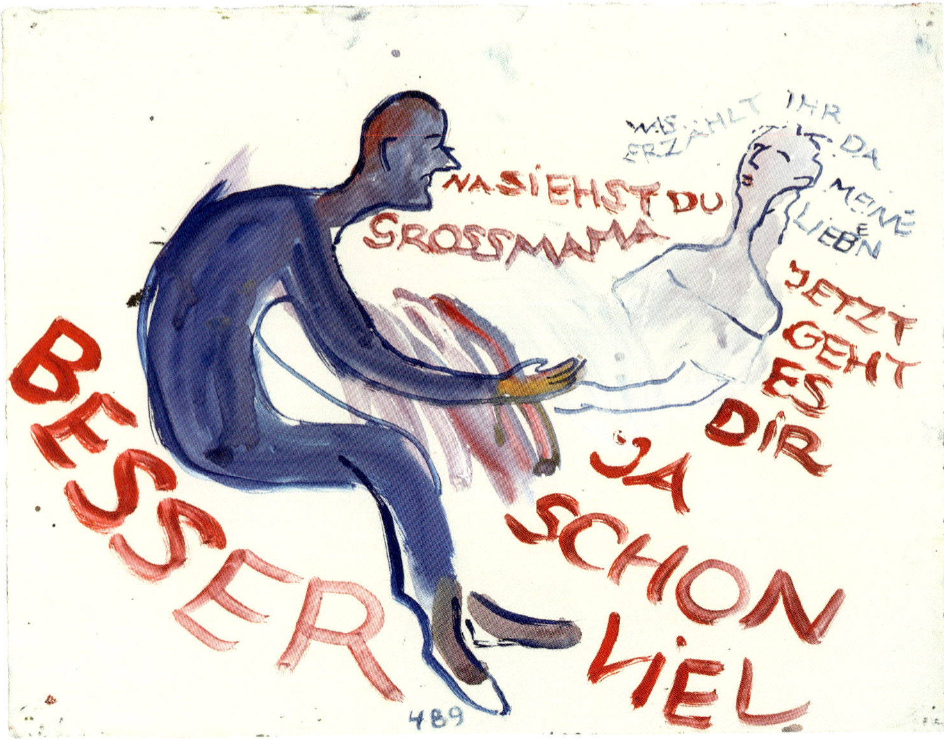

GRANDMOTHER
"What are you talking about, my dear ones?"

CHARLOTTE
"There, Grandma, you see?
You're already feeling much better."

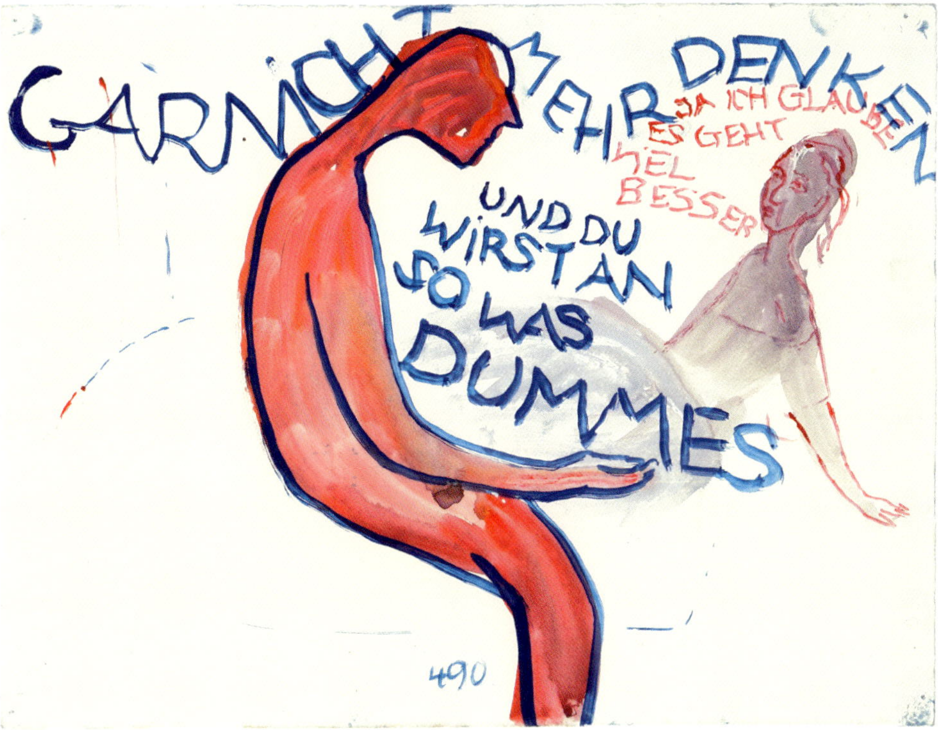

GRANDMOTHER
"Yes, I believe I am feeling much better."

CHARLOTTE
"And you'll never again have
such a silly notion."

"... that I love life and affirm it threefold. In order to love life completely, perhaps it is necessary to embrace and comprehend its other side: death.
May you never forget that I believe in you."

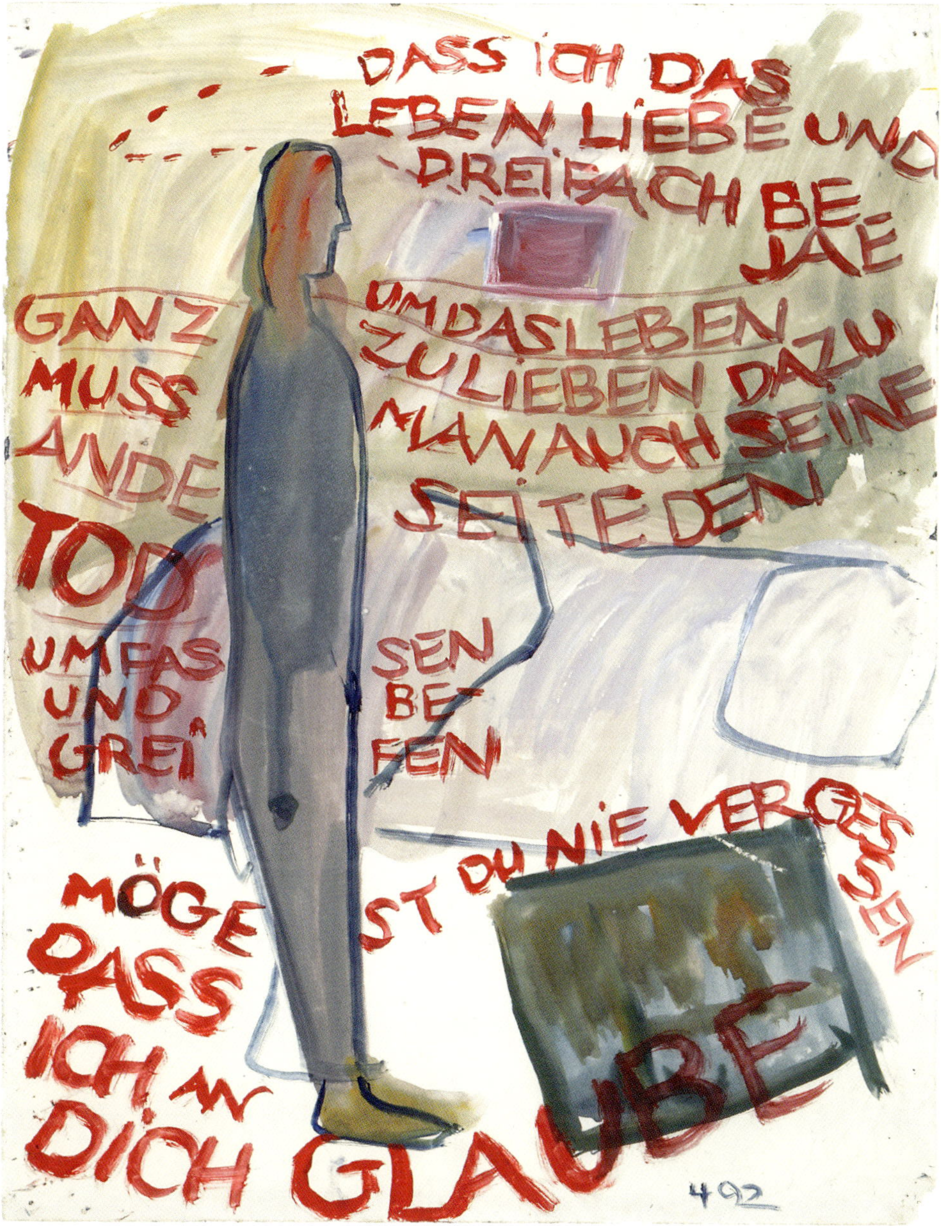
DASS ICH DAS
LEBEN LIEBE UND
DREIFACH BE-
JAE
GANZ
MUSS
ANDE
TOD
UMFAS
UND
GREI
UM DAS LEBEN
ZU LIEBEN DAZU
MAN AUCH SEINE
SEITE DEN
SEN
BE-
FEN
MÖGE
ST DU NIE VERGESSEN
DASS
ICH AN
DICH GLAUBE
4 92

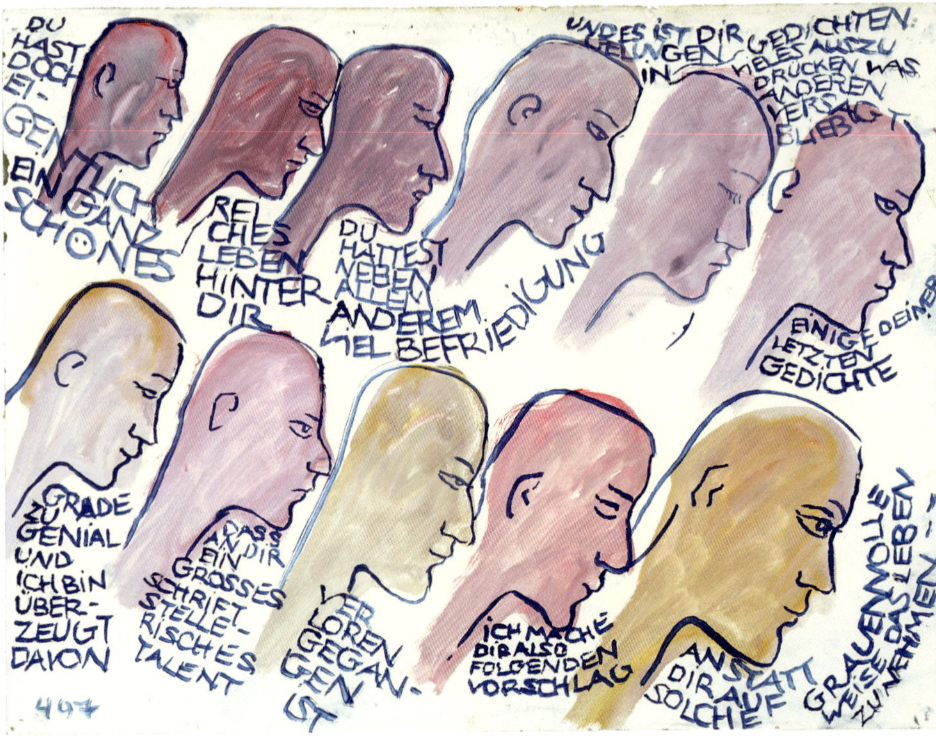

CHARLOTTE
"You can look back on a wonderful, full life. Apart from anything else, you've found a great deal of satisfaction, and you have succeeded in expressing in poems many things that have been denied to others. Some of your most recent poems are ingenious, and I am convinced that in you a great literary talent has been lost. So I'll make you the following proposition: instead of you taking your own life in such a horrible way..."

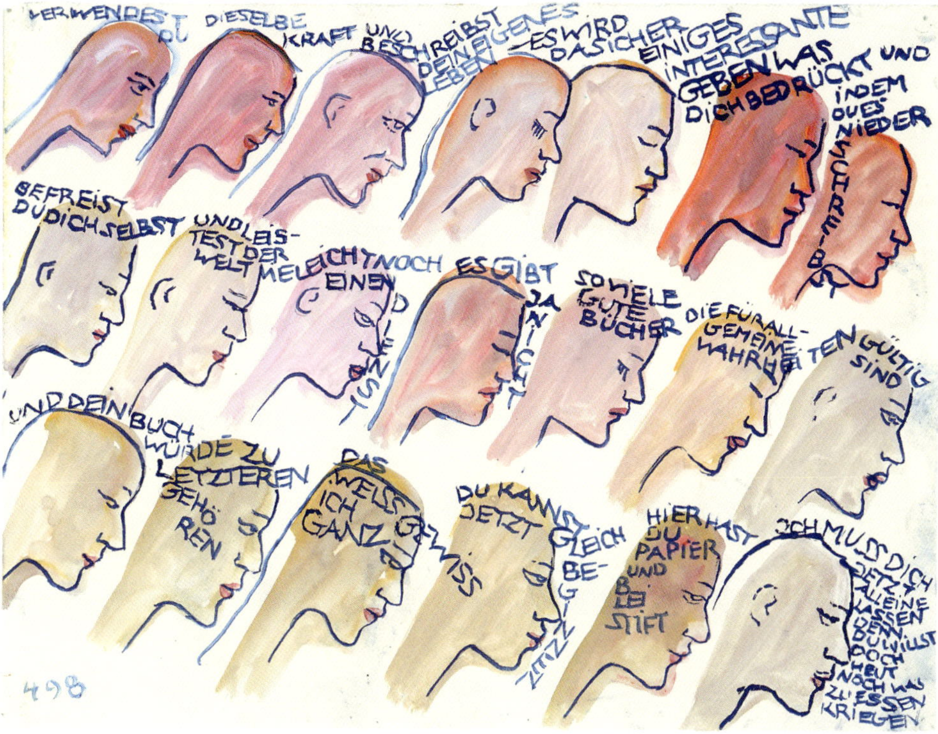

"... why don't you make use of the same powers to describe your life. There will surely be some interesting material that's weighing on you, and by writing it down you will liberate yourself and perhaps perform a service to the world. There aren't that many good books representing universal truths, and your book would be among those. I'm absolutely sure of that. You can start right now. Here you have paper and pencil. I have to leave you alone now, since I don't imagine you want to go hungry for the rest of the day."

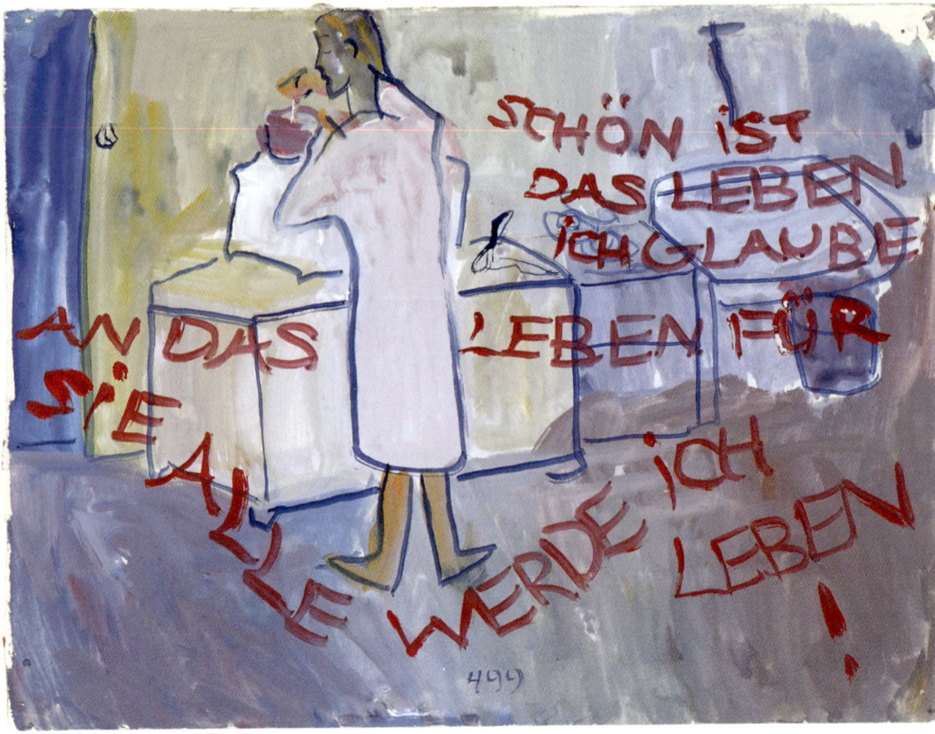

CHARLOTTE
"How beautiful life is, I believe in life!
I will live for them all!"

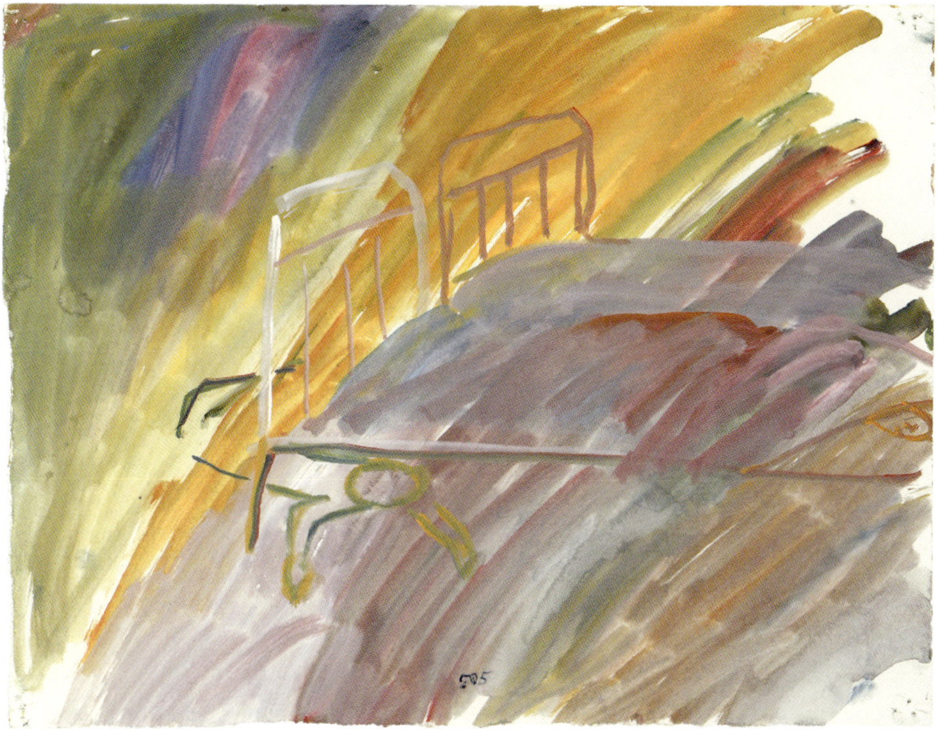

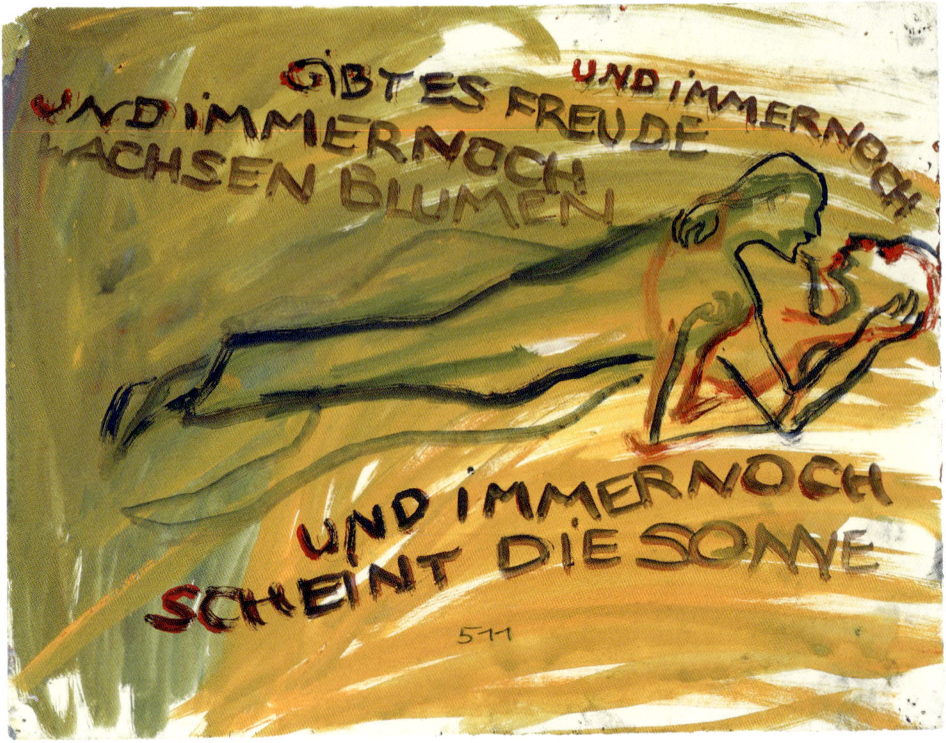

CHARLOTTE
"And still there is joy,
and always the flowers still grow,
and always the sun still shines."

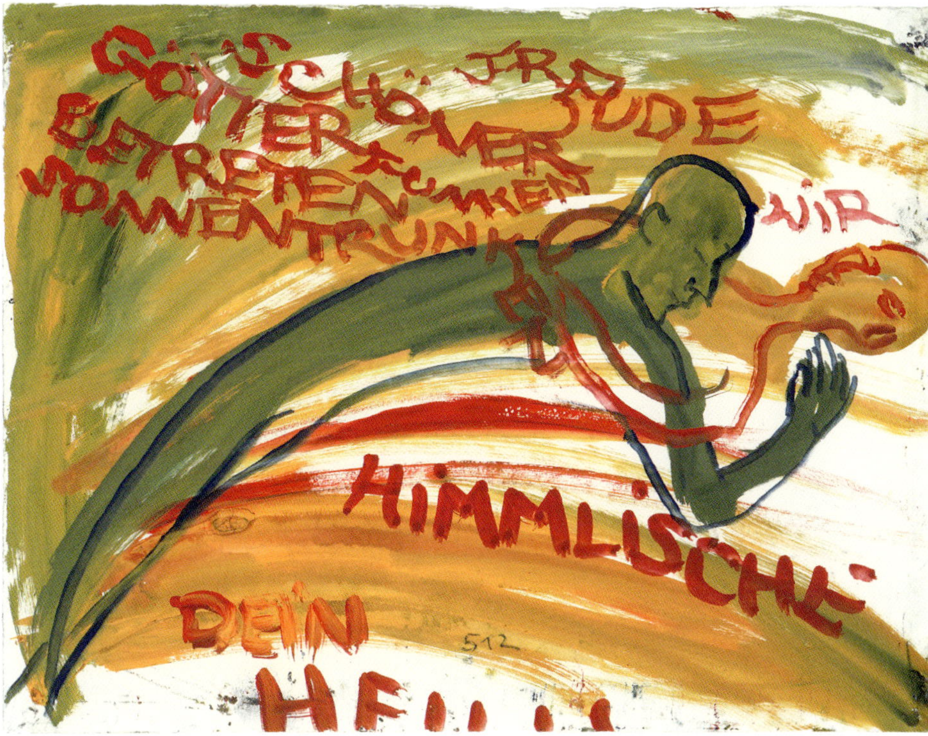

Freude, schöner Götterfunken.
Wir betreten sonnentrunken,
Himmlische, dein Heiligtum
[Joy, divine sparks of the Gods.
We enter sun-drunk, heavenly,
your sanctuary].

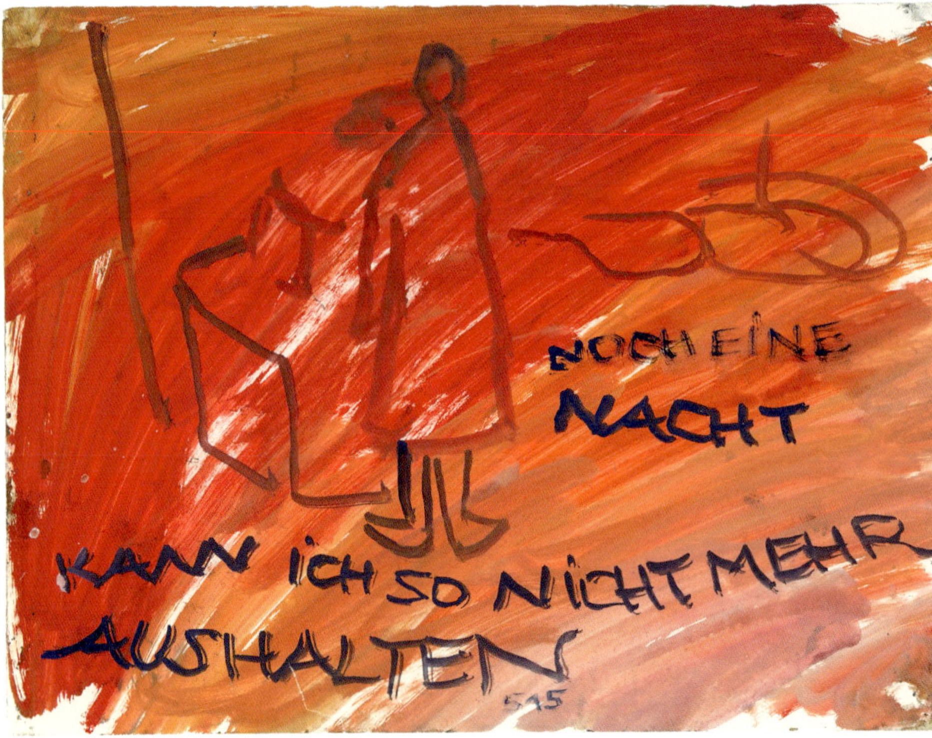

CHARLOTTE
“Another night like that
will be more than I can take.”

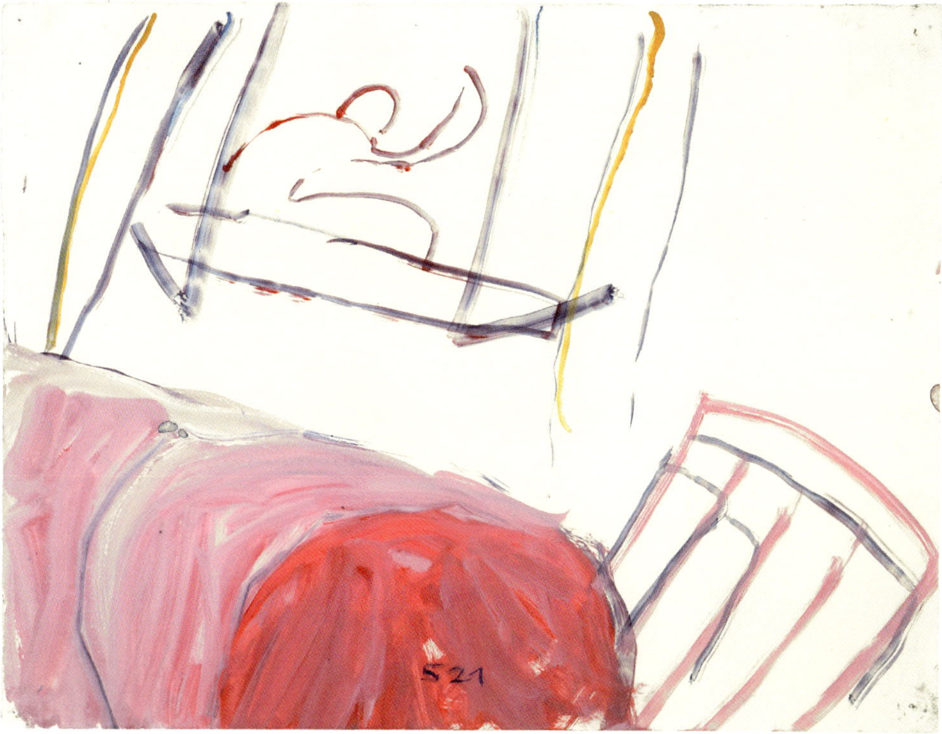
521

(bottom)

CHARLOTTE
"'May you never forget
that I believe in you.'"

(opposite)

GRANDFATHER
"Here are some carnations
I've brought for her."

CHARLOTTE
"Grandpa, it's too late."

GRANDFATHER
"So she has done it after all."

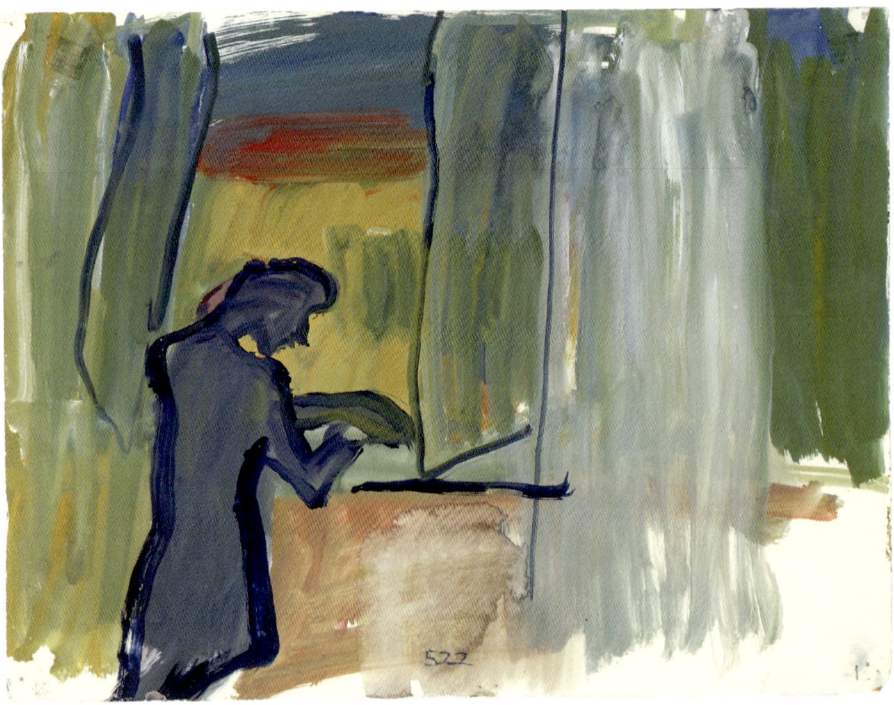

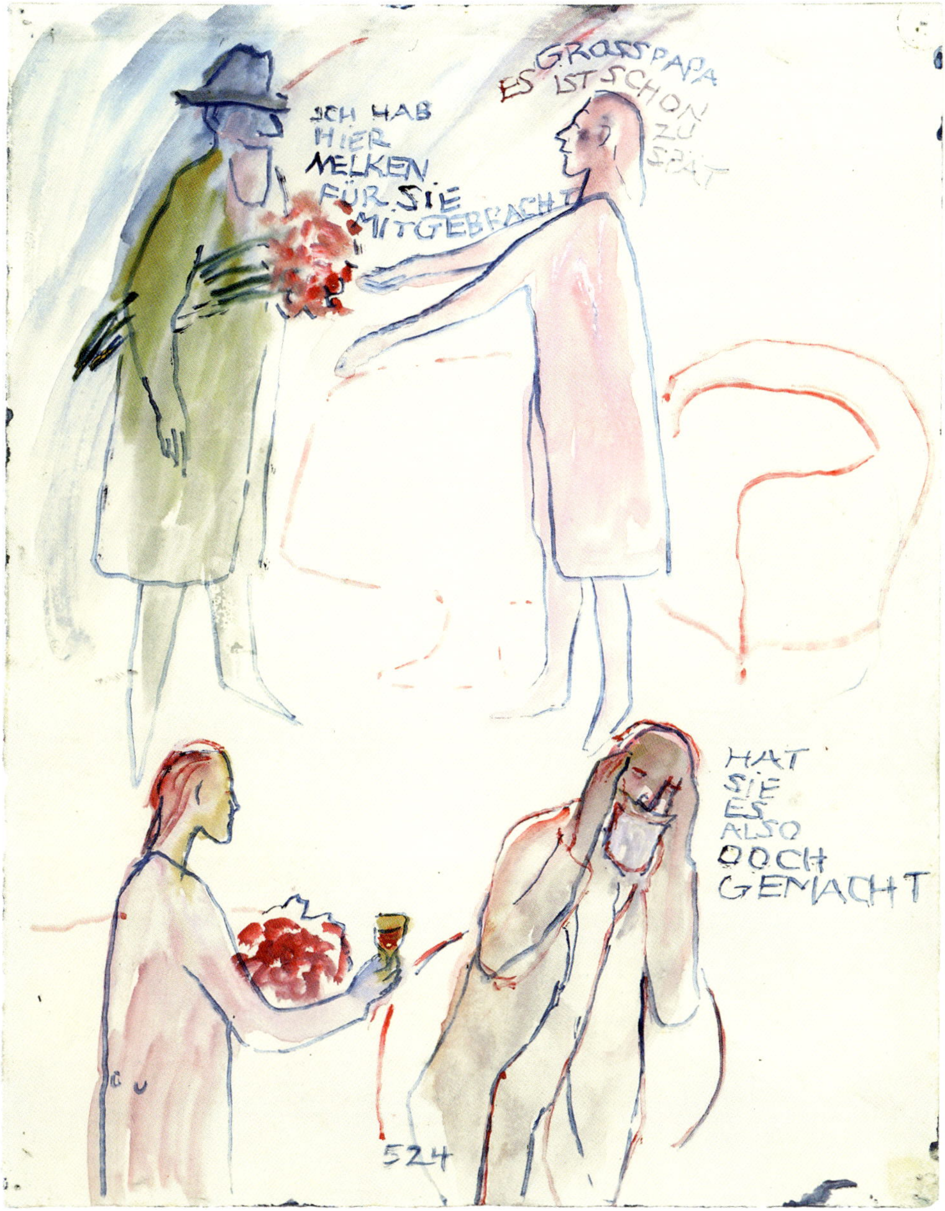
ICH HAB HIER NELKEN FÜR SIE MITGEBRACHT
ES GROSSPAPA IST SCHON ZU SPÄT
HAT SIE ES ALSO OOCH GEMACHT
524

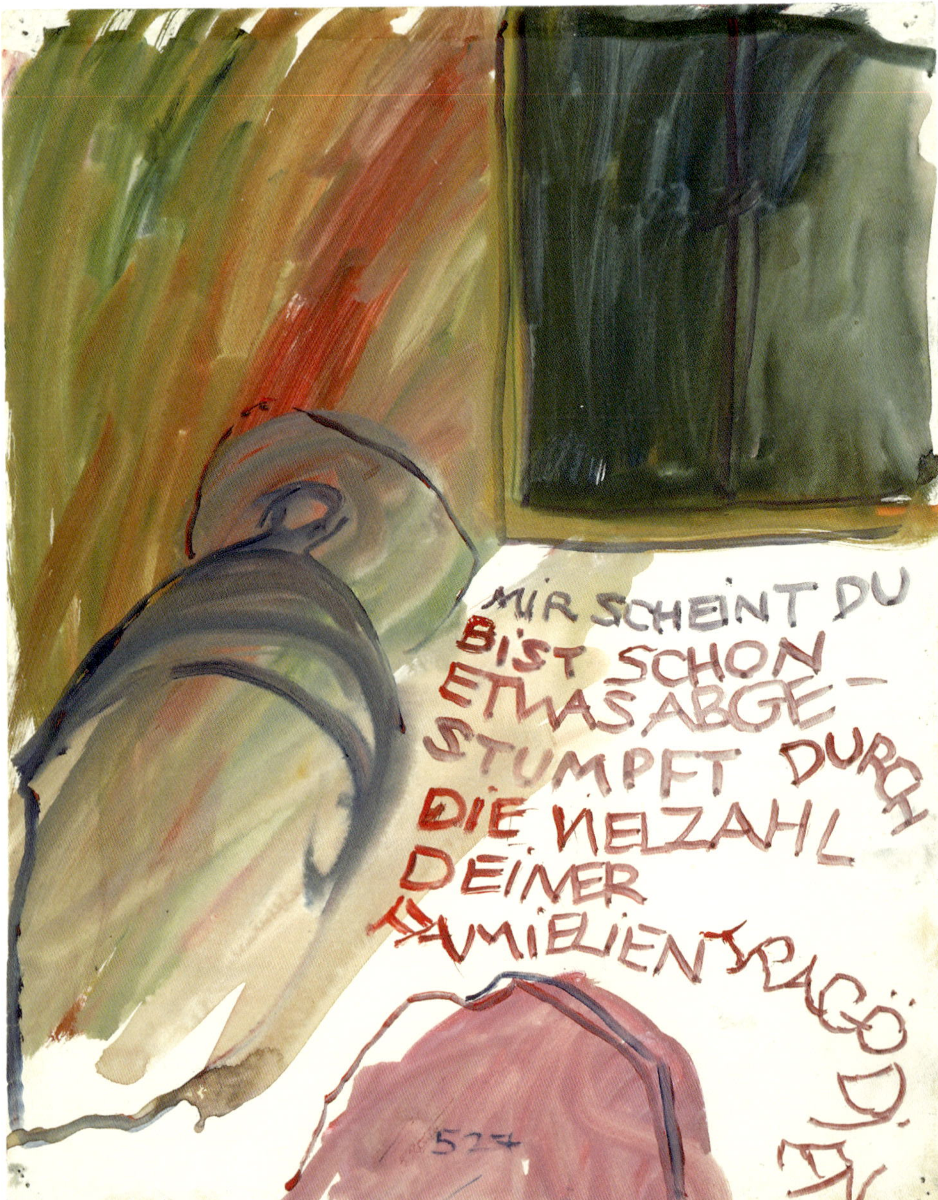
MIR SCHEINT DU
BIST SCHON
ETWAS ABGE-
STUMPFT DURCH
DIE VIELZAHL
DEINER
FAMILIENTRAGÖDIEN
527

(opposite)

CHARLOTTE
"It seems to me that all those family tragedies of yours have made you rather insensitive."

(bottom)

"Dear God, please don't let me go mad."

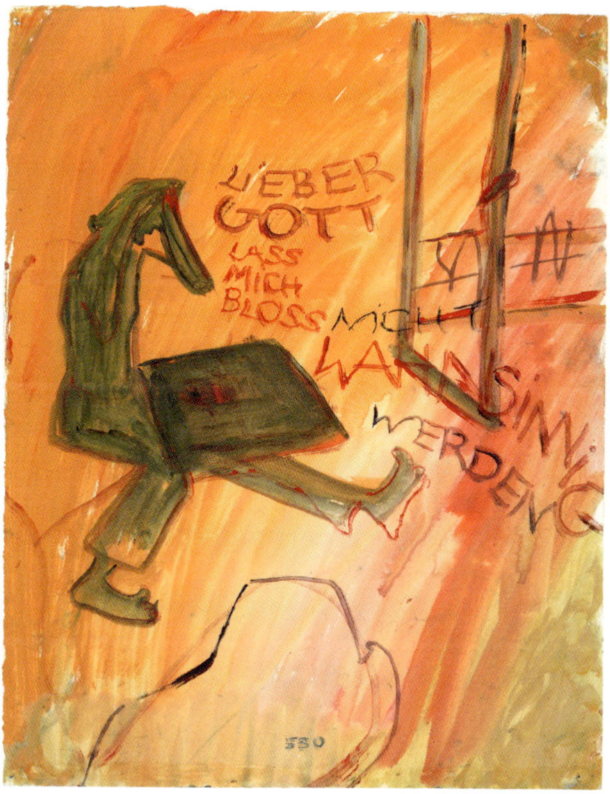

MAY 1940
DECLARATION OF WAR

"La guerre est déclarée."

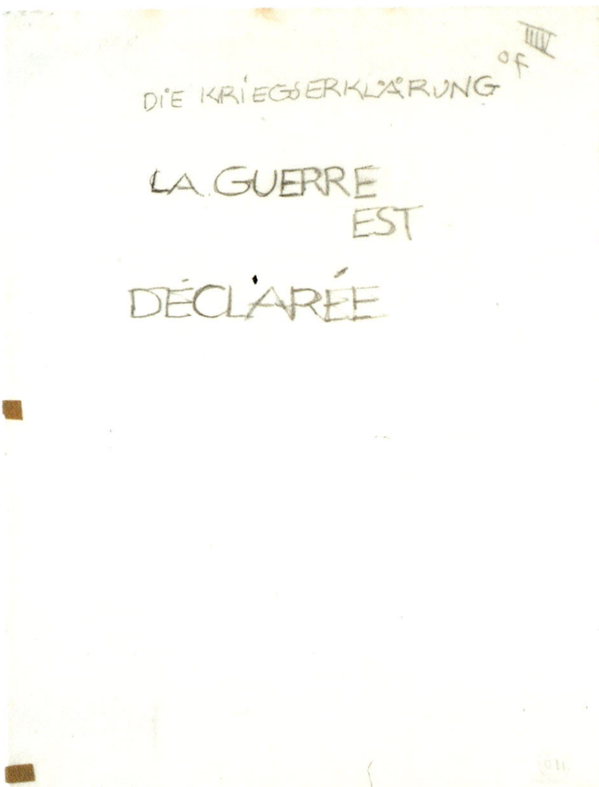

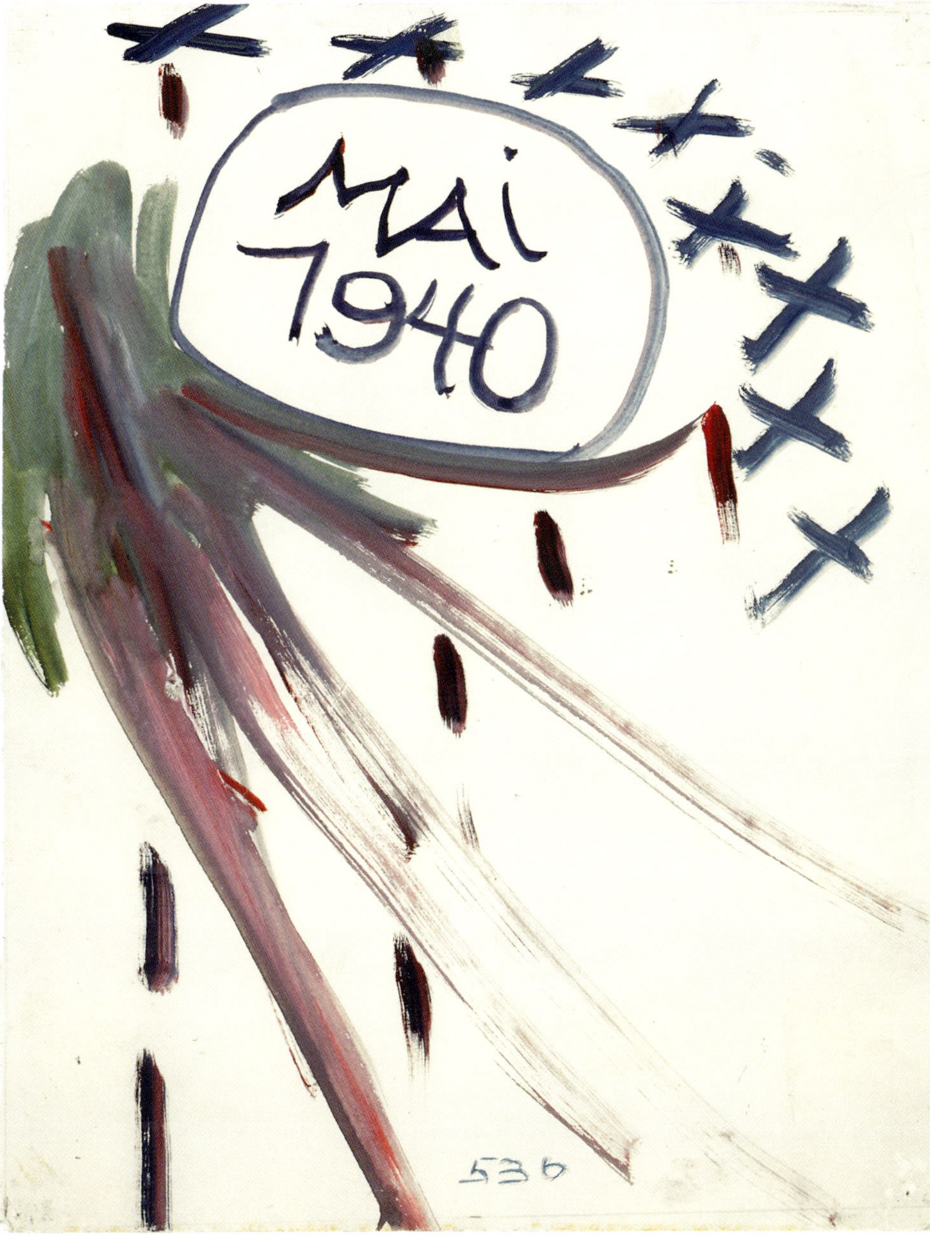
Mai
1940
530

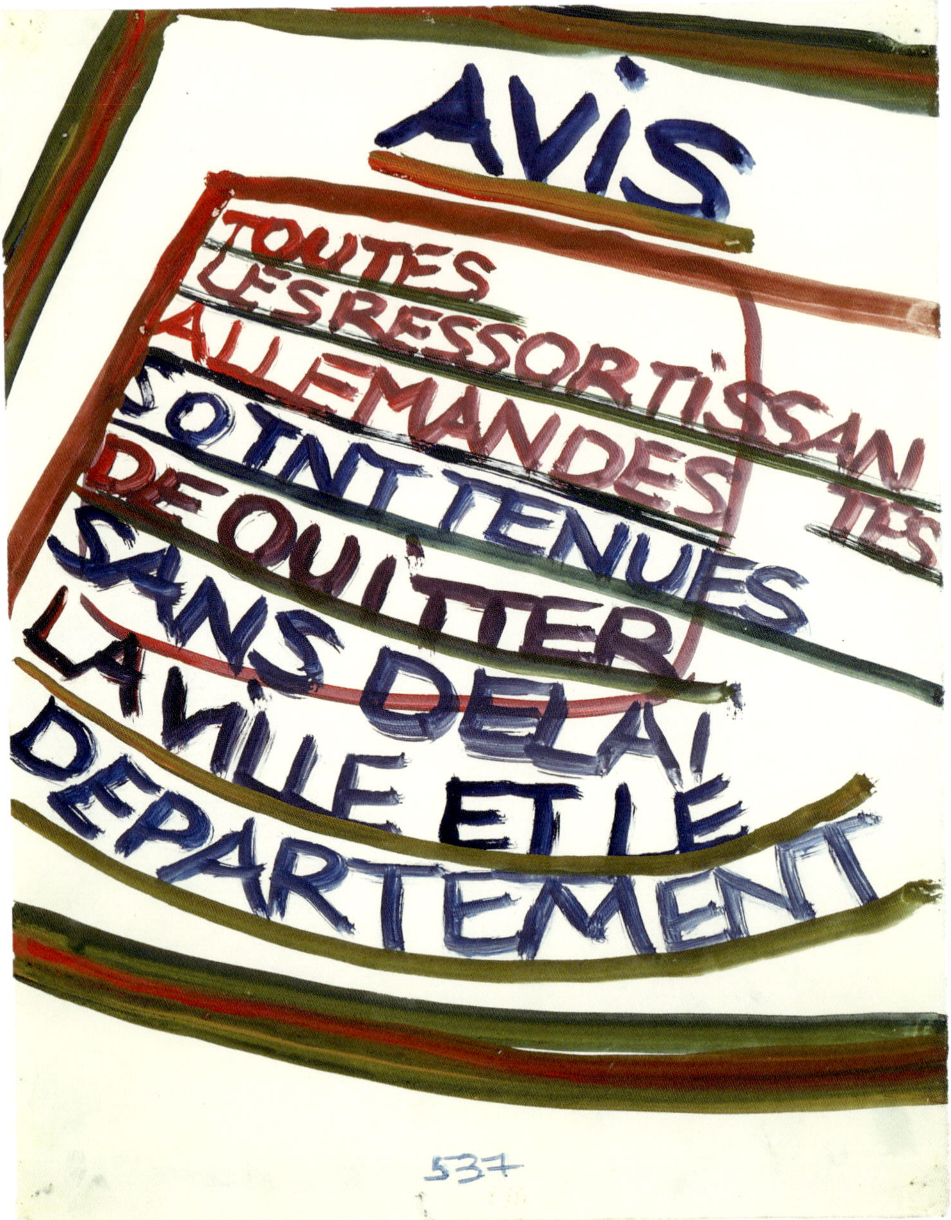
AVIS
TOUTES
LES RESSORTISSAN
ALLEMANDES TES
SONT TENUES
DE QUITTER
SANS DELAI
LA VILLE ET LE
DEPARTEMENT
537

AVIS

Toutes les ressortissantes allemandes
sont tenues de quitter sans délai la ville
et le département.

(opposite)

Mr Knarre and Charlotte have spent the last few days in a railway car crammed with thousands of totally exhausted people. Driven from the interior of the country, chased by air raids, these people have had to leave all their possessions behind in order to escape with their bare lives.

CHARLOTTE
"I'd rather have ten more nights like this than a single one alone with him."

GRANDFATHER
"I do not understand you. You can lie down in a bed with me just like that – if there's nothing else to be had. I'm always for what's natural."

CHARLOTTE
"Don't torment me. You know – I know exactly – what I have to do."

(page 574)

CHARLOTTE
"God, it's beautiful here."

GRANDFATHER
"Oh, come along, eventually. We have to find some place to sleep tonight."

CHARLOTTE
"Chère Madame, n'existe pas la possibilité – je ne peux pas dormir â côté de mon grand-père – que je puisse dormir ailleurs?"

HOTELKEEPER
"Je veux voir, Mademoiselle. Je crois ça ira."

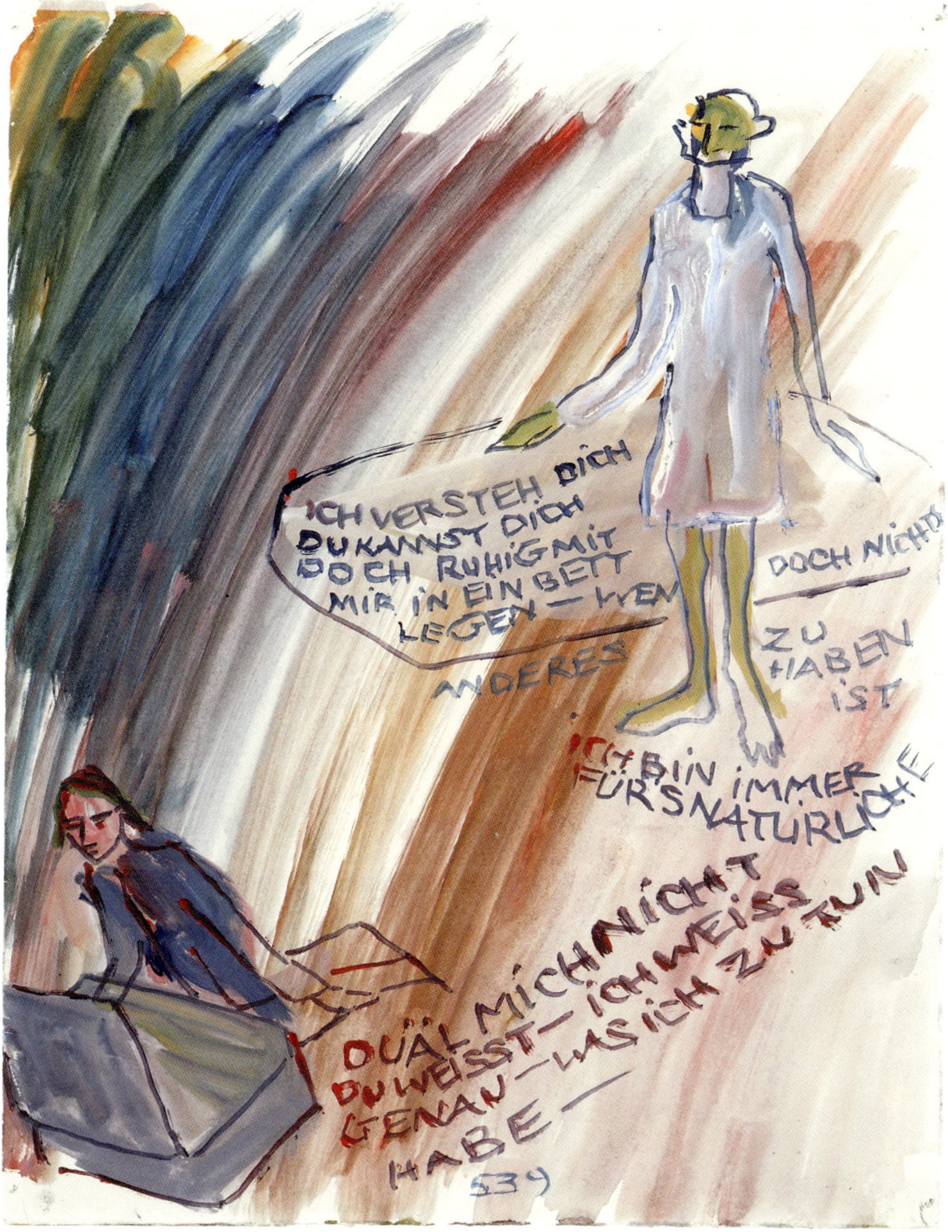
ICH VERSTEH DICH
DU KANNST DICH
DOCH RUHIG MIT
MIR IN EIN BETT
LEGEN – WENN
DOCH NICHTS
ANDERES
ZU
HABEN
IST
ICH BIN IMMER
FÜRS NATÜRLICHE
QUÄL MICH NICHT
DU WEISST – ICH WEISS
GENAU – WAS ICH ZU TUN
HABE –
HABE
534

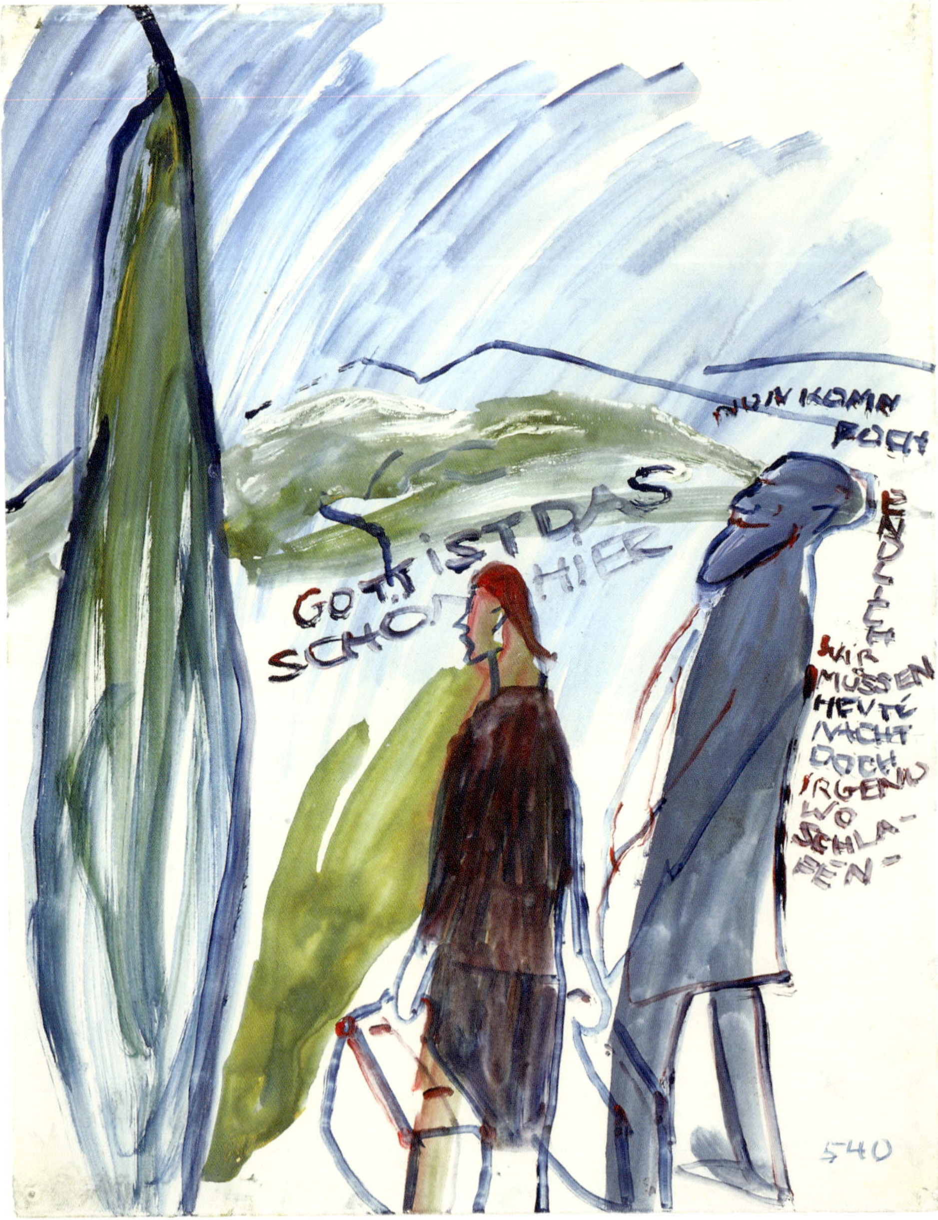
NUN KOMM DOCH
ENDLICH
GOTT IST DAS SCHÖN HIER
WIR MÜSSEN HEUTE NACHT DOCH IRGENW WO SCHLA-FEN-
540

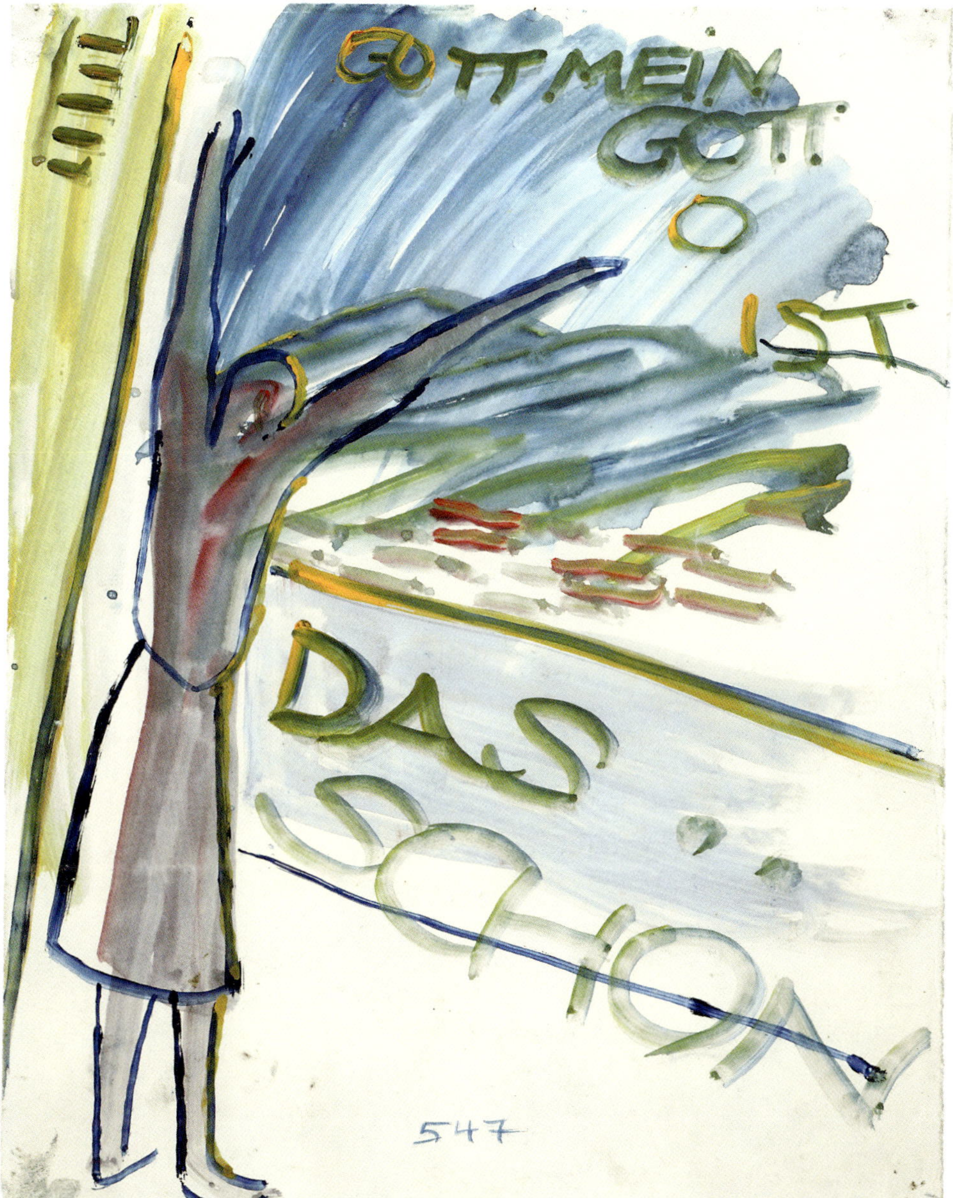
GOTT MEIN GOTT
O
IST
DAS
SCHÖN
547

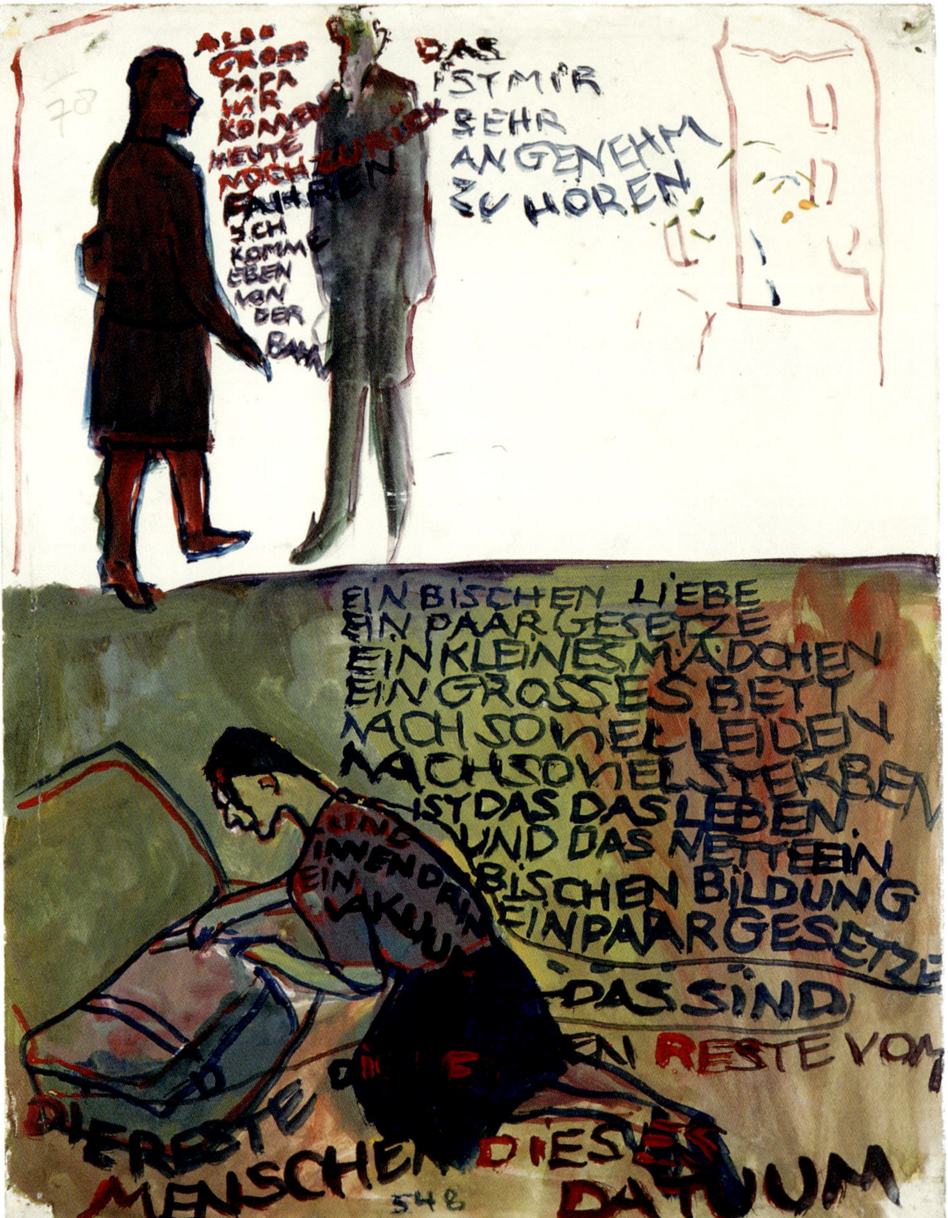

ALSO GROSS PAPA WIR KOMMEN HEUTE NOCH ZURÜCK FAHREN
ICH KOMME EBEN VON DER BAHN
DAS IST MIR SEHR ANGENEHM ZU HÖREN
78
EIN BISCHEN LIEBE
EIN PAAR GESETZE
EIN KLEINES MÄDCHEN
EIN GROSSES BETT
NACH SO VIEL LEIDEN
NACH SO VIEL STERBEN
IST DAS DAS LEBEN
UND DAS NETTE EIN
BISCHEN BILDUNG
EIN PAAR GESETZE
DAS SIND
RESTE VOM
DIE RESTE
MENSCHEN DIESES
DATUUM
548

(page 575)

HOTELKEEPER
"Mais Mademoiselle, si vous serez comme ça, ce Monsieur a à quitter ma maison immédiatement."

CHARLOTTE
"Chère Madame, je vous en prie, ne laissez rien voir à ce Monsieur que vous avez entendu quelque chose – parce que, vous comprenez, ça sera une honte pour lui – et c'est uniquement, je vous assure, chère Madame, la faute à moi, et nous allons partir aujourd'hui. Et vous aussi, cher Monsieur, je vous en prie, n'est-ce pas, on se comprend, c'est si naturel, ne laissez rien voir à ce monsieur."

HOTELKEEPER
"Qu'est ce que ça me regarde?
Parfaitement, Mademoiselle."

CHARLOTTE
"God, oh God, this is beautiful!"

(opposite)

CHARLOTTE
"Well Grandpa, we can go back today.
I've just come from the station."

GRANDFATHER
"I'm delighted to hear it."

CHARLOTTE
"A little love, a few laws, a young girl,
a big bed. After so much pain, after so much
dying, this is the life and the niceties.
A little education, a few laws, and inside
a vacuum – that's what's left, the last
remnants from human beings of this date."

(opposite)

CHARLOTTE
"You know, Grandpa, I have the feeling
as if one has to put the whole world
together again."

GRANDFATHER
"Now conclusively take your life,
so this babble finally stops."

(following pages)

This took place in July 1940 en route from a little town in the Pyrenees to Nice. One year later, during which the world fell ever more apart, the spirit of this strangely twin-natured creature was ever more crushed by the proximity of her grandfather, tragically hounded as he was by fate. And since this applied to everyone at that time, so that no one was able...

... to listen to another, but immediately begins to speak of himself, there awoke in a creature, who simultaneously suffers and is above things, a feeling of utter helplessness of all men who try to hold on to straws in the most violent of thunderstorms. Despite greatest weaknesses, however, our object refused to fall into
the circle of straw-seekers...

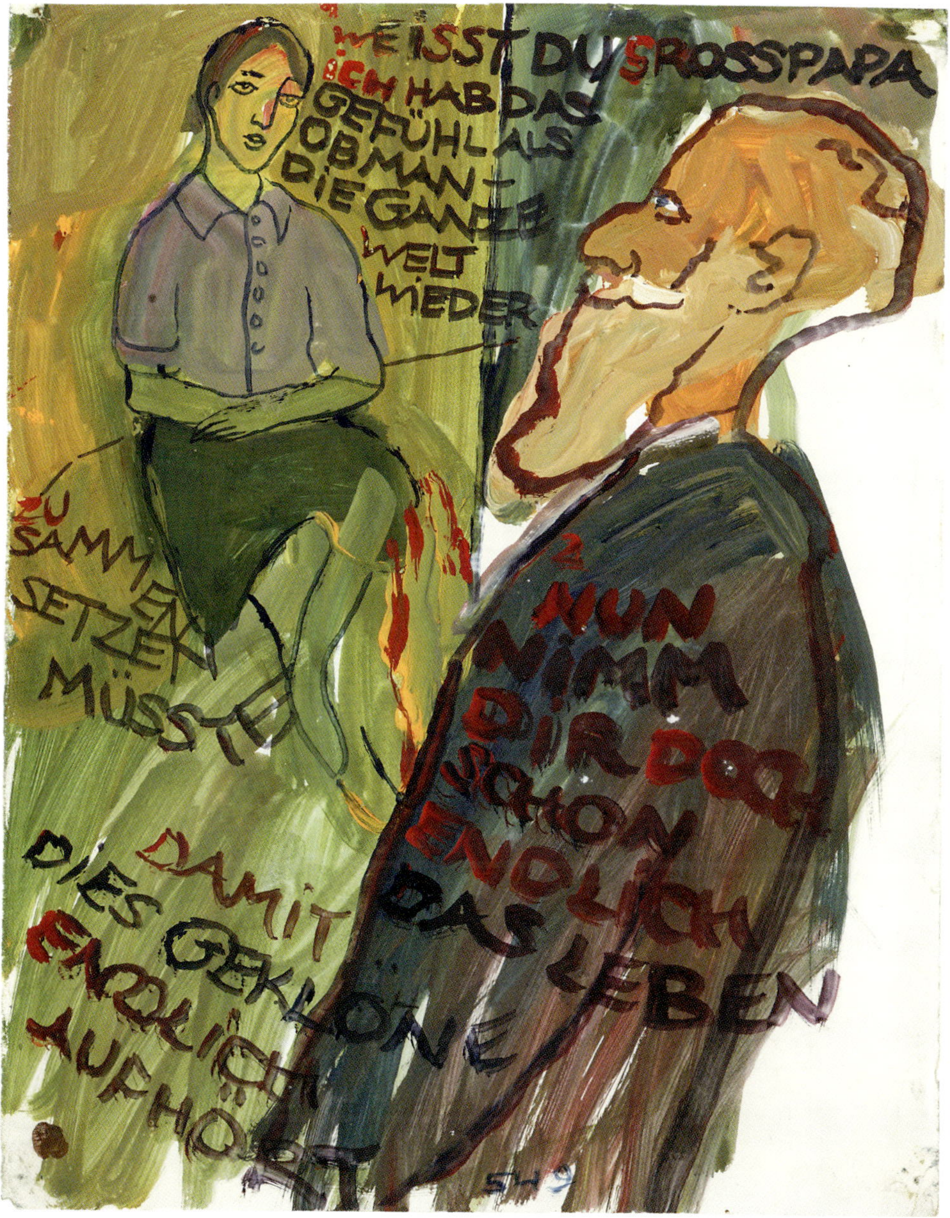
WEISST DU GROSSPAPA
ICH HAB DAS GEFÜHL ALS OB MAN DIE GANZE WELT WIEDER ZU SAMMEN SETZEN MÜSSTE
NUN NIMM DIR DOCH SCHON ENDLICH DAS LEBEN
DAMIT DIES GEKLONE ENDLICH AUFHÖRT

DIES EREIGNETE SICH
IM JULI 1940 AUF DEM
WEG VON EINEM KLEINEN
STÄDCHEN IN DEN PYRINÄ-
EN NACH NIZZA EIN
JAHR SPÄTER IN DEM
DIE WELT IMMER MEHR
ZERFIEL - WURDE AUCH
DER GEIST DES MERKWÜR-
DIG DOPPELSEITIG VER-
ANLAGTEN GESCHÖPFES
IM ZUSAMMENSEIN MIT
DEM VOM TRAGISCH VOM
SCHICKSAL VERFOLGTEM
GROSSVATER - IMMER
MEHR ZERMÜRBT. UND
DA DIES IN DIESER ZEIT
MIT ALLEN MENSCHEN
EBEN SO WAR SO DASS
NIEMAND MEHR IM STANDE

550

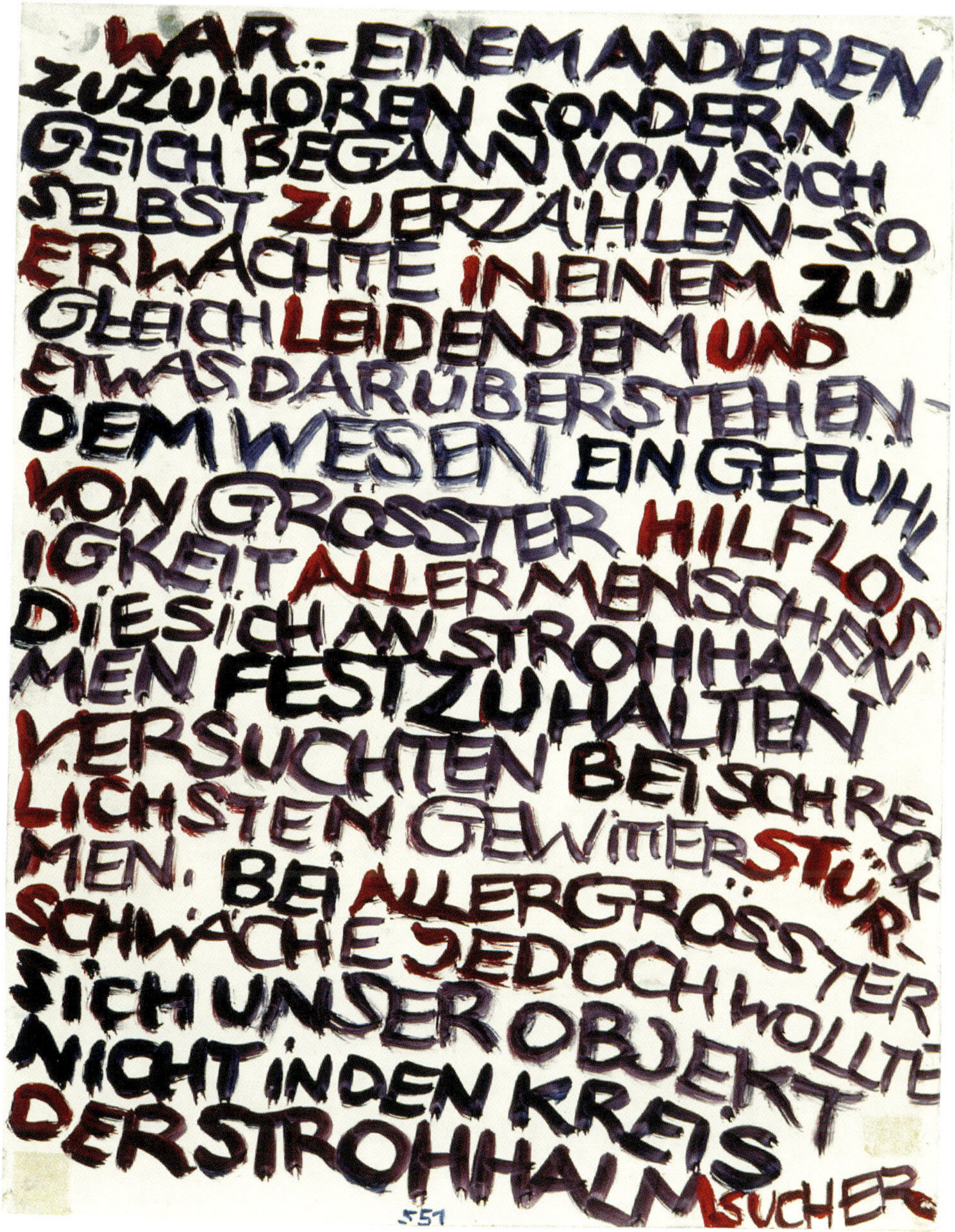
WAR.-EINEM ANDEREN
ZUZUHÖREN SONDERN
GEICH BEGANN VON SICH
SELBST ZU ERZÄHLEN-SO
ERWACHTE IN EINEM ZU
GLEICH LEIDENDEM UND
ETWAS DARÜBERSTEHEN-
DEM WESEN EIN GEFÜHL
VON GROSSTER HILFLOS
IGKEIT ALLER MENSCHEN
DIE SICH AN STROHHAL-
MEN FESTZUHALTEN
VERSUCHTEN BEI SCHRECK
LICHSTEN GEWITTERSTÜR
MEN. BEI ALLERGRÖSSTER
SCHWÄCHE JEDOCH WOLLTE
SICH UNSER OBJEKT
NICHT IN DEN KREIS
DER STROHHALMSUCHER
551

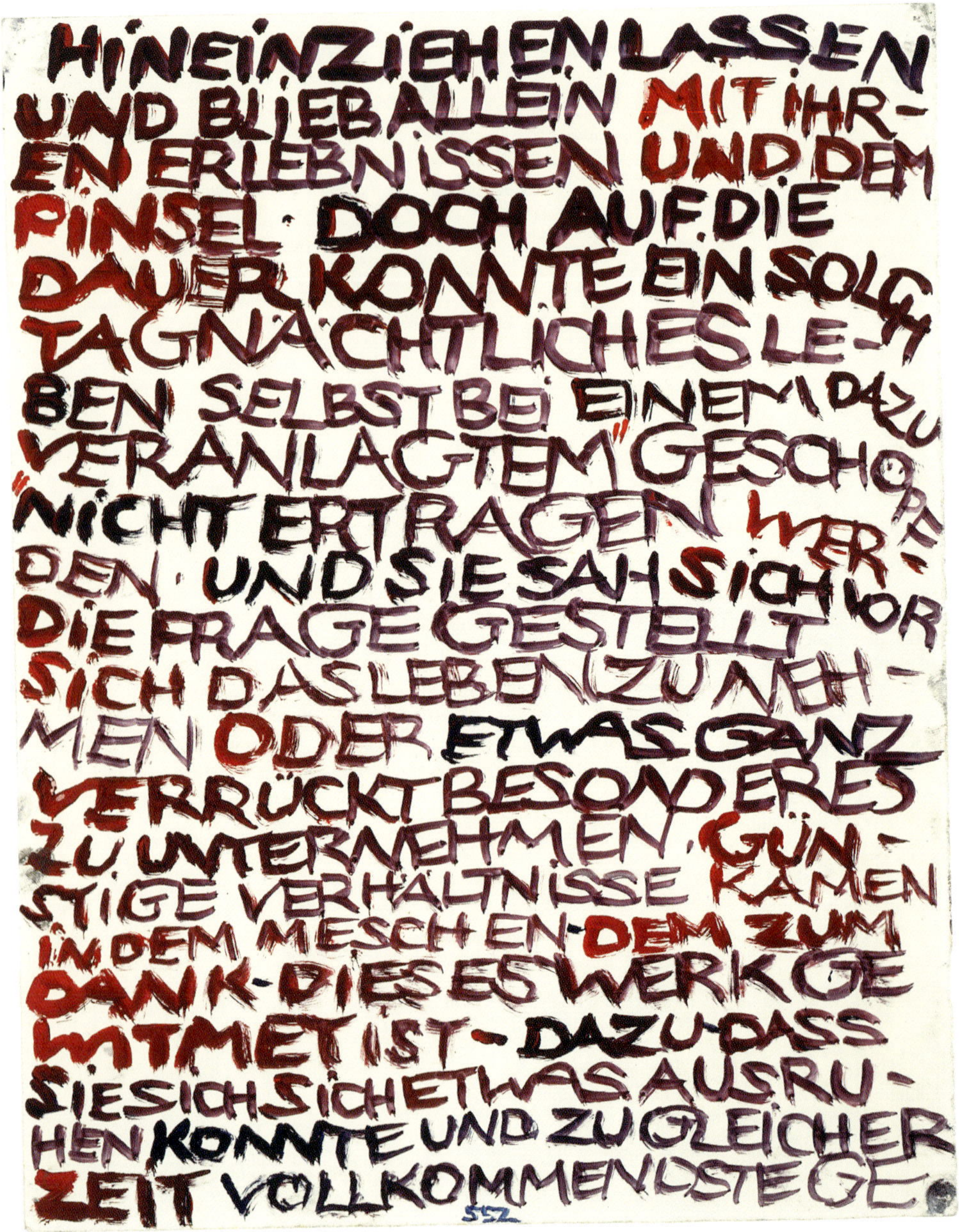
HINEINZIEHEN LASSEN
UND BLIEB ALLEIN MIT IHR-
EN ERLEBNISSEN UND DEM
PINSEL. DOCH AUF DIE
DAUER KONNTE EIN SOLCH
TAGNÄCHTLICHES LE-
BEN SELBST BEI EINEM "DAZU
VERANLAGTEM" GESCHÖPF
NICHT ERTRAGEN WER-
DEN. UND SIE SAH SICH VOR
DIE FRAGE GESTELLT
SICH DAS LEBEN ZU NEH-
MEN ODER ETWAS GANZ
VERRÜCKT BESONDERES
ZU UNTERNEHMEN. GÜN-
STIGE VERHÄLTNISSE KAMEN
IN DEM MESCHEN-DEM ZUM
DANK-DIESES WERK GE
WITMET IST-DAZU-DASS
SIE SICH SICH ETWAS AUSRU-
HEN KONNTE UND ZU GLEICHER
ZEIT VOLLKOMMENDSTE GE
552

(opposite)

... and remained alone with her experiences and her paint brush. Yet, in the long run, such a day-nightish life like this became intolerable even to a creature thus "predisposed." And she found herself facing the question of whether to commit suicide or to undertake something quite insanely extraordinary. Favourable circumstances came in the person to whom this work is gratefully dedicated, so that she was able to have some rest while at the same time having a perfect op...

(follwing pages)

...portunity to get to know the people of that era as accurately as possible and to learn to hate, love or despise them. Thus facing the most ardent sun, blue-red sea, and the most blossoming trees, she remembered an old experience of her most glowing former love. And she tried to illustrate this face, this figure. And behold, she succeeded, and she noticed that this was a very interesting occupation. For she discovered that this figure...

... might possibly preserve her from suicide inasmuch as she remembered one of Amadeus's main clauses which he was always ready to utter: Love, know thyself first in order to love thy neighbour. And then: one has to go into oneself – into one's own childhood – to be able to go out of oneself. And he felt that the movie was the machine of modern man as a means of going out of oneself. And finally she recalled the famous couple under a bathrobe, functioning as one person.

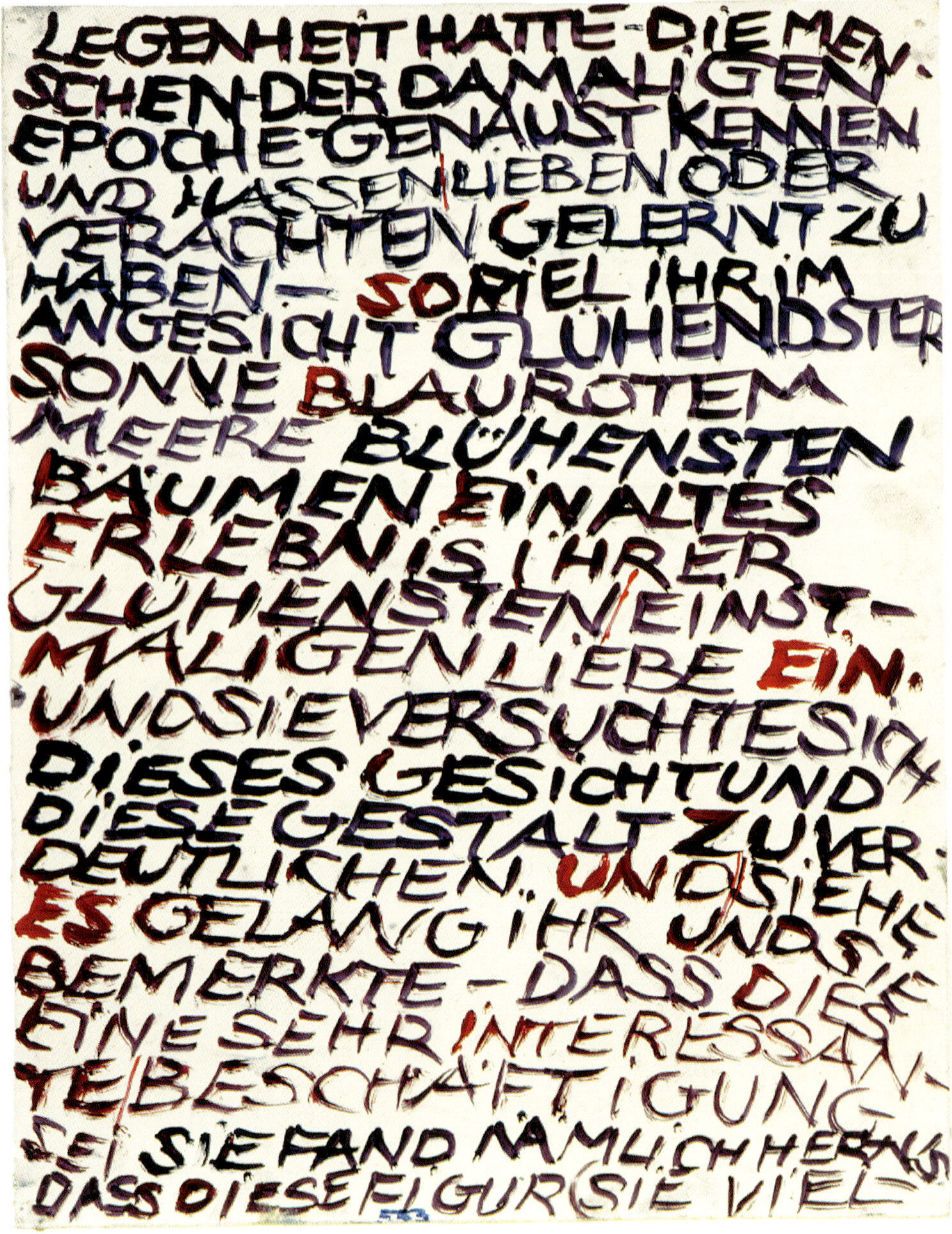
LEGENHEIT HATTE - DIE MEN-
SCHEN DER DAMALIGEN
EPOCHE GENAUST KENNEN
UND HASSEN LIEBEN ODER
VERACHTEN GELERNT ZU
HABEN - SO FIEL IHR IM
ANGESICHT GLÜHENDSTER
SONNE BLAUROTEM
MEERE BLÜHENSTEN
BÄUMEN EIN ALTES
ERLEBNIS IHRER
GLÜHENSTEN EINST-
MALIGEN LIEBE EIN.
UND SIE VERSUCHTE SICH
DIESES GESICHT UND
DIESE GESTALT ZU VER-
DEUTLICHEN. UND SIEHE
ES GELANG IHR UND SIE
BEMERKTE - DASS DIES
EINE SEHR INTERESSAN-
TE BESCHÄFTIGUNG
SEI SIE FAND NÄMLICH HERAUS
DASS DIESE FIGUR SIE VIEL

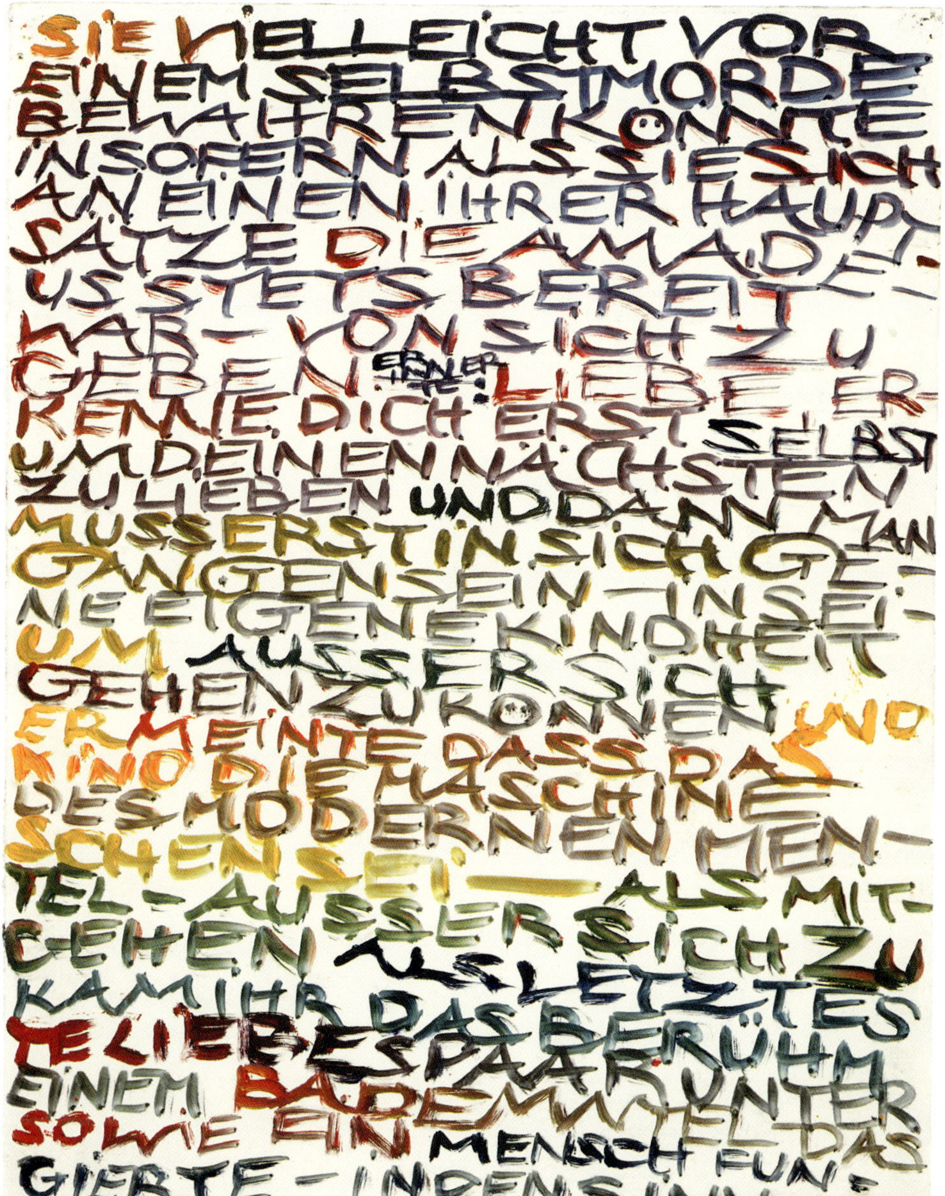
SIE VIELLEICHT VOR
EINEM SELBSTMORDE
BEWAHREN KONNTE
INSOFERN ALS SIE SICH
AN EINEN IHRER HAUPT-
SÄTZE DIE A.M.A.DE-
US STETS BEREIT
WAR - VON SICH ZU
GEBEN: LIEBE ER-
KENNE DICH ERST SELBST
UM DEINEN NÄCHSTEN
ZU LIEBEN UND DANN MAN
MUSS ERST IN SICH GE-
GANGEN SEIN - IN SEI-
NE EIGENE KINDHEIT
UM AUSSER SICH
GEHEN ZU KÖNNEN
ER MEINTE DASS DA UND
KINO DIE MASCHINE
DES MODERNEN MEN-
SCHEN SEI — ALS MIT-
TEL - AUSSER SICH ZU
GEHEN ALS LETZTES
KAM IHR DAS BERÜHM
TE LIEBESPAAR UNTER
EINEM BADEMANTEL DAS
SOWIE EIN MENSCH FUN-
GIERTE - IN DEN SINN
534

(opposite)

And now something strange happened to our Charlotte. While drawing, as always, she fell asleep in the midday sun. And when she awoke, in front of her was the painted picture of her once so beloved Daberlohn. But she tore the sheet into a hundred thousand small shreds, which she threw into the wind. Then she sat down anew and tried to fall asleep again, and the experiment succeeded anew. Again it was the face of our Amadeus, but this time in profile, facing towards a standing person – namely Charlotte – and she sought for an explanation of these strange facts. Then her glance fell on one of her old drawings representing Death and the Maiden.
And suddenly she knew...

(following pages)

... two things. First, that Daberlohn's eyes seemed to say: "Death and the Maiden, that's the two of us"; and second, that she still loved him as much as ever. – And if he was Death, then everything was all right, then she did not have to kill herself like her ancestors, for according to his method one can be resurrected in fact, in order to love life still more, one should once have died. So she was in fact the living model for his theories, and she remembered...

... his book, Orpheus, or The Way to a Death Mask, of which he had said he regretted not having written it as a poem. And with dream-awakened eyes she saw all the beauty around her, saw the sea, felt the sun, and knew: she had to vanish for a time from the human surface and make every sacrifice to create her world anew out of the depths.

UND NUN GESCHAH UNSE-
RER CHARLOTTE ETWAS
MERKWÜRDIGES. ZEICH-
NENDERWEISE – WIE IMMER
SCHLIEF SIE IN MITTAGSSONNE
EIN. UND ALS SIE ERWACHTE
LAG VOR IHR GEMALT DAS
BILD IHRES EINST SO HEISS
GELIEBTEN DABERLOHN
DOCH SIE ZERRISS DAS
BLATT IN HUNDERTTAUSEND
KLEINE SCHNITZEL
IN DEN WIND.
UND DAS EXPERIMENT
GLÜCKTE VON NEUEM
WAR ES DAS GESICHT
UNSEREM AMADEUS
DIESMAL IM PROFIL DOCH
STEHENDEN PERSON
NÄMLICH CHARLOTTE
SUCHTE NACH EINER ER-
KLÄRUNG FÜR DIESE MERK-
WÜRDIGEN TATSACHEN
DA FIEL IHR BLICK AUF
EINE ALTE ZEICHNUNG
VON IHR DIE DEN TOD
UND DAS MÄDCHEN DAR
STELLTE. UND PLÖTZ-
LICH WUSSTE SIE –

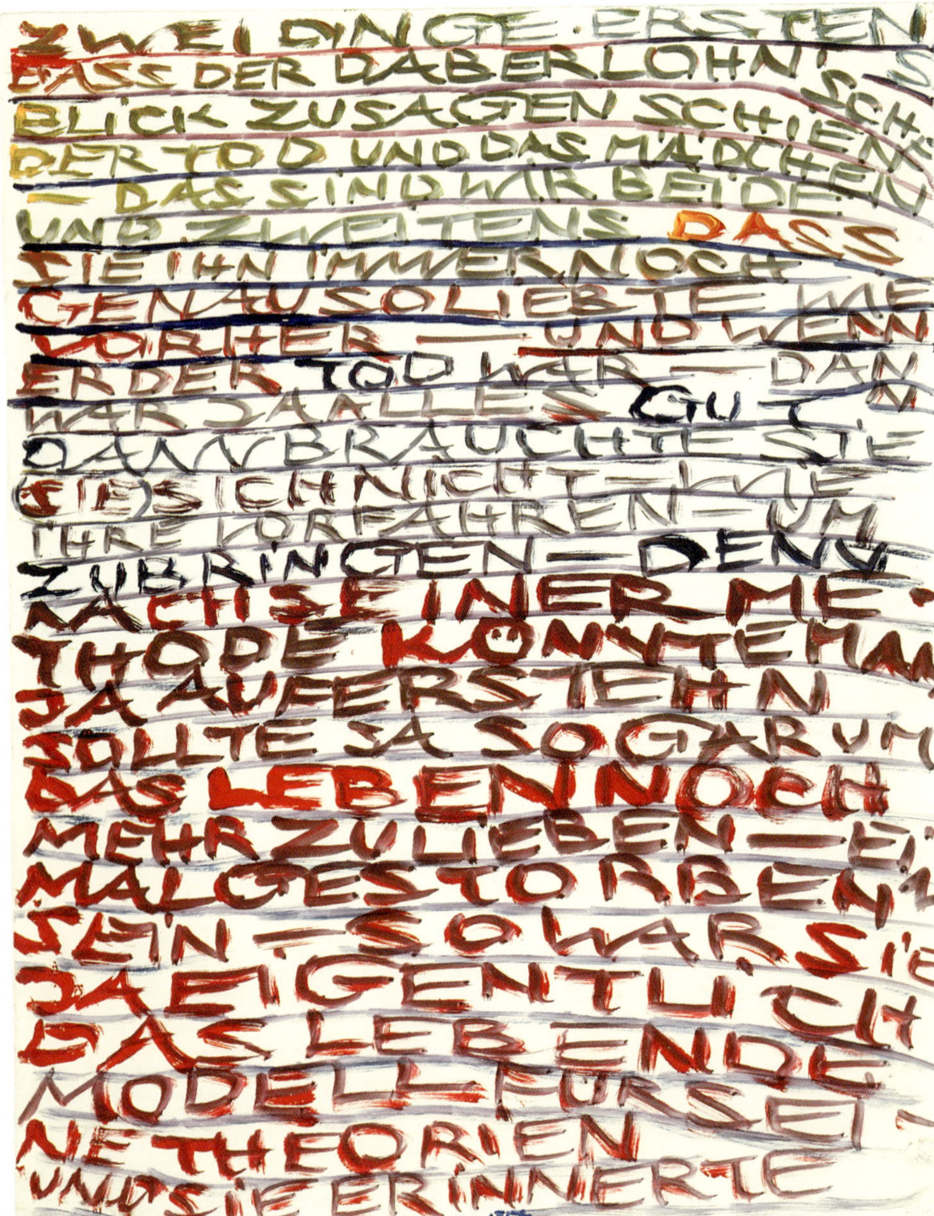
ZWEI DINGE. ERSTENS
DASS DER DABERLOHNS
BLICK ZU SAGEN SCHIEN
DER TOD UND DAS MÄDCHEN
– DAS SIND WIR BEIDE
UND ZWEITENS DASS
SIE IHN IMMER NOCH
GENAU SO LIEBTE WIE
VORHER – UND WENN
ER DER TOD WAR – DANN
WAR JA ALLES GUT.
DANN BRAUCHTE SIE
(SIE) SICH NICHT – WIE
IHRE VORFAHREN – UM
ZUBRINGEN – DENN
NACH SEINER ME-
THODE KONNTE MAN
JA AUFERSTEHN
SOLLTE JA SOGAR UM
DAS LEBEN NOCH
MEHR ZU LIEBEN – EIN
MAL GESTORBEN
SEIN – SO WAR SIE
JA EIGENTLICH
DAS LEBENDE
MODELL FÜR SEI-
NE THEORIEN
UND SIE ERINNERTE
556

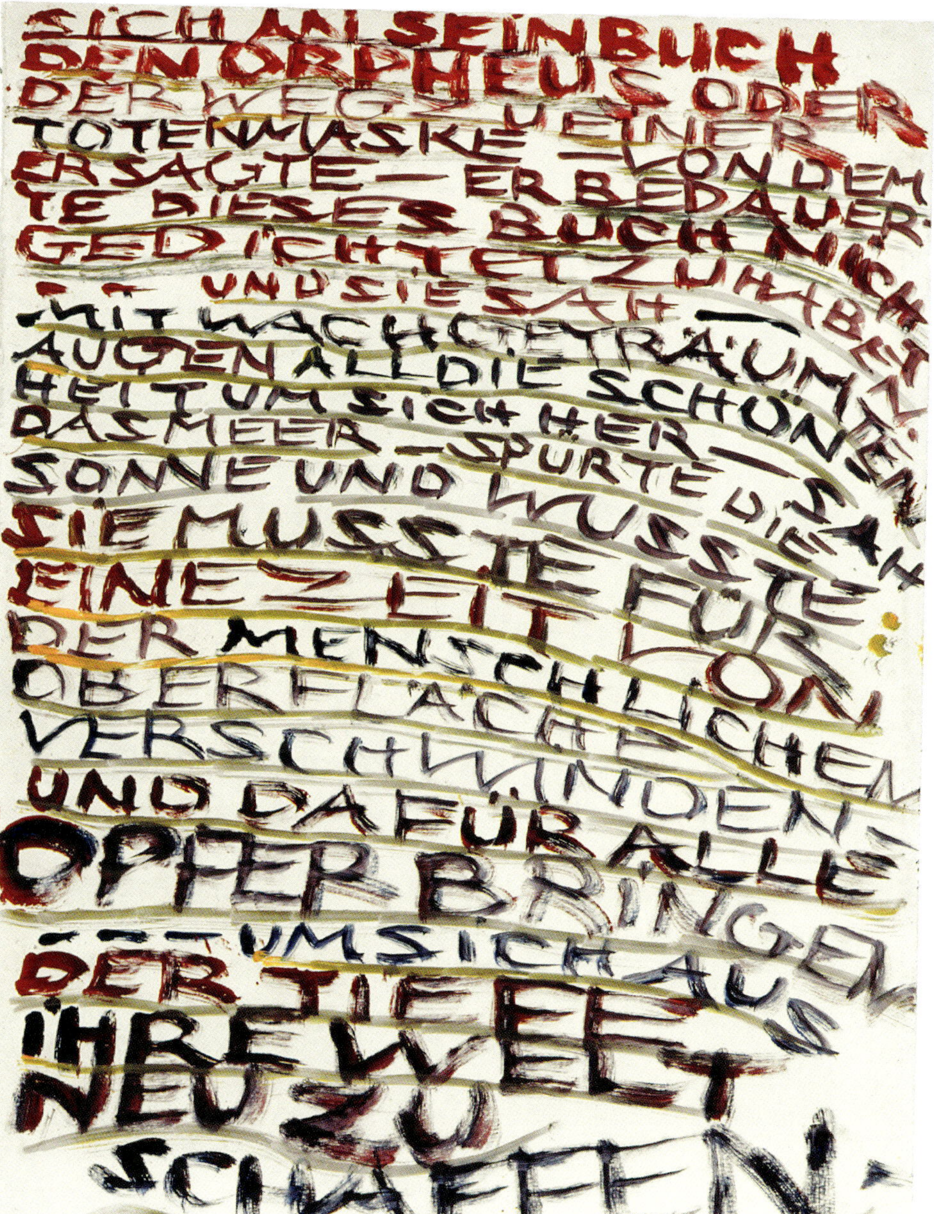
SICH AN SEIN BUCH
DEN ORPHEUS ODER
DER WEG ZU EINER
TOTENMASKE — VON DEM
ER SAGTE — ER BEDAUER-
TE DIESES BUCH NICHT
GEDICHTET ZU HABEN
UND SIE SAH —
MIT WACHEN TRÄUMEN
AUGEN ALL DIE SCHÖNEN
HEIT UM SICH HER — SAH
DAS MEER — SPÜRTE DIE
SONNE UND WUSSTE
SIE MUSSTE
EINE ZEIT FÜR
DER MENSCHLICHEN
OBERFLÄCHLICHEM
VERSCHWINDEN
UND DAFÜR ALLE
OPFER BRINGEN
— UM SICH AUS
DER TIEFE
IHRE WELT
NEU ZU
SCHAFFEN.

And from that came:
The Life or the Theatre???

Life or Theatre?

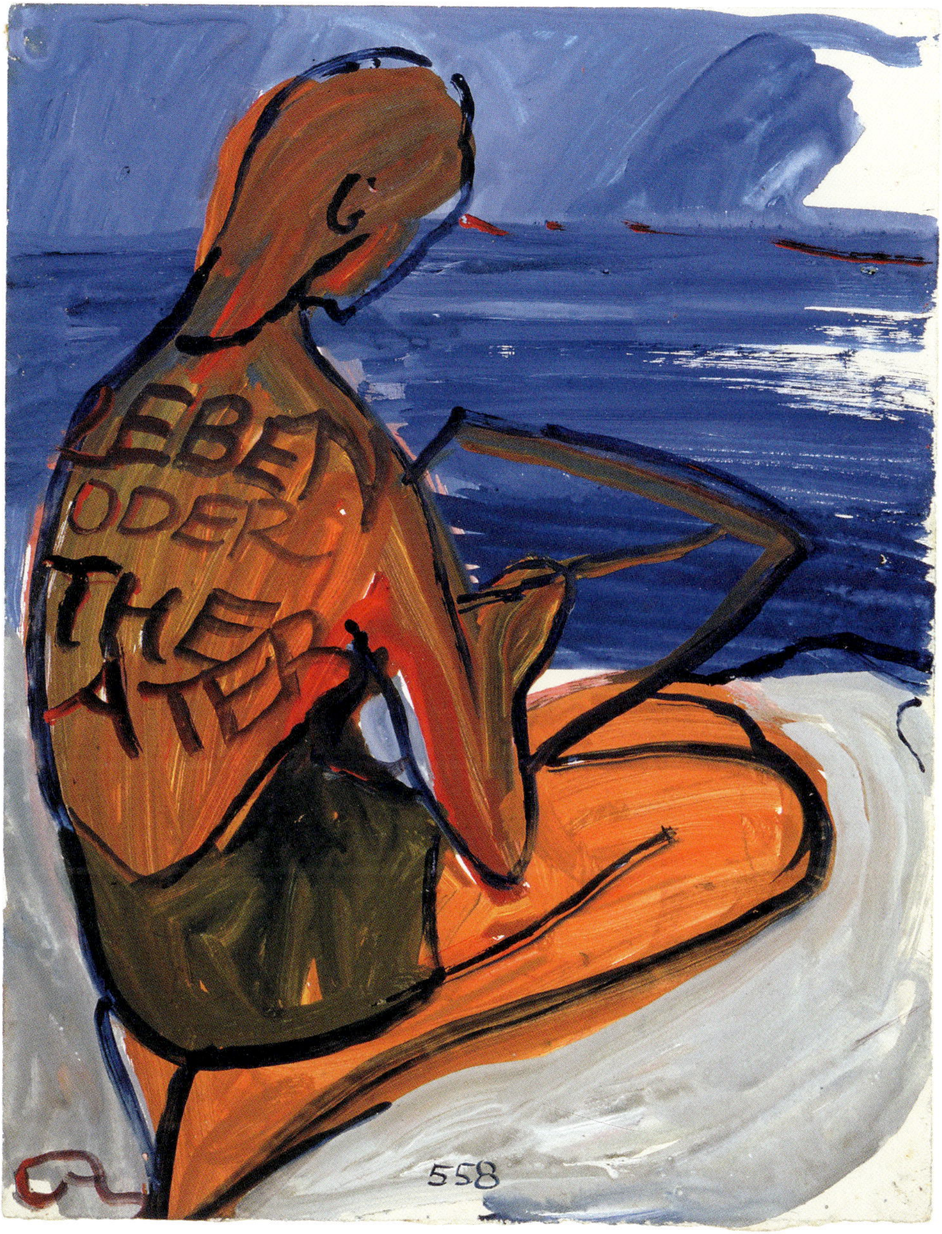
LEBE
ODER
THE
ATER
558

APPENDIX

Charlotte Salomon – A Chronology

1913 Charlotte Grunwald, the artist's aunt, commits suicide.

1915 Charlotte's parents meet during the First World War while her mother Franziska Grunwald, a nurse, is assisting her father, Albert Salomon, who is a surgeon.

1916 Marriage of Charlotte's parents.

1917 16 April: Charlotte Salomon, the only child of Albert and Franziska Salomon, is born in Berlin.

1926 Charlotte's mother commits suicide; Charlotte is told her mother died of influenza.

1927 Charlotte becomes a pupil at the Fürstin-Bismarck-Gymnasium (today Sophie-Charlotte-Gymnasium), Berlin-Charlottenburg. Albert Salomon is appointed non-tenured professor at Berlin University.

1930 September: Albert Salomon marries the alto singer Paula Lindberg.

1933 January: The Nazis come to power. Albert Salomon loses his professorship, his right to teach at German universities, and his health insurance authorisation; Paula Lindberg-Salomon is no longer allowed to perform in public. As a result, the former takes a position as head of the Jewish hospital in Berlin while the latter becomes active in the Kulturbund Deutscher Juden (Cultural Union of German Jews; later Jüdischer Kulturbund).

September: Charlotte leaves school. She takes private art lessons to prepare for the entrance examinations of the Academy in Berlin.

Autumn: Charlotte's maternal grandparents initially emigrate to Rome. Charlotte visits them there and discovers prominent works of art during her short stay, among them Michelangelo's works.

1934 Charlotte's grandparents settle in Villefranche-sur-Mer at the Côte d'Azur near Nice.

1935-36 Autumn: Charlotte starts attending the Vereinigte Staatsschulen für Freie und Angewandte Kunst (United State Schools for Fine and Applied Arts), at first on approval and from 7 February 1936 as registered student.

1937 The self-acclaimed vocal teacher Alfred Wolfsohn is sent as *répétiteur* to Paula Lindberg-Salomon by the Jewish artist's aid organisation Jüdische Künstlerhilfe. He befriends Charlotte and becomes an important figure especially for her artistic work.

1938 Summer: Charlotte is exmatriculated from art school.

9 November: Pogrom known as "Kristall-nacht" (Night of Broken Glass). The day after, Albert Salomon is arrested and interned in Sachsenhausen concentration camp, near Berlin. After several weeks of internship, Paula Lindberg-Salomon succeeds in getting Albert Salomon, who is frail in health, released.

9 December: Charlotte emigrates to her grandparents who have found refuge in the Villa L'Ermitage in Villefranche-sur-Mer of the American Ottilie Moore.

1939 Spring: With forged papers Albert and Paula leave Berlin for Amsterdam.

September: Second World War begins. The grandmother tries to take her life. Her grandfather informs her of the many suicides in her family.

1940 Beginning of the year: Charlotte leaves Villefranche-sur-Mer with her grandparents and moves to Nice.

5 March: Charlotte's grandmother commits suicide.

May/June: All German refugees residing in the south of France are interned in camps. Charlotte and her grandfather are taken to the French internment camp Gurs, which is north of the Pyrenees. The Franco-German Armistice is signed; among other things, it stipulates that all German refugees in France be handed over to the Germans. Germany occupies the north of France.

10 June: Italy enters the war on the German side.

July: The Vichy regime under Philippe Pétain is established in southern France.

After their release from Gurs, Charlotte and her grandfather return to Nice. Charlotte has a fit of nerves. Dr Georges Moridis recommends to taking up art again.

1941 June: Charlotte starts work on *Life? or Theatre?*

September: Ottilie Moore, who supports Charlotte in her artistic work in Villefranche-sur-Mer and to whom *Life? or Theatre?* is dedicated, returns to the United States.

At the end of the year, Charlotte leaves Nice for St Jean-Cap-Ferrat, where she stays at the pension "La Belle Aurore." She continues her work on *Life? or Theatre?*

1942 Autumn: Italian troops occupy the French Mediterranean coast; as a consequence, the Italian Secret Police cooperate closely with the German Gestapo.

At the end of the year, Charlotte returns to her grandfather in Nice.

1943 12 February: Charlotte's grandfather dies. On his deathbed she writes the "Letter to Amadeus Daberlohn" that she adds to the finished work of *Life? or Theatre?* She finally returns to Villefranche-sur-Mer and lives there with Alexander Nagler, an Austrian emigrant to whom Ottilie Moore left the villa in her absence.

17 June: Charlotte Salomon marries Alexander Nagler.

8 September: After Italy concludes an armistice with the Allies, German troops occupy the French Mediterranean coast.

23 September: Charlotte and her husband are arrested by the Gestapo and taken to the transit camp of Drancy, near Paris.

7 October: Charlotte and Alexander Nagler are deported to Auschwitz.

10 October: They arrive in Auschwitz. Charlotte, five months pregnant, is probably killed on the same day; Nagler dies on 2 January 1944 due to the effects of enforced labour.

1946 Ottilie Moore returns to Villefranche-sur-Mer. Dr Moridis, the physician to whom Charlotte had entrusted *Life? or Theatre?*, hands the work over to her.

1947 Charlotte's parents travel to Villefranche-sur-Mer for the first time. Ottilie Moore presents them with *Life? or Theatre?*

1961 First exhibition on Charlotte Salomon at the Museum Fodor in Amsterdam where, along with gouaches and drawings from Ottilie Moore's possession, parts of *Life? or Theatre?* are also shown.

1962 5 February: Alfred Wolfsohn, who had emigrated to England in 1939, dies in London.

1963 First book publication on Charlotte Salomon and on *Life? or Theatre?*

1971 Albert and Paula Salomon donate *Life? or Theatre?* to the Joods Historisch Museum (Jewish Historical Museum) in Amsterdam.

1972 First exhibition of *Life? or Theatre?* at the Joods Historisch Museum in Amsterdam.

1976 7 May: Albert Salomon dies in Amsterdam.

2000 17 April: Paula Lindberg-Salomon dies in Amsterdam

Notes

Comments by the author Judith C.E. Belinfante

In 2010, the Joods Historisch Museum gave the filmmaker Frans Weisz the task of creating a one-hour documentary film on Charlotte Salomon's *Life? or Theatre?* The documentary was not only to include conversations with contemporary witnesses, but also interviews with those key players that had committed themselves since 1963 to the task of establishing the work of the then still unknown artist. Frans Weisz, with the assistance of Batya Wolff, was able to collect around 50 hours of interviews for the film, which have been now fully evaluated, for the first time, for this essay. Combined with the writings and audio materials from the collection of the Joods Historisch Museum, they allow for new insights and supplement research and publications from the last 30 years. One person is missing in the interviews from 2010-12: the writer Judith Herzberg who, in 1964/65, wrote the first article on Charlotte Salomon after she had looked through *Life? or Theatre?* with Ad Petersen. She described her recollections in a 2015 television interview with Wim Brands. The interviews are cited with the interviewees' names, their date-of-birth, and their relation-ship to Charlotte Salomon or to her work. Data on date-of-death of the intare only given if the museum has been notified of this.

Judith C.E. Belinfante: What Is *Life? or Theatre?*?

1. Also known as *Death and the Maiden* is Schubert's 1824 String Quartet No. 14 in D Minor, D 810.

2. Darcy C. Buerkle, *Nothing Happened: Charlotte Salomon and an Archive of Suicide*, Ann Arbor, 2013, p. 1.

3. Prologue: nos. 1-211; JHM inv. nos. M004155-1-369; Main Section: nos. 1-456; JHM inv. nos. M004370-833; and Epilogue: nos. 457-1558; JHM inv. nos. M004835-925.

4. JHM inv. nos. M004155-5116.

5. The entire work can be consulted at https://charlotte.jck.nl/en.

6. Charlotte Salomon, *Ein Tagebuch in Bildern 1917–1943*, Reinbek/Hamburg, 1963 (henceforth referred to as *Ein Tagebuch in Bildern* 1963); *Charlotte. A Diary in Pictures*, London 1963.

7. Charlotte Salomon: *Leven? of Theater? (Life? or Theater?)*, with texts by Judith C.E. Belinfante, Christine Fischer-Defoy, and Ad Petersen, Zwolle/Amsterdam, 1992, p. 7.

8. Alfred Wolfsohn, *Die Brücke (The Bridge)*, London, manuscript, c. 1946, typoscript p. 18 (henceforth referred to as *Die Brücke*).

9. *Ein Tagebuch in Bildern* 1963, p. 10.

10. Mary Lowenthal Felstiner, *To Paint Her Life: Charlotte Salomon in the Nazi Era*, New York, 1994, p. 15 (henceforth referred to as *To Paint Her Life* 1994).

11. Interview with Eleonore Herzberger-Katz (1917–2016), a pupil at the Fürstin-Bismarck-Gymnasium, in Frans Weisz, documentary, 2012, JHM 4000549 (henceforth referred to as documentary 2012).

12. *To Paint Her Life* 1994, p. 39.

13. Letter of 14 January 1962 from Alfred Wolfsohn to Ruth Liepman, in Dossier Liepman, JHM D014978.

14. *To Paint Her Life 1994*, p. 53.

15. *Charlotte Salomon – Leben oder Theater? Das "Lebensbild" einer jüdischen Malerin aus Berlin 1917–1943. Bilder und Spuren, Notizen, Gespräche, Dokumente* (Schriftenreihe der Akademie der Künste, vol. 18), ed. Christine Fischer-Defoy, Berlin, 1986, p. 83 (henceforth referred to as *Charlotte Salomon – Leben oder Theater?* 1986).

16. *Die Brücke*, p. 88.

17. *Charlotte Salomon – Leben oder Theater?* 1986, p. 48.

18. Letter of 27 September 1981 from Marthe Pécher (in São Paolo, Brazil) to Gary Schwartz, editor and publisher; photocopy in Archiv Katja Reichenfeld, JHM D005046.

19. Interview with Gerhard Schoenberner (1931–2012), politically engaged intellectual, author of *Der gelbe Stern*, 1960. It was he who organised the first exhibitions of Charlotte Salomon's work in Germany in 1966/67; in documentary 2012, JHM 4000258.

20. Emil Straus, *Das Refugium*, unpublished introduction to *Ein Tagebuch in Bildern* 1963; dossier Liepman, JHM D114978.

21. Report no. 712, by the Commissariat Général aux Questions Juives, 16 April 1943; photocopy in Les Archives départementales des Alpes Maritimes, Nice.

22. Interview with Kika Moridis (b. 1941), daughter of Dr George Moridis; in documentary 2012, JHM 40002550.

23. Stefan Zweig, *The World of Yesterday*, London, 1943, Preface (German ed. *Die Welt von Gestern*, Stockholm, 1942).

24. Letter of 14 June 1985 from Mrs H.R. Salomon from London to Katja Reichenfeld, JHM 40002547.

25. Interview with Christine Fischer-Defoy (b. 1951), author, filmmaker, cultural historian; in documentary 2012, JHM 40002545.

26. Charlotte Salomon, *Letter to Amadeus Daberlohn*, February 1943, p. 2 (henceforth referred to as *Letter to Amadeus Daberlohn* 1943).

27. Interview with Judith Herzberg (b. 1943), poet, author of the screenplay for *"Charlotte": Leben oder Theater* in *Brands met Boeken*, VPRO 2015, JHM 40002592.

28. JHM inv. no. M004932.

29. I am grateful to Mirjam Knotter for this information.

30. The original is to be found in the Joods Historisch Museum, Amsterdam: Archiv Katja Reichenfeld, JHM D007804.

31. JHM inv. no. M004904v.

32. Interview with Christine Fischer-Defoy in documentary 2012.

33. *Charlotte Salomon – Leben oder Theater?* 1986, p. 78.

34. JHM inv. no. M004900v.

35. *Letter to Amadeus Daberlohn* 1943, pp. 4 and 17–19.

36. *Charlotte Salomon. Life? or Theatre?*, exh. cat. Joods Historisch Museum, Introduction pp. 9–13, Amsterdam 1998.

37. *Letter to Amadeus Daberlohn* 1943, JHM inv. no. M004928: "[...] collapsed – but kept believing in its existence. Really the world disintegrated more and more as time passed. While people were fighting everywhere, we lived seemingly peaceful lives on the Côte d' Azur. My love for drawing grew and grew, even more when I began to understand that it was blessed. My grandfather symbolised for me the people I had to resist. He was someone who had never felt true passion for anything. Blessed by an attractive appearance, he was able to advance in both work and other things. He married my grandmother and only out of his own ambition he imagined himself her equal in 'culture.' Then it became apparent, in that prominent family, that the grandmother had suicidal tendencies."

38. *Letter to Amadeus Daberlohn* 1943, p. 6.

Evelyn Benesch: *Life? or Theatre?* as a Mirror of Art and Culture in Berlin in the 1920s and Early 1930s

1. For a more precise dating of the individual works in the series of gouaches, see the essay in this volume by Judith C.E. Belinfante, pp. 6–48.

2. A full and precise list of these musical elements is to be found on the website of the Joods Historisch Museum (Jewish Historical Museum) in Amsterdam: https://charlotte.jck.nl.

3. Salomon, furthermore, later discarded a number of sheets, including some that had already been numbered. This explains both why there are occasional gaps in terms of numbering, with some numbers missing, but also why there are, in total, far more sheets than Salomon finally included in the numbered sequence. The numbering employed here follows that used in the aforementioned website of the Joods Historisch Museum. On this matter, see also the essay in this volume by Judith C.E. Belinfante, pp. 6–48.

4. In this context it may, however, be of significance that Salomon calls her narrative sequence a "tricoloured Singspiel" ("Dreifarben-Singespiel"; p. 83). On her use of only three colours, see also Judith C.E. Belinfante, "Leben? oder Theater? Anmerkungen zu einem Kunstwerk", in: *Leben? oder Theater?, 2004*, pp. 404–09, here p. 404 (hereafter cited as *Leben? oder Theater?* 2004). See also Belinfante's essay in this volume, pp. 6–48.

5. The Vereinigte Staatsschulen (United State Schools) were formed in 1924 by the architect Bruno Paul (1874–1968), in line with the principles of the Deutscher Werkbund. Because he was regarded by the National Socialists as too sympathetic to Jews, Paul was, in 1933, replaced as Director by a regime-approved functionary, Max Kutschmann (1871–1943), who had been charged with dismantling such art-educational institutions of the Weimar Republic and removing Jews

from their teaching staff. In 1939, the United State Schools became the State College for the Fine Arts (Staatliche Hochschule für Bildende Künste). In 2001 this, in turn, became the Universität der Künste Berlin.

6. Charlotte Salomon initially attended the class taught by the graphic designer Ernst Böhm (1890–1963); then, from the summer semester of 1936, that taught by Ludwig Bartning (1876–1956). Known as the "Primrose Professor", Bartning encouraged his students to sketch the flowers in a garden he had laid out for this purpose; he was also especially keen that they work after literary models. On this subject see, most recently, Christine Fischer-Defoy, "Charlotte Salomons Leben: eine Spurensuche", in *Leben? oder Theater?* 2004, pp. 12–22, esp. pp. 16ff., as well as earlier publications by this author: *Charlotte Salomon – Leben oder Theater? Das "Lebensbild" einer jüdischen Malerin aus Berlin 1917–1943: Notizen, Gespräche, Spuren, Dokumente*, ed. Christine Fischer-Defoy (Schriftenreihe der Akademie der Künste, Berlin, 1986, vol. 18 (hereafter cited as *Charlotte Salomon – Leben oder Theater?* 1986); and, in particular, "'Theater? – oder Leben?' Zum Leben und Werk von Charlotte Salomon", in ibid., pp. 15–28; and "Der Ausschluss jüdischer Künstler aus den Berliner Kunst- und Musikhochschulen und der Preussischen Akadenie der Künste", in ibid., pp. 95–117, esp. p. 106.

7. Christine Fischer-Defoy, "Wie ein trüber Novembertag, das war die Lotte.' Gespräch mit Barbara Petzel", in *Charlotte Salomon – Leben oder Theater?* 1986, pp. 59–75, esp. pp. 60ff.

8. Ibid. pp. 73ff, and Christine Fischer-Defoy, "Theater? – oder Leben?, Zu Leben und Werk von Charlotte Salomon", in: *Charlotte Salomon – Leben oder Theater?* 1986, p. 22.

9. Christine Fischer-Defoy/Reinhard Meerwein, "Zur Geschichte des Kulturbundes Deutscher Juden 1933–1940", in *Charlotte Salomon – Leben oder Theater?* 1986, pp. 134–56; Christine Fischer-Defoy, "'Der Mut, Dinge auszusprechen...,' Gespräch mit Paula Lindberg", in *Charlotte Salomon – Leben oder Theater?* 1986, pp. 52ff. On the role of Kurt Singer and Paula Lindberg-Salomon at the Kulturbund Deutscher Juden (and subsequently Jüdischer Kulturbund) see also Gabriele Fritsch-Vivié, *Gegen alle Widerstände: Der Jüdische Kulturbund 1933–1941*, Berlin, 2013, esp. pp. 33ff., 55ff., 59, 125.

10. Precisely when Alfred Wolfsohn (the real-life model for Daberlohn) moved in with the Salomon family in Berlin has not been precisely determined – although it is reasonable to assume that this occurred in spring 1937. On this matter, see Christine Fischer-Defoy, "Charlotte Salomons Leben – eine Spurensuche", in: *Leben? oder Theater?* 2004, pp. 12–22, esp. p. 16.

11. JHM inv. nos. M004398-T and M004651-T.

12. Alfred Wolfsohn was later to say of this work: "The central idea of the book stems from the legend of Orpheus, which, stripped of its mythological cloak [,] is the story of a singer who lost his voice and had to descend to the underworld before he could return to the world of men, to sing in a transformed voice", cited after: http://www.roy-hart.com/awesmanuscripts.htm.

13. On Salomon's time at the labour camp at Gurs (which was notorious for its frequently reported catastrophic lack of hygiene), see Monica Bohn-Duchen, "A Life before Auschwitz", in *Reading Charlotte Salomon*, eds. Michael P. Steinberg and Monica Bohn-Duchen, Ithaca, NY and London, 2006 (hereafter cited as *Reading Charlotte Salomon* 2006, pp. 21–33, here pp. 30ff.; and see p. 31 on artistic activity in the camp at Gurs. On this last subject see also Griselda Pollock, "Theater of Memory: Trauma and Cure in Charlotte Salomon's Modernist Fairytale", in *Reading Charlotte Salomon* 2006, pp. 34–72, esp. pp. 44ff. It has been impossible so far to ascertain whether Charlotte

Salomon was in contact with other artists at Gurs.

14. The present essay is only concerned with the sequence of images in gouache that form Charlotte Salomon's *Life? or Theatre?* Works that appear to have been produced earlier, possibly when Salomon was still living in Berlin, require separate consideration. These were romantically conventional illustrations to fairy tales, which Salomon may have been encouraged to produce at the Vereinigte Staatsschulen and which have no ostensible formal connection with the expressive sheets of *Life? or Theatre?* Separate research is also needed into the formal differences between the earlier and the later works, as into the marked caesura between them in terms of overall approach, which may well, if not exclusively, be explained by Salomon's experiences between 1938 and the summer of 1940 (including her stay at Gurs).

15. Werner Hofmann, *Die Grundlagen der modernen Kunst: Eine Einführung in ihre symbolischen Formen*, Stuttgart, 1978, p. 265.

16. In this connection one would, yet again, mention the repeatedly recurring sequences of talking heads or figures engaged in philosophical discussion, which Salomon liked to employ at moments of thematic intensity. There arises here the question as to whether there exists perhaps even a connection with the will to form or the language of form of traumatised individuals, such as would itself require appropriate specialised attention.

17. It is, above all, Sabine Schulze who has engaged with the question of Charlotte Salomon's sources of inspiration: "Kunst! Und Leben: Charlotte Salomons Arbeit im Spiegel der zeitgenössischen Kunstströmungen", in: *Leben? oder Theater? 2004*, pp. 393-403.

18. On one of the following sheets (p. 422), Salomon alludes again to Michelangelo, on this occasion to a work to be found in Florence: "Please compare this pose [...] 2. with that of Michelangelo's Night, sheet 308, and also with sheet 325." (Salomon here employs the numbering of the sheets that she had established, no. 308 corresponding to the sheet illustrated on p. 411).

19. Rembrandt Harmensz. van Rijn, *The Anatomy Lesson of Dr. Nicolaes Tulp*, 1632, Mauritshuis, The Hague. A further picture by Rembrandt – *Saul and David*, 1650/55, Mauritshuis, The Hague – is mentioned and described by Salomon on another sheet (p. 394), but she does not depict it.

20. On the history of Modernism in Berlin see, for example, Dieter Honisch, *Die Nationalgalerie Berlin*, Recklingshausen, 1979, pp. 33-46; also Annegret Janda, "The Fight for Modern Art: The Berlin Nationalgalerie after 1933", in: *"Degenerate Art": The Fate of the Avant-Garde in Nazi Germany*, exh. cat. Los Angeles County Museum of Art et al., ed. Stephanie Barron, New York, 1991, pp. 105-20.

21. This is the case, at least according to comments made by Charlotte Salomon's colleague at the Vereinigte Staatsschulen, Barbara Petzel, in an interview: see Mary Lowenthal Felstiner, *To Paint Her Life: Charlotte Salomon in the Nazi Era*, New York, 1994, p. 65 ("I certainly assume Lotte saw it too"), and related note on p. 251.

22. The self-portrait probably belongs to the group of portraits and landscapes on which, according to Ottilie Moore, Salomon worked while living at the Villa L'Ermitage during the months before her internment in the labour camp at Gurs. Almost none of these appears to have survived. See Griselda Pollock, "Theater of Memory: Trauma and Cure in Charlotte Salomon's Modernist Fairytale", in: *Reading Charlotte Salomon* 2006, pp. 34-72, p. 45.

23. JHM inv. no. M005090.

24. Vincent van Gogh, *Prisoners' Round*, 1890, State Pushkin Museum, Moscow.

25. JHM inv. no. M004900v. Maria Lassnig's formal language, which ultimately derives from that of the Surrealists, has in itself no demonstrable connection with Charlotte Salomon.

26. See: "'Der Mut, Dinge auszusprechen, auch wenn sie im Moment nicht schön sind.' Gespräch mit Paula Lindberg", in: *Charlotte Salomon – Leben oder Theater?* 1986, pp. 37–58; see also "Gespräch mit Barbara Petzel" (as in note 7), pp. 59–75.

27. Franz Wickhoff, "Römische Kunst: Die Wiener Genesis", in: *Die Schriften Franz Wickhoffs*, ed. Max Dvorák, vol. 3, Berlin, 1912, pp. 12–14. On the narrative principles defined by Wickhoff, see Ulrich Rehm, "Wie viel Zeit haben die Bilder? Franz Wickhoff und die kunsthistorische Erzählforschung", in: *Wiener Schule – Erinnerungen und Perspektiven*. Wiener Jahrbuch für Kunstgeschichte, vol. 53, 2004, pp. 161–89, esp. pp. 162–66.

28. See the observations of Horst Bredekamp in: Hans Dieter Huber and Gottfried Kerscher, "Kunstgeschichte im 'Iconic Turn': Ein Interview mit Horst Bredekamp", in: *Kritische Berichte*, vol. 26, 1998, no. I (Netzkunst), pp. 85–93, here p. 86. The comic strip as we now understand this form of publication became established in Germany only after the Second World War. The "principle of pictorial narrative" – that is to say, the recounting of a story through images with accompanying text – can, however, be traced back there to at least the 19th century. See Dietrich Grünewald, "Das Prinzip Bildgeschichte: Konstitutiva und Variablen einer Kunstforum", in *Struktur und Geschichte der Comics: Beiträge zur Comic-forschung*, ed. Dietrich Grünewald, Bochum and Essen 2010, pp. 11–33, esp. pp. 11–26.

29. On this matter see, above all, Christine Fischer-Defoy, "Theater? – oder Leben??", in: *Charlotte Salomon – Leben oder Theater?* 1986, pp. 20ff., who finds a sort of "flip-book" (Daumenkino), most markedly, in Salomon's rows of heads accompanied by speech bubbles.

30. Barbara Petzel, "Sicher allein, ich weiss es nicht. Ich bin auch allein ins Kino gegangen. Man ging damals oft ins Kino", in: *Charlotte Salomon – Leben oder Theater* 1986, p. 67.

31. On one sheet (p. 531) Salomon cites – albeit cynically – the then popular song "Heute Nacht oder nie, mein Schatz" (Tonight or never, my darling) from the 1932 film *Lied einer Nacht* (Song of a Night), a frivolous production intended for mass consumption.

32. Griselda Pollock (as in note 12), pp. 51 and 55. Christine Conley has also investigated the connections between Charlotte Salomon and Walter Benjamin; see Christine Conley. "Memory and Trauerspiel: Charlotte Salomon's Life? or Theater? and the Angel of History", in: *Reading Charlotte Salomon* 2006, pp. 88–104, esp. pp. 93, 98.

33. Walter Benjamin, *Berliner Chronik* (1932), Berlin, 2016.

34. Benjamin's six texts for radio were re-broadcast by Radio Bremen in 2002. They can be accessed at: https://ubusound.memoryoftheworld.org/benjamin_walter/Childrens_Radio/Benjamin-Walter_Childrens-Radio_CD01T03. They are also available as an audio book.

35. See Astrid Schmetterling, "Inscriptions of Difference in Salomon's Work", in: *Reading Charlotte Salomon* 2006, pp. 140–47, here pp. 144ff.

36. The typescript of Wolfsohn's book is now in the Jüdisches Museum, Berlin. See: http://objekte.jmberlin.de/object/jmb-obj-45567;jsessionid=B25042587D867466B077ACFC5CBB5BFF. On Charlotte Salomon and Alfred Wolfsohn, see Edward Timms, "Creative Synergies, Charlotte Salomon and Alfred Wolfsohn", in: *Reading Charlotte Salomon* 2006, pp. 105–13, here pp. 106ff

Sources

Video and audio material, collection JHM 40002542 to 40002558 raw material of the interviews for the documentary by Frans Weisz, 2012:

40002544: *Ad Petersen*, curator of the first exhibition, 1961.
40002545: *Christine Fischer-Defoy*, scholar and curator of the first exhibition in Berlin, 1986.
40002546: *Gary Schwartz*, publisher of the first complete book edition, 1981.
40002547: *Katja Reichenfeld*, staff member of the Joods Historisch Museum, music expert.
40002548: *Helga Lowenberg-Domp*, friend of Paula Salomon-Lindberg.
40002549: *Eleonore Herzberger-Katz*, schoolmate of Charlotte Salomon in grammar school (Gymnasium).
40002550: *Kika Moridis*, daughter of Dr Moridis.
40002551: *Valerie Kaempf*, child entrusted to the care of Ottilie Moore at Villa L'Ermitage 1939 – September 1941.
40002552: *Michelle Bergquist*, granddaughter of Ottilie Moore.
40002556: *Chastaing*, villager in Villefranche-sur-Mer.
40002558: *Gerhard Schoenberner*, journalist, designer of the first exhibition in Germany.
40002553: *Mary Felstiner*, biographer of Charlotte Salomon.
40001028, Paris Journal 1963: including Documentation from 1963 on Charlotte Salomon, after the publication of the book *Charlotte, ein Tagebuch in Bildern.*
40002592 *Boeken met Brands*; television broadcast of Wim Brands with Judith Herzberg on the occasion of publishing the first edition at Cosee publishers. VPRO, 2015.

Collection of documents from the JHM:

D009705 photocopy of the typescript: Alfred Wolfsohn, *Orpheus oder Der Weg zu einer Maske*, Berlin, 1930s.
D002101 photocopy of the typescript: Alfred Wolfsohn, *Die Brücke*, London, c. 1946.German original at the Jüdisches Museum, Berlin.
D007803 photocopy of the typescript: Alfred Wolfsohn, *The Bridge*, English version, London, c. 1946.
D014978, folders (2) with Correspondence of the literary agent Ruth Liepman (1909–2001) related to the publication of the book in 1963.
D007804, folder with Information by Katja Reichenfeld, JHM, on Charlotte Salomon, 1981–85.
D005046 photocopy:Copies of 4 letters by Marthe Pécher (Brazil) to Gary Schwartz, 1981–83. Originals are with Gary Schwartz.
Not inventoried:Documents from Nice and Villefranche, 1939–43.

Bibliographie

Editions of *Leben? oder Theater?*
1963, 80 gouaches

Charlotte Salomon: Ein Tagebuch in Bildern, 1917–1943, with an introduction by Emil Straus and a preface by Paul Tillich, Reinbeck near Hamburg 1963.
English edition: *Charlotte: A Diary in Pictures*, London 1963.
Dutch edition: *Charlotte Salomon 1917–1943*, Amsterdam 1963.
Italian edition: *Diario in figure di Charlotte Salomon, 1917–1943*, Milan 1963.

1981, first complete edition with all 769 numbered gouaches

Charlotte Salomon: Leben oder Theater? Ein autobiographisches Singspiel in 769 Bildern, introduction by Judith Herzberg, Cologne 1981.
English edition: *Charlotte: Life or Theater? An Autobiographical Play by Charlotte Salomon*, trans. Leila Vennewitz, London/New York 1981.
Dutch edition: *Charlotte Salomon: Leven of theater? Een autobiografisch zangspel in 769 Gouaches*, introduction and translated by Judith Herzberg, Maarssen 1981.

1992/1994, 133 gouaches

Charlotte Salomon: Leven? of Theater? – Life or Theater?, with texts by Judith C.E. Belinfante, Christine

Fischer-Defoy, and Ad Petersen, Joods Historisch Museum, Zwolle/Amsterdam, 1992.
Extended German/English edition: *Charlotte Salomon – Leben? oder Theater? – Life? or Theatre?*, Amsterdam 1994.

1998, complete edition with all 769 numbered gouaches and texts, small format
Charlotte Salomon: Leven? of Theater?, with texts by Judith C.E. Belinfante, Christine Fischer-Defoy, and Ad Petersen, introduction by Norman Rosenthal, trans. Judith Herzberg, Joods Historisch Museum, Stichting Charlotte Salomon, Zwolle/Amsterdam 1998.
English edition: *Charlotte Salomon. Life? or Theatre?*, trans. Leila Vennewitz, exh. cat. Royal Academy of Arts, London 1998 / 2. edition 2006.

2004, complete edition with varying image formats
Charlotte Salomon: Leben? oder Theater?, ed. Edward van Voolen, exh. cat. Städel Museum, Frankfurt am Main, Munich/Berlin/London/New York 2004.

2015, complete edition including all transparent text sheets in small format and *Letter to Amadeus Daberlohn*
Charlotte Salomon: Vie? ou Théâtre?, ed. Frédéric Martin, trans. Anne Hélène Hoog and Michel Roubinet, Paris 2015.
Dutch edition: *Leven? Of Theater?*, trans. Judith Herzberg and Gerrit Bussink, with an epilogue by Emil Straus, Amsterdam 2015.

Selected and cited literature
Belinfante, Judith C.E., "Leben? oder Theater? Anmerkungen zu einem Kunstwerk", in: *Charlotte Salomon: Leben? oder Theater?* 2004, pp. 404–09.
Benjamin, Walter, *Berliner Chronik* (1932), new edition, Berlin 2016.
Blom, Philipp, *The Vertigo Years: Europe 1914–1918*, New York 2010.
Blom, Philipp, *Fracture: Life and Culture in the West, 1918–1938*, New York 2015.
Bohm-Duchen, Monica, "A Life before Auschwitz", in: Steinberg/Bohm-Duchen 2006, pp. 21–33.
Buerkle, Darcy C., *Nothing Happened: Charlotte Salomon and an Archive of Suicide*, Ann Arbor 2013.
Conley, Christine, "Memory and Trauerspiel: Charlotte Salomon's Life? or Theater? and the Angel of History", in: Steinberg/Bohm-Duchen 2006, pp. 88–104.
Felstiner, Mary Lowenthal, *To Paint Her Life: Charlotte Salomon in the Nazi Era*, New York 1994 (Dutch edition: *Charlotte Salomon: een biografie*, trans. Jeanette Bos, Amsterdam 1994).
Fischer-Defoy, Christine (ed.), *Charlotte Salomon – Leben oder Theater? Das "Lebensbild" einer jüdischen Malerin aus Berlin, 1917–1943. Bilder und Spuren, Notizen, Gespräche, Dokumente* (Schriftenreihe der Akademie der Künste, vol. 18), Berlin 1986.
Fischer-Defoy, Christine, "Theater? – oder Leben?? Zu Leben und Werk von Charlotte Salomon", in: Fischer-Defoy 1986, pp. 15–28.
Fischer-Defoy, Christine, "Der Ausschluss jüdischer Künstler aus den Berliner Kunst- und Musikhochschulen und der Preussischen Akademie der Künste", in: Fischer-Defoy 1986, pp. 95–117.
Fischer-Defoy, Christine, "'Wie ein trüber Novembertag, das war die Lotte.' Gespräch mit Barbara Petzel", in: Fischer-Defoy 1986, pp. 59–75.
Fischer-Defoy, Christine/Meerwein, Reinhard, "Zur Geschichte des Kulturbundes Deutscher Juden 1933–1940", in: Fischer-Defoy 1986, pp. 134–56.
Fischer-Defoy, Christine, *Paula Salomon-Lindberg – mein "C'est la vie"-Leben. Gespräch über ein langes Leben in einer bewegten Zeit*, Berlin 1992.
Fischer-Defoy, Christine, "Charlotte Salomons Leben – eine Spurensuche", in: *Charlotte Salomon: Leben? oder Theater? 2004*, pp. 12–22.
Foenkinos, David, *Charlotte*, Paris 2014 (German edition: Munich 2015; English edition: *Charlotte: A Novel*, New York 2016).
Fritsch-Vivié, Gabriele, *Gegen alle Widerstände: Der Jüdische Kulturbund 1933–1941*, Berlin 2013.
Grünewald, Dietrich (ed.), *Struktur und Geschichte der Comics. Beiträge zur Comicforschung*, Bochum/Essen 2010.
Herzberg, Judith, "Charlotte Salomon 1917–1943", in: *Hollands Maandblad* 6, 1964/65.

Hofmann, Werner, *Die Grundlagen der modernen Kunst: Eine Einführung in ihre symbolischen Formen*, Stuttgart 1978.
Honisch, Dieter, *Die Nationalgalerie Berlin*, Recklinghausen 1979.
Huber, Hans Dieter/Kerscher, Gottfried, "Kunstgeschichte im 'Iconic Turn'. Ein Interview mit Horst Bredekamp", in: *Kritische Berichte* 26, 1998, no. I (Netzkunst), pp. 85–93.
Janda, Annegret, "The Fight for Modern Art: The Berlin Nationalgalerie after 1933", in: *"Degenerate Art" The Fate of the Avant-Garde in Nazi Germany*, ed. Stephanie Barron, exh. cat. Los Angeles County Museum of Art et al., New York 1991, pp. 105–20 (German edition: Munich 1992).
Pollock, Griselda, "Theater of Memory: Trauma and Cure in Charlotte Salomon's Modernist Fairytale", in: Steinberg/Bohm-Duchen 2006, pp. 34–72.
Rehm, Ulrich, "Wie viel Zeit haben die Bilder? Franz Wickhoff und die kunsthistorische Erzählforschung", in: *Wiener Schule – Erinnerungen und Perspektiven* (Wiener Jahrbuch für Kunstgeschichte 53), 2004, pp. 161–89.
Schulze, Sabine, "Kunst! Und Leben: Charlotte Salomons Arbeit im Spiegel der zeitgenössischen Kunstströmungen", in: *Charlotte Salomon: Leben? oder Theater?* 2004, pp. 393–403.
Steinberg, Michael P./Bohm-Duchen, Monica (eds.), Reading Charlotte Salomon, Ithaca/London 2006.
Timms, Edward, "Creative Synergies: Charlotte Salomon and Alfred Wolfsohn", in: Steinberg/Bohm-Duchen 2006, pp. 105–13.
Wickhoff, Franz, "Römische Kunst: Die Wiener Genesis", in: Max Dvorák (ed.), *Die Schriften Franz Wickhoffs*, vol. 3, Berlin 1912, pp. 12–14.
Zweig, Stefan, *Die Welt von Gestern* (1942), Berlin 2013 (English edition: *The World of Yesterday*, 1964).

Films

Feature film

Charlotte, Berlin 1980; director: Frans Weisz; screenplay: Frans Weisz and Judith Herzberg; producer: Artur Brauner; leading actors: Birgit Doll and Derek Jacobi.

Documentaries

C'est toute ma vie, Paris 1992; director: Richard Dindo.

Paula Paulinka. Die jüdische Sängerin Paula Salomon-Lindberg erzählt ihr Leben, Berlin 1996; directors: Christine Fischer-Defoy, Caroline Goldie, and Daniela Schmidt.

Leven? Of Theater?, Amsterdam 2012; director: Frans Weisz.

Concordance

The originals from Charlotte Salomon's *Life? or Theatre?*, a selection of which is shown here, are located at Joods Historisch Museum, Amsterdam. The concordance lists the page number of the present publication and the designation under which each original is inventoried in the museum. On the museum's website https://charlotte.jck.nl/en the individual pages are also to be found under these inventory numbers.

Programme

Prelude

Main Section

Addendum

The authors:
Evelyn Benesch was deputy director of the Bank Austria Kunstforum in Vienna. In her long career as an exhibition curator, she has focused on the many artists of classic modernism – from Paul Cézanne to Henri de Toulouse-Lautrec, from the Futurists to the painters of *Die Brücke*, and from Pierre Bonnard to Balthus.

Judith C. E. Belinfante studied Modern History at the University of Amsterdam. From 1976 to 1998, she was the Director of the Jewish Historical Museum in Amsterdam. After a subsequent period as a parliamentary deputy, she was a leading curator of the special collections at the University of Amsterdam Library from 2003 to 2008. She chaired the Charlotte-Salomon Foundation from 2002 to 2017.

This publication is made with the support and assistance of the Charlotte Salomon Foundation and Joods Historisch Museum, Amsterdam, the Netherlands (Jewish Historical Museum). It is based on *Leben? oder Theater?* (*Life? or Theatre?*) a dramatised autobiography in 769 gouaches by Charlotte Salomon (Berlin 1917–Auschwitz 1943).

Leben? oder Theater? (*Life? or Theatre?*) by Charlotte Salomon is part of the collection of the Joods Historisch Museum, Amsterdam (Jewish Historical Museum): https://charlotte.jck.nl/en

Photo Credits
Bibliothèque nationale de France, Paris: pp. 70, 71, 74, 75
defd Hamburg: p. 77
Joods Historisch Museum, Amsterdam: pp. 19, 20, 23, 24 right, 37, 48, 51, 73
Nasjonalmuseet for kunst, arkitektur og design, Oslo: p. 68
© Staatliche Museen zu Berlin – Preussischer Kulturbesitz, Nationalgalerie, photo by Jörg P. Anders: p. 64
Städtische Galerie im Lenbachhaus und Kunstbau München, Munich: p. 72
© The State Hermitage Museum, St Petersburg, photo by Vladimir Terebenin: p. 78 left

Front cover Detail of p. 223 (M004275)
Back cover Detail of p. 351 (M004574)
Page 2 and 5 Details from p. 125 (M004175) and p. 229 (M004288)

Project Management Ute Kieseyer, Cologne
Petra Lamers-Schütze, Cologne
Translation Elizabeth Clegg, London (essays and appendix), Eila Vennewitz (Texts of *Life? or Theatre?*)

Printed in Bosnia-Herzegovina
ISBN 978-3-8365-9865-1